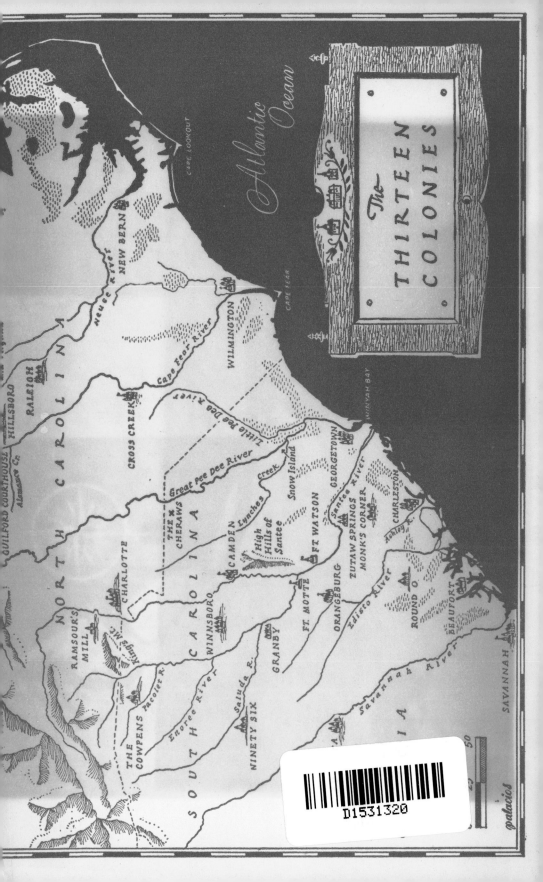

Mainstream of America Series ★

EDITED BY LEWIS GANNETT

FROM LEXINGTON
TO LIBERTY

BOOKS BY BRUCE LANCASTER

From Lexington to Liberty

Guns of Burgoyne

For Us, the Living

The Scarlet Patch

Phantom Fortress

The Secret Road

Blind Journey

FROM LEXINGTON TO LIBERTY

THE STORY OF
THE AMERICAN REVOLUTION

by BRUCE LANCASTER

DOUBLEDAY & COMPANY, INC., Garden City, New York, 1955

To

MY WIFE

JESSIE PAYNE LANCASTER

and to

MY FRIEND AND EDITOR

GEORGE SHIVELY

"And those who came were resolved to be Englishmen
Gone to the World's end, but English every one,
And they ate the white corn-kernels, parched in the sun
And they knew it not, but they'd not be English again."

from Stephen Vincent Benét's WESTERN STAR

CONTENTS

FROM LEXINGTON
TO LIBERTY

1. The World of 1764

IN the dawn of 1764 the world was spinning its way through a seeming eternity of feudalism. In the islands of Japan, Ieharu, tenth of the Tokugawa shoguns, was continuing a rule of absolutism that dated back at least a thousand years and would endure, little changed, until a mushrooming cloud would spread ruin over Hiroshima. Across the narrow seas China basked in the gentle tyranny of the Ch'ien Lung era.

In Russia the Empress Catherine was following the despotic rule of her predecessors by deftly mingling the functions of the throne room with those of the boudoir. Her neighbor, Frederick the Great, was sowing the seeds that were to grow into Prussia, the *General-Stab*, and, eventually, the Third Reich of Adolf Schicklgruber. In France the fifteenth Louis was faithfully carrying out the total rule bequeathed to him by his great-grandfather, the Sun King. Across the Channel, the personally righteous and incorruptible George III was ponderously moving to use the unrighteousness and corruptibility of others to turn England, last hope of liberalism, into a neat, one-party state. Parliament was to be a mere echo, subdued and respectful of the royal will.

And yet, under the surface, the oil of feudalism, which kept the world of 1764 turning so smoothly on its axis, was being slowly drained off. There were the liberal, inquiring Encyclopedists of Louis XV's France, and their influence was spreading into southern Germany. There were powerful forces at work in England that would struggle unceasingly against the encroachments of the Crown. But the largest and least suspected leak in the world supply of feudal lubricant lay far across the Atlantic.

When England had faced beaten France over the treaty table the year before, knowing experts in the embassies and courts of Europe had murmured approvingly or enviously that England would demand possession of sugar-rich and income-producing Guadeloupe as part of the victor's spoils. It wasn't even worth arguing. Wasn't England desperately hard up for revenue? To the shocked amazement of many, England let France retain

Guadeloupe and took instead the barren wastes of Canada and its scant trickle of furs.

It was easy for the knowing ones to point to the very bad bargain that England had made economically. None seemed to see that a major leak in the feudal oil tanks had been started. For had France and a French army stayed in Canada, it is more than doubtful that the North American events of the next two decades could have taken place. But now, with flank and rear secured, the ever-cantankerous colonies were free, knowingly or unknowingly, to set up a friction on the smooth-turning feudal axis of the world that would halt its spinning forever.

The year 1764 would see England, in frantic search for revenue, turn abruptly to the colonies with a virtual demand note for payment in direct violation of what those colonists conceived to be their sacred rights. The question of revenue for the Crown would fade into the background, and the two forces on their respective sides of the Atlantic would at last be faced with that long-deferred showdown and definition of rights of the colonists under British law. The final definition would pass beyond assemblies and law courts and hover over the crackle of musketry from the St. Lawrence to the far Savannah and beyond.

But all this lay in a slowly nearing future, and for the moment the North American colonies noted the arrival of the new year, 1764, without a hint that it was more than a date on a calendar, that it marked the faint beginning of an era.

2. The Land and Its Waters

SO North America turned its face to the new year, and its lakes and rivers, highways of a wilderness world, glittered a frosty welcome. There were names and places scattered along shore and watershed, thick-clustered in the East, where settlements had grown into towns and cities, sparse through deep forest and along mountain trail. Many names were mere indications, guideposts in untouched country. Certainly no man of 1764 knew them all, nor even an appreciable share of them. In later years they would enter into the consciousness of tens of thousands of people as, generations ahead, there would come a sudden awareness of Kasserine Pass or Piva Forks or Bastogne or Inchon. But now they lay waiting for history along the waterways and the coasts.

In the flatlands of eastern Massachusetts, the Assabet and the Sudbury wandered, lost, through endless marshes until their currents joined by an old town to form the Concord River. The combined streams flowed on, slipping under a plank structure called the North Bridge at the foot of John Buttrick's Hill. The road that crossed that bridge ran on into Concord, on to Lexington and its Green. Miles farther east, it forked and one branch led on to a choke-necked peninsula, with the Charles on one side and the Mystic on the other. There was little to note on that peninsula save the village of Charlestown and two low hills carpeted by the green pastures of Messrs. Breed and Bunker.

Deep inland, beyond the bold jut of New England, a nearly continuous waterway lay like a broken sword blade whose point was the Richelieu River, stabbing into the great St. Lawrence, and whose hilt was lost in the sea reaches south of Manhattan Island. Along much of this lake and river highway, names and places were few. There were Sorel and St. Johns on the Richelieu, but south of them began the wastes of Lake Champlain, whose waters mirrored a thousand-year-old reflection of unmarked forest and encircling mountain. Unmarked, that is, if one forgot the sagging stone barracks at Crown Point and the half ruins of the Marquis de Lotbinière's star fort, first known as Carillon but slowly resuming the resonance of "Ticonderoga."

The lake ended and a land bridge began, the break in the sword blade of water. Eternal forests were beginning their methodical engulfing of the log walls of Fort Anne, and to the south where forest gave way to meadow, the casemates of Fort Edward were settling in their foundations.

The Hudson took up the waterway again, swinging south in a channel that slowly widened and more slowly deepened. There were affluents entering the main river, like the Walloomsac, which began far to the east near the hamlet of Bennington. Farther along its course it edged past a round steep hill of little note or significance. Later the German colonel, Baum, would die there and give his name to it. Down the Hudson, the mouth of the Mohawk gaped, bringing in its current the mystery of the West and memories of its passage past another crumbling fort called Stanwix and marshy ravines near the settlement of Oriskany.

Villages and farms were gnawing into the banks of the Hudson, faintly registering neighborhood names like Stillwater and Bemis Heights and Freeman's Farm and Saratoga. Well marked was Dutch-flavored Albany, but below it the land grew wilder and rivermen watched for navigation guides like the bold, untouched masses they called West Point and Stony Point, just names along the river that told them when to shift the tiller of a Hudson sloop.

The Hudson rolled on, now vast in breadth and depth, until it reached an island where fortlike crags lowered down at the current. Later, true forts would be hewn from them and would be named first for a Virginia planter and then for a German general. The crags ended and the Hudson kept on past the gentler plains of the island where clustered houses showed their Dutch or British gables to New York Harbor.

Out of the wild tangle of the western Catskills, a stream plunged south, met a web of confluents, and became the Delaware. Clear of the mountains, it dipped smoothly south and east, losing the wilderness and bearing on its banks rich farm lands and pasturage. Life was thick along this river as it rolled to the sea. There were McKonkey's Ferry and Beatty's; there was the solid little town of Trenton and its stone barracks at the junction with the Assunpink and the road that led away to Princeton.

There were lesser streams below the Delaware, like the Schuylkill, a pleasant watercourse important only to those who throve on its banks. At one spot a confluent was swift enough to support a flour mill and the forges of Isaac Potts. Mill and ironworks lay in the shelter of soft hills and, locally, the place was called Valley Forge.

South and south again from the Schuylkill, a peninsula jutted out from the ragged west shore of Chesapeake Bay. Well to the north of this tongue of land, the Ma and the Ta and the Po and the Ni came together to form the Mattaponi, which joined with the Pamunkey to edge the peninsula's left bank. The new river was called the York and pushed on past a once-thriving town that was beginning to die on its banks. Men predicted that before many years had passed the very name of the old tobacco port of Yorktown would be lost to memory.

From the highlands of both Carolinas a great network of water spilled over into the plains, where men could scarcely tell where the riverbanks ended and where the swamps began. They were rivers with swift-running, whispering names. There were Thicketty Creek and Reedy Fork, where the brick walls of Guilford Court House rose so unexpectedly, and the Yadkin and the Deep.

Farther west the river names began to sing as they dove from the highlands. The Catawba became the Wateree and swirled on past the soft, green rise of the High Hills of Santee. McCord's Ferry and Howell's spanned the Congaree, and far down the Santee bubbled the twin mouths of Eutaw Springs.

So in the new year of 1764 the lakes and rivers of the thirteen colonies followed their ageless courses under thick ice in the North, below a frost skin in the middle lands, and free-running and clear in the South, setting the stage for the drama of coming years and for the men who would act out their parts in that drama.

BOOK 1

CHAPTER I

By Common Experience

A NATION has been defined as a group of individuals united by common experience. Most of the inhabitants of the thirteen colonies traced their origin to the British Isles and obeyed, or disobeyed, a British king or a British Parliament with exasperating inconsistency. Beyond these points they had little in common, having come to the New World for widely varying reasons and at different times, and, once settled, had been played upon by dissimilar climates, terrain, resources, and ways of life. They rarely moved in unity even when faced by dangers that might threaten them all. There was little uniformity of outlook, and some South Carolinians seemed closer to England than to New York, and a New Englander might be more aware of the West Indies than of Delaware. True, a growing system of post roads was working a subtle change by linking the colonies with an earthen chain that in time might lessen the importance of the bridge of boats to England or the Indies. So far, no single cause had appeared to unify colonial thought and act. But such a cause was being quietly and unconsciously prepared in England.

The ministry of William Pitt, which had guided England through the breakers of the Seven Years' War, had been ousted by a grateful country much as V-E Day spelled the doom of Winston Churchill's cabinet. Into Pitt's seat of power slipped George Grenville, whose plaintive, bleating voice had won him the nickname "Gentle Shepherd." Like Churchill's successor, Pitt's replacement found the joys of high office tempered by a bewildering array of problems demanding quick solution. And each problem fitted neatly into the vast, staggering major one of finance.

For example, there was the matter of nailing down the chief prizes of victory out of the last war—Canada and the so-called Ohio country. It seemed obvious to London that North America must be garrisoned by at least ten thousand British Regulars to keep the beaten French from turning speculative eyes on their lost possessions. Or, if the French could be airily overlooked, the Indian war that still flickered along the Great Lakes could not be. Such a standing army would cost over two hundred and fifty thousand pounds a year, and where could the Gentle Shepherd find such an amount when the national debt stood at nearly one hundred and thirty millions sterling?

The search for this and other revenue led Grenville and his aides to another question—who would benefit most immediately by such an army? The answer seemed, at the time, a happy one. Who but the colonists? Let them contribute to the upkeep of the great victory that had been won for them and to such other phases of the liquidation of the great debt that had been piled up. This partial solution was not illogical, since the ministry did not dare add to the burden of grinding home-side taxes. It did overlook the fact that New York and Massachusetts had financed in great part the last victorious campaign of General Jeffrey Amherst and that Pennsylvania had disbursed large sums in the cause of Empire. Also, this oversight buried the allied fact that none of this money had been repaid.

An alternative course would have been to appeal to the legislators of the various colonies to contribute to the common cause or to issue prorated requisitions in the hope that they might be honored. Little as Grenville and his associates knew of the colonies and their respective histories, they were sadly aware that such requisitions and appeals in the past had produced protestations of loyalty rather than hard cash. And hard cash was essential.

Soon colonial merchants were choking and sputtering, reeling under a succession of blows that threatened to overturn the commercial routine that had evolved with the decades. In the past, customs collectorships in the American ports had been handed out in England to party hacks, most of whom not unnaturally preferred to enjoy their salaries in London or the shires while they sent out often unsavory underlings to act for them in the colonies. Any reasonably bright merchant could come to an understanding with such deputies. Now Grenville was insisting that each appointee actually cross the Atlantic, with a stern injunction to collect to the last specified farthing. Not only were the colonial governors called upon to co-operate with the collectors, but the Royal Navy in American waters was to be turned, in effect, into a customs patrol.

All this was bad enough, but London dredged up a mass of nearly forgotten regulations known as the Acts of Trade and Navigation, and from them an added list of revenue-producing duties was unveiled. For years the colonies had enjoyed a free trade in Madeira wines, which were paid for by shipping vast quantities of barrel staves to Madeira. Now, if the colonists wanted to drink wine, they must buy it at a far higher price from British shippers only. This cut two ways, since Madeira vintners would no longer buy the barrel staves, a highly lucrative source of colonial profit. Duties were upped on French linens, and Americans were faced with the choice of meeting the greatly increased cost or buying cheaper and inferior British products. American lumber, which had always enjoyed a fine market in Europe, could still be sold there. But first it must clear through an English port for transshipment, thereby running up the cost until all profit vanished.

New collectors, new regulations, new duties, descending with little warning onto the American economy, constituted a high-explosive shell. But the detonator of that shell lay in one particular item which involved, incredibly, not an increase but a lowering of duties, for the ministry proposed to change the rate on humble, sticky molasses from sixpence per gallon to threepence, limiting the source to the British West Indies.

All through the colonies, particularly the Northern ones, molasses, almost a waste product of highly prized sugar, had assumed a vast importance. Whole fleets from their ports disposed of lumber, salt, dried fish, naval stores, Moses boats, and draft animals in the Indies, bringing back molasses, which was then processed into rum. Much of this was consumed locally, but great quantities were exported.

It may be mentioned here that the long-cherished "African triangle"— that is, New England ships bringing molasses from the West Indies to be made into rum to be carried to Africa for the purchase of slaves to be sold in the West India market for more molasses to be made into more rum to purchase more slaves, etc.—seems to belong to legend. Recent studies made by Charles H. P. Copeland of the Peabody Museum of Salem show that the Massachusetts slave trade averaged less than one ship a year over a period of more than a century prior to the Revolution.

So the molasses market appears to have flourished without an assist from the slave trade. The sixpenny duty had been on the books for years, but a mutually satisfactory arrangement had grown up in many ports whereby importers paid a surreptitious duty of one and one half pence to the collector in person and heard no more of the matter. So in effect the duty was now actually doubled, for all signs and portents indicated that the new threepenny duty was to be collected.

The cumulative effect of all these measures so suddenly imposed brought a crescendo of protest, not only from the merchants throughout the colonies, but from the thousands who would surely suffer from any slackening in the flow of the commercial lifeblood of the land. In his study looking out over the trim gardens of Province House in Boston, Francis Bernard, royal governor, chewed at a quill pen. The local uproar was such that he had laid aside work on a grandiose plan of his own for reforming the governmental structure of all the colonies and was writing to London in high agitation that the news "had caused a greater alarm in this country than the taking [by the French] of Fort William Henry did in 1757. . . . Merchants say, 'There is an end of trade in this Province.'"

Bernard's wails were echoed far and wide. Down in Rhode Island, where there had been a marked trend toward a Crown-appointed governor and council instead of the popularly elected slate which the little colony and Connecticut uniquely enjoyed, warring factions closed ranks to send up a roar of protest. The collection of the new molasses duty and the limiting of the source to the British West Indies were too murderous to contemplate. The colony imported over one hundred and twenty thousand pounds' worth of British goods each year. It exported to England a mere five thousand pounds' worth. The balance was made up by the molasses-rum trade. And even if the Rhode Islanders could afford to pay the new duty and still make a profit, the molasses output of the entire British West Indies would supply only one fifth of the demand of the incredible number of thirty distilleries crowded about Narragansett Bay.

Off to the west, New York, which usually presented the most nearly reasonable facsimile of polite obedience to the Crown, drowned out the din that rolled down Long Island Sound from Rhode Island. New York's books, so far as British trade was concerned, showed about four hundred and seventy thousand pounds in the red and, like Rhode Island's, they showed a favorable over-all balance that was due only to molasses shipped up from the French West Indies.

The frenzied clamor reached London with its volume very little diminished, but the new regulations underwent no change, and a common cause for all the colonies began slowly to emerge from the black, sticky syrup of the West India sugar mills. And these regulations became commonly known by the source of their tenderest point—the Sugar Act—although the word was scarcely mentioned in them.

So far the various colonial assemblies had skittered away from any strong official pronouncements against the Sugar Act as being a little too hot to handle. The aim of the act, of course, was revenue, but it could also be interpreted as simple regulation of trade, a parliamentary right that the colonies had pretty well admitted. But now word came through various channels of still another act, to be put into effect the next year. This act implemented what was called a stamp tax, applicable to all sorts of licenses, publications, and legal papers.

Here was a threat that could be played only one way, and the assemblies roared with surprising unanimity. Virginia stormed that it was a fundamental principle of the British Constitution that "the people are not subject to any Taxes but such as are laid on them by their own Consent." North and South Carolina paraphrased the Virginia protest with equal vehemence.

This Stamp Act, as it came to be known, was not due for passage until the next year, as has been noted. In the dead space of time a blast of rage crossed the Atlantic from west to east. But unfortunately the whole matter had gone beyond protest. By questioning the Sugar Act and the impending Stamp Act, the colonies seemed to be challenging the rights of Parliament. The whole aspect of affairs in England was changed. The many friends and supporters of the colonies in Parliament backed the ministry solidly. What did these colonials mean by denying any power that Parliament claimed? The matter of revenue was quite lost to sight. Instead there loomed inexorably that far deeper question, one that had never yet been even vaguely defined—just what were the rights of Parliament and what were the rights of the colonies?

In the meantime the measures for collecting the existing as well as new duties were running into rough seas. In addition to the blizzard of new certificates, bonds, and cockets to regulate trade, it was ruled that all violations be tried in the Admiralty courts. This provision infuriated even those colonists not engaged in trade, since the Admiralty courts did not allow for trial by jury, and the belief in the jury system was deep-seated. To make matters worse, Lord Colville, admiral in charge of American waters and hence of the Admiralty courts, decreed that all such trials be held at Halifax.

There was something to be said for his ruling. He was in charge of law enforcement and was sourly aware that a Rhode Island offender tried in a Rhode Island court would be regarded benevolently by the local judge, if indeed the judge himself were not financially interested in the seized vessel or cargo. But a suspect and his ship, taken to Halifax for trial, were due for a costly immobilization, regardless of the final verdict. As a further irritant, customs officers were immune from damage suits brought on grounds of false seizure. All the officer had to do was to satisfy the judge of the probability of guilt. Such satisfaction would have been virtually impossible in a local court but a foregone conclusion, and often a correct one, at Halifax.

The use of His Majesty's Navy as an enforcing agent brought in fresh complications, for officers from admirals down to midshipmen took the problem of enforcement far beyond the probable intent of Parliament. In addition to stopping ships at sea, in harbors, and at docksides, His Majesty's cutters and longboats paddled and fossicked about in backwaters and estuaries, pouncing on dories as eagerly as on brigs. Part of this was due to a stern sense of duty, to a high regard for the honor of the navy. But perhaps even more important was the fact that the ships' officers could look forward to a good slice of prize money accruing from the seizure of a bona fide violator—or a mere convicted one.

Such zeal exposed the Royal Navy to a most unseamanlike cross fire. From the very start the royal governors raised anguished howls over the Navy's doings, not because the governors disapproved of such seizures, but because they held that prize money should accrue to them and not to the underpaid officers of the fleet. This friction possibly went far toward nullifying the effect of Grenville's request that the governors co-operate with the navy in enforcing the acts.

The other batteries brought to bear on the Navy were more understandable, since they were manned by the merchants. Sedate William Allen, Chief Justice of Pennsylvania, wrote to a London friend, "Even the Intercourse between here and New Jersey is in great Measure interrupted, which was carried on in flats and small boats and the produce of the Western part of that Colony shipped off from this City, but now, one of those poor fellows cannot take in a few staves or Pig Iron or Bar Iron or Tar &c, but they must go thirty or forty miles or more to give Bond, the Charge of which and his travelling, makes the Burthen intollerable. This is a general complaint all over the Continent." Similar tooth-gnashings came from Charleston, Newport, and Boston, a merchant of the last place observing glumly, "No vessel hardly comes in or goes out, but they find some pretext to seize and detain her."

The merchants, from the very nature of their calling, were sharp, resourceful citizens and they found other means than the written word to underscore their protests. In many ports they coldly and effectively boycotted the pilots who brought navy ships into the harbor. Once a navy ship was berthed, the merchants chuckled sourly and, well aware of bad pay and bad living conditions on those ships, sent agents among the crews to whisper to able seamen, to skilled ratings, even to boatswains and midshipmen, that good quarters, good food, good pay, and chances for advancement were eagerly awaiting them on trading vessels soon to put to sea. Such inducements were often successful and depleted the crews of the men-of-war. And when officers sent press gangs ashore to recover deserters or to shanghai likely-looking colonials to replace them, the merchants whistled merrily to their private goon squads to break up the press gangs, rescue any men seized, and drive the sailors back to their ships.

To plague the colonists further, the unwholesome boom that had been a by-product of long war years began to fade, slowly at first, then with increasing speed. Shortly after the opening of the new year, 1765, a heavy blow struck Boston with hurricane force. Nathaniel Wheelwright, who had amassed an eighteenth-century fortune in filling and farming out war contracts, suddenly suspended payment. Boston and its dependencies reeled about as much as they were to reel in the fall of 1929. James Otis, already a marked man for his opposition some years before to the Writs of Assistance—virtual open-ended blank search warrants—gathered his breath enough to write that Wheelwright had enjoyed "such an Undue Credit that he became, next to the Treasurer, Banker General for the Province and almost for the Continent. Such was the Consternation for some little time that people appeared with pale Horror and Dread, and when a little recovered run about the City. Widows and Orphans that are ruined can only bewail their fate, the more resolute have been pulling and hauling, attaching and summoning to secure themselves, but it was too late to shut the Stable door."

There were other failures and in other cities, less spectacular but as tragic. Few of these were due to the Sugar Act, but it made a convenient target for those most pressed, as in later years the crash of 1929 would be blamed on the stock market, war debts, land speculation, and the Eighteenth Amendment. There was a definite effort to have the act repealed, as a sort of cure-all, and the colonial merchants counted not unnaturally on the help of their British opposite numbers, for the American trade accounted for a vast share of British income.

To underscore their meaning, colonial traders tried to start a nonimportation agreement. In Boston, families were urged to do without elaborate mourning costumes, to forgo the custom of giving out black gloves to the mourners, the last being more of an item than would appear, since funerals have been cited at which two hundred pairs of gloves were provided. Women were called on to shun "gaudy, butterfly, vain, fantastick and expensive Dresses." In New York, at least as hard hit as Boston, a Society for Promoting the Arts was founded, a sort of eighteenth-century WPA whereby the unemployed would be furnished with looms and spinning wheels, thus ending unemployment and providing colonial goods to replace British. In Philadelphia the patriotic fire buffs solemnly pledged themselves to eat no more lamb and to drink no imported beer, thus profoundly encouraging local wool production and local brewing.

These manifestations, while basically significant, were about as effective as snowballs thrown at Iwo Jima. Organization was lacking, community of purpose was still a hothouse growth, and the colonists as a whole were not geared materially or mentally for any sweeping changes in their economy. Peter Hasenclever, viewing the artificial stimuli applied to New York, reported to Sir William Johnson, secure in his forest mansion along the Mohawk, "This country is not yet ripe for manufactures. Labor is far too high—too much land to be settled." This last point was well taken. Who would bind himself to an eighteenth-century industry when the winds rolling down from the Great Lakes set the pines and oaks of the unsettled stretches awhisper with promises of farms to be had almost for the asking?

As to the British merchants, the colonial agents worked tirelessly and hopefully among them, keenly aware that as a class they were feeling the bite of post-war depression and certainly ought to be alive to the fear of losing the American market whence most of their revenue stemmed. The merchants showed satisfactory alarm, but the turmoil came to nothing, and Jasper Mauduit commented wearily that while they talked much there was no bringing them to action.

CHAPTER II

". . . but all of us Americans"

THE dreaded Stamp Act was to come before Parliament sometime in the middle of February 1765. But the act was nothing that Grenville had dreamed up suddenly. Long before he had mentioned its advent in 1764, Treasury experts equipped with a magnificent ignorance of the colonies and things colonial had been wearing out bales of gray goose quills and emptying stone jugs of ink as they labored over the specific provisions of the act.

Thomas Whately, secretary to the Gentle Shepherd, recommended, among other points, that the tax on admission to the learned professions be at least as high as in England, if not higher. Confronted with the exist-

ence of wilderness universities—there were already Harvard, William and
Mary, Yale, the University of Pennsylvania, St. John's at Annapolis, and
the institutions to be known later as Brown, Princeton, Columbia, Washington and Lee, with Rutgers and Dartmouth hovering in the close future
—Whately became gravely alarmed and pronounced that fees should be
raised considerably "in order to keep mean persons out of those situations
in life which they disgrace." Like Marquand's Laurence Lovell, he was
keenly aware of the difference between inherited money and earned money.

By some arithmetical magic Whately set forth that an American freshman should pay to the Crown two pounds sterling on entering a university,
while his British opposite number got off with two shillings. Graduation
fees were on the same general scale. Turning to the learned professions, he
recommended that, for admission to the Bar, a colonial must pay ten
pounds as against his British confrere's six. As such details leaked out, it
seemed to many that the Stamp Act aimed more at regulating a way of life
three thousand miles away than at raising revenue.

It was an age of pamphlets, and the approaching session of Parliament
triggered off a fine flood. It was also an age of resounding titles, and the
ministry fired its first blast, penned by a nonentity named Soame Jenyns
and carefully packaged as *The Objections to the Taxation of Our American
Colonies by the Legislature of Great Britain briefly Considered.*

Across the Atlantic an answering drumfire began its deep thunder roll.
One of the best detonations was fired by Daniel Dulany, Maryland-born,
but a product of Eton, Cambridge, and the Middle Temple. He pounded
away at the Whately-Grenville contention that since the colonists were
Englishmen they were, by the very nature of things, represented in any
elected British Parliament, pointing out glaring inconsistencies and contradictions in the ministerial claims. And not to be outdone in the matter of
title, he headed his offering *Considerations on the Propriety of Imposing
Taxes in the British Colonies, for the Purpose of Raising a Revenue, by Act
of Parliament.*

The question of representation, on which hinged the right to tax, was
largely a matter of definition. Most of the party in power in England, and
many of its opponents, seemed to look upon election to Parliament as a
close equivalent to being named to a board of directors set up to run the
country. The colonial view was strikingly different. Election to a colonial
legislature established a member as the direct representative of his particular
district. In many cases he acted under instructions from his town meeting
or its equivalent. This was especially true in the Northern colonies. In the
South, where a more scattered population made such close contact less
possible, the same theory was held, if not so widely observed.

News of the final passage of the act was sent rolling and pitching across
the Atlantic through the spring gales, the ships that bore it making their
American landfalls at widely differing times, so the impact of their news
began a slow detonation that ran up and down the coast like a chain of
land mines equipped with time fuses.

For example, there was Virginia with May a soft green cloud over the narrow peninsula between the York and the James rivers. In rose-brick Williamsburg with its hover of white spires, the House of Burgesses was in session. A Virginia law student was strolling through the mellow town, proud to show it to a French traveler. He may have pointed out to his French guest various members of the House as the pair neared the capitol, for the day's session was beginning to break up and men like Peyton Randolph, Robert Nichols, Colonel George Washington, and Richard Bland might have been calling for their horses about the wide white doors, and those men would have been known by sight at least to Thomas Jefferson.

When Jefferson and his guest reached the airy lobby of the House, only thirty-nine out of the one hundred and sixteen members were still in their seats, with Speaker John Robinson wistfully eying the slanting sunshine on the turf outside the tall, bow-topped windows. As the two men looked in at the gathering, a plainly dressed member arose and Lawyer Jefferson must have whispered to his guest that that was Patrick Henry, from one of the back counties. The Frenchman's name has not come down through the years, but his, the only known firsthand report of Patrick Henry's speech, survives.

Spelling the surname "henery," the Frenchman wrote that the member, in some heat, mentioned that Tarquin and Caesar had their Brutus, Charles his Cromwell, and he hoped that some good American would stand up for his country. Then he cooled off considerably and was going on when Speaker John Robinson cut in sharply to say that "henery" spoke treason and was sorry to see that no member was loyal enough to rise against him. Henry at once apologized. As to his own loyalty, he would shed the last drop of his blood for His Majesty George III. If he had said too much, he concluded, it was out of concern for his country. Some unnamed members backed Henry, and the matter was dropped.

There the Frenchman's narrative ends, and while it differs markedly from the drama of familiar legend, with Henry hurling hot defiance before a packed House, the main outlines remain and Patrick Henry appears earnest but level-headed. The defiant legend, incidentally, seems to have originated with William Wirt of Philadelphia, who reconstructed the scene nearly fifty years later. With the end of Henry's speech, the Frenchman seems to have left or lost interest, else he could have noted that that speech led directly into the so-called Virginia Resolves, the first official reply to the Stamp Act.

These resolves, four in number, were passed after much debate and wrangling there in the rose and white town while the May sunshine made ready to deepen into a June glow. In substance the resolves stated once more that only Virginians could tax Virginians, and stated it firmly and respectfully. So the four became history and stemmed, so far as anyone may tell, directly from Patrick Henry's speech.

But, in all the wrangling, considerably more than four resolves were pre-

sented, and those that were finally quashed and kept out of the record were
sheer dynamite. There was one shattering declaration that His Majesty's
liege people were not bound to yield obedience to any tax law that did not
originate in their own legislature. This was strong enough, but it was given
a further bursting charge in the final paragraph, which stated flatly that
"Any Person who shall, by Speaking or Writing, assert . . . that any Persons, other than the General Assembly of this Colony, have any right to
impose any Tax whatever . . . shall be deemed an Enemy to This His
Majesty's Colony." The question of freedom of the press and freedom of
speech, virtually abolished by this last sentence, does not seem to have
troubled the backers—and there were many of them—of the rejected provisions of this resolve.

But the four that were passed were quite strong enough. So appalled was
Joseph Royle, tight-laced editor of the *Virginia Gazette*, that he immediately suppressed any mention of their final form, no doubt fearing lest some
bolt from heaven strike him down for treason, lèse-majesté, and guilt by
association. And his suppression of the actually moderate though firm resolves added an unmeasured store of explosive force to the twelve other
time bombs that erupted from Kittery Point to the mouths of the Cooper,
the Ashley, and the Savannah.

At least three highly inflammatory resolves had been killed by the
burgesses, but the backers of those items, with Patrick Henry almost surely
among them, at once circulated the full bill as it had been first conceived
and said nothing about the defeat of sundry parts. The bill was picked up
in Rhode Island by the Newport *Mercury* as though it had been passed in
its entirety, and the *Mercury's* account was sent roaring up and down the
coast. Before long the Rhode Island Assembly passed virtually all the resolves, moderate and radical together, omitting chiefly those items that did
not apply to the charter of that colony. Georgia, North Carolina, Delaware,
and New Hampshire took no action for varying reasons, but most of the
other colonies followed Rhode Island in greater or less degree and formally
declared that they could not be taxed by Parliament so long as they were
unrepresented in that body. In some cases colonies actually agreed to protect and indemnify Crown officials against any penalties and punishments
that Parliament might visit on them for non-compliance with the new act.

So the dark clouds of the explosions mushroomed high as the time fuses
operated. It is probable that the blasts would have been only a little weaker
had the horrified Mr. Royle published the resolves as actually passed. It
can only be said that most people took in good faith the more radical
measures, since no correction appeared in the *Virginia Gazette*.

The heaviest echoes rose from the bays, the rolling plains and high western ridges of Massachusetts. Back in the days before the Sugar Act—which
men could almost look back upon as the good old days—the Assembly had
drafted a stinging protest to Parliament about the threatened duties. On
the advice of Sir Francis Bernard, royal governor, and his second-in-command, the brilliant, scholarly Thomas Hutchinson, they had toned their

protest down, being assured that a more violent one would only exasperate Parliament. Almost at once the Assembly and its constituents had experienced increasingly strong regret over that toning. Now they had their chance to show their real feelings and backed most of the Virginia Resolves, those that were quashed as well as those that were accepted.

But over and above this, they took a step that seems logical enough today, but in 1765 there was a magnificent daring about it. It was a step even farther-reaching than that of their Virginia colleagues and came as a direct result of it. The Massachusetts Assembly called for a congress of all the colonies to meet in New York and there to consider further measures.

Such an idea was not new. Benjamin Franklin had called again and again for such a gathering and a feeble one had even sputtered out an inglorious life during the French wars. In fact, the failure of that meeting may well have given Parliament the idea that colonial unity of purpose would be accomplished only in the Greek Kalends. But now the colonists were beginning vaguely to feel that common experience which goes to make a nation.

So the formal call went out, the agenda being most mildly set forth as the consideration "of a general and united, dutiful, loyal and humble Representation of their Condition to His Majesty and the Parliament: and implore Relief." The mention of the King before Parliament is significant. The colonies owed their existence and their charters—if they had charters—directly to the kings and queens of the past, not to the British legislature. Yet, with their backgrounds, they would not omit Parliament.

The response was surprising. Nine colonies named their delegates at once. New Hampshire declined but later endorsed the proceedings. No delegates came from Virginia, North Carolina, or Georgia, not from any reluctance on their part but because the royal governor in each case refused to summon the Assembly to name them. The governors of New Jersey and Delaware acted as did their colleagues to the south, but the assemblies stubbornly insisted on naming their delegates without official sanction or call.

Wall Street in New York City had been a busy place ever since the Dutch days, when it was marked by a wooden wall or palisade to protect the burghers of Nieuw Amsterdam from the Indian attacks that swept down from the wild tangles of middle and upper Manhattan Island. But never, in all its colorful days, had it seen such an assemblage as that which entered it in the early fall of 1765.

With gold- or silver-laced hats, with plain hats, in mulberry velvet or plum-colored or sky-blue coats or in more subdued broadcloth, the delegates walked or rode on flat saddles or in high-slung coaches, turning down the street's gentle slope just opposite Trinity Church. There were grassy banks ahead of them, the junction of Queen and State streets, and, down by the blue glint of the East River, the high bulk of the Tontine Coffee House with its tall, arched windows and graceful iron balconies. Nearby was the Merchants' Coffee House, from whose door one could look down the few feet that lay between it and the bristle of masts and spars surrounding Murray's Wharf. One by one the members of this bold Congress turned

in at the doors of the Town Hall, with its double portico and high entablature, halfway down Wall Street, on their left-hand side as they quitted
Broadway.

As they trooped into the great hall for the first meeting, tough-minded,
earnest Caesar Rodney of Delaware surveyed them appraisingly and summed
them up as "an Assembly of the Greatest Ability I ever Yet saw." Many of
the names have faded out of significance with the years, but plenty of
remembered heads, carefully dressed and powdered, bobbed above the
chairs as Rodney watched them. There was Timothy Ruggles of Massachusetts, who would later retreat to a position of "The Crown above everything" and go into exile for his credo. With him was James Otis, for the
moment a firm exponent of moderation. New York produced a couple of
Livingstons with their flavor of aristocracy, a Bayard, and a Lispenard.
There was Henry Ward from Rhode Island, Edward Tilghman from Maryland. South Carolina sent up the brilliant Christopher Gadsden and John
Rutledge.

The opening meeting dealt largely with organization. It is probable that
the sparkling but unstable James Otis hoped to be elected to the chair. But
this was a conservative gathering, at least at the start, and the past had
touched him with a lingering suspicion of radicalism despite his present
frame of mind. In the end, his colleague, Timothy Ruggles, was elevated
to the chair, a move that seemed to doom any chance of outspoken resolutions on the part of this fledging Congress. Ruggles' original nomination as
delegate had been brought about by fussy, nervous Sir Francis Bernard,
whose secret instructions to Ruggles would have shocked many of the
Congress: to induce the Congress to vote submission to the Stamp Act,
holding out as bait a pixie hope of later repeal.

So Ruggles took the chair, the meeting adjourned, and the delegates
scattered to stroll down Broadway toward the Battery, where they could
admire or look disapprovingly at the Georgian elegance of the houses facing
the ancient Bowling Green. There was the Livingston mansion, the Van
Cortlandts', the house of John Watts, soon to be first president of the
Society of the New York Hospital flourishing today, the Stevens', and
Archibald Kennedy's, which proudly bore the number 1 Broadway. Those
with a horse or carriage at their disposal might drive out into the country,
as far as St. George's Square, to marvel at the Holland-brick-and-brownstone
wonder of William Walton's three-story palace.

The work of the Congress went briskly on as October deepened and the
North River reflected the golds and oranges and the blood reds of the
autumn-touched palisades. Men of a far different temper from that of the
arch-conservative chairman, Timothy Ruggles, swung into action and a new
note was struck by Christopher Gadsden. Seeing that many delegates were
prone to move only as it affected the particular charter of the colony in
question, he called out that people should not think so much about specific
and widely differing charters, particularly as some colonies had no such
source of being. The delegates must close ranks, they must "stand on the

broad and common ground of natural and inherent rights . . . as men and descendants of Englishmen. . . . *There ought to be no New England men, no New Yorker and so on, but all of us Americans.*"

At last a Declaration of Rights and Grievances was produced, largely the work of the Pennsylvania delegate, John Dickinson, its fourteen articles stating firmly but politely that the colonies were not represented; that, unrepresented, they could not be taxed; that the colonies alone could lay taxes on themselves. In view of the feeling of the times, this was a moderate enough statement of belief, but at least the Congress, speaking not for just one section or one group, had flashed a red light of warning to Parliament, had drawn an unmistakable stop line. And for the first time they had formulated a theory of the rights of man, not of an Englishman alone.

The delegates scattered to their homes, having acted together and as officially as possible. The pen strokes on their declaration had released a force that would gather in volume and in power. But other media were setting swift currents in motion, currents that could move far more smoothly than ever before.

The postal system with its post roads and postriders, over which Benjamin Franklin and others had worked so long and so fruitfully, had shrunk the whole Atlantic coast line, had brought the inland farm and market town closer to the seaports. Men were writing to each other without regard for colony boundaries. They wrote on business, they wrote socially, they wrote as members of various organizations and clubs, from trivial to deeply philosophical. And as they could write in those channels, so they could and did write politically—whole letters on the current scene, or a hasty, hot paragraph at the end of a letter dealing with a consignment of books from Boston to New York, or a cargo of iron ore from Pennsylvania to Rhode Island. Men traveled more and more, and already South Carolinians were beginning to summer at Newport in Rhode Island to avoid the deadly coastal fevers along the Ashley or the Congaree. And all this writing and all this travel sped the spoken word as well as the written. A whisper under the low beams of the Green Dragon in Boston might be discussed in Fraunces' Tavern in New York no less than five days later.

Then there was the press, its influence widening and widening as new roads and new organization of postal services spread its range from a given town to a township, to a county, to another, a dozen other colonies. There were *Gazettes* and *Mercuries, Journals, Post-boys,* and *News-letters* that carried accounts of debates in assemblies, pronouncements of governors and mayors, letters, often unbelievably scurrilous, to the editors, accounts of shipwrecks, murders, fires, and always editorials, pungent and free-swinging to a degree scarcely credible today. And belatedly but of great importance, many British journals followed the routes of their colonial counterparts, and in distant corners of America men could read of parliamentary debates, of doings in the Old Country, could frown over indignant or conciliatory or puzzled letters to British editors. Americans could note the proprietary air with which many Britons spoke of "our" colonies, or they could chuckle, perhaps a little sourly, over the bewilderment of one Englishman who, surveying the new empire from India to North America, wrote plaintively that the Americans were "of a disposition haughty and insolent, impatient of rule, disdaining subjection and by all means affecting independence," and contrasting this frame of mind with other colonials, "the remarkably pliant and submissive disposition of the inhabitants of Bengal," seemingly to the advantage of the Bengali.

And along with the press flourished an endless white blizzard of handbills, "throwaways" that spread protests, violent lampoons, cries of alarm, of scorn, of justification over the country, and were to accomplish, in a smaller way, for the politician what a few minutes of radio time or television glitter do today. These single sheets, often bearing crude cartoons, screeched warnings against the Sugar Act, the stamp tax, the sins of customs officers; they were used for matters local as well as general and were remarkably effective.

And there were the mobs, just beginning to stir into life or to have life breathed into them. Some came into being on the heat of the times; others were there, ready to hand and needing only organization. There was Boston, for instance.

For years the men and the youths of the South End of Boston had dropped all work on the fifth of November to celebrate Guy Fawkes Day or, as it came to be known, Pope Day. The South Enders, in ceremonial that grew over the years, trundled forth from their corner of Boston a vast, heavy cart laden with fantastic dummies of a pope with a great number of satanic attendants. Howling and bellowing, the South Enders set out, rolling their juggernaut over the clanging cobbles, came up through the city with frequent halts to pass around jugs of rum or to tap barrels of beer. When they reached a point somewhere below the present North Station, the South Enders met, as though by agreement, a similar joyously bawling cortege manned by the hated North Enders. There was always a collision, followed by an utterly unrestrained Donnybrook in which each side, well drilled and organized, fought to destroy or capture the opposing pope's figure. It is likely that all significance of Guy Fawkes or the symbolism of the dummies was quite lost to sight, providing merely an excuse for a glorious free-for-all which ended only when the huge puppets were taken by one side or the other. It was, for eighteenth-century Boston, a World Series, a Rose Bowl game, a heavyweight title match rolled into one.

Sometime during the years that simmered slowly on to their eventual boil, astute, Harvard-bred Samuel Adams, with his palsied head and hands, considered the Pope Day brawls and the organization of the contestants. If only they could be brought together, controlled by a wise, shrewd mind, what a weapon the combined mobs would make for the underscoring of some strong, popular wish—or at least popular in the mind of Samuel Adams. By some alchemy of his own he approached the leaders of the two gangs, and North and South shook hands and became one. They made a formidable body, since they were made up, in addition to a certain unavoidable amount of riffraff, of reasonably solid citizens—butchers, artisans, men from the ropewalks, apprentices, mechanics, small merchants and shop-keepers, mostly highly employable people with a respectable level of intelli-gence. But there was another element, not so apparent in this mob. Often dressed like silversmiths or clerks or flax teasers, sometimes with their faces blacked, men of much higher economic and cultural levels sank into the anonymity of the mass and moved with it.

Other mobs would appear in Rhode Island, New York, Delaware, right down to Georgia, functioning with varying degrees of skill and organization and with comparable personnel, but usually lacking the characteristic co-hesiveness of the Bostonians. They were all produced by the same tensions, the same fears that had started with the earliest whispers of the Sugar Act, with the first hints that what people believed to be colonial rights were, in parliamentary eyes, only revocable privileges. Shoulder to shoulder with the assemblies, with that first tottering Congress, the people of the colonies, too, were standing close together.

The Stamp Act, while passed, was not to take effect until November 1, 1765, and in the interim the machinery to set it in motion had to be assem-bled, the official stamped forms sent across the Atlantic, and stamp officers appointed to distribute the forms and collect the resultant fees. This last item appeared like a toothsome political plum, and there were many appli-cants for the posts at first. But in the slow, uneasy months that lay between the passage of the act and the meeting of that first colonial Congress, the American coast and hinterland seethed and whirled like a shaken bottle of soda water.

The first stamp officers were named and the cap was snapped from the bottle top, fresh effervescence being added by the news that swift packets were bringing reams of stamped paper. In August the Boston mob moved and Andrew Oliver, named stamp officer by Bernard, found himself be-sieged in his house while window glass shattered and solid doors rocked on their hinges. Lucky to escape without severe personal injury, Oliver re-signed. The mob had probably gone much further in its demonstration than Samuel Adams and other leaders wished, but the mob temper was conceivably heated beyond control by the fact that Oliver was the brother-in-law of Lieutenant Governor Thomas Hutchinson, who in the eyes of many seemed bent on turning Massachusetts into a neat little preserve to be administered by—and for—himself, heirs, assigns, and relatives. Again, in the same month, the mob got worse out of hand, burned the records of the Vice-Admiralty Court—thereby effectively disposing of records of tolerated smuggling in the past which might crop up unpleasantly in the present and future—and moved north to Thomas Hutchinson's magnificent house. This they wrecked with a certain hilarious thoroughness, emptying the wine cellar, ruining the library, and scattering Hutchinson's invaluable manu-script history of Massachusetts through the alleys and side streets of Boston. The act was indefensible, barbaric, and cruel. Thomas Hutchinson had

written and spoken fiercely against the Sugar Act and the Stamp Act—and
the people for whom he spoke gutted his town house. Perhaps outweighing
his defense of the colonists was the fear, mentioned before, that the
scholarly man was aiming for family control of the colony, anticipating a
pattern that was to be set by his ilk in later generations in Upper Canada,
the tight control of all life by a group known as the Family Compact. Its
reign, too, would produce its Canadian Samuel Adams, in the person of
William Lyon Mackenzie, lead to Revolution and, by very slow and more
peaceful stages, to the virtual independence of Canada.

This Bostonian outburst seemed to presage an overthrow of law and order.
Instead, it marked the only times that the Boston mob got seriously out of
hand. The mob would demonstrate, threaten, and, having made its point,
melt away. Its doings were bad enough, but, as Esther Forbes has pointed
out in her superb study of Paul Revere and his time, the Boston mob—and
indeed all American mobs—was merely playful compared to the fearful
destruction of property and loss of life in England during the Gordon Riots
of 1780, with London in the hands of a mob for three long days. And of
course there is no comparison with the wreckage and bloodshed of the
French Revolution.

But Boston was by no means unique. As November came on, New York,
still tingling with the excitement of the now-adjourned Congress, began to
rumble ominously. The first day of the month, with the Stamp Act officially
operative, dawned like a day of mourning, angry mourning. The Merchants'
Coffee House down there near the foot of Wall Street was crape-hung, even
to its dice boxes. Many offices did not open and merchants and traders
wandered the streets, muttering uneasily. Out in the East River, in the
North, down in the Lower Bay, and off the low green dome of Staten Island,
ships lay with their colors lowered. The sun set and a dull murmur crept up
to the fading skies. A mob was gathering on the Common, today's City Hall
Park.

They came in dozens and scores, up from Coenties Slip, from Church
Street, from the Fresh Water far uptown, from the tan yards and Cortlandt
Street and the foundry up beyond Ranelagh Gardens. There were black-
smiths and cartwrights, teamsters, tavernkeepers, barbers, sailors, though
the hands of many others would not suggest close acquaintance with sledge,
maul, turnspit, or tarred rope. In the flare of torches and lanterns they began
building a mock gallows mounted on a cart. From some mysterious source
an effigy of the acting governor, old Cadwallader Colden—correspondent of
Linnaeus, Franklin, and Dr. Samuel Johnson—appeared and was hoisted
onto the gallows, clutching a facsimile sheet of stamped paper. A fearful
devil, suggestive of the Boston Pope Day effigies, was hauled up beside the
sham Colden.

There was a dull roar from Broadway and another crowd poured onto the
Common, trundling the gilded magnificence of Colden's coach, topped by
another image of the unfortunate and well-meaning lieutenant governor.
The mobs merged and set off with coach and gallows, now lantern-hung,

making a fearful din as they headed for Fort George, about where the old Aquarium used to stand.

Colden had shut himself up in the fort, clutching the stamped paper that had just arrived, since the captain of the ship *Coventry*, which had brought the stamps, did not dare keep them in his own custody. He heard the mob and the rumble of wheels pouring down past the Bowling Green, but he could feel reasonably secure for the present. Fort George had stout walls and was manned by over one hundred and eighty men in the trim blue and red of the Royal Artillery, whose mounted guns covered the inland approaches as well as the harbor.

The mob ought to have been brought up short. Instead, it acted most illogically. Fanning out over the great expanse of the Battery, it swept up to the gates of the fort, pounded them with heavy timbers, showered rocks and bricks on the parapets, and dared the garrison to fire. Major James, commanding the garrison, appeared on the walls, and the mob remembered his public statement that he would cram the stamps down the throats of the colonists if necessary, or words to that effect. There was a fresh surge forward, and the gunners at the pieces began nervously waving their everburning slow matches to coax a steady spark from them. An assault that could end only in slaughter seemed inevitable.

Then shadowy men began moving along the tattered front of the mob, pushing, shoving, butting, giving whispered commands, and the great wave fell back sullenly from the walls of Fort George and its mercifully silent guns. There was a sudden rush toward wooden-fenced Bowling Green. Posts and pickets came down, were heaped about the vice-gubernatorial coach, and soon high flames danced in the mouth of Broadway, were dimly picked up by the ruffled waters of New York Harbor. Coach, cart, and effigies crumbled slowly into ashes.

Part of the mob broke away and pelted uptown, making for the big house that Major James had leased overlooking the North River, somewhere between present Chambers and Warren streets. As though a blueprint had been sent them by their Boston colleagues, they proceeded methodically and cheerfully to take the James mansion apart, in savage acknowledgment of his high-handed threats about stamped paper. They drank up his liquor joyously, battered in doors, smashed fine furniture in wanton vandalism, shattered the windows, had a rare scrimmage in the library among good books, maps, and mathematical instruments, and ripped open feather beds. Not satisfied with their work on the house, some members rushed whooping into the broad gardens, ruined the perennials carefully sheathed for the winter, and heaved the summerhouses into the North River. Then, by two o'clock in the morning, the mob broke up and scattered, some of its members grimly aware of a righteous purpose accomplished, some cooling into jittery apprehension of what had been done and what might follow as retribution, some gloating happily over a most exciting night's work.

Cadwallader Colden was profoundly shaken by the demonstration. Still more so was the legally appointed stamp tax distributor. With the echoes of the torchlit night and the roar of the mob still in his ears, he hastily sent in his resignation to Colden, adding, understandably enough, "I find it will be attended with the greatest risk to my person and future . . . to execute the office. If I attempted it, my house would have been pillaged, my person abused."

This whole pattern, in varying degrees of intensity, was repeated in nearly every colony. In Charleston, South Carolina, the Battery, Exchange Street, Tradd Street, Broad Street echoed to the tramp of a mob that invaded several houses, including that of Colonel Henry Laurens. Much threatening talk was heard, weapons were brandished, a heart-warming volume of liquor flowed, but there was relatively little damage done. In Rhode Island there was some hacking and smashing and here, as in many other colonies, stamp officials, real or suspected, had little trouble in recognizing friends, business partners, relatives, marching under the thin disguise of hastily blackened hands or faces, a teamster's smock or a smith's apron.

So the mobs came into being, were to be a very heavy factor in the years to come as well as in the present. Their leadership and membership might vary a little in type, depending on the part of the country that produced them and the particular kinds of wrongs, real or imagined, that threatened. But they had a name in common that would outlast their organizations and the need for them. America's friend, Colonel Isaac Barré, rising in Parliament to defend the colonists against ministerial blasts, called them Sons of Liberty and the term stuck tight to the less conservative, whose fullest expression lay in the mobs.

Up and down the ladder whose steps climbed from the misty Altamaha in Georgia to the churning Maine coast, a line was becoming slowly evident. It did not mark off those who opposed the Sugar and Stamp Acts from those who supported them. In fact, there were relatively few of the latter. Cleavage was coming between those who opposed the acts but would bow, if sadly, to the will of Parliament and those who were determined that they should not be put into effect, who would fight them by fair means if possible, à outrance if necessary. And by the acts they meant, of course, the right of Parliament to tax. Let that be established just once, and any British government could extend its rule logically and by precedent into every phase of life. Charter guarantees would become worthless and the colonies might then sag back into the status of strictly regulated trading posts, a role which many in England honestly felt was the most that the transatlantic possessions ought to play.

So as 1765 ended and prepared to give way to 1766 the Stamp Act was a matter of law, but hardly anywhere did a local government dare bring out the stamped paper. Since the provisions of the act reached deep into colonial life, a sort of paralysis set in. Courts could not act for lack of stamped sheets. Ships could not be cleared or admitted. Deeds, wills, powers of attorney remained mere unofficial documents and, legally, no one was born and no one died.

Various subterfuges were employed. A judge who did not cling to the letter of the law might allow a will to be probated if accompanied by a sworn statement that the proper stamped forms were not available, which they certainly were not. Of course this involved a double risk since the sworn statement, if not on stamped paper, was of itself invalid. Ships were cleared here and there, possibly following Virginia's lead in allowing such sailing on the strength of a mere statement by the port officials that stamps could not be provided. It was a hazardous, mischancy state of affairs, for there was no telling how the next royal officer would view the absence of stamped paper. He might not honor the sworn statements or certificates. And who could tell how a will executed after November 1, 1765, would be regarded ten or twenty years hence? But business went on somehow. Courts functioned without stamps. Ships were cleared, stampless, and cargoes were bonded. However, such activity was unhealthy, abnormal, similar to the muscular reflexes of a fresh-killed animal.

The colonies stirred uneasily, restlessly, and wondered what the future held. The earlier, fumbling move toward a boycott, a non-importation agreement, caught fire as though by spontaneous combustion. Instead of Philadelphia firemen doing without mutton and imported beer or merchants wagging their fingers at Boston girls and urging them to shun "gaudy, butterfly, vain and expensive Dresses" in favor of homespun, the merchants of the Northern colonies presented an unexpectedly solid front. Nearly nine hundred businessmen, from Boston clear down to Philadelphia, banded together to import nothing more from Great Britain until the Stamp Act and the Sugar Act were repealed. Actually, the agreement was a very shaky structure. There was no way of enforcing the pact, nor even of observing whether signatories lived up to it. Some merchants undoubtedly came in under pressure or through fear of the mobs, and such would be the first to find loopholes through which British goods could be slipped. Others, faced by bankruptcy, would be forced to hedge or go under. But as an expression of general determination and feeling, the agreement was an impressive one. British merchants, in particular, felt a very real threat and began to mutter and grumble ominously, and their grumbles reached into Parliament.

There was good cause for alarm in mercantile England. The next annual governmental accounting would show a decrease of nearly 50 per cent in the American trade, and the symptoms that were forecasting such a loss set a move for repeal rolling down the corridors of the Houses of Parliament long before the Stamp Act was to take effect. And the setting was ripe for repeal.

During the turbulent summer of 1765, the Gentle Shepherd lost his flock and his party was out of power. In his place came the Marquis of Rockingham and, with William Pitt's leadership in the House, the question of repeal was trundled out. Colonial agents, British merchants, members of the old opposition worked valiantly, with Benjamin Franklin dealing some very effective blows. The act, so hated by the colonies, was killed and the news of that killing reached the shores of the New World during the late spring of 1766.

Oddly enough, the very real relief which the colonists felt was expressed with a startling moderation. Along the Battery in Charleston, in the Virginia House of Burgesses at Williamsburg, up and down Brandywine Creek in Delaware, by the Mohawk River, and in Massachusetts' Berkshire Hills the general temper seemed to be one of quiet contentment. True, the sheriff of Falmouth—now Portland, Maine—after discussing repeal in several homes and taverns, became so exalted that he rode his horse up the stairs and into the Town House, but the tempo of the day was made manifest when other celebrants sternly clapped him into the town stocks, there to meditate on the dignity of his high office.

The slow beat of the country's joy may have been due to suspicion, which would later be confirmed, that the chief reason that Pitt and the others had managed to get the repeal through lay not in any recognition of the colonists' claims. Rather, it was due to the obvious fact that, to enforce the act a sizable army would have to be shipped overseas by the Crown. There was also another bit of parliamentary however-ing wrapped up in the same package with repeal. Despite the repeated statements of Pitt and his close supporters that England could not tax the colonies, a substantial majority firmly down-planted its buckled shoes and announced in what was called "A Declaratory Act" that that right had always existed, existed now, and would always exist. And the statement was made in such clear terms that even the mildest of colonial viewers-with-alarm was sobered as effectively as the stocks had sobered the Falmouth sheriff.

The slow months of 1766 rolled by and in the late summer a ripple of increasing hope passed gently over the colonies. Their friend, William Pitt, was called upon to form a ministry to take the place of Rockingham's, and as Parliament assembled for another session the colonists and their adherents and backers held their breaths. There was a moment of disappointment when Pitt was offered, and accepted, the Earldom of Chatham. Men who had hailed him fulsomely as "the American Moses," "Guardian Angel of British Liberty," and "the Wonder of the World" took another quick look at their hero and began hedging craftily. They said that the peerage was a bribe to sell out the colonies, that "no girl could shew more impatience for a new toy than did he for a title." They wailed that he had sunk into the peerage.

Nevertheless, the new ministry quickly produced modifications of the so-called Sugar Act, concerning which, it will be recalled, the colonists did not challenge generally as a matter of right. The threepence-a-gallon duty on molasses was cut to one penny and took in British as well as foreign molasses. Rhode Island's thirty-odd distilleries could give off rum fumes to their hearts' content. Export duties on sugar shipped to the colonies from the West Indies were canceled, thereby making the commodity cheaper for the consumer. There was, unfortunately, a damper to these last moves as there had been for the Stamp Act repeal. Most goods exported from the colonies to northern Europe now had to clear through British ports, thereby cutting heavily into the shippers' margin of profit.

There was also an ominous rumble-bumble from New York, British military headquarters. Under a law known as the Mutiny Act, the colonists might be forced to pay for the upkeep of British troops, like those now quartered on Manhattan Island. Invoking that act, Governor Moore, who had taken over from Cadwallader Colden, called on the New York Assembly for several thousand pounds, covering rations, heat, light, and so on, for the troops.

The Assembly cast an agonized look about and then went into a tantrum. For one thing, the members felt that their colony was being mulcted for the entire cost of a force that was designed to protect the other twelve as well. Furthermore, if the sum should be voted, and repeated year after year, it would amount to a tax levied without colonial assent. The amount could be increased at the pleasure of the governor until the colonies could, in theory, be forced to carry the load of the entire British Army. And if the army, why not the navy? As Rhode Island had icily refrained from taking any action in connection with the stamp tax, so the New Yorkers stubbornly sat on their hands and let the demand pass by in silence.

It is possible that had Pitt's health held out, he might have been able to smooth over such rough spots as the onerous provisions of the amended Sugar Act and of the Mutiny Act. It is doubtful, however, for despite his other outstanding virtues, Pitt did not shine as a politician. His reign through most of the Seven Years' War was due to the fact that the crisis was so great that Parliament did not dare challenge him. Now matters stood very differently. Pitt began to suffer so much from the gout, a highly fashionable ailment at that time, that by the end of 1766 the real running of affairs lay in the hands of Charles Townshend, Chancellor of the Exchequer, and the slope down which Anglo-American relations had been skidding grew steeper and steeper. The Townshend Acts were hovering just over the edge of the new year.

CHAPTER III

". . . that rash and hasty proceeding"

CHARLES TOWNSHEND was an able, gifted politician who had changed sides so successfully and consistently through various governments that he was known as "the Weathercock."

Like his predecessors, he turned his quick eye on the colonies, where he also had another problem, that of disciplining the New York Assembly for its maddeningly obstinate refusal to take any action whatsoever on the demand for financial support for the garrison.

Quipping, laughing, turning out neat phrases as a hand plane rolls out graceful shavings, Townshend minced his way through committees, through the Cabinet, and finally came up with what seemed to him to be an ideal solution. He had noted that in the past the colonial opposition to revenue measures had stemmed from a violent objection to Parliament's levying internal taxes. Knowingly or not, he skidded gracefully over the fact that the colonies had picked on internal taxes to avoid a direct challenge to parliamentary rights, and proposed external taxes to be levied on certain imports the colonies received from England. They were innocent items enough—glass, lead, paints, paper, and tea. As to the insufferable New Yorkers, it must be noted to Townshend's credit that he fought off a strong faction headed by the Duke of Bedford, which clamored for the full use of the British Army and Navy to bring that impertinent colony to its senses. Instead, he sponsored a measure that merely suspended the New York Assembly until it should comply with the demand for funds.

It has been said that the British Empire was acquired in a moment of absent-mindedness. The loss of a large part of that empire would be due to that same amiable failing. The new duties, known under the collective name of the Townshend Acts, glided past the sleeping sentries of the opposition and became law. Townshend was undoubtedly helped by an understandable feeling on the part of many members that the colonies ought to be cuffed about a bit for their attitude toward the Stamp Act and similar benevolent measures and to underscore those parliamentary rights that had been formally stated in the Declaratory Act of the year before.

At first glance the Townshend Acts, which were to take effect in November, were curiously mild—if one forgot the conviction of the colonies that they were unconstitutional. A stiff duty on paper might have been irksome. Certainly a great deal of tea was being drunk, although a tax on it could be largely disregarded since tea from Holland was brought in so openly that it could hardly be called smuggling. The other items could be shrugged off.

And what about the New York Assembly? Its suspension caused a quick wave of alarm, which died away when the New Yorkers grudgingly approved the grant of a sum rather less than had been called for and worded their approval so deftly that the money seemed to come from the spontaneous generosity of a warmhearted colony rather than as a dutiful answer to the mother country.

But there was far more to the Townshend Acts than a mere levying of duty, even if the colonists were ready to agree to Parliament's right to tax, which they emphatically and increasingly were not. In this bill and in a companion measure, several hobgoblins were rushed out of dark closets and set up in full view.

The hated Writs of Assistance, those blank search warrants against which James Otis had fought so hard at the beginning of the decade, were dusted off and strongly reaffirmed. New vice-admiralty courts were established, thereby toughening up some of the provisions of the Sugar Act. Frightening to most merchants and especially to those of New England, an American Board of the Commissioners of the Customs, and directly responsible to the Royal Treasury, was to be set up in Boston. This last measure was

looked upon, in memory of past riots, with an understandable lack of enthusiasm by some Englishmen, one of them writing sourly that it was an
admirable step, assuming that the commissioners were not hanged the
instant they landed.

Worst of all was the use to which money raised by the new duties was to
be put. Such funds could be used for the defense of the colonies, certainly
an all-embracing field, since keeping the colonists in order and in their
proper place could be considered as "defense." The funds could also be used
for "defraying the charge of the administration of justice, and the support
of the Civil Government." In other words, the import duties paid by the
colonists to the Crown would be used to pay the salaries of colonial officials,
thereby making that class quite independent of the people whom, in Anglo-
Saxon thought, they served. A man from Massachusetts or a man from
North Carolina did not have to be in any way a radical thinker to cast his
mind ahead and see the colonial assemblies reduced to petty debating
societies or abolished outright, to imagine colonial affairs run from London
and guided only by the advice of men paid by the Crown and hence anxious
to give such advice as would please their paymaster.

It was by no means illogical to look forward a few years and see local
affairs firmly in the grasp of a group of families and their allies, with the
colonies themselves fading away into mere trading posts profitable to the
few. The "big house on the hill" was clearly foreshadowed by the Townshend Acts, as it had been in earlier measures; a squirearchy, a government
by landed gentry. And for the others? Kipling's lines come at once to mind:

> An' 'ouses both sides of the street,
> An' 'edges two sides of the lane,
> And the parson an' gentry between,
> An' touchin' my 'at when we meet—
> Me that 'ave been what I've been?

If such fears seem farfetched today, it is only necessary to look back at
the pattern of life that started to form in Upper Canada through the first
quarter and more of the nineteenth century, when the Robinsons, the
Boltons, the Hagermans, the Strachans and the rest, mostly able, well-
intentioned men, fought to make a private preserve of their own from the
Ottawa River on to Toronto and the West. These men applauded the
appeal of their fatuous governor, Francis Bond Head, to "stamp out that
Hydra-headed monster, democracy." And virtually every mistake that was
made by both sides in 1760 and 1770 and beyond was repeated by both
sides along the north shore of Lake Ontario. There are few falser adages
than "Experientia docet."

Yet the year 1767 trailed from the future into the present and thence into
the past with far less bubbling and simmering than might have been expected. In South Carolina, which had flat-footedly stated that Parliament
had no right to tax the colonies, a golden glow of prosperity and amity

flooded the coastal lands. In the harbor of Charleston vessels crowded along the wharves or rocked at anchor out in the stream. Carolina indigo and rice were being shipped in torrents, the rice sacks being unloaded at ports all over the world. A new governor, Lord Charles Greville Montague, arrived from England and was greeted with illuminations. He inspected Captain Gadsden's chunky black guns on the Battery and reviewed the light infantry under Captain Thomas Savage. Graciously he accepted addresses of loyalty from the Charleston Library Society, the South Carolina Society, the leading merchants, and the clergy of the Church of England.

Later the Charlestonians elected Montague president of the Library Society and applauded heartily when he received a deputation of Cherokee chiefs. The *South Carolina Gazette* devoted much space to the performance of the eagle-tail dance by Attakullakulla, the Prince of Chote, Tiftoe of Keowee, and the Raven of Toogaloo. Later, detachments of the 60th Royal American Regiment, garrisoned at Charleston, joined with the militia light infantry and artillery to parade for the Cherokees, to the delight of the chiefs if not to the privates sweltering in woolen uniforms under a Carolina sun. There was much talk, too, about the coming winter's horse racing and the points of James Ravenel's filly, Harleston's and Mazyck's and Drayton's and Horry's entries. Peaceful, contented days and months could tick off their slow passage, it seemed, for an eternity.

Of course there were rumbles from the western highlands where for more than a decade a culture alien to that of the coastal planters had been filtering down from the north. These inland settlers, hardy and mostly poverty-stricken frontiersmen, had come south along the mountains from western Pennsylvania, Maryland, and Virginia, fearing that their original holdings lay wide open to Indian attacks after Braddock's defeat in 1755, and their ways and thought did not fit into the ways and thought of the planters. Trouble was brewing and would soon turn to violence. When the break with England finally came, these pioneer people would, in perverse violation of accepted history, largely side with the Crown while most of the coastal planters, the Church of England group, were to be found in blazing opposition. But all that, along with the races to be held at Strawberry or Newcastle, lay in the future.

There was quiet in Pennsylvania, too, where Speaker Joseph Galloway and the so-called Quaker clique tried to disassociate their colony from any opposition to the Crown, to maintain a sort of pre-Nehru-like neutrality. But in the uneasy hush, John Dickinson, trained, like Daniel Dulany, in London's Middle Temple, was turning his lawyer's mind to problems that would not die. In November of 1767 readers of the *Pennsylvania Chronicle* stared bug-eyed at the first of a series of some dozen or more essays, the product of Lawyer Dickinson's thoughts. They were headed *Letters from a Farmer in Pennsylvania to the Inhabitants of the British Colonies.* From the very start these essays, known as the "Farmer's Letters," were picked up by other publications and appeared in pamphlet form in England as well as in the colonies. Up and down the coast, in the back country, in Newport's

Redwood Library, in Fraunces' Tavern in New York, the Raleigh Tavern at Williamsburg in Virginia, in the Charleston Library Society, men grew red with approbation or rage, according to the turn of their minds, as they studied out Dickinson's rather dry, legal prose. The carefully drawn arguments said little that was new, but said it authoritatively and to an audience whose range would have been incredible a few years before. Men in all walks of life who might have been fumbling clumsily toward an expression of their thoughts could now quote Dickinson. They probably skipped over the weakest part of the text wherein the Pennsylvanian conceded Parliament's right to regulate trade even if such regulation brought revenue as a by-product. But they could thunder out the declarations that Parliament had no right to tax the colonies for revenue, that the Townshend Acts were glaringly unconstitutional, and that all colonial assemblies were under a death sentence from the precedent which Townshend's suspension of the New York Legislature established. Perhaps unwittingly Dickinson had pointed out that common experience which the colonists were sharing.

Dickinson wrote as an individual. But up to the northeast a mind less trained but far more impetuous was hammering out similar thoughts that would be presented for action and receive it. For in Boston, shabby, intense, palsied Samuel Adams was writing busily, conferring with the printers, Messrs. Edes and Gill, darting into the Bunch of Grapes or the Green Dragon, buttonholing his less impetuous cousin, John Adams, weaving through Boston's twisting streets for a word with James Otis or trying out a new thought on handsome young Dr. Joseph Warren, running squirrel-like down the spiral stairs of what is now called the Old State House.

As the autumn of 1767 wore on, the Weathercock veered for the last time and died, very likely thinking that the Townshend Acts had put the colonies in their place once for all. A new ministry was formed with Lord Hillsborough as Secretary of State for the Colonies, a spectacularly bad choice. George III was to say later that he never knew of a man of less judgment than Hillsborough, and Sam Adams, writing, talking, scurrying about Boston, was providing that nobleman with a glittering chance to do the wrong thing.

The fruits of Adams' work came before the Massachusetts Assembly in February 1768, were passed easily, and entered history as the Massachusetts Circular Letter. It's more than probable that Adams' thoughts were considerably toned down by his more conservative friends, for the Circular Letter was reasonably mild. In effect, it informed the assemblies of the other twelve colonies that Massachusetts denounced the Townshend Acts as violating the principle of taxation without representation; that colonial representation in Parliament was a physical impossibility; that any move by England to make colonial judges and governors independent of the people could not be tolerated. The letter ended with a call for proposals for united action.

Many Massachusetts conservatives approved the letter as being mild, respectful, entirely loyal, and a modest statement of the reaction of the colonies to the late acts. It met with strong support save in Pennsylvania, where Speaker Galloway jumped as though bees had settled under his knee buckles. It was bad enough, he thought, to have Dickinson writing the seditious "Farmer's Letters" under Galloway's loyal nose. It was worse when rich young John Hancock journeyed to Philadelphia to sit at Dickinson's feet. And now came the Massachusetts Circular Letter, which seemed to him a trumpet call to outright rebellion. What next? He supposed the next step would be the introduction of the damnable town meeting to Pennsylvania, creating an "American bedlam for mad Whigs." He accordingly arranged to have the letter tabled, to "run it up the lane" in later congressional parlance, burying it forever. He was successful, causing a coolness between the Pennsylvania Assembly and the assemblies of the other colonies which would die hard. In Massachusetts, Governor Sir Francis Bernard sputtered out cries of treason and sedition, his frenzy mounting to the point of dissolving the Assembly out of hand.

But the harshest cracklings came from the pen of Lord Hillsborough. Without consulting his colleagues, some of whom might have soothed him a little, he sent a stinging blast across the Atlantic. The Massachusetts letter was calculated "to promote an unwarrantable combination and to excite open opposition to the authority of Parliament." Metaphorically he thumped his ministerial desk and commanded all the colonial governors to order their respective assemblies to ignore the Massachusetts action. Any bodies that approved the letter were to be dissolved at once. As for Massachusetts, Hillsborough lashed out, no Bay State Assembly would ever do one scrap of business until it had obediently stated its "disapprobation of that rash and hasty proceeding."

This was the first implied threat of the use of force by the Crown, and the answering roar echoed from the White Mountains to the High Hills of Santee. Those assemblies that had not warmed toward the Massachusetts Circular Letter now came tumbling forward to endorse it and were promptly dissolved by their respective governors. Even in Pennsylvania the letter was rescued from oblivion, endorsed, while its governor wrote in exasperation that "those persons who were most moderate are now set in a flame and have joined the General Cry of Liberty." From Virginia a most loyal colonial soldier who had fought time and again against the French and Indians wrote of his shock at Hillsborough's ukase and stated simply that he, for one, was ready to take up arms to defend colonial liberties. He signed himself George Washington.

All in all, Hillsborough had turned the relatively mild Adams-sponsored letter into a hot rallying point that must have been beyond the wildest dreams of the writer and his radical friends up and down the colonies. The Boston *Evening Post* bugled that "the tighter the cord of unconstitutional power is drawn round this bundle of arrows, the firmer it will be."

So it was in a mounting flame of hope that the Massachusetts Assembly met in answer to Sir Francis Bernard's call to disavow their act that had started a conflagration. Sure of themselves, the legislators threw Bernard's order full in his face. By a vote of ninety-two to seventeen they refused all compliance. And the political careers of those who voted to obey the governor, the "Seventeen Rescinders," were virtually over, as most of them were overwhelmed at the next elections. Their defection was the subject of handbills and broadsides. Someone drew up a cartoon showing the seventeen descending into the flames of the pit, with the caption, "SEVENTEEN such Miscreants will surely startle Hell," and had it engraved by a young North End silversmith named Paul Revere, who had a crude knack of caricature.

Nonetheless, the provisions of the Townshend Acts went into effect. Every effort was made to tighten up the customs, and most of those efforts seemed to show a remarkable ingenuity on the part of the Crown in doing things the wrong way. The port collectors were appointed from those men who basked in the favor of the royal governors, like Charles Paxton in Boston and Ebenezer Richardson in Philadelphia. Such appointments lacked the one thing that would have made them work—popular support. Then, most exasperatingly, a swarm of minor clerks, many of them Scots, were sent out to replace veterans with whom merchants had long since reached an understanding. The merchants did not object to Scots as such but to the fact that the young men seemed not only able but willing to live on their salaries and hence were poor prospects for bribery. The *Massachusetts Spy* called the whole customs personnel "a Troop of Cossacks."

The importance of popular support for the collectors was shown in April of 1768 when the ship *Lydia* berthed at Hancock's Wharf not far from the Old North Church. On the more than logical suspicion that there was contraband on board, two minor customs officers boarded her. Her owner, young John Hancock, possibly refreshed in spirit from his draughts of Dickinson's wisdom, came to the wharf and ordered his skipper not to let the customs men go below decks. Frightened, the officers left, but one of them returned during the night and managed to get below.

Amiable John Hancock was popular with his tenants living on or near the wharf, and one or more of them must have sent word to the big house up on the north side of Boston Common. Hancock came at once, probably via present Tremont Street to Dock Square to Ann Street and thus to Fish Street and the wharf. Accompanied by a dozen or so powerful young men, he boarded the *Lydia* and demanded to see the officer's credentials. The Hancock luck held good and young John was able to spot a technical omission in the warrant which, legally, nullified it. Whereupon he ordered the mate and the boatswain to hustle the poor man above decks, whence, with his heart surely in his mouth, he fled to the safety of the land. This was the first act of violence, though a mild one, against the Crown, and no shipowner would have dared it had he not been very sure of heavy popular support.

John Hancock was eventually called into court, and such was the fear of the Hancock wealth and, more important, of the citizenry of Boston, that he was let off with a light reprimand. But there was more to come. In May the ship *Liberty* docked at Mr. Hancock's wharf, out of Madeira with a good cargo of wine. The customs declaration that listed a mere score or so of kegs was certainly a masterpiece of New England understatement. A minor official later went on board, was discovered by the skipper and a select crew of muscle men, and was at once hustled below to an innocuous part of the ship and the companionway nailed up against his possible escape. Then the skipper blandly proceeded to unload the undeclared portion of the cargo. When the officer was finally released, he was so terrified that he decided to say nothing of the endless clank and clatter of unloading machinery to which he had listened while a prisoner.

In a few days' time, while the *Liberty* was loading for another happy and prosperous cruise, His Majesty's Frigate *Romney*, fifty guns, appeared in Boston Harbor. The customs official found that his heart had changed and at once told what he believed to be true, and which was true, about the rest of the Madeira. Benjamin Hallowell, comptroller of customs, appealed to the skipper of the *Romney*, a tough old sundowner named John Corner. Corner had been in Boston before, it seems, and had endeared himself to the townsfolk by snapping up likely-looking young Bostonians and impressing them into the service of the Royal Navy. Likewise he stated with a deplorable lack of tact that Boston was "a blackguard Town and ruled by mobs . . . and by the eternal God I will make their hearts ache before I leave."

The next step in his popularity campaign was to paint the broad arrow, already an ancient symbol of Crown ownership, on the *Liberty*. He then put a squad or so of Royal Marines aboard and moored her under *Romney's* guns. This process was somewhat impeded by a mob that gathered on Mr. Hancock's wharf and sent showers of rocks and bricks thudding and booming onto the *Liberty's* decks. In a rage, tough old Corner ordered the marines to fire and surprisingly, as well as luckily, they refused.

Balked in their attempt to halt the seizure of the *Liberty*, the mob of sailors and townspeople turned their thoughts inland and set off at full cry, chivvying Hallowell and his brother through the streets and ending by sending the Hallowell window glass streetward in a most satisfying clatter. The Hallowells fled aboard the *Romney* with most of their staff and finally refugeed behind the walls of Castle William in the harbor. The mob took counsel with itself and then some sharp-eyed member noted gleefully that the collector's official barge was still at the wharf. The barge was hauled out of the water, trundled and manhandled up past the Old State House, past King's Chapel and onto the Common, where in full sight of John Hancock's front windows on Beacon Street it was burned to the sounds of hearty, if untuneful, rejoicing.

Of course proceedings against Hancock reached England, and the King's Advocate recommended that an unmerciful total of one hundred thousand pounds be levied against the young merchant. To cast ahead a little, the case dragged and dragged. John Adams defended Hancock and in 1769 Attorney General Sewell, possibly with an understandable sigh of relief, announced that "Our Sovereign Lord the King will prosecute no further hereon."

The *Lydia* and *Liberty* actions should have been as sharp a warning to the Crown as were the responses of the various colonies to the Massachusetts Circular Letter. It is clear that no Crown officer could have prevailed against Hancock. Such dignitaries were learning the power of the mobs and feared that power. A customs chief, a Crown attorney could reason that, given the same conditions, New York or New Haven or Philadelphia or Wilmington in Delaware or Charleston in South Carolina would have reacted pretty much as had Boston. And they also knew that the word "mob" did not mean a roaring, bedraggled crowd of unemployable goons.

There was one simple answer to all these perplexities. The most prominent of the opposition leaders were well known. In fact, they had made no effort to work behind the scenes in stirring up violence, which in many cases went far beyond the wishes of great numbers of their associates. A royal official in Massachusetts could point at once to Sam Adams or to James Otis. In New York the spotlight played strong on Isaac Sears and Alexander McDougall. Caesar Rodney was a marked man in Delaware, though rather less radical than the others mentioned above. And there were Patrick Henry and Richard Henry Lee in Virginia, Christopher Gadsden and Thomas Lynch in South Carolina. In many twentieth-century countries a swift descent of Brown Shirts or Thought Police would have removed them at once, would have broken the mainsprings of dissension. Such raids could probably have been carried out in eighteenth-century Wilmington or Hartford. Gory and callous as the eighteenth century may appear in retrospect, no British government seems to have seriously weighed such steps. There would be no dragonnades in the Thirteen Colonies.

But a milder form of therapy was attempted by the Crown. As September 1768 faded, a mass of shipping was sighted off Nantasket Roads, maneuvering for the passage into Massachusetts Bay and Boston Harbor. The great flotilla worked on past the green islands of the bay, and Bostonians, lining beach or wharf, could see that the decks were bright with the scarlet coats of the British Army.

Platoon by platoon the troops were boated in, formed on the echoing stretches of the great Long Wharf. Bostonians who were wise in things military could recognize the pale buff facings of the 14th West Yorkshires, the yellow of the 29th Worcestershires, and, if they were particularly learned, could recall that both regiments had been conspicuous in the Low Countries under John Churchill, Duke of Marlborough, at the dawn of the century. There were also a few companies of the 59th East Lancashires and a strong detachment of the Royal Regiment of Artillery in their dark blue coats that set off their scarlet facings so well.

Drums beat, palms slapped against musket butts, the landing force wheeled and, with their field music shrilling out a quickstep, marched up past brick Merchants' Row, up King Street (now State), obliquing past the gable ends of the Old State House, and so to the Common.

Boston had seen royal troops often enough in the past. Then they had come to take the field against the French in the North and the West, usually under glitteringly incompetent commanders. The provincial troops had marched with them, fought with them, and died with them. This landing was different. The King's troops were here to act as a police force, to protect the King's officials in their usually sincere and honest efforts to carry out the orders sent them. Governor Bernard, nervous and fidgeting, defined their mission as rescuing the government and restoring the activity of the civil power against the Sons of Perdition, which was the term that he and many others used to denote the rather hysterical patriotism of some of the Sons of Liberty.

As for those Sons, they found their councils divided, once the last gunner or matross in blue and red had stepped ashore. There was a hurried meeting at the house of William Molineaux, a hardware dealer ruined—or so it was stated—by the oppressive acts of the past years. The son of a titled Dublin surgeon, Will Molineaux had worked up to the leadership of the toughest, least responsible segments of the Boston mob and undoubtedly roared on this occasion for a meeting of violence with violence. He may have remembered the comparative helplessness of the New York garrison during the Stamp Act troubles, forgetting that a handful of gunners cooped up in a New York fort could not be compared with the better part of three seasoned infantry regiments loose in a town and with a powerful fleet behind them. Had the ex-hardware dealer had his way, it seems likely that all but the most violent of the Sons would have fallen away from him and history might record the now incredible spectacle of Sam Adams, James Otis, Josiah Quincy, and Joseph Warren standing shoulder to shoulder with Sir Francis Bernard, Thomas Hutchinson, and Benjamin Hallowell.

But wiser counsel prevailed, probably through the efforts of Sam Adams, and a policy of passive disobedience was decided upon. But there were other ways in which the gentlemen of the 14th, the 29th, and the 59th could be shown just how they were regarded. The highly unpopular Quartering Act called upon any colony to provide billets for His Majesty's troops. Boston, hearing the call, merely sat on its municipal hands and looked glum. The senior colonel, Dalrymple of the 29th, had to move fast, since the day was wasting. His own regiment, alone of the landing force, had brought tents with it from Halifax, and these were pitched on the rolling slopes of the Common. Dalrymple buzzed angrily about Boston while the gunners and the men of the 14th and the 59th stood about in the usual apathy of waiting enlisted men. At last, to the horror of Boston, he forced his way into sacred Faneuil Hall and managed to get his men billeted there before dark. The next day he further offended the sensitive town by moving some of his men into the Old State House itself.

Then there was the matter of the troops themselves, that anonymous mass that would in other years be known as Tommies. Later we may take a look at how they were recruited, how they lived, and what they thought. For the moment it is enough to say that, as private soldiers, they were paid virtually nothing and, other than guard and going through the routine fatigues, they had little to do. Their officers, as in most armies of that era and well on into later years, paid no attention to the morale of their men. That would have been infra dig.

But various Bostonians noted the temper of the troops and acted accordingly. As they had tampered with the crews of His Majesty's ships, so they craftily approached the unwelcome garrison and very soon soldiers began to desert, nearly twoscore of them going over the hill in the first fortnight ashore.

Others hired themselves out for all sorts of menial tasks, glad of a copper or two for rum or tobacco or food to eke out their poor rations. As Boston had large numbers of unemployed citizens—which made mobs easier to raise—there was bitter resentment on the part of Boston laborers over the low wages for which the British were not only willing but anxious to work. A highly explosive situation was growing. Sentries were pelted with oyster shells. There were numerous fights. An occasional soldier was pitched into the Charles or into the harbor. Not even the Tories, whom they were supposed to protect, seem to have looked on the troops with favor. Thomas Hutchinson called them "generally bad fellows." For the malcontents James Otis resented the main guard placed in front of the Old State House, with cannon commanding the meeting place of the Assembly. In addition, he complained that the soldiers stank, a protest that would be repeated by Mrs. John Adams when viewing Brunswicker prisoners of war in Harvard Square.

This tension was a rare gift to Sam Adams, who wrung tears from his pen as he described the persecutions to which the Bostonians were subjected by these dreadful mercenaries. He was as indefatigable in writing as the small boys of Boston were in screeching "Bloody-back" or "Lobsters for sale" at "poor bloody Tommy."

This was not all one-sided, however, for the British soon found means of striking back. Through most of their history Bostonians had been used to come and go as they pleased. Now if Dr. Joseph Warren spent an evening at the Bunch of Grapes, or if Merchant John Rowe were detained past sundown at his countinghouse, they could be, and usually were, challenged by gruff, unsympathetic sentries, forced to identify themselves and state why they were out so late. Indignant young officers and perhaps a few seniors, resentful of the general attitude toward the garrison, took unholy delight in massing fifes and drums outside a church during service time. The most fiery sermon ever preached in Boston would have been drowned by the tweedling of fifes and sharp snapping of drums as the musicians blared out "Nancy Dawson" or "Yankee Doodle."

True to home-side custom, the officers cast about to enrich their sporting lives. There was probably a cricket pitch on the Common beyond the tents. And there was a racecourse laid out on that sacred ground, and to make sure that the greatest number of officers and men could be present to line the course and lay their bets, the races were scheduled for Sundays. Devout

members of the Boston churches raised such an outcry over this that the
Sunday races were reluctantly given up while the officers—the opinions and
feelings of the men hardly counted—cursed Boston piety and thought up
new ways of badgering their reluctant hosts.

General Thomas Gage, commander of all forces in North America, made
a flying trip to Boston, managed to get the troops safely if uncomfortably
quartered in old sail lofts, warehouses, sheds, before snow flew. An uneasy
peace settled over the town, broken only by such scuffles and collisions as
mentioned above. Sam Adams managed to keep the Sons of Liberty in good
order. There were few if any insults offered the royal officials. No Sons gathered about the Liberty Tree on present-day Washington Street, for any
such assembly would surely have brought out the garrison. What Adams
could not control was the feelings of the out-of-work dockmen and rope-
workers. No fiat of his could keep small Bostonians from whizzing snowballs at a grenadier's tall bearskin cap. The miracle is that, given the combination of resentful troops and a more than touchy town, blood did not
flow sooner over the Boston cobbles, particularly in view of the November
arrival of two more complete regiments, the 64th North Staffordshires and
the 65th Yorkshires and Lancashires. It is likely that British discipline
rather than Boston forbearance delayed any real clash.

Seventeen sixty-eight drew to a close. It had been a nagging, uneasy year,
and people watching its progress on both sides of the Atlantic found it difficult to assay. Observers who confined their researches to the ports and
their immediate hinterlands would have been partially justified in conclud-
ing that the merchants and their satellites constituted the only important
sore spots. And why not? Did not all the major swivets arise from taxes and
restrictions? How did such matters affect men in places like Worcester in
Massachusetts, Morristown in New Jersey, Skippack in Pennsylvania, or
Camden in South Carolina?

But men were profoundly affected far away from the ports and the customs houses and His Majesty's patrol boats. The taxes and restrictions,
often light in themselves, were looked upon as denials of certain basic rights
that touched everyone. The fact that they had been imposed strongly implied that they could be extended again and again until they reached the
most remote farmer in an upland clearing or a trapper feeling his way
through the dangerous forests of the Adirondacks.

And if such warnings were too ethereal for any but the most politically
sensitive, they were backed and strengthened by the spoken word, the
written word, and, perhaps most important of all, the printed word as manifested by newspapers, broadsides, and cartoons.

Editorially there was an astounding uniformity of feeling in the colonial
press. Dissent from the prevailing views was treated swiftly and harshly,
often violently, and in a way that seemed ominous for the future freedom
of the press. The Sons of Liberty did not care to spread their enlightened
mantle over any opposition Courier or Gazette. In Virginia the editor of
the Gazette, the correct Mr. Royle, who suppressed all mention of the Vir-

ginia Resolves, found himself unseated and the paper taken over as an organ of popular discontent. In Boston, Stationer John Mein fought for law and order through the columns of his *Chronicle*. Then, as the non-importation pacts were revived, he began craftily to publish attacks not on the non-importing merchants but on those patriot merchants who clung outwardly to the pacts and at the same time bootlegged legal cargoes into the port. This was too much. A mob moved on Mein's plant and he finally refugeed to England.

So the press, virtually untrammeled by opposition and often sternly disregarding truth, flooded the farmers of the interior of the country with awesome warnings. The merchant in the seaport was not really the man in peril. No. It was the farmer, the local miller or lumberman, and editors wept over his plight, and the coverage was limited only by communications and by the literacy of the hinterlands. The last does not seem to have been very important, since the spectacle of one learned man, local lawyer or schoolmaster, reading the weekly news and editorials to a gaping, rustic audience was persistent enough to flourish as a favorite subject down to Currier & Ives days.

Such word-of-mouth transmission of news and opinion undoubtedly formed a fruitful field for spectacular garbling. And yet many of the editorial arrows were so extreme that garbling could hardly sharpen their points. The Boston *Gazette* chittered like a treeful of squirrels. If a tax on merchandise went through unchallenged, only an idiot oaf in a hayfield could argue that a killing land tax was impossible. You think the land is yours? Well, the merchants thought their own property, their profits "fairly gained after many a Risque in their Trade," was theirs—and just look what happened to them. If Parliament could seize John Hancock's wharf or John Rowe's, of course they could move in on fields, barns, livestock, and harvest. Alexander Hamilton cast a sardonic eye on possibilities and wrote, "Perhaps before long your tables, chairs . . . knives, forks and everything else would be taxed. . . . Nay, I don't know but they would find means to tax you for every child you got and for every kiss your daughters received from their sweethearts." And Mr. Hamilton concluded slyly, "God knows *that* would ruin you."

It is very easy today to sum up all the verbal and written blasts as sheer demagoguery. Yet a well-read man in the America of the 1760s could shiver a little when he thought of the tax sources that prevailed on the Continent and in England, such as levies on each cottage window, on the hearth itself. Or there was Ireland to consider, bled white by taxes beyond the conception of the average American, by rents paid to absentee landlords almost equal to the yield of a given tract of land, and by commercial restrictions, rigidly enforced and strangling in effect. It was easy for a careless American to say, "It can't happen here." But it was increasingly difficult to believe it.

CHAPTER IV

Embers of Rebellion

IT was bright May in Virginia again as the year 1769 rolled back the
sleets and fogs of winter to make way for summer. Williamsburg's greens
were already lush and full against rose bricks, and in the House of Burgesses, where the anonymous Frenchman had watched with Thomas Jefferson, a tall, long-limbed member from Fairfax County asked for the floor and
the Speaker recognized Colonel George Washington, probably hoping that
the commander of the Virginia militia would bring up some uncontro-
versial point.

Mr. Speaker was toying with false hopes, for the colonel coolly but firmly
presented a set of resolves framed largely by his friend and fellow member,
George Mason. As afternoon sun sifted in through the high, arched windows and mellowed the paneling of the hall, Colonel Washington read
out the paragraphs in his full, fine voice and the rest of the House listened
appreciatively, nodding their powdered heads or tapping their feet in time
to the rich prose. The resolves were mild enough, since few people had
ever thought of the colonel as a firebrand like Patrick Henry and the Lees.
They restated the proposition that only Virginians could tax Virginians;
they added a new flavor to past actions by quietly denouncing the British
ministry for its hotheaded petulance in the matter of the Massachusetts
Circular Letter and the letters which had followed from other colonies, and
sounded one sharp warning against a proposal in England that a two-hun-
dred-year-old act be revived to allow the Crown to bring malcontents to
England for trial. Any member of the House could have drawn up a mental
slate of those who would be liable.

The member for Fairfax County finished his reading and resumed his
seat. The Speaker looked about uneasily, ready to recognize the first man
who would at least try to tone down the resolves, if he did not dare to
challenge the whole body of the document. Row by row the Burgesses sat
motionless and silent. When a reluctant vote was called for, they rose as a
man, and the wholehearted response of the House was probably far more
important, as a shadow coming out of the future, than the rather mild tenor
of the resolves themselves. Still more important was the choice of a man
to present them. The shadow of the future was growing stronger.

Lord Botetourt, the amiable, popular, and rather witless royal governor,
dissolved the Assembly the next day, possibly in the fear that more radical
measures would follow on Colonel Washington's speech. The members
drifted away to the Raleigh Tavern, clustered like a swarm of bees, and went
into informal session. There, unofficially but effectively, they voted to join

the Massachusetts merchants in a strict non-importation association. Colony after colony followed suit. Maryland, South Carolina, Georgia, North Carolina ranged themselves with their sister colonies. Others took less formal and sometimes weaker action, with Pennsylvania and, surprisingly, cantankerous New Hampshire alone dragging their feet.

A false calm settled over the country, broken only by occasional outbursts against Crown officers, volunteer spokesmen for the Crown, and against merchants suspected of clandestine receipt of banned British goods. These outbursts involved about everything from placarding the windows of suspects—"It is desired that the Sons and Daughters of LIBERTY, would not buy any one thing of him, for in doing so they will bring Disgrace upon themselves and their Posterity, for ever and ever, Amen"—to the familiar hustling, window smashing, and even tar-and-feathering, the last a hoary custom that has been traced back at least to the Crusades.

Through the Carolinas the heat lightning of growing trouble flickered along the great plateau that slanted southwest across both colonies, found answering flashes from the swampy coasts. The uplanders wanted courts, roads, schools, such as they had known in Virginia, Maryland, and Pennsylvania, and their tone grew uglier as they were denied them, in part by the planters but largely by the Crown officials, who were afraid of the watering down of sinecures through a spread in facilities. The absence of law bulked darkest in the gathering storm, for the highland people began taking it into their own hands and meting out their own hasty and rough justice. Along the coast men thought of these self-appointed guardians of the peace, these "Regulators," as they called themselves, as an even more immediate danger than parliamentary threats to civil rights.

Far away in the Boston area, people either snapped and yelped at the unwelcome royal garrison or beamed on it in smug approval as a sure shield against popular risings. But that smugness was not to last. Acting on some incredible logic of its own, the War Office suddenly transferred the two regiments that had come from Ireland, the 64th and the 65th, to foggy Halifax and its deep, hill-girt bay. Thus the Boston garrison was just strong enough to be a continued source of irritation and far too weak to be an effective force. And the irritation was by no means confined to Massachusetts Bay. Barring the small New York garrison and a detachment of the Royal American Regiment, the 60th, at Charleston, the only royal troops in the colonies were in Boston. But if they could be sent there, why not to Philadelphia or Williamsburg or Wilmington or the Cape Fear River?

The slow suspicious summer saw two highly frictional men removed from the scene. July brought unexpected orders for the immediate return to England of the increasingly irritable Sir Francis Bernard from the cool, high rooms of Province House, nearly opposite Boston's Old South Church. Sir Francis had not been a happy man for some time past, and in his anxiety to see the last of his troublesome charge he scampered down Long Wharf to his waiting ship, leaving his family, lares and penates to follow at a later date. Yet his relief at leaving must have been heavily tempered by disap-

pointment. He had hoped to climb high through his two colonial posts.
Now his grandiose plans for colonial reform were dead and his career was
over, and a far bigger, finer man, Lieutenant Governor Thomas Hutchinson, presided at Province House in his place.

The second removal involved the opposition. Able, stormy, bitter James
Otis, whose pen and tongue had played a large part in Sir Francis' discom-
fiture, entered the Royal Coffee House, a gathering place for army officers
and administrators, one day in early September. As he turned from the
street into the wide doors of the tavern, he was unknowingly making his
exit from active life. Just what did happen when he entered the dim exterior
has been told in conflicting detail. According to one account, he provoked
some army men. Swords were drawn, the lamps were overturned, and there
was a scuffle in the dark. Another source states that he came to the place to
seek satisfaction from a man who had challenged his—James Otis'—loyalty
to the Crown, and a brawl ensued. Still another story has it that John
Robinson, now collector for the port, saw Otis enter and, probably justifi-
ably provoked by articles against him that Otis had written, pulled the
patriot's nose and thus brought on a fight. Whatever the details, Otis
was badly beaten in the now darkened coffee room and took a blow
from a lamp base, candlestick, or sword hilt. He was carted home somehow, and witnesses state that the "crack in his skull was so deep a man
could lay his finger in it." As a result of the blow, his never too stable mind
was unhinged. We have a few more glimpses of him, carrying out a feverish
one-man assault on the windows of the Old State House or shouting from
his own window and firing muskets into the night. There is a last tragic
entry onto the scene when history sees him, a vacant-eyed, distracted man
armed with an old musket, wandering vaguely in the June sunlight of 1775
through the smoke clouds that billowed so strangely over the slopes of the
hills named for Messrs. Bunker and Breed across the river at Charlestown.

So the voices of Bernard and James Otis faded away into the wings as
1769 took its final swing toward a new year. The merchants in most of the
colonies still clung to their non-importation agreement and their fellows in
England became increasingly alarmed. When the complete figures for the
year were in, British exports to the colonies showed a drop of nearly 50
per cent. The alarm of the British merchants would probably have soared
higher than it did had not new markets, developed after the peace of 1763,
begun to show such amazing growth that colonial trade losses could be
pretty well written off. As it was, their fears as they watched the growth of
non-importation became so vocal that they reached Parliament and the
circles of the Cabinet. First there was a rumor, then a growing whisper that
swelled to a certainty. A new ministry under the Duke of Grafton was going to repeal the hated Townshend Acts. And, taking away those acts,
what would the exasperatingly unruly and unreasonable colonials have to
complain about? The future looked rather more serene.

So, as clerks on high stools or standing at tall, slanting desks grew used to
writing 1770 on their ledger sheets, the acts died. Relief was so universal

that many men on both sides of the Atlantic overlooked the fact that one tax was salvaged from the Townshend wreckage, a rather insignificant tax on tea. It did not amount to much, and if it did, there were always the Dutch tea smugglers. But, like the Declaratory Act that accompanied the repeal of the stamp tax, this duty, small as it was, kept the old dispute alive, for by its very presence it reaffirmed Parliament's right to tax.

To the bitter disillusionment of the more ardent men of the colonial opposition, the carefully built wall of non-importation began to sag and crack, to let loose a trickle here, a flood there. The ban on British goods was to hold until *all* the Townshend Acts had been repealed. Everywhere, save of course in cantankerous Boston, merchants sighed in relief and over-looked the tea item. Each passing month saw the abandonment of one association after another, though Virginia was to hold out until 1771. To many it must have seemed that Parliament had won in its long-distance dispute with the colonies.

But there were plenty of other points of friction, often local, from which sparks might fly to start conflagrations in other parts of the country if those sparks were suitably fanned. In the city of New York hot ill-feeling existed between the Sons of Liberty and the little local garrison. Shortly after the beginning of the year 1770, this antipathy flared up in an ugly riot that could have developed into really murderous street fighting. That it went no further was probably due to the quick thought and cool-headedness of a few British officers who managed somehow to get their men back into bar-racks with no damage to either side beyond the normal quota of black eyes, cracked heads, and sprained wrists.

As a riot, this so-called Battle of Golden Hill amounted to little, save as a forecast. No one had been killed, no shots had been fired—this time. But if troops and townsmen clashed again in New York or some other garrison city? Tempers might flare hotter in Charleston, where the 60th Royal Americans sweated under the Carolina sun. The tinder was drier in Bos-ton, where the 14th West Yorkshires and the 29th Worcestershires glow-ered at a surly town. But for the moment Golden Hill passed off as a symptom rather than an event, though a skilled propagandist might have been able to use it to inflame a whole country.

A not much worse clash was lingering in the offing, and with it a true master propagandist would know exactly what to do. It was March in Bos-ton, and a nighttime crowd of toughs gathered apparently spontaneously to devil the lone British sentry at the east end of the Old State House. Snowballs and clubs flew. A squad or so of troops raced out from the bar-racks on Brattle Street, closed in with the hard-pressed sentry. The mob swelled, surged nearer, daring the troops to fire. Captain John Preston of the 29th Worcestershires threw himself among his men, shoving them back, striking down raised muzzles, shouting at them not to fire. Then a soldier's musket slammed orange in the slushy night, another man fired, another, and five of the mob lay dead or wounded on the icy cobbles. Drums and pounding boots in the narrow Boston streets told of more troops being rushed to the scene, and a full-scale battle seemed in the making.

There was a momentary lull as the mob recoiled, stunned by the sight of its own dead. Captain Preston somehow got his men in hand skillfully and courageously. Fresh troops stormed up in the brief breathing spell. But the next rush of the crowd could set tragedy roaring again. Then Thomas Hutchinson, lieutenant governor, managed to claw his way through the streets, which were now jammed with onlookers brought out by the din, and appeared on the balcony that still looks down the length of State Street. Hated by the more radical of his fellow citizens, held up to the mob as more dangerous than any Townshend or Grenville, he stood under the climbing moon that shimmered over the slates, a magnificent target. He began to speak and wove a spell in the March night, promised justice, and the furious mob and the equally furious troops were quiet. The space below the Old State House emptied. The dead and wounded were carried away and the troops went sullenly to their barracks. Before the sun rose, it was known from Copp's Hill to the Town Gates that Hutchinson had kept his word. Captain John Preston and eight men of the guard were to stand trial for murder.

Such, in bare outline, was the "Boston Massacre," differing in few respects from the less known Battle of Golden Hill down in New York, save that in Boston the rising seems to have been in no way connected with the leaders of the Sons of Liberty and that it did produce actual casualties. It was a collision between two groups of violent men who had long smarted under mutual provocation. The only wonder is that it was so long in coming and produced as few deaths as it did. For the night itself, it is hard to find anyone to admire save John Preston and Thomas Hutchinson.

The trial of Preston and his men took place. In the face of a surge of hatred that threatened to bring on another outburst, John Adams, inflexible in defense of colonial rights against the Crown, and Josiah Quincy, Jr., quieter than either Adams but firmly sharing their convictions, amazingly took over the defense of Preston and the guard squad. Despite a fearful clamor from press and pulpit, Adams and Quincy forced their case through and obtained acquittal for the whole group save two, who were lightly branded on the hand. Adams and Quincy ran a fearful risk in taking over this case. Their stature is little less than that of Preston and Hutchinson in relation to the whole affair.

Yet the "Massacre" was local. It could have been buried as was Golden Hill. But a man was ready for the event, and Samuel Adams grasped at a torch that had been accidentally lighted and burned far brighter than any that he and his associates could have contrived. First of all, he stormed into Thomas Hutchinson's office, demanding that the troops be removed from the town. It is more than likely that the grave, troubled lieutenant governor was glad for an excuse to get the troops and the townspeople apart. Perhaps he would have made the move on his own initiative. But Sam Adams' hot warnings gave him a reason to report to his superiors in England and he moved the 14th and the 29th, the only remaining troops in Boston, to Castle William in the harbor. It was a wise move and did credit to Hutchinson. Few, however, have remembered Hutchinson's part, and the regiments have gone down in history as the Sam Adams Regiments. And Sam Adams bulked larger and larger in Boston, throughout New England and the other nine colonies.

Whether he was partly aware of the brightness of the beacon that he was lighting or whether the whole incident snowballed into importance as days, months, and years went by, Adams began to thump the Massacre drum, its roll swelling louder and louder. Few of the victims of that sudden burst of musketry in State Street had been held in any particular regard in Boston. Now they all became holy martyrs. Adams wrote and orated about them, about the cruel mercenaries who had shot them down in cold blood. He persuaded others to write and to speak. Perhaps conscious of the axiom that a picture is worth a thousand words, he or his allies had cartoons circulated. Paul Revere, whose movements on the night of the clash are more than obscure, seems at least to have been on the fringes of the fight. He produced for the trial a carefully drawn and probably accurate street plan, featuring just where the martyrs' bodies had fallen, and this was circulated. He etched a copperplate showing the moment of firing, a crudely drawn sheet that is highly accurate as to background and more than fanciful as to the actors in the foreground. Copies are a collector's item today.

Most of the newspaper accounts were heavily slanted against the troops. A Bostonian by no means biased in favor of the military wrote dryly to a Southern friend, "The number killed and wounded you will have learned by the papers"—an unconscious tribute to the circulation of the times—"being almost the only truth in them." The Boston town meeting, in formal session, voted solemnly that Preston and his men were murderers and spread their resolution in the Boston Town Records. A pious divine called from the pulpit for the executions of those same "murderers," and the press carried his sermon.

For fear lest the memory of this priceless propaganda gift might die out, the date, March 5, became an anniversary, first marked by solemn mourning and highly colored reconstructions of the scene and later, as happens to many solemn observances, by increasing hilarity.

It may be justly held that one reason for Samuel Adams' tenacious hold on the Massacre was due to the worst tragedy that can befall an extremist—a lack of vivid popular issues to embrace. Many milder patriots had become disgusted with the growing threat of the mob, whether in Boston or Charleston. In Adams' immediate circle Cousin John had suddenly grown weary of public life and announced a retirement to his Braintree farm. John Hancock withdrew to the deep rooms of his Beacon Hill mansion, which stood close to the present State House, saw less and less of his more violent friends, and was markedly cool to the unfortunate Samuel.

It was so in other parts of the country. The Townshend Acts were dead, save for the tea duty which hung on like a non-infected vermiform appendix. The non-importation associations were largely forgotten, and citizens and citizenesses of all political complexions threw off their homespuns, dumped out their home-brews, smashed up their local pottery, and welcomed the finer British-made goods. If they could afford it, they also bought up the shipments of more heavily taxed continental wares. They were emerging from a long Lenten period and reveled in the release, anticipating Bismarck's pronouncement that patriotism stops with the palate and broadening the dictum to include the human frame and the dining table.

Discouraged, Samuel Adams wrote to John Dickinson down in Philadelphia, hoping for a fresh series of Farmer's Letters. But Dickinson had grown cautious and refused to take up his quill again. Also, he had quite recently married a wealthy Quakeress, and his political and economic outlook seemed changed. Then there was Daniel Dulany off there in Baltimore. Could he be induced to come out again and thunder as effectively as he had against Grenville's Stamp Act? But there was sad news from Maryland. Controversy had arisen over taxes levied by the governor without consent of the Assembly. The dispute grew hot, and there was Daniel Dulany championing the governor's acts against the barbs of Charles Carroll of Carrollton. In fact, Dulany had taken his stand once for all and, with the firmest convictions of his rightness, was to be henceforth an avowed Tory.

New York was little help to one like Adams. A struggle for power was still going on between the two great landed families, the De Lanceys and the Livingstons, to the absorption of all else. The extreme New York leaders like Isaac Sears and Alec McDougall seemed to be waiting.

To make matters worse, local crises that had nothing to do with the Parliament kept cropping up. The colony of Connecticut had claim through bygone grants to the lovely Wyoming Valley in the west of Pennsylvania and sent settlers there. Others, not from Connecticut, had come there before them, eternally convinced of the justness of their own claims. The indignant Connecticut men harried the supposed intruders and set up a mild reign of terror through a district that would, in less than a decade, forget old quarrels in the vast tragedy of Joseph Brant's Indian raids. There was also a wild unsettled tract that lay between New York and New Hampshire, just north of western Massachusetts. Men had been moving into it from the east, often on the strength of grants issued by New Hampshire's equivocal governor, Benning Wentworth. Massachusetts men, too, felt they had a stake in this wilderness, known only as the Hampshire Grants. So, unfortunately, did east-moving New Yorkers. The New Yorkers met with resistance and began to mutter fearfully of a group known as the Green Mountain Boys, who rallied against them. The New Yorkers in most part withdrew, but they still muttered and still made their claims.

It almost seemed as though the mainspring of the opposition movement had gone slack. Tempers were flaring; incidents were occurring within the colonies themselves, diverting the energies that should have gone, in many minds, against the still unsettled assertion of rights by Britain. And worse

was about to happen. The tense situation in the highlands of North and
South Carolina sudden exploded. Uplanders took the field as 1771 ripened
into late spring. Their leader, one Hermon Husbands, had been arrested
and jailed at the German-Swiss settlement of New Bern, where the harsh
Governor Tryon was building the palace that is today in the process of
restoration. The Regulators, used by force of circumstance to taking matters into their own hands, marched on New Bern with the somewhat drastic
aim of burning the town. William Tryon, a most unpopular governor, was
surprised to find the North Carolina planters and their adherents rallying
to his support. When he had enough men he took the field, met the Regulators along the Alamance River, which would know blood again in a few
years, and defeated them utterly. There had been passed a few months
before a vicious act that turned such an uprising into treason. Backed by
this, Tryon hanged a good many of the Regulator prisoners, though not so
many as his later record along Long Island Sound would suggest in retrospect, and sent the others home. The revolt was crushed. The survivors
waited sullenly for the next chance. It did not come until hostilities were
flaming between all the colonies and the mother country. Then the Regulators, whose economic and political position would indicate them as material for violent Sons of Liberty, thought only of striking back at the low-
landers who were in revolt against the King.

The whole scene, from Maine to Georgia, must have looked hopeless to
those who felt that a showdown between England and the colonies must
come. Secure in the year 1771, an intelligent man could prophesy that the
right to tax would go unchallenged so long as that right were not exercised
too stringently. Patriot leaders waited, hoping that Parliament would
blunder again, that fresh acts would fan the ash-buried sparks to a point
where colonial rights would have to be admitted. But the months sailed
by, with England showing an exasperating tendency to do nothing pro-
vocative.

It was June of 1772 and His Majesty's armed schooner, Gaspée, Lieutenant Dudington commanding, was making itself highly obnoxious in
Narrangansett Bay, which had always been looked upon as a sort of Mare
Nostrum by the better smugglers of Rhode Island. Dudington, taking himself, his mission, and the honor of the Royal Navy very seriously, had
started a reign of terror. He halted everything that floated, damning the
eyes and blasting the souls of anyone not R.N. The indignant smugglers
and suspected smugglers reported him to be "Haughty, insolent and in-
tolerant, personally ill-treating every Master and Merchant of the Vessels
he boarded." He further endeared himself to the always intractable Rhode
Islanders by sudden descents on the green farms that sloped down to the
bay or raiding inland along white oyster-shell roads. He commandeered
without payment hogs, poultry, and provisions apparently at his whim and
pleasure, cut down fruit trees, and had the neat silver-gray stacks of firewood, the farmers' insurance against winter, lugged aboard the Gaspée.

Then to the unholy delight of the Rhode Islanders, the Gaspée most unfortunately ran aground while chasing a suspect, leaving a still unanswered question: Did the suspect deliberately lead Lieutenant Dudington into shoal water? At any rate, the local Sons of Liberty moved quickly. A flotilla of small boats left Providence; exasperated men boarded the stranded schooner. There was a scuffle; Dudington was wounded and set adrift in a dory, after which the Providence raiders pulled back to port, looking over their shoulders at the fascinating spectacle of H.M.S. *Gaspée* burning down to the water line.

This was a far bolder move than, say, John Hancock's men hurling rocks at H.M.S. *Romney* and burning the collector's barge. It could almost be set down as piracy. Sons of Liberty held their collective breath all through New England, hoping that *this* might be the unifying act which would start the sparks smoldering again. And even if England swallowed the loss of the *Gaspée*, which had certainly been on a lawful mission, why, stronger measures could be tried without fear of retaliation and perhaps those measures would do the business. The Tory uproar was even louder. At Province House in Boston, Thomas Hutchinson, now confirmed as governor, cried in alarm, "If the *Gaspée* rioters are not punished, the Friends to Government will despond and give up all hopes of being able to withstand the Faction."

The response from England was highly satisfactory to the Tories. A Commission of Inquiry was appointed to look into the *Gaspée* matter and hold all suspects for trial—in England. Tory joy was premature. Sons of Liberty all over the colonies began to stir. Many of them saw a truly unifying grievance in this setting up of what they called an Inquisition. The *Pennsylvania Journal and Weekly Advertiser* volleyed out joyously that with such a star chamber set up, the position of the American was infinitely worse "than that of a subject of France, Spain, Portugal or any other most despotic power on earth." The commissioners, looked upon by Tories as guardian angels, were called "a pack of Egyptian tyrants." Their mission was scored as "the most insulting violation of the rights of Americans that could be devised."

The commissioners sat and were soon driven to the verge of hysteria by the amazing presence of amnesia throughout the colony of Rhode Island and the Providence Plantations. No one could recollect the slightest fact about the *Gaspée's* flaming end. As in the case of John Hancock and that of the *Lydia*, the court finally was seized with a sort of mad despair, threw in its hand, and announced that there were no suspects to be found, therefore there were none to be sent to England for further trial and virtually certain hanging at Tyburn, near the present Marble Arch, Hyde Park, London.

The Tories, naturally, were crushed. Men who had worked hard and cleanly at their assigned tasks began to slump in their chairs. "There's an end," lamented Robert Nicholas, the Rhode Island collector, "to collecting a revenue and enforcing the acts of trade." Admiral Montague, evaluating the repercussions that reached quickly to Boston, confessed that he felt the

Bostonians were about ready for independence, adding that "Nothing but the ships [fleet] in Boston Harbor prevent their going greater lengths, as they see no notice taken from home of their behaviour." The good admiral should have said "*effective* notice." Modern totalitarian methods of handling unco-operative witnesses might have changed the whole picture at Rhode Island; leading patriots could have been seized as hostages. Fortunately the times were not sufficiently enlightened for such measures.

So a spark was being fanned once more and earnest men as well as the more dangerous radicals were sniffing the breeze that fanned it. Then, in Massachusetts, Thomas Hutchinson announced, before 1772 died, a new policy, and Samuel Adams could well have thanked him from the bottom of his heart. Beginning with the new year, Thomas Hutchinson reported, the salaries of the governor and of all Massachusetts judges would be paid by the Crown.

Few moves could have been more damaging to the Loyalist cause. As has been pointed out before, as soon as legal and administrative officers began to look to England for their pay and support, they at once slipped out of colonial control. Men holding such posts would be very careful to do as England wished, to report only such things as England wished to hear. The colonies would be left officially voiceless. The voices that spoke would belong to hacks and wastrels sent out from England, to men like Lord Dunmore, who was often seen disgracefully drunk in public and who further enhanced the dignity of the office of royal governor by assaulting the aide of William Tryon.

Perhaps this policy of Crown pay for colonial officials to Massachusetts alone was prompted by a hope that it could be introduced gradually, thus avoiding a general conflagration. But instead of slow fires springing up all along the coast, the result was one hot flame blaring out in the Bay Colony like a single blowtorch. It made a very willing martyr out of Massachusetts and, as Sam Adams had seized upon the Boston Massacre, so he and like-minded men pounced at once on this ruling. The jump-off spot was so obvious that it is strange that the usually calm and foresighted Hutchinson did not see it. Why did he discount the propaganda value to extremists of the issue that he had presented? It would be child's play for them to broadcast to other colonies, "Look what's happened to us. It can happen to you!"

Like so many other manifestations that cropped up as conditions grew worse, there was a precedent arising out of past disputes that lay ready to hand and ripe for revival. Sam Adams whistled up and labored to expand the Committees of Correspondence. At first in his own domain he met with resistance from his former co-workers. John Adams was more than dubious of the wisdom of Cousin Sam's course. John Hancock came reluctantly down from Beacon Hill to the town meeting that Sam had convoked. James Otis, in a brief final spell of lucidity, was in the chair. There was hot debate, but the Sam Adams forces prevailed and his opponents, for better or worse, closed up with him. A Committee of Correspondence was set up with twenty-one members and was authorized to make known to other towns of the province the Boston point of view. Then its scope was broadened to include not only the other colonies but, in a sweeping gesture, "the World." The Massachusetts towns were also to be urged to form similar committees. Soon memorials and resolutions were streaming out of Boston. Samuel Adams himself drew up a "State of Rights of the Colonists." Able and devoted young Dr. Joseph Warren penned a lengthy and compelling "List of Infringements and Violations of Those Rights." Another member, Dr. Benjamin Church, who had previously distinguished himself chiefly by setting down pro-Whig verses that were lamentable in form and meter but highly acceptable to like-minded people, joined the writers. Urbane, polished, dissolute, probably the best-trained surgeon in New England, he contributed "A Letter of Correspondence" that was praised by men who a couple of years later must have wondered how they were so taken in.

So the committee wrote and wrote, to other towns, to other colonies, and to England. The letters were immensely effective, at least on this side of the Atlantic, and the chain of committees they set up throughout the colonies was to endure as an invaluable asset to the American cause, the greatest unifier that was to be known, save only for the acts and decrees from England that brought those committees into being and gave them the common experience that makes a nation.

There were two unconscious errors in the letters and speeches of this time. The colonists quite universally protested their loyalty to the King and reserved their abuse for Parliament. In this they were wrong. George III was patiently and stubbornly carrying out his mother's stern words when he took the throne—"George, be a *King*." Little by little the control of Parliament was becoming vested in what might be called the King's men. If the process continued, as it seemed to have every chance of continuing, Parliament would become the rubber stamp that George III intended it to be. Given time, the King would not have to bother to call Parliament into session. He could rule by Cabinet and Cabinet appointments. Little of this seems to have been apparent in the colonies. When hostilities broke out, men rallied against "the Parliamentary forces" and in some American regiments the King's health was drunk well into 1776.

The second error lay in the colonists' insistence on what they called "Englishmen's rights." Conditioned to life in America since the early part of the preceding century, they had ceased to be Englishmen and had become Americans.

CHAPTER V

"Mr. Revere will give you all the news"

AFTER the wraith-like era of good feeling that had followed on the collapse of the non-importation agreements and the shying away of all but the extremists from the fear of the power of the mob, the flames of opposition were hard to fan, but the Adams committees toiled endlessly and, in most cases, selflessly. Paul Revere was more and more absent from the bench where silver was transmuted from crude bars and became glowingly alive under his skilled hands. Instead, he rode and rode, over the New Hampshire border, deep into the Berkshires, down into Rhode Island and Connecticut, along the Sound to the island of Manhattan. His saddlebags bulged with pamphlets and letters, linking Boston with a committee in Worcester, in Hartford, in Portsmouth, in Fairfield, or in Westchester County. If the outbound mail were scanty, a committee-man in a distant town might find at the bottom of a brief letter the bold words, "Mr. Revere will give you all the news. J. Adams."

So stones were cast into the pool of colonial discontent, and little by little the resultant ripples began to reach Boston. Virginia formed its own committee and would keep in touch. South Carolina answered, as did Rhode Island and New Hampshire. One by one the colonies lined up, formed a relatively smooth channel through which protests, letters of sympathy, promises of help, propaganda ideas could flow smoothly. An event, a plan hatched in New Bern, North Carolina, would be soon known in Portsmouth in New Hampshire.

In England, where ministries had succeeded each other in bewildering parade, Lord North had finally settled into the saddle as Prime Minister and would survive in that post for over a decade. Personally honest, able, but completely subservient to George III and his plans, North pursued the same course that had kept the colonies bristling since the passage of the Sugar Act. Now, in 1773, he was busily concocting another issue, a fresh, tempting one, to replace the older grievances that were being passed along from committee to committee.

The great East India Company, source of vast riches for the few and very little for the Crown, was in a badly jangled state. Its stock had recently dropped from £280 to about £160 and the stockholders were in a panic. Since many of them were influential people, North cast about for a way of easing the company's financial problems. He hit on the happy device of giving the company a monopoly on the American tea market, carefully rigging rebates so this India tea could be sold in the colonies at a figure rather lower than even the non-duty-paying Dutch and other smugglers could meet. The colonies were not fond of monopolies. They were far less in favor of a select few being appointed by royal governors to handle these new shipments and profit handsomely thereby.

The Anglo-American pattern had become so well worn that the results of almost any Crown act could be predicted. As in the case of the stamp tax, friends of the Crown were given control of the new tea, when, as, and if landed. In Massachusetts, Hutchinson, who had appointed two sons and one nephew to fatten on the stamp tax, now designated a nephew as the lucky tea recipient. And, again as in the case of the stamp tax, angry meetings were held up and down the land. As soon as the names of the tea consignees were known, either by official pronouncement or inner-circle leakage, delegations called on them and demanded their resignations, which were usually forthcoming. The appointees had not forgotten the more than harsh pressure that had been brought to bear in the case of the distributors of the Stamp Act papers. Many rock-ribbed Tories joined in with the most ardent Sons of Liberty to protest North's clever little scheme. In New York, Tory William Smith confided to his diary, "A new flame is kindling in America. . . . I suppose that we shall repeat the confusions of 1765 and 1766. Our domestic parties will probably die and be swallowed up in the general opposition to Parliament." And note that Parliament is still cast in the villain's role in the great Anglo-American drama.

Busy with his brand-new grievances, the cup of Mr. Samuel Adams must have been brimming with happiness. But still greater blessings were to fall into his nimble hands. Over in England, Benjamin Franklin, Deputy Postmaster General for the Colonies *in absentia* and recently appointed agent for Massachusetts, was toiling calmly, imperturbably, earnestly for a solution of the Anglo-American troubles. To him came a shadowy figure with a sheaf of letters. These he showed to the benevolent, wise Dr. Franklin as evidence of the type of information that was reaching governmental circles from Massachusetts. The doctor's usually serene face must have broken into a pattern of wrinkles of amazement. The letters were from Thomas Hutchinson and Andrew Oliver, the latter now province secretary, to the same Thomas Whately of Gentle Shepherd Grenville's entourage, who had been so concerned lest mean people should better themselves.

The letters seemed to show that Parliament's blunders in colonial matters were due at least in part to the fact that only one side of such questions—the squirearchy side—was being presented. (Casting once more into the future, the identical state of affairs would prevail in Upper Canada in the 1830s, when successive English ministries were to receive only the squirearchy point of view, the side of the Family Compact.)

The astute Dr. Franklin was not one to miss the importance of the letters. His visitor reluctantly allowed him to keep the originals. They could even be sent to America so long as Franklin gave his word that they would not be published or given wide circulation. In modern terms, whoever saw them in Boston must consider them as off the record, as informatory material and nothing else. Top secret. Eyes only.

Franklin shipped them to Thomas Cushing, Speaker of the Massachu-setts House. The latter, following instructions, showed them to the prin-cipal opposition leaders, a group that could not conceivably exclude Samuel Adams. After mulling over the contents of the letters for a matter of days, Samuel made his way along State Street to the Old State House, where he had summoned a secret session of the House.

There is no questioning the purity of Sam Adams' patriotism, his devo-tion to the cause in which he believed with every shred of his energetic being. But he was never too particular what road he took toward his ends nor whom he used to smooth out that road. On a June day whose sun poured into the Assembly Room and onto the golden lion and unicorn that still prance on the east gable of the Old State House, the letters were read, thus securing a wider audience than Franklin had probably intended.

As far as the bare bones of the letters went, they gave the Assembly little that was new. But the phrasing, which Adams must have carefully noted, was quite different from that which either Hutchinson or Oliver used in Boston. This was natural enough, since they were written to a man who believed as they did, and the sentiments did not have to be toned down to suit a hostile audience. The effect on most listeners was to suggest that Hutchinson and his cohorts were double- and triple-crossing their fellow Americans.

Not content with this use of top-secret papers, Adams turned to his friends of the press and soon, along the very roads which the Deputy Post-master General for the Colonies had helped bring into being, the letters went out and, by means of the chain of committees that Adams had created, enjoyed wide circulation. Emboldened by the popular response, the Assembly took a step far more drastic than it had ever dared before. It called upon His Most Gracious Majesty to remove Messrs. Hutchinson and Oliver from office.

Samuel Adams must have been an extraordinarily happy man. Not many months ago he had seen some of his most important followers drop away from him. Dickinson penned no more Farmer's Letters and Daniel Dulany had turned Tory. But now! And there was still the fascinating future just ahead, the future that would bring the tea ships to the chosen ports of Boston, New York, Philadelphia, and Charleston. What would those cities and the colonies for which they stood do now? Sam Adams must have been very sure about Boston. And the others?

There was New York, for example. In New York the Sons of Liberty took for the moment the name of Mohawks and spattered the half-English, half-Dutch town with broadsides denouncing every feature of the tea pro-gram. Each handbill and poster ended with the not very conciliatory state-ment that any New Yorker who tried to warehouse the tea when, as, and if it arrived could expect an unwelcome visit from the undersigned, the Mohawks. The weeks slipped by, and soon in the coffeehouses of New York men were spreading the news that the Manhattan tea shipment had already left England in the good ship *Nancy*. Governor Tryon, a little unsure of himself for once, called in leaders of the De Lancey faction and the Livingston group. He hoped that the tea would be landed without trouble. For his own career, he did not want another mob rising such as had greeted the arrival of the hated stamps. Perhaps Tryon was due for leave. Perhaps he sniffed the breezes that flowed down Broadway to the Battery correctly. In any event, he left for England, turning over the government of the island to unlucky, eighty-five-year-old Cadwallader Colden, who had also had to face the stamp riots.

December of 1773 came in, and still the Nancy was unreported. Down the Post Road that ran from mid-town pretty directly to Boston rode a stocky, pleasant-faced, quiet-mannered man, his saddlebags a-bulge. Once in the town, he sought out the leading member of the Committee of Correspondence and particularly those who belonged to a subcommittee that concerned itself solely with tea. He introduced himself, probably needlessly, as Paul Revere from the Boston committee and gave forth his news, verbal and written.

It was news that plunged the New Yorkers into a pool of wildly exciting thought and speculation. The Bostonians had demanded of Hutchinson that the tea be sent back to England without unloading and without paying duty. Hutchinson, smarting over the publication of his letters to Whately, was not in a mellow mood and stated flatly that the tea would be landed and that Boston would pay the duty exacted by law.

The New Yorkers exchanged glances. Their own Governor Tryon had strongly urged obedience. What did the Bostonians do? Paul Revere went on with his story. At night a number of men, many highly respected citizens among them, had smeared their faces with lampblack or with soot from the base of a kettle, had stuck feathers in their hair and wrapped themselves in blankets, Indian-fashion. Soberly they had gone to the three ships that lay at Long Wharf, boarded them, and—note this, New Yorkers —with the assistance of the British crew had dumped no less than three hundred and forty-two chests of fine tea into the harbor. Then the mock Indians withdrew, feeling that at least they had made a point.

There were other questions from the heartened New Yorkers. No, there had been no violence of any sort. The ships had been in no way damaged. Astoundingly, no one had clandestinely slipped a case or two ashore to enjoy in the quiet of the family circle. Some men who found their shoes full of dry leaves emptied the tea into small bottles, which were carefully sealed as a memento of the event. At least one of these bottles survives to this day.

Paul Revere left his audience, to rest up for the long ride back to Boston. His hosts had plenty to think about. North's tea duties, condemned by conservatives as well as radicals, had been thrown back at him dramatically. A mob had acted, but without violence, disorder, or the wholesale wanton destruction of former risings. The Bostonians seemed to have charted a new course of opposition, had created a type of resistance with which fastidious-minded men need not fear to associate themselves. Men who had drawn back from the Sons of Liberty began to edge closer.

Silversmith Revere must have made a very quick return trip, for late in December, Sam Adams wrote to James Warren, who had married James Otis' sister Mercy, "We had yesterday the Return of Mr. Revere . . . who carried the important News of the Fate of the Tea to New York. By him we are informed, that a Tea-Ship with 270 Chests arrived at Charlestown [sic] South Carolina. The inhabitants were determined she should return with her detested Cargo. Before the Arrival of this and the News from Boston, the Citizens of New York had got to be divided, many of them being for storing the Tea. But immediately they became united and determined that it should not be landed. . . . The Ministry could not have devised a more effectual Measure to unite the Colonies. Old Jealousies are removed and perfect Harmony subsists between them." Sam Adams' committees were beginning to pay handsome dividends.

Looking ahead a little, in order to dispose of the other tea chests the New Yorkers finally dumped theirs into the East River with as little commotion as the Bostonians had stirred up. The Philadelphia shipment was landed and allowed to rot away. Charleston, too, despite the warnings of capable, popular Lieutenant Governor William Bull, refused to receive the shipment. It was finally landed and stored, remaining in bond until the outbreak of hostilities, when it was sold at auction for the benefit of the patriots, this action meeting the stern approval of sundry Gadsdens, Rutledges, Lynches, Horrys, Brewtons, and Motts.

The strong renewal of opposition to the Crown and its acts that was flaring up so strongly again in the colonies did not pass unnoticed in London. Ministerial tempers flared and ministerial forces were rallied to cuff down any expression of sympathy for the colonists' claims that might arise from His Majesty's Loyal Opposition. Dr. Benjamin Franklin, appearing before the Lords' Committee of His Majesty's Privy Council for Plantation Affairs in connection with the Massachusetts petition for the removal of Hutchinson and Oliver, found himself under a furious, merciless attack by the Solicitor General, Alexander Wedderburn. The petition was not to be discussed. Instead the bland doctor was given a savage raking for his part in the transmission of the Hutchinson-Oliver letters to Boston and was allowed to make no reply. Wedderburn's attack, like the Golden Hill riot, was chiefly important for showing the temper of the times, and as Golden Hill was followed by the Boston Massacre, so a more concrete expression of British temper followed on Wedderburn.

George III was no man to accept meekly the colonists' treatment of John Company's sacred tea, and now he moved swiftly to administer suitable punishment. His move was understandable in intent but highly illogical in detail. Calmly overlooking the fate of the tea consignments in other ports, the Crown marked down Boston alone for spectacular retribution, and his ministers at once began in an atmosphere of smug righteousness to

draw up measures that were to stir up a gleeful pandemonium in the mind
of every colonial extremist.

It was May in New England and the couriers were out, bearing scalding
news north, south, and west. Letters to the key men in the vital cities of
New York and Philadelphia were entrusted to the chief of the riders, Paul
Revere, for had not John Adams once written, "Mr. Revere will give you
all the news"? So Revere headed on, possibly thinking of the plates he had
engraved for James Rivington in New York, to illustrate an American
edition of Captain James Cook's voyages. Or a bold flare for the lip of a
silver cream pitcher or a rich curve for the side of a silver punch bowl
might have been taking shape in his mind. But all this would be underlaid
by his own awareness of the news he carried.

He followed a route that was as old as mankind. First the rolling country
west of Boston, then the great surge of the tree-thick ridges that swept on
through Marlboro and Worcester lay before him. There was a sharp slant
into the broad valley where the Connecticut touched thriving Springfield
and whispered to it the mystery of the river's origin far off in wilderness
lakes to the north. The way bent south and paced the river through Hartford and on to New Haven and Long Island Sound and thence west again
to King's Bridge at the head of Manhattan Island. Five good days would
Paul Revere spend, riding on through woods, past fields seamed by the
plow, past muttering waterfalls until a windbreak of pines, a white spire
topped with a gleaming weather vane signaled an unmistakable "Halt!" to
him. There were inns with creaking signs—Blue Anchors and Gen'l. Wolfes
and Red Dragons and Marquises of Granby and a fulfilled promise of rum
and fresh-baked bread and a great joint of beef turning in a fireplace solid
as a bomb shelter. At each stop, whether for the night or for a quick meal
while his horse was rubbed down by whistling hostlers, Paul Revere spread
the word of his mission, as the other riders were doing north and south and
west of Boston. He also passed out handbills, very likely his own product,
showing skull and crossbones, mourning wreaths, and a Phrygian cap for
liberty. Mr. Revere will give you all the news. Take a sheaf of the handbills.
Read, think, spread the sheets about. The same message that riders were
giving out in Newburyport up on the mouth of the Merrimac, in Portsmouth by the Piscataqua, "river running so Intrycate," at Providence down
at the head of Narragansett Bay, at Plymouth at the root of Cape Cod.
But the silversmith was bringing tidings to the more distant colonies, where
it was important that the bearer be known, and favorably known, to the
heads of the various committees. For this was no Stamp Act crisis, touching
all the thirteen colonies. It bore only on Boston. A reasonable man could
argue that it concerned only Boston and would not trouble any other
region. How would men outside of New England look on it?

Revere rode into New York City and at once hunted up John Lamb,
ardent Son of Liberty who would later turn his skilled hand to gunnery.
For once Mr. Revere did not have to tell all the news. A ship had brought

it from England ahead of him, and New York's Committee of Fifty-one was even then in session. Its members knew all about the Boston Port Bill and its incredible measures. The whole port of Boston was closed. Even the ferries were shut down and the city could be supplied only across the narrow neck of land by Roxbury. The government and the customs were to be moved, the former to Salem and the latter to steep-rocked Marblehead. And to prevent the Boston Sons of Liberty from expressing their displeasure as forcibly as they had in the past, five regiments of infantry were to garrison the town and His Majesty's Fleet would lie in the harbor. There was a slight sweetener at the end of the bill. Boston could be reopened, the old ways could return, if the Bostonians would just pay for the tea cargoes that had been so unceremoniously dumped overboard and also reimburse His Majesty's customs for the duty that was lost through the destruction of the tea chests. Yes, it concerned Boston only. But it promised a possible bonanza to other port cities, which might compete highly profitably for Boston's vast sea-borne trade. Salem could fatten at Boston's expense and so could Providence. And there was New York, with one of the finest harbors in the world, ready to take its share—or as much as it could get, and of course Philadelphia merchants could reach out easily for slices of the old Boston trade. It was as obvious as a proposition out of Euclid. Those ports could not afford to pass up such a chance.

The courier found a fresh horse, crossed to New Jersey, and pushed on to Philadelphia, spreading his news and his handbills as he went. Again he found the Sons of Liberty in tense meetings, for the news was ahead of him once more. So at Philadelphia he entrusted the forwarding of intelligence south to local Sons and turned his horse back toward Manhattan and Boston. When Boston's spires once more lifted out of the lowland haze, Paul Revere had been gone twelve days. He could tell the Adams cousins and Dr. Warren and John Hancock that New York had put on solemn record its "detestation of the execrable Port Bill" and promised its support to Boston. The Philadelphians had acted with an un-Quakerlike firmness and while holding up a cautioning finger and whispering of "moderation" had voted to close ranks with Boston, even to "the last extremity."

Similar words came from Virginia as the Philadelphia couriers went south. North Carolina failed to appreciate the parliamentary reasoning that the act touched only Boston. In Charleston there was a meeting at Mr. Dillon's tavern at Broad and Church streets, and Christopher Gadsden and Ralph Izard and Thomas Lynch found the temper of the people in no way different from that in New York and Philadelphia and Williamsburg. Merchants who had grown rich on the indigo trade sat in packed meetings side by side with conservative planters who still looked back wistfully to the original plan for the colony with its hereditary nobility of landgraves and caciques and the country divided into baronies—Colleton Barony, Waccamaw Barony. Why were they shouting in agreement with Gadsden? The act did not touch them. But it could.

And the Carolinians did more than vote support of Boston. They could visualize their own plight should Charleston be closed. A subscription list was opened, and money and rice were not only pledged but sent to Boston. It was a generous, spontaneous gesture, for the Carolinians could not know that other colonies were acting as they themselves acted. A flock of more than one hundred sheep trailed away out of green-hilled Brooklyn, heading for the Sound and thence to Massachusetts Bay. New York uncompromisingly pledged a ten-year supply of food. Individuals stirred themselves, and out of Pomfret in Connecticut there started, as though to match the Brooklyn gesture, another flock of sheep, Boston-bound and driven by a tough old Indian fighter named Israel Putnam. Wherever a man looked in the summer of 1774, he could see indisputable evidence that the colonies as a whole could not quite accept Lord North's reasoning that Boston alone was affected.

So the Boston Port Bill was poured into the country like a reagent into a test tube, and the reaction was so typical that from the vantage point of later years it seems as though Lord North and his colleagues might well have predicted it. The old mechanisms brought into being by other crises began to turn faster and faster. The committees in every colony met, whispered, took counsel, orated, wrote and wrote again. Boston's demand for a new congress, like the Stamp Act body of 1765, was anticipated by many committees, even though Boston's hope for a revival of a non-importation agreement was deftly brushed aside.

And while committeemen were arguing, balancing, weighing, and while couriers rode from New York to Albany, from Boston to Hartford, from New Bern to Wilmington, ships that had cleared the Mersey in England weeks before brought fresh rulings. Again they were aimed solely at Boston and its hinterland, threatened to shatter the cherished political foundations of the Bay Colony as the Port Bill had shattered its economic life. The issue was being clearly, if locally, defined. The question of revenue, which had started the bubbles rising in the colonial pot, was far, far in the background, if not actually out of the picture. Through its increasingly rubber-stamp Parliament, the King's ministry was saying flatly that the colonies had only such rights as the mother country might choose from time to time to grant. And since those rights could be granted, they were also revocable at the pleasure of the Crown. And such revocation could be applied to the supposed rights of North Carolina and Delaware as well as to those of Massachusetts.

The terms of the next two acts were more than enough to set the people of other colonies atingle with apprehension. The first was the Administration of Justice Act. The trial of any Crown official for a capital offense committed in putting down a riot or in collecting revenue could, on the oath of the governor, be transferred to England. In view of the proven hostility of the colonial bench and bar to Crown officials, the act appeared reasonable enough. But it could also be taken as giving carte blanche to those officials, a blank check to use violence without fear of consequences. The action of any British court in such a case seemed a foregone conclusion.

The second act arrived with the first and sent a chill of genuine terror up and down the coast and far inland. It was known as the Massachusetts Government Act and was aimed, in Lord North's words, at "better regulating the Government of Massachusetts Bay and purging their constitution of all its crudities." Like its predecessors, this act struck only at Massachusetts and, by implication, seemed to give assurance to the other twelve well-behaved virtuous colonies that they needn't worry—so long as they continued well behaved and virtuous. But the twelve were rocked back on their collective heels as they mulled over the measures that were to discipline their errant fellow.

The act was tantamount to revoking the cherished charter of Massachusetts, to taking away all but a token remnant of the self-government to which most colonials clung. The Governor's Council, chosen in the past by the lower House, was now to be appointed by the Crown and to serve at the Crown's pleasure, responsible only to the Crown. Measure by measure the act bit deeper. The attorney general and judges were to be appointable and removable by the governor, acting in the name of the Crown. Even sheriffs and justices of the peace became virtual Crown appointees, depending on royal pleasure for their tenure of office. The very juries throughout the colony were to be chosen by the Crown-appointed sheriff. And, to many the most lethal blow, the sacred town meeting was virtually abolished. Meetings could still be held, but only when the governor gave his written consent in advance. And, if this consent were forthcoming, the meeting was shackled by the provision that the agenda had to be approved by the governor. No other topics could be brought up. A colonial of 1774 did not have to be a very profound pessimist to envision a very near future with all the colonies reduced to trading posts, administered by a small, chosen class that must look to the Crown for a livelihood as well as for orders.

These three acts, known as the "Intolerable Acts," were like high-explosive shells aimed by the North ministry to land squarely and shatteringly on Massachusetts alone. There seems to be little to indicate that the ministry foresaw that splinters from those shells would go whizzing hotly all through the colonies. It isn't likely, however, that such knowledge would have induced North to proceed differently. As it was, his ministerial battery, turning from high explosive to shrapnel, loosed a round that burst high in air and sent its pellets singing down in a pattern that blanketed the continent.

This was the Quebec Act, launched with intent only of ordering matters in Canada, which had been on a very makeshift basis since the peace. This act confirmed French law, very different from the Anglo-Saxon form, for the French inhabitants of Canada. It allowed the use of the French language for official matters. The Catholic Church, to which French Canadians were devoted, was left unmolested. These were surprisingly wise measures to have come from the ministry of North. But they set the colonies seething still more, just as the Intolerable Acts had stirred men far away from Target Boston. The sorest point was the encouragement given the Roman Catholic Church. While most of the colonies preened themselves on their religious tolerance, this was too apt to mean, "You tolerate my sect and don't come crowding in with yours." Then, too, most colonies had a bristling aversion to a union between Church and State. This generous gesture to Canada was to some people a forerunner of a flood of Anglican bishops with official status, looking to London for orders rather than to the wishes of their parishes and sees. The clamor over this point was loud, bitter, and continuous. But even more dangerous was the final part of the Quebec Act, which extended the boundaries of Quebec, and hence the provisions of the act, south as far as the Ohio. Thus all the cultural, legal, linguistic, and religious blessings bestowed on the habitant could also be forced on Protestant Anglo-Saxons who might move into that area. And more, Massachusetts, Connecticut, and Virginia had valid, if confusing, claims to vast slices of the territory. Great stretches had been set aside for veterans of the French wars. Long-sighted men, Colonel George Washington among them, had bought or were trying to buy into that area.

Certainly the year 1774 had more than filled its quota of ministerial blunders and grist for the mills of the colonial extremists. But the North ministry seemed determined to break all known records and followed the Quebec Act with the Quartering Act, a logical military measure but one that sent most colonials, extreme, moderate, or ultra-Tory, into a gibbering wrath. An earlier act had made it mandatory to quarter royal troops in buildings otherwise unoccupied. Now troops could be moved into a crammed warehouse, a church, or a private home at the whim of the upper brass.

It was time to stand up and be counted, and lines invisible but very real began to make themselves felt in city and hamlet, market town and countryside. On one side of the division stood those who felt that the Crown must be right and its rightness unquestioned. There were those who identified themselves with the Crown and subordinated all else to it, looking on dissidents as brabbling mutineers.

Some men were convinced that ministry after ministry had bungled colonial affairs badly, but time would heal all, they held. Wait. Wait. Don't protest. Bad mistakes have been made, but the Crown will see that and correct matters. As many shades of opinion ranged themselves on the other side of that invisible line. England must be shown all these errors. How else can we make our case known? But don't go too far.

We must resist or cease to exist as free men. The cost of resistance? It doesn't matter. We must take our rightful place in the empire. How many people on that side of the line followed their thoughts through? Resist? But how? And if the Crown shows no signs of seeing its errors and correcting them? The ultimate answer had surely formed in Samuel Adams' mind by now, and that answer spelled out the word "independence."

But the word had been in other minds, too, long before. Back in '69, patriot George Mason of Virginia had intently scanned a letter that ended, "That no man should scruple or hesitate a moment to use a—ms in defense

of so valuable a blessing (freedom) is clearly my opinion." The words and
the sense of the words were enough to make careful George Mason read
and re-read the letter, which had come from no firebrand, no hothead. Its
writer had been a regular attendant at the House of Burgesses, where he
spoke seldom but listened long and carefully. The man who had written so
plainly of arms and the defense of freedom had signed the letter with his
boldly characteristic flourish, "G. Washington." And to what could an
appeal to arms lead save to independence?

Now, in 1774, the Virginia House was deliberating again, and most of its
thought centered on those acts that affected only that lone colony away to
the northeast. There was an echo of the Washington-Mason letter in one
resolution, which held the significant phrase, "A Congress should be appointed . . . from all the Colonies to concert a general and uniform plan
for the defense and preservation of our common rights and continuing the
connection and dependence of said Colonies upon Great Britain under a
just, permanent and constitutional form of government." On the surface
that resolution was mild enough, but an ominous rider took most of the
balm out of it. For, said the Virginians, this congress must be bound to
issue a "humble and dutiful remonstrance to the King, who was to be conjured and besought to reflect that from our Sovereign there can be but one
appeal," thus setting down an unmistakable "Or else!"

So quick words were flying up and down the country, were becoming deeds as colony after colony voted to send delegates to a Continental
Congress to be held at Philadelphia in the coming September. In some
cases there was little trouble in arranging such a vote. In others all sorts of
steps had to be taken to get around the royal governor and his powers of
dissolution. The South Carolinians, for instance, met at a hideously early
hour in the morning, complied with all legal forms, and authorized delegates and ample funds for their expenses. So when the respected lieutenant
governor, William Bull, arrived on the scene all important business had
been done and Bull could only hurl the thunderbolt dissolving the session,
a bolt which the members had avoided just long enough by their early
session.

While other colonies debated and resolved on measures that as yet hardly
touched them directly, Boston was feeling the full impact of the Intolerable
Acts. Under a cold May rain Boston's militia turned out to stand, sodden
and shivering, the length of Long Wharf. There was Colonel John Hancock
at the head of his Boston Cadets, the same unit which figured in World
War I as the 101st Engineers, 26th Division, and as the 211th Anti-Aircraft
Battalion in World War II. The Boston Grenadier Company was in formation, a strapping lot of young men, most of them six feet tall or better.
They were commanded by Captain Joseph Pierce, and chief among his
lieutenants was burly young Henry Knox, owner of the London Book-Store
up there on present Washington Street. The Ancient and Honorable
Artillery turned out, blue coats standing out from the red mass of grenadiers
and cadets. To this day the Ancients hold their drumhead election of officers

on Boston Common. Beyond the Ancients were the little fieldpieces under Captain Adino Paddock. Boston was changing rulers, and the militia was turning out to welcome General Thomas Gage, "Vice-Admiral, Captain-General and Governor in Chief of Massachusetts," who was to replace Governor Thomas Hutchinson. Hutchinson was sailing soon for England but hoped to be back in his cherished Massachusetts during the next year, 1775. It was a vain hope. Never again would Thomas Hutchinson hear the breakers lashing at the Roaring Bulls near the harbor mouth, nor would he see Blue Hill, in whose shelter he had built his country house, shimmering vaguely over the green of the lowlands.

A boat put out from a British man-of-war in the harbor to bear the vice-admiral, captain general, and governor in chief to the rain-dappled steps of Long Wharf. Thomas Gage and his staff came gingerly ashore, received the salutes of the militia officers, and inspected the unhappy, drenched ranks. Then fifes began their shrilling; the militiamen wheeled and formed an escort for Gage up streaming cobbles of State Street and on to the rain-washed brick of the Old State House. In the second-floor Council Chamber the man with the triple title presented his credentials and the high sheriff read a proclamation from the outer balcony for the edification of the dripping citizen-soldiers and a large press of civilians. The crowd answered with three cheers, the infantry fired three volleys, and the Ancients whanged away with their brass fieldpieces. Or so contemporary reports say, without explaining how powder was kept dry in the downpour. Later there was a reception, at Boston's expense, in Faneuil Hall; toasts were drunk and warm speeches made and at last Thomas Gage was trundled off to Province House in a smart carriage.

An uninformed onlooker might be excused for thinking that the city was welcoming a beloved leader to its midst. And he would have been right so far as the die-hard Tories were concerned. As to the rest—a typical Tory wrote a friend in England "You . . . must not imagine there was any honesty in those marks of joy these Bostonians showed the General . . . no sir, it was hypocrisy all." Much depended on the point of view. To this Tory, Gage and the troops who would follow him were a protection against the radical Whigs. But to many, Whig and Tory alike, a new governor was not being welcomed. Rather, they were receiving a soldier who had come not to govern but to enforce a set of laws that struck most as being incredibly harsh and tyrannical. As to the reception, it may not have been entirely hypocrisy. An Englishman, in this same year of 1774, wrote of Boston, "In this land of bustling am I safe arrived, among the most social, polite and sensible people under heaven. To strangers friendly and kind—to Englishmen generously so." Perhaps what the Tory took for "hypocrisy" was merely the proper Bostonians being very proper, maintaining due form in observing the arrival of an accredited official to their city.

CHAPTER VI

"... *a new and grand scene open before me*"

WHILE British troops were embarking for Boston or being sculled from calm anchorages to land at Long Wharf as part of the Crown experiment in coercion, another experiment, vividly daring, was being renewed. The shell splinters that had buzzed hotly out of Massachusetts to reach far corners of the continent, the ministerial shrapnel of the Quebec and Quartering acts which had rained down in an all-embracing pattern, were producing their effect. From South Carolina to New Hampshire, men were packing saddlebags, crowding into coaches, or embarking in swift coastal vessels as the call for another and more vital congress of the colonies was answered. Only Georgia, newest and most thinly settled of all, lay in a deceptive quiet which would not last long.

On a brilliant August morning the people of Boston forgot the red coats that dotted their sacred Common and crowded down toward Bromfield's Lane and the big house of Thomas Cushing, Speaker of the House. James Bowdoin's glittering coach with its red and yellow wheels stood at Mr. Cushing's mounting block. There were four chestnut horses, nicely matched, a liveried driver and groom on the box, two very correct Negro footmen behind, liveried like their fellows. Four servants, heavy pistols bulging in leather holsters, sat their single mounts grimly, waiting for the Cushing front door to open.

Through the windows the Bostonians could catch a flash of powdered heads, braided coats, and a heaped-up buffet table. They could try to pick out words from the buzz that drifted out into the summer air. Through other windows there was a glimpse of a quieter room that held white bonnets, yards of flower-sprigged chintz, taffeta bows setting off dark hair, graying hair, brown hair, as the wives of the men about the buffet waited. Abigail Adams was there and Mercy Warren, pleasant-mannered Mrs. Sam Adams, and James Bowdoin's wife making conversation with Mrs. Cushing.

Then the Cushing door flew open and the Massachusetts delegates, leaving for the congress in far-off Philadelphia, appeared. There was John Adams in sober traveling clothes, Thomas Cushing, Robert Treat Paine. The crowd gasped as Sam Adams emerged into the August sunlight. There he stood in gorgeous claret-colored broadcloth and fresh white ruffles. Silver buckles glinted on his shoes, and the sun caught the gold top of his long cane as he settled a glossy hat on his head. Earnest, devoted Sam Adams could labor effectively for everyone except himself, was always in debt. Then someone whispered that his whole outfit had been contributed anonymously by the craftsmen of the Sons of Liberty and their emblem was stamped on the gold-headed cane as well as on the buttons that glinted from his cuffs.

Other prominent Sons stepped into the still air. There was James Bowdoin, a delegate but unable to leave his ailing wife. Dr. Warren appeared, smiling and handsome, with Josiah Quincy, whose unfortunate squint masked one of the best minds of the colony. Tough Will Molineaux was followed by John Hancock. Many thought it odd that John had not been made a delegate. Was the rift between him and Sam Adams, which dated back to the lull of a couple of years ago, still gaping? A cabinetmaker in the crowd could answer that, for he had seen the matching portraits of Hancock and Sam Adams which the former had commissioned Johnny Copley to paint. Side by side they hung now in the Hancock drawing room, up over the other slope of Beacon Hill, where you saw them the first thing when you entered. More likely Sam had wanted Merchant John to stay and watch matters in Boston.

The crowd parted as grooms brought up more single mounts, as other, plainer coaches rolled in behind Bowdoin's. There was Dr. Warren mounting, and Will Molineaux. Josiah Quincy was getting into a light chaise, and John Hancock was helping an elderly Son into the Hancock coach. First and last, nearly a hundred men would ride or drive as escorts.

The crowd swayed back again. Someone shouted; the shout was caught up. No! No! They were not leaving by the North Ferry and Cambridge. Get back! Clear the street. They're going smack-dab down Treamount Street, right past the camps, past the soldiers. Wheels grumbled, hoofs clacked on the cobbles, and the procession moved off, skirting the tented Common where sentries stood with fixed bayonets, where the tap of a drum could bring a small army to its feet.

Frederick the Great or his Russian neighbor Catherine would have known just what to do in this case. So would a later Prussian king, who admitted delegates of the people to a palace courtyard, closed the gates while his infantry, forewarned, mowed down the petitioners. But the hoofs and the wheels, stirring up a cloud of dust, passed the Common under nothing more deadly than the probably uncomprehending stares of grenadiers, light infantrymen, and their fellows of the line companies.

There was a banquet at Watertown, and the delegates pushed on over the well-worn road that would take them to New York and thence to Philadelphia. The coach rolled on alone now and the delegates were left to each other's company and their own thoughts. Of the four, only Robert Treat Paine had spent much time out of Massachusetts. Sam Adams had never crossed its borders, so far as anyone knew. And the quartet were to match their wits against men from colonies whose very names were strange; they were to oppose a rule that originated three thousand miles away in a country where none of them had been. Articulate John Adams must have thought back to a talk he had had with his lifelong friend, Jonathan Sewall, now a devout Tory. In answer to Sewall's able arguments, John had said,

"Sink or swim, live or die, survive or perish, I am with my country from this day on." Fully conscious of the task ahead, as his less diary-minded fellows must have been, John Adams wrote in all humility, "There is a new and grand scene open before me. . . . I feel myself unequal to this business."

The life of a big-scale operator of Virginia lands had a fine surface opulence. Underneath lay constant tension. There was a ready market, principally in England, for the tricky tobacco crop. Wheat grew well and could be absorbed locally or in neighboring colonies. To maintain output, land and more land had to be controlled. And that meant slaves and more slaves, and these two factors added up to cash and more cash, which was very scarce in Virginia, as it was in most of the other colonies. A good tobacco crop might meet a sagging market in England. A devastating blight or rust on narrow leaf or broad could wipe out the yield of a good year and leave an unsatisfied demand in Britain, with merchants turning to other sources to meet it. There was an added peril and a keen one in that British buyers and their Virginia domiciled factors were more than willing to advance cash or credit to assure themselves of an eventual crop, and even careful Virginians often found themselves casting so far into the future that a virtual mortgage lay on a growing crop or even on one not yet planted.

Most fortunes lay in land and slaves, and a respected, solid man, experienced in such matters, was apt to find himself named trustee for the estate of a deceased neighbor or relative. In that case land and slaves must be disposed of quickly and profitably, for Virginia bonding of trustees was tight, and heavy penalties could accrue to a trustee who was no worse than unlucky.

All these worries lay on the shoulders of Colonel George Washington in that summer of 1774 as he stood on his porticoed porch and surveyed Mount Vernon, which, incidentally, was named for Admiral Edward (Old Grog) Vernon, R.N., a close friend of an earlier Washington. The estate and its development lay very close to the colonel's heart, yielding precedence only to his country and his family. Summer was the time when the keenest eye was needed on acres and slaves. Then, too, there was the troublesome Savage estate, a good part of whose disentangling lay in his hands, along with possible penalties.

The colonel was a taciturn man and seems to have left no particular record of his feelings as he saw the always smoldering Patrick Henry, now a marked man among the Virginia burgesses, riding in along the dusty, reddish road from the east. Henry was expected, but with him came the colonel's old friend and correspondent, George Mason, and Burgess Edmund Pendleton. The visitors brought an unneeded reminder that there were other matters than those of Mount Vernon to claim the colonel's time.

Henry and Pendleton, along with Washington, had been appointed delegates to the same new congress to which the sober Yankees had ridden with such panache out of Boston. And that congress could conceivably hold far

sharper and more deadly perils than drought-crisped tobacco crop or tor-
tuous trusteeship. As for George Mason, whom Henry called "the first man
on this continent," he was present only in his role of elder statesman, giving
wise counsel to his younger colleagues and probably regretting that the
health of that rising young lawyer and burgess, Thomas Jefferson, had pre-
vented him from joining the other delegates.

The four men dined, talked far into the night, took up the thread the
next day, their words probably having much the same tenor as those in
James Bowdoin's glossy coach. It is a pity that none of the four had John
Adams' memorandum habit. Mason was a man always worth listening to,
and no one could hold the thoughts of the others to be much less enlighten-
ing. There was another dinner, and at the end Mason accompanied the
delegates down to the Potomac and watched them as they crossed over and
rode away into the north. Before the trio returned, they would have watered
their horses at strange rivers—the Brandywine, the Schuylkill, and Wis-
sahickon Creek as it flowed to a suburb called Germantown. Those names
sounded odd to Virginia ears. Time and blood would make them more
familiar.

So up and down the colonies delegates stirred and, like beads of quicksilver, flowed away to join the gathering mass at Philadelphia by the
Schuylkill, where the bells of all the churches, Episcopal, Lutheran, Roman
Catholic, Presbyterian, tolled in welcome. The city, awe-inspiring metropolis
of some thirty thousand, was new to many of the members and to them
spread out its display of humming wharves and countinghouses. There
were mellow tree-shaded squares, wide streets, and men accustomed to
errant soft dirt roads now walked straight over smooth brick. The most
pious of the newcomers had to be impressed by the chains that were
stretched across the streets each Sunday and left there as long as services
lasted. Men of business cocked their heads each Tuesday night to hear the
bells of Christ Church chime softly the "Butter Bells," which reminded
citizens that the next dawn would bring market day.

Some delegates found lodgings at the City Tavern, famous for its cellar
and its table. Others, with an eye on a limited purse, took rooms on
Chestnut Street or Front Street. The Adams cousins stayed at Mistress
Jane Port's house on Arch Street nearby, while Colonel George Washington
was put up by an old friend, Dr. William Shippen.

The great gathering began in prophetic tension. Brilliant, conservative
Joseph Galloway, a Pennsylvania delegate, had secured for this, the First
Continental Congress, the use of the Georgian majesty of the State House,
now Independence Hall. But as other members arrived in town, muted
whisperings arose and the rather perplexed Mr. Galloway found that the
newcomers had joined with local colleagues in accepting the gemlike Carpenters' Hall, newly built by master craftsmen for master craftsmen. This
building, for all its fine entrance, exquisite proportions, and unrivaled wood-
work, was much smaller and less convenient than the State House. The
gesture of acceptance had psychological undertones, for by avoiding the

seat of government, all connection with the Crown was done away with. And by moving into the seat of the powerful Carpenters' Guild, a century old already, tacit notice was served that the business of the congress concerned those who worked with their hands as well as those who rolled in leisurely carriages.

With a minimum of shuffling and side-stepping, the delegates, some forty strong until other colleagues still en route should make up the full fifty-six, settled themselves in the East Hall. To set matters moving, they elected calm, deliberate Peyton Randolph of Virginia as president. A member called for recognition, and the new president gave the floor to Thomas Lynch of South Carolina, a veteran of the Stamp Act Congress. Mr. Lynch proposed the name of Charles Thomson of Philadelphia as secretary, adding that he was a "gentleman of family, fortune and character." The nomination was carried over the rather flabbergasted objections of the ultra-conservatives, like Galloway of Pennsylvania and Duane of New York, for some men called Charles Thomson the Sam Adams of Pennsylvania.

Through these initial steps the delegates watched their fellows curiously. Some of them had met before during the Stamp Act Congress, but many were making their first appearance. A delegate from the interior of New Jersey might look askance at a fellow from far-off Rhode Island, or an aggressively rustic man might sniff mentally at the sight of a bland, urban type all prinked out like a jibby horse in peach velvet and boots shining as if a cow had licked them. But slowly they all became oriented.

A congressional freshman like Major John Sullivan from Portsmouth by the winding Piscataqua could listen to comments whispered to him by his fellow New Hampshireman, Colonel Nathaniel Folsom. It was like a tour of the colonies to hear those names. Over across the hall was oak-tough Roger Sherman from Connecticut, and nearby Maryland's Matthew Tilghman was running fastidious fingers over the carved paneling that flanked the high windows. There was conservative George Read of Delaware and fiery-cool Christopher Gadsden of South Carolina. Folsom could indicate among the New Yorkers the high-nosed Livingstons standing a little apart from James Duane and John Jay, who were known to be far to the right of the middle of the road. Fat, genial Benjamin Harrison of Virginia was close by, and near the president's dais sat gray old Stephen Hopkins of Rhode Island in Quaker dress, who had actually participated in that first feeble congress at Albany in '54. That was "Farmer" John Dickinson listening absently to his fellow Pennsylvanians, George Ross and, of course, Joseph Galloway. Off to the right was steady-minded Caesar Rodney of Delaware and Samuel Chase of Maryland. In a very short time John Sullivan's lawyer mind would have all the personalities sorted out and neatly docketed.

Day by day, as September glowed gold along the Schuylkill and the Delaware, the congress, now fifty-six strong, examined credentials and listened as the spokesman for each colony detailed his instructions. To John Sullivan fell the honor of speaking first in the mellow, airy, bright room. The men of New Hampshire, meeting at the little hill town of Exeter despite the efforts of the governor, had instructed him and Colonel Folsom "to devise, consult and adopt measures to secure and perpetuate their rights, and to restore that peace, harmony and mutual confidence which once subsisted between the parent Country and her Colonies." Many delegates found the use of the past tense most interesting. Massachusetts set forth her aim as "The restoration of that union and harmony . . . most ardently desired by all good men." The New Yorkers had come with no instructions at all, but most of the others showed an amazing uniformity of purpose. Thomas McKean, with a bow to his colleague, Caesar Rodney, spoke for Delaware, and while settling his finely cut coat ripped out against the "taking away of the property of the Colonies . . . for new-modelling the Government of the Massachusetts Bay."

This was all heartening fare for the Adams cousins, Cushing, and Robert Treat Paine. But the Bay State delegation kept silent, knowing that the lukewarms and the conservatives were expecting fireworks from it. Members began to murmur in wonder, saying that the Massachusetts men were milksops compared to the Southern planters. The roll call went on, and Thomas Cushing must have allowed himself at least to nudge Sam Adams in silent glee as a South Carolina voice proclaimed that "the Acts and Bills of Parliament in regard to Massachusetts Bay affect the whole Continent of America."

There were a hundred questions to resolve, any one of which might have split the congress as wide as Delaware Bay. Tempers rose in the East Hall. Members paced up and down the wide, cheerful central corridor of the hall in hot if muted discussion. Impromptu debates took place about the famous pump just outside in the cobbled court, where Colonel Washington might listen to Mr. Chase, or Mr. Galloway might take Charles Thomson to task for his careful omissions in his minutes.

There was the question of representation, of the number of votes alloted to each colony. Should it be on a per capita basis? And how about property? Why should a small colony's wishes offset those of a larger, richer one? Here John Sullivan was on his feet, quick temper flaring. "A little colony has its stake as well as a great one!" He had strong backing, but Patrick Henry was crying in tones that shook men's deepest emotions that there were no more colonies, that the old structure was gone and the continent in "a state of nature." He ended his blast with a perhaps unconscious quote from the Gadsden of 1768: "Let freemen be represented by numbers alone. The government is dissolved, landmarks are dissolved. Where are now your boundaries? The distinctions between Virginians, Pennsylvanians, New Yorkers and New Englanders are no more. I am not a Virginian but an American!"

Leaving the hall after Henry's plea for vote en masse and not by colonies, John Adams confessed to Cousin Sam that he had been deeply moved by the Virginian. But his legal mind, cramming down emotion, approved of the final act of the session, proposed so ably by that young New York lawyer, John Jay, which awarded one vote to each colony, regardless of wealth and population. And on this basis the sessions continued.

It was slow going, this work of shaping an inter-colonial statement to Parliament. There were dozens of factions showing. Mercantile against agricultural, Congregationalist against Presbyterian, Presbyterian against Episcopalian, Quaker against Roman Catholic, conservative and middle-of-the-roader against radical. Richard Henry Lee was often on his feet, as was John Sullivan. Christopher Gadsden and Thomas Lynch spoke and were followed by Stephen Hopkins and Joseph Galloway. Sam Adams kept surprisingly and cleverly quiet.

No one who had known Colonel Washington in the House of Burgesses expected orations from him, but his tall, rather narrow-shouldered and broad-hipped figure was always seen among small groups about the pump, strolling over the pinkish brick sidewalks, listening, interpolating a brief word here and there, a nod, a negative gesture. Once with his old friend Dr. Shippen he spent an afternoon with the Massachusetts delegation in Adams' quarters at Mistress Port's.

Sam Adams, whose fine claret-colored coat, present of the Massachusetts mechanics, was showing signs of very hard usage—for he was as untidy externally as he was neat-minded—poured wine for the doctor and the colonel. When the guests left, they carried two strong impressions with them. Robert Treat Paine, in answer to the doctor's question, had said, "Independence? A hundred times no." And John Adams, to whom the colonel listened most carefully, had said flatly, "There is no man among us that would not be happy to see accommodation with Britain." Did it occur to the guests that the reputed firebrand, Sam Adams, had said nothing?

In fact, things were not marching to Sam Adams' liking. The conservatives, even the ultras, seemed to be in the saddle, and he feared that some watered-down document, as bland as the one that had been toned down under Hutchinson at the time of the Sugar Act, would be sent to England, and then the Congress, to his way of thinking, would have been in vain. There was no real, immediate issue for his genius to seize onto and fan into flame.

Life in Philadelphia flowed quietly on outside Carpenters' Hall. Snows and pinks and schooners glided about the wharves. Each Tuesday night the chimes of Christ Church foretold a new market day. Through the daylight hours vendors cried fresh vegetables or scrapple or pepper pot. Pretty Philadelphia girls skimmed along the brick sidewalks under colored parasols or, if the day was very bright, sheltered behind little green masks they held in place by a bar gripped between white teeth. Rural delegates thought the girls Frenchified. Inside Carpenters' Hall, debate dragged on, inconclusive if acrimonious.

Then gallop-gallop-gallop! With a timing that was almost melodramatic, into town rode Paul Revere, his saddlebags bulging with news from Boston and, in particular, with a set of resolutions drawn up by Dr. Joseph Warren for a convention of Massachusetts towns. For Sam Adams and men whose thoughts kept step with his the resolutions were as timely as the Boston Massacre had been. They became known as the Suffolk Resolves, and as Peyton Randolph read them slowly and ominously to a plenary session of the Congress, a hush fell over the East Hall, the conservatives stunned and the radicals almost incredulous with gratification. Under the sculptured ceiling the words rumbled out: ". . . the arbitrary will of a licentious Minister . . . the streets of Boston thronged with military executioners . . . murderous law . . . We therefore advise . . ."

There was not even a hint of restraint in the phrases that Joseph Warren had penned. When Peyton Randolph had finished, the dullest delegate could summarize what had come out of a house in Suffolk County in Massachusetts. The Coercive Acts that had been launched against the Bay Colony were declared to be unconstitutional and hence not to be obeyed. The people of Massachusetts were urged to form a government of their own to collect taxes and withhold them from the royal government until the Coercive Acts had been repealed. They were strongly advised to arm and to form their own militia. The most stringent economic sanctions were recommended in terms that Charles Thomson could not have bettered.

There was a heavy pause as all this was assimilated. Then a shouting swarm of delegates engulfed the Massachusetts men. Men from the Carolinas, from Virginia and New Jersey and Rhode Island, thumped the nearest Adams back, wrung a Cushing hand, beamed at Robert Treat Paine. The mad surge of enthusiasm boiled higher and higher, and the congress formally adopted the Suffolk Resolves, without a comma changed or a thought toned down. A few shocked ultra-conservatives like James Duane and Joseph Galloway dissented bitterly, insisted on their high disapproval being certified in the minutes, but their cause was gone.

The rest of the congress could have been accurately predicted from that day, September 17, 1774. Joseph Galloway, fighting hard and cleanly to the end, tried to have a plan of his adopted, a carefully reasoned Plan of Union that had many good points and none that was petty. But he was too late. The hoofs of Paul Revere's post horse had trampled the plan into the cobbles of the Philadelphia streets.

By mid-October, still under heavy conservative fire, the congress adopted a series of resolves. Not only were the Coercive Acts denounced as roundly as they had been at the Milton meeting, but revenue measures dating back to 1763 were blasted. The keeping of a standing army in the colonies was blistered, as were the various parliamentary measures dissolving colonial assemblies. Then, in a set of ten resolutions, various rights of colonists were set forth. There were the rights of life, liberty, and property. There was the right of colonial assemblies to have exclusive power, subject dutifully to royal veto, in all matters of taxation and internal polity. All in all, no less than thirteen acts of Parliament were declared illegal, with the rider that economic sanctions were to be applied until those acts were repealed.

A few days later, as the congressional term waned, a Continental Association was formed, modeled not on any fire snort of Sam Adams, but on a measure first framed in Williamsburg in Virginia. This association provided that as of December 1, 1774, all imports from Great Britain were to cease. The slave trade, from which British merchants largely profited, was to end. Other shafts were launched against British commerce. But perhaps more important were the recommended ways and means for carrying on life in the face of this change. A committee was to be elected in every county, town, and city to implement this association. Committees of this type would meet far up the Merrimac, along the Mohawk and the Brandywine and the James and the Congaree. The committees were given power to punish local violations and, should the higher colonial echelons be delinquent, they would be boycotted by the others.

Few men, possibly not even Sam Adams, could have dreamed of so solid and sweeping a closing of ranks as the resolutions and the articles of association. Joseph Galloway, shaken to the depths of his loyal soul, nearly helpless with rage and frustration, signed the final document with the other delegates. But he must have wondered at the unity. From Delaware north, the colonies could do fairly well without England. There were other markets. But the Virginians, the Carolinians, and the Marylanders! Trade with England was their lifeblood. It did not mean merely prosperity. It meant the roots of existence. It had not been mere oratory when Christopher Gadsden and Patrick Henry, Southerners both, had trumpeted out that they were Americans, not men of one colony or another.

On October 20 there was a great dinner at the City Tavern on Walnut Street to mark the end of the Congress. Colonel Washington was magnificent in blue and gold braid. Thomas McKean wore deep maroon velvet with sweeping skirts. Sam Adams managed somehow to freshen up the mechanics' gift of claret cloth, and Cousin John, handsome in blue and canary with a superb wig, was talked into dancing a minuet with Mrs. Thomas Lynch. There were mounds of Philadelphia baked oysters in their shells, deft colored servants who really understood the art of waiting on table. Madeira glasses were filled, emptied, and filled, over and over. Someone proposed a toast, "May the sword of the Parent never be stained with the blood of her Children." A Quaker guest observed that it was more of a prayer than a toast and felt that he could properly join in. The dinner broke up very late, and despite an admitted quantity of Madeira, John Adams told his diary that he had not a trace of a hangover.

So the delegates prepared to leave the city by the Schuylkill. They had thrown out a bold and momentous defiance. Some voices had been raised louder than others. Some men had spent their time lobbying so that others spoke their thoughts on the floor. But the fruits of this Congress cannot be said to belong to any one man or group of men. It was not Sam Adams' Congress, nor Caesar Rodney's, nor Christopher Gadsden's. A phrase spoken by a Massachusetts jurist more than a century later describes it best. For the Congress had expressed "the felt necessities of the times."

CHAPTER VII

They Were Known as Minutemen

D URING the long days and weeks that the Congress had been sitting
in Philadelphia, the needle of revolution, of which that Congress
was only an expression, held steady on the compass, rose and bore
always to the northeast. Before the delegates had even started for the city
by the Schuylkill, the Coercive Acts were manifesting themselves in Massachusetts and particularly in Boston. Through the spring and summer His
Majesty's transports had been heading in to Boston Harbor, bringing troops
and more troops to bolster the original tiny police garrison and to see to it
that Bostonians accepted the new order peacefully if not cheerfully.

Company by company they tramped ashore at Long Wharf or were
lightered in from anchorages among the green of the harbor islands. Interminably they came, men of the line companies, grenadiers, light infantry,
fusiliers. History, past, present, and future, landed with them. Most of the
regiments had battle honors from Minden or Dettingen or Fontenoy.
Others had served at Culloden or Quebec or Gibraltar. Here and there units
might be invisibly branded with the shame of Prestonpans. Soon all would
write scores of New World names into their regimental histories. And
descendants of the Bostonians who sourly watched them make their camps
on the Common would stand in an unguessed future with those same regiments along French rivers, in bleak North Africa, on Normandy beaches and
the bitter ridges of Korea.

Those descendants would know the 4th Foot as the Royal North Lancashires, or the 14th as the West Yorkshires. Up from New York came the
23rd, the Royal Welch Fusiliers, clinging fiercely then as now to odd prerogatives. They defiantly substituted a c in the word "Welsh." They ate
leeks on St. David's Day and their field music was always headed by a
cynical goat with gilded horns. A 1917 version of music and goat was on
hand to add dignity to the debarkation on British soil of an American
general named Pershing.

But the Boston garrison of 1774 was firmly embedded in the eighteenth
century. For the moment most troops camped on the soft slopes of the
Common, but cold weather would come and, under the hated Quartering
Act, Gage could herd his men into warehouses, tanneries, and, of course,
into private homes. Open, in the King's name. You will lodge, furnish with
heat and light one sergeant major, one sergeant, and a regimental clerk. You
will also make places for them at your table.

To back up the army, a strong fleet under petty, niggardly Admiral
Samuel Graves lumbered into the harbor, moored at strategic points to

make sure that the closing of the port of Boston existed in fact as well as on paper. With Graves came a few hundred Royal Marines, whom Gage promptly landed, to the disgust of Graves, who hoped to turn a penny or two for himself through providing quarters and rations for them on his ships. An officer did not need to wait for winter to find billets, and tailor Francis Shaw, bitterly anti-Tory, complained to his silversmith neighbor, Paul Revere, that a marine major was under his roof. The major's name was John Pitcairn, an amazingly gentle and understanding man to have been a marine, for that service in the eighteenth century was far different from that of the nineteenth and twentieth. In the few months of life that remained to him, John Pitcairn won solid trust and affection from Whig as well as Tory. It is odd that legend has painted him as the savage ogre of the nineteenth of April.

Nearly as popular as Pitcairn was young Lord Percy, camped with his Northumberland Fusiliers along the edge of high Beacon Street, popping in and out of John Hancock's house, which faced his tents, making himself agreeable to Hancock's friends and, according to legend, carrying on a mild flirtation with Dorothy Quincy, whose name the merchant prince hoped to change to Hancock. It is even said that the young earl managed to melt tough old Will Molineaux, mob leader and Hancock's neighbor.

But there were few Percys and Pitcairns in Gage's garrison, or if there were, Boston nerves were too tense to perceive them. A shipmaster or a merchant could stand by the beacon that gave its name to a street and a hill and look down on wharves that berthed only the King's ships. He could train a glass over harbor and inflowing river and see them unscarred by keel or oar that did not belong to the Royal Navy. The closing of Boston was a fact, even to the ferries themselves; and Thomas Gage, along with the local Crown adherents, could sit back and with tolerant amusement wait for this most cantankerous of cities to be starved into submission, to watch with approval the sudden growth of Salem and Marblehead, which would surely fatten on the trade denied Boston.

But the script was written differently. The Marbleheaders and the Salem men placed their facilities at the disposal of the Boston merchants. More, they began shipping fish and other supplies overland to Boston, and the north-running roads became thick with carts, which the country people called "Lord North's Coasters." Inland towns began sending supplies, even luxuries, over the choke-neck of Roxbury into the city. Down across the New Hampshire border came food and clothing. Loaded carts rumbled up from Connecticut and Rhode Island. And if Gage and the Tories were disconcerted by the response of New England, they must have turned turkey-red as post riders brought news of the quick rallying of the Carolinas, of New York and Delaware and New Jersey and Virginia and Pennsylvania. Transshipped from Manhattan or from Sound ports came rice and fish and clothing and money. The crowning touch must have been the receipt of actual specie from London itself.

There were other alarming symptoms to be noted by Loyalists. New faces began to be seen along Tremont Street, drifting in vague worry in and out of Province House, putting up in the Tory inns. Among the provisions of the Coercive Acts was the appointment by the Crown, not election by the people, of the Council. Many sincere and able men, notified of their appointment, accepted eagerly. Perhaps they could do their part in righting times that were far off center. It seems odd that experience had not taught, that the lesson of the fate of those men who accepted the duty of distributing the hated stamps had been forgotten. Actually, it was like playing over an old record. Mobs rose throughout the colony, acting not always on the purest of principles and often showing a violence that Will Molineaux would have applauded. One by one the appointees, who survive in history as the Mandamus Councilors, gave up the fight and took refuge in Boston under the muskets of the King's troops.

Up from Marshfield came Nathaniel Thomas, abandoning a fine river property. From far-off Hardwick in the shadow of Potopaug Mountain, Timothy Ruggles, brigadier general of militia, made his way. There were Epes Sargent from red-rocked Cape Ann and John Murray from the Rutland ridges, and hundreds of others. Only a few were councilors, but all thought alike. Nor were they all important men, for the bulk were small traders, farmers, mechanics, men perhaps with no great stake in the triumph of the Crown but with an unshakable belief that that triumph was right.

This exodus cannot be assayed in terms of wealth, education, ability, or breeding. High and low, families split. When Nathaniel Thomas left Marshfield, his wife and son stayed on, kept the property, part of which Son John was later to sell to Daniel Webster. Epes Sargent's sons, Paul Dudley and John, followed sharply diverging courses, the former serving under Washington and the latter under the British flag.

Another manifestation became evident as time slipped uneasily by. One by one militia officers of known Tory tendencies were persuaded, coerced, or induced by physical force to toss in their commissions. The colonels were the chief targets, since the officering of militia formations lay pretty much in their hands. In Worcester, in Springfield, in Barre, in Taunton, in big towns and in small, the old formations melted away, were replaced by units considered reliable by those who were clinging desperately to what they felt to be their rights.

From the Berkshires to Cape Cod, matters were not moving as Thomas Gage could have wished. And, like mosquitoes rising from a marsh, a cloud of minor irritants buzzed thicker and thicker about his head. He needed civilian labor, skilled and unskilled, to work for the fleet and the army. Barracks must be built, storehouses, bake ovens. He called for artisans and was answered by a cold silence. Angered, he applied to Rhode Island, New York, Connecticut, and a trickle so feeble as to be useless was the result. At last he had to send to Nova Scotia, but the men who came down were either impeded by their Boston colleagues or showed a most annoying sympathy with them.

There were odd accidents. Hay barges sank in deep water. Provision carts began to suffer from a plague of broken axles or wobbly wheels that went skimming off at the first bit of rough road. A newly raised brick wall might crumble in a very mild shower. Countrymen, surprisingly supplied with money, slipped over Roxbury Neck, bought drinks for privates off duty, did their best to persuade them to desert or, failing that, to sell their muskets and bayonets.

Through these wearying days it must be said that General Thomas Gage, possibly softened by his American wife, a Kemble from New Jersey, was good-humored, tolerant, and forbearing. Harsher methods could have snapped the spine of active dissent a dozen times in the past. Now Gage had a sure weapon, given him with the Coercive Acts. He had only to reach out a hand, send out a sergeant and a squad of infantry, authorize a mounted party of young officers to ride out into the countryside, and he could have seized Warren, Hancock, Benjamin Church, the Adamses, and shipped them to England for a quick trial and almost certain death by hanging. He held his hand, kept his temper, gave his dinners and receptions at Province House, hoping always for a better turn of the tide.

There were lighter, happier sides to life in Boston. The London Book-Store, which fat, likable Henry Knox had opened for himself on Cornhill, just across from Williams' Court, was becoming, despite Henry's known Whig views and activities, very much of a social center. Young Tory girls were brought there by watchful mamas to observe the shelves of edifying literature and to be observed by handsome young British officers of the Royal Irish or the Lincolnshires. By midmorning the shop took on the air of a more than fashionable salon, with ruddy colonels bowing to dowagers and slim girls flirting their fans at captains and ensigns.

The proprietor seemed on good terms with everybody, soldier or civilian, but he sought out the former and could be found, deep in the shop, poring over works on gunnery or field fortifications with an officer of Royal Artillery and an infantry subaltern or two, asking keen questions, listening, reaching for another leather-bound tome to verify some point. The officers agreed that, for an American and civilian, young Knox had an amazing grasp of things military.

He did not neglect the rest of his clientele entirely, however. With his shattered hand carefully wrapped in a white silk scarf—he had lost two fingers and part of another on a gunning expedition in the harbor—he made himself agreeable, and more than agreeable to the mothers who had brought their daughters to see the bindings and the uniforms. Henry Burbeck, a contemporary and, later, a fellow artilleryman, noted more than once that little Miss Lucy Flucker, daughter of Thomas Flucker, dyed-in-the-wool Tory and secretary to the province of Massachusetts, seemed tireless in her quest for new titles, which necessitated long talks with Proprietor Henry Knox. He and many others, except possibly for Flucker père, could have been little surprised to read in the Gazette of June 20, 1774:

Last Thursday (the 16th) was married, by the Rev. Dr. Caner, Mr. Henry Knox of this town, to Miss Lucy Flucker, second daughter to the Hon. Thomas Flucker, Esq., Secretary of the Province.

This match, with its flavor of elopement and Gretna Green, gave Tory Boston and Whig Boston plenty to buzz and rustle about. Perhaps it took Whig minds off the troops on the Common and the Tories' off the hustling of the mandamus councilors out in the hinterland. However the town may have felt about the wedding, there is no doubt about fat Henry and his Lucy, their marriage being one of the happiest in Bay State annals.

Sometime after the wedding Henry Knox had another young visitor, this time from out of the province. He was nearly as tall as Knox, though not as heavy. He wheezed a little, as though with asthma, and as if to match his host's maimed hand, he walked with a slight limp. He introduced himself —Nathanael Greene, from the west shore of Narragansett Bay in Rhode Island. Knox recognized the name, for he had been shipping out parcels of military books to Nathanael Greene, Esq., of Warwick, for the last two or three years.

Young Greene, heir to a small family empire on which hundreds of Rhode Islanders depended for a livelihood, and member of the Rhode Island Assembly, had come to Boston on an odd mission. In the inner fast- nesses of the shop he told about it in a low tone, wheezing a little as he talked. He knew Knox's reputation as a good Whig and hoped that the young man could help him. On the west shore of Narragansett a militia company, a new one, was being formed. Jim Varnum was at the head of it and Nathanael's cousin Kit was most active. The names were new to Henry Knox. Later Colonel James Varnum and Colonel Christopher Greene would be well known to him. But about the militia company, to be called the Kentish Guards. Nathanael wanted to join it too. There had been some difficulty about his stiff knee and growing asthma, people saying that he was just not cut out to be a soldier. But that had been cleared up, and now what Nathanael wanted, what he had come all the way from Rhode Island to find, was a musket. It was useless to think of enlisting unless he could furnish his own weapon, and firearms were terribly scarce in Rhode Island. Did Henry Knox know of safe channels through which one might be pro- cured?

That night Nathanael headed back to Warwick in Rhode Island, riding on a load of straw that hid the good British musket to which Knox's advices had guided him. A day or so later young Greene must have given a shudder of relief. Another man had tried to smuggle a musket through the Roxbury lines, had been roughly handled, tarred, feathered, and ridden through Bos- ton on a rail. If legend is correct—and it certainly is not incredible— Nathanael had more than the musket as basis for his retrospective shudder, for it is said that he also brought with him a deserting British sergeant to teach the Kentish Guards and other Narragansett units the manual of arms and such esoteric matters as "the Column of Attaque and Plesion."

Nathanael Greene and the Kentish Guards were symptomatic of activi- ties elsewhere, of the reorganization of the militia. This was not too diffi- cult a matter. Militia units went back to the seventeenth-century Train Bands. Ninety-nine years before, they had swarmed out of their villages to answer the call for King Philip's War. Later the French wars, Indian raids, and incursions had sent them into the field. They existed as a matter of law, and old statutes required a certain amount of drill by all able-bodied men and the possession of a musket, powder, and shot by each member.

This was true in virtually all the colonies. New York was refurbishing its old cadres, and its neighbors south along the coast were as busy. At first glance this matter might have seemed more difficult in the slaveholding areas, where few important centers of population existed to form available reservoirs of man power. But in those colonies, particularly in the Carolinas and Georgia, a peculiar system made the gathering of local forces almost easier than in the more thickly settled North.

Since the earliest days, the colonists had found it advisable to organize and maintain an almost constant patrol, particularly at night, to guard against possible slave uprisings. This soon became highly systematized, with districts set up on a military basis, with command of the patrols rotating from plantation owner to plantation owner. Thus a large holder might serve as colonel for a given number of weeks with legally appointed majors, captains, and lieutenants under him. His term expired, he turned command over to the next colonel on the roster, the latter bringing his own subordinates with him. This plan, while held necessary, was regarded as being highly onerous and was avoided whenever possible. Nonetheless, when 1775 rolled around, those colonies had ready to hand a trained force of mounted musketeers ready to take the field under proven officers.

Carolina historians have claimed that the patrol system was essential, saying that their forebears had not had the judgment shown by slaveholders farther north, who bought only docile, well-trained slaves from the West India plantations. To the Carolinas and Georgia were sent jungle-fresh, war-like Negroes whose womenfolk would hardly inspire a mammy song. This may be true, but in the late 1760s Colonel George Washington advertised for a runaway slave distinguished by tribal tattooing on his cheeks and cannibalistically filed teeth. The runaway also spoke little or no English.

Military and civil stirrings outside of Massachusetts were important, if smaller, bubbles about the rim of the caldron whose spiritual center was Boston, where matters were coming to a faster, more ominous boil. Thomas Gage, properly concerned about the health and morale of his ever-growing garrison, began sending units out over Roxbury Neck on practice marches that carried the red files sometimes as far as Watertown or even Waltham. British subalterns were quick to notice the intense interest on the part of the townspeople and the drivers of country carts. Flippant young officers were amused at the antics of the peasants. Their more serious-minded fellows sensed a unity and a purpose in squads of farmers drilling near a tavern in Dedham and returned to their quarters quietly frowning.

Without warning, one march turned out not to be for practice. A few red-coated companies swung over what is now the Larz Anderson Bridge in Cambridge, seized a store of powder and arms belonging to the province, cut out into Charlestown, nobbled up more province supplies, and returned in triumph to Boston. Militarily Gage's act was a sound one. Psychologically and practically it was an error. Powder and arms belonged to the province, and Gage's men had snapped them up without a trace of formality. A dispassionate observer could reason that the British commander had shown fear by his hurried move. More than that, he provided the Massachusetts militia with a superb dress rehearsal that would pay big dividends in the future.

From the Boston area, riders went out. Bells rang and alarm guns were fired. From the North Shore, from the Merrimac, from oak ridges of the interior, farmers left their fields, lawyers their clients, shopkeepers and tavernkeepers their customers. Individuals flowed into squads, squads into platoons, and platoons into companies. There is no accurate count of the numbers who turned out that day in early September 1774, but all estimates run into the thousands. Distance seemed to mean nothing. Merchant John Andrews wrote to his friend, William Breck, Philadelphia agent for Messrs. Amory & Taylor of Boston, "Though they had an account at Marlborough [sic] of the powder's being removed, last Thursday night, yet they were down to Cambridge (which is thirty miles) by eight o'clock Fryday morning with a troop of horse and another of foot, both under command of Gib. Speakman." This is the same Speakman whose white-coated company would later march with John Glover's Marbleheaders, the amphibious 14th Massachusetts.

Fortunately there was no clash and the militia returned peaceably to town and farm. Thomas Gage had unwittingly given them a practical lesson in quick mobilization by which all ranks would profit. The close-knit web of the Committees of Correspondence, which had sent out the word, had been well tested. The laggard and the disaffected had been shown up and could be weeded out. New means of communication could be developed, better mobilization routes explored, leaks deliberate or unconscious could be stopped. In a smaller way this test was as valuable to the future of the Massachusetts troops as was the sudden dispatch of the whole country's National Guard, direct heirs of the militia, to the Mexican Border in 1916, a move without which the formation of the A.E.F. of 1917 would have been far more difficult, perhaps impossible.

A restless hush fell over Massachusetts and its fellow New Englanders. In Salem, where Gage had gone to observe matters, the Provincial Congress met despite all bans and decrees, seemingly unperturbed by the presence of the purple-trimmed ranks of the 59th East Lancashires. Joseph Warren, Elbridge Gerry, Benjamin Church, Nathaniel Appleton, Richard Devens, Azor Orne kept firm hands on large districts and small. They debated, argued, and perhaps most important, kept a stream of letters going out to Committees of Correspondence at Stonington and Norwich in Connecticut, to Newport and Warwick and Providence in Rhode Island, to Portsmouth in New Hampshire, and, until the Continental Congress ended, to the Adamses and Cushman and Paine in Philadelphia. All that the Provincial Congress did was important, but the driest tinder was embodied in an act that set up a Committee of Safety. Headed by John Hancock—had he not been colonel of the Boston Cadets?—it was empowered very broadly to call out the militia of the province when, in the committee's judgment, such a summons was necessary. To implement such a call, a special group was set up within the usual militia cadres, men who could be counted on to answer at once, armed and ready. The idea was not a new one, something of the sort probably dating back to the Train Bands. But the name given these men was new and they kept that status until war forced the formation of a true field army. Then they passed into history, but their name has survived. They were known as minutemen.

Fall painted the trees of Massachusetts, set long ridges and steep, pond-bottomed valleys ablaze with blood red and gold. Then it stripped bough and limb, leaving them silver-drab against oncoming winter. But the change of seasons brought no added color, no marked increase in comfort to Boston, puffing irritably under the effects of the Port Bill and the presence of the garrison that seemed to grow with each sail that broke the horizon off Minot's Ledge.

All supplies for the townspeople were hard to come by and increasingly hard to pay for. It was all very well for the Marbleheaders to send sweet oil and fish and woolens. Gage, interpreting the Port Bill rather strictly, refused ferry rights to the shippers, and the added miles involved in carting clear around to Roxbury Neck ran up all prices. As in the days of the Sugar Act and its enforcement, the Royal Navy scudded about among the islands of the harbor, holding up mud scows, seizing the most battered dories and rowboats. Trade, of course, was dying and unemployment grew ominously. In a WPA gesture Gage set as many out-of-work men as he could clearing the wharves and warehouses, but he could pay them little, and sullen men, hands in their pockets and growing despair in their hearts, lounged along Lynn Street or Ship Street, glowering at the empty wharves that had once pumped life into the crooked streets of the city.

Winter came on warm and stayed warm. Not once did the Charles freeze over, and there were light coatings of snow cloaking the escarpments of Dorchester Heights and the twin hills across in Charlestown. But even with the mild weather, life in Boston became worse and worse. For years past the countryside for miles around had been deforested and much of the town's firewood was shipped up from Maine. Now only wood for the garrison could be brought in by water, prices jumped dizzily and the unemployed shivered under the nor'easters that whipped down across bleak Noddles Island. Even the garrison felt the pinch, for little space could be spared for warming the enlisted men. Guards at Roxbury Neck, at Charlestown Ferry, looked wistfully out through bone-chill December dusks and saw warm orange lights show in the houses outside the lines. It is more than possible that cold hearths lay behind the windows' glow, but that would scarcely be apparent to unimaginative sergeants and enlisted men. Murky evenings and somber sunrises, those home lights pulled at the shivering men.

One night there was a whispered betrayal and a sergeant and eight men of the Royal Welch were arrested as they made their final plans to break away into the interior, taking their regimental standards with them. Before the end of the year the guard post at the Charlestown Ferry was abolished. Too many men had slipped away from there, probably aided by appropriately bribed sailors from the fleet. Gage was genuinely afraid that his force might desert from under him. In this he underrated the essential toughness of the British soldiers. There were constant desertions, but they added up to no significant total. The bulk of the garrison grumbled, fumed, did as little work as possible, fought with the Bostonians, and took great delight in hacking at the handsome fence around John Hancock's house up on the hill.

There were far more important things than random desertions for Thomas Gage to worry about had he turned his rather sluggish mind to them. He might have reflected on the surprising turnout of the militia in September. He needed no spies to tell him that the militia was still drilling and drilling faithfully, "when the Parson as well as the Squire stands in ranks with a fire-lock." He could have learned that Colonel William Lee of Marblehead "Was not asham'd to be taught the manual exercise in particular."

There was the question of the militia cannon in Boston. Those in Charlestown had been secretly trundled away into the interior by far-sighted patriots. That must not happen in Boston. A double guard was placed over the Old and New Gun Houses. To Gage's wrath, feather-footed miscreants found a side door to the Old Gun House, craftily took the pieces out through Frank Johonnot's garden. When this loss was discovered, Gage decreed that the guns remaining in the New Gun House—"which stands directly opposite the encampment of the 4th Regiment and in the middle of the Street near the large Elm tree"—be placed inside the camp itself the very next night, the house to be under heavy guard until that time. In the morning gunner officers threw open the house and found it empty. So Gage's staff, totting up relative strengths, could reckon that in addition to unguessed numbers of passably armed militiamen, the rebels-to-be could count now on several highly serviceable fieldpieces.

Up in New Hampshire sleet-coated snow lay thicker than around the great U of Boston Harbor, but big-voiced John Sullivan kept the militia companies churning the fields and pastures into sloughs of ice-riddled mud. Long after a red sun had dropped back of the rising western ridges he cheerfully squelched back to the graceful white house, still standing, that he had built for his Lydia at Durham, not far from Portsmouth, along the twist and flow of the Oyster River. It was a house that was quite in key with the fine homes of that area, with the Purcells', the Whipples', Thomas Wentworth's with the golden pineapple of hospitality over the broken pediment, even with the classic splendor of Lady Pepperrell's on the Kittery shore. John Sullivan had come a long way from his first start as chore boy for Sam Livermore over in Portsmouth. Most of the mansions

had been open to him, but now some of the traditionalists were looking at
him uneasily, if not hostilely. John Wentworth, serious, able royal governor, could not be expected to approve his old friend's course, nor could
Peter Livius with his flavor of European universities and his honorary
degree from Harvard College down there near Boston. Of course cantankerous Wyseman Claggett, notary and tabellion publick by act of Parliament, had been one of the first to turn from him. But the Irish redemp-
tioner's son had set his course, would hold to it for the rest of his life.

His energetic mind must have turned often to Boston, where dissent
had switched from the theoretical to the highly practical. Down there
things were *happening*. Up in New Hampshire no British troops stopped
the traveler with weary requests for passes to be shown. The Royal Navy
threw no blight over Portsmouth's wharves and warehouses. Gundalows,
scows, skiffs eased down the many-branched Piscataqua without let or
hindrance. But John Sullivan could recall conversations with men from
unbelievably remote colonies in the broad sunlit corridor of Philadelphia's
Carpenters' Hall. It *has* happened in Massachusetts. It *could* happen in
North Carolina—or New Hampshire. So far it hadn't, but John Sullivan
always preferred action to debate. There was no action along the Piscataqua
or the Oyster.

On a soggy December afternoon a spent horse was reined in at the white
house on the Oyster River. Sullivan surely knew the chilled man who dismounted by the front door. Paul Revere was bringing word from the Boston Committee of Safety, bringing it to a man who wanted action. The
silversmith had had a bad time leaving Boston. Controls were tighter than
ever, and an outbound traveler had to satisfy all sorts of military dignitaries in order to leave town. Unless, of course, he had a *laissez-passer* from
Gage, but such were only for proven Tories, not for a North End silversmith. The roads had been bad, too, Revere went on in his good-humored
way, but the news was worth a far worse trip. In Boston taverns, in grog-
shops, perhaps at British headquarters itself, right-minded men had learned
that Tom Gage planned to slip out a boatload or two of infantry to take
over Portsmouth's Fort William and Mary. So far the fort held only a
token garrison and—surely John Sullivan would know this—powder and
arms.

Paul Revere had to tell the restless Irishman nothing more. Then, probably refreshed and dried out, the silversmith headed his horse south for
Boston. John Sullivan was a man to whom little had to be explained or
expanded.

In a few days' time even those Bostonians who were not in the confidence
of the inner councils of the dissidents could note a stewing and a flurry
around Province House. Some damned rebels up in New Hampshire had
swarmed into Fort William and Mary, sometimes called Newcastle Fort,
seized the tiny garrison, carted off all stores, and had pretty well dismantled
the fort itself. John Andrews noted that the "affair at Portsmouth . . . has
caus'd the General to send the *Scarborough* there to keep 'em in order." It

was all the general could do, considering his relatively small force. If Sullivan's coup did not make him more thoughtful, it should have. Gage could reason uneasily that, as a mere word from Boston had set New Hampshire moving at once, so a whisper from New Bern in North Carolina could react in Charleston or Williamsburg.

Wearily Boston sweated out the end of the year 1774. More troops, more marines were landed, and it was rumored in the markets that the contractors for the Royal Navy alone were signing up for "a Tun weight of Mutton every day." At that rate, how much mutton would appear on civilian tables and at what price? Why, already housewives were paying half a dollar a pair for partridges that not so long ago cost only eightpence!

CHAPTER VIII

". . . to act solely on the defensive"

FAR eastward across the Atlantic the detonations that had been rumbling out along Tremont Street, down State Street, on the Charles and the Piscataqua echoed sharply in the British Parliament. The ailing Pitt came up with a plan for conciliation which was soundly beaten. Then, surprisingly, Lord North offered his idea of a neat, peaceful settlement. A few years earlier it might have been considered. Now it left too many recent questions unanswered. More, it gave no assurance that a whim of the increasingly rubber-stamp Parliament might not hopelessly reverse any immediate concessions. Parliament passed North's bill and then, as though to compound its futility, was busy with another act which, when known, would swing many American moderates to the side of Gadsden, Rodney, Henry, and Sam Adams. But that act still lay in the mists of the future.

In Massachusetts, committees and congresses buzzed away as diligently as their British opposite numbers. In February of 1775 the Committee of Public Safety—a body that has been revived in virtually every crisis down to and including World War II—was sitting in the relative security of Charlestown, just across the river from Gage's guard posts. John Hancock was there, handsome Dr. Joseph Warren, Dr. Benjamin Church with his air of bland sophistication, Colonel William Heath, who in his post-war memoirs would scorn the pomp of the pronoun "I" and refer to himself as "our General." Azor Orne came from Marblehead and was joined by Richard Devens. With amazing unanimity it was voted that "all kinds of warlike stores be purchased sufficient for an army of fifteen thousand men." A form letter was prepared for emergency transmission to all commanding officers of militia and minutemen to assemble, on receipt, "one fourth part of the militia." The purchase of twenty hogsheads of rum was authorized, to be delivered to the town of Concord, a spot, of course, far out of the reach of Gage's men. Set routes were prescribed for all couriers. The committee also asked Joseph Warren to get in touch with Major Adino Paddock in Boston and find out quietly how many of Paddock's officers and gunners could be counted on "to form an artillery company, when the constitutional army of the province should take the field."

Across Charlestown Neck, in Cambridge, the Provincial Congress was sitting, humming with similar resolves. A committee was set up to "observe the movements of all who should attempt to carry into execution the Regulating Act" (the Boston Port Bill with all its trimmings) and, if the committee thought such an attempt was in the air, "to alarm, muster and cause to be assembled with the utmost expedition" an adequate force of militia. As for the militia itself, the shadow of a true military framework was set up, a measure which might, in time, transform the local city, town, and village companies into an actual army of the province of Massachusetts. Under this, Jedediah Preble, Artemas Ward, Seth Pomeroy, John Thomas, and William Heath were to be general officers, with a cautious rider to the effect that the appointments would hold "so long as it [the militia] should be retained by the Committee of Safety and no longer." The Congress had no intent of creating a military hierarchy for Massachusetts. Like most emergency appointees, these men were picked on past performance and were beyond their prime. Seth Pomeroy had distinguished himself at the capture of Louisburg in 1745 and was now nearly seventy. Ward, already "sick of the stone," had done well under Abercrombie at Lake George in 1758. 1745 and 1758! Back in the good old days, before Sugar and Stamp Acts, before the Boston Port Bill.

In Boston, where drumbeat and sentry's challenge were becoming a part of the local flavor, adherents of the Congress carried on their daily lives as best they might, listened, watched, sent fact and rumor to the nearest point for transmission to Congress or committee. An unofficial sort of Civilian Defense Corps of spotters took form, meeting in great secrecy at the Green Dragon. There were Joshua Bracket, keeper of the Cromwell Head on School Street; Ben Edes, the printer; Joseph Ward, distiller; Paul Revere, silversmith; and Thomas Crafts, painter, to mention a few of the more prominent. Despite their secrecy—nearly all of them were Masons—they found that news and plans had a way of leaking to Gage's headquarters. They sought in vain to plug that leak, but it dribbled away secrets like a leaky tap. Had none of them noted that Dr. Benjamin Church, member of the Provincial Congress and the Committee of Safety, seemed very thick with some of the people about Gage? The doctor was questioned, answered frankly that he was much in Tory and army circles, thus finding out plans and measures against the patriots. His statement was accepted, but no one seemed to think it worth while to follow up an observation of one of Church's medical students who had noted that the perennially hard-up but high-living doctor was suddenly chucking golden guineas about and taking up with a new and expensive mistress.

There were also leaks at Province House. In February, Thomas Flucker, ultra-loyal secretary to the province, must have dropped a word about troop movements in the hearing of Daughter Lucy, now Mrs. Henry Knox of the London Book-Store on Cornhill. Lucy could have repeated this innocently to Henry, who might have related the information to chance words dropped by various of his officer friends who crowded his shop. Henry would find it easy to tip off Josh Bracket, who, with his colleagues, would take appropriate steps.

But Gage remembered the leak that led to the Portsmouth fiasco and began casually juggling his troops. In these moves the 64th North Staffordshires were moved to Castle William and its island. Paul Revere and some of his friends rowed across, landed, and were at once thrown into the brig and kept there through a long week end. It is interesting to note that they seem to have made no complaint over their arbitrary arrest. So while they looked wistfully through the bars of their cells, the North Staffs embarked and sailed out of Boston in all secrecy.

They were led by Colonel Thomas Leslie, known to all sorts of Bostonians as "an amiable & good man . . . his soldiers look up to him with respect and affection . . . he's of a Noble Scotch family, but distinghused [sic] more by his humanity and affability." Perhaps Gage should have picked a more swashbuckling ruffler for this job.

Military stores at Salem were Leslie's objective, but he and the North Staffordshires might just as well have stayed in Boston. They landed at Marblehead, and with the sight of the first scarlet coat with its black facings the whole countryside boiled into action. By the time the British column reached the North River in Salem, the stores were quite out of reach, unless Leslie was willing to resort to violence. So the colonel accepted defeat and tramped his men to Marblehead and the transports, his mission quite decidedly not accomplished.

If this sally was a British fiasco, it was one more highly valuable laboratory test for the New England alarm system. Without benefit of any advance tip-off from Boston patriots, the call to arms went out swiftly and was not confined to the immediate locality. As far away as Amesbury, away up there beyond the north bank of the Merrimac, minute companies swarmed out, ready to march. And the venture served notice to Gage and his staff that very little warning was needed to alert the militia of a whole colony.

It was March, and Tory Boston was glowing with rumors of fresh legislation by Parliament. Those acts, mentioned earlier as due to follow North's feeble reconciliation move, were due to pass, people said. They were right, although the actual news of passage would not reach America until the long-awaited, long-dreaded, and final explosion had thundered out. By one act all the New England colonies were forbidden to trade anywhere save with the British Isles and the British West Indies. More, New England ships were to be strictly barred from the North Atlantic fisheries. No more Gloucestermen would clear for the Grand Bank. Marbleheaders might troll or net in narrow Marblehead Harbor, but that was all. A later, futile rider threw the ban at New Jersey, Pennsylvania, Maryland, Virginia, and South Carolina. Men in other colonies would learn that "it could happen here."

Another act, still not passed but so sure that people could write to American correspondents about it, gave the commander of the British forces in North America the power to use force in the execution of the Coercive and related acts, even if this meant open hostilities. Authority for the seizure of the Adamses, Warren, and Hancock was also in the air. Harsh as these measures were, they came too late to play any part in men's decisions, save to show dissidents how matters would have run had the ultimate outburst been delayed.

As it was, it was common talk in Boston that the leaders of the opposition walked with halters about their necks. Those leaders seem to have accepted their foot-of-the-gallows status with remarkable equanimity. They may have counted on Gage's known distaste for positive action or his rather bumbling good nature. Or Mr. Secretary Flucker may have mentioned to Daughter Lucy that he had heard Gage say that he would take no steps to round up the brabbling leaders.

The usual March ceremonies for observing the anniversary of the so-called Boston Massacre were held in Old South, diagonally across from the foot of School Street. The airy white nave with its mahogany-railed pews was packed, and a glance from the pulpit should have been enough to make even Sam Adams speak moderately and softly. Sprinkled about among the civilians was an alarming number of epauleted red coats. One officer of the Royal Irish even sat defiantly on the steps leading to the pulpit.

There was a mutter, half deeply admiring, half bitterly hostile, as Dr. Joseph Warren mounted to the pulpit to deliver the oration, always the pièce de résistance of the day. Other prominent leaders were well to the front. The dullest member of the audience could not have avoided the thought that here was a chance to snap up most of the motive power of opposition in Massachusetts. Ample troops were within call and plenty of officers to call them.

Joseph Warren began to speak. "My ever-honored fellow citizens. It is not without the most humiliating conviction of my want of ability that I now appear before you; but the sense I have of the obligation I am under to obey the calls of my country at all times. . . ." Tension slacked off like a damp fiddle string. Warren probably could not be classed as a great orator, but he was at least competent and he faced a group of Bostonians that was as devoted to oratory as a modern radio audience is to a molasses-voiced commentator. If the unexpected British listeners had originally cherished a notion of starting a free-for-all or of snaffling up Warren and other leaders, either his voice or the setting or perhaps a what's-the-use feeling kept them far quieter and more orderly than might have been expected. They were apt to hiss when the Bostonians applauded, often thumped their sticks on the floor in disagreement.

There were a few jagged notes as the oratory rolled on. The officer perched on the pulpit steps held up a handful of pistol or musket balls. According to legend, the speaker neatly dropped a handkerchief over the hand. At the end, when a vote of thanks was offered Warren, the officers again hissed, stamped, and banged their canes on the floor, voicing stinging (eighteenth-century) disapproval by yelling, "Fie! Fie! Oh, fie indeed!" This was mildly disrespectful, but it nearly had disastrous results since a good many in the audience, still on edge, took the words for "Fire! Fire!" and started a quite respectable *sauve-qui-peut* via doors and windows. But order was restored; the meeting went on to a reasonably orderly close. The officers tramped out, probably in none too sweet a temper. The rest of the audience left, feeling that they had paid solemn respects to the martyrs of the Massacre, extraordinary as those martyrs may seem to us today.

The roads were drying out and Gage's regiments pushed their route marches deeper and deeper. One day the 23rd Welch slogged as far as Punchbowl Village in Brookline. The 10th and the bear-skinned 5th pushed west and south. In true cloak-and-dagger spirit, Ensign Henry de Berniere and one Captain Browne disguised themselves "in country cloathes" and went far into the flatlands and on to the ridges where Framingham still stands. There, from a tavern window, they watched a militia group drill.

The two officers were not impressed, Ensign de Berniere writing: "We arrived at Buckminster's tavern about six o'clock that evening, the company of militia were exercising . . . they performed their feats before the windows . . . ; we did not feel very easy at seeing such a number so very near us; however they did not know who we were." (This last prompts a query: Were the Framingham people obtuse or the officers naïve? It seems incredible that speech, manner, and bearing, if nothing else, had not betrayed them within seconds after their arrival at Buckminster's.) "After they had done their exercise, one of their commanders spoke a very eloquent speech, recommending patience, coolness and bravery (which, indeed, they very much wanted) particularly told them they would always conquer if they did not break . . . quotes Caesar and Pompey, brigadiers Ward and Putnam and all the battles they had gained for his majesty in the last war and observed that the regulars must have been ruined but for them. The whole company came into the house and drank until nine o'clock, and then returned to their respective homes full of pot-valour." Ridiculous as the ensign seems to have found the general tones of the muster, it is interesting to note that he found no fault with the drill, which must have been at least passable to escape jeering professional comment.

During these days a new listener seems to have appeared at the more informal patriot gatherings. He was a well set up, carefully dressed, good-looking young man with a marked foreign accent and may have been sponsored by Dr. Joseph Warren. The newcomer had arrived in Boston a few years before and had settled down to trade. With the death of trade, he stayed on and must have caused raised eyebrows among the rougher of the patriots, who would surely have expected him to frequent Province House rather than the Green Dragon or the Bunch of Grapes.

His story was well known. He was a Dane and had come to the Danish West Indies as secretary to his uncle, the royal governor of those islands. The post seems to have been a sinecure and the young man had drifted into trade, finally winding up in Boston. Bostonians had trouble remembering his, to them, odd name. But in a few years American regimental and brigade circles would find no trouble in recalling Christian Febiger, one of the very first to become American by choice and not by birth.

Christian Febiger heard many other grave matters discussed besides politics and the hell-brewed machinations of British ministries. The troops had brought all sorts of plagues and fevers with them, many of them known by attractive names such as "bloody flux" and "putrid throat." Garrison funerals were frequent, and a great lot was set aside for burial along the now Boylston Street side of the Common. All these ills, of course, spread to the townspeople, Whig and Tory alike, and contemporary letters are filled with accounts of some disorder "wich has been very prevalent among us, and carried off a great number of the inhabitants as well as soldiers."

Yet there were amenities, even between townsfolk and troops. British officers and enlisted men who were Masons were received into the local lodges or at least attended lodge meetings. The 47th North Lancashires seem to have received a virtual mass invitation. Merchant John Andrews' cherished wife "Ruthy" dabbled in the arts and "had lately finished a landscape which she drew with a pen, that's equal to any copper-plate that I ever saw. . . . It is so much admir'd, that it is sent for to all quarters to see. She has received the compliment of Earl Piercy [sic] upon the occassion, who express'd his very great admiration of it."

On a more somber level, people noted that "Several young tradesmen have left town to join the American Army [an almost incredibly early use of the term] . . . and others of a higher sphere in life, am told, have sent their names to congress for commissions. I hear they [the Congress] have provided stores, ammunition, tent equipage and provisions for an army to consist of thirty thousand men."

Near the end of March there was a great flurry. Earl Percy led out not merely a single regiment but a whole brigade, making a great circle through Watertown and Cambridge. This was a real alarm. Militia cannon appeared in Watertown. In Cambridge the ancestor of the bridge that now leads down to the stadium was ripped up. Fences were broken down by the marching troops, plowed and seeded fields were trampled into mud, but no great harm was done and no physical outburst occurred. At least Gage and Percy had given the militia one more highly beneficial lesson in mobilization.

Far off in Concord, where the reconvened Provincial Congress was sitting, a more ominous view was taken of the foray. Leslie's weak party at Salem had been no great menace. A few companies of the Tangier regiment skirting the Rocks of Menotomy could be handled. But a whole brigade, with transport! Out of congressional misgivings came a highly important resolution.

"Resolved that: whenever the Army under command of General Gage, or any part thereof to the Number of Five Hundred, shall march out of the Town of Boston, with Artillery and Baggage, it ought to be deemed a design to carry into execution by Force the late Acts of Parliament [again, the Coercive Acts], the attempting which, by Resolve of the late Honorable Continental Congress, ought to be opposed: and therefore the Military Force of the Province ought to be assembled, and an Army of Observation immediately formed, to act solely on the defensive so long as it can be justified on the Principles of Reason and Self Preservation and [no] longer."

This resolve, wisely invoking the authority of the Continental Congress as well as that of the Provincial gathering, was sent as a matter of record to other local congresses. In addition, a plea was made to New Hampshire, Rhode Island, and Connecticut to form similar armies of observation and to treat a British incursion in Massachusetts as though it had occurred on their own soils.

Logical as this step was, in effect it removed the already loose lid from the powder keg of events and made a clash inevitable. Gage would continue to send his troops out of Boston. The Army of Observation would rally. When these two forces should come into violent collision lay in the hands of time.

INTERLUDE

The Opposing Forces

ONCE again two armies, not yet in actual collision, faced each other on the American continent. Unlike earlier wars, the opposing forces were of the same general stock and spoke the same language. Yet each had its own marked characteristics, or would develop them. Traits based on long conditioning or newly acquired were to set the two armies as sharply apart as though they had nothing in common save membership in the human race.

As April of 1775 came on, there was little to say about the American Army, whether units in New Hampshire or South Carolina were considered. It contained a fair sprinkling of veterans of the French and Indian struggles, men who had known the forests about Lake Champlain and Lake George as well as those who had sweated through the Carolina brakes in the old Yamassee wars. Its brand-new regiments had no traditions. Uniforms, except in a very few instances, did not exist. Weapons were limited to what was available. Drill, even down to squad formation, consisted of what a given commander could puzzle out of texts like *The Norfolk Exercise*. A captain in Williamsburg in Virginia might, and probably did, rely on a drill book that ran at utter variance with that used by an officer in Yorktown, a few miles away. And the past could contribute little. Colonial formations in the old wars had been used largely as irregular troops, as rangers. Now the new army would have to fit itself to meet regular troops in formal, European-type warfare fought out mostly over a cleared, settled terrain. The lessons learned in flushing a Franco-Indian scouting party in the forest tangles above the big bend of the Hudson were useless now.

The transition from homespun citizen-rangers into uniformed, well-drilled, well-armed soldiers was never completely realized. Traditions were acquired, some of them excellent, many of them damaging. American uniforms, battle painters to the contrary notwithstanding, were not common, though from time to time uniformed outfits did appear. Drill became fairly well standardized, as did weapons. What uniforms, what drill, what arms the American Army did acquire were owed to European sources more often than to local. It is worth noting that most of the unquestionable American victories were won in wilderness terrain—King's Mountain, Cowpens, and Saratoga. When the colonists went up against His Majesty's forces in the open, a Long Island, a Brandywine, a Germantown was very apt to result.

The British Army, on the other hand, was a well-established, solidly based organization, a going concern that had to do a minimum of improvising on taking the field. Like most of the relatively small professional armies of the day, it had strong characteristics that sprang from a long life through wars and, militarily, the more difficult times of peace. Some of the British military traits strike us as so odd, so crippling today that it is hard to understand how, shackled by them, that army was able to function at all. History shows that it did function, and function very well.

The British infantry was made up of royal regiments and proprietary regiments, the former raised by order of the King and the latter by specified men at the King's command. These last were virtually the property of the colonel who raised them. A clever man could make quite a good thing financially out of a regiment. It often happened that a colonel commanded only on paper, drawing what profits there might be and leaving the actual running of the outfit to a lieutenant colonel. If the colonel went up to general's rank, he still kept titular command. When the Norfolks sailed for America, their true colonel, Lord Ligonier, waved to them from the dock, he being "too demm'd grand for such capers" as leading his men against colonials in the wilderness.

A valuable perquisite for the colonel, or for the Crown in the royal regiments, was the matter of commissions. These were available, with a few exceptions, only through purchase, and the cost was high. A man wanting to command a company in a given regiment might pay as much as two thousand pounds. To advance to the rank of major would cost still more and, in most cases, required influence at the War Office or at court. Lord Bute's son wrote his father from Boston that he had bought a majority in the 43rd Oxfordshire Light Infantry for twenty-six hundred pounds "without making use of your name or being obliged to Lord Barrington." When an officer was killed, the commission was part of his estate, and his junior could buy it if he had the means. If not—no promotion. This most pernicious system, barring most men of modest means from any but the lowest grades, held on until 1871. The Victorian novels are full of young so-and-so's father "purchasing him a cornetship in the Lancers," or of someone "selling out" from the Blues.

The regiments themselves followed a quite uniform pattern. Ten companies made the norm, eight of these being called line companies or battalion companies. The remaining two formed on either end of the regimental line and were known as the flank companies, specially drilled, trained, and equipped. There was the grenadier company, made up of big, powerful, active men. The other flank company was light infantry, whose men were carefully chosen for intelligence, agility, and swiftness of foot. In modern sporting terms, the grenadiers were the guards and tackles of the team, the light infantry the fleet backs and shifty ends. In the field, these flank companies were almost invariably detached from the parent unit and made into a separate corps along with their fellows from other regiments, making a corps d'élite, a body of shock troops. This massing of the flank companies of all regiments will show very clearly in the opening stages of the nineteenth of April and in Burgoyne's march down the lakes and the Hudson in 1777.

Formation of regiments, purchase of commissions, company organization—these matters are hard to visualize today. Still more difficult to understand is the eighteenth-century enlisted man. Pay was not worth mentioning, and "poor bloody Tommy" even suffered numerous deductions from the miserable sum that was his on paper. Many articles of dress and equipment were actually charged against him, and there were many fines for infractions of rules. The British Army was undergoing a siege of Prussia-worship and many of Frederick the Great's ultra-rigid rules were in force. Hair was to be carefully dressed and powdered—at Tommy's expense—a good part of the time. The nearly universal white breeches, spatterdashes, and slings had to be pipe-clayed daily to avoid fine and/or flogging. This meant, since pipe clay is a moist paste, that Tommy was rarely dry. If the whitening did dry out, the garment shrank, constricting leg and shoulder muscles. Little brass or pewter buttons, brass, silver, or black japanned cap plates must catch the sun properly when the regiment passed in review or when guard was mounted. It is probable that a good many hours of the soldier's off-duty time had to be given to complying with uniform regulations. Overcoats were rarely provided, each regiment owning a few which were issued to men on guard during inclement weather.

Rations were poor and never plentiful, the enlisted man being utterly at the mercy of commissary officers and sergeants who were noted for feathering their nests out of ration funds. That anyone should concern himself with a private's welfare was virtually unheard of. Drill was carried out by cane-bearing sergeants, for an officer would only earn the scorn of his fellows by instructing the enlisted men. This last was also characteristic of the American Army until old Von Steuben horrified the rank-conscious by seizing a musket and demonstrating the manual of arms to the ragged privates at Valley Forge. Flogging was no worse than in most armies of the day, who were busily copying the outward manifestations of the Prussian Army. The French of that day stand out in insisting that flogging degraded both flogger and floggee. The one British voice raised against it was that of lovable, often exasperating Gentleman Johnny Burgoyne, who really laid his career on the line by banning all corporal punishment in his commands, beginning with the 16th Light Dragoons.

Under such conditions it is impossible to visualize any great crowds about recruiting offices. There were no crowds. To get recruits, company officers and sergeants, usually with a noisy drummer, combed the countryside, resorting to bribery, the anesthesia of rum, and often violence to get their men. Press gangs, such as the navy used, were not permitted under the law, but that law seems often to have been winked at. Justices of the peace sometimes offered an offender a choice between jail and enlisting. Men without visible means of support could be picked up and rushed into a uniform. Discharged convicts, finding employment impossible, came into the ranks. The mentally deficient, the unemployable were gladly taken, for if a regiment were not kept up to strength it would be disbanded and its titular colonel would lose a neat little source of income. More, the officers' commissions would probably lapse and become worthless. It seems incredible that soldiers so officered, so starved, so badly handled could have been anything but a sullen mob. Yet these were the men who charged again and again in the slaughter of Bunker Hill, who rallied in the fog of Germantown. In a later generation, comparable men would beat off magnificent French infantry and artillery at Albuera, would stand firm under the smash of Napoleon's cuirassiers at Waterloo—and Wellington, for whom they won the battle, would refer to them as "the scum of the earth."

Cavalry, artillery, and engineers bore up under virtually the same conditions, though commissions in the last two branches were not for sale, possibly because genuinely skilled and trained officers were needed and possibly because few men in their senses would have paid to serve in those arms.

Only two regular cavalry outfits served with the British during the war, Burgoyne's old 16th, briefly, and the 17th Light Dragoons. A good deal of their time was frittered away in outpost duty and courier service, though toward the end of the war in the South the 17th aided various units to function as mounted infantry. Both sides, in fact, badly bungled their use of cavalry, much as the North and the South, particularly the North, misused this arm during the first two or three years of the Civil War.

The unfortunate gunners for the most part had a dragged-out, poor-relation sort of life, being considered not quite soldiers by the infantry and cavalry. Promotion was far slower than in those branches, and a man did very well to retire with field rank. The highly skilled commander of Burgoyne's German artillery, Georg Pausch, was a seasoned veteran and only a captain.

The artillery of those days was organized into battalions, made up of a varying number of companies. It is hard to follow professional references of the times, but it seems that the battalions constituted a pool of cannoneers from which men were drawn to handle a given number of guns. The men were the artillery company, the guns the battery, in contrast to the later and current practice of making the battery a self-contained entity embracing men, guns, carriages, and horses or, now, tractors and half-tracks. As a further elfin quirk, the limbers in the Prussian service had to carry at all times a miniature library including a Greek lexicon and a treatise on papermaking.

The engineers fared even worse than the gunners. They had almost no enlisted personnel, for the most part, and had to depend for actual labor on men detailed to them—never the brighter citizens, of course—by infantry outfits that wanted work done. Montrésor and Twiss were highly skilled men, but Twiss carried on his functions as Burgoyne's chief of engineers with the rank of lieutenant and Montrésor went no farther. Considering these facts, and those appertaining to the gunners, it is not surprising that there was no market for such commissions.

Turning over the pages of Charles M. Lefferts' fine book of Revolutionary uniforms, or studying the excellent plates which Colonel Harry M. Larter has been making for the Fort Ticonderoga Museum, the twentieth-century eye is struck by the use of vivid color on the part of those who authorized or designed uniforms of that time. An eighteenth-century eye would have been less impressed. Sartorially it was a colorful age, and men, in the cities at least, pursued their daily rounds in peach and emerald and orange and puce. There was little distinctive about the military cut, and a line officer strolling down Mincing Lane in London would not be conspicuous save for a metal gorget dangling over his collarbone or a gold or silver epaulet. It was not until about the Napoleonic era that truly smashing uniforms began to appear. We have completed the cycle today. General Sir William Howe looked much like a London merchant so far as dress went. Our modern generals in field dress are virtually indistinguishable from telephone linemen, garage workers, or week-end duck hunters.

Except for certain specified units, the cocked hat, differing very little if any from a civilian hat, was de rigueur. It was probably the most useless bit of military equipment ever devised, with the possible exception of the cap worn by the early A.E.F. of World War I, which, with the rest of that ghastly uniform, has been described as the invention of the worst tailor in the world in collaboration with the worst soldier. The cocked hat was merely a low-crowned, broad-brimmed headpiece with the brim caught up against the crown at the back and in two places in front, thus giving no protection to the back of the neck and none to the eyes.

Other types were little better. The grenadiers wore a cap with a high brass or black metal front plate, just back of which rose a tapering expanse of bearskin, smaller and rather neater than the present busbies of the Coronation. Light infantrymen wore a leather skullcap faced with a metal plate a little lower than that of the big grenadiers. Both these caps left the eyes and the back of the neck unprotected but offered some token cover against heavy blows on the crown. There was logic to their shape. We have noted the grenadiers and the light infantry as the shock troops of the army. They were often called upon to cover very rough country, to tear down an abatis or scale walls under fire. In such tasks they would need free hands and could sling their muskets over their backs more easily than could wearers of the spreading cocked hat. The grenadiers had another valid, if obsolete, reason for their headgear. They had been originally trained to go ahead of an attacking column, throwing grenades as they went, and certainly needed the hands free for this, though the grenade had gone out of use well before 1770, not to be revived until 1914–15.

The regiments designed as fusiliers—the name still clings to many British units today—wore the grenadier's bearskin or a rather higher version of the light infantry cap. The dragoon regiments had some time before dropped the cocked hat in favor of a brass helmet with a Greek crest and a red horsehair plume that suggests the later splendor of Napoleon's cuirassiers as they thunder interminably across the canvas of Meissonier's "1807."

The coat was pretty well standardized, a clumsy, long-skirted garment with an unnotched lapel that ran down to the waist or even to the full length of the swallowtail. The light infantry and some of the cavalry wore a rather short jacket, but with the same lapel. This lapel was to the British soldier what the modern divisional patch is to the G.I. The coat itself was the familiar scarlet, but the colors of the lapels—the facings, as they were called—varied from unit to unit. Depending on the taste of the colonel, this colored lapel could be quite plain or it could have its buttonholes elaborately worked out in varicolored thread and it could be edged with some contrasting tape. These facings and their often minute variants were a source of pride to officer and enlisted man alike. The color of the facing was the color of the regiment, and from this use comes the word "regimentals" to denote an entire uniform.

All the royal regiments had blue facings. Other units followed the choice of their colonels, and the dyers of the day turned out not only fine shades but invented some fascinating names for them. Thus we find the 5th Northumberland Fusiliers glorying in "Goslin green," the 24th South Wales Borderers wearing "Willow green," the 54th Dorsetshires with their "Popinjay green," while others settled for such shades as "Philemot yellow." The colors were often carried over to the cuffs and might appear on the cloth back of the grenadier's cap. Breeches and waistcoats were usually white—more pipe-claying for poor bloody Tommy—or buff or yellow might be used.

The true bursts of color, however, were to be found among the regimental musicians. Oddly enough, the drabbest of these were in the royal regiments, which wore the cocked hat, red coat, and blue facings of their fellows. But elsewhere the spectrum fairly whirled. Not only did the fifers and drummers wear a grenadier bearskin, but their coats showed the colors of the regiment reversed. If the regiment wore scarlet faced with orange, then the musicians wore orange faced with scarlet; if scarlet and popinjay green, they marched in that green faced with scarlet. And over their coats ran arabesques of colored braid, and their arms were streaked with chevrons from shoulder to wrist. As in the case of the shape of the grenadier and light infantry hats, there was logic here too. Many commands were given by drumbeat in action as on parade, and the men in the ranks could spot the source of the racket at some distance owing to the fantastic coats. Men could rally in action about the musicians with little danger of mistaking a drummer of the Tangier Regiment for one of the Buffs.

Gunners of nearly all armies, and the British with the rest, wore blue faced with red, the color surviving today in our own army in the red piping along the seams of the muffinlike cap. The doleful and forgotten engineers were decked out in scarlet faced with black, the colors of our own Engineer Corps in the year 1954.

Roughly, this is what the army in Boston was in April 1775; this is how it was officered, recruited, dressed, and fed. All these factors played on the individual, affected what he thought and did, how he acted and reacted. Little or nothing has been said about training. In a modern sense there was none. The companies were drilled and drilled to attain a precision of maneuver, to keep aligned. They were even drilled to the beat of metronomes in an attempt to synchronize the smallest ordered movement of each man. To load their clumsy muskets, drill sergeants intoned no less than sixteen orders, which the man in the ranks followed with forty-seven distinct and abrupt motions. He was never encouraged to think. He was not taught to aim. All that was asked of him was that he march in tight, rigid order toward the enemy and, at a command, raise his musket to shoulder level, shut his eyes, and fire. This type of drill, too, had its effect on the British officer and soldier, on every man who would be roused secretly on the night of the eighteenth of April, 1775.

BOOK 2

". . . a grait many Lay dead and the Road was bloddy"

THOMAS GAGE, so comfortably lodged in Province House, had more than enough on his mind to switch his thoughts from their normally convivial channels to more somber paths. He had been sent out to enforce the Coercive Acts, had been given what Parliament deemed to be an ample army, and still more troops were on the way. He had finally been given a pretty free hand in the use of force and the power of arrest. Obviously, he must do something, but when he discussed steps and measures with his second-in-command, the Swiss Haldimand or Earl Percy or his senior colonels, he had only to close his eyes to visualize Leslie's Salem fiasco, which had set the militiamen stirring up and down the province. He could recall written reports from column commanders that told of peaceful route marches through a suddenly bristling countryside.

His aides were making briefer and more noncommittal entries in his Orderly Book, fearful of leaks. Yet the very terseness of the orders set people speculating. Young Ensign John Barker of the light infantry read the "Genl. Orders, April 15th. The Grenadiers and Light Infantry in order to learn Grenadrs. Exercise [i.e., drill] and new evolutions are to be off all duties 'till further orders," and commented, "This I suppose is by way of a blind. I dare say they have something for them to do." Others besides Barker knew of the orders, and the Reverend William Gordon of the Third Church of Roxbury noted that they "made the Bostonians jealous." Paul Revere and the other Volunteer Watchers knew of them, absorbed what was between the lines, and sharpened their eyes and wits for future omens. At midnight of the fifteenth the Watchers saw strange doings in the Charles and in the harbor and reported, "The Boats belonging to the Transports were all launched and carried under the sterns of the men of War. . . . From these movements, we expected something serious was to be transacted." Something serious and amphibious.

The next day, Sabbath or no Sabbath, Dr. Joseph Warren, still carrying on cheerfully almost within sight of Province House, sent Silversmith Revere to Lexington, where Sam Adams and handsome John Hancock were staying with the Reverend Jonas Clark. Casting about for probabilities and possibilities, they reasoned that Gage was sending an expedition to seize the Concord military stores, now reaching very fair proportions, and that the expedition would skirt Cambridge and keep to the back roads and lanes to avoid observation, a rather naïve hope on Gage's part.

From Lexington, word was sent to Concord, and the whole village labored long and tirelessly, rounding up carts, packing stores and supplies, which, load by load, rumbled off west to the rolling ridges where Worcester lay. Apparently on his own, pleasant Mr. Revere reasoned that Gage might throw a scarlet curtain about Boston if the troops did march out, might clamp down a censorship that would prevent further word. So he stopped off in Charlestown on his way home and sought out Colonel William Conant and some other local leaders to arrange that "if the British went out by water, we would shew two lanthorns in the North Church Steeple, and if by land, one, as a signal; for we were apprehensive it would be difficult to cross the Charles River, or git over Boston neck." Revere did not have to explain that if the expedition were dumped in Cambridge marshes, near the present Lechmere Point, the mission might be deadly; if the troops marched out over Boston Neck, however, they would be plodding on through or near important centers of population and would be easy to pick up.

Other than the to-ing and fro-ing of the drilling light infantry and grena-diers, there was quiet for a few days. On the afternoon of the eighteenth Gage sent a few mounted officers out to the northwest. The weather was fine, inns and taverns at least passable, and the young officers could have a good country gallop, dinner by a cheery fire, and then return through a spring evening over familiar roads. They could also intercept any suspicious riders and place them under arrest.

Boston and its uneasy garrison turned in as usual that night of the eight-eenth. Darkness swallowed up the city as regimental drums beat tattoo—a beat then commonly, and correctly, spelled tap-to, since it had originally been the signal for turning to—or off, in modern usage—the taps of the kegs in regimental pubs.

There is an unearthly hush about a barrack full of sleeping men. A cor-poral snores heavily and rhythmically. His neighbor coughs, stirs, turns on his cot or on his heap of straw, and sleeps again. Men from late details creep in, stow their equipment, exchange muffled whispers, settle into their blankets. Someone murmurs through the veil of a dream, and the weird silence falls again.

Into such a hush on this evening of the eighteenth came sergeants of the light infantry and grenadier companies, slipping into the doors of ware-houses, "Distil houses," commandeered homes. Their voices were barely audible as they went from man to man. Get up. Dress. No talking. No smoking. Got your rations in your haversacks? Hurry. No talking. No smoking.

All over Boston, companies of irritable, half-awake men were forming, tramping through sleeping streets, over the Common or along the hill past John Hancock's scarred fences. Near the foot of the Common the leading files smelled water, heard the sullen drub-drub-drub of moored boats, found a whole flotilla waiting at the present western side of Park Square. On came the troops, the grenadiers' brass- or silver-fronted bearskins glinting to match the shimmer from the plates of the light infantry. At the water's edge their sergeants and officers chivvied them about, raising a subdued clatter with the reiterated hiss of "Silence." The files stood, with grounded arms, disdainful of the orders. They had marched quietly enough, almost in dead quiet, if one could forget the occasional strangled yelps of the dogs which the sergeants, under orders, had bayoneted to still their betraying barks. This was a feature that distressed the basically humane Gage, as a few years later it would distress a young Pennsylvanian named Anthony Wayne as he led a secret mission toward a British fort on the Hudson.

The dogs might just as well have lived. Paul Revere, who had slipped out perilously by skiff, gliding under the very stern counter of H.M.S. Somerset, was waiting by his horse on the Cambridge shore. One lantern, then another, glimmering in Old North's steeple, sent him into the saddle, his horse's head turned toward Menotomy (now Arlington), Lexington, and Concord. The regulars were out, were surely heading for the country roads to Concord. Revere raced off through the night, stopping to pound on a door here, to chuck gravel at a window there. After each brief halt he knew it was safe to go on. The man he had awakened would keep the word spinning on through the night by prearranged plan, would set up a chain reaction of alarm. Revere did manage to get to Lexington, where he roused John Hancock and Sam Adams. But that was the end of his ride. In a field toward Concord a knot of Gage's young sportsmen cornered the silversmith and sent him back to Lexington on foot. Luckily young Dr. Sam Prescott of Concord, who had been courting one of the Milliken girls in Lexington and who knew of the Revere mission, broke away and galloped on to Concord to report to the town notables.

From the foot of Boston Common the loaded whaleboats pushed out and headed over calm water toward Lechmere Point, following the route of present Arlington Street. Someone had miscalculated the tides, and the troops had to go over the sides of the boats into knee-deep water, the men grumbling and cursing. What a job they'd have the next day cleaning their white breeches, now mud-smeared! Fate would relieve many of them of that detail.

The companies were formed on the bank, and the men scowled as they recognized the leader of the expedition, fat, stupid, bumblepuppy Francis Smith, lieutenant colonel of the 10th Lincolnshires. Gage could hardly have made a worse choice. It was so bad that he must have been forced into it by some rigid rule of seniority. The grenadiers and light infantrymen probably did not know the second-in-command. If they had known him, they ought to have been cheered, for he was strong, likable Major John Pitcairn of the Royal Marines. In choosing Pitcairn, despite the fact that there were no other marines along that night, Gage must have had a free hand. It has been noted before that the major was immensely popular with Whig and Tory alike. With him on the expedition, a clash might have been averted owing to the respect in which he was held. He could have parleyed well with the colonists.

The waiting, drenched men could make other observations, nearly as disquieting as those about Smith. A great many of the company officers were strangers to them. Their own known and probably trusted officers were sick or on detached service—"on command" was the term used then— or had traded jobs with friends for the night. In their places were volunteers, adventure seekers, subalterns who had just come along for the ride. Some of them were not even from flank companies and wore the silly cocked hat of the line.

There was plenty of time for such thoughts and qualms. For two hours Frankie Smith kept the men standing on the far bank of the Charles. When someone—possibly Pitcairn—asked about the wait, Smith said that rations were coming across by boat. It was then pointed out to him that the men had drawn rations before they left their barracks, and at last commands snapped out, the companies swung from column into line, the light infantry in the van, and plunged into night-shrouded Middlesex County. As an added snafu to an already fouled-up night, someone had miscalculated the route, and the wretched men had to ford a backwater of the Charles, waist-deep. At last, sodden, chilled, and squelching, they started off along what is now Somerville Avenue, which joins Massachusetts Avenue—direct road to Lexington and Concord—just beyond present Porter Square.

They marched on through silent country, a cluster of houses here, a well-fenced farm there. They maintained a well-disciplined silence which was as needless as the bayoneting of the dogs, for Paul Revere had been ahead of them. Eyes watched them from behind curtained windows. Sleepy-faced men slipped from back doors, sprinted off into the night to spread the word. Revere is right. The Regulars are out.

On past Menotomy went the column, marching through an unreal world in which they alone were alive. They alone? As the route continued, the fox-terrier light infantry up in the lead began to turn their heads right and left, inquiringly. Shots? But who would be hunting at this time of night— or rather morning, thanks to Smith's delay at Lechmere Point? Bells, too, sending out their call to worship at a strange hour.

Smith seems not to have taken in the meaning of shot and peal. Pitcairn surely must have, along with alert-minded young officers like Barker and De Berniere. Musket, saluting cannon, and church bell were sending on Paul Revere's summons, each in its own way. Men who had been out on the practice marches, who had tramped to Salem behind affable Colonel Leslie could, without too great a mental effort, picture a dozen, a score of village greens, a hundred, with shadowy companies lining up in their cocked hats, their smocks and hunting shirts. It was no mark of a weak spine if a captain or a private kept glancing uneasily toward the black fields. That oak grove, that pine windbreak might be sheltering the men of two or three villages, armed and watchful. What lay behind that low hill to the left?

Gage's mounted patrols began materializing out of the night toward the head of the column, drumming down in a flurry of hoofs and barking questions at the leading files. When they reached Smith and Pitcairn, there was no need to wonder about musket, cannon, or bell. The countryside was rising ahead of them, and the expedition's surest weapon—surprise—was gone irretrievably.

There were halts on hollow lanes where the men tried to ease the grip of shrinking breeches and leggings. At muffled commands they were on their feet again, hobbling and limping along until the soaked cloth stretched enough to revive circulation. Slowly the eastern sky paled, showing the outline of a tree already budding in the unusually early spring, the pitch roof of a house, or the eerie shimmer of a pond where the pinkle-tinks were shrilling. They were not alone. Across that field to the right a cluster of men hurried away, muskets slung across their backs. Another group, leaving the shelter of that walnut grove by the white house, was hurrying too.

Francis Smith, John Pitcairn, and their seven hundred-odd men were well past the halfway mark of a twenty-mile battlefield, a stretch of country so extended and to be the scene of such fluid action that no one can pinpoint a spot on the map and say, "Here was the main struggle."

The sun was getting up above the horizon as the leading files headed for the last slope that led down into Lexington and whatever the little town held. Pitcairn moved up closer to the head of the column, probably followed by some of the mounted officers who had spent the night patrolling, and surely by the guides identified as "several of the inimical torified natives." The road wound down a fairly gentle hill and Lexington lay before the column, fresh in the first touch of slanting sunlight.

The town could have held no surprises for those of the British who had been there before. There was the spreading Green, fringed with mellow white houses, some of which, along with Buckman's Tavern, are still there. The little church and its detached belfry on the Green, to the British left front, caught the first rays of the sun. The elms and oaks showed a budding froth of jade. Everything looked calm and predictable.

Less calm, but surely predictable to anyone who had taken in the message of musket, cannon, and bell during the night, who had heard the reports of the mounted officers and seen the shadowy armed groups slipping on through the fields, was the tense stirring on the Green. The Lexington Minute Company was drawn up there in order, with Captain John Parker and his officers at the flank. The Alarm Company, made up of the older, less fit men, was there too. About one hundred and thirty men faced the tramp and glitter of the seven hundred-odd from Boston. The leading British files could see more than the two militia formations. Uncounted numbers of armed men were standing about the Green, moving in the fields beyond the white houses and their smoking chimneys, springing up from

idle seats on stone walls. These were the unattached men, belonging to no
particular formation, men from outlying villages and farms, strays and laggards with probably a fair number of the simply curious, like many of the
volunteer officers who marched with Smith and Pitcairn. John Parker was
in command of the only organized formations and he must have been a
very puzzled man. Mobilization orders, so often rehearsed in the past, had
thus far worked quite smoothly. His unit was there. But there were no
specific instructions to him concerning what to do when, as, and if the
British did arrive. Nor was there any real central authority to which he
could appeal. Taking in the strength of the British, he very wisely ordered
his companies, Minute and Alarm, to disperse and not to fire. There seems
little basis for the various more moving but far less sensible oratorical commands that legend gives him.

John Pitcairn must have been pleased at his first glimpse of the Green.
The two militia formations were slowly breaking up. There would be no
resistance to the King's troops. But, under orders, he was to disarm the
militia. The British column was strung out far back on the road, and only
six companies of light infantry were under the marine's orders. Very properly, he swung them from column into line, obliquing them far out to his
right to get around the flank of Parker's men—a "right front into line," in
more modern usage. His men swarmed on in very good order, the sun
bright on scarlet coats, on blue facings, yellow, white, black, brighter still
on the metal plates above the leather caps and on the needle-glint of leveled
bayonets.

In their ordered rush the light infantry raised a thin flurry of dust. A
heavier dust of rumor, hearsay, conjecture, and supposition has risen over
these few moments and heavily blurred history's picture of what really did
happen. There were hundreds of eyewitnesses to this curtain-raising, but
very little satisfactory evidence. Each side, naturally, accused the other, but
few of the accusers were in a position to see what actually occurred. Some
British reporters were out of sight of the Green at the moment. Patriot
affiants often were not even present. Historians have been able, in all
honesty, to season to taste. So thorough a worker as the late Douglas
Southall Freeman states flatly that Pitcairn called on the militia to disperse
and, when they moved too slowly to suit him, ordered his men to fire. This
is in keeping with the fiery, brutal Pitcairn of legend, but not with the
steady John Pitcairn of fact.

The testimony of the man best placed to see just what did happen, to
control events, to restore order, was buried for a great many years. So far
as I know, it was first unearthed by the late Allen French, master researcher
and chronicler of this period. In the Gage papers he came across a report,
written a few days afterward, a routine report to General Thomas Gage
that was signed "Your most obedt humble Servant, John Pitcairn." The
major was not writing for history. He had nothing to gain by altering what
he saw, said, and did. And, from what we know of him, no considerations,
no pressure could have colored his account. Gravely he reported to his

chief, "I gave directions to the Troops to move forward, but on no account to Fire, or even attempt it without orders; when I arrived at the end of the Village, I observed drawn up upon a Green near 200 of the Rebels; when I came within about One Hundred Yards of them, they began to File off toward some stone Walls on our Right Flank—the Light Infantry observing this, ran after them—I instantly called to the Soldiers not to Fire, but to surround and disarm them, and after several repetitions of those positive Orders to the men, not to Fire &c, some of the Rebels who had jumped over the Wall, Fired Four or Five Shott at the Soldiers, which wounded a man of the Tenth, and my Horse was wounded in two places from some quarter or other and at the same time several Shott were fired from a Meeting House on our Left—upon this, without any order or Regularity, the Light Infantry began a scattered Fire and continued in that situation for some little time, contrary to the repeated orders of both me and the [other] officers that were present."

This bare, matter-of-fact account presents a vivid picture between the lines. The militia companies breaking up, probably to avoid the flanking movement which threatened to envelop their own left; the men from the companies getting mixed up with the unorganized militia whom we have noted; the wave of light and color sweeping across the Green, bayonets aslant; a militiaman in a panic, trigger-happy in modern speech, blasting off into the blue, a few shots following. These are surely panic shots, since the target was a perfect one and only Pitcairn's horse and a man from the 10th were hit, neither seriously.

Unsolicited and unofficial support is given Pitcairn's account in the narrative of Ensign Jeremy Lister of the 10th Lincolnshires, whose story lay buried until 1931. Lister was with the light infantry company of the 10th, the first to enter Lexington, and must have had a fine view of what happened. He writes, "Major Pitcairn . . . call'd to them to disperce [sic], but their not seeming willing he desired us to mind our space [this must refer to the move from column into line] when they gave us a fire then run off to get behind a wall." This suggests that Parker's men fired *before* they broke ranks.

Lieutenant Sutherland of the 38th South Staffordshires, a volunteer who was out in front with Pitcairn, also supports the story of the random shots not from the Green but from behind the stone wall. He also tells of Pitcairn shouting again and again, "Soldiers don't fire, keep your Ranks, form & surround them."

There was no reason for Pitcairn, Lister, and Sutherland to set down anything but what they saw. It is hard not to accept as true the steady, disciplined sweep of the light infantry, a moment of panic among scattered militiamen, and then—a strange pandemonium. Despite the efforts of Pitcairn and other officers, the highly trained light infantry kept up their fire—which ironically struck down not those trigger-happy men who had fired, but Parker's men who had *not*—and were soon joined by the oncoming grenadiers. For a few moments all order left the British. Men were shouting that the town should be burned. There was a ragged rush to break into Buckman's Tavern, whence some shots had come. At last the men were quieted. They re-formed and, without wasting more time, pushed on up the slope at the far end of the Green, where a ribbon road led on to Concord.

The question of why first-class British troops—and there were probably none better in the world of 1775—got so out of hand on the Green seems to have attracted little attention in the past and, so far as I know, no one has tried to explain it. Yet the matter is important, not only so far as Lexington is concerned, but as an ominous shadow trailing off toward the unborn hours of the nineteenth of April. We may think back to the more than trying months—and in the case of some outfits, years—spent in cantankerous Boston. There was the sudden nighttime call of the eighteenth, the drenching at Lechmere Point, the two-hour wait, the second drenching in the Charles backwater, and then the long black march through a muttering countryside. Any one of these factors ought to have been taken in stride by a reasonably well trained unit. Added up, they could, and probably did, affect the morale of the enlisted man most adversely. Nor must the absence of known and trusted officers be forgotten. In many cases, strangers with alien facings on their coats were yapping orders at the men. Francis Smith was no man to inspire profound confidence, either.

The resumption of the march spiked another hard-dying legend set down in many accounts, including that of H. G. Wells in his *Outline of History*: the legend that the purpose of the whole expedition was the arrest of the patriot leaders known to be in the vicinity. No written line of Gage confirms this even vaguely. The stores at Concord were the objective, and the brush at Lexington was entirely incidental. If Francis Smith had had verbal orders to seize Adams and Hancock, he would not have set out at once for Concord as soon as the Lexington Green was cleared. A book soldier who would obey the least comma of a precise order, he would have camped at Lexington, dully and routinely combing the neighborhood until formally recalled by unmistakable orders.

So the long scarlet column in its bright metal-fronted caps, bold against the spring hues, stepped briskly out to cover the last five miles to Concord. Even Pitcairn's horse and the wounded private of the Lincolnshires went with it. There was no need to hurry. Smith's two-hour delay at Lechmere Point had seen to that. But for that dallying, grenadiers and light infantrymen would have swung through Lexington in the dark, avoiding the great spray of late militia arrivals. They would have come into Concord well before light, with nothing but the Concord companies near them. The picture was different now, and to get at least a rough idea of what lay ahead, watches must be set back a few hours and a view be taken of the dark-cloaked countryside that lay west of Lexington.

We have followed young Mr. Revere of Boston up to the time of his capture in the fields between Lexington and Concord. Other riders were out, spurring into less sensitive but equally important territory. Hoof, musket, cannon, and bell sent their messages rolling through the April night, setting up a chain reaction that touched the far ridges of the Berkshires. Marlboro might receive a rider, hear an echo from Sudbury, and from Marlboro word would go west or south or north. A Worcester courier might arouse Paxton and Rutland, and the men he warned would send on to Barre and Petersham. The call knew no boundaries, and men assembled on greens in Rhode Island and Connecticut and north into New Hampshire.

It was no impromptu swarming of suddenly angered men. They were angry enough, but each man knew where to go, to whom to report, and what to bring with him. Squads could head at once for the next assembly point where other squads might meet, and soon a whole company was trudging off under the soft dark sky. All through the night of the eighteenth, through the unseasonably hot hours of the nineteenth, through another nightfall, a dawn and nightfall again, they kept working east toward the point of danger.

Their two vital weaknesses were supply and the lack of a directing force to employ them wisely, once action was reached. For supply, each man carried what was available to him for rations and ammunition. Little or no provision had been made for seeing that an empty cartridge pouch, a flapping haversack could be filled. As for the directing force, when action was finally joined, companies frayed out into squads and squads into individuals. There was no one to shout, "This way!" or "Billerica Company, join on with Medford, circle out and hit the head of the column." The rising of the provinces was not individual. The fighting was.

There is no reliable account of numbers. By dozens and scores, men must have straggled, have become weary or discouraged or timid and turned back. Not all left their homes in a spirit of grim dedication. Two men, probably from the North Shore-Cape Ann area, trudged into the town of Saugus, Concord-bound. In Saugus, in present Chestnut Street, they found the inviting doors of what they described as "the Blew Anker," where there was food. Likewise rum and a tame bear chained outside. "We stopped at the Blew Anker to cut the dust," one of them wrote. "Well, we surely got drunk and give the bear a hot flip. You never see such a funny sight as that drunken bear. We were late in getting here [to Concord] and was glad old John [probably their commanding officer] didn't catch us."

Shifting attention from this over-all reconnaissance flight through time and space, we find the sensitive point, Concord, sweating out the night. The local militia gathered on the Green near still-standing Wright's Tavern—and waited. They had solid, experienced men in command. Colonel James Barrett had come down from his farm to the northwest of the town where the last of the supplies were being hastily shipped out or hidden. Major John Buttrick was there from his farm across the Concord River and above the echoing planks of the North Bridge. The Reverend William Emerson, musket in hand, had been the first man to report, tramping up from the Manse down by that same North Bridge. He would later die at a stone fort on Lake Champlain, leaving behind him a family from which would come, in another generation, Ralph Waldo Emerson. Modest Lieutenant Joseph Hosmer, a cabinetmaker, noted in a critical town for the purity of his English, had come up from his house across the Concord, and Reuben Brown, the saddler, was there. Buttricks, Emersons, Barretts, Hosmers, Browns—their houses still stand within the town limits, so well preserved that today's date comes as a shock to a visitor.

There, terrain is almost as little changed. Just at the edge of the town a low, steep-sided ridge runs east-west by the Lexington Road, breaks at a point in mid-course, slants away again to die not far from the North Bridge. North of the ridge is a table-flat stretch of land still called the Great Meadows, and to the south another flat, rather marshy stretch which once held a very small mill and which is still cut by Mill Brook. A light infantryman of the Lincolnshires or a grenadier of the South Staffordshires would have no trouble in orienting himself in the Concord of 1954. Few sites of great clashes between men and ideas have changed as little as has this.

All through the night the Concord men waited, wondering. There had been false alarms in the past. This could be, probably was, another. Militiamen dozed against the Meeting House, crowded into Wright's Tavern. A few went home. From the higher ground to the west an occasional rumble told of another cartload of province stores heading for Worcester. In the street, at the foot of the ridge, people came and went, ghostly, impersonal, their voices flat in the hush of the night.

Very close to dawn a general consultation was held—how many others had taken place during the night?—and it was decided that Reuben Brown had better ride the five miles into Lexington to see if the committee over there had any late news. Brown clacked off down the Lexington Road and his fellows took up the endless task of the soldier—that of waiting. Brown was back far sooner than they had expected, and his story ended the last bit of drowsiness in the Concord streets. The Regulars were out! The saddler had gone no farther than the brow of the hill that looks down onto Lexington Green. He had seen the leather caps of the light infantry, the sheen of their scarlet jackets. Then he had wheeled his horse about as smoke, a rattle, and a flash swelled out in the still April dawn. He had seen some Lexington men fall. He was sure of that. He could tell the Concord men no more, but he had told them enough. The King's troops had fired!

There was another impromptu town meeting there in the fading darkness along the flank of the ridge. A sober decision was taken. Some threat of unknown strength lay off there along the Lexington Road. Whatever it was, they would march to meet it. Commands echoed hollowly about the Meeting House, against the walls of Wright's. The Concord minute companies formed, swung into column, and headed east along the Lexington Road. With them marched the men from nearby Lincoln, who had come in during the night. Those not in formation waited by the Meeting House or climbed to the prow-like nose of the ridge that looked east toward the route of the King's troops.

To solemn drumbeat the militia kept on over the always lightening road that led to Lexington. In the flatlands a mile and more from the edge of the town they saw the sheen of red, the wink of metal. Trained eyes in the column made a rough estimate. A force far greater than their own hundred-odd. In good order, the militia countermarched, headed decorously back into town, almost as though serving as escort of honor to the scarlet column a hundred rods behind.

Stand at the prow of the ridge today and it is easy to reconstruct the scene. First the orderly if drab militia with their strangely unhurried step. Behind them—the light is strong now—a blaze of color. Smith had massed his musicians at the head of his force, a moving dazzle of the bright coats which have been noted before, black coats, white coats, dark blue and sky-blue coats, orange and buff and yellow coats, laced and arabesqued, and over all, except for the musicians of the royal regiments, the metal-fronted bearskins. The light infantry came on, scarlet and white, scarlet and white, blue facings, buff facings, white and black and blue again, with the sheen of fixed bayonets a-glitter in the new sun. Rank after steady rank they flowed by, and then the soft wind blowing across the fields rippled through the glossy bearskins of the grenadiers coming on endlessly.

A drum hammered in preparatory warning. Other drums joined in, their thick tones carrying the shrill notes of the fifes high into the blue. The militia music was playing. So was the British in this pageant-like approach to the town of Concord. Long afterward, Minuteman Amos Barrett was to recall the glitter and the pathos of this opening scene, to remember how his company "march'd before them with our Droms and fifes agoing and also the B[ritish] we had a grand musick."

Watchers at the prow of the ridge could see a sudden change in tempo. The British music stopped. The musicians doubled back right and left along the column to rejoin their companies. There were more drumbeats, and the light infantry suddenly fanned out across the fields to their right, heading for the ridge, an excellent military precaution to guard the right flank of the expedition. With open fields to its left, stretching away and away, such a move on that side was unnecessary.

So some of the light infantry companies came on, covering the ridge like an inverted V, from the Lexington Road to the crest and down to the Great Meadows on the north side. The few watchers on the high ground hurried away to the hillside cemetery, which still rolls in slow gray cascades down the south face of the ridge. There they found another general debate in progress among the men of the companies that had led the British into Concord. Reverend William Emerson was all for standing fast and meeting the scarlet flood. More prosaic but wiser counsel prevailed, and the whole militia force trailed west to the break in the ridge, took the road again, and followed it past Elisha Jones's house, down the sharp bend that led to the Concord River, across North Bridge, and up to the old Muster Field out of sight on the high ground beyond.

The light infantry, finding nothing on the ridge, rejoined the main force near Wright's Tavern and the Common. The expedition that had toiled over the night roads had lost no strength, save for one mounted officer. Before reaching Lexington, Francis Smith had one clear flash of logic and sent the horseman back to Boston. He was to tell Gage that the countryside was up in strength and to pray, in eighteenth-century fashion, that Lord Percy follow at once with the rest of the garrison, the line companies in their cocked hats and what marines could be found. A piece or two of artillery, complete with gunners and drivers, would be highly acceptable.

Establishing his command post at Wright's, a pleasant spot then as now, Smith emphasized the need for haste by holding a review of his entire force —a rather puzzling move which was to be repeated by Gentleman Johnny Burgoyne in his retreat up the Hudson two and a half years later. Then he and Pitcairn went up into the cemetery and stared fiercely at the surrounding country through telescopes, as they still stare, above their marching men, in the crude but fantastically accurate Amos Doolittle prints.

Then Smith returned to the tavern with his staff. It was then about eight o'clock in the morning and he was ready to contemplate action. He sent some light infantry to seize the South Bridge and, having nothing to do, these men pass out of history for a few hours. To the North Bridge he sent first six companies and then a seventh. Three were to hold the bridge, and the others were to push on to Colonel Barrett's farm a mile or more beyond and snap up the stores supposed to be there. The grenadiers in their pointed fur caps were set to searching the town itself, a few of them mounting guard at strategic spots. Concord lay in the grip of the brutal, bloodthirsty, and licentious soldiery.

Even legends agree that they failed to live up to such a reputation. In fact, they behaved with remarkable restraint and consideration. There is a story of a tapster at Wright's cuffing an officer who complained about service. No retaliation is rumored or recorded. A determined old lady, finding a grenadier entering her house under orders, chased him out with a mop and her house went unsearched. An officer in another house, asking to have a closed chamber door opened for him, was told that the room was occupied by an invalid. It actually was occupied by military stores, but the officer accepted the explanation courteously and left the house. With joyous yelps some searchers found wooden gun carriages in the Town House and proceeded to set fire to them. A Concordian pointed out that the Town House, too, would burn, whereupon the detail dragged the carriages out in the street by the Common and rekindled them. The events of the rest of the day might have been incredibly altered had the men smashed them up with sledges. As it was, the carriages burned and their smoke sifted up through the elms and oaks, high into the warming sky. It is surprising that these troops, conditioned as they were by their life in Boston, by their killing night march, and by the brush at Lexington, behaved as they did. Substitute S.S. officers and some tough Feldwebels for Smith, Pitcairn and the rest and both Concord and Lexington would have burned, with a heavy casualty list.

By the millpond that lay behind Wright's, grenadiers were throwing sacks of bullets into the water, cheering at the splash that heavy flour barrels made—legitimate military stores, not town supplies. Carelessness took most of the value from this coup of Smith's. The bullet sacks were not cut. The flour barrels were not staved in. When the British finally left, most of the stores were salvaged.

At the North Bridge, the Light Infantry Guard took solid station. The 43rd Oxfordshires stayed on the Concord side. The 10th Lincolnshires and the 4th Royal North Lancashires, also known as the King's Own, spread out over the hillside across the bridge. Militarily the position would have been stronger had all companies stayed on the Concord bank, but the senior officer, Captain Laurie of the 43rd, had to think of the other four companies who had plunged off into the hinterland after the Barrett stores.

There was little for the bridge guard to do. On the skyline they could see a few militiamen, observers for the main body massed on the hidden Muster Field, but these watchers seemed content to keep their distance. The road to Barrett's, like the bridge itself now long out of use, curved away to the left around the foot of the hill.

There was a sudden stir on the sky line. Cocked hats, bayonetless muskets showed. In column of twos the militiamen topped the crest and began a steady march down the steep fields, heading straight for the bridge. Captain Laurie had to think fast. His whole force numbered less than one hundred and twenty men. As the militia came on, it seemed to him, standing on the sandy planks with the slow rustle of the little river below him, that their numbers had increased notably since the brief meeting beyond the prow of Concord Ridge. He recalled the Lincolnshires and the North Lancs and took up a formation designed for street fighting on the Concord side. The so-called street-fighting tactics called for simple if smart maneuvering. The command was formed in a column of fours. At an order the front-rank men fired, then peeled off right and left down the column to take their places in the rear, where they were supposed to reload at once. The peeling off exposed the second rank, which fired and ducked back in the wake of the four front-rank men. Thus a continuous fire could be kept up with rank after rank peeling off until the original front rank was back in the van again. These were good troops, none better. The bridge and its approaches were narrow. They should have been able to shatter innumerable attacking waves, especially as the assault would lack artillery support.

Yet something was wrong. There was an inexplicable uneasiness in the tight-formed ranks. Perhaps the morale factors mentioned before played their part. Good officers could have steadied them down, and good officers were present. But many of them were strangers. Even at the last moment, when the other four companies passed over the bridge, bound for the unknown, officers who should have stayed behind joined the little sub-expedition either under orders or through a sense of adventure.

The militia column came on, headed by Captain Isaac Davis, the gunsmith, with his Acton men. Little Abner Hosmer was close by him, thumping manfully at his drum. The column was long, but it should not have seriously concerned troops like the light infantry there on the Concord side with the Old Manse sunning itself in their left rear. Lieutenant Sutherland, whom we met with Pitcairn at Lexington Green, a carefree and spirited volunteer with no responsibilities for the day, jumped out on the bridge and began tearing up the planks. His action, a brazen interference with town property, drew a shout of indignant protest from someone in the militia ranks. Sutherland left the bridge and there was silence. Nothing but the ripple of the slow Concord River, the rustle of the budding trees, and the steady drub-drub-drub of the militia boots.

This time there was no question of who fired first. A volley blanketed the leading light infantry in smoke. Isaac Davis was down. Abner Hosmer rolled dead on the soft grass, his clumsy drum bumping along and his now useless drumsticks slithering out of his hands. The militia formation, two abreast, made any real volume of answering fire impossible. Whether by instinct or by order, men broke ranks, fanned out right and left, and returned the blast.

A few men dropped on the Concord side. Volunteer William Sutherland, who had slipped over into the Manse fields to get a flank shot at the militia, was slightly wounded. Then, inexplicably, unless all blame is laid on morale, Laurie's men broke. It was not a retreat but a rout, a racing scarlet column that poured back to the bend in the road that led on into the town, incredibly abandoning their dead and severely wounded comrades. Their flight—and it can be called nothing else—continued along present Monument Street until the fugitives met a body of grenadiers sent out by Smith in reply to an earlier request from Laurie. Had the grenadiers kept on, they might have changed the whole aspect of the nineteenth of April and of the days and years that followed it. They were tough, well-trained men and they would have taken badly disorganized militia in the flank. Instead, they opened their ranks, let the light infantry through, wheeled, and went back to the Common and Wright's Tavern.

If panic struck the British, a sort of premature battle shock seems to have fallen over the militia. They had seen the best troops in the world in sudden flight. They had only two men killed. The North Bridge was theirs. But they made no attempt to follow up their stroke. Instead, a good many of them went back to the Muster Field, some of them helping the few wounded. The rest kept straight on until they reached the sharp bend in the road, crossed it, and took up a position on the slope to the right of the Elisha Jones house and above the present parking lot. Then they waited. Perhaps their luck amazed them beyond the point of coherent action. Many were later to recall the ineffectiveness of the British fire, with British bullets splashing into the Concord River. Amos Barrett, with his "grand Musick" still in his ears, wrote that "It is straing their warnt no more killed but they fird to [sic] high." This must place Barrett well to the front in the column, since the high fire did wound men in the following companies. But most paralyzing of all must have been the unspoken thought hanging like a pall over all of them. "We've fired on the King's troops!"—a vastly different matter from writing inflammatory letters, making treasonable speeches, dumping tea at Griffin's Wharf, hustling a customs officer, or chivvying a mandamus councilor.

What had sent these men marching two by two down the slope of John Buttrick's hill? When the Concord and the Lincoln men had climbed it earlier in the morning, they had found waiting for them the Bedford and Acton companies. Villages too small to support companies had sent their quota—Carlisle and Chelmsford and Littleton—and the force probably numbered about four hundred men. These new arrivals were only an earnest of what was to come. The Sudbury men and the Westford contingent were close by and would report within an hour or so. Watchers on the high points about Concord like Punkatasset Hill eyed the now sunlit approaches to the town and guided the fresh arrivals to the assembly points.

Colonel James Barrett had gone back to his farm to see to the bundling off of the last of the supplies, and Major John Buttrick was in command with Lieutenant Joseph Hosmer as adjutant. Guided by what they could see from the Muster Field and by what the scouts down the slope reported, the Concord leaders and the out-of-town commanders took counsel. Captain William Smith of the Lincoln company optimistically offered to take his men down the hill and chase the British off the bridge. The consensus, however, was that the colonists should commit no overt act, a view supported by Colonel Barrett returning to the field from his farm.

So events were given, for the moment, into the hands of time. It is quite possible that had nothing else occurred Smith would have taken his command back to Boston with little damage to the colonial cause to report— if one forgot the handful of dead on Lexington Green. But an observer, or someone on the Muster Field, saw smoke welling up from Concord. The quite understandable inference was drawn from that smoke that the town was burning. There was an end to hesitation, and the whole militia body marched off to save Concord from a fate that did not threaten it, since the smoke came from the gun carriages being burned before the Town House. So now most of them lay up on the hill by Elisha Jones's house and waited.

They could not see the town. Directly ahead of them, down the elbow bend of the road, was the North Bridge with scarlet-coated, white-breeched bodies lying just short of it or on it. Most of the watchers saw a gangling figure in civilian clothes crossing the bridge, ax in his hand. One of the scarlet coats stirred, tried to raise itself, and the civilian shied, struck out with his ax, and then took to his heels. The soldier fell back. The road to the bridge was silent again. The silence was broken by the sound of boots, and bayonets gleamed among the trees. The four companies under Captain Parsons of the Lincolnshires—whose company stayed to guard the bridge and its approaches—were returning from their search at Barrett's. They had found nothing, which had not improved their tempers. They may have heard the brief exchange of fire at the bridge, which would have added to their uncertainty. When they saw the British dead and the still-living man with the ax wound in his head, their pace quickened, and when they reached the sharp bend toward Concord they were at a full double. There they went —four companies, passing under the muzzles of the muskets on the hillside to their left. One concerted blast would have thrown them into deeper confusion, might even have shattered them, in view of their morale. It might have been because there was no one in command of the militia to give the order to fire; it might have been that the men were still so shaken by the thought of having fired on the King's troops that the idea of repetition did not occur to them. Whatever the reason, not a trigger was drawn, and Parsons' men reached Concord with a report of a fruitless search and of Yankee mutilation of the wounded, a yarn that grew into a charge of scalping. The actual blow seems to have been struck by a panic-stricken man who had been cutting wood in the Manse fields and who had strayed out onto the bridge through curiosity. He had been frightened by the move of that severely wounded man, had lashed out convulsively and fled. As to scalping, Allen French has pointed out that probably not a man in Massachusetts was familiar with the process, or would have had such an act in mind or have had the skill to carry it out.

The North Bridge lay quiet in the sun with its freight of British dead. Later the villagers would bury the dead just to the left of the bridge where a plain solid stone with Oliver Wendell Holmes's verses marks the grave. It is a quiet spot, and on each nineteenth of April the British and American flags go side by side under the pines and British and American ex-servicemen fire a salute over those lost light infantrymen.

The hours of the morning ticked on. Probably under Pitcairn's prompting Smith hired carriages and chaises, loaded his wounded into them, and started them off toward Boston. It is interesting to note that the fat, slow Colonel Smith voluntarily paid the rebel owners of these conveyances. Then at noon he lurched into action, formed up his whole command, and took the road that led back through Lexington Green.

At the first warning of the evacuation, the militia force, with probably many additions, left the slopes by Elisha Jones's house, filed out through the gap in the ridge, and headed east through the flats of the Great Meadows, the ridge at their right masking both town and road. Ahead they could see the light infantrymen once more forming their inverted V to comb that ridge. When the last scarlet coat had gone, they swarmed up and followed along the crest. It is impossible to say what they had in mind. To judge from the temper of the day, their sole aim was to see the invaders off the premises. Certainly there was no one in command to tell them to follow in pursuit or to stop where they were.

The firstcomers at the prow of the ridge, from which the British dawn advance had been watched, looked down on what might well have been the final act of the day. The light infantry had spread out to the left again as flankers, with some detachments doubling to the head of the column. The last of the grenadiers were filing over a little bridge that spanned Mill Brook. It was a very narrow bridge, replaced today by a culvert, and the grenadiers naturally jammed up crossing it, making very slow time. At the foot of the prow was the Bedford Road, leading from the north into Lexington Road. Merriam's Corner it was, and still is, with the Merriam house that today looks out on swift motor traffic along the Battle Road. To the right were the flats, marshy and treeless. A militiaman who had been up since midnight, had fired his first shot in anger and seen his comrade and enemy fall, could well lean on his musket and wonder numbly about the events of the day.

But there was more to see than the grenadiers crowding across the narrow bridge beyond Merriam's Corner. The Bedford Road was thick with militia, headed by the companies from Reading and Billerica. Some unidentified but highly experienced eye took in the scene and in surprisingly good order the newcomers fanned out, lapping about the Merriam house and making for the stone wall that lined the Lexington Road. (British officers insisted on referring to this New England feature as a stone hedge.) The flats to the south were suddenly full of men. The companies and squads from the Sudbury area were coming in to report. They did not bother to report but pressed on toward the south wall of the road.

Up to this very instant the rest of the day might have passed without further event. The fresh arrivals knew nothing except rumor. In many cases they had not even heard of the firing in the two villages. Their first rush could easily have petered out. But the last of the grenadiers turned at the bridge and fired. It must have been a gesture of exasperation and defiance, for there was no target within musket range. It triggered off the real, the irretrievable results of the day. Militiamen closed in on the rear and flanks of the column. One of them noted in awe that "A grait many Lay dead and the Road was bloddy." For miles the British were to march in a funnel of musketry, and with each mile more militia closed in at the head. Men who had been out since the first call dropped out, bullets or rations or courage exhausted, but always new men took their places. Rarely if ever did the militia fight as units. They sighted the road, broke ranks, fired, moved on, fired again.

By some orange-brown stone bluffs west of Lexington a stand was attempted, with Pitcairn on his black horse very much in evidence. A militiaman wrote later, "An officer, mounted on an elegant horse, and with a drawn sword in his hand, was riding backwards and forwards, commanding and urging on the British troops. A number of Americans behind a pile of rails, raised their guns and fired with deadly effect. The officer fell and . . . his horse ran directly toward those who had killed the rider." Pitcairn was not even wounded and fought the rest of the day on foot. His horse was captured; his pistols were carried through the war by Israel Putnam and are now owned by the Lexington Historical Society. The retreat went on.

The British were hard pressed but were striking back hotly. The light infantry had recovered its poise. Like a well-trained pack of hounds, the companies swept along the flanks of the retreat, dropping into hollows to fire, breaking up knots of militia, swinging away from the road, circling back, and taking incautious rebels from the rear.

The pace told more and more on Smith's command. The afternoon of the nineteenth was wearing on, and very few of the men had had any real sleep since the night of the seventeenth. Signs of panic showed. Francis Smith himself was wounded in the leg. Observant young Henry de Berniere wrote bitterly afterward, "[The rebels] kept the road always lined and a very hot fire on us without intermission; we at first kept our order and returned their fire as hot as we received it, but when we arrived a mile from Lexington, our ammunition began to fail and the light [infantry] companies were so fatigued with flanking they were scarce able to act . . . so that we began to run rather than retreat in order . . . we attempted to stop the men and form them two deep, but to no purpose."

When the flight reached the long slope that leads down to Lexington Green, men were dropping their equipment and the scarlet-and-white flood rolled on toward the scene of the morning's brush. It really began to look as though there might be a mass surrender, as complete in its way as Dupont's yielding up Napoleonic eagles to Spanish irregulars at Baylen in 1808.

Relief came with flamboyant suddenness. The hill beyond the Green was black with cocked hats, bright with more scarlet and white. Up on the shoulder of the hill by the present high school a fieldpiece was being dragged into place. Major General Percy had arrived with the rest of the Boston garrison. Smith's men plunged on to safety, and Earl Percy's lines opened to let them through. The harried fugitives "were so exhausted," wrote British Stedman, "that they were obliged to lie on the ground, their tongues hanging from their mouths, like those of dogs after a chase." Another fieldpiece was trundled up and joined its fellow in sending a few rounds down at the more than disorderly pursuit, which slackened and finally halted.

It was now nearly three o'clock. This part of the pursuit was over, but the lull was only a breathing spell. The second half would begin soon. Onto the Green, out of cannon range, came the only American general to be present during the whole day, William Heath, the modest "our General" of the autobiography. With him was Joseph Warren, who had, in some amazing fashion, followed Percy's men out from Boston, leaving them to detour toward the sound of the firing. There was little that Heath could do. As has been noted, most units broke up to act as individuals on arriving at the Battle Road. The one thing that he might have done, that leaders back in Concord might have done earlier, was overlooked. Axmen could have been circled round ahead of the British to fell trees across the road. Had this been done, the expedition would never have returned to Boston. Two years later, Philip Schuyler, rebel New York patroon, was to set his woodsmen blocking Burgoyne's route south of Lake Champlain, and their activities, if not decisive, played a big part in Gentleman Johnny's ultimate disaster.

From his position on the hill beyond the Green—or the Heath, as some

diarists called it—Earl Percy could watch the militiamen falling back under
the threat of his two little cannon and could justly say to himself, "I had
the happiness of saving them [Smith's men] from apparently inevitable
destruction." What was his next move to be? He had brought, along with
the guns, over a thousand fresh men. How about a quick counterattack?
But he had only to look at Smith's refugees, to talk to Smith and Pitcairn.
He would not fail to note, being an excellent soldier, that the rebels, while
keeping out of range, were not leaving the field. Rather, he could detect
cautious parties trying to work around his flanks. The most that he could
safely do was to allow the briefest of rests and then strike back to Boston.
Some of his wounded were treated at Munroe's Tavern, close by his left
rear, and the ceilings there still show the marks of bullets fired by disgruntled patients. Then Percy gathered his forces, sent Smith and Pitcairn
with the spent men ahead of him, and took the road, the two guns and the
eight line companies of the 23rd Welch covering his rear.

As soon as Percy stirred, those militiamen who had stayed the course to
this point lurched after him and the blazing horror of the road from Concord was repeated. Militiamen dropped out, were replaced by fresh arrivals.
Companies from distant towns and villages came on the scene, broke up,
and, as individuals, sank back of stone walls, glided behind trees, made
sudden rushes to close in for a moment, shouting, according to Lieutenant
Frederick Mackenzie of the Welch, "King Hancock forever!"

Over and over the scene was repeated, sometimes clear and sharp for an
instant, sometimes blurred like a bad film. Smoke rolled back to show the
little fieldpieces being tugged along by the patient horses, while wounded
and malingerers clung to the guns and their carriages like swarms of bees.
When the pursuit pressed too close, the gunners roughly pushed the pas-
sengers off, unlimbered, fired, limbered up again, only to have trail and
limber and barrel buried under a heap of scarlet coats.

There was a stand, much like that attempted at the Bluffs, near the Rocks
of Menotomy, but it frayed out and the battered column reeled on. The
ammunition of the rear-guard Welch began to run low and their place was
taken by tough marines.

The force was clear of the high ground at Menotomy and flowing out
into the flats that led on to Cambridge and Charlestown and the river.
Percy had first come out the longer but easier route via the single Cambridge
bridge. Now he had word that the planks had been torn up and a strong
militia force stationed on the far bank. Supply wagons that were supposed
to have followed him had been snapped up by some elderly men, probably
belonging to an Alarm Company. (The men of the Supply Company, deep
in enemy territory, are said to have surrendered themselves to old Mother
Batherick as she peacefully gathered up a mess of dandelion greens in Cambridge.) Clearly, Percy would run into trouble if he headed back along his
old route. He decided to take Smith's Massachusetts Avenue-Beech Street-
Somerville Avenue course.

The tortured march went on and his men began understandably to get

out of hand, galled by an enemy against whom they could not strike effectively. Men broke ranks, set fire to houses, looted, destroyed wantonly, shot
at any civilian they saw. They should not be blamed too much for this.
They had been fired on from houses along the route; therefore, to them, any
house was a snipers' nest, any male a sniper. Ensign Barker, making no
allowances for what his own men had been through, complained bitterly,
"The plundering was shameful; many hardly thought of anything else; what
was worse, they were encouraged by some Officers."

The column was into Cambridge, its course marked by a rolling smoke
cloud, and out of that smoke another problem emerged to face Percy.
Striped by the afternoon shadows of oak and elm, a large, fairly solid body
of militia loomed over the approaches to Beech Street and the road to the
Charles. The earl was a man of decision and usually of sound decision. He
ordered an abrupt change of course and swung off past Prospect Hill and
Winter Hill in present-day Somerville and urged his men on toward Charlestown, militiamen still snapping and worrying at the desperate column.

And here Fate gave a grudging nod to the earl and his men. Unknown
to him, the Salem militia, reputedly the best of the province, trained and
led by Colonel Timothy Pickering, who in the past had probably bought
many military texts from Henry Knox's London Book-Store, was closing
in, threatening the tormented men of Smith's original force, the grenadiers
and light infantry. But Pickering, knowing that Heath was at least in
nominal command, had halted and sent a courier to "our General" for
instructions. Heath fumbled badly. He told Pickering that, as Percy had
cannon, the Salem men could do nothing against him unless they too were
so equipped, a surprising bit of logic in view of what mere musketeers had
been doing all through the day. Pickering was not to engage. His losses
would be too heavy. "Our General" was reasoning, or failing to reason,
like McClellan, who in a later war would let a small fraction of his force
be shredded by Joe Johnston or Lee and refuse to throw in his heavy, untouched reserves for fear that they might suffer casualties.

So Percy's men and Smith's finally stumbled onto the narrow-necked
peninsula of Charlestown, and militiamen, following cautiously, could see
British warships close to the shore, their gun ports open and muzzles
pointed inland, masts high and golden in the sunset.

The day of Concord and Lexington was over. From it a long, tragic succession of tomorrows stretched out into the future. The first year of the
Revolution had begun.

Night crept in from the sea, spreading lavender, then purple, then black
over Charlestown and the restless inland reaches. Along lanes, along highways, weary men began tramping off to the homes they had left a seeming
eternity ago. But hundreds stayed, guided by the vaguest of orders, guided
more, perhaps, by an uneasy sense that their time of service was not up.

A homing militiaman topping the Heights of Arlington, near where the
water tower stands today, could look out over a great and moving panorama

that revealed little by little an immense, growing horseshoe of scattered lights closing in an arc about Charlestown and Boston—the campfires of the men who had followed that long April road, an arc that was thickened and deepened by the fires of companies from the central and western parts of the province, still arriving.

Those fires burned on through the summer, fall, and winter, into the spring. They saw the British fleet carry away those troops who had burned a few gun carriages in Concord, who had pulled their triggers by that little bridge near Merriam's Corner. The fires died away. But they reappeared, not the fires of a provincial army or a New England army, but of an American army on Long Island, on Manhattan, below Quebec and in Montreal, in the Jerseys and Pennsylvania, and at last before Cornwallis' lines at York-town in Virginia.

They were durable fires. From time to time they flare up again. They burned at Lundy's Lane and New Orleans; at Gettysburg and Appomattox and San Juan. Carefully shielded, but still bright under their cover, they burned along the Marne and through the Argonne, on African and Nor-mandy beaches and on sinister islands of the Pacific and among the iron mountains of Korea. Fires of conviction and not of conquest, fires that were first lighted at the end of that winding Battle Road in Middlesex County.

Few military men of any era and of any army, given the nature, training, and equipment of the opposing forces, would have correctly forecast the outcome of the nineteenth. On paper it was an upset and, like most upsets, produced damaging results for both sides. The British High Command seemed to suffer from a form of combat fatigue which would be intensified by events in Charlestown a few weeks hence. They feared the sudden rallying power of the province—and if Massachusetts could so rally, why not New York or North Carolina or Delaware? They also became gun-shy, although they seem to have argued themselves out of this frame of mind long enough to send their men up the Charlestown hills, after which their fear, in many cases, became an obsession.

For the American side, the nineteenth encouraged a sort of lazy reliance on a spontaneous levee en masse, a comforting but treacherous manner of thought which discounted the true lessons of the day. It blandly disregarded the weeks and months of organizing, planning, weighing, training that made this and other turnouts possible, imperfect as they were. It led men to sit back and contemplate surface results without making any serious attempts to correct glaring flaws. It produced unsound national thinking that had ghastly effects on national defense down to World War II and perhaps beyond. Why have an army? If need be, the nation will rise over-night. To challenge this view was, to some, a deadly insult to the men of 1775.

Militia fire power deluded America nearly as badly as did the matter of spontaneous mobilization. A legend was bred that all Americans, from the very nature of things, were deadly with firearms. Remember how those farmers left their hearths and rushed into the fields to blast the clumsy British from the roads with their unerring rifles?

Many people still remember this, without stopping to think that that memory has almost no foundation. Based on cold figures, the American marksmanship was not merely terrible, it was virtually nonexistent. All that may be said for it is that it was better than the British, who were not trained to aim but only to point their muskets in a rather general direction. There is no reason why the Americans should have been good shots. Few had been in actual warfare. Big game had gone from the region years ago. The area was largely agricultural and commercial, and few men had to depend on musket or fowling piece to keep the larder full. Occasional duck-hunting trips would afford no worth-while preparation for armed combat. Powder was scarce and expensive, and when the militia began drilling there was little if any ammunition to spare for target practice, particularly after Gage's men went scuttling off with the stores from Cambridge and Charlestown.

Then there was the musket, the almost universal weapon of the day. The more accurate and longer-ranged rifled piece may be forgotten; there probably was not one north of Pennsylvania. The smoothbore firelock was not a weapon of precision. It had a very short range. One hundred yards would be a long shot. It was heavy and clumsy. When the trigger was pulled, a sluggish hammer fell, striking against the flint and igniting a little loose powder that sent flame through a vent into the chamber where more powder and the bullet lay. If all went well, the real powder charge was exploded and the bullet went away on a cheerfully erratic course. The quality of powder varied and bullets were irregular in size, shape, and weight. A man could be a better shot than his neighbor, but he could never be particularly accurate.

A glance at the British casualty lists ought to have squelched this legend at the start. From Merriam's Corner, where the only serious action of the day started, until Charlestown was reached, nearly two thousand British, counting Percy's reinforcement at Lexington, struggled along narrow roads, often overlooked by high ground. There is testimony that they marched between walls of living fire—walls that were not too close to the road, however, owing to the efforts of the light infantry in protecting the flanks. In such a setting a few companies of Morgan's riflemen probably could have wiped out Smith's force before it ever reached Lexington. What was the score of the musket-armed farmers and townsmen? Gage's reports show that in the whole day just over seventy British were actually killed and about one hundred and seventy wounded, many of these last very lightly. This is not an impressive figure. Yet, in a larger view, the militiamen of Massachusetts touched military heights rarely reached by better-trained, -armed, and -led armies. They did what they could with what they had.

CHAPTER X

"We do now pledge ourselves to each other . . ."

THE events of the nineteenth of April, from their very inception, dislocated the machinery of the Provincial Government of Massachusetts. Some members, while knowing of the alarm, were in ignorance of later developments. Others, like "our General" and Dr. Joseph Warren, were active participants. Of the Committee of Safety, only one man appears to have been functioning in that role. Early on the morning of the clash Colonel Joseph Palmer of Braintree rode into rich black-soiled Watertown, a bend and a twist and a bend up the placid Charles from Cambridge. Some unknown hand brought him news of the march-out of the Boston troops and of the haphazard musketry on Lexington Green.

Palmer hurriedly obtained a quill, ink, and paper and, on his own responsibility, began to write.

Wednesday Morng near 10 of the Clock.

Watertown

To all friends of American Liberty let it be known that this Morning before break of day a Brigade . . . marched to Lexington . . . where . . . they fired without any Provocation and killed 6 Men and wounded 4 others . . . we find that another Brigade are now upon their March from Boston. . . . The bearer Israel Bissel is charged to alarm the Country quite to Connecticut, and all persons are desired to furnish him with fresh Horses, as they may be needed. I have spoken with Several who have seen the dead and the wounded. . . .

J. Palmer—one of the Comy of Sy.

Iz Bissel was a veteran postrider of the Boston–New York run. He also must have been a man of rare determination, for he far exceeded Colonel Palmer's prayer to carry the news "quite to Connecticut" and in his zeal must have set some sort of a record for speed. In two hours he had covered the roller-coaster road to Worcester and delivered his news to the local authorities, tradition claiming that his spent horse died under him close to present Worcester City Hall. The next day found him spurring into the low, swelling hills of Connecticut, stopping off in Pomfret for a hasty word with a grizzled, round-faced man on a quiet farm. There would be no better man to hail south of the Connecticut line than the old ranger and Indian fighter, Israel Putnam.

Bissel was off again, south and still south, down the long green valley of the Thames, and at last sighted the spires and wharves of New London, lavender and gold in the April sunset. There were delays at most of his stops. The local committees were made up of cautious men. Copies of Palmer's letter, duly witnessed and attested, had to be made for further distribution. Searching questions had to be answered and querulous minds satisfied.

Delays and all, the twenty-first brought him into New Haven, and on the twenty-second he rode along the dune grasses of the Sound, pausing briefly at Fairfield, then up and to horse again. On the twenty-third, Sabbath or not, Israel Bissel crossed the King's Bridge onto the island of Manhattan and sent his horse pelting toward the bright little city at the far end. "Between the forenoon and afternoon service" he shot on past the Bowery, the high windmill, the reeking tanyards, and reined in on the Common with the smell of fresh brick and mortar coming to him from the nearly finished Georgian grace of the New York Hospital.

There were many people about, returning from one service or waiting for the next in the warm April air. From the saddle, Bissel shouted his news. The ministerial troops had fired on the people of Lexington, a small village up there in Massachusetts. The postrider and his horse were jostled and shoved by a tidal wave of shouting people. Men clawed at his stirrups, demanding proof, and he showed his papers, signed by Palmer and endorsed by a dozen committees in Connecticut. New York caught fire. Isaac Sears, John Lamb, Alex McDougall started a procession down Broadway under the snap and flaunt of impromptu banners and to the thick rustle of drums. Householders along the line of march stared at the gathering from their windows, vanished, reappeared, running down their Dutch stoops, musket in hand. It would have been something to see, that sudden rush of citizens toward the Battery and the wharves.

Iz Bissel had no time for gaping. Before the next dawn his horse drummed along the New Jersey flats, passed the college at Princeton, kept on and on until the low stone barracks at Trenton marked a longer halt. The twenty-fifth brought Germantown and Philadelphia creeping up over the horizon toward him. In five days and some hours he had gone from Watertown by the Charles to the capital of Pennsylvania. Under ideal conditions the fast stagecoaches used up a good six days in getting only to New York.

This ride was no mere speed test, for out of the dust plume that marked his long passage a new country was to emerge. Israel Bissel could be content to end his journey at Philadelphia and drop out of history. He had played his part, and sure hands would urge his words southward. Scrawls on copies of Colonel Palmer's letter tell their own tense story. "Forwarded to Col. Thomas Couch, Esquire, who received it this moment, and he to forward it to Tobias Randulph, Esquire, Head of Elk, in Maryland. Night and day to be forwarded." . . . "For God's sake send this man on without the least delay and write to Mr. Marion to forward it by night and by day." . . . "I request, for the good of our Country, and the welfare of our lives and liberties and fortunes, you will not lose a moment's time." . . . "We send you momentous intelligence, this instant received."

While messages and endorsements winged south, Virginia was angrily astir, stung into turmoil by local events. The clownish, bibulous Governor Dunmore, blinking over maps that showed land grants made to Virginia soldiers who had served in the last French war, stunned the colony by suddenly ruling that, through a technicality, those grants were null and void. They took in huge tracts of undeveloped lands far to the west, reaching out beyond the Great Kanawha River in present West Virginia, and grantees had spent much money and pledged still more to establish titles and make surveys. This was a blow to present solvency and future prospects that rocked many Virginians, Colonel George Washington among them, back on their heels. The colonel wrote courteously to Dunmore, whom he had entertained at Mount Vernon, only to receive a reply that was insulting in its coldness and brevity. Apparently the nullification of the grants would stand.

Plantation life went on uneasily. Spring plowing was over. Wheat was showing green in the fields that sloped down to the Rappahannock, the North Anna, and the Potomac, and slaves were sowing corn. Blossoms were opening in formal gardens and in cutting gardens, and men were watching the rivers for the annual run of herring. To Mount Vernon came the usual flow of guests. A retired British major, neighbor to Samuel Washington, rode up for a visit. His name was Horatio Gates and he had been a company commander on Braddock's blundering, bloody expedition back in '55. A wandering British general, the incredibly thin and ugly Charles Lee—general by pronouncement of the King of Poland—repeated an earlier visit from his seat in Berkeley County. With the general came another Lee, no kin, young Harry Lee, son of Henry Lee of Leesylvania. He was just nineteen and a graduate of the college at Princeton in New Jersey, an unusually handsome, magnetic young man. All these guests would serve with varying degrees of sincerity and success under their host, and young Harry's son, born late in the father's life, would in his mature years be ranked with that host as a great Virginian and a great patriot. He would bear the name Robert Edward.

Into this setting whose pastoral calm overlay hot tension came an express rider with a hurried letter to Colonel George Washington from Hugh Mercer, written at Fredericksburg on the Rappahannock and giving startling news. Dunmore had acted again with even less than his usual tact and judgment. Fifteen royal marines under Captain Collins of the schooner *Magdalen* had landed near Williamsburg at night, had snapped up the province powder stored there and carted it away.

"The gentlemen of the Independent Company of this town," wrote Hugh Mercer, "think this first public insult is not tamely to be submitted to and determine with your approbation to join any other bodies of armed men who are willing to appear in support of the honor of Virginia. . . . Expresses are sent off to inform the commanding officers of Companies in the adjacent Counties of this our resolution and we shall wait prepared for your instructions and their assistance."

"Your approbation"—"your instructions." Men were leaning more and more on the judgment of the quiet master of Mount Vernon. What answer could he give? He and the other Virginia delegates to the Continental Congress could recall the gust of alarm that swept over the country at the news of Gage's march through Cambridge and Charlestown the September before. Nothing had happened, despite the deep fears at the time. So wait. Things might settle down in Virginia as they had in Massachusetts. Dunmore might have an unexpected ray of sense and release the powder. In any event, it amounted to only twenty-odd barrels. So hope for an amicable settlement—or at least delay. Yes, by all means keep the militia in hand, though in all probability they would not be needed. For himself, the colonel had every hope of leaving for Philadelphia and the new session of the Continental Congress early in May.

Other expresses than those of Hugh Mercer were riding through the late April days and nights. At least by sundown of the twenty-eighth, Washington knew of the fight that had rolled savagely along that Massachusetts road. Other Virginians had learned of it, and there were reports of more militia musters, of companies making ready to march on Williamsburg. Somehow they managed to wait until they knew what advice Washington and other trusted leaders had to give. These men now had to reorient their thoughts. The news from Massachusetts showed them that now they must study their own troubles from a national, not a local, point of view. An explosion in Virginia might bring on undreamed-of complications. Wise Peyton Randolph, probably voicing Washington's thoughts as well as his own, urged the companies to disperse, to forget about Williamsburg. "Violence may produce effects which God alone knows the effects of."

The militia broke up, but not before passing a resolution that ended, "We do now pledge ourselves to each other to be in readiness, at a moment's warning, to reassemble, and by force of arms, to defend the law, the liberty and rights of this or any sister Colony, from unjust and wicked invasion." This was blazing, unequivocal speech. To underscore it, the officers who read out the resolve to their companies omitted ominously the customary coda of "God save the King." Instead, the phrase "God save the liberties of America" sailed boldly out into the Virginia air. Bloodlessly but unmistakably the Southern militiaman closed ranks with the minuteman of Massachusetts.

The last and southernmost ripples of the shots that splashed into the Concord River by the North Bridge rolled into the harbor of Charleston in South Carolina on the eighth day of May, riding ahead of the prow of the brigantine *Industry*, Captain Allen, twelve days out of Salem in Massachusetts. The ripples finally died away against the stone facings of the Battery, but their soft sounds were clearly heard in the quiet elegance of the big houses of the town and in the smaller dwellings of the mechanics.

The road that led across Lexington Green was unimaginably far from the

Ashley and the Cooper rivers, from Charleston and Monk's Corner and Purrysburg and strangely named Round O. The sparks that had fallen in the powder barrels of Virginia and New York and Massachusetts were cold embers along the Santee. South Carolinians, with almost nothing to gain and virtually everything to lose by even tacit sympathy with those Northern colonists, could have been expected to view the news from New England with academic detachment.

Such expectation, however, would have overlooked the former spontaneous and instant dispatch of supplies and credits to the port of Boston. Acting in complete harmony with that earlier generous gesture, Carolinians went into action at once. The timid, the ultra-conservative, the men who clung to the Crown regardless of royal acts, began to drop out, to speak in lower and lower tones. Names like Brewton, Laurens, Pinckney, Drayton, Bee, Huger glowed with an increasing luster that they would never lose. The Provincial Congress of South Carolina voted to raise at once two infantry regiments of seven hundred and fifty men each and a squadron of four hundred and fifty mounted rangers. Then, as though to emphasize that this was more than an emotional gesture, the sum of one million pounds sterling was appropriated. In the years to come, no colony would be more torn by war, not even battered New Jersey. No colony would stand more unflinchingly to the end.

The house of Artemas Ward still stands on the east slope of the great Shrewsbury Ridge, looking down through its narrow-paned windows on the lift and climb of the Boston–Worcester road. Ward, senior active general of the Massachusetts army, lay "sick of the stone" in an upper chamber when the news of the fighting of the nineteenth was brought him. Stone and all, he managed to heave himself into the saddle—he was a big, heavy-set man—and made his way grimly through Northboro and Marlboro until he reached Cambridge and the Charles River. There he reported to the Committee of Safety and, with understandable reluctance, took over command of the wrack of men that the tide, set in motion by Smith's march and the subsequent alarm, had swept into an arc about Boston.

What Artemas Ward found would have horrified a modern recruit of ten days' service. The Shrewsbury general, while better conditioned by eighteenth-century life in general and Massachusetts military life in particular than any modern could have been, must have felt his shoulders sag under the impact of the task ahead of him. Another six months of peace would have eased his burden tremendously, for, as has been noted, the Massachusetts plans were still in the roughest of paper stages. The Hutchinson appointees in the militia, the unshakable Tories, the unreliable had had to be weeded out of the militia and a whole new structure built. What had been accomplished up to date had been sufficient to launch a great mass of men against Smith's and Percy's columns, to bring a still larger number hurrying to the scene long after the last shot had been fired. But what organization there existed was held up by the shakiest of scaffolds.

The militia and minute companies that had swarmed along the Battle Road were now massed haphazardly across the northern and western approaches to Boston, their formations in unutterable confusion. The breakup that had occurred as they joined action on the nineteenth had left individuals embedded among strangers, had found officers trying to give orders to a score or so of men from different villages and counties. There was more coherence from the center of the line along to the southwest and south, since many of the units stationed there had arrived too late for the fight and had not undergone the disintegration of battle, save for the usual wastage caused by those who lagged, got lost, or went home.

Artemas Ward, gnawed at by his stone, followed the example of the men of the nineteenth by doing what he could with what he had. He divided the living arc into two great halves and took command of the northern part. The southern, which ran on looping through Roxbury, he entrusted to a man from Plymouth County, giving him virtual autonomy in that sector.

This Plymouth County general was a man to rely on. Like Leonard Wood of a later generation, John Thomas had begun as a doctor and had served in the 1746 expedition into "Cannady" as "second chirurgeon." Later came the provincial grades of lieutenant and surgeon's mate, then captain-lieutenant and surgeon. By the end of the French wars he had turned from medical duties to combat and had been a full colonel during operations in Nova Scotia and Canada. He was a well-set-up man with rather saturnine, dead-pan features and had the full trust and respect of the men of the southern counties. Like Wood, he showed a great aptitude for things military and might have been one of the outstanding names of the period had not smallpox struck him down in his last foray into "Cannady" in 1776.

Little by little a vague semblance of order was brought to the Massachusetts army. The problems of arms, powder, rations, pay, rank were never solved, but a solution was approached nearly enough to keep the flimsy organization in the field. Diatribes have been launched against militia demands for pay and rations, and most unjustly launched. We have seen how the officers and men turned out on the night of the eighteenth and through the days following. They had answered a hurried call, leaving law office, shop, farm, sawmill, gristmill, tavern to get on as best they might. There had been little or no provision made for the morrow. Most were willing to stay in the field, but while they stayed, how about that farm or that mill? For their own livelihood the men could not let them rot. More than that, the army and the province needed what these men produced.

Out of a welter of frustrations and contradictions, a new army was formed. There was little or no precedent to go by. The authority of the Provincial Congress and the Committee of Safety was shadowy in the extreme. More than that, this transformation took place under the very guns of a powerful, well-organized and -equipped British force. This achievement was, in its way, a miracle. A far greater one would occur when the new year of 1776 came in.

The minute companies were disbanded and passed out of history. Actual regiments were formed, officers and men agreeing to serve to the end of the year, thus gaining the name of the Eight Months' Army. Congress and the committee in a deep fog of perplexity juggled the size of the companies, issued orders, canceled them, set up one framework to serve as a model, discarded it, and went on to another.

There were many honest if, to us, stupid obstacles in the regiments themselves. There was the intense spirit of localism that shackled plans basically sound. We think nothing today of a man from North Dakota or Colorado serving with Vermonters or Floridians. In eighteenth-century Massachusetts, and indeed in all the colonies, an incredibly smaller, narrower spirit was horribly manifest. Men wanted to serve with their immediate neighbors and with no others. A company from Sturbridge might march beside one from Petersham, but each unit seemed to regard the other as a dubious ally rather than as a group of comrades.

The archives are thick with petitions to the committee and to Congress. There was one "desiring that the men raised in and about Newbury might not be annexed to Colonel Gerrish's regiment, or any other where it would be disagreeable to them." Regiments shied away from having surgeons appointed, not because the surgeons were not competent, but because "they might not be agreeable to the Officers and Soldiers"—in other words, a stranger, a foreigner. In York County, in present-day Maine, the men would not serve under Alexander Scammell, who was to fight superbly through the whole war, only to meet a tragic end at Yorktown on the threshold of victory. The Maine men wrote that "Mr. Scammell lives in New Hampshire and has no property in Berwick or the County of York." From Suffolk County came a similar wail. "And we are apprehensive that we, or part of us, shall be put under command of officers from other Counties, which will be very disagreeable not only to us, but to our Companies also." A letter to the committee warns, ". . . and am credibly informed that 3–4 Cos. that are raised, wil refuse to serve in the regt. & perhaps be the means of ruining the Regiment entirely."

The financial problem is well spotlighted in a letter addressed to "Colony Congress of the Massachusetts Bay." Eight captains of James Scammon's regiment humbly showed "That whereas there is no provisions made for the money that we, our subalterns & soldiers have advanced for their support from the time of enlistment to arrival at Cambridge, humbly pray [that Congress] contrive some way that is most agreeable for their being refunded the several sums advanced." These men of all ranks had apparently financed themselves and were now asking, mildly enough, that their expenses be indemnified.

A strange twist in what was known as military honor threw congressmen and committeemen into gibbering frustration. The code then prevailing in all armies insisted that once an officer had held a given rank he could not honorably serve in a lower one. The reshuffling, and the re-establishment of the Massachusetts army inevitably meant some officers would find themselves without commands. Colonel A, a proven and respected man, might find himself without a regiment. He could, however, serve valuably as major or even captain in one of the new formations. But to drop a grade would tarnish his honor. So only two courses remained open to Colonel A. He could go home and hang up his sword and his uniform if he had one, or he could mouse about Congress, lobbying for the establishment of a new regiment with himself as colonel.

There was another turmoil involving the New Hampshire troops, who had made a remarkable march by companies and squads, the first representatives of an "allied army" to assist that of Massachusetts. With them came a tough, ultra-cantankerous Indian fighter and ranger, John Stark, who, reversing the usual procedure of the day, refused to serve as a New Hampshire man and demanded and received a Massachusetts commission, though leading New Hampshire troops. When the time came to form these northerners into regiments on the Massachusetts pattern, the men showed little inclination to go home but an illogical distaste for serving under their own colonels. This impasse was solved by appointing a Massachusetts man as one of the colonels, Paul Dudley Sargent. This seemed to satisfy the New Hampshire men.

Just as Ward and the Congress settled back with weary sighs, New Hampshire erupted again. One Captain Espy claimed that Ward had told him that the New Hampshire troops were neither needed nor wanted. He passed this not exactly flattering statement on among his men. Huge, competent, well-liked Andrew McClary, with only a few weeks of life left to him, wrote home to New Hampshire of Espy that, "by the insinuations of himself and his busy emissaries, about five or six hundred of our men inconsiderately marched off for home." Worse, they managed to turn back a few parties of men hurrying toward the Charles.

At last two full New Hampshire regiments were formed, one under Stark and one under James Reed, but there was little smoothing of the waters. New Hampshire appointed Nathaniel Folsom, the man who had ridden to the Continental Congress the year before with John Sullivan, as commander of all the troops of that province. At once Stark slashed and struggled like a trapped bear. He may have disliked Folsom personally. He most certainly disliked serving under him. It is quite in keeping with his honest, turbulent, undisciplined character that when he appeared on the field on the bloody seventeenth of the coming June he had angrily thrown up his commission, had no military status, no actual command—and fought magnificently.

The story of the days and weeks and months that followed that red sunset of the nineteenth of April is infinite, and only a few of the difficulties that formed a mile-deep morass for the struggling Congress, committee, and army may be indicated. More tractable, though no less valuable, allies moved in from the south, not losing their numbers in an American army, but joining hands with a Massachusetts army.

From Connecticut came nearly three thousand men under the scarred old Indian fighter, Israel Putnam, with whom Postrider Bissel had talked at Pomfret on the twentieth of April. Company by company they crossed the border and marched on toward Boston. Some of them were uniformed, notably the company from Wethersfield, trim and well-disciplined in blue coats faced with red. From New Haven came the Governor's Foot Guards, outshining even the Wethersfield men in British-like scarlet coats faced and trimmed with buff, with black half gaiters sharp against white breeches. Their commander was a stocky, soldierly man with a roving hard eye. On the news of the Lexington fight he had forcibly seized the New Haven supply of military stores for his men, and for this and later acts Connecticut would not forget the name of Benedict Arnold.

From the southeast, as May came on, another ally appeared, the compact, almost self-sufficient army of Rhode Island. It came to help against the King's troops and yet, gravely and soberly, the men had been enlisted and the officers commissioned "in His Majesty's Service and in the pay of the Colony of Rhode Island and the Providence Plantations for the preservation of the Liberties of America." Patriotic merchants, Providence gentiles and Newport Jews, had seen to it that it marched with ample tents, wagons, supplies, and a complete train of artillery, whose gunners wore blue faced with red and a leather skullcap with an oddly twisted front plate, like the cap still shown at Fraunces' Tavern in New York. The Rhode Islanders, including the Kentish Guards, who had nearly refused him a few years before, poured into Roxbury behind young Nathanael Greene, brigadier general and commander-in-chief for the province. Greene, ex-Quaker and heir to that empire of sloops and mills and bog iron near Warwick, must have pored endlessly over those military books he had bought from Henry Knox, must have drilled hard with the musket that young Henry had helped him smuggle out of Boston. His quiet star was ascendant as he reported to General John Thomas at Roxbury. It never ebbed until his task was done and he saw the British pinned fast in Charleston in the far Carolinas.

As for Thomas Gage and his scarlet battalions, they remained fairly immobile, crammed into the pear-shaped peninsula of Boston, sheltered by the very narrow pear neck near Roxbury and by the fleet, which controlled the water approaches. In and out of Boston there flowed a pitiful systole and diastole. Through the close-guarded fortifications on the Neck came distraught Tories, singly, by families, by districts, not daring to linger in the hinterland out of reach of the protecting shield of His Majesty's forces. Outbound, sometimes furnished with a grudgingly given pass, sometimes slipping over night waters in breath-holding suspense, went those who still stood firm against the Crown. Whig and Tory, outbound, inbound, they usually went with what they could carry in their hands or on their backs. A smithy near Milton, a mansion in Brookline, a snug house in the North End, or high-ceiled residence on Beacon Hill—each was left behind. Yet exodus and influx were by no means complete. Patriot families like Paul Revere's stayed on unmolested in Boston. Tory women—patriots, too,

though not in legend—lived on the far outskirts of the makeshift blockading army and appear, from their letters, to have felt no fear of molesta-
tion. All these would have been fair game for a modern gauleiter or com-
missar, but they seem to have been singularly untroubled in that rougher
age.

Watertown, spread along the lovely bends of the Charles, had turned
into the provincial capital, would remain so for nearly a year. Through the
spring and summer it throbbed to the life of the new government, which
was very sure why it had been called into being, by no means sure of what
it could or would or ought to do. Joseph Warren was there, shuttling between the capital and Ward's Cambridge headquarters, which had been
established across from the Harvard Yard in the "gambrel-roofed house"
where Oliver Wendell Holmes would one day be born. The Adamses
and Hancock appeared, then set off with the other Massachusetts delegates to the new Congress in Philadelphia. Urbane, handsome Benjamin
Church walked gracefully about, basking in the memory of the admiration
shown by the Adamses and Joseph Warren—none of whom liked him—
over the bloodstained stockings that he claimed to have worn on the nineteenth.

To the rage of the ultra-Tory Fluckers, Lucy had gallantly ridden with
her handsome Henry Knox in a chaise through the British lines, and legend
says that Henry's sword was sewn into her petticoats against the certain
British search of the chaise at the Roxbury lines. Henry had left Boston un-
hesitatingly; his thoughts must have been tinged with the deepest black.
He had merely walked out of his beloved London Book-Store. What would
happen to his well-stocked shelves? And there was at least one big shipment from England for which he had not yet been billed. The businessman
half of his mind had ample grounds for worry. The London Book-Store was
pillaged and his books, paid for or not, vanished. A merchant could have
been forgiven for writing off this debt, caused by the fortunes of war. It
gives a warming touch to our knowledge of Knox to recall that he settled in
full, making his final payment to the British firm of Longman in the last
month of the year 1793, a payment of nearly one thousand pounds on a
debt incurred in 1774.

Benjamin Edes, the printer, came to Watertown and kept up his Boston
Gazette, using blurry, makeshift type that must have hurt his craftsman's
soul. From Brattle Street Church came Samuel Cooper, following many
of his congregation. Paul Revere, finding engravers' tools somehow, began
striking off fiat money for the Massachusetts Congress, using the backs of
some of his more famous plates, like his "View of Harvard" and "The Boston Massacre," for lack of fresh metal.

In this swarming scene in Watertown along the Charles the Provisional
Congress creaked and clattered and toiled, a dozen new problems leaping
up for each one solved or dismissed as hopeless. Handsome Dr. Joseph
Warren was emerging more and more as the sure prop for failing hearts

and sagging wills, as the man who could make a quiet decision, give steady advice, bring clashing factions together. He must have missed his old friend and associate, brilliant Josiah Quincy, in these days. But Quincy, with his crossed eye and the clean scalpel of his mind, had died on his return trip from England with the toss of the surf along Cape Ann sounding in his ears as his ship edged in to Gloucester. So Warren, never pushing himself forward, found the tiller of events tighter and tighter in his hand.

It is hard to chart a course ahead when helmsman and crew must always be looking over their shoulders to the wake astern. What would the rest of the country do? The other three New England colonies stood in line with Massachusetts. The rest were so far away. Could it be that New England would be left to fight a war with the British Empire?

Here was a question that could hardly be put bluntly, but one that had to be answered. The Continental Congress was already in session, and to it the Massachusetts Committee of Safety addressed a letter, a calmly worded one that must have been sweated out syllable by syllable. New England, said the letter, had an army but no civil power to provide for any control of it. The idea was enlarged, embroidered, shaped to a final conclusion. As the army was for the general defense of the rights of America, it was suggested that the Congress of all the colonies take over the regulation and general direction of it, that the operations might more effectually answer the purposes designed.

There had been a Massachusetts army. Now there was a New England army, for Rhode Island and New Hampshire had put their troops under Ward, while Connecticut agreed, tacitly if not formally. This letter is the first appeal for an American army. The signers must have had damp foreheads and unsteady hands as they thought fearfully of their fate in the event of a negative answer from Philadelphia. A sure hand must take the letter to the Congress and a skilled tongue must plead between the lines. Possibly on the strength of his Concord and Lexington stockings Dr. Benjamin Church was chosen to go. He set out for Pennsylvania, assuring his associates that he would do his best. And of course it was only courteous—and no business of his friends—to write a letter to another friend, Thomas Gage, Commander of His Majesty's forces in America, telling him where he was going and what he was going to do.

CHAPTER XI

". . . a gentleman from Virginia who is among us here"

BRIGHT dogwood dappled its white blooms through the green of the swelling Pennsylvania hills, and the Schuylkill rolled a gentle flood that varied from cobalt to misty gray on past the wide streets and the brick houses of Philadelphia. From the far Carolinas and from New Hampshire, where snow still lingered along lichened stone walls in upland pastures, from every colony except Georgia, the delegates to the Second Continental Congress trooped into the city under tender May skies.

Now they were to hold their sessions in the Georgian splendor of the State House, and to it the delegates headed. There was a faint flavor of schoolboys returning to a beloved school as they settled themselves in the finer and larger building. From the first timid, apprehensive Congress, a background of tradition and precedent had subtly grown. Charles Thomson, clerk to the Congress, could now sail through the task of verifying credentials that formerly had been so irksome. He could look up from his papers and ledgers to see well-remembered faces coming toward him: Peyton Randolph and Patrick Henry from Virginia; hot-tempered, earnest John Sullivan from New Hampshire; John and Sam Adams, bringing with them a handsome, able-looking newcomer, John Hancock; here was tall, silent Colonel George Washington from Fairfax County in Virginia and steadfast Caesar Rodney of Delaware; Farmer John Dickinson and Joseph Galloway, uneasy lest too much be ventured, were fellow Pennsylvanians. The South Carolinians arrived and Thomson registered Thomas Lynch, tried old veteran, and the Rutledges. John Penn and William Hooper were seen, weary from their overland journey from North Carolina. From neighboring New Jersey, John Witherspoon set down his calling as "College president" and spoke warmly of the spirit of his students at Princeton.

One new delegate needed no introduction as he sat benignly in an armchair, silver-headed stick in his hand and his long hair grayed with his sixty-nine years. Benjamin Franklin had returned from England and men pressed about him, heavy with questions. Some men might spend years in a foreign country and bring back dross. But Dr. Franklin, spectacles up on his forehead and a deceptive placidity in his eyes, could be trusted to carry into the State House the very essence of thought and act in England, be they ministerial or mercantile. His presence was like a fresh, well-led army corps arriving at a crucial battle point.

The Massachusetts delegates had left a citizen army blockading rather than besieging Boston. They must have been taut with worry over what they would find in Philadelphia. The first glimpses, well before the Congress opened, sent even sober John Adams into something like a delirium of joy. In the very State House grounds he could see the Pennsylvania Associators standing in fine formation, the distinguishing bucktails in their hats rippled by a morning wind. Nearly a century later other hard-bitten, hard-fighting Pennsylvanians would wear that same bucktail badge in northern Virginia thickets. Out in the country the Adamses and John Hancock could marvel at a whole company armed with long, deadly rifles, a weapon virtually unknown in New England, lean shirted men who could also use the throwing axes that they carried. There was even a Quaker company, the Blues, a well-drilled formation whose men were grimly aware that, by taking arms, they would be read out of meeting, like asthmatic Nathanael Greene now with his Rhode Islanders in front of Boston. There was even a Silk-Stocking Company, sponsored by John Cadwalader, a flashy, determined outfit that wore light green uniforms topped off with an incongruous green jockey cap, a type of headgear that some hundred and seventy years later would be much favored by fighter pilots, mechanics, and carrier-borne admirals.

John Adams was not a man to catch facile contagions, but he wrote home lyrically, "Oh, that I were a Soldier! I will be. I am reading Military Books. Everybody must, and will, and shall be a Soldier." Symbolically, one other military touch must surely have impressed itself far deeper in the minds of all the New Englanders than massed groups of Silk-Stockings or Bucktails. At the very first session that quiet, thoughtful Virginia delegate, Colonel George Washington, appeared in full uniform, complete with sword of rank, not, it seems, the blue and buff of legend and tradition, but in scarlet faced with blue, the same colors he had worn as commander of Virginia troops a decade before. Waverers and doubters in the Congress could see that striking red-and-blue figure out of the corners of their eyes and be reminded that, in some parts of the country at least, peace did not reign.

The New Englanders found a deep and understandable hesitancy on the part of other members to commit themselves on New England matters beyond an expression of sympathy and concern. But the Yankees were patient men. John Adams wrote to his Abigail, "America is a great unwieldy body . . . It is like a large Fleet sailing under Convoy. The fleetest Sailers must wait for the dullest and the slowest."

Without the slightest warning a piece of stunning news shook the elaborate crystal chandelier that hung over the heads of the delegates, rattled along the high windows that covered two sides of the hall, rumbled in the twin fireplaces. The delegates, horrified, triumphant, vaguely worrying, toothed over the utterly unexpected capture by provincial troops of the old bluestone fort that De Lotbinière had built for Montcalm on a point called Ticonderoga on Lake Champlain. It had been a military man's nightmare, that expedition against the fort. Ethan Allen of the Hampshire Grants, which are now Vermont, acting under the authority of the province

of Connecticut and accompanied much against his will by Colonel Benedict Arnold of Connecticut, acting under Massachusetts authority, had,
with a handful of Green Mountain Boys, surprised the token garrison of
the fort and taken it, presumably, in the name of the United Colonies,
which were by no means united.

Just as the Middlesex County men, after the first brush at the North
Bridge in Concord, must have been obsessed by the thought, "We've gone
and fired on the King's troops!" so many of the delegates, particularly the
New Yorkers, seemed paralyzed by a similar phrase: "We've gone and
captured one of the King's forts!" New Englanders had captured the fort,
but it lay well in New York territory, and no overt act had been committed
against that province. Aghast, a dozen proposals were made. It was even
suggested that it be respectfully turned back to the Crown. And if not, who
owned it? New York? The amorphous Hampshire Grants? Connecticut?
Massachusetts?

The question was allowed to ride along for the time being, with a few of
the wiser heads indicating that while there might not be much value in
bluestone walls and a grassy point of a northern lake, those walls held a
wealth of artillery, an arm in which all the colonies were weak.

The Congress settled into its work after this interlude and the New
Englanders felt, if they did not show, qualms. There appeared a growing
and strong tendency to appease the Crown, almost to apologize, and the
leaders of this trend were Farmer John Dickinson and James Duane of
New York. Dickinson, exasperated by speeches by John Adams and stormy
John Sullivan of New Hampshire, even threatened an actual break with
New England.

Then into Philadelphia, beginning to bake in early June, came bland,
smiling Dr. Benjamin Church, bearing with him the letter which the
Massachusetts Committee of Safety had drawn up. Its urgent plea, it will
be remembered, boiled down to: Adopt the New England army as that of
America. Set up a civil government to run things. Implicit in this last was
the deep-seated American fear, apparent through all history right down to
the presidential election of 1952, of the military growing supreme over the
civil arm. Still more implicit was the idea of an independent America, living under its own Constitution.

This letter met with a disheartening and widespread growl of disapproval, for the tide of appeasement was running stronger and stronger.
Even the member from Fairfax County in Virginia was voting for very
mild measures despite his inner conviction that none of them would work.
A committee, which sensibly barred all New Englanders, studied the plea
from Watertown and came up with renewed murmurs of sympathy. But
New England, as wise old Benjamin Franklin had written from London
the year before, must not be allowed to drag the continent into war without
the unanimous consent of the whole thirteen colonies, and there were
thirteen now represented, since Dr. Hall from Georgia, with the backing
of only one Georgia county, had taken his seat.

John Adams, moving into quiet leadership of the New Englanders, spent sleepless nights, his weary head thumping with the great problem. The rest of the country must not split away from New England. Nor must New England, through the accident of war within its borders, try to shoulder and butt its way into a dominant position. A union of the thirteen, not nine tagging along after four.

Soon the Braintree lawyer was on his feet again in Congress. Skillfully he painted a picture of the British breaking out of Boston. There were scores to be settled with New York, with almost any colony that could be named. What could stop such a foray of bloodshed and desolation? Calmly he envisioned a Grand American Army made up of all the colonies. As commander? Well, British-born Charles Lee, an occasional visitor at Mount Vernon, with his shady title of general and his wild service in Poland and Portugal and in America, with his known deep friendship for the colonies, might be the man. But it would be better, all things considered, John Adams went on, that the commander be a native-born American, and he had just such a man in mind.

Here John Hancock, presiding in the absence of Peyton Randolph, looked self-conscious. After all, had he not been a strikingly martial figure as colonel of the Boston Cadets? But his colleague had other names in mind. "A gentleman whose skill as an officer, whose independent fortune, great talents, and universal character would command the respect of America and unite the full exertions of the colonies better than any other person alive"—John Adams was building up to his climax like a keynoter at a modern nominating convention—"a gentleman *from Virginia* who is among us here, and well known to all of us——"

At the mention of Virginia, the member from Fairfax County slipped out of the hall as unobtrusively as a man standing six feet two inches may in an age when a mere six-footer was a rarity. When Adams had named George Washington of Virginia, he ended his speech. A swelling hum bridged the actual nomination and the debate that followed. Men began arguing that, since New Englanders had done all the work so far, the commander should come from their ranks, and such thoughts were by no means confined to New Englanders. There were other objections, notably and amazingly from Edmund Pendleton of Virginia, who thought that the colonel was a good enough man but, after all, he'd lost every major affair that he had ever engaged in as commander.

The debate trailed on into another day, another. Then John Hancock, with George Washington present for the first time since Adams' speech, rapped for silence. "The President [of Congress] has the order of Congress to inform George Washington, Esq., of the unanimous vote in choosing him to be General and Commander-in-Chief of the forces raised and to be raised in defense of American liberty. The Congress hopes the gentleman will accept."

George Washington, master of Mount Vernon, was no orator. But his thoughts were never in need of gilded speech to touch other men's hearts and minds. He drew a paper from his scarlet pocket and read:

"Mr. President: Tho' I am truly sensible of the high Honour done me in this appointment, yet I feel great distress from a consciousness that my abilities and Military experience may not be equal to the extensive and important Trust . . . exert every Power I possess . . . for the Support of the glorious Cause. . . . I . . . declare with the utmost sincerity, I do not think my self equal to the Command I am honored with. As to pay, Sir, I beg leave to Assure the Congress that as no pecuniary consideration could have tempted me to have accepted this arduous employment at the expence of my Domestic ease and happiness, I do not wish to make any proffit from it: I will keep an exact Account of my expences; those I doubt not they [Congress] will discharge and that is all I desire."

There was applause, a few more speeches, then hurried measures taken to appoint lesser generals to serve with the Virginian, and at last the new commander-in-chief left the hall and went to dine with his old friend Dr. Thomas Cadwalader. He has left no record of his thoughts at the moment. Did his mind turn to the broad reaches of the Great Kanawha where he had vast land claims and where, in black moments, he thought he and his friends might retire in case Crown and Parliament combined to make life unbearable along the settled Eastern seaboard?

It may have been some such frame of mind that led him to defer writing of his momentous news to the one person who loomed most important in his life. It was Sunday, June 18, 1775, when his quill traced out the letter that would go to Martha Washington, back there in Virginia keeping a careful eye on beloved Mount Vernon. The new commander began: "My dearest: I am now set down to write you on a subject which fills me with inexpressible concern, and this concern is greatly aggravated and increased, when I reflect upon the uneasiness I know it will cause you. It has been determined in Congress that the whole army raised for the defence of the American cause shall be put under my care, and that it is necessary for me to proceed immediately to Boston to take upon me the command of it." He then expresses more fully than he had to Congress his doubts about his own fitness. But his chief concern is the thought of "my dear Patsy," as he called her, being left alone. If she wants to close Mount Vernon and move to Arlington nearby, why, Cousin Lund Washington will see to putting that property in order. He has made provision for her in case of his death, provision which, he trusts, "will be agreeable," and ends, "My dear Patcy [sic], Yr. affecte. Go Washington." The letter is held up for a hurried postscript, to say that he has bought for her "two suits of what I was told was the prettiest muslin. I wish it may please you. It cost 50/ a suit that is 20/ a yard."

In the new week Congress went on in a welter of hassles and swivets. There were the new generals to be appointed, and ideas ran utterly unrestrained. It may have been the Philadelphia heat, so unseasonable that some delegates wrote to Hartford, way up north in Connecticut, to see what the facilities were like there. It may have been sheer weariness. In any event, the final slate was drawn up and served as a satisfying, durable basis for squabble, recrimination, and intrigue for years to come.

There were the major generals, and no colony grudged that the senior appointment went to heavy, sick Artemas Ward, trying earnestly and quite successfully to build a dam against the British flood with the wickerwork of his army. Then came British Charles Lee, self-proclaimed master of both war and literature. Now the choices must move west and upper New York State be considered as well as Manhattan. Here was a man ready-made, of old Dutch patroon stock and living a feudal life that made that of a Virginia planter seem like a sharecropper's. Philip Schuyler had had some military training, was influential from the mouth of the Hudson to the source, and might be able to pull the whole vast area into a unit. The last choice went, oddly enough, to another New Englander, and scarred, prematurely old Israel Putnam was named major general and Connecticut's claims were satisfied. One may wonder whether Israel truly was. His service had been that of a ranger, like Stark and Allen and Robert Rogers. Putnam probably was the greatest of the rangers, but now he would be called upon to take up a field command in an army hopefully destined for formal warfare. In a way, barring honors, it was an unfortunate turn of the wheel, for at war's end the comments on him sounded much like a paraphrase of a gibe at a World War II American general—the best two-star company commander in the army.

Then the new commander would have to have an adjutant and one was ready to hand, tailor-made, on paper, for the job. Horatio Gates, friend and not too distant neighbor of George Washington, ex-major in the British Army, and veteran of the French wars, was not only available but ready. His long professional experience, like Charles Lee's, would turn the American militia into steady fighting men, it was hoped. It would have been better if neither of these professionals had been willing to take up arms against their old comrades. Lee, at best, turned out to be an unpredictable eccentric of more than dubious loyalty and with an insatiable thirst for rank and power. Gates was more balanced, often able, usually good-hearted, and apt to be liked by his men. But a mean, if not a treacherous, streak of intrigue ran through him, not meanness to his cause, in which he never wavered, but toward those about him, up to and including his commander-in-chief.

There were brigadiers to be created, and here the posts were plentiful enough to glut every colony in quantity if not in quality. Some were so superannuated that they do not appear in history. Others dropped out, wavered, clogged progress. But the general run was surprisingly good. So the Congress busied itself with questions of rank, building the framework of a true American army, since the appointment of a commander-in-chief implied the establishment of such a force and the civil authority to control it. If not to the letter, the plea of the Massachusetts Committee of Safety had been answered in spirit.

Then, to test the new unity, news came from the always threatening northeast and Boston. The King's troops had come out again and there had been fighting.

This was no mere demonstration like the powder march of the year before, when exaggerated reports had sent the delegates scurrying about like a nest of mice. In his headquarters at the edge of the Harvard Yard, Artemas Ward had made a decision and the British had reacted to it. This decision, sound in intent, led to a series of glitteringly wrong steps. There were two masses of high ground that commanded Boston, the first being the Heights of Dorchester and Roxbury and the other the twin hills of Charlestown with the pastures of Messrs. Breed and Bunker across the Charles River.

The fortification of the Dorchester mass was highly logical, militarily. Strong works there would have seriously slowed down, if not blocked, any sudden British foray out over narrow Boston Neck. So the American High Command blithely plumped for Charlestown, which Gage had evacuated shortly after Percy's retreat in April. Charlestown was shaped much like a smaller edition of Boston, a fat polliwog of land swelling out into the Charles and linked to the shore by a long and very narrow strip that was sometimes overflowed by the Mystic on one side and the Charles on the other. Thus any garrison on the peninsula blob could be very neatly cut off by an opposing force which controlled the river approaches, and His Majesty's Navy was ready to hand for such control. Strong posts on Winter Hill and Prospect Hill in present Somerville would have served far better and with infinitely less risk. But the decision was taken.

In the early evening of June sixteenth, while the stirring leaves of the elms around Harvard Yard still glowed in a summer sunset, some eight hundred men gathered about where Memorial Hall now stands. Colonel William Prescott was there with his regiment and details from Frye's and Bridge's. While light played on the soft brick of Massachusetts Hall and Harvard and Hollis off to the right, the detail uncovered and President Samuel Langdon of Harvard offered up a prayer. Then Prescott marched his men away, wagonloads of picks and shovels rattling after them. Somewhere near present Central Square the detail was joined by two hundred Connecticut men under Captain Thomas Knowlton, a gifted soldier who was to die the next year near Martje David's Vly in far-off Manhattan. Colonel Richard Gridley, an engineer with a record dating back to the capture of Louisburg, picked up the column and with him, bursting with more energy than judgment, Colonel Israel Putnam.

The diggers headed off toward Charlestown as dusk deepened into night. No one at headquarters seems to have taken thought of them beyond telling them where they were to go and what to do when they got there. No provision had been made for relief of the men, who had a major entrenching job ahead of them. No ration dump was established to look after the detail once it had consumed what little it brought with it. Most fatally, no one thought to send out reserve supplies of ammunition in case Gage found out what was going on and decided to interfere.

As has been noted, there were two hills on the Charlestown peninsula, Bunker's and Breed's. Bunker's, a little to the northwest of Breed's, was the higher and looked straight down onto the summit of its lesser neighbor. Breed's was closer to the water, and on its right-hand slope the village of Charlestown clung, solid and pretty enough to win approval even in supercilious British eyes. Ward's orders had stated that Bunker's Hill was to be fortified, a highly correct decision if anything were to be done on the peninsula. But one more blunder was made, either through confusion in the darkness or because Putnam, ever a fighter, preferred the eminence nearer the British. In any event, the main redoubt was sited on Breed's. And so the Battle of Bunker Hill was fought on Breed's Hill.

All night long the men dug, and when the sun came in with the blue dawn tide the works were in a fair way toward completion. There was the strong redoubt cresting Breed's Hill, but the position could be easily flanked on either side. A boggy stretch in the gap between it and Bunker Hill gave some protection, and Prescott ran out earthworks to make that side— his left—stronger. Running down to the Mystic, still to the left from Breed's, was a rail fence, and some efforts were made to bolster this up by stacking hay against it.

There was amazement in Boston when sentries and officers in the North End and on the waterside of Beacon Hill, virtually all pasture land at the time, saw the stir and bustle and the fresh-turned earth across the river. At sunset of the sixteenth the hill had been bare. Now, in an incredibly short time, it was fortified, and a lesson was stamped indelibly and perhaps too deeply into the consciousness of most British commanders: never give the Yankees time to dig.

Thomas Gage reacted with a swiftness that was by no means characteristic and may have been due to the presence of a group of newly landed generals. At his elbow was Sir William Howe, whose brother was Vice-Admiral "Black Dick" Howe, R.N. Another brother, Lord George Augustus Howe, had been closely associated with New England troops until his death at Ticonderoga in '58. Lord George's name was held in profound affection by all New Englanders, the Bostonians going so far as to put up a monument to him. Sir William had had a brilliant record in the British Army and particularly in the development of the light infantry had shown a daring, energetic mind. Sir Henry Clinton had landed with Howe, a highly capable soldier. And with handsome presence and purple pen ever ready was Gentleman Johnny Burgoyne. These three may have put Gage on his toes. At any rate, the British ships in the river, the land batteries along the shore at Copp's Hill in the North End began to send their round shot whining over the water to thud and skitter among the still-toiling troops.

These men were in understandably bad shape. They were exhausted, weak with hunger, throats itching with thirst. During the night many of their comrades had taken advantage of the darkness to slip along the little causeway that led to the mainland. Officers disappeared, usually on vital and legitimate business, but the men knew only that they were gone. Israel Putnam's military training finally conquered his overwhelming combativeness and he sent men and tools to scratch about on Bunker's crest. It did not help those who stayed to realize that a good part of the men who left for the higher crest merely kept going and ended up near Prospect Hill. And now land guns and naval guns were dropping live shot among them. A digger named Peter Brown wrote hotly, "The danger we were in made us think there was Treachery, and that we were brot here to be all slain. and I must and will venture to say that there was Treachery Oversight or Presumption in the Conduct of our Officers."

Artillery fire is the worst of nightmares to green troops, and those on the Charlestown hills were, as indicated, of very shaky morale. By rights, the first salvos from Boston and the river should have sent them scurrying to the mainland in desperate and shameful panic. Many amazing things were to happen before sundown. Not the least amazing was the fact that the weary, hungry, suspicious men kept on digging, possibly encouraged by the example of Colonel Prescott walking along the growing parapet, Louisburg sword buckled over a banian, a sort of half topcoat, half dressing gown. So they dug and began subconsciously to realize that cannon fire is often more noisy than effective. A few light fieldpieces were dragged in from Cambridge, mounted on hills, and a few rounds went screeching off into Boston. The diggers cheered. The American fire ceased and the shovels plied resignedly on.

The perfection of a New England June morning wore along, with soft, towering cumulus clouds sailing slowly across a deep blue sky. Bostonians began crowding into church spires, lining windows of hill houses that looked across the scant mile of water to Charlestown and the stir about the fresh earthworks. Hopefully or wrathfully they saw long columns of men spill along the causeway to the peninsula. It was a drab picture they witnessed, for all marchers were in dull civilian clothes. Even the blue-and-red magnificence of the company from Wethersfield in Connecticut was hidden by long, brownish smocks to make the wearers less conspicuous. There was nothing to distinguish a Worcester company from one that had marched down from the sweeping uplands of Exeter across the New Hampshire border.

Then there was color along the Boston water front. Barges and whaleboats manned by sailors from the fleet began to fill with scarlet and white, scarlet and buff. Blue facings, popinjay-green facings, white facings, and black facings could easily be made out. Gunners in the blue and red of the Royal Regiment of Artillery manhandled light fieldpieces into the heavier barges. Cockades were fresh on glossy cocked hats. Black and silver and brass glittered under the bearskins of the grenadier companies, against the skullcaps of the light infantry. Fifes raved and drums beat in a throaty mutter as a floating pageant, royal and regimental colors high, began its slow glide across a Massachusetts river. With the other watchers, official and unofficial, was Gentleman Johnny Burgoyne, probably shaping in his mind some fine sonorous passages that he would use in writing of the affair to England. Before the day was over, John Burgoyne's rich voice was to be dulled and his infectious, rolling laugh stilled by the sheer tragedy of what he was to witness.

The Boston batteries and His Majesty's ships *Lively* and *Falcon* increased their fire as the barges worked across the mirror of the Charles, and watchers on the Boston hills could see slow puffs of dirt kicked up along the slope of Breed's. One by one the barges grated ashore, spilled out their gleaming cargoes on the beaches, mostly on the northern and eastern edges of the Charlestown bulge.

Sir William Howe, commanding the expedition, looked up the rolling ascent with its tangle of rail fences, its clumps of blackberry bushes and brambles. He could see clearly the American works and must have wondered why they stayed so silent, why no smoke gushed out from fence or parapet. He took counsel with his second-in-command, General Robert Pigot, and sent back for reinforcements. Quite soon the 47th North Lancashires and the Royal Marines were tumbling ashore on the face of the peninsula. At last the command was given and the assault started, long scarlet lines three deep flowing ponderously up toward the works or along the northeast beaches where the hay-stuffed rail fences touched the water's edge. Sir William was ordering a direct frontal attack against entrenched infantry of unknown strength. As though seeking to handicap the attackers still further, someone had decreed that each man should stagger under the June sun bearing a load estimated at one hundred and twenty pounds per man and including three days' rations and blankets. And this with their base of supplies a mere mile away.

Far afield and far ahead in 1899, at Colenso on the rolling brown South African veldt, the United States military attaché, Captain S. L. H. Slocum of the 8th Cavalry, watched General Sir William Butler prepare a frontal assault against entrenched, hard-shooting Boer farmers. Slocum asked rather dubiously "if there were not a way around." No one seems to have noticed his question and Butler's men were smashed by Boer fire.

At Colenso there may or may not have been another way around, but at Charlestown there was. Covered by the fleet, Howe could have landed his men at the base of the Neck and waited until the garrison of the hills was ready to surrender, which should not have been long. But custom and tradition, by no means confined to the British, decreed the frontal attack as being more consistent with military honor. Good soldiers, none too friendly so far as Gage and Howe were concerned, watched all this from Boston and found nothing to criticize. Burgoyne wrote frankly that "Howe's disposition was exceedingly Soldier-like, in my opinion it was perfect."

On paper perhaps it was perfect, as Gentleman Johnny wrote. The men in the redoubt on Breed's Hill, those behind the earthworks that stretched down from its left, the men sheltered behind detached arrowheads of earth

called flèches, those back of the hay-stuffed rail fence that ran down to the
beach were not, in theory, the stuff to beat off a massed attack of British
Regulars. Most of them had worked all through the night and into the
day. They had not been fed and their ammunition supply was alarmingly
low. They had been cannonaded off and on since daybreak. No one man
was actually in command. No reinforcements had come into the works.
True, the crest of Bunker Hill was black with more troops, but they seemed
content to stay where they were and there was no one to order them into
action.

Now they could hear the British drums rattling off their staccato commands. Through the knee-high grass along the crunching sand of the
beaches came the grenadiers and the light infantry, the line companies and
the marines. This was no field day like those April hours when desperate
men in scarlet and white slogged heavily along country lanes. The picked
might of Britain moved steadily toward the works, officers to the front and
little drummer boys flailing their sticks at the flanks. Scarlet lines were
thrown into confusion as white-breeched legs clambered across the brown
of rail fences. In the green of the long grass, order was restored and the
living, bayonet-tipped wall rolled on. The psychological impact on the defenders must have been terrific. No one could blame them much had panic
seized them, as raw troops of the 1940s broke at the first sight of tanks,
dive bombers, or flame throwers.

They did not panic. Something inexplicable kept them steady. In the
redoubt a gray-haired farmer prayed aloud, "I thank thee, O Lord, for spar-
ing me to fight this day. Blessed be the name of the Lord." And he and the
others waited, incredibly patient, struggling against raw fear as the red lines
came closer and closer until faces could be distinguished, details of equipment like the little brass matchboxes worn on grenadier chests.

Who finally gave the command that set trigger fingers tightening? Who
saw to it that the best shots lay forward while men behind them waited to
pass up a steady flow of fresh-loaded muskets? However it happened, that
first blast, delivered according to British sources at less than fifteen paces,
ripped out in smoke and flame, and through the smoke grenadiers' bearskins could be seen flying high. Scarlet-coated bodies were suddenly bright
on the trampled green of the grass, and mouths that had been shouting
were jammed down among the little white and blue flowers that grew at
the grass roots. White breeches showed quick crimson spots. Then powder-
blackened eyes in the works stared incredulously as disordered wreckage
broke back out of the smoke, not dashing over the last few feet to the
parapets, but pounding in real flight to the beaches and the waiting boats.

The pattern of the day had been set and would repeat itself with little
change as the scenes along the Battle Road of April repeated themselves.

On the beaches, Howe fought against the shock of combat. He had been
up with the leading files, had seen row after row of men blasted away under
the short-range fire from the works. All about him on the beaches veteran
officers were muttering shakily that never had they faced such a deadly

volume of musketry. Sir William, a fine man in any kind of action, got hold
of himself, rallied his men, and formed for another try. He sent a boat to
Boston with an urgent plea for more troops, along with a message that hot
fire was hitting John Pitcairn's marines from the houses of Charlestown.
Something must be done about that.

More men were sent him, with Sir Henry Clinton in command. The note
about Charlestown and the snipers came to Gentleman Johnny Burgoyne
at a big shore battery. He at once sent a storm of incendiary shells whizzing
down on the unfortunate town, while ships out in the stream joined in.
There can be no criticism here. Charlestown was a legitimate military
target.

The shells landed and the town went up in a flame-shot mantle of heavy
smoke. Gentleman Johnny, his dramatist's mind struggling against the
horror of the slaughter which was becoming increasingly apparent, recorded
his impressions. "And now ensued one of the greatest sights of war that
can be conceived; if we look to the height, Howe's corps ascending the
hill in the face of entrenchments . . . strait before us a large and noble
town in one great blaze; the church steeples being of timber, were great
pyramids of fire above the rest . . . the roar of cannon, mortars and mus-
quetry, the crush of churches, ships upon the stocks, and whole streets falling together in ruin, to fill the ear . . . made the whole a picture and a
complication of horror and importance beyond anything that ever came to
my lot to be witness to."

Howe massed his men, took them up the bloody slopes himself, and once
more the living wall of fire shattered solid grenadier companies, shredded
the light infantry, sent the line and the marines reeling back to the water's
edge. More artillery was brought up, but it was useless, since some gaily
careless soul in Boston sent along ammunition too big for the barrels of
the guns.

There was a panting hush over the Charlestown bulge. Blackened faces
peered cautiously over rail fence and parapet. Men who had known Louisburg or the echoing glades about Champlain thought that it might be safe
to draw a long breath. What troops in the world could rally after two such
murderous smashings that left Breed's field red with a litter of dead and
wounded? The answer was before their eyes. Once again the scarlet and
white and buff formations were massing. All élan, all dash was gone down
there on the beaches in the lower fields. Nothing remained except sheer,
raw courage. The drums of the King were beating once again, and limping
officers, some with bandaged hands or heads, were giving orders. In the
redoubt, where Prescott and Joseph Warren were in unceasing evidence,
men were slipping shaky fingers into their cartridge pouches. Four rounds
left? No, only two. Perhaps none.

Down by the rail fence to the far left, John Stark's New Hampshiremen
and Knowlton's Connecticut troops were grim. They had begun the day
with about a gill of powder per man and had blazed most of it away at the
oncoming light infantry. They, like the men in the redoubt, could throw

rocks at the next attack. They could swing their clubbed muskets. That was all. There were few, if any, bayonets, the infantryman's last deadly weapon, to meet the steel-tipped charge of the British.

The last attack came on. There was one, perhaps a second, blast that shook the attackers. Then grenadiers and light infantry, bayonets aslant, were among the defenders and hideous slaughter loomed. As inexplicable as the impromptu, unrehearsed American fire control, exhausted men with empty muskets made an orderly retreat. Burgoyne commented, "The retreat was no flight; it was even covered with bravery and military skill and proceeded no further than to the west hill where a new post was taken and new intrenchments instantly begun."

Sir William Howe has been blamed by old-time and modern writers for not annihilating the American army, for not turning the retreat which Burgoyne praised into rout and slaughter. Probably several factors played their parts in his failure. First of all, it must be remembered that his men had made three murderously punishing assaults. There are plenty of British tales of big grenadiers collapsing once they were inside the redoubt. In all probability they were in no shape to do more than hold the immediate ground they had won. A second factor must lie in the unexpected stubbornness of virtually unarmed garrisons of all the works who refused to panic. A final reason may possibly be found in the action of one man, who had been forced into a spectator's role through most of the fighting. It has been noted that swarms of men were massed on Bunker Hill and held there immobile, largely through the lack of formal orders from higher up or through the lack of one man of rank to say, "Come on, boys!"

Among these wasted men on Bunker was Gerrish's regiment, and its adjutant was a man whom we have met before, listening quietly in the various patriot taverns—Christian Febiger, the Dane, with his flavor of courts and governors' palaces in tropical islands. So far as the record may be traced out, Febiger, entirely on his own, rallied enough men there on Bunker's crest to form a strong party and led it down into the hollow between the hills, thus probably putting it between the retreating garrisons and any possible British pursuit. The appearance of fresh troops in a smoky June dusk would surely make any commander with nothing but utterly exhausted men pause long before resuming his offensive.

So Sir William Howe had won for Thomas Gage an utterly useless peninsula. Colonel James Abercrombie, commanding all the grenadiers, was dead and so was John Pitcairn, to top off a ghastly roll of killed and wounded. So many had fallen that the mind became mercifully numbed trying to grasp the tally. A British officer wrote shakily, "Some had only eight or nine men a Company left; some only three, four or five." First and last, nearly twenty-three hundred men had struggled through the blackberry bushes and over fences in the June sun. The casualty list was totted up by Gage's headquarters at one thousand and fifty-four, most of them killed or wounded in the first two attacks. Only British troops could have mounted to that last grim assault—or to the second. Howe himself escaped unharmed, despite his reckless exposure at the head of his men. But something went out of William Howe, vanished for good in that sunny June afternoon between the Mystic and the Charles. Trained by the immortal Wolfe, Sir William had been a daring innovator, a brilliant champion of the quick, deadly attack, a man never dismayed by the unexpected, but some flame in him died up by the redoubt on Breed's Hill, and for the rest of his service in North America he was at best mediocre, slow, hesitant, letting opportunity slip through his fingers again and again.

Nothing could kill the spirit of the British Army as a whole, but its thinking in all ranks was affected by what it had been through, a sort of universal combat fatigue that muddled thought and dulled reaction. Gentleman Johnny Burgoyne remembered all too well what he had seen from the Boston water front, and it tripped him badly when he had an independent command. Sir Henry Clinton, even closer than Burgoyne to the events, could never get the picture of shattered grenadiers out of his mind. Where drive and initiative are displayed by the British command for the whole duration of the war, it will usually be found that the officer responsible had not toiled up the slopes that led from the beaches to Breed's Hill or else had not watched others on that hideous ascent.

The defenders of the peninsula, active and passive, fell back as far as Prospect Hill on the mainland—which must have been the "west hill" of Burgoyne's letter—and took stock. There is no sure way of telling how many Yankee troops were present that day, but the usual estimate is about twenty-eight hundred, which seems high. Losses of all kinds, killed, wounded, and missing, are given as about five hundred, and most of these must have taken place in that last pounding British rush when spent, battle-shocked men at last came to grips with a virtually defenseless adversary. The two deaths most keenly felt occurred in those ghastly closing moments. Dr. Joseph Warren, dressed in a light banian with sprigged buttons, a fringed white waistcoat, and a neat tie wig, had fought through the whole day as a private, although he had a colonel's commission in his pocket. He stood fast with the defenders of the redoubt and vanished in the murky cloud of dust and smoke and evening shadows. Big, magnetic Andrew McClary of New Hampshire made his way safely across the Neck to the mainland with the last of his men. Fearing that some might still be left on the peninsula, he started back through the dusk, striding out to an unguessed rendezvous with a chance British cannon ball.

There were bitter recriminations among the troops who huddled wearily on Prospect Hill. Why had Artemas Ward stayed snugly in Cambridge all during the fight? This question was asked with increasing vehemence as men looked about for someone to blame. They were not seasoned enough to realize that Ward's place was in Cambridge, since the Charlestown fight involved only one wing of the army that he commanded. There was every chance that Gage might use his first attack as a feint and then strike at the Roxbury lines, where success would bring him in a wide sweep along the flats into Cambridge with its invaluable supplies as well as the makeshift heart of a makeshift army.

Officers and men snarled about Ward's failure to reinforce the Breed's Hill works. Gradually they found enlightenment that should have made them feel less bitter toward the sick man from Shrewsbury. Reinforcements had been sent and had been as poorly led and as ineffective as the aimless swarms on Bunker's Hill, some of whom Febiger, the Dane, finally managed to get into action. Regiments and companies had started for the peninsula, but conflicting orders, no orders, orders misunderstood anchored them far out of the fight. Hundreds and even thousands of men had stood idly along the approaches to Charlestown and its hills, sitting out the fight. James Scammon's Massachusetts regiment, bedeviled by orders issued, counter-manded, changed, and issued again, had spent the whole day wandering from place to place, heading toward Roxbury, veering back to Lechmere Point, where Smith and Pitcairn had landed their men an infinity of time ago, in April. Like D'Erlon's corps on the day of Quatre Bras and Ligny in 1815, like Halsey's fleet at Leyte, a good force, willing to fight, had been wasted and merely set adrift in the Middlesex County flats.

There was no reason why all this should not have been so. Companies and regiments may be hastily formed and made to look at least presentable. To create a staff to pass down the will and direction of a High Command, to see that both will and direction are obeyed are far more difficult. The failure to reinforce, the failure to get what scant ammunition there was to Breed's Hill showed no defects that might not be remedied in the future.

Far harder to cure was the psychological effect of the seventeenth of June on the army, on the country, and particularly on members of con-gresses and committees. Note has been taken of the utterly false conclu-sions drawn from events on the April road. Just as dangerous trends of thought arise out of the smoke that curled so sullenly from the Charlestown slopes. And who could argue against such dangerous conclusions? Had not hasty civilian levies entrenched in the full blast of land and naval gunnery and then, so long as a shot remained to them, wrecked the heavy, formal attacks of picked veteran troops? Just whistle up a swarm of farmers and townspeople, give them picks and shovels, and their deadly marksmanship would do the rest.

This frame of mind was apt to dump its owners headlong into very deep pitfalls. It utterly discounted the very obvious British mistake of the frontal attacks. ("Isn't there a way around?") Worse, it repeated the comforting but damaging legend of unerring Yankee marksmanship that had hung over from April's running fight. There was no need for marksmanship at Breed's Hill. What was needed, and what was unaccountably present, was the impromptu discipline which sprang from God knows where and held the great mass of fire until the very last second. At this range a man had only to hold his piece level, shut his eyes, and pull the trigger. But such discipline was not a constant, ever-present asset. Often as the war went on, American troops, faced with far weaker attacks, fired one hasty, scattered volley and fled. But such instances were forgotten and Breed's Hill was remembered. The optimistic lessons which our people drew from Breed's Hill were as deadly, if not more so, than the too great fears instilled into the British.

The moon came up over Boston Harbor and the broad estuary of the Charles, and the two armies lay on their respective hills, weapons ready, while the night air was filled with the chunk and clink of busy pick and shovel. Tardily, the wounded were gathered up and sent in limping processions to Cambridge or in pitiful boatloads across to Boston. The stars came out to blink impartially down on sleeping men, digging men, sentries whose eyes smarted with the effort of keeping awake. Starlight and moonlight touched still heaps, anonymous in their sprawl along the slopes and in the earthworks. Night faded civilian drab and scarlet regimentals to a somber darkness. Only dancing lanterns in the hands of surgeons and burial parties made fleeting distinction as they passed among men from Worcester and Leicester and Framingham and their silent neighbors who had come from the deep lanes of Somersetshire, the tors of Dartmoor, or the Mull of Kintyre. Down toward the water's edge the embers of Charlestown glowed like clusters of red planets.

CHAPTER XII

". . . he fully answers to the character you have given him"

INTO Cambridge, a few days after the fight on Breed's Hill, marched a strange formation that brought into the quiet college town a strong flavor of the sea and the mutter of the surf along the rocky North Shore. The 21st Massachusetts Infantry was arriving. With rolling gait they tramped down Massachusetts Avenue in cocked hats, short blue jackets of good sea cloth, and loose nautical white trousers; and the shoulders of the men were bent and their hands crumpled by a lifetime of sail and oar. Their company rosters bore names like Brimblecome and Trefry and Orne and Blackler and Cash and Sedgebard, and they spoke a language that was alien to Cambridge ears. A stern man was "hord-horted." A barrel of tar was a "tor-borrl" and their equipment followed them in a "cort." An unhandy man they described contemptuously as "a froach." Virtually born at sea, they knew the Grand Banks and could handle anything that floated. Now there was deep bitterness in their hearts, for the impending Fisheries Act would shut them off from the cod-thick waters of the north and ruin their town of Marblehead and most of its families.

Behind their colonel, stocky, watchful John Glover, they filed off past the college buildings and pitched their sailcloth tents—why worry about sails when fishing was doomed?—on the estate variously known today as the Vassall or Craigie or Longfellow place on Brattle Street. John Glover and his lieutenant colonel, the Huguenot Gabriel Johonnot, set up their head-quarters on the ground floor of the mansion, using a room that would one day be the study of Henry Wadsworth Longfellow, and proceeded to run a very tight ship. Discipline was an easier matter than in most regiments. A farmer or a townsman might feel that a curt order somehow struck at his independence. But a seaman, though he might have served on nothing more than a small Marblehead fishing boat, understood in his very marrow that a crew must work together, that a command to reef or let out sail, to hold to a set course, to stand watch until properly relieved could mean the difference between sighting the rocky islands of the home harbor and death in the tossing foggy waters of the Banks.

This is a long look to take at one of scores of regiments. But the Marble-headers, through the whole war, made up one of the most efficient, the most skilled, and the most quietly colorful of all the American outfits. Once the commander-in-chief was to reach out for its skill afloat and use that skill to save the army from unfathomable catastrophe. Again he would call on Glover and the Ornes and the Speakmans and the Brimblecomes to ferry the army in an unexpected attack across a stormy, ice-choked river that, militarily, was utterly impassable. All this, of course, lay in the future. For the moment, the rest of the army in the great arc about Boston took silent note of the taut Marbleheaders, approved, and in some cases strove to follow its example.

Far to the southwest a cavalcade wound across the Jersey flats as Cap-tain Philip Markoe's swank Philadelphia Light Horse and a cloud of un-official riders escorted the new commander-in-chief on the first leg of his long journey north to Cambridge, where his arrival would immeasurably outweigh that of any regiment or even corps. With General George Wash-ington trotted ugly, saturnine Charles Lee, very possibly dourly dreaming of the day when the tall Virginian would take his proper place as deferen-tial aide to Lee's self-acknowledged military genius. Young Major Thomas Mifflin was there and Major Joseph Reed, two able men who were to bolster up the commander's stiffness with the written word. One drafted his speeches and addresses and the other his letters. Stern, aloof Major General Philip Schuyler from his up-Hudson barony of uncounted acres would continue with the group until it reached New York, where he would take command of the area.

It was the first time that a genuine American staff, small as this one might be, was unveiled in a land which still thought largely in terms of reconciliation with England—after various moot points had been cleared up. And for the first time George Washington stood forth in the guise that would be stamped indelibly on the consciousness of America and of the free world. As the general tossed back a light cloak, the Jersey sun lit up not the scarlet-and-blue regimentals which had known the halls of the

Congress, but a coat of dark blue faced with buff, a buff waistcoat, and white breeches. This uniform was to be peculiarly his and through him extended by American thought to clothe his entire command, with the phrase "regulation Continental blue and buff" entering the American language. Actually few besides Washington wore it, and the reasons for his choice of the combination seem lost to knowledge. He may have adopted it as a graceful compliment to the light infantry company of Philadelphia, whose city had been his host. Such a gesture was typically Washingtonian. Less known, and certainly less pleasing to the color-conscious, was the purple sash about his waist, the sash which was as distinguishing a mark of commissioned rank as was the Sam Browne belt of later American forces.

The exit from Philadelphia and the passage across New Jersey had been tumultuous, and now New York was close at hand. There was a moment of embarrassment when it was learned that harsh William Tryon, royal governor, was due to land at the Battery in New York at about the same time that Washington's party would be on Manhattan. Violence, even a regular battle, might break out. But time favored peace this day and the new commander-in-chief was met by uniformed companies of New York militia and rode through streets where bunting flew, handkerchiefs waved, and citizens yelled themselves hoarse. It was an impressive welcome, particularly as one never could be quite sure that New York might not suddenly rush over to the side of the Crown. It was less impressive to the Loyalists, and crusty, irritable die-hard Judge Thomas Jones, who left such venomous memoirs, snarled about "the shouts and huzzas of a seditious and rebellious multitude," with "everything conducted in the same tumultuous and ridiculous manner."

Philip Schuyler and Markoe's men were dropped off outside New York, and the procession, picking up and shedding escorts, pushed hard across Connecticut. He had Yale undergraduates shouting with him as he left New Haven. Then there were solid farmers to meet, and what was a planter but a farmer? The commander-in-chief called his companions' attention to wide village streets through which produce wagons could roll so easily, good houses set well apart in gardens where red and white and gold and orange blooms nodded to the summer air. Grazing, he thought, would be much easier and more profitable here than at home, and wrote about "a great deal of delightful country covered with grass in a very different manner to what our lands in Virginia are." If people who cheered could have read his mind or listened to his observations, they would not have needed the assurance which he had given outside New York, using rather touchingly an almost regal pronoun in a simple, honest thought, "when we assumed the soldier, we did not lay aside the civilian."

The party was across the border and into Massachusetts, where the pines were thicker, the hills higher, and the stone walls formed of rough boulders instead of the flat slabs of Connecticut. At Springfield there was a delegation of two, appointed by the Massachusetts Congress, to receive the generals Washington and Lee "with every mark of respect due to their exalted characters and stations." One was a stranger to Washington, Moses Gill, the devoted Boston printer, but the other he surely would have remembered as the man who brought Joseph Warren's plea to the Congress. A charming man, Dr. Benjamin Church, graduate of Harvard and familiar with England, where he had married a Hertfordshire girl.

Then, with Gill and Church, to Worcester and on to Marlboro, where a troop of cavalry—probably mere mounted militiamen—joined them for the last lap to the Charles and Watertown. Records of the meeting at the provincial capital have a hurried, breathless tone. The commander-in-chief was met by James Warren, now president of the Massachusetts Congress, Elbridge Gerry of Marblehead, chairman of the Committee of Supply, and a fat lieutenant colonel named Benjamin Lincoln, of Hingham, who may or may not have known that a lost cousin was in the Virginia militia, Captain Abraham Lincoln, later to be grandfather of another Abraham.

The commander-in-chief presented a quite unnecessary letter of introduction from the Continental Congress, was welcomed eagerly by the Massachusetts Congress in session, and was tendered a written address from that body which was most cordial in spirit, though tapering off into a description of his new command which many felt was far too pessimistic. Actually it could have been called glowing with optimism, disheartening as it was.

So the Massachusetts legislators faced for the first time this Virginian, almost a foreigner, to whom they were entrusting the New England army. He, in turn, was having his initial close glimpse of the men who, through tense years, had been thinking so much as he himself had thought, as he had sat with the burgesses at Williamsburg or ridden slowly along the heights of his beloved Mount Vernon. What did the legislators think of the man and he of them?

Washington's mind must have been tormented by an overriding eagerness to get on to Cambridge and see at first hand the material with which he would have to work. The Massachusetts Congress could only have been deeply impressed and moved, since that was the way men reacted to George Washington. James Warren wrote to John Adams of "the sage, brave and amiable General Washington . . . he fully answers to the character you have given him." Warren spoke for all New England when he added, "We find a great relief in the General's presence."

But on this, the second day of July, 1775, the main task lay ahead in Cambridge, and Washington and his staff pushed on as soon as manners allowed. Their arrival in the little college town was a sodden anticlimax. It had rained heavily in the morning and Artemas Ward, jumping at conclusions, had made up his mind that the general and his party would not make Cambridge that day and canceled whatever measures he had planned for a reception. So Washington rode into a town and an army that were yawning and lounging through a Sunday afternoon.

This, of course, runs counter to legend and legend-inspired paintings of a colorful taking over of command under the Washington Elm on Cambridge Common. But the commander-in-chief's timetable and various negative entries in diaries of the day do away with any such scene. One James Stevens, a soldier on duty in the town, made a single bored entry in his own record: "Nothing heppeng extroderly," which seems to show that not only was there no turning out of the garrison but that the average G.I. was unaware of the all-important arrival. It may be added that the story of the elm and the review first appeared as late as 1837.

Washington must have thought it more than "extroderly" that there was no one to meet him. Someone had presence of mind to guide the little group to the quarters commandeered for it by the Congress, mellow Wadsworth House with its fine doorway, then the residence of President Samuel Langdon. Aides were sent scampering wildly about Cambridge and out to the stubby little turf forts that squatted along the green bank of the Charles. Stern, slow-spoken Artemas Ward came in, followed by hard-chinned Israel Putnam, grizzled Billy Heath, and others.

Artemas Ward was a disappointed man. After all, he had been in command since the very start and had done about everything that a mortal could to keep an army in being about Boston. His earlier military service was at least as extensive as Washington's and he did not relish turning over command, particularly to a man who was not even a New Englander. His manner toward Washington was entirely correct, but he could not or would not feign a warmth that he did not feel. It is to his credit that, for the rest of his service, he supported the Virginian loyally, if coldly, never criticized him, never intrigued against him.

The meeting at Wadsworth House did not last long. Washington was in the saddle again, riding with his staff along the outer curve of the American lines from the posts before Charlestown, where he could look out on scarlet-coated pickets and patrols, to the far tip of the works that shut off Boston Neck at Roxbury.

Then he returned to Cambridge, his devoted mind heavy with what he had seen and what he had not seen. A stream of papers began to funnel out from Wadsworth House. How many units were there and what was the strength of each? How much powder was available? Was there a reserve? What was being done about a medical service and did rations and supplies flow smoothly into the camps? Artemas Ward's paper work had been his weakest point. Or perhaps there simply had not been time to set up the proper channels. Whatever the reason, the commander-in-chief was kept waiting, restless and more than uneasy, for day after endless day.

There was a very bad snarl that threatened the very structure of command. Washington had brought with him several congressional commissions for the ranks of major general and brigadier general. In some cases the new national rank awarded an officer was lower than that which he held from his own province. Wooster and Spencer of Connecticut retired in wrath, their military honor hopelessly stained in their eyes. Spencer later came back, but Wooster remained unappeasable. Dr. John Thomas, in command of the right of the whole American line, was also left out and

Cambridge gossipers nudged each other knowingly. Thomas would go home, of course.

John Thomas seems to have agreed with those gossips, but with reservations. He was deeply attached to his family down there in Plymouth County, an attachment that Washington, with half his heart at Mount Vernon, could understand. Thomas wrote his wife, "I am not Sertain but I may visit you herelong which would give me much pleasure to Return to my Dear Famely," which suggests a retirement from military life. He added, to confound Cambridge whispers, "Liveing with my famely . . . is the only Happy way of Life that I am acquainted with and Never shall Injoy my Self untill that Happy Day Shall Come, but as my Country Calls me I must obey." His mind was made up. If he lost his command, he would go home, straighten out his affairs, and then return to serve, in the ranks if he must.

The command problem, which might have wrecked the whole fabric of the army, was eventually solved—largely, it would seem, by the quiet impact of Washington's personality and the immensity of the sacrifices he was making in the common cause. These he did not mention, but they were deep in men's minds. A Continental commission as brigadier general was somehow arranged for John Thomas and he kept his post by Roxbury and the Boston Neck. Into Cambridge rode another one-star officer, John Sullivan of New Hampshire, to add his fire and determination to the men about Washington. On a ride with Charles Lee out to Roxbury, the commander-in-chief met a fresh-faced young man, tall and fat, with his left hand muffled neatly in a white silk scarf. That evening, in some excitement, the young man wrote to his wife, "Yesterday as I was going to Cambridge I met the Generals who begg'd me to return to roxbury again which I did when they had viewed the works they expressed the greatest pleasure and surprize at their situation and apparent utility, to say nothing of the plan which did not escape their praise." Henry Knox must have spent many profitable hours over the works of Vauban back there at his London Book-Store, for while Washington's engineering eye was amateur, Charles Lee prided himself on being the hard-bitten professional, and praise from him had to be well earned.

Slowly the army was being molded into shape. Artemas Ward commanded the right wing, with Thomas and the now repentant Spencer under him. Israel Putnam and Billy Heath reigned in Cambridge, while the far left wing was entrusted to Charles Lee, with John Sullivan and Nathanael Greene as his brigadiers.

As Washington signed each order, made each move, his keen blue eyes were always turned toward Boston and Charlestown. He was forced to shuffle and juggle his formations, to shift men from one command to another. What if Thomas Gage sallied out across the Neck while such shifts were being made? Suppose the garrison on the Charlestown hills erupted onto the mainland just while Nathanael Greene was bringing up his smart Rhode Islanders? Did Washington dare move powder from one dump to another? Desperate men might be calling for ammunition at the very moment when the precious stuff lay immobilized in moving carts. The decisions that Washington had to make were as vital and taxing as any battlefield decision could ever be.

Partly because Wadsworth House was small, partly because its usual occupant, President Langdon of Harvard, was limited to one room by the needs of the military, the commander-in-chief cast about for other quarters. Then Colonel John Glover vacated the spacious splendors of the Vassall house on Brattle Street and Washington and his staff took over. Wisp-thin Charles Lee, wishing to be nearer his new command, set himself up in the Royall mansion in Medford, a house which soon became known as Hobgoblin Hall, possibly in recognition of its new tenant's rather extraordinary features.

If the setting was vastly expanded, so were the commander-in-chief's worries. He had time to look closely at his basic raw material, the infantryman with his musket and his pack, who would be the true determining factor in success or failure. What he saw bit deeply into his mind. The New Englander did not embrace military discipline with any perceptible ardor, save in particular units like John Glover's. The principle of equality, entirely understandable in a population that had been largely self-employed, stressed and overstressed the fact that one man was as good as another, with the added thought that he was probably a sight better. Virtually all military ranks subscribed to this, voluntarily or because they had no choice if they wished to exercise any kind of command. Israel Putnam, major general in the Continental Army though he was, never attempted in these days to set up a mess. He stood in line with the rawest privates to draw his rations from the commissary, carried raw meat back to his quarters in his bare hands, and cooked it himself. A company commander who ordered one of his men to get a truss of straw might be told pleasantly enough to get it himself. A tried, veteran army can get along somehow with such informality. It is death for green troops.

Washington, bred up to the more feudal life of a big planter, was profoundly shocked. He called the army "a mixed multitude of people here, under very little discipline, order or government." He wrote in alarm to Patroon Philip Schuyler, "Mine must be a portrait at full length of what you have had in miniature. Confusion and discord reigned in every department." The camps themselves must have been a fearful sight to the military eye. Flimsy shelters had been constructed with no thought for order, neatness, or sanitation. Men pitched half-eaten rations outside their huts to rot in the sun, adding to the usual camp reek. Where there were exceptions to such slovenliness, they could be traced to the efforts of some one man who moved through instinct or training, a nameless company commander or a brigadier like Nathanael Greene.

Civilians strolling through their first camp looked on matters very differently. The Reverend William Emerson, who had wanted to attack Francis Smith's column as it moved into Concord, wrote his wife at the Old Manse,

" 'Tis also very diverting to walk among the camps . . . every tent is a portrait of ye temper and taste of ye persons that encamp in it. Some are made of boards, some of sail-cloth . . . others are made of stone and turf . . . some are thrown up in a hurry and look as if they could not help it— mere necessity—others are curiously wrought with doors and windows done with wreaths and withes in the manner of a basket. Some are your proper tents and marquees and look like ye regular camp of the enemy. These are the Rhode-islanders, who are furnished with tent equipages from among ourselves and everthing in the most exact English taste. However, I think that the great variety of the American camp is upon the whole, rather a beauty than a blemish to the army."

This was strictly a civilian view, and the camps about Cambridge, seen by a military man, would appeal to his sense of disaster rather than of beauty. Filthy huts, haphazard latrines, then known as vaults, rotting food could only mean a dull, sickly army. Washington had to contend with such conditions through most of the war, and his labors began here in Cambridge. But for the moment his main concern had to be with security rather than health. His very dreams must have been filled with pictures of sudden, heavy rushes of scarlet-and-white columns out of Charlestown or over the works that shut off Boston Neck.

Unlike Ward, who seems to have issued few orders and done little personal reconnaissance, the Virginian and his generals issued floods of commands, few of them superfluous, and were tireless in riding about the lines. For every digger in the works under the old regime, ten now appeared and dirt began to fly by four each morning. Slowly the sensitive points were thickened and strengthened.

There were repeated orders calling for exact discipline and obedience, for universal refraining from "profane cursing," and for compulsory attendance at divine service twice a day. The Reverend William Gordon, stalking through the camps, commented, "The regulations of the camp have been greatly for the better. . . . Every officer and private begins to know his place and his duty."

What uniforms there were began wearing out, and Washington urged Congress to provide ten thousand smocklike hunting shirts. This eminently sensible suggestion, however, produced no action, and men went about in shredding uniforms or civilian tatters. In a move to distinguish those entitled to give orders from those permitted only to receive them, various scarves, cockades, token epaulets were prescribed. Available colors must have been strictly limited, for one group crept forlornly about branded with most unmilitary pink.

Slowly and uncertainly an army was taking shape. Its combat education was greatly advanced by an unexpected teacher. As the early divisions of the American Army of 1917–18 learned valuable lessons by serving in so-called "quiet sectors" opposite seasoned German veterans, so the army of 1775 was schooled by the blockaded garrison. The British guns under Burgoyne's command blasted off vast amounts of artillery ammunition against the American works. Like the diggers on Breed's Hill, Washington's men learned that an alert soldier had little to fear from a bombardment. They found out what types of fieldworks were proof against heavy guns, found out when and how to take shelter, and their knowledge grew with each salvo out of Boston.

Their own guns were pitifully few and light, and ammunition was lacking. The ever-energetic Iz Putnam watched spent shot skittering over the ground and offered a hearty tot of rum for each round recovered. The more daring men tracked down explosive shells, stamped out the clumsy, slow-burning fuses, and turned in their prizes for a double ration. A few thirsty souls tried to stop rolling balls with feet and sometimes lost both foot and leg through misjudging speed. But these accidents do not seem to have acted as a deterrent, and on a pleasant afternoon clouds of men could be seen scampering along the banks of the Charles, pushing, shoving, hauling at each other in the hope of carrying a twelve-pounder to Iz Putnam and the rum stores.

On the Neck, among the harbor islands, both sides staged small-scale raids aimed at feeling out the strength of a position or in securing poorly guarded stores. None of these affairs amounted to much, except that they contributed more lessons for the school of the soldier. Washington's men found that they could actually stage small offensives and, especially among the islands, come off very well indeed.

As July rounded into August and the smoke of the camps sifted over the brick buildings in the Harvard Yard, Washington and his staff watched the roads from the west. Then there was a thick dust plume winding over the flats from Sudbury and its Wayside Inn, a thick plume that worked on toward Watertown and Cambridge. Swinging along with a loose, flowing stride came companies of tall, lean, leathery men in hunting shirts, double-caped, with sleeves and edges adangle with leather thrums. They and their fellows, a day or so's march in the rear, were ending a memorable hike that had begun for many of them in far-off Virginia, for the rest in Pennsylvania and Maryland. The riflemen had arrived. No sick. No stragglers. Some of the companies had covered more than seven hundred miles in three weeks and seemed to think it nothing of a feat as they poured smoothly over a Massachusetts road. They wore broad hats and cocked hats and fur caps with pendent ringed tails, and every man balanced a long-barreled rifle on his shoulder or tucked it familiarly under his arm. They were rare-spoken men whose eyes ranged north and south of the road as though habit turned them to the farthest horizon, and thus they came in to the theater of the blockade of Boston.

First and last there were some fourteen hundred of them, picked men from the Western frontiers with every frontier virtue and some frontier faults. Their rifles were accurate at astounding ranges, two hundred or even three hundred yards, and they handled those weapons with an almost contemptuous skill. In the April fight a few of these companies could probably have broken up both Smith and Percy beyond hope of salvation. In June they could have wrecked Howe's forces as they left the Charlestown beaches.

Now, faced by a pseudo-siege, they were wasted. There was no scouting to employ their unsurpassed woodlore. Targets were few and far between, as the British quickly learned to take cover and to show themselves as little as possible. Vigorous, skilled men, they rotted in the camps to which they were so ill adapted, and unwelcome idleness made them riotous and insubordinate. So they hung about in a state of growing demoralization until the fall of the year brought more suitable employment for them.

As long as their military existence endured, the riflemen were generally wasted or misused. Their very background, their highly individualistic natures did not fit them to serve in line of battle with the less colorful, formal organizations of the army. They were more like the Commando and Ranger formations of World War II and might well have been used as such. Their very armament rendered their employment in close combat highly dangerous. The rifle, for all its accuracy, took two to three times as long to load as the smoothbore musket and it could not be fitted with a bayonet. Hence, in the face of a charging enemy, the rifleman was helpless once he had fired his piece. Combat would not allow him those precious minutes necessary for reloading.

Nonetheless, these could have been invaluable troops, but like Berdan's United States Sharpshooters in the Civil War, their undoubted talents and skills were frittered away. Just once, in the summer of 1777, were they given full scope and, as they chewed up Burgoyne's British and Brunswick units in the thickets and clearings along the Hudson, showed magnificently what might have been done with them in the past and what could have been done with them in the future.

So the summer wore on with the two armies snarling and snapping at each other and doing relatively little damage. From the Vassall house Washington's orders poured out, exhorting, commanding, pleading, reasoning, commending. The camps must be kept clean or the army would sicken. Rations must be fairly distributed. Gambling must cease at once and officers and men must refrain from profane cursing. And powder must not be wasted. A man must not fire as much as a single round without written permission from his commanding officer. More comforts must be provided for the sick and wounded in the hospitals, and to ensure this, a director of hospitals was appointed. The appointee was handsome, affable Dr. Benjamin Church.

It was killing work for the master of Mount Vernon, who sometimes felt that New Englanders were hopeless material for soldiers. This opinion he would later alter most emphatically, but in the summer of 1775 neither he nor they had grown used to each other. He distrusted more and more what men called "the leveling spirit," which allowed a private to regard himself complacently as the full equal of a general. The privates and many officers found the Virginian's insistence on rank and military caste to smack almost of Toryism.

Yet some New Englanders struck the commander-in-chief as soldierly, and more and more often he directed that the Headquarters Guard about the Vassall house be drawn from John Glover's blue-and-white Marble-headers. The men might hold themselves as though they had just stepped ashore from fishing smack or dory, but they did not seem to feel demeaned by saluting smartly and they walked their posts as alertly as though they were standing watch. And then there were Nathanael Greene's Rhode Islanders under the pouched, watchful eye of Charles Lee at Hobgoblin Hall. They were really shaping up very well, and Greene was showing himself more and more as a man to rely on.

Any optimism on the part of Washington could have had only a brief life. Many units were improving. What of it? At the end of the year all enlistments ran out. A new army would have to be formed under the very muzzles of the British guns. Washington may have turned for comfort to the letter that Governor Jonathan Trumbull of Connecticut had written him some weeks before. "Now, therefore, be strong and very courageous. May the God of the Armies of Israel shower down the blessing of his divine providence on you; give you wisdom and fortitude; cover your head in the day of battle and danger."

Those about Washington, civilians as well as military men, must have had a good many dark moments as they surveyed the slow turn from summer into fall. They were true rebels now, for their party had fired on the King's troops, had captured one of his forts, and was now penning up one of his armies in the city of Boston. The families who had fled from that city, from the protecting arm of His Majesty's forces, would certainly be written down as in opposition to the King by that very act of flight. And even if the rebellion collapsed and men and women could show that they had not taken truly active part in it, their livelihoods were gone.

Men who lived by skills, like Silversmith Paul Revere, could probably set themselves up again somehow. Printers and publishers like Messrs. Edes and Gill could probably make do with a font of type and some paper. But we have seen how Henry Knox, not yet truly of the army, had turned his back on the fruits of careful years of building, on his profitable and well-stocked London Book-Store near the Old South Church. How could he start again? John Hancock was, of course, a marked man in royal eyes and the Hancock fortune was vested in Boston wharves and Boston properties and Boston shipping, now completely in the hands of the army and the Royal Navy. John Adams wrote resignedly, "Of the little Acquisitions I have made, five hundred Pounds Sterling is sunk in Boston in a Real Estate, four hundred Sterling more is completely annihilated in a Library that is now wholly useless to me and mine, and at least four hundred Sterling more is wholly lost to me in Notes and Bonds, not one farthing of the Principal or Interest of which I can obtain."

It is hard to picture just what such men had to look forward to. The Crown might weary of the struggle and yield most of the points for which the colonists had fought for a decade and more. What then? Would the thirteen colonies take their old places in the British Empire? There were very few hints of a conciliatory attitude drifting across the Atlantic. Would moderates and conservatives make secret deals with the Crown, compromise, and possibly sell out the more radical? The Crown would surely want its price for any concessions made. What if Gage's army did suddenly smash out from Boston and scatter the American forces? Every prominent rebel, especially those in Congress or in the arc about Boston, walked daily with a rope about his neck. Most people still shied away from the thought of a victory leading to independence, but men's inner minds must have kept swinging back to it as the one logical conclusion.

Yet life went on somehow with at least an outward placidity. John Hancock, one of the most vulnerable of all as president of Congress, forgot a gloomy future in present joys, for his long courtship had come to an end and, at the Burr mansion in Fairfield, Connecticut, Dorothy Quincy finally became Mrs. Hancock. Henry Knox, now weighing close to two hundred and eighty pounds and still a theoretical civilian, rode cheerfully about the lines, examined fortifications, and combed his memory for bits of lore gleaned from the pages of the master engineer, Vauban. He came back each evening to regale Lucy with tales of his wanderings and whom he had seen as the pair dined in the Watertown house they shared with other Whigs. John Adams, starting off for Philadelphia again, genially badgered Cousin Sam into learning how to ride, an accomplishment that the town-bred Adams viewed with deep trepidation. John reported that the lessons were a success, adding with mock chagrin that others of the party thought Sam the better horseman of the two. Sam, with characteristic ill luck in matters sartorial, managed to split his only pair of breeches while in the saddle. John persuaded him to buy "two yards of flannell, which we carried to our Landlady, who with the assistance of a Taylor Woman in the House, made up a Pair of Drawers which . . . entirely healed the little Breach which had been begun."

Insecure and ominous as life was outside of Boston, within the city Whig, Tory, and soldier found their prospects no sunnier. Thomas Gage labored to strengthen his works opposite Roxbury, along the river, and in Charlestown, but his men showed a marked aversion, in contrast to the enemy, to pick-and-shovel work and he could get little or no civilian labor. Clinton, Howe, and Burgoyne watched him sardonically and sometimes offered advice that may possibly have been well meant. Gage felt, despite his near ten thousand troops, that he was too weak to take the offensive and contented himself with the optimistic and utterly ungrounded hope that Washington might make a frontal attack on his works.

Supplies of all kinds were harder and harder to find, and the garrison went on very short rations. Even the water routes, which Graves and the Navy should have kept open, became highly hazardous, and armed sloops began snapping up smaller craft bearing food and fuel for the city. Officers and men suffered alike, and the Earl of Percy, giving a dinner to friends in the magnificence of John Hancock's house overlooking the Common, served roast colt as an entree. Officers wounded at Bunker Hill complained bitterly of hospital diet. "Broth of salt pork!" raged one of them. "That's impossible. Yes, we get sometimes a piece of an old cow at the rate of fourteen times as much as we paid last summer."

Enlisted men fared much worse, and the death rate mounted fantastically. The incessant pealing of church bells for funerals beat louder and louder in the ears of weakened men, like heavy, ominous steps that drew nearer and nearer to the heaps of sour straw on which they lay. A Bostonian noted, ". . . the chapple bell toled almost all day for people that died . . . which was so Malincully that the General has stopped the toling of bells for funerals."

Then there was the civilian population, some sixty-five hundred souls. Nearly a third of these were Tories, either Bostonians or refugees. This third might have strengthened Gage's hand appreciably, for most of them were devoutly for the Crown and had bitter, personal scores to settle with their erstwhile Whig neighbors in the hinterland or in Boston. Timothy Ruggles, who had presided at that First Continental Congress of 1774, had a fine record from the French wars and was greatly respected by all American friends of the King. On the nineteenth of April he formed a military body called the Gentleman Volunteers or the Loyal American Association. Quickly there followed the Loyal Irish Volunteers and the Royal Honorable Americans.

Here was a weapon that might well have been expanded into a really valuable auxiliary to the King's forces. But Gage dallied and temporized, was reluctant to issue them arms on the not unjustifiable grounds that such units might contain secret Whig elements, so little by little these allies were allowed to slip away. The British Army as such regarded them in a very dim light, as indeed it had regarded all colonial units in the past. Virtually any royal commission was superior to one of colonial origin, and any callow British captain could have given orders to Brigadier General Timothy Ruggles. There were other items, such as pay, allowances, and eventually retirement, in which the Tory officer was placed in a most inferior position, if not barred altogether from such benefits. So what could have been the nucleus of a most useful body withered.

There was also an odd sort of cantankerous inertia that kept the Tories from forcing themselves into action. This was not merely true in Boston. It was to show itself time and again through most of the rest of the country. The Tory, generally speaking, seems to have been static, while opposed to him ideologically was the dynamism of the rebel Whigs.

From a civilian standpoint, the Tories did not fare too well, though on paper they should have constituted a privileged minority. There was the question of food. Attorney General Jonathan Sewall wailed, "How times have changed! If a quarter of a poor, half-starved dead sheep is carry'd thro' the street, people fly to their doors and windows to view the wonderful sight, in the same manner as they formerly did to see the funeral of a person of distinction, while in return a funeral passes along as unheeded as ever a

panier of pigeons did in the afternoon of a hot day when the morning price
was a half penny a dozen." There were other matters to plague Loyalist
Sewall. "My pew in church is converted into a pork-tub. . . . I have just
parted with my coach horses for £24 sterg. which cost me £40 last fall and
£20 more in keeping. I parted with them because they were starving in the
midst of British armys and British fleets in the most plentiful country in the
world."

The Whigs may be viewed as the enlisted men of the occupation of
Boston. They had what the army and the Tories left, "Salt beef and salt
pork, much the greater part of which is hard as wood, as lean as carrion and
as rusty as the devil." Just as Gage might have put the Tories to good use,
so he might well have bettered his whole position by allowing the Whigs
to leave town. As it was, they could leave only by written permission. Once
this was obtained, a Whig could take with him no more than five pounds
sterling, what possessions he could carry or, in favored cases, could load into
a small cart. No silverware could be taken out of Boston, a mild enough ban
unless it is remembered that eighteenth-century Americans often used the
fine work of men like Hurd and Revere as a sort of safe-deposit box. The
purchase of a silver pitcher would employ idle capital. In case of need the
pitcher could be melted down and the metal used for currency. So a Whig
who passed the Roxbury lines was virtually penniless and without possessions.

The abandoned Whig houses were, despite orders, quite systematically
looted, and Merchant John Andrews could write sadly that they had
"strip'd your uncle's house of everything . . . some of the china and principal part of the pewter is the sum of what he has left." And there was
"poor Ben." "A party of soldiers got in, went into his cellar, took liquors
from thence and had a revelling frolick in his parlour, carried off and destroy'd of his furniture &ca to the value of two hundred sterling." This was
less, concludes Andrews, than losses suffered in fifty or a hundred other
houses.

A good deal of the Whigs' trouble was probably unknown to Thomas
Gage but was due to and vastly aggravated by two of his civilian appointments. The first and worst of these was one William Cunningham, a brutal,
vicious clod of a man who was named provost marshal, which made him
virtually civilian chief of police. In modern days Cunningham would have
been known as a fast man with a shilling and at once he began to turn a
neat profit through the clandestine sale of stores given over to him to maintain his prisoners. Other opportunities soon came under his questing eye,
and chance gave him a suitable partner.

Joshua Loring, Jr., was a very proper Bostonian and his very pretty wife
was seen more and more about Province House until she really seemed part
of Sir William Howe's entourage though with quite unofficial status. But
Husband Joshua became highly official, with the titles of sheriff and vendue
master. Armed with this twin authority, he began seizing the properties
of absentee Whigs and selling them at public auction. Then he expanded

his activities to non-absentees and finally to Tories of some means but little influence. These sales were attended only by his own deputies, by Cunningham and his deputies or assigns, which kept the bidding on the seized goods at a figure highly satisfactory to the bidders, who would later offer them to the public. When scarcity of food in Boston led to rationing and to the issue of stores of usually damaged edibles to the Tories, Cunningham and Loring felt that they could not, in fairness to themselves, sit idly by, so they started a very healthy black market that allowed some few to live reasonably well while jails, hospitals, and civilians suffered cruelly.

News of American events reached England in tardy if unmistakable echoes. Each side had rushed its own version of the clash of the nineteenth of April to London, with the colonists winning the race. Bunker Hill was officially reported by Gage alone. But busy pens, Whig, Tory, and British Army, scuffed and scratched over paper and sent their own tales of life in the colonies to the old country. Soon peers, merchants, and army officers were drawing out sheets of paper, with the blotting sand still rough on the surface, in clubs and coffeehouses. "My sister-in-law, married to a Scottish tobacco factor in the Virginias, writes me that the rebels are the most contumacious set of scoundrels ever whelped. She says here . . ." "My nephew, a cornet in the 17th Light Dragoons, has lately come to Boston and discloses that our generals—— Here, just listen to this."

Evening Posts and Chronicles and Advertisers were highlighted by letters "from a gentleman in Philadelphia, to his correspondent in London." "Genuine extract of a letter from New York." "Letter from a Sergeant of Foot in the King's Troops to his Relation in the Isle of Ely, dated at Boston." "Letter from an Officer in the Camp on Bunker's Hill." Many of these make odd reading, since several, notably from officers in the King's army, are bitterly critical of the administration and express sympathy with the colonists in rebellion.

Most, however, reflect the correct Royalist view. Some are sternly critical of American methods of making war. A British lady in Boston confessed that she was not at all competent to judge from a basis of international law and military jurisprudence but felt strongly that it was contrary to civilized practice for the Americans "to take aim at Officers with rifled muskets." No doubt poor bloody Tommy was fair game.

Dispatches and letters, official and unofficial, from the New World set many Englishmen thinking, some of them fuzzily, some soberly and logically. William Phillips, an artilleryman who held for that arm the unusually high rank of colonel and lieutenant governor of Windsor Castle and who would later roll down the Hudson as Burgoyne's chief gunner, wrote to his friend Sir Henry Clinton at Boston, "I see the American War full of horrors. . . . I see that so large extensive a Continent cannot be conquered by a handful of Men but, My dear friend, depend on it that administration see it quite otherwise, they see it as when you were here, that is, to speak to you plainly, they do not see it at all. They attempt to carry on a War of such magnitude without a serious consultation of any military man."

Honest, tough-souled Billy Phillips was certainly seeing straighter than many Londoners, military or civilian. But apparently he was not close to the ministerial gossip parties. Thought was being taken by the administration, and it went much farther than the "*handful* of Men." How could that handful be increased? Inefficiency, corruption, and a most shocking disinclination on the part of the masses to enlist in the armies of the King made recruiting a highly difficult problem to solve. But there were other sources of the raw, human materials of war, and soon agents of the Crown were whispering discreetly to German landgraves, dukes, crown princes, and counts. They flitted about the petty courts in Brunswick, Waldeck, Anspach, Hesse-Cassel and Hesse-Hanau, and their whisperings and flittings were to bear fruit. All these minor monarchs maintained marketable armies which they would hire out to any power willing to pay in good gold. To them and to the hirers there was nothing sordid or underhanded in this buying and selling of companies and battalions. Time and usage had sanctified it for centuries, and in some small states it almost amounted to a major industry, maintaining beautiful castles and gardens and theatrical troupes and mistresses for the ruling princes. A glance at the order of battle at Fontenoy in 1745, theoretically between the British and French, will prove illuminating on this score. There on a Belgian plain, British, Dutch, French, Sardinians, Neapolitans, Swiss, Scots, Irish, and men from many German states brawled cheerfully under either standard.

Was it not an ideal solution, this hiring of foreign troops to fight against the contumacious American rebels? Even so relatively modern a historian as Sir John Fortesque defends the hiring for this particular war and is quite cross with American writers who denounce it.

But the colonists were never able to take such a broad-gauged view of the practice. When the news of the German treaties reached America, it solidified military resistance to the Crown as had few other factors, and this struck many British ministers and military men as further proof of the cultural backwardness of those transplanted Englishmen who had become Americans.

Then there was still another source of strength for the Crown, another type of treaty that might be neatly executed. This source had nothing to do with obese German princes, but rather with swift, lean, copper-colored chiefs in northern New York and Canada and about the Lakes. Such treaties would be made and would backfire even more than those with the landgraves and princes and dukes. But so far, no shadow of Mohawk brave or Brunswick grenadier hung over the theater of the siege of Boston.

CHAPTER XIII

"I most heartily wish it, though . . . I may be the greatest sufferer"

TO most people clustering about the great arc so loosely clamped around Boston, the eyes of the world seemed focused on the Charlestown hills, Roxbury Neck, and the Heights of Dorchester. But far to the west life was stirring strongly if uncertainly.

Armed men were camped and clumsy boats moved along the great broken sword blade of water that reached from the Narrows about Staten Island north and north until it reached the far St. Lawrence. And all this activity stemmed from a resolution passed by the Continental Congress in the early days of the summer of 1775:

"Resolved, That if General Schuyler finds it practicable and that it will not be disagreeable to the Canadians, he do immediately take possession of St. Johns, Montreal and any other parts of the country, and pursue any other measures in Canada, which may have a tendency to promote the peace and security of these colonies."

There is something pathetic and at the same time splendid in this simple yet sweeping order to a general with virtually no army to take possession of the greater part of a continent if it will not be disagreeable to the inhabitants thereof. Militarily, this proposal was not as fantastic as it may seem at first glance. General Sir Guy Carleton, British commander in Canada, had a very small force at his disposal. Traders and American agents had brought word that the Canadian French would welcome release from the British yoke—probably one of the lightest in history, though Congress does not seem to have looked into this phase of Canadian life. Even more encouraging, the Northern Indians were said to have declared for strict neutrality, with death to any brave who fought on either side. So there would be no scalping parties slipping down Lake George or bursting out of the thickets along the Mohawk. Nothing but Carleton's scattered posts stood between the American forces and the conquest of Canada.

All this might have been worked out as planned, and so it very nearly did work out. But it is hard to see how such a conquest could be held. Let the Americans take Montreal or even Quebec. What then? Holding those cities would mean tying up garrisons and maintaining an immensely long and vulnerable line of supply. So long as England held control of the sea, its ships could always sail up the St. Lawrence and smash or starve out the American garrisons. Congressional vision does not seem to have gone beyond the possibility of initial success.

Philip Schuyler was on many counts an obvious choice to be over-all commander. While he had never had combat experience, he had a good all-around mind, ability in the abstract, unshakable integrity, and a profound belief in what he was fighting for.

As second-in-command was designated Irish-born Richard Montgomery, till 1772 a full captain in the British Army and more lately a devoted delegate to the First Continental Congress of 1774. Now an American brigadier, he brought to the cause a devotion equal to Schuyler's, a professional military background, a driving yet controlled energy, and an inventive mind that was not easily discouraged. Though a newcomer, his marriage into the wealthy, powerful Livingston family made him highly acceptable to the most clannish New Yorkers.

With headquarters at near-ruinous Ticonderoga, the two settled down to make what preparations they could, to build the flotilla that was to take them down Sieur de Champlain's lake, and to wait for an army to command. Somehow a little fleet was hastily cobbled together, though Schuyler complained that he had no nails, no oakum, no planks. Like the naval stores, troops trickled into camp, first a few companies under Philip Van Cortlandt, then a few more New Yorkers under Rudolph Ritzema. Turbulent John Lamb, the fires of the Sons of Liberty days still blazing in him, brought up some artillery and with it a set of very odd notions concerning the prerogatives of gunners. He explained coldly that "artillery companies, in every country, are always looked upon in a superiour light to other foot companies." Schuyler and Montgomery were unable to see this nice distinction, and Lamb, feeling himself degraded by being classed with infantry, resigned in a fair-sized tantrum and asked to be reimbursed for his expenses in raising the company.

High hopes had been pinned on the Green Mountain Boys, across there in modern Vermont, but meetings designed to raise companies raised only a fearful row, with the result that Ethan Allen reported at Ticonderoga as a Vermont expeditionary force of one. More New Yorkers came in, bringing a great store of enthusiasm, courage, and almost no equipment. Then Congress sent Schuyler Colonel David Waterbury's Connecticut regiment. A Massachusetts contingent appeared and some New Hampshire Rangers. Schuyler and Montgomery actually had a command, makeshift and ill equipped though it might be.

Schuyler hurried down to Albany to attend a council fire of some of the New York Indian tribes, leaving his Irish second-in-command in charge. Pacing about the sagging stone walls of the fort, prodding the shipwrights into speed and still more speed, bringing order and sanitation into the noisome, unhealthy camps, Montgomery received a letter from one John Brown, written deep in Canada. Brown should have been a buckskin, a wiry, slow-spoken man of the woods, to do the work he had set himself. Instead, he was a Yale graduate, a full-fledged lawyer, and, in calmer days, King's attorney for the province of New York; yet, with the tang of cities and law courts about him, he moved skillfully and efficiently among the Indians and habitants of Canada. John Brown's letter was a model of military reporting, and the writer, civilian though he was, realized the importance of controlling the waterways leading north. He had seen good-sized craft being built under Carleton's orders along the Richelieu and did not miss the lesson they taught. These boats, he wrote, "can easily sweep the Lake. I therefore humbly beseech that some effectual measures may be immediately entered into to keep the command of this lake."

Montgomery would have been justified in merely passing this plea on to Schuyler at Albany, but that was not his way. He moved swiftly, embarked Waterbury's 5th Connecticut and Ritzema's 4th New York and a few gunners under Samuel Mott. By sunset of August 28 the little force of some twelve hundred men pushed off into the narrows by Ticonderoga, turned north down widening Champlain. Schuyler, warned by a hasty letter, might follow with the rest of the force as soon as he could. But Richard Montgomery, so long as there was a chance of forcing victory or staving off defeat, was going to strike swiftly and surely with such weapons as he had under his hand. A true soldier, he realized that days and hours could sometimes be more important than the matter of numbers, supplies, and equipment.

So the schooner *Liberty*, the sloop *Enterprise*, and the lesser flock of gundalows, bateaux, row galleys, piraguas, and canoes headed north up the lake, with the Green Mountains already cloaked in somber dusk at the right and the Adirondacks catching the last gold of sunset on the left. Montgomery's flotilla was heading into the night. Canada lay far ahead down the lake, and in its unmeasured immensity lurked Carleton's men, the Indians, who might or might not remain neutral, and—had Congress thought of this in prescribing the whole coup?—the Canadian winter.

As though the winds that swept east out of the Adirondacks, across Champlain, and over the rounded summits of the Green Mountains had brought a hint of distant activity to the arc of the blockade about Boston, ripples began to stir, gathered strength, and flowed out in a quick, harsh stream. In a bright September noon, soldiers and townspeople lined the Harvard Yard and the fringes of Cambridge Common to stare at a lithe-moving column that swung steadily on, pointing to the northeast.

It was an American column, such as few people a decade or five years before could have conceived. In the van were three companies of riflemen from Virginia and Pennsylvania, their killing tools balanced nonchalantly over sinewy shoulders and their long linen hunting shirts swinging like kilts to their easy stride. After them flowed companies of musketmen from all the New England states, and some of them had uniforms and some had hunting shirts or clothes that suggested a hayfield or a sleepy town square. However they were dressed, they stepped smartly out, eyes to the northeast, and kept up with the free-striding riflemen ahead.

These units had been in the area long enough to assume identities, to draw nods of quiet recognition from the crowds about Yard and Common. Individuals in those units stood out in their own right, and ripples of subdued whispers from the bystanders must have marked their passage.

"That's Dan Morgan a-leading of that rifle company. Biggest feller I ever clapped eyes to. Seen him swimming in the Charles, and his back looks 's a body'd jammed a red-hot grid on it." Back in '55, Daniel Morgan had gone with Braddock's fatal expedition as a volunteer teamster, and a stupid martinet had had him flogged. His back still showed the twenty-year-old weals and his mind bore scars, too, to remind him of the army that had triced him up and beaten him, a freeborn man.

"Look yonder, Dr. Winthrop. There is young Captain Henry Dearborn with his large dog, which is said to be a most sagacious animal." The sagacious animal would be killed and eaten on the horrible march that lay ahead, but his master would live to fight again and again.

"Kit Greene, cousin to General Nat over in the Rhode Island camp. People say he's a sound man and a stirring one, but I always think an army out of Massachusetts ought to be Massachusetts-officered."

"That's Benedict Arnold, the Connecticut colonel, Tabitha. His eyes burn through you and they do say that he's devil-driven." Devil-driven or not, Arnold rode on as commander of this force of some eleven hundred men, bringing to it an indomitable will, a striving that always glowed at fever pitch, and a nagging, almost visible sense of always being pushed aside in favor of his inferiors.

So the whole command passed by. Aaron Burr, almost girlishly handsome and driven by an ambition nearly as great as Arnold's. Christian Febiger, the Dane of Bunker Hill, adjutant to Benedict Arnold. Return Jonathan Meigs of Connecticut, an able soldier who could foresee very clearly what lay ahead of him and his men. Dr. Isaac Senter, surgeon; Captain Simeon Thayer; Mathias Ogden; privates like Rifleman John Joseph Henry and Caleb Haskell—all tramped on northeast as people named them and called to them from under the Cambridge elms.

They were off on an expedition that would have ripped the heart out of most armies. Their route lay through Newburyport and thence to the mouth of the Kennebec, where bateaux hastily hammered up out of green wood were awaiting them. Thence they were to push off into untouched and largely unknown wilderness, portaging their bateaux and supplies past falls and rapids. High, forested land, lost rivers, unknown swamps were to be faced after leaving the sapphire Kennebec and then, after a last lunge, the angry, boiling Chaudière would lead them on and on until they reached the St. Lawrence with the blanket of Canadian winter masking them in its freezing folds.

And at the St. Lawrence? Quebec, the cliff-high fortress, lay across that river, the towering prize at which the little expedition aimed in its sublime venture.

Arnold's eleven hundred men were gone, but the main army still swarmed about the fringes of the blockade and its problems grew from day to day. Lights burned late in the Vassall house and shone across its gardens to the golden leaves of the autumn elms along Brattle Street as the one man who must solve them all fought his way stubbornly on. He must have felt himself agonizingly alone, this Virginian suddenly in command of a New England army, this man who had not given a military command in more than sixteen years. Occasionally he burst out, setting forth on paper the words and the thoughts which he must choke back in public. "Such a dearth of public spirit, and want of virtue, such stock-jobbing and fertility in all the low arts to obtain advantages of one kind or another . . . I never saw before and pray God I may never be witness to again. . . . Could I have foreseen what I have, and am likely to experience, no consideration upon earth should have induced me to accept this command."

Yet for the most part he curbed his naturally quick temper, set his chin, retired behind a mask of stern gravity. He rode about the lines, talked with John Sullivan and Nathanael Greene and John Thomas, took counsel with his adjutant, Horatio Gates, late of the British Army, with unpredictable Charles Lee, late of many armies, with honest, combat-minded Israel Putnam. There was strength to be drawn, in one way or another, from all these men, from colonels like John Glover, Loammi Baldwin (who was later to give his name to an apple), John Nixon, or James Varnum. From their varied skills, abilities, confidence, prudence, energies, and devotion he could fortify himself, the more so as the New Englanders among them ceased almost imperceptibly to be strangers and turned into friends.

Large in the back of his mind must have been Virginia. Lord Dunmore, bibulous and coarse royal governor, was racketing about the lower Potomac. What if the noble lord should take it into his head to raid into the upper reaches of the river, burn Mount Vernon, and seize Martha Custis Washington as hostage? But the commander-in-chief seems to have kept such fears from interfering with the task to which he had not too willingly or confidently set his hand.

When George Washington trotted past Cambridge Common, through the Harvard Yard, or along the flats by the lower Charles, there was always one overriding problem to leap at him. There were his troops. How long would he have them? The fall was wearing on day by day, dragging him closer to the end of the enlistment period for nearly all his force. So far, cautious polls taken among officers and men showed a discouraging reluctance to extend their terms or to sign on when the present tour of duty should end. Other exasperating quirks were manifesting themselves. From what day did the eight-month term date? The Connecticut men and some of the Rhode Islanders claimed that the day of their original summons marked the start of their service, and if they held to this, the first of December and not the first of January, 1776, would see them marching home, leaving a fatal gap in the lines about Boston.

If new units could be formed in December and January, how were they to be armed? Most of the men at the first call had brought their own weapons. If they went home, their muskets would surely go with them, and the same fate would probably befall such firearms as had been issued from scanty public stores or captured from the British. Blankets, overcoats, uniforms, if any, haversacks, and the invaluable cartridge pouches could be counted on to trickle away with the time-expired men. Why not? These are American stores and I'm an American, aren't I? Looking ahead to that day, Washington and his consultants evolved a plan that was drastic in that time and in that place of uninhibited individuality. No discharged man should leave camp with a musket. If he could prove personal ownership, he was to be given a receipt and paid a fair valuation of the weapon. There would be numerous leaks to such a plan, but it assured to the new army, if it really came into being, firearms in quantity. Quality was another matter.

As the man from Mount Vernon rode over the plank bridge that led into Cambridge, the least hint of northeast storms rolling down from Cape Ann brought another problem sharply before him. New England winters were harsh. How was the army to be sheltered? Barracks must be built in the face of a great dearth of nails, tools, and cut lumber. Harvard College had agreed to house many of the men. Abandoned buildings were to be requisitioned. Christ Church, with its off-center tower facing the Common, must be used. But all these places must be heated, and the country about Cambridge had been deforested for a generation or more. Even now with the weather still warm, men fought for clumps of scraggly bushes along the Charles for their cook fires, and the losers often ate their rations raw.

These were just a few of the more apparent difficulties which the commander-in-chief faced, and none of them took in the reason for the army's being in existence—Gage and his men in Boston. It was obvious that Washington's men would not merely sit in front of the town while weeks trailed into months and months into years. The role must be defined somehow. Perhaps it might be best, in the long run, if harbor and river froze solid and Graves's fleet were immobilized, to make a sudden dash over the ice and carry the city by storm. Or passivity might be the wise course, since rumors from overseas hinted that conciliation was in the wind, that there might be a change of ministry as well as heart. Either course meant that enlistments must be kept up and weapons supplied and so on through the whole crushing cycle of intense worry.

Racked by deep concern and pressed unbearably by the slow march of time that seemed to promise nothing short of disaster, Washington stayed outwardly calm and assured. No waverer would ever be precipitated into panic by the example of the commander-in-chief. The Vassall house took on more and more the air of an orderly, competent headquarters where tension was rarely allowed to show its head. The Virginian may even have had a deep laugh out of a letter that Charles Lee ("a great sloven, wretchedly profane and a great admirer of dogs") had written in a whimsy-struck moment to Iz Putnam. It was dated at Hobgoblin Hall and read, "Dear General,—Mr. Page, the bearer of this, is a Mr. Page. He has the laudable ambition of seeing the great General Putnam. I therefore desire you would array yourself in all your majesty and terrors for his reception. Your blue and gold must be mounted, your pistols stuck in your girdle; and it would not be amiss if you should black one half of your face. I am, dear general, with fear and trembling, your humble servant, Charles Lee." Such a light, fleeting moment could drive the shadows out of the forefront of Washington's mind for a little. And then it was always comforting to think of the army hospitals. Their management had improved immeasurably. Even touchy John Sullivan, who had drawn up lawyer-like charges against them, had apologized handsomely. It was increasingly obvious that a wise move had been made in the appointment of Dr. Benjamin Church as director.

One evening on the last of September the commander-in-chief had a surprise visit from Nathanael Greene. The handsome Rhode Islander had with him a civilian, one Godfrey Wainwood, a baker from Newport, who in the past had probably bought milled flour from the Greene empire across Narragansett Bay. Wainwood, for whose status Greene vouched, had a story and a letter, both of which troubled him.

In the summer there had come to Newport a young and presumably pretty woman with whom, Wainwood confessed, he had dallied pleasantly on various trips to Boston. Now she wanted the baker to put her in touch with prominent Tories, whom she named, or else with the captain of a British ship lying off the town. Wainwood, profoundly shocked, had enveloped himself in a smoke screen of words, dilating on the dangers and difficulties of any such encounter. The woman had given up and vanished, leaving a letter which she had hoped to give to the people mentioned.

Perplexed, Wainwood took letter and story to a trusted friend, who promptly opened the sheet, only to find it covered with code-like signs, quite unintelligible. So Wainwood, while keeping the letter, dismissed it from his mind. But it came to life again. The young woman wrote from Cambridge, asking about its fate and stating very clearly that someone in British-held Boston was concerned over its non-arrival.

The inferences of Wainwood's story were shocking. Someone in or about Cambridge was sending letters in code by a circuitous route to Boston. The writer had been careless enough to set down the address en clair—"For Major Cane in Boston on his magisty's sarvice." Shaken as he was, Washington may well have found a certain relief. Here was a problem that could be attacked at once without the deadly hazard of time and other people's actions. Armed with such intimate descriptions as Wainwood could give, searchers were sent out to find the girl. They had to act very quietly, for she was an obvious pawn, and any disturbance would warn her principal or principals. A legend in the Greene family states that somehow Iz Putnam managed to seize her, hoist her behind him in the saddle, and gallop off through the night to the Vassall house and up the drive. Dismounting, Putnam flew up the steps and into the house, dragging her after him.

At first she refused to talk, but Washington's stern and unyielding insistence finally induced her ("a subtle, shrewd jade," by James Warren's account) to confess that the letter had been given her by her present bel ami, Dr. Benjamin Church, director of hospitals. Her confession virtually broke the case. Failing to make out the code, Washington turned it over to

Colonel Elisha Porter of the Massachusetts militia, the Reverend Mr. West, and to Elbridge Gerry of Marblehead. How these three qualified as cryptographers is not known, but working together until they found a reasonable key and then separately, they produced identical decodings.

The letter was more than odd. The greater part of it vastly magnified Washington's strength, as though warning the British that an attack against him would be fatal. It ended, however, with instructions for answering and a terse, damning sentence, "Make use of every precaution or I perish."

There were examinations of Church and then a court-martial, and all through the proceedings the gifted doctor defended himself brilliantly, as might have been expected. The end of the trial brought a verdict of guilt and a sense of profound embarrassment. Under the hastily drawn military code there were no provisions for Church's offense. What was to be done with him?

This was finally solved by sending him out of the sensitive area and placing him in the custody of Governor Jonathan Trumbull of Connecticut, "without use of pen, ink or paper, to be conversed with in the presence of a magistrate only, and in the English language." For some years Church was shifted from jail to jail and at last allowed to leave the country. He is said to have been exiled to the West Indies and, about 1782, was lost at sea.

Church had a few champions at the time and more later. His guilt for years was never actually proved, though it seemed certain enough. Then the indefatigable Allen French, going through the Gage papers in the 1930s, came on material that shows the doctor as the principal leak into Gage's headquarters, the man who told Gage the location and extent of the Concord stores and of the plan to move them west out of British reach. Had Church's information reached Gage more promptly or had fat Colonel Francis Smith of the Lincolnshires not made so many blunders on the nineteenth of April, the course of history might have been different. But the doctor would not have been different. The Allen French researches show clearly that Church was no misguided patriot hoping to bring about peace in his own way. Like a slightly later villain, he wanted cash on the line. He was under a regular subsidy from Gage and was not the least hesitant in reminding the general, in the course of his letters, that another payment was due.

Whatever shock Washington may have felt over the apostasy of his director of hospitals, of the man who had greeted him at the Connecticut line in the name of Massachusetts, he managed somehow to choke back wrath and disgust and disillusionment and to present a coldly unruffled front to the people for whom he was rapidly becoming a symbol.

Then the world outside this alien New England reached out to him. Up from Philadelphia came a committee from the Continental Congress to remind him that if he were responsible to thirteen colonies, those thirteen stood solidly back of him. One by one the three men of the committee came up the drive of the Vassall house and passed through its lovely doorway. There was Benjamin Harrison, a Virginia friend of long standing.

There was Thomas Lynch, a world away from his beloved South Carolina, Lynch the unshakable veteran of many congresses. Last of all came the wise, silvered head of one of the greatest men of the age, and Benjamin Franklin, benign and gently smiling, entered headquarters.

A conference of the senior officers was called, and Nathanael Greene wrote immediately afterward, "I had the honor to be introduced to that very great man, Doctor Franklin, whom I viewed with silent admiration the whole evening. Attention watched his lips and conviction closed his periods." The doctor, whose mind was apt to miss little, may have made silent note of the young general, for Greene's wife, the former Kitty Little-field, was the niece of Franklin's lifelong correspondent, Catherine Ray, and Catherine would surely have written him about Kitty's husband.

There were endless conferences that ate away nights and gnawed at long days. What the trio had to tell Washington was that the Congress of all the colonies had complete confidence in him. It was hoped that he would feel strong enough to shift the British out of Boston, the when and how being left to him. One of the committeemen brought up the possibility of finding enough heavy artillery to shell the city. What did the commander-in-chief think would happen if incendiary shells fell in close-packed, largely wooden Boston?

The answer came, convincing and unexpected, a true laboratory report. From Falmouth on Casco Bay, just north of present Portland, Maine, came one Pearson Jones. A small British fleet under Captain Henry Mowat, R.N., had appeared off Falmouth and, after a delay that allowed most of the inhabitants to make a hurried exit, opened fire. Nearly one hundred and forty homes and close to three hundred other structures had gone up in flames on the threshold of a Maine winter, said Jones. The firing of Boston, with its many resident Whigs, was left in abeyance. The matter was so important that the committee felt that Congress alone should pass on it.

The delegates were gone, but they must have left the commander-in-chief with the feeling that he did not stand alone on Massachusetts Bay. November brought in uncertain trickles of news from the twin expeditions into Canada. Schuyler wrote of countless difficulties, dwelling on the hot tensions that arose between New Yorkers and New Englanders. "If Job had been a General in my situation, his memory had not been so famous for patience," stormed Patroon Schuyler. But his field commander, Richard Montgomery, kept doggedly on, doing what he could with what he had. St. Johns fell to him, and among the prisoners was a fantastically hand-some young officer of the 7th Royal Fusiliers, John André. Stone-walled Fort Chambly, now a museum, had fallen earlier into American hands. Arnold's column, fighting natural conditions far more vicious than any mortal enemy, checked in from Dead River, well beyond the Kennebec. The dynamic Arnold wrote cheerfully of frightful difficulties overcome, with more ahead. Then news that Montgomery was certain to take Mont-real. The great gamble showed signs of paying off.

Bright flashes from the sea dispelled gloom about headquarters. Some of John Glover's officers had put out in small armed ships and were making serious inroads on British sea-borne activities, though of course they were far too weak to challenge morose Admiral Graves and the main fleet. But a load of lumber here, of flour there, fell into Yankee hands. Then the schooner *Lee*, Captain John Manly, pounced on the British brig *Nancy* off Cape Ann. When the brig's papers reached Cambridge, Horatio Gates was shrill with glee and announced that he could not have dreamed up a better invoice himself. There was no powder, but the holds were crammed with two thousand stand of small arms, barrels of flints, enough musket balls to ballast a frigate, and a vast mortar weighing nearly a ton and a half and with a muzzle that yawned a full thirteen inches. It is a cheery note in a dark time that when this giant was dragged into Cambridge, Iz Putnam used its capacious interior for a punch bowl and Colonel Thomas Mifflin broached rum to christen it the *Congress*. No one seemed downcast over the fact that the mortar blew up at its first shot fired in anger.

Early December brought the last fine glow of the year. The New England skies seemed to turn softer, the thin winter air was gentler, and the bare elms along Brattle Street shed for the moment their grim starkness and traced graceful arabesques against the blue. An elaborate chariot rolled up the drive to halt before the Vassall house, and the young Virginian, George Baylor, flung open the carriage door and handed out a serene-faced woman whose eyes were suddenly bright through the fatigues of a long journey as she looked up at the blue-and-buff figure under the Vassall pediment. Martha Custis Washington had come to Cambridge, and for her coming the bleakest camps would take on a different air and men, counting the days until their enlistments were up, would forget to count.

There were others with her. Out of the depths of the chariot came motherly Mrs. Horatio Gates and Mr. and Mrs. Jack Custis, Virginians all, not paying a visit to an alien and distant colony but merely to a distant part of a common country.

So Martha Custis Washington settled herself as the hostess of the big Brattle Street house, presided at the long table for two o'clock dinner, received callers, and returned calls in company with her daughter-in-law, Eleanor Custis, and Mrs. Gates. Cambridge life, other than military, centered about her and is preserved in many notes in which "Mrs. Washington presents her respectful compliments" . . . "Mrs. Washington cannot help wishing for an oppertunity of shewing every civility in her power . . ." usually ending, "The General begs that his best regards may be presented to . . ."

There was need for her influence in the Vassall house and in Cambridge. The few flickers of light, such as Manly's capture of the *Nancy*, were soon cloud-wrapped, and hopeful prospects faded and faded. The commander-in-chief was faced with disheartening court-martials, notably that of Colonel Roger Enos, who with his men had turned back from Arnold's column in high north Maine. The court-martial properly acquitted Enos, for had his command stayed on to eat what rations were left, Arnold's whole force must have vanished forever in the hideous country beyond Dead River. But Enos brought back stories of men having to eat their roasted cartridge pouches, their moccasins. Dearborn's sagacious dog had gone into the common pot. Men died, miles from any mortal enemy, their hearts bursting as they forced their way up sodden forest ridges or slipped and floundered in boiling rapids. The tough frontier riflemen were dying, along with their comrades from New England farms and towns. There was only one amazing hopeful fact that Americans could work out of Enos' report. So far as he knew, the skeleton men were still driving north and west toward the St. Lawrence.

Mercifully the British stayed quiet, despite a change in command that had taken place in October, when the King graciously permitted "Blundering Tommy" Gage to return to England. Sir William Howe now reigned, but owing perhaps to his Breed's Hill combat fatigue, perhaps to a growing natural inertia, and perhaps to the delights of his definitely on-the-record ménage with Mrs. Joshua Loring, he did little.

If Howe had moved! In Washington's lines, polls were taken among the men whose time ran out in January. Barely one thousand out of the near twenty thousand who blockaded Boston allowed that, under certain conditions, they might not be averse to tarrying. The response from the Connecticut and Rhode Island troops was shattering. In the 8th Connecticut a test was made "to see who would stay in the service till the first of January, but not a man would engage." Stubbornly these units clung to their belief that their time was up on December first, and they would not wait until the discharge of the Massachusetts and New Hampshire men, let alone sign up for 1776.

Knife-like northwest winds, deep frost and snow seemed to play into Sir William Howe's hands. It looked more and more as though one day soon might find the rebel lines deserted and the leaders of the rebellion fleeing west past the dead campfires of their commands.

Strength and salvation came from an unexpected source. New Hampshire and Massachusetts called on their militia—Home Guards and State Guards, they would be termed now—and surprisingly the men turned out by hundreds and by thousands. The Continentals, the regulars, with their time about to expire and with little intent of renewing their enlistments, watched the home levies pour into the theater of the blockade with derision. They called them "the Long-faced People." As time-expired troops marched off, apparently careless of what might happen to the rest of the army, the militiamen (Sam Adams, always weak in spelling, wrote them down as "melitious men") took their places. The commander-in-chief had a breathing spell in which he could form a new army, as one had been formed in July, under the very muzzles of the British guns.

More and more news began to come in from the outside to show the men of the blockade, as the visit of Franklin, Harrison, and Lynch had shown them, that they were one fragment of a vast unity. From Philadelphia came word that the Congress had deliberated over giving Washington permission to burn Boston if that were the only means to drive out Howe. He was given a free hand to act as he saw fit. John Hancock, who surely might have been forgiven for thinking of his own huge holdings in the city, wrote Washington, "This passed, after a most serious debate . . . and execution referred to you. I most heartily wish it, though individually I may be the greatest sufferer."

News of mixed content came from another source. In November, Washington, who had been watching Henry Knox with increasing attention, had pulled him off his civilian status as sort of engineering consultant and installed him as chief of artillery with the rank of colonel. Now Henry had had to say au revoir to his Lucy and was at ruinous Ticonderoga on a very special mission. Many men had turned their eyes to the artillery in the star-shaped fort, but no one had made a move toward this gunner's treasure that would vastly strengthen the weakest arm of the American forces. Henry Knox, virtually alone, was faced with the problem of shifting this mass of ordnance from the west bank of Champlain, in the dead of winter, across a nearly roadless wilderness to western Massachusetts and thence over the heartbreaking ridges to the blockade of Boston.

This was a task equal in magnitude to Arnold's march through Maine to the St. Lawrence, but the ex-bookseller faced it calmly. In early December he wrote Washington that all was going well. General Schuyler was helping him. The guns were being dismounted and would be floated down Lake George and there transferred to sledges. In the hiring of help, oxen, and vehicles of all kinds, Schuyler was tireless, but the burden of the task remained squarely on Henry Knox and his well-padded shoulders.

To know this much was heady news at the Vassall house. The guns of Ticonderoga were starting east. But there were grimmer reports in the same letter. Knox had learned that Arnold had actually reached Quebec, had tried to storm the town from the famous Plains of Abraham, where Wolfe had struck back in '59. The attack never came off, and Arnold was now below the citadel and Montgomery was on his way east to complete an impromptu pincers movement. Yet many people with whom Henry Knox had talked were more than dubious of success.

This must have taken much of the edge off the news of Knox's own progress. The twin expedition might be lost for good. And—ominous note —the year was running out. All but the three companies of riflemen under Arnold's command would be free men, out of military service at midnight of the thirty-first of December. It must have taken deep, hard courage for any man to turn his thoughts as far ahead as January 1, 1776.

CHAPTER XIV

"... with a noble train of artillery"

ACROSS the Atlantic, George III could survey the new year of 1776 with a comfortable feeling that, despite the American troubles, he was drawing close to his ideal of what royal rule should be. He had a most obsequious Parliament and, more important, a Cabinet made up largely of yea-sayers, the eighteenth-century version of yes-men. He was particularly pleased with his latest ministerial acquisition, which was to turn out to be one of the worst choices possible. It is odd that the King's good memory did not snap out a danger signal and remind him of a court-martial sixteen years before.

The records of that trial set forth how one Colonel Sloper, being duly sworn, did depose and say that at the Battle of Minden in 1759 orders were sent to the leader of the British cavalry to launch his squadrons against the shattered French. The leader fumbled and mumbled, made excuses, and not a trooper rode out. Later another officer appeared and, Sloper went on, "I said . . . 'For God's sake repeat the orders to *that man*, that he may not pretend not to understand them. . . . You see the condition he is in.'"

Here the court instructed Witness Sloper to explain the phrase "*that man*," and the sturdy colonel answered, "My Lord George Sackville." There was more damning evidence. Sackville was clearly "alarmed to a great degree." He was in "the utmost confusion." A verdict was officially rendered that said Sackville be judged "unfit to serve His Majesty in any Military Capacity whatever."

It was lucky for the rebels that this sentence specified military capacities only. For, with his name changed by an inheritance to Lord George Germain, "that man" was taking office as Secretary of State for the American Colonies and for the American war. His many blunders and omissions were to be worth many battalions to those rebels.

The King felt no qualms about the appointment. Germain would follow royal thought and direction, and nothing else mattered. The American business would be wound up quickly and satisfactorily. There was a plan for making Quebec a major base as soon as the ice left the St. Lawrence and, with no climatic hazards, a strong fleet would be sent to blast out that nest of ungrateful vipers at Charleston in South Carolina. Prospects looked very good off there in the South. Governor Martin of North Carolina had assured him that the whole area swarmed with countless devoted Loyalists who would sweep out the rebels at the first glimpse of the Royal Navy along the sandy coast.

As for the rebels themselves, the King could chuckle a little. Allowing for Atlantic storms, January ought to bring to those perfidious people copies of his October message to Parliament. He had stigmatized that distant rising as "a desperate conspiracy" and declared that it was carried on for the purpose "of establishing an independent Empire." The gracious royal patience was at an end and would be replaced by strong measures of suppression. Not only were the army and navy to be enlarged, but treaties with foreign powers—the petty German princes—were under way.

George III was quite correct in his estimate of time. He was less fortunate in forecasting American reaction. Copies of his message were duly sent through the British lines, and the High Command in Boston settled down, with their honest, puzzled Tory backers, to watch the result. From the outposts on the Charlestown peninsula came reports of a strange new flag that had been raised suddenly on Prospect Hill in present Somerville. It had the familiar combined crosses of England and Scotland as a canton, and the rest of the banner was covered with thirteen alternate red and white stripes. A thrill of pleased expectancy ran through military and Loyalist circles in Boston. This new flag must be a sign of submission. Washington was quitting! Then came disillusionment. Out of the scanty powder stocks came a deep-throated artillery salute of thirteen guns. Perhaps Washington wasn't quitting after all.

If Boston Whigs and Tories could have looked over Washington's shoulder as he wrote, the former would have been greatly heartened and the latter profoundly depressed. Setting aside gnawing worry and discouragement, the outwardly calm and always unshakable Virginian put on paper his views of the King's message. "It is full of rancor and resentment against us, and explicitly holds forth his royal will to be, that vigorous measures must be pursued, to deprive us of our constitutional rights and liberties. These measures . . . will be opposed by more vigorous ones, and rendered unavailing and fruitless."

So Royalist Boston had to give up its feeble hopes of an end to the blockade and face again the grim struggle of existing, which occupied all waking hours and filled the nights with terrifying dreams. Life was becoming a very desperate matter, even for the most favored. Fuel was so scarce that it was virtually off the market, even though Howe ordered the fine elms along the Common to be chopped down for firewood. Food consisted, beyond a scanty and hazardous black market, of salt rations out of which Cunningham and Loring still managed to turn a profit. The sacred town bull, a venerable gentleman of twenty years or more, was slaughtered. The Boston Whigs were further dispirited by what was happening to their town. The North Meeting House was ripped down for fuel. In hallowed Faneuil Hall, Gentleman Johnny Burgoyne presided blandly over amateur dramatics. His gaudy 17th Dragoons, a fine body but as useless as the American riflemen in the blockade, cleared the pews out of the Old South Church and used the nave for a riding school. In the graceful white balcony the officers set up what would be called today a cocktail bar.

Merchant John Andrews wrote that for a Whig wood was twenty dollars a cord when you could get it. He himself had been forced often to burn horse droppings. Cheese and butter were two shillings a pound. "Milk, for months without tasting any." George III might have found the closing lines of Andrews' letter far more illuminating than reports from royal governors telling of vast armies of Tories ready to rise for the Crown. Andrews wrote simply, "Notwithstanding which, Bill, I can safely say that I have never suffer'd the least depression of spirits . . . for a perswasion that my country would eventually prevail, kept up my spirits and never suffer'd my hopes to fail."

Had our merchant been able to look at the other side of the fourteen-mile line that shut Boston off from America, he might have had to cling still harder to his "perswasion." The whole American army was breaking up as the Connecticut contingents had broken, and re-enlistments were mortally slow to materialize. Letter after letter went inland from the camps telling how "this Day we have ben In an uprore about packun our Things up In order to go Home a monday morning." Muskets were still in terribly short supply, and many men were issued spears or pikes for weapons. Benjamin Franklin seriously suggested reviving the bow and arrow as being very cheaply made, silent, and allowing rapidity of fire far beyond the musket or rifle. His idea was not as fantastic as it sounds today. Well into the nineteenth century some quite high British brass toyed with the same notion, recalling the glories of the British bowmen at Crécy and Agincourt.

But one major worry found relief. Agents in Europe and in the West Indies had been busy, and powder began to flow in from France and Spain and the Sugar Islands. And as January drifted along under its gray skies, a tremendous and largely forgotten epic was being played out. Henry Knox was coming east with what he described as "a noble train of artillery" from Ticonderoga.

The corpulent young Boston bookseller loaded heavy pieces on makeshift barges and started them up Lake George. A barge sank, but Knox grubbed the cannon up from the bottom of the lake cheerfully and efficiently. Sledges were ready to start him overland from the head of the lake, but a sudden thaw immobilized sledges, oxen, and horses. Patiently Knox waited, consulted with the ever-helpful Philip Schuyler, perfected his plans for keeping his hired teams and teamsters on the go, sent letters warning and rewarning the members of the various Committees of Safety that lay along his route. There must be food and shelter for man and beast. Horses and oxen might give out, sledges might smash on roof-steep slopes, so there must be replacements available. He foresaw a hundred eventualities and provided for them as best he could. The guns must go through.

Snow fell, the roads froze, and the long train of artillery, carefully packed on the sledges, was under way again. Knox crossed the Hudson at Claverack, plunged on east. The rolling Taconics were ahead of him, and somehow his teamsters worked their panting beasts through the low passes. He was in Massachusetts, at Great Barrington with the high Berkshire Hills about it, and he wrote to Lucy of his activities, saying that he was bouncing about like a tennis ball.

Great Barrington was passed, and he watched his endless string of sledges crawl up the very eaves of the Berkshires and was amazed at the relative speed of his progress. There were snowy slopes, twisting ridge roads which hoofs and runners churned into glue, narrow trails that clung to a pine-thick hillside with a white torrent snarling over slick, black rocks just below the other side of the trail. The teamsters swore and cursed and panted as they prodded their animals on. They became homesick for Old York State and demanded to be released. Knox argued and cajoled and pleaded with them. They remained dissatisfied, swore louder—but stayed on with their teams. Somehow, big smiling Henry had conveyed to them his one dominant credo. The guns must go through.

Out onto the floor of the Connecticut River Valley the convoy lurched, and at Springfield, according to contract, the Yorkers and their beasts were sent home. Then another thaw struck and there was trouble engaging Massachusetts teams and teamsters. Patiently, calmly, as though tracking down a rare title for a valued customer, the young colonel of artillery waited out nature and soothed ruffled committeemen. Cold weather came and the train moved out, heading for the last high bastion of hills. At Palmer he delighted the townsfolk by squandering enough powder to fire a salute from one vast Ticonderoga mortar, known to history as the Old Sow. If the Palmerites needed heartening, it was there for them in the knowledge that the huge, squat weapon would soon be thundering just outside Boston.

Through Leicester and Worcester, up the great escarpment where Marlboro lay, Henry Knox cheered on his crews and kept hoof and runner gliding from dawn to sundown. Then on January 18, 1776, the long column wound into Framingham, after a little more than ten days on the road, counting from the crossing of the Hudson. At Framingham the whole train was halted, teams and teamsters dismissed, and the colonel of artillery made out his last inventory. There were fifty-nine pieces of ordnance, ranging from squat little coehorns to twenty- and twenty-four-pound cannon and giant mortars like the Old Sow. The "noble train of artillery" was ready to take its place along Washington's thin fourteen-mile line. No one could have guessed it at the time, but Knox's feat, although actual results were delayed, wrote the final chapter to the blockade of Boston.

Late winter lay bland on Philadelphia. In the towered State House the logs of the twin fireplaces set up a muted perfunctory crackle as President John Hancock ruled over the Continental Congress. There was hot and increasing tension on the floor, and members spoke long and earnestly or burst into florid oratory as their tempers might dictate. They passed carefully written notes from seat to seat. During recesses they leaned against the paneled walls, walked with bowed heads through the wide corridor, arguing, pleading, denouncing, riposting. They climbed to one another's lodgings to talk late into the night, paced soberly along Market Street, probably unaware of glaze-hatted sailors, carriages that ground over the cobbles, housemaids clattering about in pattens, or boys from the bakeshops with their loads of warm, richly scented loaves. Broadcloth elbow and homespun elbow, gold-laced beaver and shabby felt hat rubbed and bobbed side by side as the delegates walked, talked, and supped together. Slowly these men of conscience felt their way step by step, fumbling ahead through mists where there was no precedent to guide them toward a rational form of life to be sought for the thirteen colonies now frequently termed states.

A tremendous upgrade lay ahead of them, and not even the wisest or the most obstinate could be quite sure which was the right and just path to the summit. Few people could say that the ascent might not be by-passed. Divisions in the Congress were sharp and often bitter. It was no longer a matter of Whig against Tory, of rebel against Loyalist. The last true Tory, Joseph Galloway, no longer sat with the body, and even some of the more radical regretted the loss of his integrity and wisdom, misguided as he might seem to them. But other alignments were making themselves felt. What was the true relation between the States and England?

On one side of the widening gulf stood John Dickinson, James Wilson, and Robert Morris of Pennsylvania, with James Duane of New York. This quartet drew the support of those who felt that while the position of the Crown was wrong there should be a return to amicable relations—as soon as American grievances were redressed.

Their opponents, in the main, seem to have been as anxious for a reconciliation but felt that it was now impossible, that it lay beyond the utmost purple dream. Here were aligned John Adams, opposition spokesman in Conservative eyes, backed by Christopher Gadsden, the Virginians George Wythe, Richard Henry Lee, and Francis Lightfoot Lee. Samuel Adams, so prominent before, was now in the background. Not only was he thought too radical, but men felt that he spoke as a Massachusetts man, not as an American like his cousin John.

One word bobbed up increasingly in the debates, to the deep distress of the conservatives. Independence. When John Rutledge first saw it in a resolution by the South Carolina Provincial Congress, he broke into uncontrollable tears. The South Carolina resolution, which had shocked Henry Laurens, president of the legislature, nearly as much as Rutledge, seemed a mild enough document to many congressmen, a permission given the South Carolina delegates to use their own judgment. A step farther north up the coast, the North Carolina Assembly flat-footedly instructed its delegates to "apply to Mr. John Adams for his views on the form of government they should assume—if independence be declared."

The harassed conservatives wheeled up their heaviest guns. The states could not survive if independent. Separation from Great Britain meant suicide. And anyway, Parliament and the Cabinet were the villains, not the King from whom all charters sprang. Why, look at George Washington up there before Boston. Didn't he call the enemy "the Ministerial Soldiers"?

He wrote that he could not bring himself to refer to them as "The King's Troops." One exasperated voice cried, "I feel like a child being thrust violently out of his father's house!" Less scrupulous conservatives, recognizing John Adams as the focal point of the independence movement, began a smear campaign in Philadelphia and in the states themselves. Adams had been in league with Benjamin Church. He had fled Philadelphia and was on board a British ship, London-bound. He was secretly and skillfully working to undermine Washington.

Through debate, counsel, and slander, John Adams moved steadily on. He knew exactly where the one sure road into the future lay and, in his sureness, took on a sort of arrogance, the exasperating self-confidence of the man who feels that he is right. His strong voice rolled on and on, hammering his message home. "Nothing can save us but discipline in the army, governments in every colony and a confederation of the whole." John Jay or John Dickinson might rebut every point brought up, but when they had done, Adams was on his feet again, shouting, "A union and a confederation of thirteen states, independent of parliament, of minister and of king!"

John Adams was not playing a lone hand, nor was he dominating a group of lesser minds, molding them to his own will and thought. Able and devoted as he was, he was only expressing the dynamism of America. He was effect and not cause, as Cousin Sam had been in Massachusetts. Now, unexpectedly, his words were underscored heavily and sent broadcast over the country.

Sponsored by Benjamin Franklin, an Englishman in his late thirties had come to America and, looking about him, had somehow found the phrases to express in non-congressional terms those "felt necessities of the times." His name was Thomas Paine and his forty-seven-page pamphlet, entitled with striking brevity *Common Sense*, was caught up in the mysterious air currents of the year 1776 and swept blizzard-like into every state. A man or woman did not have to be a jurist, an expert in political economy, to follow Paine's message.

British-born and -bred, he could express himself with a freedom that might be denied a writer who had known only America, and he attacked royalty with a vehemence that made some radicals wince. But mere abuse is a tricky weapon, and the pages of *Common Sense* soon soared above it. Wherever men could read or listen to reading in the thirteen states, phrase after phrase rang out, bit deep, and was remembered. " 'T is not the affair of a city, a country, a province or a kingdom, but of a continent. . . . Now is the seeding time of continental union, faith and honor. . . . Time hath found us. Time hath found us! O! ye that love mankind, stand forth. . . . Ye that dare oppose not only the tyranny but the tyrant, stand forth! O! receive the fugitive, and prepare in time an asylum for mankind."

There was much in Paine's work that was easily rebutted. He made flamboyant overstatements, wild charges and claims. The ideal state that he outlined was definitely alien to American thought. But clamorous trumpets sounded through his words, and the drums of the future beat deeply and heavily as men read or listened. And when the reader had turned the last page, a single line of huge, bold black type stood out in his memory, a simple, daring line that read: THE FREE AND INDEPENDENT STATES OF AMERICA.

In the whirling tempo of Philadelphia the delegates to the Congress may well have been anesthetized against bad news from the outside by their absorption in the one great problem of independence, an absorption that may have enabled them to roll with the punch. There was Canada, for example, and the high hopes in the twin expedition.

Now it was known that Arnold and Montgomery had met before Quebec, had attacked the Lower Town in a blinding blizzard—and failed utterly. Bit by bit details came through to the State House and its brick walls. Richard Montgomery was dead, killed at the very start of the assault. Benedict Arnold was badly wounded. Huge Captain Dan Morgan of Virginia was a prisoner. Captured, too, were Henry Dearborn of New Hampshire, Return Meigs of Connecticut, Christopher Greene of Rhode Island, and Christian Febiger, the Dane. And these were mere samplings from lists that trickled in to the Congress.

This might have been a time to cut losses, withdraw what was left of the two expeditions and return them to the parent main army. Instead, it was resolved to send more troops, bolster up the forces in Canada, and try again. Somehow or other, Canada must be secured. New England could spare a regiment or two for the cause, and a more truly American flavor was given to that Northern army by the inclusion of Pennsylvania troops to join the New Englanders and the New Yorkers.

With the Pennsylvania decision, two figures at once stepped out of the local picture and, for all time, into the national. Commanding one of the Pennsylvania regiments was a tall, red-haired native of Scotland, Arthur St. Clair, like Gates and Lee and the dead Montgomery, late of His Majesty's service. St. Clair was competent, inclined to be morose, prone to overestimate his enemy. Worst of all, he was unlucky. In vivid contrast to the Scot, young Colonel Anthony Wayne marched out in command of the 4th Pennsylvania. Scion of a wealthy stock-breeding family of Chester County, Wayne brought a much-needed dash of color to the grim expedition. He was above average height, well built, and remarkably handsome. His wavy dark hair was usually powdered, and his deep-set hazel eyes could snap out natural fire as easily as they could laugh. A self-taught soldier like Knox and Greene, he had been very active in Whig politics in Pennsylvania, and there seems to have been little or no opposition when the thirty-year-old was jumped into command of the 4th Pennsylvania. He was to show a natural flair for soldiering, with emphasis on the attack, but he was level-headed enough on most occasions to allow for possible retreat in his most violent onsets. He had an almost Gallic flair for word and gesture, for true panache, and was frankly fond of display, but always with a keen eye on the effects of such trappings on the men he was to lead. Later he was to write Washington, "I must acknowledge that I have an insuperable bias in favor of an elegant uniform and soldierly appearance; so much so that I would rather risk my life and reputation at the head of the same men in an attack, clothed and appointed as I could wish, merely with bayonets and a single charge of ammunition, than to take them as they appear in common with sixty rounds of cartridges. It may be a false idea, but I cannot help cherishing it."

So the new forces set out for Canada and a campaign that was to trail off and off in disaster until its remnants were carried up the Richelieu, up Champlain, until they came to a panting halt by De Lotbinière's star bastions at Ticonderoga. It may be wondered what Congress would have decided about Canada had the searing question of independence been settled. There is almost a hint of absent-mindedness as this military problem was waved away, a mere interruption in the main trend of congressional thought.

There was another annoying non-political interruption. Washington reported that Sir Henry Clinton had left Boston Harbor with five ships. Where was he going? Congress gave the impression of looking up irritably from its papers and finally prayed that the skilled book soldier, Charles Lee, be sent with a force to whatever point Clinton might threaten. There were no troops to spare, so Charles Lee set out gaily alone on a ride that would take him through Connecticut, to New York, where the little fleet showed itself momentarily, and at last to South Carolina and the flat ground between the Ashley and the Cooper where Charleston lay.

It was February, and the clans were out in North Carolina with bagpipe and kilt and bonnet and claymore and musket. From dozens of settlements they had rallied as surely as they had rallied for Glencoe and Killiecrankie and Prestonpans and Culloden, and now they poured over the hillocks and marshes that drained off into the Cape Fear River. Most of them were men who had cast their lot with the Stuarts in '45 and had been virtually deported by families, by whole villages, out of their beloved Highlands by command of Hanoverian George II. To them had come in 1774 their heroine, Flora Macdonald, who had saved Bonnie Prince Charlie after Culloden. Her counsel and that of her husband Allan weighed heavily with them but, oddly enough, seems to have played little part in the present foray.

It might have been thought that claymore and musket would be taken up to strike a blow against the hated victors of Culloden, against the royal house that had driven the clans out of the purple Scottish hills. But, impelled by some logic or emotion peculiar to themselves, they carried the royal standard and their objective was Wilmington on the coast, where they hoped to make contact with the King's troops as allies. On their way they expected to brush aside a reported rebel force marching northwest toward them.

So the Highlanders came on, McDonalds and McGregors and Camerons and McLeods and McDowells, led by one Donald McDonald. Hardship, faintheartedness, lack of conviction thinned their ranks, but there were still more than fifteen hundred of them when contact was made with a major rebel force near a plank bridge across Moore's Creek, a tributary of the South River that, in turn, flowed into the Cape Fear.

The rebel force of a thousand-odd, which had grown by slow accretions under Colonels Richard Caswell and John Lillington, gouged trenches among the laurel and myrtle bushes that sprang out of the sandy soil, siting them on the creek bank toward the Scots' advance. Someone, probably Caswell or Lillington, realized that it was not good practice to fight with a body of water at one's back and fell back to the far side, where works were again thrown up.

In a soft February morning, in the uncertain light that hovers between dawn and sunrise, Donald McDonald's advance came to the abandoned works by the creek, reasoned falsely that empty trenches meant empty countryside, and rushed the bridge. Caswell and Lillington were more than ready. Musketry smashed into the head of the attacking column, shattered it, sent it reeling back. With surprising promptness for hastily raised troops, a counterattack was launched and the sun, coming up from over the misty sand bars at the mouth of the Cape Fear, lit up flying knots of kilted men, climbed higher to glow somberly on ghastly drifts of kilted dead. McDonald's coup was ruined and his force irretrievably scattered.

Caswell and Lillington and their well-handled men had won an immensely important victory. The rising of the Highlanders was just as much a Tory move as though Brigadier General Ruggles had knifed through Washington's works at the head of the Massachusetts Loyalists. The rising had failed utterly and dismally, and for months to come the Tories of North Carolina were to be a negligible factor. Their sympathizers in South Carolina were affected nearly as deeply. When Henry Clinton and Admiral Peter Parker finally joined forces off the sand bars that hem both Carolina coasts, they found no Loyalist tide rushing to meet them. Had the fight at Moore's Creek Bridge turned out differently, the Tories might well have been in the saddle, the rebels in full retreat, and the Revolution in the South might have come to a sudden end. As it was, the rebel cause in those states was vastly strengthened. So were the hands of their representatives in the Continental Congress, where the word "independence" was being uttered more and more boldly and where Carolinians could mention with deep pride the date February 27, 1776.

The Carolinas relapsed into an uneasy calm, but with the advent of March, activity flared unexpectedly in another and distant theater of war, for about Boston, George Washington was initiating a quick and far-reaching move.

A British private in a post facing south out of Boston saw that move at last. The private, impressed, reported to his corporal—or so events may be plausibly reconstructed—and the corporal told the nearest sergeant, who told his appropriate subaltern, who told his field officer, who flew at once to the brigadier general in charge of the sector, bursting with his news.

The field officer would have done better had he jumped the routine chain of command and gone straight to William Howe, for the brigadier was none other than that same Francis Smith of the 10th Lincolnshires, who had led the expedition into Middlesex County nearly a year ago. Smith's promotion was, of course, by purchase and utterly unhampered by any absurd question of merit, and Francis Smith was the same lethargic man he had been before his elevation. He received the news, which was certainly alarming—and sat on it.

Lacking any warning, Howe must have thought that he was seeing the day of Breed's Hill all over again, though its focus was shifted geographically. Working with amazing speed and still more amazing silence, Washington had fortified the Heights of Dorchester, which had been neglected by both sides up to now. Howe and Percy—Burgoyne was back in England and Clinton was bucketing about somewhere at sea—could look out onto the Heights and stare in wonder. The British commander was stung into observing that the American troops had done more in one night than his whole force could have accomplished in a month. There were fine, solid entrenchments, well sited and apparently well manned. Many of the guns that Henry Knox had dragged from Ticonderoga were cunningly emplaced and, facing the steepest slopes, great barrels and hogsheads of rocks were delicately poised, ready to be sent pitching headlong down the hill and onto any attacking column. With a good glass Howe could pick out the long weapons of five companies of riflemen, in addition to countless musket-bearing formations. Heavy booming told him that more of Knox's guns had gone into position across the Charles at Lechmere Point and on Cobble Hill, facing Charlestown.

Most of this had been made possible by the Boston bookseller's "noble train of artillery," the freer flow of powder to the army, and the slow but steady build-up of the new regiments.

There was little that Howe could do. Dorchester Heights presented him with another Breed's Hill, but a hill far better fortified, manned by plenty of well-led men, and, most important, backed by formidable artillery. Those guns commanded Boston itself and a good part of the Royal Fleet. Howe's own cannon, while in ample supply, were unable to make even a gesture toward shelling out this new threat. From their low battery positions the British guns could not even reach the most advanced outworks up there on the Heights.

The British commander, with the shock of Breed's Hill strong upon him, showed that his military courage was still intact. He massed his flank companies, his shock troops, and made ready for a water-borne attack against the Heights of Dorchester, but what was locally termed a "Hurrycan" swept up from the south and he called off the coup, more than ever convinced of its suicidal nature, weather or no weather.

Now, possibly to his relief, his decision was made for him. He had to get out of Boston and chose Nova Scotia as his next base. To move the army was simple enough, but how about the swarms of Tories who had fled to Boston and the protection of the British flag? Harbor and coast line were combed and every craft that could possibly face the stormy Northern voyage was commandeered. Sir William would not abandon those who had placed their faith in him and in the Crown.

By hundreds and by thousands the unfortunate Tories pigged in on board the ships assigned to them. Other ships were crammed with their possessions, and the tonnage devoted to such transport seems surprisingly large in view of the fact that so many had come to Boston empty-handed. But there were unscrupulous people among those Tories, as in any group of hundreds and thousands. Also, there were acquisitive men like William Cunningham, and many a Whig returning to Boston found his house or his warehouses gutted despite promises of protection.

Early on the morning of March 17 American outposts began shouting. All Boston seemed strangely abandoned. Small boats, deep-laden with black hats and red coats, were seen pushing out into the harbor mists. Someone sent for General John Sullivan, who stared through a glass at the Charlestown works. No action. No motion. But he could see a few red-clad sentinels and pickets about. He may have scented something in the air, or it may have been the stimulus of St. Patrick's Day. Whatever the cause, Sullivan arranged for a strong reconnaissance party and led it with commendable caution over ground that would have been death to cross a few hours before. He and his men entered the first works and found crude dummies draped in worn-out scarlet. One of them bore a placard reading, "Welcome, Brother Jonathan."

Joyously John Sullivan reported his mission. "I sent for a strong force to follow us onto the hill, to assist us in running away (if necessary). . . . I then brought on the party to secure what we had so bravely won and went down to the other works, where we found all abandoned. . . . We then informed the General."

The thoughtful Virginian seems to have indulged in no particular outburst of joy over the news. Perhaps he had expected evacuation when Howe's attack on the Heights failed to materialize. He may have felt that any exulting was premature, since the great flotilla lay off Nantasket Roads for some days and its commander might be contemplating a descent on some other part of the New England coast. Or he may have considered rejoicing a waste of time. He issued a few swift orders and then remained in Cambridge, applying himself to the unending task of command.

As a result of those orders, Sullivan's men swarmed into Charlestown. At the other end of the line Iz Putnam issued a call for pock-marked men only, as there was known to be smallpox in Boston and such men would be immune to it. Some five hundred good infantrymen, suitably scarred, were gathered under Artemas Ward, who had seen the blockade of Boston open and who would now close it.

His column went onto the Neck, where Colonel Ebenezer Learned of the 3rd Continental Infantry made a ceremony of throwing open the main gates of the big barricade. Headed by a young ensign carrying the flag with the British Union in the canton above the thirteen stripes, the column filed in over the narrow Neck. Progress was slow, for the British had sprinkled the road with iron caltrops or crow's-feet, nasty spiked objects that presented a sharp point upward no matter how they were thrown.

More men under Putnam himself were landing at Sewall's Point, and Bostonians began emerging timidly from their houses at the sound of marching feet and the shrill of fifes and the snap of drums. They stared hesitantly, almost unbelievingly, and then began to cheer, though to some of the troops the cheers sounded thin and feeble. James Thacher, surgeon to the 6th Continentals, noted that while the people seemed happy and relieved they were in a state of shock, as though the long months of virtual captivity, short rations, and harsh discipline had dampened some spark in them.

Once in the city, Putnam flew about with his usual energy, taking stock. There was less actual damage than he had expected, barring the conversion of several churches into barracks, riding halls, or firewood. There had been a good deal of last-minute looting, and the contents of grocery shops near the wharves had been dumped into the streets, along with a gruesome mixture of molasses and salt. There were gutted houses and storage buildings, but it might have been worse. Odd omissions were exclaimed over. There was John Hancock's house, for example, the home of that arch-rebel and president of the rebel Congress. It was virtually untouched, and some of his warehouses were marked with the royal seal by way of special protection.

Then "Old Put" was crying out over abandoned royal stores. Over three thousand blankets in excellent condition, stand after stand of small arms, powder, shot, shoes. What sort of commander was Billy Howe to leave such stuff behind when his whole flotilla, off there in the harbor mouth, numbered over one hundred and seventy sail? There was more good news, and John Sullivan, still riding the crest of St. Patrick's Day, galloped up with the gleeful report that nearly seventy pieces of ordnance in good condition were now available to Washington's army.

Israel Putnam was a Connecticut man and a New Englander. But he took great care to assume possession of this treasure in the name of the "United Colonies."

The next day General George Washington quietly entered Boston, that city which had been hardly an entity to him through the long blockade, just the name of a place that lay somewhere over beyond the Charles or behind the barriers on the Neck. He made, so far as we know, no dramatic speech or gesture in taking over the town. He attended divine worship, asking Dr. Eliot, dean of the Boston clergy, to preach a sermon of thanksgiving and not of war. Dr. Eliot thought of Isaiah, and the commander-in-chief may well have bowed his head as the old minister announced his text: "Look upon Zion, the city of our solemnities: thine eyes shall see

Jerusalem a quiet habitation, a tabernacle that shall not be taken down."

Strength and comfort could be drawn from those words. But even a man in prayer must think about that flotilla off Nantasket Roads and wonder where it would make its next landfall.

CHAPTER XV

Men and Palmettos

AS each month accumulated its events and dumped them into the next month like a growing rockslide, many eyes that were neither British nor American began to turn more and more west across the Atlantic. Moving elegantly between Paris and Versailles, Charles Gravier, Comte de Vergennes, erstwhile Ambassador to the Sublime Porte and to Sweden, now Minister of Foreign Affairs for Louis XVI of France, found the world growing perceptibly brighter.

As a good foreign minister, his chief aim was to recoup the French losses that came out of the Treaty of Paris, signed thirteen long years ago, and the only true path to such recouping lay through the destruction of British power, a somewhat ambitious project, as other ministers and rulers have found. But the dire troubles that England was suddenly facing over there in North America suggested to the astute count that there might lie the lever and fulcrum to topple the ancient cross-Channel enemy.

Vergennes could always find able, pliant agents when he needed them, and now he seized upon the rather equivocal person of Caron de Beaumarchais, courtier, dramatist, financier, whose immortal *Le Barbier de Séville* had been unveiled the year before. Beaumarchais was sent to England to take the stolid British pulse, a mission which he accomplished in the midst of balls, minuets, elegant snuff-taking, and candlelit salons. His final report to Vergennes was more than satisfactory.

With royal assent, the Count opened deft and polished negotiations with Grimaldi, his haughty opposite number in the Cabinet of Charles III of Spain. Grimaldi was receptive, in a rather icy way, for Spain had suffered along with France in that treaty of 1763.

These negotiations had to be handled most delicately, for if wind of them came to the ears of Viscount Stormont, British Ambassador to France, there would be exquisitely, acidly polite notes in which it would be stated that His Britannic Majesty's Government found itself unable to view with equanimity such plans as were brewing. But the secret seems to have been well kept, and in May of 1776 France and Spain decided jointly to furnish the colonists with one million livres' worth of munitions, an immense sum at that time. This was not a helping hand stretched out to further the ideals of the American rebels, nor did either of the High Contracting Powers view it as such. Both owned colonies and hence could hardly relish the example of any overseas possessions revolting against royalty. Nor could either power actually relish the idea of aid to a potential nation that was then largely Protestant. But for the moment the important thing was to nibble away at any prop that held up the British Empire.

Of course both nations were on terms of official amity with England and munitions could not be sent openly. So Vergennes and Grimaldi craftily set up a dummy company and thereafter blandly ignored its existence, though not its purpose. The company was prosaically chartered as Roderigue Hortalez et Cie., a commercial undertaking without the faintest of governmental connections. And since in the manner of the times there would be innumerable clusters of ripe financial plums to be plucked as a side issue, who was more worthy to head this trading concern than one Pierre Augustin Caron de Beaumarchais?

These coldly practical negotiations between Vergennes and Grimaldi may be looked upon as one of the solidest blocks to be built into the eventual structure of American success. It is hard to see how the colonies could have carried on without the war supplies that poured in a dozen American ports. And from such sub rosa aid it was only a step to the last clinching act which brought French fleets and French armies to North America and to that swampy, hot peninsula between the York and the James where the old tobacco port of Yorktown lay slowly dying.

So great was the flow of munitions during the year 1776–77 that some 80 per cent of the powder used by American troops came from Hortalez et Cie. and its charming, frivolous director, Beaumarchais. And this powder was none other than the incomparable product of the great scientist Lavoisier.

Sir Henry Clinton, weeks afloat with his small flotilla, was finding that the frustrations of the blockade of Boston could be repeated at sea and offshore. He had touched near the mouth of the Cape Fear River in North Carolina, expecting the hordes of Loyalists of whom Governor Martin had spoken and written so hearteningly. Had the clans delayed their march, Sir Henry might have found valuable reinforcements and a solid core of supporters of the King. But Richard Caswell and John Lillington had scattered the Highlanders and other Loyalists beyond any hope of rallying. To the south the royal cause looked no better, for there Colonel Richard Richardson had paralyzed the Crown adherents and seized many of their leaders in his grim "Snow Campaign" that had swept up beyond the rushing Enoree.

Sir Henry could only lie off the North Carolina coast, waiting for seaborne reinforcements that he believed to be on their way to join him. To hurry the slow days, he wrote long letters to his sister in England, unrolling for her the great living map of the New World. He told her of swamp and cedar grove, of heavy stretches of myrtle and grassy meadows called savannas that bloomed with wild "hunnisuckle." And there were "prickle-paires" for her to wonder at and "offencive animals" like the "wipping snake that lashed men unmercifully and two of which would kill a horse!" About his keels were endless shoals of fish that grunted like hogs, "of great Size, but well-tasted."

Then over the horizon masts bristled and sails glowed golden and Sir Henry's nature studies came to an end. Admiral Peter Parker had arrived with warships and transports, the troops being under command of Major General the Earl of Cornwallis. The choice of Charles Cornwallis Cornwallis probably seemed an odd one to most Britons. His beginnings had been impeccable—Eton, Clare College at Cambridge, the Grenadier Guards, service in Germany, A.D.C. to the King, Gentleman of the Bedchamber, and Member of Parliament. Then he abruptly left the rails of right thinking, came out very heavily against the right of taxing the colonies —not the expediency—and, when that right was upheld, dropped out of political life and retired to the country, marrying a girl with the delightful name of Jemima Tullikens. Yet despite his opposition to the Crown policies, here he was, a full major general, en route to suppress those very colonists for whose rights he had jeopardized his career. He was the ablest of the British high brass and, after the Revolution, went on to notable triumphs, military and civil, in India and Ireland.

So the two fleets headed south, lurching through the bright days and soft nights of late May, bowsprits dipping through palm-green waters and masts tracing invisible arcs against the blue curve of the sky. Out of sight to the west was the coast of South Carolina, sheltered by an endless chain of narrow sandy islands that lay like yellow daggers touched with the green patina of palmetto and wild myrtle. Beyond the islands lay the true shore line, edged with deep blue lagoons and livid green tidal marshes. More than halfway down the coast was the objective of this task force, the city of Charleston ashimmer in the sun on the flattish tongue of land between the Cooper and the Ashley rivers, the only great American port south of Philadelphia.

It was the first dawn of June, but already Charlestonians were peering from the little round windows set high in the soaring white spire of St. Michael's Church on Meeting Street. The city below them, where "houses stand sidewaies backward into their yard, and only endwaies with their gable toward the street," looked much as it had five years or a decade ago, much as it does today. There was the stuccoed elegance of the Miles Brewton house on King Street, the Horry house on Meeting Street, the Mottes' on Church, or the Alstons' on Tradd. Men in white planters' suits and broad straw hats moved antlike, the rap of their boots on fresh-washed stone swallowed up long before the sound reached the little tower windows.

There were few about those windows or lower-level openings who dropped more than a quick glance at the familiar street pattern below, for along the water front and far beyond it were sights that could not have been seen five years—or five weeks—ago. Charleston voices, rising muted within the spire shell, made grave comment. "Can see right down to the water now." . . . "All those warehouses, lofts, store sheds, ripped down or shoved into the harbor. Rebuilding will take a lot of money." . . . "Can't be helped. They masked the old batteries and bastions. Our gunners have got to have a good field of fire." . . . "Right. It had to be done. The cost doesn't count." Already Charleston was unconsciously establishing title to the later state motto: *Animis Opibusque Parati*, which might be roughly translated as "Ready with Mind and Means."

As one looked farther out, the dazzle of the new sun made eyes water and eyelids flick, but off to the left front, some two miles away, men could make out a black-yellow smudge that was the lower tip of Sullivan's Island, shutting in the upper harbor end. The familiar landmark was changed. "Cleared away all that scrub myrtle on the spine of the island." . . . "Yes, most of the palmettos down, too. Don't see much but sand, when you can see anything." . . . "The fort looks close to finished, but they say not." . . . "Lot of work to be done. Star-shaped walls, double, made of the palmetto logs, and the space between filled with sand. Sounds flimsy." . . . "Nothing else to build with. Palmetto or nothing." Inside the spire, below in the belfry and past the four-faced clock, pigeons muttered angrily over the invasion of their domain, swooped out in wide, fluttering cartwheels through the still, dawn air.

"Make out any of our people yonder on Sullivan's?" . . . "Too far. There are boats putting out from Haddrell's Point for the island, though." There was a silence in the high tower as memories recalled "our people yonder." Days ago the 2nd South Carolina Foot had marched through the streets, file after file of faces that were mostly familiar as Granville's Bastion or Vanderhorst's Creek. The sun had flashed on visored skullcaps, their high front plates marked with a silver crescent. Women had leaned from Church Street windows to exclaim over the dark blue jackets and red facings, the immaculate sheen of white waistcoats and breeches, the lift and drop of well-greased boots. The South Carolinian rarely counted pennies or pounds, whether he was betting on horse races, sending thousands of guineas' worth of supplies to unknown people in far-off Boston, or demolishing a water front in time of crisis, and he had not stinted the early state regiments. Like the others, the 2nd was a smart, well-equipped, and well-drilled outfit, though the Carolina ideal of organization—"officered by gentlemen with hired soldiers in the ranks"—would have shocked egalitarians in some states farther north.

Mentally, the watchers in the tower were calling the roll of the regiment out there. There was the Colonel, William Moultrie, able, affable, and inclined to be indolent, his heavy face always ready to break into a smile that was known from the Bay Street to the High Way. His lieutenant colonel was as much a part of Charleston as St. Michael's spire, from which people could look down on Isaac Motte's house at Tradd and Church streets. Motte's value in these times was increased by prior service as an officer in His Majesty's 60th Foot. Like Moultrie, Motte was a neighbor, a known quantity.

It was a little different in the case of the 2nd's major. He was not a Charlestonian, did not even come from a neighboring county or parish. Berkeley County, some people said, or even the Waccamaw area. Not a military-looking man like Moultrie or Motte. Very small, almost frail, and wizened and swarthy, a man who didn't look hearty enough to be a soldier. He was known to speak very little, and then in monosyllables. Just the same, he'd had a good record in the Cherokee Wars and his men obeyed him quickly and with respect. A Huguenot, of course, like the Horrys and the Manigaults and the Trapiers. Marion—Major Francis Marion. They said he had a little plantation up the Santee not far from Eutaw Springs. So the silent roll call went on.

Off to the right James Island lay, closing off the lower end of the harbor as Sullivan's blocked the upper, and on its near tip crouched the almost finished Fort Johnson. And here again Charlestonians could satisfy themselves with familiar, reassuring names. Christopher Gadsden, who had marched shoulder to shoulder with Yankee John Adams, was now out of Congress and serving as colonel of the 1st Foot, blue and red like the 2nd. Charles Cotesworth Pinckney and William Cattell filled the other field ranks and with the "hired soldiers" guarded the lower approaches to the city.

The 1st on James Island and the 2nd on Sullivan's were not merely precautionary garrisons. An alarm from the north, weeks ago, had set men digging, hauling cannon, clearing fields of fire, and now the alarm had materialized into reality and had sent Charleston civilians climbing to every high point to stare eastward through the rising sun. Far out to sea, ghostly through the tinted mists, showed clouds of sailcloth. Peter Parker's fleet had arrived and dropped anchor off Five Fathom Hole. And the favoring winds that brought the flotilla, the bow waves of frigate, bomb ketch, and transport, pushed on into Charleston, and the city and the far lands behind it detached themselves from the local scene and slid into the national, as Boston and its hinterland had done before them. Parker, Clinton, and Cornwallis threatened an American port, not a port of South Carolina.

June days glided by and still the combined fleets lay idle at their anchorage. The commanders had arrived at their goal and then suddenly discovered that they had no idea of what to do now that their voyage was ended. In eighteenth-century warfare this lack of planning was not unusual. Years before, a powerful naval and military force had closed in on a rich Spanish-American port, with no step planned beyond the dropping of anchors. A series of heated military and naval conferences followed aboard the admiral's flagship, conferences, oddly enough, not concerned with the next steps but with the sharing of the vast plunder that would fall to this force when, as, and if the port were taken. Proceeding more directly, Parker and his fellows actually set to work to map out a concerted plan of attack, but agreement always hung over the horizon and the ships rocked sluggishly at anchor.

Every day wasted by the British command showed heavily on the credit side of the Charleston ledger. Along Tradd Street, in front of the Dock Street Theatre, under the columned portico of St. Michael's, people passed tense comment on the progress of the defense. Moultrie was stirring out there on Sullivan's Island, and heavy palmetto logs were being spiked down along unfinished walls. More guns, bargeloads of powder were being ferried out across the narrow stretch that separated the island from the mainland. Gadsden was working miracles in the sands of James Island.

And over the rough, river-scored roads from the north, more strength was pouring down to the Ashley and the Cooper, fresh, quick-stepping formations that planted South Carolina more firmly than ever in the national picture. General Robert Howe brought in a solid contingent of tough North Carolinians. After Howe, grimly alert despite a much longer march, came five hundred Continentals of the Virginia line. In command was a grave-faced man who had recently made a dramatic entry into American military life. Son of the Patriarch of the Lutheran Church in America, he had been sent to study in Germany. The rigid atmosphere of a European theological seminary was too much for a young, free-ranging Pennsylvanian and he left his books, joining, according to some, a German dragoon outfit, while others place him with a British unit. Whatever his enlistment, he finally made his way home and despite his theological truancy was somehow ordained. Assigned to a largely German parish in Virginia's Blue Ridge country, he mixed fiery preaching with equally hot espousal of the colonists' cause.

In January 1776 he mounted his white pulpit in his somber Lutheran robes. His congregation thundered out Martin Luther's magnificent *"Ein Feste Burg Ist Unser Gott"* and, as the deep echoes died away, the pastor flung aside his robes to reveal the uniform of the 8th Virginia Line, with the shoulder badge of colonel. The pastor was gone and Colonel Peter Muhlenberg stood in his place. Drums beat; the colonel spoke earnestly and fervently and swept a good part of the able-bodied men of his congregation into the ranks of the 8th. Now, Pennsylvania-born, German-trained, he encamped an American regiment drawn from Virginia on the South Carolina coast not far from Sullivan's Island.

Another reinforcement of a more dubious nature also arrived. Into the city rode angular, ugly, cantankerous Major General Charles Lee, completing the long ride that had begun away off in Boston. In earlier service in America, Charles Lee had been adopted by an Indian tribe whose direct-minded chiefs had christened him "Boiling Water," a name which he at once began to justify under the Carolina sun. Forgetting that most of the troops in the area were state and not federal, he assumed command of everything that moved, issuing orders, criticizing, objecting, decreeing new dispositions. An ugly rift threatened, for local pride was strong, but John Rutledge, president of the Council and *de jure* in supreme command, labored endlessly to smooth over sore points, spoke of common aims, soothed ultra-touchy officers, and by deep wisdom and devotion averted a clash.

Out at the anchorage the ten ships of war and their thirty transports rocked idly while the leaders mulled and mumbled over what to do and how to do it. On the scorching decks "poor bloody Tommy" gasped and panted in the heat that was so different from an English June and waited patiently for orders. There were seven regiments aboard, East Yorkshires and Gloucestershires (the same regiment which, over one hundred and seventy years later, was to stand firm in magnificent wreckage on a Korean mountainside), the West Ridings and the Duke of Cornwall's men, to name a few—twenty-five hundred hard, trained fighting Englishmen.

The fleet began to stir, moved into the outer roadstead—and anchored again. British officers who had not watched Americans at work on Breed's Hill or the Heights of Dorchester trained their glasses on Sullivan's Island and bitterly cursed the speed with which the rebels toiled. They stared again and cursed their High Command and its delays. Each hour gained by the defenders might mean more English lives when the attack finally came. Days later, boats were launched and over the transport sides went the fur busbies of the grenadiers, the skullcaps of the light infantry. More landing craft swung in to load the yellow facings of the 15th East Yorks. In crawling procession the boats moved on toward Long Island, just north of Sullivan's, the oar blades of the sailors biting sluggishly into the oily waters. The troops were landed. That was all. They were merely given a different place to wait—the sandy island instead of the pitch-bubbling decks.

At last a plan was agreed upon, sound and soldierly—on paper. The frigates and auxiliary ships were to curve in around the south end of Sullivan's Island and smother that little makeshift timber fort with gunfire at very close range. Simultaneously the force on Long Island was to ford the narrow gut onto Sullivan's, brush aside the light defenses, and storm into the fort itself. It was thought that there would not be much life in that fort after the terrific concentration of naval gunfire, a grave miscalculation which was to be repeated by naval and military men off the islands of Tarawa and Iwo Jima in the far Pacific and in another century. Perhaps there was greater reason for optimism back there in 1776. That log fort was only as strong as its garrison, and that was composed of willing, able, but untrained men, of gunners who would have to stand to their pieces and return the fire of onsweeping ships whose gun ports would be flashing and thundering steadily. Perhaps the first few rounds, fired by trained British gunners, would bring a white flag to flutter over the works in place of the green palmetto banner.

Even with plans perfected, there were still delays, and it was not until the morning of June 28 that Charlestonians in their high vantage points saw the men-of-war stand in toward the palmetto fort. (In 1861 and again in 1863 Charlestonians would watch hostile ships move futilely over those same waters.)

From the start, everything went wrong for the British. The infantry attack that was to sweep away Colonel William Thomson and his command of North and South Carolinians never got started. Very tardy reconnaissance showed the gut to be unfordable, and Thomson's men beat off whatever hesitant attempts were made. At the south end of the island matters were even worse. Ships collided, went aground, fouled one another's range, mistook the channel. When they were able to fire, the spongy palmetto logs absorbed the heavy shot easily, and there were no long, deadly wooden splinters to whirl down among the gun crews of the fort.

Within the fort, William Moultrie kept a firm hand, undaunted by the steady, ominous procession of ships that bore down on him, a psychological hazard that must have been even more unsettling than the gunfire. Somehow, he and his gunner officers managed to keep their crews firing slowly and coolly. Powder began to run low, and imperturbably the usually indolent colonel saw to it that his rate of fire slackened, that his men fired only when they had a sure target. General Lee, whose shortcomings did not include a lack of physical courage, crossed over from the mainland under heavy fire, saw that Moultrie and his men were doing all that could be expected of human beings, returned to his quarters through the fire again. More powder was brought into the fort and the rate of fire quickened. A British shot carried away the palmetto flag, and Sergeant Jasper of the 2nd achieved immortality by scrambling down outside the works and setting the colors in place again.

Moultrie's gunners were not merely burning powder. Out in the slow-moving procession of ships, wooden walls shook and shivered, masts wavered, sagged, crashed overboard. Decks were swept with shot of all calibers, and officers and gun crews were shattered as the vessels glided close to the fort batteries. An officer of H.M.S. *Bristol* wrote shakily, "No slaughterhouse could present so bad a sight with blood and entrails lying about, as our ship." The *Experiment*, which with the *Bristol* seems to have been the chief target of the green gunners ashore, was in nearly as dangerous a condition. Admiral Peter Parker, grimly driving his fleet again and again into the stinging fire, suffered the gross indignity of a splinter that "Ruined his Britches . . . quite torn off, his backside laid bare, his thigh and knee wounded."

Slow sunset glowed behind the spires of Charleston, deepened, faded, ebbed, and the rank swirls of gun smoke drifted more and more sluggishly across the water to the watching city. Each tack of Parker's fleet took it farther from Sullivan's Island and its shaken but still intact log fort. There was a last reluctant thud or two, and quiet settled over harbor, fort, and city. Years were to pass before gunfire was heard again along the Ashley and the Cooper, before sweating armies pushed up the banks of the Congaree or mounted scouts rode out over the High Hills of Santee.

Parker's amphibious attempt had resulted in one of the most complete defensive victories won by the Americans in the whole course of the war. In many ways this action was even more remarkable than Breed's Hill. The

green gunners, hastily instructed by Grimball and Masson, were every bit
as steady as the raw levies in the redoubt on the Charles River. Their fire
control was still more marked. At Breed's, Prescott's men were facing recognizable human beings, men like themselves and armed like themselves. But
the gunners in the palmetto fort—Fort Moultrie from that day to this—
were crouched in stifling casemates that allowed only quick glimpses of the
sweep and plunge of impersonal frigates whose walls were smoke-wrapped
and thunderous. Infantry and gunners facing the first tanks of 1916 may
well have felt as had those South Carolinians. The Southern gunners stood
firm, served their pieces like skilled veterans, refused to panic through those
agonizing stretches when powder ran low, leaving them with silent muzzles.
And they managed somehow to achieve the maximum damage with minimum expenditure of ammunition.

It must be said that their courage and steadfastness were matched by the
men who manned Parker's ships. Time and again those frigates had swept
back to the attack in a sort of dogged splendor while gunners and helms-
men, topmen and officers were blasted from the decks. And there was the
added psychological pressure of seeing their best shots sink harmlessly into
the boggy walls of that palmetto fort.

Panting at his anchorage, Peter Parker served out well-earned commenda-
tions to his men and sent the worst of his crippled ships to Halifax for
refitting. Then he retrieved the landing force that had rotted so uselessly
on Long Island and at last put out to sea, his sails standing off into the
northeast, fading through the soft sea shimmer that masked the horizon.

Couriers from Charleston took the news north, and Americans could
hardly be blamed for wondering if possibly a pattern for this odd war had
not been set. Up in Massachusetts a heavy British column had been riddled
with musket fire and sent reeling back to its Boston base. There had been
slaughter at Breed's Hill that might have ended in a crushing American
victory had powder lasted. The whole country had watched a solid British
army rot helplessly in Boston for nearly a year, immobile and impotent,
then evacuate the port under the threat of the guns that Henry Knox had
dragged down through winter-bound trails from Ticonderoga. And now
Charleston. An optimistic patriot of 1776 might be led to reason that any
royal attack could be beaten off, that all the American forces had to do was
stand fast and fire. Such reasoning might be justified if one overlooked
various underlying military factors. And particularly if one kept one's mind
away from the far North.

Along the St. Lawrence that first bold if somewhat flimsy stroke had
fallen into slow disaster. Supplies were few and smallpox was raging. There
was bitter ill feeling among the officers and men of the various states who
made up the expedition. Egalitarians from western Massachusetts and Connecticut were sniping angrily at Philip Schuyler, who seemed hopelessly
feudal to them. Sulky, difficult David Wooster of Connecticut had been
recalled from his command of the combat army and had grudgingly obeyed.

Stalwart, able John Thomas had taken his place, only to die of smallpox by the thick stone walls of Chambly, and John Sullivan of New Hampshire now struggled with the crushing problems of morale, health, transportation, and local feuds. Benedict Arnold had finally withdrawn his command from captured Montreal and added his troops to the general wreckage that was sullenly moving up the Richelieu to the great Champlain waterway. The whole venture had turned into a pool of quicksilver that no man could gather up in his hands and control.

There was no help from Canada itself. The habitants, the peasants—an odd term in North America—politely receptive at first, had grown increasingly difficult, reluctant to part with supplies of any kind, especially when they were paid in a ragged paper currency which they did not understand and which they could not redeem for broad gold and silver pieces. The clergy, from the start, had been understandably hostile, seeing no health in this largely Protestant invasion. As for the seigneurs, the lords of the land, who had been confirmed in most of their sweeping rights and privileges by the British, they could only read chaos in the American proclamations. And worst of all, Sir Guy Carleton, heavily reinforced, was driving west, turning the American retreat into a rout. By the time Peter Parker's ships had closed their gun ports and stood away from Charleston, the northern American forces were straggling up Champlain, blundering toward the deceptive shelter of the walls of "Old Ti."

Yet the Canadian will-o'-the-wisp danced as alluringly as ever before the eyes of Congress and of General George Washington. Instead of cutting losses, of massing the main army into one compact body, orders kept going out for more regiments, like Enoch Poor's 2nd New Hampshire or Elias Dayton's 3rd New Jersey, to take the road toward Lotbinière's fort on the lake. Horatio Gates, now a major general, was sent up to take command and at once became embroiled, politely and with much punctilio, with Philip Schuyler over who was in charge of what. The whole Northern theater threatened to become what Spain and Portugal were to be for Napoleon, an endlessly bleeding wound that drained strength from the main effort.

And that main effort? Its direction and purpose lay shrouded in Nova Scotia mists as the British fleet and British army that had left Boston earlier now received more ships of the line, more frigates, more scarlet regiments with vari-colored facings. Sir William Howe and his admiral brother, Lord "Black Dick" Howe, held the great trump card of mobility. What the bulk of the American army under Washington could do lay in where, when, and how the brothers played that trump, backed by other very strong cards in their hands. Would Boston sight again the heavy flotilla of warships and transports? Would the fleet break the horizon by Sandy Hook? And what about rich Philadelphia, where the American Congress still battled over the extent and the intent of the new rebellion?

CHAPTER XVI

"From This Hour, Freedom"

AS spring came green along the Schuylkill and swelled gently into early
summer, the surface of Philadelphia exhibited a bland courtliness.
The Congress sat; committees sat. Members wined and dined each
other in the better taverns, strolled through the corridors of the State
House, or basked in the green yard outside, preparatory to a sally into
Market Street or along the river. Dorothy Quincy Hancock—"Damsel,
damsel Dorothy Q." of Oliver Wendell Holmes's poem—held court in her
apartment in Mrs. Yard's house at Fourth and Arch streets. The almost
regal air which she gave to the lodgings of the president of the Congress
was enhanced by a vivid spread along one wall where the standard of His
Majesty's 7th Fusiliers, captured in the days of early successes along the
Richelieu, glowed like a Roman trophy—*spolia opima.*

There were new faces to appear through the superficial unconcern of the
city, faces that had been unknown or unseen at the first hesitant beginnings
of the Congress. Distant Georgia, newest and supposedly most royal of all
the colonies, was at last represented, and the old-timers eagerly sought out
young Button Gwinnett, Lyman Hall, and George Walton with their flavor
of far-off rivers like the Savannah and the Ogeechee. Benjamin Franklin,
eternally wise, eternally inventive, and always benevolent, studied the scene
through his small-lensed spectacles. Tall, redheaded, rawboned Thomas
Jefferson had early set his mind, one of the best equipped of his age, to
sorting and weighing and evaluating what he saw and heard, and found his
closest intellectual kinship with John Adams.

A committee had been appointed, enthusiastically by some delegates,
reluctantly by others, to reduce to proper legal and parliamentary form the
sense of what thirteen states had approved. The little group of five met in
the second-floor sitting room of one of their members. There was Benjamin
Franklin, grave under his urbanity; John Adams, feeling like a pilot whose
ship had skirted past shoal and reef into a harbor mouth; Roger Sherman
of Connecticut, his last doubts dispelled by the strength of the rising tide;
Robert Livingston, calmly sure of himself and of his stand, a New York
patrician not ill pleased at following a course that would goad the equally
patrician De Lanceys into a blind fury; last of all the host, lessee of the
sitting room in the house at Seventh and Market streets, the thoughtful
syllable-and-word-weighing Thomas Jefferson, Thomas Jefferson of Virginia.

The five had met to shape words and build them into sentences, to plane
and chamfer and bevel their raw material into a giant, soaring structure
whose unadorned splendor would make men in far ends of the world

catch their breaths with awe and wonder. Who first suggested the name of
the man to be the master builder and architect? It might have been Franklin with his uncanny gift of penetrating deep to the very essentials of a man.
Whoever the chooser, the heart work of this committee was placed in the
hands of Thomas Jefferson. The Virginian, very likely with his mind on
Monticello, where no less than thirty-four whites and eighty-three slaves
looked to him for a livelihood, objected. For one thing, at thirty-three he
was the youngest of the group, except for thirty-year-old Bob Livingston.
Messrs. Franklin and Adams and Sherman were obvious choices.

John Adams laughed away the Virginian's objections. The issue was such
a delicate one that no New England radical—the Wise Men from the East,
Robert Morris had called them in glum sarcasm—should touch it. Besides,
Adams added thoughtfully, Jefferson wrote ten times better than the rest
of the group.

So the Monticello planter was left largely alone in his task, pacing his
Seventh Street sitting room, roaming past the moored ships or out into the
country toward Germantown and its stone houses, while the structure took
shape in his mind. Mentally he added a story here, sketched out a colonnade
there, rejected an entablature, removed lines from a pediment. His colleagues occasionally walked with him, climbed the narrow stairs to his room,
made suggestions, enlarging a dome, adding to the sweep of approaching
steps.

The word structure grew. "When in the course of human events it becomes necessary——" An interpolation: "You have here 'to advance from
that subordination in which they have hitherto remained.' I wonder now—
suppose you say 'to dissolve the political bands which have connected them
with another.' There are implications—currents of thought in admitting the
subordination." Benjamin Franklin's steady, all-seeing eye fell on a sentence
that began "We hold these truths to be sacred and undeniable." "Why not
merely say that we hold them to be self-evident?" asked the doctor, peering
benignly over his spectacles. These corrections stood.

July the first, 1776. The hall of the Congress was full, for the underlying
reason of Thomas Jefferson's structure in words was under debate. Farmer
John Dickinson spoke out in anguished negative. "My conduct this day will
give the finishing blow . . . to my . . . popularity. Yet I had rather forfeit popularity forever, than vote away the blood and happiness of my
countrymen. . . ." On he went, and there could be no doubt of his soul-
deep sincerity.

With a sort of hard despair he slashed out in sharp, powerful strokes.
Independence meant all-out commitment to a war which England could
and would intensify to a degree beyond imagining, a war for which the
states were unprepared economically and militarily. Independence was like
"destroying our house in winter . . . before we have got another shelter."
What would all-out war mean? In future, an evacuated city like Boston
would be burned. Indians would be turned loose along the frontiers, which

would shrink and shrink until war whoops might be heard along Broad Street. Such war could ruin England, and France could sweep back among the weak fragments of the old British colonial empire. By all logic and reason, John Dickinson's forecasts were right. What he predicted should have happened and in many instances did happen. No sensible man could have guessed the actual course of the tides of the future. But history is seldom sensible.

By common consent John Adams rose to answer the Pennsylvanian, and history must record another "lost speech" to stand beside Abraham Lincoln's. Against a storm that rolled thunder and lightning outside, against still more ominous rumblings from the opposition, the Braintree lawyer hammered out his case. Adams himself thought little of his efforts. To him, his speech was a rather weary repetition of dozens of other speeches that had been heard in that hall, and afterward he could recall little of what he had said. It was "an idle mispence of time," as he remarked to Samuel Chase of Maryland. But Thomas Jefferson had far different memories. "He came out with a power and thought and expression that moved us from our seats," said the Virginian.

The debate was ended. In order to sit with his New England colleagues, John Hancock had turned the chair over to Benjamin Harrison of Virginia, who now called for a vote. The roll call of the states began, the names echoing through the crowded hall: "Massachusetts . . . New Hampshire . . . Rhode Island . . . Connecticut . . . New York . . ." The reverberations of Harrison's voice quivered through the July air, forecasting future roll calls that would begin: "Alabama . . . Arizona . . . Arkansas . . . California . . . Colorado . . . Connecticut . . . Delaware . . ." The old familiar names intermingled forever with those of lands undreamed of in July 1776.

In the practice of the times, Harrison read out the resolution that had been under debate. He read slowly, giving full weight to each word. "Resolved: that these United States are, and of right ought to be, free and independent States; that they are absolved from all allegiance to the British Crown, and that all political connection between them and the State of Great Britain is, and ought to be, totally dissolved."

A strong resolution, but the vote was indecisive. The next day a few absentees appeared. Caesar Rodney rode eighty miles through a storm-battered night and stood, still mud-splashed, beside Thomas McKean to set Delaware with the ayes. By the end of the session the ayes were unanimous, despite cleavages within individual delegations.

That night John Adams wrote to his Abigail, tending farm and family off in Braintree, that the second of July "ought to be commemorated, as the Day of Deliverance, by Solemn Acts of Devotion to God Almighty. . . . Posterity will triumph in that Days Transaction, even though We should rue it, which I trust in God We shall not." To Adams, as to now silent Cousin Sam, the day's vote confirmed an existing state of affairs—Inde-

pendence. True, the labors of Thomas Jefferson and his committee were
still to be acted upon, but in his mind that one great fact had been established.

July 4, 1776, a day of increasing heat that left seasoned Philadelphians
gasping. The high grace of the State House arched windows let in floods of
baking air as the members of Congress took their places, but thermometer
readings were forgotten in the impending weight and solemnity of the
day's business. The law of averages had decreed that in this Congress, as in
any large gathering, there would be self-seekers, charlatans, potential turn-
coats, and glib trimmers, but in the main it was a serious-minded, devoted
body. Most of the members were keenly aware that, as twentieth-century
Christopher Fry has said, "affairs are now soul-sized."

Benjamin Harrison was in the chair again and in his hands, as in the
hands of the delegates, was a copy of the final plans of the structure that
Thomas Jefferson and his committee had laid out. Congressmen muttered
to their neighbors, ran fingers along striking sentences or underscored them
with fingernails, pursed their lips, raised their eyebrows, gestured in disapproval, or shrugged in resignation. The vote of July 2 had established the
fact of independence. Jefferson's work set forth why that vote was justified,
explaining to the whole world, to nations friendly or bitterly hostile, how
the magnificently daring conclusions had been reached. And since Jefferson
was speaking in the name of the thirteen states, his thoughts and words
must be as acceptable in Georgia as in New Hampshire.

The immortal preamble of the Declaration of Independence went
through virtually unchallenged. Then the main body of the work was unrolled and tempers began to flare. Members found within themselves unexpected reservations, glowed hotly when cherished beliefs or institutions
seemed to be challenged or maligned, cooled suddenly at the sound of a
thought that was too bold, too sweeping.

There was the matter of the slave trade, of slavery itself. Here Jefferson
had made a bad tactical blunder. Himself a slaveholder by heritage and by
force of circumstances, he blasted the institution as "this assemblage of
horrors; this market where men are bought and sold." But he included his
blast in a long, detailed tirade against the Crown, seemingly charging the
King with having imposed slavery on the unwilling colonists. Many men,
North and South alike, might have gone along on a general denunciation
of slavery, but they pulled up short at blaming George III for it.

The point was lost, along with various other charges which seemed to
emanate from Jefferson's red hair rather than from his cool mind. His
demand for "eternal separation" from the British Crown and the British
people, by implication branding them as all-time enemies, was upset by
Benjamin Harrison himself, who altered the explosive words to read that
the United States would consider the British people, like the rest of the
world, "enemies in war, in peace friends."

Other articles underwent modification or sheer erasure, but when the
debate ended, the general sense of the grand statement was little changed.

Sitting wearily in his uncomfortable chair—it must have been a strain, hearing clause after clause altered or ripped out—Thomas Jefferson could well close his eyes and reflect with humble gratitude that a mission of magnitude had been placed in his hands and that he had not been unworthy of the trust. He could listen in grave relief to the last paragraph of the resolution by which the Congress of the United States adopted a great instrument: "And for the support of this Declaration, with a firm reliance on the protection of divine Providence, we mutually pledge to each other our Lives, our Fortunes, and our sacred Honour."

Other resolutions followed, and the Declaration was ordered to be duly engrossed on good parchment, since most available copies were by now scored with deletions, interlineations, and sharp carets, too confused a jumble for the delegates to sign. Someone thought of the matter of an official seal for the new United States, and the Congress characteristically turned the question of designing an appropriate design over to a committee composed of Messrs. Benjamin Franklin, John Adams, and Thomas Jefferson. Such steps took time, and the formal copy and its seal were not ready for the ceremony of signing until August.

But the country at large did not have to wait for such niceties. Philadelphia presses struck off copy after copy, and mounted messengers rode out to all points of the compass, their saddlebags bulging with sheets on which the ink was still wet. On the eighth of July, Colonel John Nixon of the Philadelphia Associators (a unit that Franklin had helped to form during the old French troubles, now nearly thirty years in the past) read the Declaration in a parade-ground voice from a platform built in the green yard of the State House. The city seems to have greeted the reading with a calm acceptance rather than jubilantly. After all, every question remotely touching that document had been tossed and bounced about in most of the local homes and taverns. It was pleasing, but hardly news.

In other parts of the country, matters went differently. In New York, where the main army under Washington had been slowly assembling since the evacuation of Boston, commanding officers of regiments representing half a dozen states formed their men into hollow squares. Drums rolled. In camps at the King's Bridge, at present City Hall Park, on the Battery, across on the Brooklyn hills, the same words rang out, delivered in Massachusetts, Connecticut, New York, New Jersey, Pennsylvania, and Delaware accents: "When in the course of human events it becomes necessary for one people to dissolve the political bands . . ." There was much cheering from the ranks, but there was also deep, searching thought. It was one thing to read certain phrases in a Philadelphia tavern. But as officers and men filed away to their quarters, each could put a personal application to "we mutually pledge our lives . . . and our sacred Honour . . ."

Riders went deep into Massachusetts, and on the bright nineteenth of July in Boston, people pressed close against the east end of the Old State House, trampling and jostling and shoving over the very ground of the Massacre. There was a stir at the second-floor windows and huge, bull-strong Thomas Crafts, ex-house painter, friend of Paul Revere and Sam Adams, stepped out into the little balcony that still looks down toward the harbor. Abigail Adams, rapt as one who sees a cherished vision turn to reality, was there in the great crush of people, heard Crafts roll out sentence after sentence, heard a shout from the balcony, "God save the American states!" With jubilant cheers still ringing in her head—Boston, alone of all American cities, had lived under martial law and the rule of the King's troops—Abigail wrote to John, "The Bells rang, the privateers fired, the forts and batteries, the cannon were discharged . . . & every face appeared joyfull. . . . After dinner the kings arms were taken down from the State House & every vestige of him from every place . . . and burnt. . . . Thus ends royal authority in this State, and all the people shall say Amen." Would Abigail be shocked today to see the gold lion and unicorn still prancing at either side of that stepped east gable of the State House, or would she be angry to find on the second-floor Council Chamber the portraits, life size, of George III and his Charlotte, at the restored royal arms? Perhaps. But surely she would forget shock and anger at the sight, each Fourth of July, of a chosen Boston high school pupil standing on Crafts' balcony to read out those same words to the crowd below on the Massacre site. Each year an immature figure steps out—D'Agostino, O'Brien, Purcell, Pereira, Ducharme, Schultz, Pappas—and an American schoolboy or schoolgirl reads out an American heritage to an American crowd.

Far down the crescent of the Atlantic coast went the news of the action of the Congress. On August 2 a sweating express rider crossed the Cooper River and limped into Charleston, the very day that Peter Parker finally raised anchor and stood away to the northeast. On the fifth there was a great procession, civil and military, led by President John Rutledge, a review of state and Continental troops, and under the Liberty Tree that had spread its boughs over so much tumult and striving, Major Barnard Elliot of the 4th South Carolina Artillery read out the Declaration.

The Charlestonians cheered, sang, prayed, drank like their fellows in other American cities. Yet there was a strong undercurrent of protest against the Congress and its latest and most dramatic act, a protest that was certainly present in varying degrees in the twelve other states, but most marked here. There were worried mutterings, with a good deal of justification, that the South Carolina congressmen had far exceeded their powers in agreeing to independence. Rutledge spread unofficial but reassuring rumors that the Declaration was only intended to set up a workable government pending a final reconciliation with England, at which time the old status quo would be resumed.

Henry Laurens was so shocked at final separation that he wore mourning. "In truth, I wept that day. . . . I thought and openly declared that . . . Congress had been too hasty in shutting the door against reconciliation." So Laurens wrote later, and many must have felt even more strongly than he. For, as indicated earlier, South Carolina had always been a highly favored colony in the eyes of the Crown. More, its original inhabitants had not come from England, but up from the West Indies, bringing with them a well-rooted way of life. They had settled not as refugees or liberty seekers but as farsighted planters seeking wider fields for their proven talents. Their chief quarrel with the Crown had been the denying to native-born South Carolinians the top-crust jobs of governing. Politically they had been treated as virtually second-class citizens.

The Parker-Clinton coup against Charleston, against a state that had not formally taken the field against the Crown, was a vast blunder. Had the fleet not appeared off Five Fathom Hole, it is quite possible that South Carolina would have repudiated its delegates to the Congress and remained benevolently neutral. And it is equally possible that such action might well have drawn North Carolina and Georgia along with it. As it was, the news of the Declaration reached the city while the hostile fleet was still almost in sight. Parker's attack probably killed any chance of limiting the Revolution to Virginia and the states to the north, a war against ten United States and not thirteen.

The United States of America had announced their existence to the world and to themselves. But mere announcement was not enough. It must be implemented by material strength, and that strength must be concentrated in the right place.

Slowly the eyes of the new nation turned toward Manhattan Island. Since the first rushes of the more rowdy adherents of Whig and Tory, the turmoil had taken on the aspect of a violent, uproarious sport with bitter undertones. Peter Elting crowed to Captain Richard Varick: "We Had some Grand Toory Rides in this City. . . . Several were handled verry Roughly, being Carried trugh the Streets on Rails. . . . There is hardly a toory face to be seen this morning." In districts where the Crown sympathizers predominated, the roles, of course, were reversed.

But New York ceased to be a glorious hunting ground for rival gangs and turned into an armed camp. After the British evacuation of the waters about Boston, Washington began sending the regiments of the siege to that area. There were more serious matters afoot than rails, tar buckets, and feathers. Through the spring and early summer the army from the Boston theater poured slowly onto the land between the North and East rivers, lapped over the western fringes of Long Island.

There were familiar units and well-known faces to be seen on Harlem Heights, down by the Battery, or on the green hills above Brooklyn. A New Englander might find himself among the shelters of the 20th Connecticut, the 26th Massachusetts, or the Rhode Island Brigade. Israel Putnam was here, there, and everywhere. Henry Knox had brought his artillery clattering overland and now established his headquarters in the elegance of No. 1 Broadway. Over the highlands about Brooklyn rode New Hampshire's John Sullivan, freed from his Canadian burden by the arrival of Horatio Gates. Nathanael Greene could be found scouring the terrain about Gravesend and the far southwest shores of Long Island, his growing military flair picking out possible enemy landing beaches, casting up logical approaches that might bring attacking troops against the inland heights.

The commander-in-chief was lodged in the Abraham Mortier house in Lispenard's Meadows, now the corner of Charlton and Varick streets. Martha Washington was with him for a while but soon left for Philadelphia and thence the Potomac. Departing, she could feel secure about her tall husband, for she could see John Glover's Marbleheaders, still trim in their nautical blue jackets and white trousers, mounting guard in the Meadows as they had at the great Vassall house in Cambridge.

There were crushing problems ahead for all these transferred units, but for the moment there was a new city to be stared at by men, many of whom had never been out of their own state or even county before. Colonel Loammi Baldwin of the 26th Massachusetts wrote his wife: "The city is grand, the buildings lofty and elegant." The streets did not strike Loammi as "so fine as those in Boston," and the manners of the New Yorkers "differ something from the natural inhabitants of Boston, having Jewish, Dutch and Irish customs." It was all so different from Boston or Newport or Portsmouth.

But the chief wonder of most must have been the rest of the army, which they were seeing for the first time, for the New England troops under their Virginia commander had not taken over the defense of New York. They had merely marched or sailed to join the most completely American force yet assembled. Massachusetts troops could recall how they had turned out alone in '75, then had been joined by Connecticut, New Hampshire, and Rhode Island. And there had been the shirted riflemen from Pennsylvania, Maryland, and Virginia.

But now the Bay Staters stared at men in brown coats with green or yellow or red facings, at hunting shirts that were brown or black or gray. They saw New Yorkers and New Jersey men and the solid files of the Pennsylvania line. In August, music shrilled by the western ferries, and onto the streets poured drummers and fifers in bright red, faced and laced with blue, and the musicians were followed by company after company of swinging infantrymen in blue jackets with red facings, black skullcaps with a high, crested plate. The Delaware Continentals, under Colonel John Haslet, were taking their place in the American army. And soon after marched Colonel William Smallwood's Marylanders, drawn, it was whispered along the Broad Way, from the sons of wealthy families of Baltimore and Annapolis by the Severn. They wore red coats with buff facings, soon to be discreetly hidden under brown smocks.

One of Glover's Marbleheaders, on guard at No. 1 Broadway, could find plenty of food for reflection in what he saw. All New England and New York and New Jersey and Pennsylvania and Delaware and Maryland signed on for the same cruise, and with a Virginian at the helm!

The build-up was gradual there on Manhattan and Long Island. National and state troops marched in, made their camps, or took over sheds and warehouses much as the army had done the year before outside of Boston.

The men drilled, drank, squabbled, complained about rations, and whenever possible avoided regimental fatigue and guard duty in the timeless manner of all troops.

Military police, as we know them, did not exist and their functions were loosely performed by hastily appointed provost guards. Debauchery and violence gnawed at the strength and morale of the makeshift army. Out in the country, perhaps as far north of the city as present Washington Square, was a tangled tract known cynically as the Holy Ground, a festering tent-and-shack village of sordid bordellos and blind tigers. Loammi Baldwin wrote his wife of vicious fights, knifings, clubbings with which the provost tried vainly to cope. In the Holy Ground an unwary man from New Hampshire or Delaware could disappear without a trace, and sometimes did. Many such were listed as deserters, of which there was a growing number, but when the tract was finally cleared, unidentifiable bodies were dug up. Some desertions had been perhaps involuntary and certainly final.

From the start the main activity of Washington's force was digging. From the King's Bridge south to the Battery, dirt flew, boulders were rolled away, trees came crashing down as forts, redoubts, and flèches took slow shape. There was, for example, a battery at the foot of present East Eighty-ninth Street to cover the Hell Gate Channel. At Kip's Bay, where the East Twenties now reach the river, the shore was scored with trenches and log breastworks walled in heavy cannon that might have begun their military careers at Ticonderoga. Near the brick walls of the New York Hospital other works commanded the broad North River. Men sweated and cursed along the high spine far up the island to carve Fort Washington out of the solid rock that still shoulders up through the soil of the West 180s.

There was more activity across on Long Island, where Nathanael Greene traced out works along the Heights and down into the flatlands below them. His chief engineer was Iz Putnam's cousin, Rufus, a quiet man who mastered his profession rapidly. Rufus Putnam was to serve through the whole war with great credit and later would lead a colony of Washington's veterans to open up the Ohio Valley.

From an engineering standpoint, Greene and Putnam planned well and built well. Their lines began with a natural tidal moat at Wallabout Bay and along Gowanus Creek, above the twin hamlets of Brooklyn Church and Brooklyn Village. Thence they ran east through what was, in many places, densely wooded country, broken by little Dutch farms that lay like islands of cultivation among the trees. The fortified sites have been long since swallowed up by sprawling Brooklyn. There was Fort Putnam on the heights south of De Kalb Avenue, zigzag works that ran via Bond Street and Fulton Street. Modern Washington Park, Prospect Park, Greenwood Cemetery—even the soil of Ebbets Field—knew Putnam's picks and shovels. Fort Stirling covered the East River approaches near Pierrepont and Hicks streets, and there was a strange conical hill, known locally as the Ponkiesburg, in the Atlantic-Pacific Avenue area, to serve as observation post and signal center.

These lines were long and deep, and to supplement the labor of the troops, local leaders proclaimed a virtual draft of able-bodied men from the settlements and farms east of Brooklyn. The order was backed up by highly effective force, and sullen Tories swung their picks side by side with convinced Whigs; slaves and masters drove their shovels into the sandy Long Island soil. Continental, militiaman, Whig, Tory, white, Negro were preparing a setting for a great tragedy that could easily have been the hasty final act of the drama of American freedom.

There was a good deal of confidence in the general situation so far as American brass on Manhattan was concerned. The growing army would soon have a paper strength of nearly twenty thousand men. Supplies were ample and could be augmented from rich Westchester County beyond the King's Bridge and from western Connecticut. Of even greater importance was the powder situation. Lavoisier's fine product seems to have been flowing in steadily from France. In early July, Washington could nonchalantly order the transfer of a few hundred barrels of the silky black stuff to Norwich in Connecticut for safekeeping. Hundreds of barrels to spare! About Boston, powder had been rationed almost by the cupful.

These amateur soldiers felt that their artillery was more than adequate. Henry Knox, always learning, rubbed his hands as he surveyed the batteries that covered the water approaches. He wrote to Brother William: "If Howe comes up like a man and brings his ships before our batteries, there must the finest fight ensue that ever was seen. We shall be able in that case to bring a great number of cannon and mortars to bear on the ships at once." The ex-bookseller was falling into a tragically common military error, one that has blinded professionals as well as amateurs. He was basing probable results on what he wanted the enemy to do rather than on the innumerable alternatives open to that enemy.

On one major count the British command did what most American leaders expected. Early on the morning of June 29, one Daniel McCurtin, busy on the upper floor of a sea-facing house, glanced out of a window, blinked, started. He had "spied as I peeped out the Bay something resembling a wood of pine trees trimmed. I declare, at my noticing this, that I could not believe my eyes, but keeping my eyes fixed at the very spot, judge you of my surprise when in about ten minutes, the whole Bay was full of shipping as ever it could be. I declare that I thought all London was afloat." What McCurtin was marveling at was the Halifax force under Sir William Howe, which was arriving at its objective, New York, or its inland-reaching waterways.

The fleet of more than one hundred sail anchored in the Lower Bay, then moved into the Staten Island area, shifted, maneuvered. Each day saw it in a new place, which left men ashore guessing wildly at its target. Would Howe land on Manhattan? On Long Island? Or would the whole flotilla beat up the North River and the Hudson and join that force under Carleton which hung menacingly at the far tip of Lake Champlain?

For the moment Sir William Howe showed no disposition to rush his fences. He occupied undefended Staten Island, pushed a few patrols across the Kill van Kull to the Jersey shore, withdrew them. Then, under a flag of truce, he tried to open negotiations with Washington, the aim being the ending of hostilities. Two meetings resulted, but the terms that Sir William was able to offer were found to be utterly unacceptable. The bowings and posturings, the courteous exchanges of compliments—"Your servant, sir," "Yours, sir"—that accompanied these conferences, one of which Washington attended in person, have an odd flavor of unreality today. Yet Howe's attempts and Washington's final response to them were justified. Each was in duty bound to see what the other would or could offer. And there were more immediate, practical considerations facing both commanders.

Washington could be quite sure that the British would take no offensive step while the shadowy negotiations were in progress. Each day consumed by letters received or by letters rejected meant more troops pouring down over the King's Bridge, more epaulements, bastions, trenches thrown up on Manhattan or about Brooklyn. And Howe? He could count on the unlikelihood of any American move during the same period. Washington, lacking a fleet, could not attack the British, but he could easily have withdrawn his army into Westchester County, where Howe would have to seek him out and where the British fleet could not reach him. And each day that Washington stayed on his two islands brought added British strength closer and closer, riding on the winds of the Atlantic. And some of that strength was very close as Patterson made his last bow to George Washington and Henry Knox.

As the third week of July wore on, clumps of masts stood bold against the eastern skies. Transports and warships began to close in on the original Halifax fleet, and "Black Dick" Howe brought a huge convoy to anchor in waters about New York.

Admiral Lord Howe had ferried an entire fresh army from Europe and by doing so injected a new element into the war. Strong glasses could scan the decks of his inshore transports and see them packed with heavy masses of men in dark blue coats. The sun was dazzling on rows of high, miter-like brass helmets or dull on black cocked hats. The hired troops from the German states, so carefully bargained for by George III's agents, were arriving.

This new fleet had been pretty much expected by the Americans, and its arrival produced little shock. But early August dealt their hopes and plans a stunning blow. Out of the southward mists and blue-green dazzle of the Lower Bay, still more sails glinted golden in the sun, masts bristled, and anchors shot huge spouts of spray into the air among the wheeling sea gulls. Perhaps this added force should have been foreseen by Washington and his generals, but it had been unaccountably left out of all calculations. Its coming was to Joseph Reed "as unexpected as though it had dropped from the clouds." For Admiral Peter Parker, his outraged backside thoroughly healed, had brought the three thousand men under Clinton and Cornwallis up from Charleston, eager to wipe out the disgrace of the bloody repulse off Sullivan's Island.

So the might of England and Hesse lay massed off New York, poised above the principal army of the United States of America. That army waited for the next hostile move with seeming confidence, perhaps brought on by the fact that few of its men had ever seen action. Those who had witnessed the slaughter at Breed's Hill clung to memories of that day, infected others with their accounts of it. And how much stronger the army was now in 1776! Nearly twenty thousand men, perhaps more. And there was powder, so much powder that its storage had become a problem. What if nearly all the uniforms had been worn out in the arduous labors of digging and entrenching? The men were there. That was what counted.

The men were there. But why they were there on Manhattan and Long Island, the gravest question of all, seems to have troubled the American mind of 1776 very little, if at all. The rawest soldier could see that Washington's force was scattered from the King's Bridge to the Battery and across on Long Island, with some units over on the New Jersey shore. Water between Manhattan and New Jersey, water between Manhattan and Long Island, and above Long Island another great waterway, the Sound. To concentrate, the army would have to cross a river or a bay or a sound, and there, lying thick about Staten Island, was a vast flotilla that could easily forbid any such passage. Even lightly armed vessels could cut Brooklyn off from New York. Where Manhattan was narrowest, naval gunfire could control the roads that ran north and south between the King's Bridge and the Battery. It did not do to look at the muzzles of Knox's guns frowning out over the East and North rivers. Already British ships had sailed up the North River as far as Haverstraw Bay, and the American guns had thundered in vain.

In fact, the commander-in-chief had placed the backbone of America's military strength in a trap that could have been deadly even for trained troops. For an army in the present position to have a reasonable chance of success implied control of the harbor, the rivers, and the Sound. That control he could never have. Clinging to the New York area was Washington's worst blunder of the war and it could very well have been his last. There had been some pressure from Congress to hold the port, but the decision was a military one, and he had made few, if any, objections to the political arguments. Nor do any of his generals appear to have been more farsighted than their chief. They all were facing formal war for the first time, and what training they had and what studies they had made did not fit into this new pattern.

Another curious blind spot appeared in the military thinking of Washington and many of his subordinates. The entire American army was composed of infantry and artillery, a badly balanced force. Governor Trumbull of Connecticut sent a regiment of some four hundred or more "light horse," not a haphazard collection of farm boys on plow horses, but, as Washington himself wrote, "men of reputation and property." These could have been whipped into shape to serve as a screen on his flanks, particularly on Long Island, where they could have provided prompt intelligence of enemy moves. But the commander-in-chief sent them home rather abruptly on the strange grounds that there was not enough fodder for the mounts and that the men were not willing to serve as infantry. With unusual testiness he wrote: "They can no longer be of use here, where horses cannot be brought into action, and I do not care how soon they are dismissed."

It seems likely that Washington was thinking back to wilderness service against the French and Indians, to the tight-grown forests near the junction of the Allegheny and the Monongahela. In such terms, he was right. He was also right in assuming that Trumbull's horsemen could not have been brought into action against the British 17th Dragoons. But they could have patrolled far in advance and on the flanks of the Brooklyn lines, where the speed of their horses would have more than quadrupled the value of any news they might send.

August wore on and the commander-in-chief found himself swamped in a welter of petty detail that plagued him in his quarters at the Mortier house or at his downtown headquarters, which may have been on Pearl Street. He was desperately shorthanded for aides. His original adjutant general, Gates, was now politely squabbling with Schuyler in the north. Stephen Moylan had left him to become quartermaster general, and Joseph Reed was still new to staff work. Washington had to handle correspondence that a modern staff sergeant or T/5 would dispose of as routine. Such work, for a field officer, struck Nathanael Greene as confining "my thoughts as well as engrossing my time. It is like a merchandise of small wares."

Rather pathetically, the commander-in-chief, always deferential to the civil powers that had created his rank, wrote to Congress, asking authorization for "an increase of my Aid de Camps." He must have struck the delegates when they were in a niggardly mood, for their president, John Hancock, wrote in hardly lavish response, "I have the pleasure to inform you, the Congress readily agrees to your having another Aid-de-Camp."

Along with the trivia that flooded the Virginian's field desk came a startling communication from Long Island. Major William S. Livingston, late of Lasher's New York militia and now aide to Nathanael Greene, was sorry "to inform your Excellency that General Greene had a very bad night of it and cannot be said to be any better this morning." Some camp fever had caught up with the Rhode Islander as he labored cheerfully and ably about the lines with his slight limp and his incessant asthmatic wheeze. This was on August 17. A few days more and Greene was completely out of action, hospitalized in a New York house at Broadway and present East Ninth Street.

This meant a complete reshuffling of the command, and Washington plowed distractedly through his rosters in search of a replacement, a maddening task since there was only one Greene. At last a partial solution was cobbled together somehow. Over to Long Island came Israel Putnam to take charge inside the main works. Major General John Sullivan, his second star now bright on his blue-and-gold epaulets, was given command of the troops posted in the woods and farmlands to the south and east, the zone where any blow delivered at Long Island would probably fall. To take over Sullivan's earlier assignment, the right half of the advanced American lines, Washington finally settled on William Alexander of New York, a brigadier general. Alexander was noted at the time chiefly for being the probably sincere claimant to the Scottish title of Earl of Stirling. He had military ability, courage, and a deep belief in the American cause, but nearly all his contemporaries agreed that he was apt to be useless after sundown, owing to an insatiable curiosity as to what might lie in the bottom of a bottle.

So the immediate chain of command on Long Island was established, for better or worse. It was new and it was shaky and the division of responsibility between Sullivan and Putnam was very hazily defined. There was no time for further adjustment or tightening. The Howes were beginning to move.

CHAPTER XVII

". . . with a Red and angry Glare"

THE rising sun of August 22, 1776, brought on clear, hot weather, good farming weather, and the early breeze off the bay stirred the tall wheat tops on the fields about New Utrecht and Flatbush and Flatland and rippled the waters under Schoonmaker's Bridge. It would be a good day to work in the plains that sloped away southeast from the fortified Heights.

There would be no harvesting on August 22. From the waters about Staten Island, frigates and bomb ketches spread their sails and stood in toward the Long Island shore, covering the beaches at Red Hook on the western tip and spreading well to the east. Then a slow procession of barges put out from Staten Island and nosed over the lazy swell in the wake of the warships. There were eighty-eight of them all told, manned by sailors from the fleet and packed with troops. Lookouts and idlers on the American shore could only gasp as oar and sail drove the blunt prows closer.

There was shrill music and the nibbling sound of drums that floated over scarlet coats of the skullcapped light infantry and their high, bright bayonets. The wind ruffled the fur of the grenadiers' tall caps and the sun glinted from the plumed brass helmets of the 17th Dragoons. There were flat caps jaunty with angled feathers and the dark kilts of the 42nd Black Watch and, beyond the Scots, the cocked hats of the 33rd West Ridings. There was a darker blur in the water as the drums and hautboys brought on Graf von Donop's contingent of Hessians. High, tapering helmets of bright brass topped with woolen pompons, blue coats and white breeches told of picked Hessian grenadiers drawn from the Von Mirbach Regiment, the Erb Prinz, or the Alt Lossberg, for the Germans designated their regiments by the commander's name instead of a number. Leading barges made bands of green on the blue shore waters as the Jaegers came on, vast cocked hats casting a shadow over red collars and red facings, short, deadly rifle barrels glinting in the sun. On they came through the August morning, scarlet and blue and green, and spilled ashore in smooth waves as the blunt bows grated on Long Island sands.

The barges headed back to Staten Island, refilled with dense cargoes of red facings, blue facings, buff and amaranth and white facings, headed for the invasion shore again. By the end of the day, with frightening smoothness, nearly fifteen thousand troops were ashore, with Clinton and Cornwallis and Von Donop watching them flow into perfect formation.

Ahead of the beaches lay a neat network of roads that wound through little Dutch villages and thick woods on to the passes that notched the Heights where Israel Putnam and John Sullivan watched. Off from the attackers' right, from their center, and from their left, the roads wound and loitered away on their lazy courses to the Heights. Clinton sent some of the light troops, British and Hessians, to probe the farmlands and woods on his front. They collided with Edward Hand's Pennsylvania riflemen, exchanged a few shots, caused and suffered a few casualties, and withdrew, as did Hand's men. Later Cornwallis pushed on and occupied Flatbush, spread out his camps from Gravesend and New Utrecht on the west to Flatland on the east. By nightfall there was nothing to mark the first day of the invasion save the campfires of the opposing forces, just the fires with a black-shirted Pennsylvanian stiffening in a grove, a Jaeger from the banks of the Kinzig lying in his green coat before a step-gabled stone house, or a grenadier from Shropshire by a calm little brook.

New York had been alerted by the very first passage of troops from Staten Island to American beaches, but even so no one seems to have grasped the importance of the East and North rivers. A wind, God-sent for the Americans, kept any British from tacking up between Manhattan and Long Island, and Washington, either from the Mortier house or from his mysterious downtown office, was able to ferry troops over to Brooklyn. Miles's Pennsylvanians and Atlee's were embarked; Gold Silliman's and Chester's raw Connecticut men joined them with Lasher's and Drake's New Yorkers. These were mostly green troops, but he did not dare commit more.

Actually, his decision hardly mattered. Surrounded by water, cut off by water, he was bound to be beaten by any major landing. Safety lay, if one may be wise after the event, in giving up Long Island and Manhattan and withdrawing his army, intact and unbeaten, to Westchester on the mainland.

The weather changed, and until the twenty-fifth the wind kept Howe from reinforcing Clinton and Von Donop. Partially convinced that the major stroke was to be aimed at Brooklyn Heights, Washington sent more and more men to Long Island. Fresh Connecticut men came over. Lord Stirling was exuberant when barges unloaded the blue-and-red files of the Delaware Continentals in their high-plated caps and sent them into the lines under his command. It is likely that they were about the only completely uniformed outfit on Long Island. Still more strength was poured in to him when the brown-smocked Marylanders took their places beside the Delaware companies. All this must have been immensely encouraging to the men about Brooklyn Heights. Actually, Washington had split his army in two, with a waterway that could be controlled by the enemy between the two halves.

The wind changed again. Barges began their sinister shuttle between Staten Island and the landing beaches. Old Philip von Heister, the agonies of his long voyage forgotten, was now champing and prancing, the battle light strong in his faded eyes. He must have purred deep in his throat as he watched his brigades of Hessian grenadiers, bullied and whipped and badgered into efficient military automatons, actually standing in their craft with shouldered muskets "and in column of march, preserving the well-considered pomp of German discipline."

All during this time, and for hours afterward, the American units mentioned above were still crossing the East River or making ready to embark. Those in position must still have been blinking or wetting dry lips as they took in the extent and quality of the force that would sooner or later move against them. Whether they realized it or not, their main hope lay in a second Breed's Hill, with ordered enemy columns marching against earthworks whose garrisons might be steady enough to hold their fire as Prescott's men had held it.

There was to be no Breed's Hill. On the night of the twenty-sixth men began falling in around the Flatland area, whence roads led straight to the heart of the American works or, fatally, in a wide curve that ended in Iz Putnam's left rear. The unit formed, and through the night went the 17th Dragoons, red plumes astir in the soft air, and after them company on company of neat-stepping light infantry; another massive column behind these —grenadiers, the West Ridings, and then the kilted swirl of the 71st Highlanders. Still more troops. The Guards themselves, twelve other regiments, ten thousand seasoned British troops strode off in the darkness while no less than twenty-eight field guns clanked and rumbled. In the lead was Clinton, with his memories of Breed's Hill and the siege of Boston. Cornwallis commanded the next group, his thoughts bitter with visions of wasted chances at Charleston. In the rear, Lord Percy may have thought of the Lexington Green and a broken British column as he rode on beside Sir William Howe.

There was a crossroads, a sandy fork or two. One turn would have taken bearskins and skullcaps, Highland bonnets and dragoon helmets toward the strong American center. The massed column went on, veered in the night, and headed northwest along the great curve that would swing it through Jamaica Pass and into the American rear. There was no one to give warning, no Connecticut "light horse" to interfere with the advance or, far more important, to send messengers galloping off to find Putnam and John Sullivan.

The "way around," about which Captain Slocum, U.S.A., was to inquire more than a century later, the "way around" which the British command had so fatally neglected at Breed's Hill, had been found and would be put to use. With Tory guides, Howe's ten thousand cleared Jamaica Pass and debouched onto the general east-west course of the night-shrouded Bedford Road. Militarily speaking, the battle was over.

Well before sunrise a general cannonade broke out along the British front, a good part of its volume concentrated on the American right, far away from the unsuspecting, threatened positions and Howe's men hidden in darkness. Roaring muzzles spouted orange-red into the haze of the summer night. Muskets popped flatly and light formations began to probe cautiously into the American right and center. The raw units beat off the tentative thrusts, stood remarkably steady under the bombardment, which was so new to most of them. Thus far there was little to disturb Israel Putnam and John Sullivan.

The sun rose "with a Red and angry Glare" and the false sense of security was shattered. Howe's attack smashed into the American left rear, rolling in almost panzer fashion between the army and the fortified heights behind it. Highlanders, grenadiers, line companies ripped hard into unready formations.

There was panic and flight, for, as Chester Wilmot has written of 1940, "nothing in war is more unnerving than the unexpected." It is probable that steady, seasoned troops would have been broken by this sudden, utterly unexpected onrush that came from the rear. The reaction of these green regiments on the eastern slopes of the Brooklyn massif was entirely predictable. Units broke, scattered, raced for the safety and comfort of earthworks and gun pits. By squads, by platoons, and by companies, terrified men, many of whom may have stood firm and cool at Breed's Hill, threw down their arms. Here and there was recovery and grim-faced Americans held their ground, slugged out the issue toe to toe with clubbed muskets against slick, cold bayonets. But always they were being pushed and harried back toward the American center. No doubt a few sanguine officers visualized a rally, a stand on a counterattack when that center was reached.

There was a signal gun, and tough old Von Heister sent Von Donop with his green-coated Jaegers and miter-helmeted grenadiers against that center. It broke, as the left flank had broken, and Americans falling south from the first British onslaught found Hessian bayonets coming up behind them. Some unwilling fugitives may have remembered that there were strong units of Pennsylvania riflemen there in the center and tried to rally on them. The riflemen were gone. Their clumsy weapons took so long to load that kilted Scot and blue-coated Hessian were on them with the bayonet before they could reload. Riflemen were caught in swamps, in thick woods, in undergrowth. Bayonetless, they were pinned to the ground, skewered against trees by long-armed Hessian or British lunges.

American gunners abandoned their pieces in the face of red-and-blue lines that rushed toward them, bayonets aslant, although here and there cannoneers stood firm, as had some of the infantry.

Sometime during the morning Washington came over from Manhattan, still with half an eye on the possibility of an attack being made there. There was nothing that he or any man could have done. As the day of slaughter and capture wore on, the commander-in-chief, watching from the strong Brooklyn works, could find only two cheering points—rather remotely cheering. Units of the British fleet were trying to work up into the East River past Red Hook and its fort, but a steady wind, a "divine wind" for the Americans, kept frigate, sloop, and bomb ketch beating about impotently. Then there was the right of the American line.

The position could be clearly seen from the forward works. It was anchored on Gowanus Bay and ran inland over the Gowanus Road along a partly wooded ridge. Men in hunting shirts could be made out among the trees, men in long waistcoats with an occasional soiled and tattered uniform here and there. But down toward the blue of Gowanus Bay, troops stood in formal line of combat. An observer would have had to know the order of battle to identify William Smallwood's smocked Marylanders, but shoulder to shoulder with them, vividly conspicuous and recognizable, was the blue and red of John Haslet's Delawares, their high cap plates catching the August sun, winking like mirrors against the green of the turf. In command of this sector was Lord Stirling, whom Iz Putnam had routed out of his tent when the night cannonade had first started.

Stirling's men were in action but holding firm. Facing them was the British left, heavy masses of fur-capped grenadiers, the jaunty bonnets and swinging sporrans of the 42nd Black Watch with their dark tartans. Thus far the British commander in this part of the line, General James Grant, had not pushed home any attack, but the guns of the Royal Artillery were thudding and rumbling and there was an endless pop and snap of skirmishers' muskets. It was heavy fire for green troops to face, but they set their chins and took whatever Grant chose to send.

So the colonel of the Delawares, John Haslet, found them as he hurried over from court-martial duty in New York, and for the rest of his tragically short life he remembered how they stood, "with a firm, determined countenance, in close array, their colors flying, the enemy's artillery playing on them all the time." Mercifully Haslet and Smallwood, like Lord Stirling, were unaware of the extent of peril and slaughter that was raging out of sight far off to the left.

There was a signal gun deep within the British lines, and Grant's Highlanders and grenadiers swung into full action, ending the semi-static warfare on this part of the front. The Pennsylvania and Connecticut troops were smashed, scattered, and in the rout a hideous new threat appeared. Down from the more distant attacks came the 33rd West Ridings, the Scots of the 71st, more grenadiers. Hautboys and deep-toned drums announced the arrival of some of Von Donop's men, and the high ground was cleared with tragic speed. But below it, toward the Gowanus Road and the sparkle of the bay, a solid mass still held firm and an Englishman particularly noted the Delawares with "their ranks full, their uniforms smart, their courage high."

Lord Stirling acted quickly and surely. In his rear were marshes, broad Gowanus Creek, little ponds, a virtually impassable barrier, militarily speaking. Across creek and marsh he sent Smallwood's and Haslet's men in orderly retreat. By all logic they should have panicked, broken ranks, blundered about in wild confusion, and finally been lost, the usual fate of green troops. But they defied logic and survived.

Not all of these troops started off on that watery march. Lord Stirling held back Major Mordecai Gist and two hundred and fifty immortal Marylanders. Ahead and to his left front, British and Hessians were re-forming, making ready to renew their attack, which might have swallowed up the still retreating bulk of Smallwood's and Haslet's men.

"The American fighting man has his failings. He is prone to many regrettable errors . . . [But] . . . when he . . . has someone to say 'Come on!' to him, he will stand as much killing as anyone on earth." So wrote Marine John Thomason of the army of 1918. It was true in 1776. There was Lord Stirling to say "Come on!" and the pitifully small force of smocked men drove with him against the blue-and-red lines that were forming near the gray stone gables of the Cortelyou house.

Cornwallis was there to command in person, and his troops were first-rate men, flushed but not disordered by victory. Five times the claimant to the earldom of Stirling threw himself and his grim men against Highlander, grenadier, and Hessian. Mordecai Gist was to remember afterward that Stirling "encouraged and animated our young soldiers with almost invincible resolution," a pretty fair New England understatement for a Baltimorean. Another wrote that his lordship "fought like a wolf." In one wild onset the scarlet-and-blue lines wavered, but fresh troops were rushed up to meet the sixth attack, and what was left of the Marylanders fell back, broke into small groups, tried to reach their own lines.

It had been a remarkable exhibition, this action fought in an atmosphere of panic and defeat, more infectious than the deadliest plague. It also established a precedent which was to repeat itself through the whole course of the war. Time and again, after shattering defeats or wasting stalemates, men of all the thirteen states who made up a wrecked or rotting army somehow managed to rally to deliver a stinging attack. Sometimes a smashing blow would have an importance that was only psychological, that showed that the offensive spirit still burned high. At others, definite results were to accrue. In this case, Lord Stirling, at his very highest, and his two hundred and fifty must have secured the unimpeded retreat of many hundreds, even thousands, of men in that part of the line.

There was a heavy price to pay. Only Mordecai Gist and nine others reached the safety of the Brooklyn lines. The rest were killed or captured. As for Stirling, he came upon irascible old General von Heister on a wooded slope and surrendered to him. The Hessian veteran had had a lifetime of soldiering and must have accepted many conquered swords. He never received a more honorable one than this.

This action, in the sunshine of August 27, had been surprisingly brief. Noon found the last of the American survivors scrambling, breathless and shaken, into the Brooklyn works, while out on the sloping plains Sir William Howe sat down to compose a long and rather glittering report to be sent at once to Lord George Germain, Secretary of State for the Colonies.

His actual accomplishment does not add up to very much, largely through his own hesitancy. Just what had he accomplished? He had cleared the approaches to the Brooklyn works of a badly placed and badly commanded American army. That army was intact, if inclined to be panicky, and now lay exactly where he did not want it—behind good earthworks. And for once there was no "way around," for the fortifications curved in a rough horseshoe from water to water and, as long as the adverse winds held, his fleet could not take the Americans in the rear.

So he withdrew his troops out into the flats again and set engineers and sappers and digging details to work constructing trenches and redoubts, pushing them closer and closer to the American lines. When he did attack, he wanted to be sure that his men had a minimum of open ground to cover. The Breed's Hill complex was strong on him, backed by his own growing tendency to indolence.

Within the American lines there were chaos and bitter, deep discouragement. Men wandered about, lost and disheartened, looking for known units or known faces, blundered in and out of formations where strange men cursed them in unfamiliar accents. Bloodshot eyes kept turning east, looking for a stir and bustle in the distant scarlet and blue and green lines that might foreshadow another attack. It was clear to the most obtuse private that he and his fellows could not stand up to Howe's men in the open field unless there was assurance of such controlled American fire power that the bayonet-wielding attackers could be broken up before they had a chance to close with their dreaded weapons. There was nothing else with which to counter. There were few bayonets in the American lines and fewer still were the men who knew how to use them.

Yet some semblance of order crept back into the works about Brooklyn, for George Washington was there, outwardly calm, imperturbable, and confident, whatever doubts and rending anxieties may have been preying on his mind over this, his first big test as commander-in-chief. Men could see his towering figure dismounting to inspect a gun position, bending from the saddle to speak to some distracted junior officer. His presence by no means told the whole story of recovery, but it must have written a very bold chapter. Units sorted themselves out, guards were posted. By late afternoon some enterprising officers sent parties of riflemen as much as one hundred rods from the outer works, where they fired, without retaliation, on the nearest enemy posts.

Riding from point to point, Washington still clung to his conviction that his position was tenable. In his mind it *had* to be. He was going to hold New York, and to do this he had to deny the commanding Brooklyn Heights to the British. Thus he must have reasoned, forgetting or discounting the fact that the "divine wind" must eventually shift and send British warships up the East River, between Manhattan and Brooklyn. So in a gesture that seemed to invite future disaster he ordered more regiments over from New York. They were not strong enough to strengthen his position appreciably; they seemed destined only to swell the eventual prisoner account that Howe would one day send to Germain.

Yet there was hidden salvation for Washington and the army in the choice of units to cross over from Manhattan. Along with John Shee's 3rd and Robert Magaw's 5th Pennsylvanians came a unit whose selection might have been attributed to divine guidance. Rowing clumsy flatboats and barges across the East River were the blue-and-white Marbleheaders under command of stocky, dogged John Glover. They disembarked, took their places in the Brooklyn lines. They would not stay there long. A crisis was developing slowly and the men of the old 21st, now the 14th Massachusetts, would be ready to meet it.

The wind shifted with the next sunrise, still mercifully favored Washington and his men by bringing down a howling nor'easter that set Glover and his Marbleheaders sniffing wistfully. The rest of the force suffered, for even in August such a storm can be icy. An officer of Shee's regiment wrote numbly: "We had not tents to screen us from its pitiless pelting." Food had to be eaten raw and muskets were drenched and useless. It did not do to complain. William Howe's men were immobilized by this same storm. So, more importantly, were his brother "Black Dick's" ships. The East River was still an American lake.

The storm roared its long course, and camp rumors—"shaves," the G.I. of 1776 called them—rode on the slanting rain. A message had gone out to General Billy Heath up there at the King's Bridge to gather boats and send them down-river to the Brooklyn wharves. Oh no. Long Island wasn't being given up. But the sick and wounded were to be evacuated and if anyone thought that they wouldn't need so many boats as had been ordered, why, General Hugh Mercer was sending fresh regiments over from the New Jersey camp. They'd relieve an equal number of regiments now in the line. The lucky ones would be ferried back to New York.

It was all in orders and all of it false, except for the fact of the boats that Billy Heath was sending. Despite the storm, Howe's covering works were being pushed closer and closer, until Washington dared hold onto his Brooklyn positions no longer. For Howe to learn of the evacuation would have been fatal. So Washington's own men must not know. One prisoner, one deserter could have thrown the commander-in-chief and his entire garrison into the British bag. There was another factor. Morale. The outer lines would have to be held during embarkation. Were any regiments steady enough to stand there until the very last moment, knowing that the rest of the army was slipping away from them through the night? It was too much to risk. Washington must lie to his army to save it.

By dusk of the twenty-ninth a flotilla of scows, barges, bateaux, anything that could float and carry men and supplies, bumped hollowly against the Brooklyn wharves, grated onto beaches. Down from the advanced lines came a silent procession of white-trousered, blue-jacketed men. John Glover's Marbleheaders were filing out to place their peacetime skills at the service of the army. Near the wharves and beaches they found seafaring neighbors, Salem men from Israel Hutchinson's 27th Massachusetts, to handle embarkation and crossing with them.

Far away in the Brooklyn works, alone, unsupported, with open flanks and no reserves, the pick of the army waited out the night. John Haslet's men were there, along with what was left of Smallwood's command. Shee's and Magaw's Pennsylvanians kept watch with them and linked onto John Chester's Connecticut command. Down the slopes to the water, line after endless line of men filed away, were quickly herded into the boats to be rowed in the deadest of hushes across to the New York landings. Trip after trip the Marbleheaders and the Salem men made, expertly dumping their living cargo, swinging about in the dense night, and heading for Brooklyn again.

Ashore, the steady and, in the main, orderly stream came in a slow flood from the Heights. There were moments of tense danger when crowds of stragglers and shirkers took panic, tried to rush the boats, the men actually clambering over each other's shoulders to get aboard, brawling and fighting like the mobs at the Berezina bridges in 1812. Order was restored somehow and the boatmen kept up their endless, backbreaking shuttle across the East River. The round trip was more than two miles, measuring from landing to landing. The oarsmen had had few rations and less sleep, yet there is no record of any break in the slow, steady passages, made in silence and without benefit of lights.

Another factor must have weighed heavily on the stooped shoulders of the boatmen. It is not likely that they knew of the extent of the evacuation until well past midnight. But the Marbleheaders, at least, were fully aware of the thin fringes that held the lines in the face of the British, for they had manned a part of it until the very last moment. Now, dragging with numbing wrists at their oars, they must have kept their eyes on the hidden Long Island Heights as they headed for Manhattan, or snatched furtive glances over their shoulders on the return trips. What was Howe up to? At any instant the night-shrouded slopes by Brooklyn might show a spatter of orange-red stars, with muffled reports coming nearer and nearer to the water front and twinkling out the doom of the waiting regiments. And Glover's men would be in duty bound to swing their craft in close, to snatch away from under muzzle and bayonet as many of their countrymen as they could—as many as they could until they themselves were snapped up or until their clumsy barges sank under them, splintered by gunfire. In the performance of Glover's men and Israel Hutchinson's there is none of the intoxication of a desperate charge like that of Lord Stirling and the Maryland two hundred and fifty, none of the cold heroism, perhaps, of the unnamed and unnumbered men who turned to face bayonet with empty, useless musket. But there is in it a sort of grim, dogged glory of its own.

The night held still more perils. A hideous snafu of blurred orders, of misunderstood instructions, brought the Delawares and the rest of the little garrison out of the lines and down to the embarkation area. Not a single man remained in the works, and the shore was thick with waiting troops. Haslet's men and Shee's and Smallwood's commands stood on the lower slopes, almost within reach of the craft that would take them to the safety of New York. The tangled orders had to be corrected.

Even with tightly disciplined men an order to return to the dangers of those outer works might have brought on mutiny. And these still green men? It is in the record that they countermarched, climbed the bitter, muddy slopes back to their posts, and resumed their tense vigil, with the British picks and shovels working nearer and nearer, with British voices more and more distinct. It was close to daylight when word finally brought them to the wharves, where weary Marbleheaders and Salem men nudged the barges in close.

And still catastrophe hovered over the lightening river. Suspicious of the silent works, British patrols began nosing in over trench and gun pit. One swift rush by a small striking force would have been the end of this last contingent. Then, miraculous as the winds that had blown down the river and denied passage to the British fleet, a sudden dense fog blanketed shore and river, and the British patrols could only report back that the Yankees were gone. No sign of them anywhere. Must have embarked somehow, sir.

So the blanket of mist clung thick over the East River and the boatmen toiled away through their sixth consecutive hour of steady rowing, of snatching a whole army away from defeat and capture. They took more than the army. No food, no equipment, no arms had been left behind, save for a few heavy cannon whose pitted bores and rust-caked muzzles made them more deadly to their cannoneers than to an enemy.

In the stern of one of the last of John Glover's boats young Lieutenant Benjamin Tallmadge turned his striking profile back toward the Brooklyn shore. He may have been wondering if his close friend and Yale classmate, Captain Nathan Hale of the 19th Connecticut, was still on the dock. He did not see Hale, who must have crossed in an earlier boat, but the lieutenant's last glimpse of the embarkation point showed him a very tall man, cloaked and booted, coming carefully down some slippery steps while a Marbleheader stretched out a blue arm to guide the commander-in-chief to the boat below.

The whole accomplishment was magnificent. In a British magazine of the time a military critic wrote with stern enthusiasm: "Those who are best acquainted with the difficulty, embarrassment, noise and tumult which attend even by day and with no enemy at hand, a movement of this nature, will be the first to acknowledge that this retreat should hold a high place among military transactions." But retreats, even those which "hold a high place among military transactions," do not win battles or campaigns. Often they only postpone defeat.

It was a drenched, dismal New York into which the ninety-five hundred-odd were poured from Glover's and Hutchinson's boats. In a chill dawn, exhausted men squelched up the cobbled streets from Coenties Slip or other landings higher up the island. The sullen reaction following their escape from the Long Island trap was strong on them, and what they saw did nothing for their spirits. There were piles of dripping supplies disintegrating in wide puddles. Abandoned arms, tossed away by earlier arrivals, tripped up stumbling feet. In side streets and gloomy, sour alleys, furtive-looking men edged away, broke into a heavy trot at the slightest hail from troops in formation. The tap of a soggy drum sent more of them drifting nervously toward the exits of the city, tossing away the remnant of a coat that bore regimental markings, ripping out a shabby cockade that might have linked them to a unit. The smell of defeat and disintegration was strong in the air.

The army as it landed looked little better than the city to civilian eyes. Lutheran Pastor Gustavus Shewkirk heard "no merry tones of drums and fifes. . . . It seemed," he thought, "that a general damp had spread. . . . Many looked sickly, emaciated, cast down . . . everything seemed to be in confusion. Many, as it is reported for certain, went away to their respective homes."

Probably neither city nor army was as bad as it seemed. Any town under military occupation and in a war zone is a dismal spot, especially in a rainy dawn. The fringes of any army, whether shattered or triumphant, suggest rout and panic. The experienced Baron de Marbot, crossing the rear of a Napoleonic army, was so depressed by what he saw that he read defeat into an 1813 French victory. For the moment New York and Washington's force were in passable shape. The question was what to do with that city and that army.

Major General Nathanael Greene, now recovered from the fever which had so unfortunately taken him out of the Long Island action, came up at once with the conclusion that seems so utterly logical from today's vantage point. City and island were of no conceivable use to the Americans as long as England controlled the waterways. Therefore, evacuate at once. Also, they could never be recovered without "a superior naval force." Therefore, burn the city and deny its shelter to the British Army. Adjutant General Joseph Reed and Chief Engineer Rufus Putnam loudly supported the Rhode Islander, as, surprisingly enough, did John Jay, whose New York holdings were roughly comparable to John Hancock's Boston empire.

A more than startled Congress came down heavily on the idea of burning but left the question of evacuation to the commander-in-chief. The latter's reasoning is hard to follow. He admitted Greene's frank admonition that "the country is struck with a panick" and that a major military reverse at this time "may ruin the cause." He agreed that there was grave danger to his entire force if the enemy "should enclose us . . . by taking post in our rear . . . oblige us to fight them on their own Terms, or surrender at discretion." This was precisely what the Howes could be expected to do, with their wide choice of point or points of attack. Notwithstanding this, Washington feared that evacuation "would dispirit the Troops and enfeeble our cause." More than being trapped on the island?

There was a Council of War at the Mortier house and a bewildering plan was produced which scattered the army all over the island, with the least battle-worthy generals in command at key points. To this Nathanael Greene protested so loudly that a second council was held and Washington at last agreed to evacuation. He began to move the vast stores that had been accumulated, but transport was scarce and he wrote the Congress: "I fear we shall not effect the whole before we shall meet with some Interruption." Unfortunately that "Interruption" was looming close as mid-September edged on.

And ominous doubts were spreading through the army concerning a respected but unsuccessful leader. Colonel John Haslet wrote to Caesar Rodney, "The Genl I revere, for his Character for Disinterestedness, Patience and fortitude will be held in Everlasting Remembrance, but the Vast Burthen appears to be too much. W'd to Heaven Genl Lee were here is the Language of officers and men." John Haslet was barely to live out the year, but before he died he surely would have admitted that if the "Vast Burthen" were too much for Washington, then it was too much for any living mortal.

CHAPTER XVIII

"The men . . . . feel a confidence which before they had quite lost"

THE dramatic American Dunkirk which spirited a beaten army from Long Island to Manhattan had taken place during the night of August 29–30. For some days Sir William Howe made no move to follow up his success. Then as September came on and American generals fumbled over their plans, heavy bodies began to move on Long Island. British and Hessians flowed along the west shore, and Washington's lookouts could easily make out scarlet coats and blue, bright in the sunlight, about present-day Long Island City and Astoria. Blackwell's Island, now cut by the towering Queensboro Bridge, was occupied. Hessians and British dug gun pits near the present Randall's Island stadium and on Riker's Island. Hidden from Manhattan, scarlet and blue pushed up to Flushing

Bay. The divine winds veered, became hostile, and British shipping appeared in the North and East rivers. And Sir William still stayed his hand.

There was his natural and growing indolence, added, perhaps, to a conviction that the American army was in such straits that a mere token attack, delivered at his leisure, was all that would be needed. But there were also his pro-American leanings, heightened by his awareness of American reverence for his elder brother, Lord George Howe, dead at Ticonderoga in 1758. He still had his rather sickly and fast-withering olive branch from Parliament. What if he, despite his courteous rebuff at Washington's hands, could bring about conciliation with these people who had actually set a monument to his dead brother in Westminster Abbey?

At Sir William's invitation, a congressional commission from Philadelphia met him on Staten Island. There were Benjamin Franklin of Pennsylvania, Edward Rutledge of South Carolina, and John Adams of Massachusetts, and the trio listened rather noncommittally to Howe's proposals. Their host began by saying that if America fell he would lament "as for the loss of a brother," whereat Franklin observed gently, "My Lord, we shall use our utmost endeavors to save your Lordship that mortification." The rest of the conversation went on courteously and fruitlessly, since Howe was empowered to speak of nothing save pardons, and at the end of the day the comissioners trooped back across the Kill van Kull with nothing accomplished. Sir William sighed, mentally dusted off his hands, and turned to his next task.

The bulk of the American army by now had been moved up near the Harlem Plains in the neighborhood of present 125th Street, and Washington established his headquarters in the vacant house of an old comrade in arms, Colonel Roger Morris, now a Tory refugee. The house, better known as the Jumel mansion, still stands white and graceful above the towering red cliffs of Coogan's Bluff, seemingly unaware of the maniac screechings which rise from the Polo Grounds just below. At the end of Manhattan Island, in the heart of the three-mile-long city of New York, Israel Putnam, Henry Knox, and some four thousand men still lingered in the face of that "Interruption" which Washington feared.

It came on the fifteenth. There had been British activity here and there for a day or two before, nothing to alarm Washington unduly. But on this morning, a clear, hot day typical of Manhattan, a glasslike clarity that was blurred now and then by a slight haze. There were five British frigates in the East River. As though to point up Nathanael Greene's urgings on the score of vulnerability, one or two more slipped up the North River. A pincers movement, one prong driving east and the other west across the island, might be in the making.

There was no need for such subtlety. All through the morning the East River flotilla pounded the shore line from the modern mid East Twenties up to the East Forties. Noon, and there was activity about the mouth of Newtown Creek across on Long Island. Barge after barge pushed out, brightly flowering with British scarlet or alive with clear Hessian blue. An observer with a poetic turn of mind compared the loaded craft to "a clover field in full bloom."

The British and Hessian officers were enchanted with the sight. "The hills, the woods, the river, the town, the ships and pillars of smoke, all heightened by a most clear and delightful morning, furnished the finest landscape that either art and nature combined could draw or imagination conceive." In fact, it was "altogether grand and noble."

Not to the men posted in flimsy, shallow works ashore. They were mostly militia, Connecticut militia, frozen there behind the loose-earth parapets. Somewhere in the rear were Massachusetts militiamen under General John Fellows and General Samuel Holden Parsons with his Connecticut Continentals, who had stood quite well on Lord Stirling's left over on Long Island. The men along the water front saw big Hessian grenadiers in towering, bright helmets leap ashore, saw catlike British light infantry spring from grounded barges. The ships' guns kept on, stunning the raw troops, and when the gunfire lifted, there were smoothly moving lines forming along Kip's Bay, not volleying, but lowering their heavy muskets, bayonet-tipped.

There was utter rout. The landing force lost hardly a man and the fugitives from the works fled inland, toward present First and Second Avenues. Suddenly Washington was there, roaring at them to stand, to take cover in the nearby orchard, behind good stone walls. Iz Putnam, never one to hold back in a good fight, was smashing his horse into groups of flying men, while Thomas Mifflin kept close by Washington, adding his voice and example to that of the commander-in-chief. Parsons' men and Fellows' were brought up from the reserve, thrown into the action. They caught the always infectious panic and soon were running in terror, not running because they were afraid, but afraid because they ran, and each step deepened their unreasoning fear.

Washington was a puzzled, overworked man that day and his usually calm poise was shattered. He lashed out at fugitives with cane and sword, seemed bent on hurling himself into the nearest British or Hessian formation. Mifflin and Putnam and others finally got him away, almost speechless with rage and frustration. Just one American line formed, just one volley fired, and the rout might have been checked. But no line was to form, no volley was to be fired. The terrified, broken men streamed away to the northwest and their commander-in-chief was hustled along in their wake.

As for the British and Hessians, they formed up calmly and unhurriedly, pushing inland a little way, spreading north perhaps as far as Forty-second Street. Then they halted, to wait for orders. Sir Henry Clinton, task-force commander, came ashore, set out with his staff, and trotted quietly on until he reached the variously spelled Inclenburg, better known as Murray Hill, and set up his headquarters in the house of Robert Murray. He did not want to rush matters. A Continental brigade commanded by broad-browed John Glover had come down from the Harlem area. His mission was to cover the wreckage of the retreat, but Clinton couldn't be sure and wanted to wait until he had more men ashore, lest Glover should attack.

More men came, filed up from Kip's Bay, and grounded their arms in the fields that used to spread out just below the present Grand Central Station. Sir William Howe soon joined Clinton, bringing with him the resentment-bubbling Sir William Tryon, Loyalist governor of New York. Mrs. Murray saw that her guests benefited from the Murray kitchens and wine cellars and thus entered legend so firmly that her delicate imprint has pressed down into history itself; by enchanting Howe and the others with good food, good wine, and good talk, she paralyzed all British activities, shouts legend.

But Howe needed no outside stimuli to fling him into a fine frenzy of lassitude. And anyway, plans and orders called for a penetration just so far. He had reached his self-prescribed D-day objective. In good time he would re-form his troops and swing on up the island, and certainly no events of the day suggested the least opposition.

Of course it would have been a very simple matter to push British and Highlanders and Hessians right across to the North River itself and cut Manhattan in two. But the troops would be all the better for rest and rations, there were reports to be received, routine orders issued while he and his brass beamed over the Murray wine and brandies. Is it possible that he thought the entire American force had been withdrawn to the north of the island, north, say, of present Fifty-ninth Street? If so, his Tory agents in New York had served him very badly.

Far south, in the city itself, there were several thousand Americans. They would have made a handsome addition to his bag of prisoners. And with them was the tall, fat Boston bookseller, Henry Knox, of far greater value than his then rank of colonel might suggest. Presently he was joined by Israel Putnam and from him learned the full details of the Kip's Bay tragedy and the completeness of the landing.

As Knox got the picture, most of the roads north were blocked by the enemy. Skimming back though his mental card index that was stocked with what he had read and seen, he came to the conclusion that it was up to him to fight his way out, in the faint hope of salvaging at least some of his force. Iz Putnam, who would have cheerfully tried to claw his way through an entire army, using nothing but clubbed muskets, rocks, or fists, agreed with him.

But there was, on Bayard's Hill, an aide, girlishly handsome, foppish, frail, rather sly-looking. For all his dainty appearance, he had made the frightful march to Quebec with Arnold, arriving there fresh, smart, and smiling. Now he had a plan. He would have plans all his life and they would usually point to great gains for him and much trouble for others. But this time Aaron Burr's glib, slick mind held salvation for all. There was a way out, he said. How this rather eely macaroni had acquired a knowledge of hidden New York lanes and wooded stretches that sloped out of British sight to the west is impossible to say, for Burr was, like Habakkuk, "*capable de tout.*" His seniors listened to him and he led out men destined otherwise for capture or slaughter. There was, of course, nothing to do about the remaining stores and all the invaluable heavy guns in the New York works. They were lost, but the men might, with luck, reach the main army.

By this time a good part of the army had been drawn up on Harlem Heights and the high ground that ran west from them clear to the North River. It is still a commanding stretch of clifflike highlands lying a little north of 125th Street. From it, one looks down on the west end into a weird scoop of a giant trowel leading down to the North River. Then it was called Martje David's Vly, or the Hollow Way. South was more high ground where the buildings of Columbia University and Barnard College now loom. To the southeast there was a quite regular, broad notch called McGowan's Pass, and right down the center of the island a rolling, wooded wilderness stretched on and on. This wilderness tract was bounded on the west by the Bloomingdale Road and on the east by the Boston Post Road. Call the tangle of woods, swamps, and low hills Central Park, the west road Amsterdam Avenue, the east highway Second or Third Avenue, and you have the main features of this terrain as they are today.

The weather stayed fine and hot and the hazes began to lift as the afternoon wore on. From the Point of Rocks, almost midway in the northern or Harlem Heights, lookouts had a superb view of the southern reaches, the two bounding roads and forest maze between them. Some watcher, officer or man, militia or Continental, had his attention drawn to the east, or Boston Post Road. For a long time it had stirred with sullen trickles of stragglers. Then it had lain empty under the baking sun. Suddenly men were shouting that that road was full, jammed from edge to green edge. Wisps of music drifted up toward the Point of Rocks, and scarlet was bright against the brown rutted surface. Sir William was moving toward the northern heights and what was left of the American army.

Another shout, high in the afternoon air. The western road, Bloomingdale Road! There was movement, but no color. Just a steady drab flow, spent men lurching on and nothing but the sound of their own broken boots for drumbeats. Aaron Burr was bringing Henry Knox, Israel Putnam, and their forgotten men back to the army.

It must have been a breath-catching sight. Two hostile forces, one victory-strong and one beaten, plodding on parallel roads, heading in the same direction, each screened from the other by some two miles of trees, swamp, and undergrowth. If the quick-stepping scarlet light infantry poured through McGowan's Pass and out onto the flats that scored east and west across the island, the drab, weary men to the west were lost. It was a deadly race. Who would win?

The life-and-death drama unrolled its slow course. Once the British halted, threw out flankers in the rough country to the west, resumed their march. The flankers beat their way doggedly over the broken ground. If they had spread out a little more, they might have caught a glimpse of the column on the Bloomingdale Road. By chance they never reached any good observation point, and Knox and Putnam went on, hampered only by fatigue and the depression of defeat.

All at once the fugitives were spilling out into the deep scoop of Martje David's Vly. To the east, scarlet showed suddenly about McGowan's Pass and disaster loomed. Once again Smallwood's Marylanders were called on to risk their lives or liberty to save a part of the army. They went out steadily, engaged the British, still in some slight disorder as they funneled out of the narrow Post Road and deployed onto the flats. There was musket smoke. Gunfire rattled and stuttered in a hesitant engagement. American drums beat and Smallwood's men disengaged, fell back to the northern heights in good order. On the high ground the rest of the army opened ranks, allowed the panting Knox and Putnam to pass their spent men through to the rear where safety lay.

The action of September 15 was over. Night fell and both armies lay on their arms, facing each other and separated by the broad hollow that ran from the Vly to the East River. Campfires began to wink, north and south. Lanterns sailed like slow stars through the night as aides probed about in the darkness, gathering reports, carrying orders, seeking out company or regimental or brigade commanders. On the British side, Howe consulted with Clinton and Cornwallis, with Von Heister and Von Donop. One strong push across the Hollow Way during the following morning, or perhaps not until afternoon or even the next day, and the campaign would be over.

There could have been found many to agree with him north across the broad, deep scoop. The Kip's Bay panic spread a heavy fog of depression, of discouragement, through the whole American force. Sectional friction rasped and grated among the weary units. The New England troops had started this war, hadn't they? And what was their record? Smashed and routed on Long Island. A mass of screeching fugitives during the bay landings. It was hard to argue against known facts. They simply were no good. And it had to be admitted that the only units to come out of the campaign with any credit were the Southerners—Haslet's Delawares and Smallwood's Marylanders, green troops without even the mild seasoning of the siege of Boston, which should at least have taught the New Englanders how to face cannon fire. Suppose that shaky palmetto fort on Sullivan's Island had been manned by such troops! There were hot waves of contempt, of resentment. The army seemed ready to break up from within, without waiting for Howe's attack. It was probably far too disorganized to be able to stage a successful retreat.

It was all true, but it was not the whole truth. A great many weights, unseen in the twilight of discouragement, lay in the American tray of the scales and tended to restore a proper balance. There were men like John Glover, for example. The men he led had done a job in bringing the army to Manhattan that a professional army might have envied, and their leader had driven himself to the cracking point as he worked with them. It was his brigade that had come down to stave off wholesale disaster at Kip's Bay, much as Lord Stirling had sent Smallwood against the Cortelyou house and as Christian Febiger, the Dane, had rallied disorganized men to cover the retreat from the redoubt at Breed's Hill.

None of this superb work of Glover's had been done with a clear mind. Many Marblehead fortunes and livelihoods had been wrecked by the various acts that led to the Revolution. This Marbleheader, now an acting brigadier general, had been in service for over a year, and many letters from home told him that his large family was destitute, that it would become a public charge unless he came home to provide for it. A Glover on relief! Some days before the Long Island engagement he had actually written out his resignation, each stroke of the pen costing him as much anguished effort as any oar stroke in the East River during the night of the evacuation. Providentially, another letter had come from home. Brother Jonathan Glover had managed to sell some property for him. John Glover's family was safe for some months. After that? It was the "some months" that counted. Wife and children were safe in the white house on the Marblehead hillside and the father was still solidly planted in the night above Martje David's Vly with his brigade and his regiment. Such a man would be fully able to retreat or attack or stand fast. And there were thousands like him.

But the heaviest weight of all was represented by a tall, cloaked Virginian, now fully recovered from his utterly understandable loss of temper by Kip's Bay. By a lantern George Washington conferred with the men whom fate had assigned him to lead, men like Nathanael Greene and Henry Knox, belligerent Israel Putnam, James Clinton of New York, and Joseph Spencer of Connecticut. He spoke to them and others calmly, fully realizing that he did not have much of an army and keenly aware that he must do what he could with what he had—do what he could to the utmost.

There was the question of Howe's intentions. Would he attack during the next morning? How were his troops disposed? High ground and thick woods south of 125th Street hid answers to all such questions, but the Virginian knew that he could not wait until those heights and woods began a sudden eruption of scarlet and blue down into the Vly and up the northern heights. Someone must go and see, in command of a small, compact, and reliable force, and where could such a force be found on the night of September 15, 1776?

Someone, possibly Spencer, mentioned young Major Thomas Knowlton of Connecticut. He had been outstanding at Breed's Hill and the rail fences that trailed down to the slow Mystic. He was "six feet high, erect and elegant in figure and formed more for activity than strength . . . courteous and affable in manners . . . cool and courageous in battle . . . the favorite of superior officers, the idol of his soldiers." He led a sort of commando formation of more than one hundred men, mostly picked by rigid standards from various Connecticut regiments. The job was his. He was to take his Rangers at dawn across the Vly and up the southern heights.

He seems to have had his command in excellent shape for the work, though he probably regretted the absence of one of his best company commanders, Benjamin Tallmadge's friend and classmate, Nathan Hale. On many counts it was a pity that Hale was not present, that he could not be recalled to his outfit. At that very moment the young Yale man was in the heart of New York City, hoping that his disguise as a teamster would frank him through while he made highly indiscreet notes about the British Army and its heavy-bodied allies.

Dawn of the sixteenth, and Knowlton took his men in extended order up the south slopes. At once he collided with two battalions of British light infantry under the same General Leslie who had led the futile march to Salem in 1775. The Rangers stood firm until the high defiance of bagpipes brought on the Black Watch through the early morning. Carefully and in excellent order Knowlton broke off the action, retired in a leisurely fashion down to the Vly.

In an instant the southern heights were thick with scarlet coats. So the Yankees were running again? There were coarse and deep-biting jeers. Mounted officers blared out insultingly with hunting horns. A jolly good fox hunt, this, chivvying the Yankees around again!

The notes carried across the Vly, and Joseph Reed remembered later that he had "never felt such a sensation before—it seemed to crown our disgrace." The horn blasts may have stung Washington, a "hard man to hounds" himself. There seemed to be no attempt at pursuit, but if—just if he could draw the light infantry off the heights and down into the Vly! Orders snapped out. Lieutenant Colonel Archibald Crary of Rhode Island led out some hundred and fifty New England volunteers. Major Andrew Leitch of Virginia charged out at the head of about as many riflemen from Colonel George Weedon's 3rd Virginia to support the Connecticut Rangers and their tall major.

There was contact at once. The eager British poured down into the Hollow Way, were abruptly checked. Then, incredibly to both sides, they began to fall back, back. The Yankees were attacking, and in the open! More troops were poured in. John Nixon's Massachusetts men came up, General Reazin Beall's Maryland militia hard on their heels. Colonel Paul Dudley Sargent's New Englanders were there, Colonel George Weedon, a Fredericksburg tavernkeeper, got the sign from Washington and raced the rest of his command into the echoing smoke. Then, with a magnificent gesture, the commander-in-chief committed to action the very militiamen who had panicked so shamefully the day before at Kip's Bay. Iz Putnam, of course, was ramping and shouting happily all along the line. Nathanael Greene was in action, and General George Clinton hurried up a pair of Henry Knox's cherished guns.

There must have been shattering disbelief on both sides of the Hollow Way. The ragged, shaken men of the Fifteenth were standing almost toe to toe with grenadiers, guards, Scots, Hessians, with the men of the 33rd West Ridings, who had cut such a swath on Long Island. Ammunition began to

run low and there was a retrograde movement. A retrograde movement by
the British! Through a field of buckwheat on the site of Barnard College,
through an orchard went kilt and bright Hessian helmet, with New Englanders and Marylanders and Virginians pressing them hard but coolly.
George Clinton brought his guns into action, and through the far fringes of
the smoke men could see the last of the British and Hessian reserves being
hurried up from their billets at the double.

This little reconnaissance by Knowlton and his hundred-odd men was
developing into a general engagement, perhaps a major one. This was more
than Washington dared risk. Through the smoke went his military secretary, young Captain Tench Tilghman of Pennsylvania. His order to retire
was greeted with derisive jeers, for "the pursuit of a flying enemy was so
new a scene that it was with difficulty our men could be brought to retire
... [but] they gave a Hurrah and left the field in good order."

Eighteenth-century musket and cannon smoke was heavy and inert and
the men must have stumbled over half-seen rocks, splashed through unsuspected puddles. The smoke hid more than the terrain. It masked two of
the best men in action that day. Thomas Knowlton, "courteous and affable
in manners," and Andrew Leitch, who had so coolly handled his Virginia
riflemen, lay somewhere under the sullen smoke pall. They had gallantly
led this first American attack, which was the last for both of them.

The action was over and the units that Washington had committed
withdrew to their lines and outwardly the positions of the two armies remained unchanged. Psychologically the picture called for a complete reappraisal. There was angry bewilderment in all ranks of Howe's forces. The
Americans had not followed the script. They had ad-libbed outrageously.
The same men who had performed, on the whole, so feebly on Long
Island, so contemptibly at Kip's Bay, had suddenly turned, slugged it out
with some of the best regiments, had actually driven them for more than
a mile! Then they had retired, in good order and unmolested. The Hessian
Von Donop went so far as to report that if his Jaegers had not come up just
when they did the British and Scottish troops would have been captured. It
was certainly something to think about.

Over on the American heights some men actually dared to hope, and
their hopes reached the Congress at Philadelphia. To Brother Thomas in
Wilmington, Caesar Rodney wrote that the New Englanders at Kip's Bay
had "behaved in a most dastardly, cowardly, scandalous manner . . . but
that courage is not always to be found the same, even in the same person,
is equally true . . . for some of them the day following were in the other
engagement [Martje David's Vly] and behaved with great bravery."

The action also gave men from different states a chance to see each other
under hot fire, and they could realize that there was little to choose between
them. Of course one's own are always the best, and Captain Gooch of
Varnum's 9th Rhode Island clucked happily that the "first Lawrels" belonged to New England. Tench Tilghman of Pennsylvania, a "Southerner"
in New England eyes like all those who came from south of New Jersey,

gravely stated that "The Virginia and Maryland Troops bear the palm." Both Tilghman and Gooch were right. The achievement was national, not sectional. Something of this was glimpsed at headquarters by Adjutant General Joseph Reed. "You can hardly conceive the change it has made in our army," he said. The army, not the New England troops or the Virginians or his own Pennsylvanians. "The men have recovered their spirits and feel a confidence which before they had quite lost." Of course such gains were not self-perpetuating. They could evaporate, as Reed realized when he added dubiously, "I hope the effects will be lasting."

For a great many days the revivified army was not to be put to the test. Sir William Howe eyed the Harlem Heights, saw Henry Knox and Rufus Putnam emplacing more guns, throwing up more solid works. It is likely that he envisioned another, and worse, Breed's Hill, with the Hollow Way stacked with scarlet heaps and blue. There were, of course, several attractive "ways around," thanks to his vast naval strength, but his mind moved slowly among them. And in the early hours of the twenty-first he had a fresh worry, no less sharp for being non-military.

The "Sentry at Genl Smith quarters at Mr. Elliot's house" roused Lieutenant Frederick Mackenzie of the 23rd Welch. New York was burning and Mackenzie could see a terrifying mass of smoke and flame to the south. He dressed and ran the two miles down into town, but the fire, which had started in a shed near Whitehall Slip, was completely out of control. There was a high wind, and the flames lunged into Dock Street and Bridge Street and Beaver Street and up to Fulton Street. Great mansions and sleazy hovels shot fire from roof and window. Dutch houses that Peter Stuyvesant might have seen became glowing ovens. Citizens, troops, and sailors turned out, but Lieutenant Mackenzie noted that the fire engines were in very bad shape, that buckets were few and water, except along the wharves and slips, in very scant supply. Parson Shewkirk, who had commented so unfavorably on the army as it returned from Long Island, joined a bucket line but saw that the fight was hopeless. "If one was in one street and looked about, it broke out already again in another." St. Paul's Church, which still backs up to Broadway, was threatened, but men climbed to the gentle slope of its roof and beat out the flames, which rolled back as though frustrated and then plunged on into Barclay Street.

There was mob frenzy abroad. Men, probably wrongly suspected of setting or spreading the fire, were seized. Some of them were hanged at once. A few screaming wretches were tossed bodily into the fires. And still the flames roared on. Beloved Trinity Church at the head of Wall Street blazed furiously, and Mackenzie, although sick with horror at what he had been seeing, found a sublimity in the death of this steepled church, which, "when completely in flames, was a grand sight, for the spire being entirely framed of wood . . . a lofty Pyramid of fire appeared with every separate piece of timber burning, until the principal timbers were burnt through, when the whole fell with a great noise."

At last the wind shifted and the fire was under control. But the city was pretty well gutted and chance had accomplished what Nathanael Greene had recommended and Congress had forbidden. It was going to be a hard winter for the returned New York Tories, who wandered singly and in family groups through the charred streets, for the troops, and especially the officers, had to be housed, didn't they?

The next day our Welch lieutenant witnessed another tragedy. A spy had been captured, a very amateur spy who had incautiously jotted down damning intelligence notes. He was not tall, but built like a fast welter-weight, with a very fair complexion, blond hair, and blue eyes. He was hanged, of course, on what is now Fifty-second Street, a little east of First Avenue, where Howe's artillery was parked. Mackenzie noted that the spy "was about 24 years of age, and had been educated at the College of New-haven in Connecticut. He behaved with great composure and resolution saying he thought it the duty of every good Officer, to obey any orders given him by the Commander-in-Chief; and desired the spectators to be at all times prepared to meet death in whatever shape it might appear."

The noose tightened and it was all over. Like his immediate commander, Thomas Knowlton, he would never answer the Rangers' roll call again, and Benjamin Tallmadge, up on Harlem Heights, would wait in vain for the return of his old friend Nathan Hale.

The September days dragged on, ripened into October. Howe sat quietly south of the Vly, or Hollow Way, seeming to weigh with ponderous care the various "ways around." On the American side, the effervescence of their successful raid in force dulled and flattened, and inactivity made men remember Long Island and Kip's Bay rather than the glittering sweep up the southern heights. Desertions became more and more frequent. Joseph Reed, recalling his reservations on the resurgence of American spirit, lamented that "A spirit of desertion, cowardice, plunder and shrinking from duty . . . prevailed too generally throughout the whole army." Per-sonal equipment was very scarce, and this lack was heightened when fresh New England troops appeared, bringing with them little beyond their muskets and cartridge boxes or powder horns. And one did not have to be a pessimist to dwell a little on the fact that by the end of the year most en-listments would run out. Washington stated somberly to Cousin Lund: "Such is my situation that if I were to wish the bitterest curse to an enemy this side of the grave, I should put him in my stead with my feelings."

A decision had to be made without waiting for Howe to call the signals. Formal councils of war were held in the Morris house up there on the red-brown bluffs. Lord Stirling and John Sullivan, newly released from cap-tivity by exchange, were there. Up from the South came gaunt, ugly Charles Lee, mentally munching on the intoxicating laurels hung on him for Peter Parker's naval mishaps and William Moultrie's unshakable heroism at Sullivan's Island. For once Lee's advice was sound, the same advice given long ago by amateur Nathanael Greene: Get off Manhattan and up into Westchester. Get off quick.

By October 16, Lee's counsel was adopted. But there was one little reservation, small and deadly. Not long ago the Congress had "desired, if it be practicable . . . to obstruct effectually the navigation of the North River." This had been attempted by a line of sunken ships and underwater obstacles. If this obstruction were to be maintained, Fort Washington, high in the present West 180s, and Fort Lee on the Jersey shore opposite must be held, for they covered the east-west anchors of the line. But from the start British ships had sailed happily back and forth over all these obstacles, thereby canceling, it would seem, the "desire" of Congress.

So in deference to this rather vague civilian suggestion it was decided to leave some two thousand men to garrison Fort Washington while the rest of the army withdrew across the King's Bridge. The works were to remain like an island, deep in British territory, cut off from reinforcements, supplies, intelligence, like an eighteenth-century Bastogne or Dienbienphu. Some optimistic officers spoke of keeping up communication via the North River and the Jersey shore, conveniently forgetting that His Majesty's ships could easily choke off any such contact.

The decision to evacuate had been sparked, at least in part, by a sudden move by Sir William Howe. Some days before the adoption of Charles Lee's advice, the British commander had thrown the greater part of his force into a great flotilla of some eighty craft of all kinds, had threaded his way up the East River, through Hell Gate and into the Sound, to land on Throg's Neck, a long nose of jutting land. Thus his striking force was placed deep to the left and rear of the American army. The term had not yet been coined, of course, but Howe had succeeded in making an "end run," a forecast in miniature of Mark Clark's Anzio landings or MacArthur's descent on Inchon. As on Long Island, he had found his "way around," though by water this time. From Throg's Neck he could strike west toward the King's Bridge, sealing up most of Washington's command in Manhattan. He could also cut the invaluable supply roads leading in from Connecticut and the rest of New England.

His intelligence and reconnaissance must have been highly faulty. He found that the Neck, owing to a creek and marshes at its base, was virtually an island. To cross marsh and creek, which were guarded by Edward Hand's black-shirted riflemen, was quite possible. It could also be very costly, since the barrier of swamp and water would keep his bayonetmen from closing quickly with the rifles on the other side. So probably from fear of heavy casualty lists Howe kept his men on the sandy Neck day after day. But his very presence there in the vulnerable American rear could not be overlooked.

Washington's retreat into Westchester started, a cumbersome, weary move, since he lacked transport and had to leapfrog his few shaky carts and gaunt horses. And while precious time creaked on, Howe moved again in the misty dawn of the eighteenth and his destination was Pell's Point, not far to the north and east of Throg's Neck.

On the high ground near the village of Eastchester, which guarded the roads leading west toward the retreating main army, John Glover lay like a wary old bull seal. In the dawn he was suddenly barking orders, for he had spotted "upwards of two hundred boats all manned and formed in four grand divisions," and knew that as acting brigadier over four small Massachusetts regiments he was facing his first independent action. He lacked Greene's natural flair for war, the feeling for combat that marked out Anthony Wayne or Harry Lee. But he did not lack common sense, courage, and a bone-deep belief in his cause. He took action as inevitably as though sending a crew aloft to take in sail in a gathering storm off Cape Ann.

John Glover had no dreams of martial glory as he led out his little brigade to meet whatever had to be met. He wrote, "Oh! The anxiety of mind I was in then for the fate of the day—the lives of seven hundred and fifty men immediately at hazard . . . I would have given a thousand worlds to have had General Lee . . . to direct, or at least approve of what I had done." He needed no sailing master at his elbow, for "I did the best I could and disposed of my little party to the best of my judgment."

His men stood firm, met heavy British and Hessian attacks, gave ground grudgingly and in good order. Pressure slackened and Glover pulled his whole command back across the little Hutchinson River without being pursued. After dusk, he bivouacked near Mile Square, "after fighting all day without victuals or drink laying as a picket all night, the heavens over us and the earth under us," Glover wrote later.

It had been a small action. Like the confused melee about the stone Cortelyou house on Long Island, like the dramatic counterattack across the Hollow Way, its benefits were largely psychological, which does not diminish its importance. It showed Howe and his commanders once again that, no matter how punch-drunk and reeling Washington's army might outwardly seem, some part or parts of that army were more than likely to bounce back off the ropes, striking hard and dangerously.

Yet there may have been something more tangible in this clash at Pell's Point. Six miles away the main army was still writhing in its snail march into Westchester. Had Glover's brigade disintegrated as other units had at Kip's Bay, the pursuit could easily have brought Howe's dreaded bayonet-men smashing into Washington's straggling and disorganized columns on the march. Did Glover's regiments, which yielded ground only when they chose, once again fill the British commander's touchy mind with stacks of casualty reports? It is possible. At any rate, he took no decisive steps for some days, lolling about New Rochelle and finally venturing as far as Mamaroneck.

There were also inertia and lack of decision on the American side the day of the Pell's Point action. Cannon fire and musketry must have been clearly heard by the main army, and yet there is no record of any attempt to find out what the old bull seal from Marblehead was up against, no despatch of reinforcements to him. Dr. Stimson of General John Fellows' New England brigade noted, with almost a veteran's detachment, that Glover's men were "briskly ingaged," adding complacently that "we was cunning a nurfe [enough] not to meddle . . . but bore away . . . to Mile Square whare we incamped and left the above named Regiments to box it out."

The move into Westchester went on. Washington settled his army in the hills about the village of White Plains and waited for the next hostile move. The October nights were growing chill, but his men could warm themselves over the coals of memory, glowing if small, of the Hollow Way and Pell's Point. British and Hessians could be attacked and broken by Americans. Steady muskets in the hands of steady American infantry could beat off those deadly bayonet sweeps after all. There was encouragement in the very sight of the nearly fifteen thousand men massed about the White Plains hills, an immense host to eyes not used to estimating numbers in the field. And there was Howe's continued inactivity to hearten and to mislead the unschooled American officer or private. Maybe Howe was in no hurry to bloody his nose again.

Howe must have figured that he had plenty of time. Certainly he had plenty of men, for on the very day of the Pell's Point action one hundred and twenty sail had come into New York Harbor, a flotilla that brought him more than three thousand replacements for his not too sorely tried British regiments. But there was much more than mere replacements. Lieutenant General Baron Wilhelm von Knyphausen was there with over four thousand seasoned Hessians to add to old Von Heister's troops, as well as several hundred men picked up by the King's agents at bargain-counter rates in the little principality of Waldeck. Most of the Germans were sent at once by water to New Rochelle, where more time was spent assimilating them into the already swollen army. Perhaps Howe excused his endless delays by remarking genially to his staff that he had never heard of a general losing a campaign by being too strong.

At last he moved over the very same ground which he might have covered just after Pell's Point on the eighteenth, which on that day would have brought him onto the flank of Washington's limping, strung-out retreat. In ten days Howe had marched just seventeen miles and now faced an army well entrenched and strong as it ever would be. There was the Bronx River ahead of him, with Chatterton's Hill rising on the opposite bank, Purdy Hill and Hatfield Hill. And there, in the full sunlight of the twenty-eighth of October, was General Joseph Spencer of Connecticut leading out some fifteen hundred New Englanders to meet him, much as John Glover had led out his little band of forty on the eighteenth.

Colonel von Rall's blue-and-red Hessian grenadiers (who had unknowingly begun their march toward the tragedy that would hit them a few weeks hence on the banks of the Delaware) charged, found that they could not come to grips with their shabby foe. There were too many stone walls, too many lines of drab infantry firing, peeling off through the smoke to shelter again, in an imitation of Pell's Point strategy that was probably unconscious, intuitive. One section of Von Rall's line, carrying the morning light through the smoke on their towering brass helmets, was badly shaken. An officer in Spencer's ranks exulted that the Hessians scurried off "like leaves in a whirlwind; and they ran so far that some of the Americans ran out to the ground . . . and brought off their arms and accoutrements and rum that the men who fell had with them, which we had time to drink rounds with before they came on again."

But this was only the thin point of Howe's spearhead. The main force was coming up, and Spencer's men fell back across the Bronx and up Chatterton's Hill. From the high points of their lines Americans could look down on cool groves, on rolling green meadows and the pale gold of wheat fields. They had been empty at sunrise, but now they were checkerboarded with squares of bright scarlet and deep blue. Cavalry made its first real appearance in the war as, with a toss of red plumes, a glint of brass, the 17th Dragoons jingled up on one flank. (This same regiment, generations later and then known as the 17th Lancers, was to pound down a Crimean valley to immortality and death, the very first wave of the tragic Light Brigade.) A Connecticut officer surveying the sunlit terrain below him noted in awe: "The rich array of dress and military equipage gave an imposing grandeur to the scene as they advanced in all the pomp and circumstance of war."

Then a heavy body of British and Hessian infantry moved off toward the American right as Howe once more probed for his "way around" that would avoid a frontal attack. American watchers were amazed to see that the rest of the Anglo-German force "all sat down in the same order in which they stood, no one appearing to move out of his place." There was a prolonged hush broken only by the scuff of thousands of boots through the waving grasses, sharp commands, and the muted ruffle of drums. A lone fieldpiece slammed, the signal for a score of guns of the Royal Artillery to blast out in covering fire for the infantry. Hessians and British floundered across the rippling Bronx River and started up the wooded slopes of Chatterton's Hill.

On the crest, round shot fell heavily, plowing up the turf, skidding off stone walls. Clumsy explosive shells fizzed and smacked, sending hot fragments of iron whining high through the blue air. Alex McDougall, spirit burning as hotly as in the days of the Sons of Liberty, was in command at Chatterton's and he must have wondered why this hill, which dominated the rest of the American position stretching off to his left, had been assigned such a relatively small garrison.

He had about sixteen hundred men. There were militia formations from New York and Massachusetts, of dubious quality. His own 1st New York was in line with Ritzema's 3rd and Webb's 19th Connecticut, sound enough units but still under the shock of Long Island. But with them were the reinforced ranks of Marylanders and Delawares, grimly proud of their record to date.

The Royal Artillery lifted its covering fire, and action was joined. There was a long, confused struggle for the crest, with some of the green regiments showing surprising cohesion and stamina. Then out of nowhere came a pounding of hoofs, the hollow boom-boom of kettledrums, and the 17th Dragoons roared down on the militia in a sweep of red plumes, the glitter of brass helmets, and the silver whirl of sabers. It was the first time that American troops had faced cavalry, and the impact on the militiamen must have been like the terror spread by the first Stuka dive bombers on the Allied troops of 1940. Once again the unexpected was showing its power to unnerve. The militia broke for the nearby woods and John Haslet's right was uncovered.

The Delawares finally retired, the last American troops to leave the field, unhurried and unbroken. Enemy observers noted this and one of them commented gravely, "The Delaware regiment, which had learned on Long Island that prisoners are not made unless they make themselves . . . fought sullenly and composedly."

So Howe had won the two-hundred-foot summit of Chatterton's Hill and there he sat, waiting for reinforcements from Lord Percy. He had not even come near his true objective, the destruction of Washington's army. He had not moved on to block those vital supply roads that led from New England. Nor did he try to interfere with the American shift, on the night of the thirty-first, to the high ground about North Castle, not far to the rear.

In the American lines, spirits rose quickly. All ranks felt that, though they had had to give up one unimportant hill, they had slugged it out once again with strong British and Hessian formations and come out rather well, as on company and regimental levels they certainly had. More important, the distrust in the abilities of their high command, so marked after Long Island and Kip's Bay, largely vanished. They were, in all ranks, still green, and there seems to have been little disposition to question why dominant Chatterton's Hill had been so lightly held, why there had been only two fieldpieces there, and why no help from the main army had been sent until the action was over. They quite understandably looked only at the box score without analyzing it. And in the meantime roads from the east were thick with supply trains as New England acknowledged the food and money that had come to her from as far away as South Carolina in the days of the Port Bill. The army received "good flour, beef and pork in plenty, with grog to wash it down."

During the night of November 4, American outposts heard heavy wagon traffic back of the British lines. The morning of the fifth allowed American patrols to wander at will through deserted British lines. Howe was gone with his formidable twenty thousand men. But where? A council of war guessed that the objective was New Jersey, with a possible containing force to watch that tragic American garrison on Manhattan, Fort Washington, where Colonel Robert Magaw lay helpless with about three thousand men. The council decided that "it would be proper to throw a body of troops into New Jersey immediately." There should also be a force at Peekskill on the east bank of the Hudson and in the passes of the highlands on the west.

The council's guess was wrong. Howe plunged straight down into Manhattan, threw some eight thousand troops against Fort Washington and the lines that had been optimistically drawn about it. The result was a foregone conclusion, with British naval control of the Hudson. It cost Howe over

seven hundred casualties but netted him over twenty-eight hundred prisoners, who marched glumly into captivity after turning over to Baron von
Knyphausen their colors, which were described as "yellow, red and light
blue." Two Hessian regiments were drawn up to receive the surrender, and
by an ironic choice they were the Von Rall and the Alt Lossberg, the latter
magnificent in dark blue and orange. For Alt Lossberg, along with Von
Rall, was to know tragedy on the banks of the Delaware in a little more
than a month.

Fort Washington was a ghastly blow to the Americans, and another,
nearly as bad, followed two days later on November 16. The Hudson
formed an easy crossing for the British, who pounced on Fort Lee on the
Jersey shore, nearly capturing Nathanael Greene in the process. Psychologically these twin blows offset much of the build-up that had taken place
in American morale since Kip's Bay. Valuable troops had been lost for
good, units like Colonel Moses Rawlings' Maryland and Virginia riflemen
and the remains of Thomas Knowlton's Connecticut Rangers, who had
sparked the attack across the Hollow Way. Hundreds of cannon of all
calibers fell into Howe's hands, nearly three thousand muskets and four
hundred thousand cartridges, twelve thousand rounds of artillery ammunition, tools, tents, blankets, whose loss was to be felt bitterly in the coming
months.

And none of this need have happened. That the forts were held was due
to fatally bad estimates of the situation. There was Colonel Robert
Magaw in command at Fort Washington and stating resolutely that he
could hold out till the end of December in the face of a siege. Had he forgotten that water for the garrison had to be brought up by hand from the
Hudson far below? There was Nathanael Greene, cheerfully assuring the
commander-in-chief that he "could not conceive the garrison to be in any
great danger . . . it could be brought off any time." Washington seems to
have been more dubious, but ended by leaving the question of evacuation
up to Greene. In the last analysis, this was a command decision and lay with
Washington.

So the entire island of Manhattan passed over to royal control. Tories
flocked in droves into the charred ruins of the city, swarmed through eastern
Long Island with its British garrisons, badgered and harassed any remaining
patriots as they themselves had been earlier knocked about, and set up a
heaven-reaching clamor to Sir William Howe for immediate reparations to
make up for their losses, real or imaginary.

Prices within the city of New York began to skyrocket and there were
uncounted ways for a smart man, British or American, to turn quick and
dizzying profits from the distress of the Tory refugees. A sort of pseudo
court life began, centering about headquarters, where honest petitioners,
people with grievances, grafters swarmed. A feverish gaiety seized the city.
Those able to afford wines and brandies poured them lavishly. For the less
prosperous, rum did quite well. The usual train of eye-catching hangers-on
appeared, apparently all-pervasive. A British visitor went to St. Paul's to

hear a "Military Sermon. . . . This is a very neat Church and some of the
handsomest and best-dressed ladies I have ever seen in America. I believe
most of them are Whores."

Beneath this overlay of rotting tinsel, which usually flourishes in any war-
zone city where the military rules, was stark tragedy. The fire that had
gutted hundreds of houses had been bad enough. There had also been the
American occupation, with buildings of all sorts put to military use and
badly knocked about under such tenure. Estates that had been show places
were scored with trenches and gun emplacements. Great mansions and ordinary dwellings had been thoroughly looted. It probably eased the minds of
returning Tories to fall on the abandoned possessions of the Scotts,
Schuylers, Clintons, Duanes, and Jays, but such acts only spread the earlier
desolation wider. Relief committees had to be formed quickly to see to the
food, clothing, and shelter of destitute Loyalists, committees on which devoted people worked endlessly and on which a horde of eighteenth-century
five-per-centers joyfully battened.

There were the prisoners from Long Island, Kip's Bay, and a dozen lesser
engagements. How could they be handled, kept alive? Unfortunately the
British command found a quick answer. There was good old William Cunningham, who had proved himself so useful during the siege of Boston. He
was made provost, and the pen that signed his commission signed the death
warrants of thousands of patriots, or perhaps merely of people who had
incurred Mr. Cunningham's displeasure. New York had jails—even one
built by a royal governor not long before the war for "the accomodation
of the better class of prisoners." There were other landmarks, like the
Debtors' Prison. The North Dutch Church and the French Church were
also pressed into service, as was the notorious Sugar House on present
Liberty Street. But still there were ragged, sullen men, picked up perhaps
by the 17th after Chatterton's Hill or seized across near Fort Lee. What
better place to put them than in old, rotting hulks anchored in the harbor,
like the *Jersey?*

This reassertion of Crown power may seem at first glance like a "return
to the old order," so far as New York was concerned. Yet it was hardly that.
The rich and the great returned, representing new wealth or old family.
With them came the loyal middle class and the loyal humble. But parvenu
and patroon, comfortable burgher and steady craftsman of the city were
about as heavily represented in the ranks of Washington's army and in the
Congress of the new nation. It was a resumption of an old rule, not an old
order.

The returning or emerging Tories were as American as the men who
had hauled down George III's statue on the Bowling Green or voted
soberly for independence. Their convictions were as deep-seated and as
honorable as those held by people who had beggared themselves to send
supplies to Washington or who had stood on the Brooklyn Heights while
Howe's army deployed before their eyes. Here, then, was a great chance to

form another American army, wholly American, to fight loyally and devotedly for the Crown and against their dissident fellow countrymen.

Such an army never materialized. Units were formed throughout the war
years under men like the De Lanceys, Emmerich, Robert Rogers, and the
English John Simcoe. Long lists of smaller units may be found in the old
records, complete with details of imposing uniforms. But many of these
existed only on paper or as skeleton formations, short-lived. In proportion
to the thousands available, the turnout was strikingly small. Up and down
the country a few exceptions may be found. Tories fought hard and in respectable numbers in the Carolinas, but their motivation is hard to separate
from that of the local disorders that had flared and flared again before the
Revolution. In upper New York State solid Tory formations appeared, but
here again they often seemed to be fighting for the regional feudal domain
founded by Sir William Johnson, to be opposing the settler waves that had
been working up the Mohawk Valley since the end of the French wars and
which threatened to end baronial rule by the very existence of smaller free
holdings which their advent implied.

True, the American Loyalist could have had a great deal more encouragement from the royal forces, who were inclined to look down on him and his
efforts, as the royal forces had endlessly snubbed colonial levies and commanders in the old wars. But it may be pointed out that the Loyalist was
given far more encouragement, at least materially, than his brother or neighbor or friend who slipped away to enlist under Washington.

It is very hard to avoid the general impression that most Tories, in New
York City and elsewhere, were far more eager to resume their old lives and
let His Majesty's forces take care of the rebellion. In New York, trade was
being resumed, the city was obviously marked as the great military and
naval base for the war. Why shouldn't a good Loyalist take this heaven-sent
opportunity to recoup the fortunes that had been lost to him solely by his
unswerving adherence to the Crown? The years would show outstanding
exceptions to this strange passivity, but in general the Loyalist proved static
in the face of rebel dynamism.

CHAPTER XIX

"It will be a terrible night for the soldiers"

DECEMBER was edging close, advancing behind a curtain of cold
rain and colder wind that beat down on the American army, which
was now split in three parts. Gaunt Charles Lee clung to the heights
about North Castle on the Croton River, guarding the approaches to New
England. Comfortable Billy Heath lay with another group at Peekskill on
the east bank of the Hudson. Across in New Jersey, Washington and

Greene with the balance of the troops were hurriedly withdrawing beyond the Hackensack, the Passaic, on to Newark, with the Watchung Mountains somber through mist and drizzle on the right.

The commander-in-chief was driven to set a smart pace, for energetic Lord Cornwallis was after him with strong columns of Hessians and British that pounded south, covering as much as twenty-five miles in a single day of downpour over vile roads and living off what flour they could commandeer locally. Newark could not be held, and the American rear guard filed out just ahead of an onrush of Hessian Jaegers whose green coats were black with rain. South again across the Raritan and Washington was able to catch his breath for a moment at Brunswick.

All through the retreat he kept relays of messengers posting to Charles Lee. Lee must break up his camps, cross the Hudson, and circle to join the commander-in-chief. The need was desperate. A bare three thousand marched with Washington. Let Lee join him, picking up other units, and the American army would total nearly ten thousand men—at least on paper.

Sometimes Lee condescended to reply to his chief. Sometimes he wrote to the adjutant general, Joseph Reed. Again, the rain-blurred dispatches lay unanswered in his ultra-professional field desk. When he did write, he seemed to take Washington's courteous orders as mere suggestions, which he dismissed with accounts of the immense value of his Westchester position, tartly criticized Heath, gave broad hints that he himself could accomplish wonders if only he were made dictator for a few days, just a few days. (Here he was anticipating a fervent wish expressed by one George Brinton McClellan, writing from Virginia in 1862.) At last, in a letter to Reed, he spoke vaguely of crossing the Hudson, adding modestly "for to confess a truth I really think my Chief will do better with me than without me." And still he delayed his move.

Had he forgotten his calendar? On December 1, 1776, some two thousand enlistments would run out. And on January 1, 1777, virtually all the rest of the army, whether with Washington or Heath or Lee, would automatically revert to civilian life. Of course many men in the ranks had also thrown away their calendars. In tens and twenties and hundreds they slipped away, casting off from an army that could not feed, equip, or clothe them. Their plight was beyond exaggeration, as their enemies noticed. A British officer was horrified to find that "many of the Rebels who were killed in the late affairs, were without shoes or Stockings, & Several were observed to have only linen drawers on . . . without any proper shirt or Waistcoat. They are also in great want of blankets . . . they must suffer extremely."

The future looked as black as the clouds that rolled sullenly down over the Watchung Mountains and onto the sodden plains. The only consolation, if it could be so regarded, was that no British stroke from the far North had to be reckoned with until the spring of 1777.

All through the summer and fall a strange war had been waged by two armies quite out of touch with each other, one lying along the Richelieu

River and the other at Ticonderoga, where Champlain narrows in its southern reaches. It was a war of axes and hammers and mauls and adzes and nails as Sir Guy Carleton, commanding the British forces in Canada, and General Horatio Gates at the southern fort strove to create a navy that would control the long lake waterway with its virtually impassable banks.

Gates, that puzzling mixture of broad vision and pettiness, already had four schooners under his command, but the reports that his scouts brought him from St. Johns, far north on the Richelieu, were enough to tell his soldier's mind that he would need far more vessels afloat. His problem was to build his navy in the tree-cloaked wilderness of northern New York State without tools, without shipwrights, skilled carpenters, joiners. There was no solution, if he limited his imagination to what was immediately at hand.

Horatio Gates was not given to panic or despair. Pacing the crumbling bluestone ramparts of Ticonderoga, he or members of his entourage calmly took in the fact that this new nation was seafaring, that it was bred to the use of tools. If sailmakers and riggers and carpenters were not to be found at Champlain, they must be brought there. So an appeal, first for tools, was sent out, and General Philip Schuyler down at Albany sent up more than a thousand felling axes. Governor Jonathan Trumbull rushed up nearly as many. Then for the men to use them a call was sent to the seaboard towns and cities.

The call was answered. From Massachusetts, Connecticut, and Rhode Island, even from distant Philadelphia, strange-looking companies took the wilderness road to the Northern lake. There were more than two hundred of them, skilled men, wise in the ways of shipyards and sail lofts, and they brought their tools with them. File by file they tramped up to the shores of Champlain, ready to set to work. They were not popular with the ragged, underfed garrison at Ticonderoga, nor in the works across the narrow strip of lake at Mount Independence. These newcomers were privileged souls, and privates of Anthony Wayne's brigade or Johnny Stark's New Hampshire units snarled at the "prodegious" pay these picked workers drew, five dollars a day in cash, they said. It was an unhealthy condition and one which, in this country, has recurred in almost every war. Navy ratings of World War II handling the guns on merchant vessels manned by highly paid civilian sailors could sympathize with the gripings of Greaton's men or Wynkoop's back there in 1776.

But the fleet took shape somehow, hammered and banged out of green timber, a great flotilla of row galleys and gundalows ranging from some fifty feet in length to almost eighty. Backing up the four schooners that had formed the nucleus of Horry Gates's navy, they could at least do something to block hostile progress up the narrow lake.

We are sometimes inclined to look upon know-how, resourcefulness, and efficiency as peculiarly American qualities. A glance at the north-running river, the Richelieu, in 1776 tends to dispel that rather pleasing illusion. Sir Guy Carleton had, of course, those parts of the Royal Navy now in the

St. Lawrence at his disposal. But he also had ten long miles of churning, white rapids denying passage from the St. Lawrence via the Richelieu into Champlain. There was the three-masted *Inflexible* with two schooners. Knock them down. Lug the parts by oxcart, by hand up the river and past the rapids. Set up stocks and rebuild the ships. There were a thirty-ton gundalow, thirty longboats, and no less than four hundred troop-carrying bateaux on the wrong side of the white waters between St. Johns and Chambly. Fell trees, improvise rollers out of logs, haul, drag, tug until the rapids were past, forty men to a load, seventy, a hundred. Out of the hold of a frigate rocking idly in the current of the St. Lawrence came strangely shaped beams and timbers and fittings that were at once manhandled over-land to still water, and there the awkward-looking parts became ten gun-boats, prefabricated in England and shipped out to Sir Guy.

Carleton had good men under him, clever, inventive men like Lieutenant Shank, R.N., who in '74 had designed and perfected the first centerboard. With only sixteen men to swing maul and hammer, Shank launched his first boat in less than a month. A huge raft, usually known by its French name, *radeau*, was built. It was christened *The Thunderer*, and heavy guns thrust lakeward through embrasures in its thick wooden walls, the plan being to tow it astern of a regular ship and into the enemy formations.

The last nail was driven, the last mast stepped, and this inland British navy was ready to move south against whatever might venture forth to meet it. But with all the advantages that had lain with Carleton, all the skills and knowledge at his command, it was not until early October that he was able to embark his troops. They were to be all British, commanded by flamboyant, affable Gentleman Johnny Burgoyne, save for the Hesse-Hanau gunners who manned the *radeau* under the tough eye of Captain Georg Pausch, battered veteran of the Seven Years' War.

Gates's fleet was ready, at least in part, far earlier than Carleton's, but it was vastly inferior in structure and personnel. He had no formations like Glover's or Hutchinson's to draw on. Instead he had to draft men from inland regiments for his deck hands and gun crews, amateur sailors who were as green as the timbers that made up galley and gundalow. At least he could give control of his lake-borne force to a fairly seasoned mariner, for the commander of his first division, Benedict Arnold, had cruised in his own ships from the West Indies to the St. Lawrence in eager and often dubious pursuit of pre-war commerce.

Arnold's natural combativeness was increased by the irritation of his Quebec wound and by the humiliation of the long retreat from the great rock fortress to Ticonderoga. Another matter galled him about as much. A good businessman himself, he was feverishly impatient with civilian govern-ment bodies that kept asking him for an accounting of public funds en-trusted to him and expended by him. His replies to such questions were often rude and never explicit. He would have understood perfectly a nine-teenth-century Hungarian colonel who was given a sum to build a road and, when pressed for a detailed accounting, wrote testily, "Thirty thousand florins received. Thirty thousand florins expended. Anyone who doubts this is a blockhead!"

So with his makeshift fleet and worse than makeshift crews Arnold headed north up the lake, cruised about, received occasional additions to his flotilla, wrote bitter complaints to Gates about the quality of his men, cruised some more. When Carleton's force appeared, Arnold took station in the lee of Valcour Island just off the west shore of the lake and some fifty miles north of Ticonderoga.

On October 11 the British fleet passed Valcour, whose odd contours hid the American ships, overran its objective and had to double back. There was a confused and bloody action for the rest of the day. The timeless shores of Champlain echoed to the boom and whang of big guns and light. Galleys and gundalows nosed about under a pall of greasy yellowish smoke, their light-cannon-mounted bow or stern blasting at anything that moved over the battle-fouled waters. By nightfall Arnold had taken a very bad pounding, but adverse winds kept the heavier British units, including the deadly if clumsy radeau, from closing in for the kill. Under a gathering mist he tried to slip out south through the heart of Carleton's flotilla, but dawn caught him in a tragically helpless position, and one by one his ships were hunted down and sunk. Arnold himself, with a few followers, managed to get ashore and made his way back to the walls of Old Ti. He had inflicted relatively little damage and, while inflicting that little, had lost the whole American fleet. The lake lay open, a smooth water highway that led straight to the fort.

Carleton landed his troops at Crown Point, not far north of Ticonderoga, and then, after some futile maneuvering, strangely re-embarked his nine thousand-odd and sailed back north, almost exactly one month after sallying so boldly forth from the Richelieu River. His professed reason was that the season was too far advanced to mount an attack, an explanation that must set critical eyebrows lifting.

If this reason is sound, then he should never have started in the first place. Some authorities, notably Admiral Mahan, have claimed that the Valcour action was the deciding factor, a view which seems very hard to justify, since Carleton had suffered few casualties and had lost little or no time at Arnold's hands. The over-all picture remained unchanged.

So the whole British force and Pausch's gunners in their radeau went back to Canada with Carleton honestly murmuring, "Wait till next year," and for that next year he began planning. He might have spared himself the trouble. Already, in London, Lord George Germain, Secretary of State for the Colonies, had decided otherwise. He had long hated Carleton, with the bitter, piercing hatred of a proven poltroon and sneak for a far more able, courageous, and honorable man. Sir Guy might stay in Canada and keep house for the forces that would be sent to strike south and cut the colonies in two. But no combat command, no chance of glory for him. Another man must be found.

Germain was not alone in this idea. In the delightfully casual habit of high brass in the eighteenth century, Gentleman Johnny Burgoyne went home to England. He had no idea of damaging Carleton, but he really owed it to the Crown to lay before the proper authorities a plan of his own for terminating the rebellion. And since it was *his* plan—— Germain, associating Burgoyne with the hated Carleton, managed to freeze him from his presence. But Burgoyne's sunny magnetism opened other avenues. The King himself pored over a flamboyant sheaf of manuscript characteristically entitled "Thoughts for Conducting the War from the Side of Canada," which Germain had been forced to send on to him.

The "Thoughts" were adopted enthusiastically, and of course it was only fitting and proper that command of the operations set forth in their flowing pages should go to the author. Sometime later, at ultra-fashionable Brooks's Club in London, a group of members was watching the opening of a new betting book. A handsome, florid man with an infectious laugh and genial manner was making the first entry while an old crony of the gaming tables approved. The entry read—and still reads, if that book survived the blitzes—"John Burgoyne wagers Charles [James] Fox one pony [fifty guineas] that he will be home victorious from America by Christmas Day, 1777." So the bet was made, with Fox warning his friend, "Be not oversanguine in your expectations; I believe when next you return to England, you will be a prisoner on parole," a far more accurate statement than the egregious Fox was given to making.

The "Thoughts," consideration of which must be postponed for a later page, were eminently sound. But, ironically, they were to bring chaos out of order, to turn victory into defeat. They were to lead to the most significant triumph of the young years of the United States, the most vital—barring possibly the activities of an able French sailor (thoroughly discredited in France in 1776) off the Chesapeake Capes in 1781. The chief architect of the wreckage of the "Thoughts" was Lord George Germain, with author Gentleman Johnny Burgoyne running him a close second.

This gift of the gods of war was hidden in the mists of the future from the dwindling columns of ragged Americans who still reeled hopelessly back through the southern fringes of New Jersey. It is doubtful if that lesser gift, Carleton's fiasco on Champlain, cheered them much. And one very real smile of fortune struck them as a dire calamity.

They knew that Charles Lee had at last crossed the Hudson and was, they hoped, on his way to join them with his strong and rested columns. Then came the word of Colonel Harcourt's patrol of the 16th Dragoons. At a grisly hour the dragoons, possibly tipped off by a local Tory, surrounded a tavern at Basking Ridge. Their quarry had finished breakfast and was writing a letter to Horatio Gates in which he stated flatly that "entre nous, a certain great man is most damnably deficient," the context leaving no doubt who that "damnably deficient" man might be. So rough troopers hauled Charles Lee from his writings and bundled him off, a prisoner of war, to New Brunswick and thence to New York. Ironically, the 16th was the very regiment which he had led across the Tagus in a smashing coup against the Spaniards in 1762.

American officers and men were stunned. They had lost their seasoned major-leaguer, their "old pro," and Washington, that "certain great man," observed somberly that Lee's loss was "almost universally bewailed as one of the greatest calamities which has befallen American arms." British reaction was quite different. King George exulted, "I shall take care of Colonel Harcourt; leave his future to me," no idle promise, since William Harcourt ended his career as a field marshal. Even the little village of Tring in Hertfordshire, which had some claim on Harcourt, plastered its market place with joyous posters: "This is to give Notis that Thursday next will be held as a day of regoicin in commemoration of the takin of General Lee, when their wil be a sermint preached, and other public demonstracions of joye, after which will bee a nox roosted whole & everery mark of festivity & bell ringing imaginable, whith a ball & cock fiting at night in the Hassembly room at the black Lyone."

Actually, the "nox" could well have been provided from United States military stores, since Lee would have undoubtedly disapproved of the next American military moves and very likely have managed their cancellation. An immediate benefit was the arrival in Washington's camp of Lee's old division, brought promptly from Vealtown by Lee's second-in-command, sturdy John Sullivan, though the five thousand men who had started off from North Castle had shrunk to a bare two thousand.

Other troops appeared, slogging wearily over the slime of the New Jersey roads. Horatio Gates sent some five hundred down from Ticonderoga, Colonel John Cadwalader brought up a thousand Philadelphia Associators, while Nicolas Hausegger marched in with his Pennsylvania Germans.

Now out of New Jersey and across the Delaware, Washington could count nearly six thousand men. But many of these were militia or utterly green replacements. Washington noted grimly that a lot of the army was "entirely naked and most so thinly clad as to be unfit for service." And with this phantom army the commander-in-chief must cover some thirty miles of the Delaware River, a line that could be attacked at one or a dozen places. Congress, in an understandable swivet, asked him if he thought he could keep the British from crossing and swooping down onto Philadelphia, seat of government. "Happy should I be if I could see the means of preventing them," he answered with devastating frankness. "At present I confess I do not." Far more candidly, but privately, he stated that unless more men were available "I think the game is pretty near up."

So thought Sir William Howe. With unconscious magnanimity he decreed that active operations were over for the year. The real cleanup would come in the spring, assuming that there was anything left for the military brooms to sweep. And besides, no army in its right mind campaigned in the winter. So he pushed a chain of posts out into New Jersey, running from Amboy and New Brunswick on to Princeton. The Delaware was held by the Black Watch at Bordentown and, post of honor, Trenton, where

Von Rall's, the Alt Lossberg, and Von Knyphausen's regiments were stationed as reward for past services. Militarily the whole command relaxed.
Cornwallis began packing for a touch of home leave. Sir Henry Clinton
might have followed him, but he had been sent with Peter Parker's fleet to
seize Newport in Rhode Island, where he could winter very pleasantly.

And in this air of military well-being the allied armies set to work to cancel out a good part of the capital they had amassed through their late con-
quests, especially in New Jersey. This was considered one of the most
Royalist of all the states and, in the glow of royal triumphs, Tories came
flocking in droves to attest their fidelity. With them came thousands of the
hither-to undecided, the waverers, the fence-sitters, the morally vanquished.

There was an oath to be sworn to or, in the case of Quakers, attested: "I
. . . do promise and declare that I will remain in a peaceable obedience to
his Majesty, and will not take up arms in opposition to his authority." In
return for this, such signers were promised the fullest of full protection.
Pardons were also granted for "all treasons . . . all forfeitures, attainders and
penalties for the same." It looked as though the thirteen states might soon
become twelve.

But the Army of Occupation had been brought up in a tough, merciless school. The enlisted man was paid little, if anything. In the long wars
that had ravaged Europe, the civilian in a military zone had no rights.
Plunder was regarded as a perquisite of the man in the ranks, since little
else was done for him. When a city fell, a day or two was usually set aside
for looting and violence, after which a tighter rein was held. This was particularly true of the German troops, a good part of which were conscripted,
kidnaped, jammed into the ranks without the least chance of redress.
When such a soldier was finally worn out, some of the more enlightened
princes granted these faithful, broken old servants of the state a license to
beg. This last practice held in Prussia well into the nineteenth century.
Among the British, where most of the men were, at least nominally, volunteers and not nearly so brutally treated, this attitude toward civilians and
their property was not so marked. But there were always barrack tales of
old so-and-so of the 9th or the 23rd who had set himself up as an innkeeper
or lord of a pothouse through the plunder amassed in the Low Countries.

A British officer wrote in bitter disgust: "No sooner had the army entered
the Jerseys, than the business (we say business, for it was a perfect trade) of
plunder began. The friend and the foe, from the hand of rapine, suffered
alike." A Jersey farmer could show a Jaeger sergeant a signed promise of protection from Sir William Howe, but the sergeant could not read English, if
he could read at all. Loot was loot, whether under a Tory or a rebel roof.
Such a state of affairs brought demoralization to the troops. Along the
Delaware, facing Washington's pathetic camps that lay on the right bank,
the Hessians were absent "on pillaging expeditions, and those who were on
the spot were more busily employed in securing their plunder in waggons
than in putting the town in a proper state of defence," says the same
Briton. So it was a pleasant enough life for the allied G.I., raiding a hen

roost here, twisting the thumbs of a Jersey farmer there to make him reveal the hiding place of probably nonexistent treasure. But the most ardent Tories began to wonder, to look askance at the bits of paper whereon Sir William vouched for their loyalty.

Despite the well-proclaimed British intent to go into winter quarters, the Congress still felt that Philadelphia was too close to the actual seat of war and moved its sittings down to Baltimore. This shift was not popular with all members, who seem to have pretty well dug themselves in at Philadelphia, and the lovely Maryland city was blasted by some as "too dirty and too dear," by others as "a dirty boggy hole." Nonetheless, the sessions went on and some acts were passed to strengthen the military establishment. The intent was doubtless good, but there were features included in the measures that sent chills down the spines of civil as well as military observers. New regiments were to be raised, which was not only admirable but essential. However, many of these were to be officered by men chosen by commissioners in the several states. In other words, trained and tested officers now serving would be thrust aside and commissioned rank would probably go by political favor. Presumably, old units would be broken up and replaced by new, green levies for these green officers to command. It has been said already that the old tag, "Experience teaches," is a lie as old as the world. This same method of keeping an army at strength, horribly inefficient and wasteful, was followed by the federal government through most of the Civil War. Back in the dying days of 1776 the whole system struck Washington as so unsound that for a moment he forgot his habitual deference to the Congress (an overdeference that was to be repeated by his fellow Virginia immortal, Robert E. Lee, in the 1860s). He protested hotly, for him, and then tempered his disapproval by adding, "It may be thought that I am going a good deal out of the line of my duty . . . to advise thus freely; a character to lose, an estate to forfeit, the inestimable blessing of liberty at stake, and a life devoted must be my excuse." But the Congress bumbled on along its own inscrutable path.

So the commander-in-chief could only hope for the future, if there were to be one for the new nation. He could not be sure that Howe's plans for winter quarters were bona fide, and for the moment only the breadth of the Delaware protected the flickering American army. To bolster this protection, before crossing to the south bank, he sent details to snap up every boat, big or little, and move them to the Pennsylvania shore. But the Delaware could freeze, and men and heavy guns could cross safely on good thick ice, could cross when and where they pleased. As though further to devil the commander-in-chief, the weather became coy. There were thaws that turned the roads into rivers of mud and halted supply columns from the south. Cold snaps succeeded the thaws and the stone-hard roads cut to pieces the shoes of those American troops lucky enough to own a pair. And the river began to skin over with ice. High-piled clouds rolled down from the northwest. Cutting winds blew. Ice on the Delaware thickened, became soggy and pitted under a warm rain, froze again. How could any soldier formulate a plan, a last, desperate, essential plan to keep his army alive and a striking force under such conditions?

For there was a plan, by now well formed behind the commander-in-chief's outwardly calm and steady eyes, a plan so top-secret that it seems to have been known only to the very highest brass about him. Henry Knox must be consulted, of course, for the plan involved artillery. Nathanael Greene's mind must be brought to bear. By good luck, or so Washington felt, Horatio Gates had come down from Ticonderoga with the small force from the fort. Gates's seasoned military thought must be used. An aide brought a letter to the commander-in-chief. Horatio Gates, without even asking leave of his superior, had gone buzzing off to Baltimore, there to bask in the admiration of those civilians who deferred so delightfully to his vast stock of military lore. And who also had the power to remove one commander and appoint another, perhaps more seasoned one. And Lee was gone, a prisoner. Did Washington, like John Glover at Pell's Point, wish that he had "some experienced officer present to direct, or at least approve," of what he was about to do? If so, he kept such thoughts to himself. Like Glover, he "did the best" he could and went ahead "to the best of my judgment."

The plan unfolded, taking in more and more of the higher officers. There was a meeting at William Keith's house on Knowles' Creek. Greene was there and John Sullivan, Lord Stirling sat near Hugh Mercer and red-haired Arthur St. Clair, late of Ticonderoga. There were colonels present: Paul Dudley Sargent, whose Massachusetts family had been hideously split by the war; rangy John Stark with his memories of Breed's Hill; Henry Knox, to whom hardship seemed only to add weight; and quiet John Glover.

The commander-in-chief spoke, briefly as always. The army would recross the Delaware, strike swiftly at the Hessian posts, retire as swiftly to the south bank. There seem to have been few if any objections to the plan, possibly owing to the absence of Gates and Lee. John Stark stirred in his chair, explosively approving. Get the men away from their reliance on damned picks and shovels! Show them what muskets and sheer guts can do!

There was the vital question of crossing the river. If the Delaware froze, then all plans were off and an Anglo-German attack might be expected. As it was, the river was in full flood, jammed with great sheets of thick ice broad as threshing floors that whirled down from the upper reaches. Was a crossing possible? John Glover, studying his scarred hands in the candlelight, murmured that the general needn't trouble about that. "My boys will get the army across." That terse statement apparently ended any discussion of the feasibility of crossing. To the generals and colonels about Mr. Keith's table a river plus boats plus the Marbleheaders added up to success.

There would not be one crossing, there would be three. The main body was to take off from McKonkey's Ferry, some nine miles above the Hessian post at Trenton, under the direct eye of the commander-in-chief. General

James Ewing would cross a little below McKonkey's with Pennsylvania and
New Jersey militia while, down by Dunk's Ferry, Colonel John Cadwalader
took over a mixed force of Continentals and militia. Any further questions,
gentlemen? Then we cross on the night of December 25–26, taking advantage of the fact that the Hessians will still be bibulously celebrating
Christmas. In the meantime, maintain the utmost secrecy. No orders until
the last instant. There must be no leaks.

Christmas night was hideous on the south shore of the Delaware. From
camp little regiments formed, left the warmth of their still-burning campfires, and filed off toward the river. A biting wind howled down from the
northeast, gathered rain and sleet, flung it into the chapped faces of New
Hampshiremen, Virginians, Pennsylvanians. It was easy for a straggler to
pick up the line of march even in the dark, a black, unwavering line beaten
through thin snow, "tinged here and there with blood from the feet of men
who wore broken shoes," wrote Major James Wilkinson. And some had no
shoes. There were wads of rags bound insecurely over callused soles; there
were sandal-like strips of the rawest of rawhide, made from the skins of
cattle slaughtered that very day. "It will be a terrible night for the soldiers,"
wrote another officer. "But I have not heard a man complain."

There was a booming and a banging from the dark, ice-choked flood
itself, where thirty-foot Durham boats, pointed bow and stern, shouldered
each other with the rise and fall of the waves. There were sinister splintery
crashes as ice slabs collided, piled high, freed themselves, went spinning
and lurching on down the frigid, tossing current. Hollow thuddings and
thumpings told of boots or rag-wrapped feet filing onto the broad Durham
bottoms where Glover's men wielded oar and pole, shouted to Abel
Brimblecome or Adam Cash or Japhet Trefry not to be a froach but to
keep that damn "cannon borr'l" pointed aft. For Henry Knox's guns were
coming down from the artillery park, dragged by gaunt horses or shoved by
panting cannoneers to be manhandled aboard. And always the stream of
men poured on from the camps, the flick of a dark lantern lighting up a
reddened face, a broken cocked hat bound tightly by a handkerchief passed
under a rough chin.

High up the bank near McKonkey's, the commander-in-chief stood by
his chestnut sorrel and shouted orders into the teeth of the storm. Halfway between him and the icy brink a vast figure stood, picked up the sound
of his chief's voice, and sent the message battering on through the lance-
drift of the sleet. What a voice, mastering the yell of the storm and the
boom of the river! Could it be the same courteous, pleasant voice that had
recommended Richardson's *Pamela* or that new translation of Livy back
there at the London Book-Store close by Province House in Boston so
many years ago? Henry Knox was playing the part of an eighteenth-century
walkie-talkie for George Washington on the banks of the Delaware.

There was Glover's bull-seal bellow among the rocking boats. If Captain
Speakman's craft were loaded, then cast off! How about Captain Blackler's?

Had a hail from Captain Orne's? Hold up the head of that Virginia company! Number 5's loaded to the gun'ls. Bring Number 6 in closer!

The Durham boats began to shove out into the flood, and Marbleheaders drove furiously at their oars, sensing the butt and heave of the current, keeping the sharp bows in their proper course. Bow, stern, and flank, men stood with long, heavy poles, eyes straining into the gnawing sleet, watching eternally for the lift and heave of the vicious ice slabs. The quick brush of a ragged blue sleeve across ice-caked eyes. A warning shout: "For Christ's sake, look to port!" A whitish mass shouldering up out of the river swirl, climbing over other slabs, rising high and high until the last despairing thrust of the poles had to be made almost overhead. An endless, shivering five seconds, ten. The blind fury of the ice slab eased off. The river closed over the frozen menace, wrapped it in sullen froth that broke immediately to drive another twenty-foot cake amidships.

Glover's boats made the far shore, unloaded, battered their way back, and there was Henry Knox's voice through the sleet: "Bring on Tom Forrest's battery. You men there, stand by the horses' heads. Ready, Colonel Glover?" So the night wore on. St. Clair's men were loaded, and John Stark's. Hands crept around the dials of bulbous watches. Midnight was passed, the hour at which the commander-in-chief had hoped to have the whole force on the north bank. One o'clock, two, three. The last man and the last horse and gun were ashore and shivering; drenched men bent their shoulders to the ever-swelling blast of snow and sleet and rain. Companies formed, became regiments, and regiments formed into brigades and divisions. Drivers and cannoneers felt the cold-tightened skin of their hands crack and spread as they fumbled with trace chains and doubletrees, ice-coated, in the dark. The march began. Nine long miles to cover before daybreak. A stirring pace would have to be set.

Men stumbled on through the knife winds that now blew into their smarting faces, stumbled and staggered over frozen ruts on the road that skirted the river. Officers with drawn pistols paced beside the columns, and the men in the ranks did not have to be told that there were orders to shoot any stragglers. On through the hissing, crunching darkness. No smoking. No talking. Wrap something around the lock of your musket. Want to go into action with a dead pan? Cover it. Anyhow. Rip a foot of cloth off your shirt. Take the rags off your feet if they're dry enough. Keep the sleet out of your pan.

Somewhere the long column split, though it is doubtful if the men in the straining ranks were aware of it. John Sullivan led the brigades of Glover, St. Clair, and Paul Dudley Sargent, backed by the batteries of Neil, Hugg, Moulder, and Winthrop Sargent, along the river road. Nathanael Greene branched off inland, took the upper road, the Pennington or Scotch Road as it was called, and after him came more brigades, Stephen's, Mercer's, Stirling's, and that of the Frenchman, La Roche Fermoy. The helmets of Morris' troop of the Philadelphia Light Horse glistened dimly under a frost sheet, and Bauman's, Forrest's, and Alexander Hamilton's fieldpieces bobbed and clanked with the column.

Company commanders began sending whispered reports to their colonels, who passed them on to their brigadiers, and the storm could not mask the alarm in their tones. The reports reached John Sullivan. Wrappings or no wrappings, the muskets were useless, the primings in the pans a wet, gummy paste. The infantrymen might just as well be shouldering staves or fish poles. The New Hampshire lawyer snapped, "Never mind. Tell them we'll use just the bayonet." A similar report reached Washington, now with Greene's upper column. His reaction was like Sullivan's: "Use the bayonet. I am resolved to take Trenton." And, for once, bayonets were available.

The killing miles went by with mortal slowness. On the Scotch Road ice began to form and marching men slithered, slipped, fell in a crash of accouterments, pried themselves to their feet somehow. Overhead and in the east the sky began to lighten, turned from black to dirty gray to smudged pearl, and still Trenton lay hidden in the sleet wraiths ahead. Muttered words were sent down the column and the men broke into a struggling lope, a "long trot," as one marcher noted later.

Trenton was a pleasant little town back there in 1776. Its hundred-odd houses were widely spaced, and about a third of them lay across the Assunpink, which idled on into the Delaware. There were picket fences and orchards and winter-locked gardens, a stone post office, a neat tavern, and close by the north bank of the Assunpink a great square stone U, two-storied, barracks that had been built a decade and more ago to house His Majesty's troops in the old French wars.

Under the gray, biting skies of December 26, Trenton awakened to thundering post-Christmas hangovers on the part of Colonel von Rall's garrison. Outposts were weak and unready, probably relying on the hell-driven storm to keep any self-respecting enemy snug by his own campfires. A few blue-coated men in tall helmets moved about, showing the red facings of Von Rall's regiment, the black of Von Knyphausen, and the orange of the Alt Lossberg.

Hauptmann Ernst Eber von Altenbockum of the Alt Lossberg regiment had a post just outside the village on the Pennington Road. About eight o'clock he was roused by muffled shots in the distance, then the sound of running feet and deep shouts of "Der Feind! Heraus! Heraus [The enemy! Turn out! Turn out]!" It was the first real warning that the Trenton garrison had. Or rather, it was the first observed warning, for the night before a Tory had sent an alarming note to Colonel von Rall. But the colonel was deep in a hand of skat and shoved the paper into his pocket unread. Doubtless he meant to look at it later, but he seems to have achieved an advanced degree of decomposition during the Christmas festivities, and the words that might have saved him were carried into oblivion on a rising tide of alcohol.

Von Altenbockum tried to form up the men under his command, but front, right, and left through the still-driving sleet, long blurred lines of running men came on. He fell back toward the V junction of King and Queen streets, roaring out the alarm, but his voice was drowned by a horrible din from the south, down by the river. John Sullivan and his brigades had kept pace with Greene's and Washington's and the trap had closed on the Hessians. Once more an American army had been able to bounce back off the ropes, its guard up and a fist poised for a stinging blow.

Trenton village boiled furiously. Hessians tumbled into the streets, half awake and half dressed, while booming drums and guttural commands fought to bring order into the sleet-filled morning. Henry Knox's guns began to slam at the junction of King and Queen streets. Down by the river Sullivan's fieldpieces answered as John Glover threw his brigade at the Assunpink bridge, crossed it, and smashed in among the dazed grenadiers.

Washington, with his staff, galloped up to a patch of high ground on present-day Princeton Avenue, took in the situation, and threw in Lord Stirling's brigade. George Weedon, in the lead, brought his 3rd Virginia in fast. Two Hessian fieldpieces had been rolled out, but a group led by Captain William Washington and Lieutenant James Monroe (who would later assume a far higher title and give his name to an immortal doctrine) cut down the gunners. On the right of St. Clair's brigade, John Stark, utterly in his element, roared and thrashed about like a wild moose and "dealt death wherever he found resistance and broke down all opposition before him," as an eyewitness reported.

Colonel von Rall, aroused at last, tried to organize a counterattack with his own and the Alt Lossberg regiments, but Americans had infiltrated everywhere and, having had a chance to dry out their muskets, fired from cellars and windows and roofs. Captain Thomas Forrest's guns joined in. Von Rall's command was badly shaken and the colonel struggled hard to rally his ranks, his voice shouting, "*Alles was meine Grenadiere sind, vorwärts* [Forward, my grenadiers]!" Then he was down, mortally wounded. Sullivan's brigade began pushing up from the south and St. Clair swung down from the north. Caught between two fires, galled from in front, the Hessians streamed away in twos and threes and by whole companies. Stark led a final rush and the Trenton garrison downed its arms in a bleak, sleet-swept orchard east of today's Montgomery Street, north of the Assunpink.

The whole affair had lasted at most three quarters of an hour, and three fine regiments were virtually eliminated from the allied strength. Washington reported to the Congress that the Hessian loss was a little over a hundred killed and wounded, with more than nine hundred prisoners. In addition, there were six brass fieldpieces, three ammunition wagons, four heavily loaded baggage wagons, a thousand stand of arms, twelve drums, and fifteen flags, which last figure surely must include company guidons as well as the formal and often beautiful German regimental standards.

One item among the captured stores held a menace which, if unleashed, could very well have nullified the sweeping success. Deep barrels of rum and brandy were found, and shivering Americans must have turned longing eyes on them, hoping to be able to drown the memories of the killing night crossing and march with one hand while celebrating their victory with the other. The commander-in-chief issued quick orders, and sorrowful details staved in the heads of all the casks. The move was a wise one, if rather stern. In 1781 Nathanael Greene was to have brilliant success changed to dull stalemate entirely because his men got loose among British stores and were busy unplugging rum casks while the British rallied for a counterattack.

The triumphant brigades reassembled in Trenton village while Washington conferred with his generals. There was some talk of moving deeper inland, but the commander-in-chief realized that the New Jersey road network would allow the British to rush strong bodies to any threatened point. So at noon the whole command re-formed and tramped off on its nine-mile trek to the ferries where it had landed in the bitter night hours. Shepherding the prisoners and the captured stores, the columns labored on. The river was in no better shape for crossing than it had been the night before. In fact, a rising wind had made matters worse, if possible. No one save the German officers, who viewed the ice-choked flood with horror, seems to have been much worried about the return trip. Weren't Glover's men still there?

Glover's men! The army never forgot them, either for Long Island or for this day. An officer watching them wrote, "There was an appearance of discipline in this corps . . . it possessed an apparent aptitude for the purpose of its institution and gave a confidence that myriads of its meek and lowly brethren were incompetent to inspire." Years later Henry Knox stood before the Massachusetts Legislature when unwise measures seemed to threaten the New England fisheries. His voice boomed out as it had boomed along the banks of the Delaware. "Sir! I wish the members of this body . . . had stood . . . in that bitter night . . . and seen the men from Marblehead and Marblehead alone stand forward to lead the army along the perilous path. . . . There, Sir, went the fishermen of Marblehead, alike at home upon land and water, alike ardent, patriotic and unflinching whenever they unfurled the flag of the country." Probably John Glover would have found Knox's eulogy overdrawn. He had promised that his boys would get the army across and, unflinchingly, they had done it.

The coup at Trenton acted as a rare tonic on the army and on the nation. Here was no mere counterattack as at the Hollow Way. A real offensive, if a limited one, had been mounted by the American army. In camps and in distant cities men commented, almost in awe, on the fact that the victory had been won largely with the bayonet, that very weapon in which most Americans had hitherto stood in understandable terror. Of course it was too bad that neither Cadwalader nor Ewing had managed to get across, but then, the Marbleheaders couldn't be everywhere. As it was, the success was rightly heartening. If Washington could have kept the Trenton force as the core about which to build his army for the rest of the war, he could have presented a very formidable threat to the British plans by the summer of 1777. But a veteran army he would never have. Even as he totaled up the score of the twenty-sixth of December, 1776, days were flicking off the calendar toward the mass expiration of enlistments.

Then without warning and certainly without his solicitation Congress placed sweeping powers in his hands, almost as though to make up for the unsound provisions that had been adopted for maintaining the army. The act, passed before the news of Trenton had reached Baltimore, specifically authorized Washington to take several steps without further reference to the civilian authorities. First he was directed to raise no less than sixteen regiments or battalions of infantry (the Congress used the terms interchangeably) in addition to those already authorized. The appointment of officers remained in his hands. Three thousand cavalry were to be recruited, officered, and equipped. The artillery was to be reorganized and a corps of engineers created. He could call on the several states for militia as he saw fit. He was allowed to appoint or dismiss any officer under the rank of brigadier. Stores could be commandeered if people refused to sell to the army at a reasonable price, and those who refused to accept the shaky Continental currency in payment could be arrested.

These powers, limited to a maximum of six months, represented a drastic change in congressional thinking and acting. A few months before, no member of the Congress would have entertained for an instant such a delegation of authority to the military. But the honorable members for the several states knew their man. In the letter of transmittal the Congress wrote Washington: "Happy it is for the country, that the General of their forces can safely be entrusted with the most unlimited power, and neither personal security, liberty nor property be in the least degree endangered thereby." This simple sentence expressed not a hope but a fact.

BOOK 3

CHAPTER XX

". . . foot-falls lightly planted"

IT was January 1777, and the army still held together somehow. A few new units had arrived, but most important, Henry Knox and Thomas Mifflin had worked long and hard, going from unit to unit of the ragged Continental Army, arguing, wheedling, expostulating. Just six weeks more, boys. The country's *got* to have those six weeks. You've done a soldier's job, and new regiments are on the way to relieve you. But—they aren't here yet. The British and Hessians are. Is it much to ask? Hang on until the new regiments get here. Another thing, Congress has voted ten dollars— and in *hard* money—to every man who signs on for that time.

Enough men agreed to stay, and now Washington's force was across the Delaware again. But this time he was in a deadly trap, seemingly discounting the fact that his opponent was not leisurely Billy Howe, basking in New York. Instead, he was faced by energetic Lord Charles Cornwallis, whose home leave had been abruptly canceled as a result of the Trenton coup in December.

Here was the shabby little army, entrenched along the south bank of the Assunpink and quite completely hemmed in by the solid well-fed and well-clothed force that Cornwallis had rushed over from the strong point at Princeton. The night of January 2 fell and the men who had stormed down King Street or Front Street on the twenty-sixth peered warily into the mist-wrapped gloom. Hessians and British had made tentative attacks during the day, but steady outfits like Edward Hand's had beaten them off. The allied strength was there, though. A flanking march or a heavy, direct thrust and Washington's army could easily be nothing but a bloody memory.

Cornwallis, for once, stayed his hand. General Sir William Erskine was dubious. "Sir," expostulated Erskine respectfully, "if Washington is the general I take him to be, he will not be found there in the morning." My Lord Charles, however, was sure that he had "the old fox in a trap. We'll bag him in the morning, my boy."

For some hours it looked as though Cornwallis were right. Mists steamed up from the thawing ground, and the muddy roads were "half-leg deep," miry gutters in which wagons and gun teams would bog down. Then, like the divine wind that held off the British fleet at Long Island, the weather changed and biting winds hardened road and field minute by minute. The army *could move*—if the freeze held.

But move where? A retreat down-river would bring Cornwallis snarling at the rear guard, would very likely crash into more British strength by the Delaware mouth. There was no chance of falling back to the old camps on the south bank of the Delaware, for the Durham boats were not at hand. In a night council of war, while the blessed knife of the wind snapped at officers' cloaks, someone, his name lost to history, made a suggestion so daring, so utterly unconventional that the most hidebound of Washington's brass could only gasp in amazed agreement. The suggestion might have come from Greene or perhaps Joseph Reed or John Sullivan, but in that case it is odd that none of them mentioned it in their not inextensive writings. So credit must go to the unknown officer who dared to recommend that the army slide out by the flank deep into British-held territory and fall hard and fast on the garrison at Princeton, now known to be weakened by the dispatch of so many men to Trenton.

Whispered words rustled in the shallow earthworks along the Assunpink. Details crept out into the night, hauled down fences and tossed the bars onto the dying campfires. Occasional shots were fired into the crisping darkness. Guard posts were changed with a maximum of noisy challenge. British patrols, now confined to the upper part of Trenton, could report to their officers that the bloody Yankees seemed to be making themselves bloody comfortable with their bloody fires and all. And these reports added up to a decision by the British High Command to rush the whole American line at dawn.

At one in the morning the desperate march began, the entire army almost tiptoeing along the night roads, with wheels muffled in old sacking and cannoneers walking beside the gun teams, holding the trace chains in their hands to muffle the slightest clank. A few devoted souls were left behind to tend the fires and make an unholy racket with pick and shovel as though the works were being strengthened.

No one below the rank of brigadier knew the objective. Thomas Rodney told Brother Caesar: "Some thought we were going to attack the enemy in the rear; some that we were going to Princeton . . . but no one knew what the Gen. meant to do." On through the freezing night went the army of scarecrows. "Orders were given in a whisper; muskets were gingerly handled and foot-falls lightly planted."

Spearheading the march was Thomas Rodney with his Dover men and the Philadelphia Red Feathers. After them crept Mercer's brigade, with St. Clair close behind and the rest of the army trailing. One familiar element was missing, a unit that had been outstanding since Long Island. The Delaware Continentals were dead or captured or at home as time-expired men. There is no shame attached to the absence of the survivors from this wearing, bitter march. In their home state they were busy recruiting and would soon be in the field again, would always be found in hard action till little more than a company of them stood with Nathanael Greene in his last battle in 1781.

Yet in a sense the Delawares were still of the army and with the army. For trudging over the frozen ruts, clutching at Hugh Mercer's stirrup leather to help his pace, was the Delaware colonel, John Haslet. With his friend Mercer he faced the bite of the night wind.

It was no highroad that the little army followed. In fact, it was far worse than the average abominable back road of the era. Newly surveyed, newly opened, the surface was still studded with tree stumps, against which men stumbled in the dark, on which horses barked legs, and into which the rag-swathed gun wheels thudded to exasperating halts. Many men compared this night with that of December 25–26 for sheer, eroding hardship. "We moved," wrote a marcher, "slow on account of the artillery, frequently coming to a halt . . . and when ordered forward again, one, two or three men in each platoon would stand, with their arms supported, fast asleep; a platoon next in rear advancing on them, they, in walking or attempting to move, would strike a stub [stump] and fall."

Yet they were lucky to have such a road, which trailed over the back country, apparently unknown to the British, and out of sight by day and hearing by night of the regular Post Road that roughly paralleled it in its sweep to the northwest and Princeton. Its existence had been pointed out to Washington, surely before this January crossing had been made, by someone like Joseph Reed of his staff, born and brought up in the neighborhood.

Officers and men lost track of time, being utterly absorbed in the task of raising and planting one foot, bringing up the other, while butting against jagged stumps or tripping over fallen comrades. There was gray in the east and then a hard, sharp sun that struck Captain Thomas Rodney as a good omen, like the sun that shone down on Frenchmen over the heights of Pratzen near the village of Austerlitz in the year 1805. Major James Wilkinson, who often approached a Burgoyne purple in his prose, remembered that "the morning was bright, serene and extremely cold, with a hoar frost which bespangled every object."

Other eyes than Wilkinson's were taking in the new day. In the village of Princeton, quartered in and about Nassau Hall of the College of New Jersey, lay the 17th Leicestershires, the 40th South Lancashires, and the 55th Border Regiment. They formed in the bright hardness of the dawn, line on line of scarlet coats with grayish-white facings, buff facing, dark green facings. They were old America hands by now and had sweated through the grim discomfort of the siege of Boston.

Now the 17th and the 55th were to take the road where ruts crunched brittle under their feet, for a message had arrived for them during the night. They were to hurry to Trenton and help the Earl of Cornwallis to

"bag the old fox," Washington. Drums beat, ranks flowed and shifted from
line into column, and the march began. In command, Lieutenant Colonel
Charles Mawhood of the 17th paced along on a favorite plump brown
pony, and a pair of spaniels, drunk with the glory of the swish of black
gaiters about them and with the keen bite of the dawn wind, yelped and
yiped and scampered about their master and his little mount.

Then off to his left Mawhood was sure that he caught the glint of musket
barrels, clusters and clusters of them, heading for the bridge over Stony
Brook on the Trenton Road, a vital link in British communications. He
checked his observations and then swung his column into action. The
musket barrels he had spotted belonged to Mercer's column, which Washington had detached to swing off to the west and destroy the same bridge
about which Mawhood was concerned, and the confused clash known as
the Battle of Princeton was on.

Mercer's men and Mawhood's collided violently in William Clark's neat
orchard beyond a Quaker meetinghouse. From the higher ground to the
east the commander-in-chief saw the collision, the firing, and much confusion and at once sent Cadwalader's militia brigade forward. Then the
echoing world seemed to turn upside down. Many of Mercer's command
had the mortally slow-loading rifles, and the Borderers and the Leicesters
were among them with the bayonet. There was a gradual but still orderly
retirement from the orchard, and the retreating men were mixed in with
the raw militia.

The militia were basically good men. But the inexperienced soldier is
always concerned about what the man on his right and the man on his left
are going to do. Cadwalader's command wavered, shivered, and broke,
carrying Mercer's hard-bitten Continentals along with them. An inland
Long Island or Kip's Bay hung on the edge of history. Off to the far right,
brass glittered and a troop of the 16th Dragoons seemed to be forming for
a charge.

Between the two armies galloped the commander-in-chief with an aide,
Lieutenant John Fitzgerald of Virginia, close behind him. Nathanael
Greene pelted out into the melee, labored with John Cadwalader to bring
order out of the panic. Slowly the militia recovered, managed to form some
sort of line, their eyes on the big man on the white horse who seemed so
oblivious of the scant thirty yards between him and the British advance.
There were two volleys, and smoke blotted out the bright glory of the
morning. John Fitzgerald threw an arm across his eyes to shut out what he
took to be the sure death of the commander-in-chief. The smoke cleared
and Washington was still calling encouragingly to the Pennsylvanians,
gentling his white horse.

Off to the right and rear, Henry Knox's guns began to bark. Over a ridge,
in swift assault, flowed the smooth ranks of Dan Hitchcock's Rhode Island
and Massachusetts brigade, with Edward Hand's shirted Pennsylvanians on
their right. Mawhood's lines halted, shook, frayed out, blasted off a harm-
less volley or two, and then broke in a flight as wild as that of the Pennsyl-

vania militia. These Pennsylvanians were new men now. Washington led them in person across the frosty meadows south of the orchard, shouting, urging them and Hitchcock's men and Hand's after the wreck of the Princeton garrison, which was in full flood down the Post Road toward Trenton. And for once the unshakable Virginian forgot that he was the commander-in-chief. The rest of the army could look after itself while he led the yelling, pounding press that surged on after Mawhood's men. He stood in his stirrups, swung his hat, and roared, "It's a fine fox-chase, boys!"

Good British troops rarely panic and, when broken, are apt to be at their most dangerous. Mawhood, his officers and non-coms exposed themselves recklessly, infected their men with their own unshakable, reasoned courage. Fluid companies solidified, closed up, became bayonet-hedged blocks, and cut their way through the not too orderly American fringes that tried to get between them and the bridge that fed into the Trenton Road. Tight ranks of the 16th Dragoons clattered up. For an instant a British counterattack might have been possible, but the Philadelphia Light Horse checkmated the sweep of brass helmets, and Mawhood's regiments went south down the road in undisguised hurry.

Washington saw the grave danger of pursuing too far, with the definite possibility of a strong force racing up from Trenton and catching the Americans in the disorder of victory, which can be as fatal as that of defeat. Flushed and triumphant, he returned to Princeton, where more good news awaited him. The South Lancashires, unnerved by the defeat of the rest of their brigade, had made a barely perfunctory stand. Most of them went streaming north along the road that led to the base at New Brunswick on the Raritan. A few squads took refuge in Nassau Hall. Henry Knox began shouting orders and Captain Alexander Hamilton trundled up one of his guns, sent a round or two—there are scars on Nassau Hall today— against the building, and nearly two hundred men piled out, weaponless and hands held high. The American army leaned panting on its muskets, hardly daring to believe in this, its second victory in the valley of the Delaware. A Princeton resident remembered afterward that they were "laughing outright, others smiling and not a man among them but showed joy in his countenance."

Close by Nassau Hall, Washington sought out Daniel Hitchcock, thanked him warmly for his advance. Then there was sobering work to do. The day must be militarily assessed. The action had been even briefer than Trenton, as little as fifteen minutes by some estimates, and losses had been quite light, quantitatively. But Hugh Mercer would never take his men into action again, nor would his strong voice ring out eagerly when his chief sent for him. When the Delawares marched into camp once more, recruited to at least a semblance of their original strength, there would be no John Haslet to put spirit into them. They would look in vain for that remembered necessary man to say "Come on!" to American fighting men. There were other losses. At the initial encounter down there in the orchard Captain John Fleming of the 1st Virginia had called to his company,

"Gentlemen, dress [your ranks] before you make ready [to fire]." He lay somewhere off there on the stiff brown grasses. Captain Daniel Neil and his New Jersey gunners had stood coolly under heavy fire at Trenton and shattered Hessian formations. Today his pieces had pinned down a dangerously advancing scarlet line. When the rush was broken, Neil lay dead across the breech of his gun.

There were the living to think of. What had the capture of Princeton netted materially? There was disappointingly little; shoes, blankets, rations, but not much of any one. These were issued to those who needed them most, it is hoped, but it is likely that here and there the 1777 model "yard-bird" managed to outslick the issuing officer. And there was the question of "What next?"

New Brunswick, a fairly big supply base, lay within striking distance and there was the dazzling bait of a military chest containing some seventy thousand pounds sterling to tempt bold men flushed with victory. But the regiments were exhausted. Two nights without sleep and the wicked march from the Assunpink to Princeton had practically canceled out this American army as a combat force, at least for a day or two.

There was a council of war. Reluctantly it was decided to push on, avoiding New Brunswick, toward Somerset Court House and thence to the natural bastions about Morristown and its rich hinterland. And there was need for haste. The firing of the morning had been heard at Trenton, and Cornwallis had at once sent a strong force to the little college town. It was bitterly disappointing to have to pass up New Brunswick, known to be lightly guarded, but at least the plodding Americans could chuckle with Henry Knox over the British arrival in empty Princeton, too late for pursuit, "in a most infernal sweat—running, puffing and blowing, and swearing at being so outwitted."

So the striking force of the American army, unfed and unrested, struck out for the western highlands and the heights about Morristown. New England, New York, New Jersey, Pennsylvania, Virginia, Maryland escorted victory for their country along the darkening roads.

That victory was important. Sir William Howe pulled back his far-flung chain of posts until the whole state of New Jersey was virtually cleared of royal troops. The Jersey people, Tory and rebel, who had seen themselves stripped of their possessions, their persons grossly abused, their houses burned by the Hessians and in many cases by the British as well, began to look more and more trustingly on the new nation. The heavy core of Royalist feeling had softened markedly, even if it had not melted away entirely.

News of the double coup of Trenton and Princeton swept over the rest of the country, and earnest men on recruiting duty found it at least a little easier to fill up companies and regiments. Continental currency was not quite so hard to put into circulation. Men in ports and farming centers seemed rather more willing than before to release foodstuffs to the commissary officers. The Congress itself took heart and moved back from Baltimore to Philadelphia.

Yet it is very simple to overrate the importance of the twin victories. They were, at most, promising. But their effects could be canceled out for good and all by just one bad reverse. Trenton and Princeton cannot be called, as some have called them, the turning point of the war. At most they gave strong hope for the continued existence of the armed forces of the thirteen independent states. They showed once more that an American army could roll with a series of hard punches and come up fighting again. But in no way did they forecast ultimate victory or obliterate the fact that a good deal of American success was due to Anglo-German carelessness, complacency, and underestimation of an enemy.

Morristown was well chosen as the winter quarters of a dwindling army. It lay on a steep-sided plateau, and the only approach from the east, the one channel by which the enemy could advance, was through broken, wooded ravines in the low hills, a sure death trap for the rather inflexible British regiments and their ponderous German associates. The plateau itself was dotted with a church, an inn, and some twoscore well-built houses, some of them brick and others of clapboard over brick. Behind the village rose the two-hundred-and-fifty-foot bulk of Thimble Mountain, a vantage point which commanded the interminable flats of the Passaic River and the reddish roads over which any hostile force must move. From plateau and mountain Washington intended to "watch the motions of the enemy and avail myself of Every favorable Circumstance." Intended at first only as a bivouac, comfortable Morristown became the five-month home of the American army.

There was little that the commander-in-chief could do save watch. It is virtually impossible to fix the strength of his force at any given time, but there were days when barely a thousand men fit for action could be counted. Fresh troops came in, but their arrival always seemed to trigger off a departure of men whose bounty time had run out, of militia who usually interpreted their enlistment dates to their own benefit. It is hard to believe that Howe and Cornwallis and Von Knyphausen were blind to this numerical weakness, yet their actions show that they must have been. The snow-covered bastions of Morristown defended a secret as well as an army.

Washington established himself in Freeman's Tavern, sometimes identified as Colonel Jacob Arnold's, a well-built house on the northwest edge of the Common. The army threw up log huts on the south slope of Thimble Mountain and set itself to endure doggedly another winter in the field. Clothes were in very short supply. Provisions came through in the thinnest of trickles from the rich land that lay beyond the western passes through which the winter sunsets burned a cheerless red. Smallpox, as was to be expected in those days, broke out and the staff labored endlessly, setting up isolation areas, struggling with the then almost insoluble problem of camp sanitation. Inoculation with "kine pox" was used, but not on a large scale.

Yet the memories of Trenton and Princeton still gave a warm glow to the icy gray dawns that flooded sullenly over the Jersey flats, to the ice-blue noons that hung over plateau and mountain, to snow-muffled dusks when bare feet padded silently from hut to hut. Henry Knox wrote, "For my part, my Lucy, I look up to heaven and most devoutly thank the great Governor of the Universe for producing this turn in our affairs; and the sentiment I hope will so prevail in the hearts of the people as to induce them to be a people chosen of Heaven, not to give way to despair, but at all times and under all circumstances never to despair of the Commonwealth."

Nathanael Greene, whose asthma was so much improved by the Morris-town air that he wore out horse after horse in his endless rounds, con-fided more philosophically to his Kitty back there in Rhode Island, "The smile of heaven has changed the face of affairs. Respect and courtesy flow in on us from all quarters. This is a picture of human life. I see the dif-ference between moving on with the tide of success, or sinking under a load of misfortunes." There was sad news to send to the Narragansett shores, however. Colonel Daniel Hitchcock and his brigade had struck the deciding blow at Princeton. Now Hitchcock's lion heart had finally worn out in the frail body that held it and he died on the Morristown heights. "We buried him," Nathanael wrote, "with all the honors of war, as the last mark of respect we could show him." And did Kitty remember his speaking of the Virginian, Hugh Mercer? Well, Mercer was "dead of the wounds received in the Princeton action. He was a fine companion, a sincere friend, a true patriot and a brave general."

As for the army itself, it had to do more than hide its weakness from British eyes. An idle force rots quickly, so the men were set to work hacking at the frozen New Jersey soil, felling trees, heaving great boulders along the outlines of a fort traced by the army engineers. It was an odd fort. It was never meant to be completed, and its sole end was to give employment to the troops. Appropriately, it was named Fort Nonsense in the top-secret orders that set pick and shovel in action.

There was other work, without the faintest trace of nonsense about it. Parties began to slip down from the Morristown heights into the plains below. British and Hessian supply trains were ambushed, shot up. Droves of cattle were diverted from their destinations and sent, lowing and tossing their horned heads, up the roads that led to the American lines. Howe tried to counter these raids with cavalry, and Washington decreed that hay and grain were to be the highest of high-priority targets. Very soon Colonel William Harcourt of the 16th Dragoons was wailing to headquarters that his mounts were unfit to take the field, and as a result the American raiders ranged far and wide over the Jersey flats. Soon Henry Knox was writing to "my Lucy" again that "we had a battle . . . with a party of ours and sixty Waldeckers who were all killed or taken." Jersey farmers, many of whom had looked with very cloudy glasses on the American cause, began to send in word to the nearest outpost of a convoy assembling up the Raritan or the Passaic. Often these same farmers joined with the raiders, spurred on by bitter memories of abuse at the hands of the allied troops. Howe's hold on the trans-Hudson theater was shrinking and shrinking.

Life in and about Morristown became smoother. Washington used his powers of commandeering and the army began to feed much better. New troops came in. Old formations stayed on, and his numbers swelled rather than shrank. There was even room for the amenities, and into the New Jersey hill town came Martha Washington, cheerful and brisk as ever, full of tales of doings along the Potomac and of how well Lund Washington was running Mount Vernon. The commander-in-chief's wife always, and unconsciously, attracted a court about her. Her husband's young aides were at her service and she began entertaining quietly for the wives of other officers who had managed to reach Morristown.

Mrs. Theodorick Bland, a fellow Virginian, wrote at length about this little court. There was John Fitzgerald, who had ridden between the opposing lines with his chief at Princeton, "an agreeable, broad-shouldered Irishman." She thought Alexander Hamilton a "sensible, genteel, polite young fellow, a West Indian." Tench Tilghman was "a modest, worthy man who in his attachment to the General . . . acts . . . without fee or reward." And for the home folks, there was Robert Harrison, "brother of Billy Harrison that kept store in Petersburg and as much like him as possible." Caleb Gibbs, who commanded a troop of the commander-in-chief's guards, she found "a good-natured Yankee who makes a thousand blunders in the Yankee style and keeps the dinner table in constant laugh." They were all, despite Gibbs's blunders, "polite, sociable gentlemen who make the day pass with a great deal of satisfaction to the visitors." And as the weather improved, the two o'clock dinner was followed by long rides, and at least once Mrs. Bland seems to have had the commander-in-chief to herself, for she told her sister that he was a "chatty, agreeable companion—he can be downright impudent sometimes—such impudence, Fanny, as you and I like."

In March there was wonderful news from the coast. The year before, Congress had sent Silas Deane of Connecticut to France to plead for arms and supplies. Benjamin Franklin joined him in Paris, and the two men found that the wheels of the ghost firm of Hortalez et Cie. had begun to turn even before Franklin's recent arrival. To John Sullivan's town of Portsmouth in the month of March came the brig Mercury out of Nantes. The cargo was a dazzling one, and James Warren in Boston set down a rough inventory in a letter to "My dear Mercy." There were 364 cases of arms, which James broke down into 11,987 firearms, 5 bales of "Cloath," 24 Ditto Coarse Woollens, 10 do. Woolen Caps and Stockings. There were thread and printed linens, cases of shoes, of handkerchiefs, 5 boxes of buttons and buckles, Lawns, needles, silks, Necloathes. And inserted modestly in the list were eleven thousand gun flints and, most important of all, a full thousand barrels of the superlative powder now being turned out by the gifted Lavoisier.

Nor was that all. Warren wrote Mercy that he had learned of no less than thirty-four other ships which had cleared French ports for the United States. Such shipments would go far to answer the national problem of how to equip the army of 1777. Many men who had thrown themselves unreservedly into the cause may have breathed wistful prayers that their own problems might be as neatly answered.

There was John Adams, for example. A top-flight lawyer in civil life, the man from Braintree had not received a legal fee since 1774. While he never seems to have entertained the thought of giving up his efforts for the cause in which he so strongly believed, he was keenly aware of his deteriorating financial position. Some of his concern came through in letters to Abigail. There was the question of living, and prices were high in Philadelphia. His board, he wrote, came to four pounds a week, and this did not allow for such expenses as candles, firewood, liquor, tobacco and clay pipes, or the services of a barber. A servant cost thirty shillings a week, and John Adams observed wryly that such servants generally ate twice as much as the employer and caused twice as much trouble. Shoes were five dollars a pair; salt, twenty-seven dollars a bushel; butter, ten shillings a pound; and punch, twenty shillings a bowl. "As to sugar, molasses and rum," he told Abigail, "we must leave them off." But John had just discovered an alien drink called whiskey and admitted in all frankness that he couldn't see why it wasn't just as good as New England rum.

Many other delegates, and army officers too, found themselves harassed by the same worries besetting John Adams. Personal problems, far more galling than matters of economics, were solved for a few officers. During the last months of 1776 and on into 1777 well-remembered faces began to appear in the camps. Men who had been captured in the blizzard hours of 1775 about Quebec had been released through exchange. There was the "Old Waggoner," Daniel Morgan, who had marched his rifle company from Virginia to the siege of Boston and thence to Canada. Morgan was far too good a man to be kept idle and soon was made colonel of the newly raised 11th Virginia. The Connecticut man, Return Jonathan Meigs, who had been outstanding on the killing march up the Kennebec, reported and was appointed lieutenant colonel in Henry Sherburne's new regiment, one of the groups which Washington had been authorized to recruit and which were never assigned numbers. They were known collectively as the Sixteen Additional Regiments and, like the Hessian and Brunswick units, were identified only by the colonel's name. Morristown began to hear good English spoken with a marked North Europe accent, and the quiet elegance of Christian Febiger, the Dane, was seen crossing the muddy Common. Febiger already had Breed's Hill and the Canada expedition on his record and soon settled down as Dan Morgan's lieutenant colonel. Somehow, on the march to Quebec and during the months of captivity, a strong friendship had sprung up between these two men of such widely differing backgrounds, a friendship that was to endure until the Old Waggoner's death in 1802. There were other experienced men in this same exchange cartel, and most of them fitted back into the slowly reviving army, bringing a leaven of military maturity that was far out of proportion to their numbers.

From Thimble Mountain the commander-in-chief watched the main threat to the existence of his country and his army, which was Howe's main force in and about Manhattan. He was sure that the real menace lay in that quarter. For reasons that are hard to understand he felt convinced that there would be no movement up Champlain and Lake George by Carleton. The American sector in the North would not, he thought, be severely tested. He was right, so far as Carleton's participation was concerned. But all through the winter pens had been scratching and scraping in London and unmeasured quarts of ink dried in fine, spidery lines on sheets of foolscap and parchment.

Lord George Germain, Secretary of State for the Colonies, always acted deviously. It seemed to be a matter of principle with him not even to let his right hand know what his right hand was doing. The flamboyant "Thoughts for Conducting the War from the Side of Canada" which Gentleman Johnny Burgoyne had submitted was being implemented. It was a sound plan, though differing very little from Carleton's general idea of the year before, which had stalled so strangely at the very gates of Ticonderoga. In Germain's hands it became Operation Snafu.

As minutely detailed by its author, the stroke against the colonies was to be no isolated, unkeyed move south from Canada. A compact force of British, Brunswickers, and Hessians was to strike down at Ticonderoga, drive swiftly thence to the great bend in the Hudson and on to Albany. The aim, of course, was control of the great inland waterway that led from New York Harbor up to the St. Lawrence, the sword blade broken only between the Hudson and upper Champlain. And this was not all. Down the Mohawk from Oswego a smaller group of British, Hessians, Tories, and Indians under Colonel Barry St. Leger would plunge east to the Hudson and link up with Gentleman Johnny at Albany. And here would come the sledge-hammer smash on the anvil formed by Burgoyne and St. Leger. Sir William Howe with the strongest force of all would come up the Hudson and the last American resistance might be battered out of existence, caught in the three-ply onslaught.

Even if the main American army should escape, the war would be as good as over. New England would be cut off from the other states. Any important flow of men and supplies could be thinned to a mere trickle by establishing a few posts along the Hudson, which the Royal Navy could also patrol as far as Albany. The rest of Howe's army could be used to track down and disperse the discouraged fugitive fragments of the rebels. For it was thought certain, and not illogically, that Washington would be compelled to bring his command up from the Jerseys in a desperate and surely futile attempt to check this shattering move.

What a stroke! It would be bound to mean a title for Gentleman

Johnny and very likely the supreme command in North America for the pleasant and profitable task of sweeping up the last bits of opposition. It could not help working. Why, King George himself had written to Burgoyne's certain knowledge that, "as Sir William Howe does not think of acting from Rhode Island into Massachusetts, the force from Canada must join him at Albany." There it was, all neatly tied up. And Germain had written to Sir Guy Carleton of the plan and of able Sir Guy's shelving, this last probably giving Germain an added thrill of pleasure. He told Carleton just what troops would be left in Canada, just how many would make up Burgoyne's task force. And he stressed the need for speedy action, saying that it had become "highly necessary that the most speedy Junction of the two Armies should be effected"—that is, the junction of Howe and Burgoyne at Albany. There was one final line to this letter: "I shall write to Sir William Howe by the first Packet." Burgoyne cannot be blamed for rubbing his hands and chuckling richly on his voyage out to take command. His "Thoughts" had been turned into a sure-fire plan, one that could not possibly miss. And, Jove, it would be fun to see Charley Fox squirm when he paid over those fifty guineas, as entered in the betting book at Brooks's.

It will be remembered that Germain had cost the British a crushing victory at Minden when, in a state of utter funk, he would not turn his cavalry loose on the beaten French. Once again he was to serve his country very badly, and this time through carelessness and stupidity. That letter that was to go to Sir William "by the first Packet" never left London.

Many versions have been given of the actions of Germain, Howe, and Burgoyne, some authorities even taking up the cudgels for that almost fabulous oaf with the bad Minden record. Others have tried to show that Burgoyne had misunderstood the part that Howe was expected to play in the year 1777. It seems difficult to go back of the material unearthed by the late Francis Huddleston, librarian of the British War Office. When Gentleman Johnny returned to England, a prisoner on parole as Fox had prophesied, he was granted the most grudging of hearings, as might be expected under the regime of Germain, who would be most careful to suppress any evidence that reflected on his lordship. William Knox, Germain's Under-Secretary for the Colonies, testified that when all Burgoyne's orders had been drawn up and were being checked over by Knox's staff Germain "came down to the office on his way to Stoneland (in Sussex), when I observed to him that there was no letter to Howe to acquaint him with the plan or what was expected of him in consequence of it. His Lordship stared and [Deputy Secretary] D'Oyly started, but said he would in a moment write a few lines. 'So,' says Lord Sackville [Knox uses the earlier title interchangeably with the later one], 'my poor horses must stand in the street all the time, and I shan't be to my time anywhere.'" (This last seems to have been most important to my lord, as he was on his way to a week end in the country.) "D'Oyly then said he better go, and he [D'Oyly] would write from himself to Howe and enclose copies of Burgoyne's instructions which would tell him all that he would want to know, and with this His Lordship was satisfied as it enabled him to keep his time, for he would never bear delay or disappointment." But D'Oyly must have had a week end on his mind as well as Lord George. He seems to have forgotten all about the letter to Howe, for it was never written. As a result, the real hammer blow of the "Thoughts" was omitted. Gentleman Johnny went gallantly to Canada, not knowing that he would fight with his hands virtually tied behind his back, and the United States was handed a victory that has been rated as one of the Fifteen Decisive Battles of the World.

The slow descent of spring on Lower Canada, the breakup of the ice in the St. Lawrence were watched with relief by a thickset German in light blue faced with buff. Nearing forty, he had Teutonic blue eyes with a tendency to twinkle and something almost Hibernian in the tilt of his nose and the length of his upper lip. Major General Baron Friedrich Adolph von Riedesel, shuttling placidly between Trois Rivières, Montreal, and Quebec, commanded not only all the Brunswick troops in Canada but some contingents from Hesse as well.

During the winter months the baron may have thought a little enviously of Von Knyphausen and Von Heister, with other German troops, enjoying the season in the doubtless semi-tropical latitudes of New York. He had been more than a little worried about how his men from central and southern Germany would stand the blizzards and hard freezes along the St. Lawrence. But the baron had worked, with an adaptability surprising in a professional soldier of his day, to adjust his command to the climate instead of fighting the strange conditions. No longer did the German camps glitter with brilliant facings on dark blue coats or green. A party of Brunswickers on a woodcutting detail suggested a highly modern week end at Mont Tremblant, for the stolid Germans wore white mackinaw-type coats edged with bright colors. In place of high brass helmets or heavy cocked hats they grinned complacently from under Canadian stocking caps that would not have looked out of place on a ski tow. Some of them, like the Von Specht regiment, took pride in Dan'l Boone fur hats, complete with trailing raccoon tails. They even ventured out in the pine forests on snowshoes and, under Canadian tutelage, glided with increasing expertness over drifted fields and snow-masked ponds. All in all, the baron's command had come through a Canadian winter in very good shape.

Another factor favored them. The winter of 1776–77, while bitter enough in the minds of these newcomers, was actually very mild. For years afterward the local inhabitants remembered the relatively high temperatures and their strange guests, and the period became "the German winter" in mind and speech.

Snow patches shrank and shrank under the pines and the white birches. The eastward flow of ice in the great river grew less, and in the baron's camps blanket coats and fur caps and mittens were seen no more. Drill-book officers drew sighs of deep relief as their men stepped out once again in proper uniforms, in helmets and cocked hats. They would have done better had they managed somehow to learn a lesson from the despised winter clothing, to see that adaptability might be an essential in all seasons.

There were various underlying trends and tendencies that must have given the baron a good many thoughtful moments. Amenities were observed in the higher brackets between the British and the Germans, but in general they did not get along very well. Germans resented the fact that, while a British officer could command German troops, no Hessian or Brunswicker, no matter how high the rank, could give an order to "poor bloody Tommy." There was friction in the ranks, and Georg Pausch wrote bitterly to the Count of Hanau about the case of the assault on Cannoneer Nantz by an English private. The German enlisted men were by no means averse to brawling, but they felt that the British did not fight fair; in fact, they struck the Germans with their clenched fists instead of trying to fell them with an alehouse bench or a wine jug. The British were rather contemptuous of German docility in obeying commands. And they were dumfounded at the sight of Hessians drinking like respectable seasoned topers but singing *hymns* while they drank. British and German units passed each other on the march, and while the British trolled out "The Darby Ram" in raucous joy, the Germans intoned Martin Luther's "Prayer of Thanksgiving."

There was tension at the very heart of the German contingent. Lieutenant Colonel Friedrich Baum, commanding the horseless Brunswick dragoons, was a stout, fair, florid German of respectable service in European wars. Heading the elite of the German contingent, the grenadiers and the light infantry, who were invariably detached from their parent regiments to serve as a single tough unit, was Lieutenant Colonel von Breymann, probably the best soldier in the baron's command, taking the word "soldier" in its most limited sense. In contrast to Baum's blondness, Breymann was lean and very swarthy. These physical traits, according to family tradition, go back to a survivor of the massacre of Varus' Roman legions at the Teutoburg Forest in A.D. 9, that survivor being somehow accepted by the victorious Germanic tribes. In addition, Breymann had a bitter, brutal nature which, added to his undoubted military gifts, would probably have given him high rank in the legions of Adolf Hitler. Between Baum and Von Breymann there smoldered, and often flared up hotly, a savage personal feud that seemed to dominate both men to the exclusion of duty itself and was to play an important part in the first major and bloody reverse of 1777. Compared to this vicious hatred, the discord that raged between Lord Lucan and Lord Cardigan in the Crimea in 1854 appears an evanescent teen-age tiff.

Yet the man from Wolfenbüttel could survey his force of some three thousand men with reasonable equanimity, particularly as he seems to have made little effort to find out anything about the terrain which that force would have to face in the inevitable spring campaign. The troops were rigidly, even ferociously, disciplined and were probably more afraid of their regimental and company officers and non-coms than of any enemy. Most field officers had had wide experience in European warfare and had their units well in hand. They could be counted on to carry out orders to the letter, unflinchingly and efficiently, unless tripped up by undreamed-of problems that were bound to arise out of a wilderness campaign.

Militarily he could also be cheered by the promised return to this theater of his friend, John Burgoyne, whom he seems sincerely to have liked and who liked and respected him. It was common rumor that Gentleman Johnny would be in supreme command and then Von Riedesel would merely have to see that his ponderous contingent carried out the leader's ringing directions. Some of the baron's pleasant anticipations would not be realized in full. Burgoyne and his staff, as the months went by, would not be above using their German auxiliaries as a convenient receptacle for blame when the going became rough below Champlain.

On non-military grounds, Von Riedesel could view the immediate future with deep contentment. The spring fleet was scheduled to bring to Canada, subject to the whims of gale and tide, a small Dresden-china figure of a woman with very deep blue eyes and distracting rosebud mouth, his adored Baroness Frederica, whom he called "Fritschen." And with Fritschen would come three very young daughters, Frederica, Gustava, and Caroline, the last literally a babe in arms. Deep blue eyes and rosebud mouth masked a most indomitable spirit that must have been passed on to the daughters, for the four Von Riedesel ladies went gallantly through the whole disastrous campaign, through years of most uncomfortable captivity, and did not see Wolfenbüttel again until the year 1783. At least one direct descendant returned to America in the person of Graf Johann-Heinrich von Bernstorff, who, as Imperial German Ambassador, was handed his passport by American Secretary of State Robert Lansing in the significant year of 1917.

The British troops to be affected by Gentleman Johnny's sonorous "Thoughts" and Germain's solicitude for his horses and his week end in Sussex managed their lives quite well. Many of them had put in long service along the St. Lawrence and conditions were quite familiar to them. Also, the average Englishman, especially in the ranks, was not conditioned by the background of virtual serfdom that influenced his German opposite number. He was far more inventive, more adaptable and independent, a factor which was bound to influence those who ranked above him, if only indirectly.

This English force of some four thousand men was favored by two facts. There had been a snafu at some British port and no new uniforms had been sent out to the Canada garrison. To repair worn-out equipment, the long, trailing coattails worn by all save the light infantry were cut off and the cloth used for patches. The brims of battered cocked hats were trimmed and the felt crowns turned into skullcaps. Such tampering with cherished regimentals must have set some of Burgoyne's military purists gobbling in protest. "The Army's going to the devil, Sir. Pass the port!" But owing to this shipping failure, the British infantry found itself quite sensibly dressed for a wilderness campaign.

The second, even more unconventional than tampering with uniforms, had to do with Von Riedesel's opposite number, the commander of the British contingent. Here was no converted cavalryman from a smart regiment, a type usually chosen by the British War Office down to 1940. Many an officer must have choked over his brandy at the thought that William Phillips was nothing but a ruddy gunner! It was almost unheard of for an officer from the "learned services" to command real soldiers. Phillips had served with distinction in the Seven Years' War. He was flawless at Minden. At Warburg he had introduced an innovation nearly as startling as the use of tanks on the Somme in 1916. He had actually brought his guns into action at a gallop! It was unorthodox, and purists might have considered it not quite sporting. Phillips had thrown himself into this action with such vigor that it is recorded that he broke no less than fifteen canes, personally flogging the unfortunate horses of the gun teams to a greater speed. How a conventional soldier like Gentleman Johnny ever saw the true value of Phillips, particularly in view of the former's conviction that high command should have "no damned nonsense about merit attached to it," is hard to understand. The gunner turned out to be an energetic, forceful commander, and it may have been lucky for the American cause that his talents were employed here in the North rather than in Pennsylvania. Perhaps credit for the appointment should go to Carleton, a clear-thinking man, but at least Gentleman Johnny welcomed it.

So the stage was being set and the cast assembled for the tragicomedy entitled "Thoughts for Conducting the War from the Side of Canada," by J. Burgoyne, Esq. Only the male lead and a few supporting characters were missing.

CHAPTER XXI

"Thoughts for Conducting the War from the Side of Canada"

IT was May 6, 1777, and the ship bearing Major General John Burgoyne dropped anchor in the apple-green light that still floods down the fjord-like reaches of the St. Lawrence by Quebec, with the scarred, towering reddish cliffs of Levis to the south and the fantastic, castle-crowned rock mass of the citadel on the north. It was a setting that must have appealed to Burgoyne and he may have quoted to an impressed aide:

> This castle hath a pleasant seat; the air
> Nimbly and sweetly recommends itself
> Unto our gentle senses.

Once ashore, hugging his top-secret "Thoughts," he was borne to the summit of the rock and, on the way, suffered a stunning shock. From hints, then words, then whole sentences, he learned that every detail of the grandiose plan was almost stale news to Quebec! He further learned that Montreal, Trois Rivières, and St. Johns on the Richelieu knew about as much as Quebec. It should have been expected, especially from an office run by Lord George Germain. Probably letters had gone out to favorites in Canada, who could benefit by advance knowledge, long before the King had backed it. Yet the leak was not serious, as it turned out. No hint seems to have reached the American Congress or the army, but of course Burgoyne could not have been aware of this consoling news.

At the citadel Burgoyne found Carleton understandably disappointed at being shelved but magnificently and unreservedly co-operative. This was a point that Gentleman Johnny could not miss and he paid orotund tribute in a letter to Germain. "I should think myself deficient in justice and honour were I to close my letter without mentioning the sense I entertain of General Carleton's conduct," he wrote, "his zeal . . . [is] manifest, exemplary and satisfactory." This is a generous tribute, though it probably accomplished little more than to cause Germain to write Carleton off as a naïve fool.

Sir Guy had news for Burgoyne, clear and valuable intelligence of American dispositions, quite unlike the military fog that rolled before American eyes. Ticonderoga, the key to lakes Champlain and George and the wilderness tangle south of them, was held by General Arthur St. Clair, late of His Majesty's army, with about two thousand effectives, in bad health and badly supplied.

This was a good omen, but Burgoyne found that there were great gaps to fill in his expedition before he could think of starting it rolling down the forest-cloaked avenue of the lake. How about the projected corps of Tories? Carleton was sorry. There were very few enrolling, despite heavy inducements. Canadians? Worse yet. They just want to be let alone. Indians? Not a great many; what there were could not be thought too reliable if the going became heavy.

This was discouraging. Now about transport. Surely Sir Guy had seen the requisition for horses and wagons sent from London. The answer was worse here. The Canadian farmers refused to sell or lease their animals and carts. Gun carriages? The requisition was late, but they were being built out of green wood. Wheels, of course, would play no part until the move south from Ticonderoga had begun, since east and west of Champlain there were no roads, only the thinnest of Indian trails. But once beyond Champlain—— So an order was sent out at once to build five hundred two-wheeled carts, flimsy little fellows and of green timber like the gun carriages. The country would be scoured for horses, but General Burgoyne would remember from his previous visit that Canada was not a horse-breeding country.

Carleton may have asked why Burgoyne planned to lug so many cannon through the wilderness, as men were to ask at the inconclusive hearing accorded him when he returned to England on parole. The genial general does seem to have been overartilleried, but he would surely have told Carleton that, while he deferred politely to the latter's wide experience, nonetheless Sir Guy had not seen that extraordinary affair at Breed's Hill. Rebels back of earthworks were dashed prickly, and Burgoyne intended to smother any enemy earthworks with artillery fire before committing his infantry. So the horror of that June day on the Charlestown peninsula was still influencing the thoughts of those who had witnessed it.

And what had Sir Guy heard from the south? What about the heaviest, the major stroke of the Howe-Burgoyne-St. Leger combined operation? Carleton had a little information for him. The New York command and that in Canada should have been working together, but in actual fact they functioned as two separate and distinct armies, almost alien armies. Connection between the two was far more tenuous than that between the American, European, and Pacific commands from 1941–45. But Howe had written one of his very rare letters to the Canadian theater. He told Carleton that the '77 campaign would find the main British force in Pennsylvania, although a very weak demonstration or two might be made a little way up the Hudson. Pennsylvania! Little Hudson River raids! This might well have chilled Gentleman Johnny's ever-present optimism. But he probably thought that Howe had written Carleton before receiving Germain's orders to implement the "Thoughts." He surely had them by now. And at any rate, Burgoyne had found a New York-bound ship before sailing from England and had sent by it a full copy of his own orders to Sir William. Nothing to worry about.

So Gentleman Johnny left Quebec and headed west, picking up the force that would muster along the Richelieu River. And he charmed wherever he went. Lieutenant William Digby of the grenadier company of the 53rd Shropshires jotted in his diary, "General Burgoyne alone engrossed their warmest attachment . . . idolized by the army, his orders appearing more like recommending subordination than enforcing it . . . he was the soldier's friend."

Gentleman Johnny's soul expanded in this atmosphere of good-fellowship that widened his genial smile and deepened his infectious laugh. And his always roving eye glowed ever more warmly as he noted some uncommonly pretty faces under the high, powdered heads that bobbed in curtsies before him. That Mrs. Commissary now. He must remember to tell one of his young aides to make sure of her name. Might be a good idea, too, to have her husband attached to the expedition.

The journey had actually begun in May of the year before, when a heavy traveling carriage rolled out of Wolfenbüttel in Brunswick. It contained Baroness Frederica von Riedesel and daughters Gustava, not quite five, little Frederica, about two, and Caroline, all of ten weeks. Riding inside with them was the maid Lena, and on the box, driving with careful speed, was the baron's grizzled old Jaeger servant, Rockel. The party was boldly heading across the north-central German plains on a rather long trip—to the heart of Canada.

There were highwaymen about, and Rockel drove only by day, when possible. But there was a grisly moment in the Netherlands near Maastricht, even then a war-weary city that in distant 1944 was to be captured by an American army. Night overtook the indomitable six and, as the baroness wrote, blue eyes wide at the memory, "Some object hanging in the air struck me through the open window of my carriage. Thereupon I seized it and as I felt something rough, I asked what it might be. It was the body of a man hanged [to a tree by the side of the road] in woolen stockings!" This must have been most unpleasant, but there is no indication that she thought of turning back to comfortable Wolfenbüttel.

They were in England, but there was difficulty in getting passage to Canada, a land where, the baron's letter assured her, there was nothing to eat but oats and horseflesh. So the little baroness, with that calm acceptance of things as they were that was to act as a tiller in all her future voyages, settled down in London to wait with her young ladies and the servants. She was presented to the royal family, and kindly, obstinate King George, carried away by the deceptive solemnity of the blue eyes and the rosebud mouth, kissed her paternally. "At which," confided the baroness, "I became fiery red, it was so sudden." Her eyes bothered her, and the Queen's oculist himself treated her with some drops which "hurt horribly." More, he charged her three whole guineas for this unpleasant if effective therapy.

Canada at last, and a mad dash west from Quebec in search of the baron. The route lay along the north bank of the St. Lawrence. There was a start through June blackness at two-thirty in the morning "in calashes [calèches] which are very small and uncomfortable but very fast. Our calash was small and open so I tied my second daughter Frederica in one corner, took my youngest, Caroline, in my lap while my eldest, Gustava, as the most discreet, sat between my feet on my purse."

Near Trois Rivières there were rivers to cross, and the delicately reared Fritschen found that "I would be obliged to make use of . . . a very light canoe, made of the bark of a tree. . . . It was horrible weather. . . . Seated on the bottom of the canoe in one corner I had my children on my lap. . . . We had to maintain equilibrium, the necessity of which I did not learn from our boatman until we were overtaken by a severe storm; whereupon Frederica became alarmed, screamed and wanted to jump up. . . . The boatman told me that the canoe would be overturned by even the slightest movement. I was obliged to hold her very firmly . . . and in this manner we finally arrived at Trois Rivières."

They were in calashes again, hard on the trail of the baron, who was on the move in consequence of Gentleman Johnny's orders. But there was no sitting down and waiting for the baroness. "My children and the faithful Rockel kept a constant watch on the high road that they might bring me news of my husband's arrival. Finally a calash was descried, having a Canadian in it. I saw the calash stop, the Canadian get out, come nearer and fold my children in his arms. It was my husband! As he still had the fever, he was clothed . . . in a sort of cassock of wool, bordered with ribbons to which was attached a . . . fringe of blue and red, after the Canadian fashion."

So the Von Riedesel family was reunited, the combined ladies having journeyed some three thousand miles by carriage, ship, and canoe. The baroness does not seem to have felt that she had accomplished anything unusual. She probably wrote mentally, "Mission accomplished," and that was that.

The reunion was not to last long. Oboes were wailing, deep-toned drums were throbbing along the green banks of the St. Lawrence. The invasion force was forming and the campaign was about to begin. The baron, now magnificent in his horizon blue and yellow, kissed his ladies good-by. They were to wait in Canada until the campaign, probably a short one, was over.

In the false dawn that crept over the high shouldering of the Green Mountains on the first of July, a vast flotilla pushed out from the Anglo-German camps at Crown Point, swung into a thick line across the mile-wide throat of Champlain, and hung poised, as though waiting for a signal. Never since glacier or terrific subterranean convulsion had ripped out its bed had the deep blue waters of the lake mirrored such a force. Keels of uncounted bateaux, gundalows scored its surface. The winds that sighed down from the lift of the Adirondacks in the west swerved against the sails of ships that were almost frigates, of smart pinnaces, sloops, ketches.

The waters also reflected a foretaste of autumn. There were Indians painted ocher and crimson and saffron and green and blood-red. The images of scarlet coats with willow-green, buff, yellow facings danced erratically along the port and starboard ripples of small craft. The blue of the Brunswickers and the Hessians glanced back from the surface with greenish overtones, almost the jade of November pines, while the lighter green of the Jaegers suggested lichened rock in a pale sunlight.

On the deck of the largest pinnace in the center of the mile-long line Gentleman Johnny Burgoyne could preen himself in the growing dawn light and survey his command with a certain amount of well-bred satisfaction. He could count no less than four British or Scottish titles among his officers, as well as a comfortable number of younger sons, like Acland of the grenadiers, whose family had been "gentle" in Somerset for over six hundred years and who was suitably married to the daughter of the Earl of Ilchester. There were also four Members of Parliament, including himself. And there was the good old Baron von Riedesel—whom the British enlisted men insisted on calling Red-hazel. German, of course, but then one could hardly disregard a title that went back to the year eleven hundred and something.

Looking aft from the pinnace at boatload after boatload of scarlet British and blue or green Germans, the military eye could be satisfied as well as the social. The Germans might be an unknown quantity to the commander of the expedition, beyond the fact that those troops had always fought well in the past and that the baron had brought this contingent up to standard. But in the gently rocking lines of boats rode British history. Take those men of the 21st Royal Scots Fusiliers, whose organization dated back to the days when infantrymen carried a long pike. Formed in 1678, the Royal Scots had fought at Bothwell Bridge and Killiecrankie, at Blenheim and on to Malplaquet. And the 9th Norfolks and the 20th Lancashires were nearly as venerable. Of the junior formations, the 47th North Lancashires had stormed Louisburg and Quebec, had marched over the tragic road that led from Boston to Concord, and had struggled up the still more tragic slopes of Breed's Hill. Gentleman Johnny was well aware of the very real value of drama in history as well as the value of history in drama. With such a force at his command he cannot be blamed for feeling supremely confident of victory—and a title—waiting for him at the narrows of the lake not far below him.

As he looked forward, a frown may have clouded his exuberant assurance. Ahead of the whole thick line glided fourteen long war canoes freighted with hideously painted allies of the Crown. More Indian paddles sliced the water at the far flanks. The color-daubed redmen were born warriors. They required little in the way of supplies and munitions, and it would never do to forget that the rebel settlers to the south lived in mortal terror of them. Savages, of course, but then they added a touch of raw elemental to the ordered formalism of the rest of the force, and this stark contrast may have appealed to Burgoyne's theatrical mind. There would be wonderful stories to tell of them when he returned to Brooks's to collect that fifty-guinea bet from Charles James Fox, like that one warrior back at Putnam Creek whose sole uniform consisted of a blackbird dangling loosely from a cord about his waist.

Yet members of the club might ask awkward questions. Could a gentleman possibly make war in association with a lot of savages, especially when those savages were to be turned loose on transplanted Englishmen, wrong-headed and rioting as those transplantees might be? Gentleman Johnny could merely refer such doubters to his speech to the assembled Indians. He had told them distinctly, emphasizing each point, that they were to fight as civilized men; they were to kill only in action; wounded and prisoners were not to be scalped or tortured; noncombatants were to be in no way harmed, especially women and children. Could a man speak fairer or plainer than that? And the Indians had all shouted and waved their weapons and rushed to the rum kegs that the sutlers were opening. A contemporary critic referred to the speech to the Indians as containing "all the tinsel splendor of enlightened absurdity," a phrase which Gentleman Johnny may have secretly envied.

It is an odd instance of self-delusion. There was the history of all wars in America where Indians had been used. And if this were not enough to guide him, there were the constant words of one of the strangest figures of this expedition, the leader of all the Indians, La Corne St. Luc. Now nearly seventy, he was of a noble French family and had spent most of his life in Canada. Among his own people he was said to have been a polished courtier, suggesting Versailles rather than Quebec. But out on the trails he dressed, lived, spoke, and thought like an Indian, viewed human life as they did, had been notorious on raids down into the old British colonies. To him, a scalp was a scalp, a settler's house something to be burned. A settler of any age or either sex was fair game. His woodcraft was amazing, as was his strength, and he could survive when the toughest Indian died. And from his first meeting with Burgoyne his one chant was, "Il faut brutaliser les affaires." Did this tell Gentleman Johnny nothing?

Another odd point about the painted men in the war canoes—black on white, white on black, ocher on green, vermilion on black—was their employment. There were many men in the British Army who had served with Indians, knew something of them, spoke a little of their tongue. Yet by some incomprehensible reasoning the Indians were assigned to cover the left wing of the advance, the wing composed of Von Riedesel's Germans. The baron's own letters show that he had had little or no contact with this strange covering force, and it is doubtful if any of his officers knew more about them than he. How could he be expected to command them, direct them, much less control them or see to it that they obeyed the incredibly naïve speech that Burgoyne had made to them? Yet there they were, rocking on the light Champlain waves, the bow- and sternmen holding their paddles poised, waiting for the signal.

The sun crept over the crests of the Green Mountains, lit up the glossy scarlet and white of Gentleman Johnny's uniform. On the quarter-deck of his pinnace Burgoyne raised his arm, dropped it. A signal gun slammed flatly, sending its echoes over the lake toward the Adirondacks. Paddles dipped and flashed, oars cut the water in sparkling eddies, sails filled; from the bateaux drums boomed, horns and oboes blared out, and the whole thick line glided south. The leap to Ticonderoga had begun.

Ticonderoga, the vaunted wilderness Gibraltar of America, was to gain no luster through withstanding a long siege. Its fall was hardly an incident, and in that fall Burgoyne's 138 pieces of artillery, lugged along at the cost of heartbreaking toil, played little part. The British went ashore on the west side of the lake, some four miles above the bluestone fort, and the bulk of Von Riedesel's ponderous Germans were dumped on the east bank. The German mission was to plunge ahead, circle a little to the east, and close in on the American works that crowned Mount Independence, just across from Lotbinière's rather overrated masterpiece on the Ticonderoga point.

No troops could have been worse prepared for the east bank than the Brunswickers. They were faced with primeval forest, with deadfalls and windfalls where colossal tree trunks were stacked like the jackstraws of a mad giant. There was East Creek, oozing evilly into the lake, its banks melting into a nauseous gumbo in which a man could neither walk nor swim. In loops and arms and angles this morass wove erratically north and south and east and west, and a soldier used to the ordered stretches of wood and water about Halberstadt could, and did, crack physically and mentally as he manfully tried to beat his way forward. Through moisture-sodden air that was like a steam room, the Germans thrashed on. Faces became scarlet under the high brass of grenadiers' helmets, under the heavy cocked hats of the line companies. Sweat pattered down on yellow, white, or red facings. Deep cuffs were clammy tortures about galled wrists, and white breeches, ever tighter about heat-swollen legs, were splashed to the waistband with gummy black mud. Useless sabers caught on limbs and branches; haversacks dangled and bumped; muskets became entangled in mazes of dead, crackling wood; men tripped and fell sprawling in rank, dripping weeds. And always the air was aquiver with the high, merciless whine of mosquitoes eager to feed on swollen faces, necks, and hands. Silent, but even more deadly, the almost invisible black flies added their quota of agony. The few miles along the east shore to Mount Independence stretched away, endless as the north German plains. Time and the wilderness were fighting for the thirteen states.

On the west shore, terrain was rather better. Burgoyne, screened efficiently by some Indians, made fair progress. He could have moved a little faster could he have guessed that red-haired Arthur St. Clair, in command of the Americans, knew only that a hostile force had been landed. Of his opponent's strength and intentions he did not have the remotest idea. So, unaware of St. Clair's ignorance, Gentleman Johnny moved more cautiously than he needed, fearful of finding the equivalent of Breed's Hill instead of victory at this throat of the lake.

Contact was made. A small American blockhouse that dominated the thread of water leading west from Champlain to Lake George was taken without much trouble. There were one or two rather noisy clashes between outposts, but no real trial of strength. Axes rang in the woods; vast trees crashed to the ground as roads were slowly chewed out and corduroyed for the passage of Burgoyne's guns. A formal siege seemed hovering on the edge of the records of the campaign.

Lieutenant Twiss, Royal Engineers, had been prowling about the terrain to the west and south of the fort, translating what he saw into workable and usable knowledge. Sometime on the third or fourth of July he called

the attention of Major General Phillips to a high peak, known as Mount
Defiance or Sugar-loaf Mountain, which Twiss had scaled. From its summit
there was a magnificent view. Without a glass Twiss had been able to look
right down into the fort itself and onto the narrowing thread of lake that
ran south to the final terminus by Skenesboro. That thread was thick with
Yankee barges and even larger craft. Also, the peak was neither defended
nor fortified.

It should have been. The year before, John Trumbull, son of the governor
of Connecticut, had demonstrated Defiance's threat to Ticonderoga very
simply and unanswerably. To the delight of young Anthony Wayne, then
a Pennsylvania colonel, he had fired a cannon from the fort and had seen
dust and rock fragments fly from the peak of the mount. Then he pointed
out to Horatio Gates that if a gun fired from the fort could hit the summit,
one fired from the summit could hit the fort. Gates, in the sureness of his
vast knowledge and experience, had good-naturedly waved off the eager
young amateur.

William Phillips treated Twiss's information far differently. Defiance
had, unquestionably, a rugged slope, but as the old gunner observed tersely,
"Where a goat can go, a man can go. Where a man can go, he can drag a
cannon." A road was hastily hacked out, weaving and twisting up a face
that was hidden from American eyes. Somehow, guns were manhandled to
the very peak and a battery installed. This battery was to be ultra top-secret.
When the time came, its guns could hammer right down into Ticonderoga,
batter the works across on Independence, smash any evacuation attempt
down the canal-like end of the lake. But until the signal was given, St. Clair
must not guess that there was any life on Mount Defiance.

Gentleman Johnny must have rubbed his hands. No Breed's Hill. True,
good old Red-hazel was mortally slow over there on the east bank, but as
soon as the Germans could strike at Independence the British would rush
Ticonderoga while the hidden guns on Defiance would drive home the last
nails of St. Clair's military coffin. Of course it was a pity that the secrecy
covering the German move had broken down. The baron's Indians had lit
fires, and the garrison of Independence was thoroughly alerted. No matter.
With the guns of Mount Defiance, the fate of Old Ti was as good as
settled.

Then a cruel trick of fate flattened the chilled champagne in Gentleman
Johnny's always filled glass. It may even have dimmed momentarily the
allure of the same Mrs. Commissary whom he had noted so favorably up in
Canada and who now shared his mess, his abundant stores of wines, his
card table and various other appurtenances. There was a flash high on the
crest of Mount Defiance, a gush of smoke, and a crackling boom spilled
out over the lake. Some careless hand had fired one of the guns. Or it may
have been the hard July sun playing on the vent of a piece loaded and
primed. Whatever the cause, St. Clair was now fully warned that his avenue
of retreat by water to the south was commanded by artillery. Burgoyne's

neat set piece was spoiled. He recovered his poise quickly and exuded his customary infectious, cheery optimism. No change in plans. Carry on.

Sometime before daybreak on the early morning of July 6 a message was brought to Brigadier General Simon Fraser, in command of the British Advanced Corps—the massed light infantry and grenadier companies of all regiments. The night had been quiet, almost suspiciously so. Cautious scouts had worked close to the American lines and found that Ticonderoga was deserted, that the more than two hundred boats of the garrison had slipped south down to Skenesboro. All at once great fires burst out on Mount Independence across the lake and sent ghastly orange flickers racing over the dark waters of Champlain.

The movement of veteran troops by night is a very risky operation. Somehow, St. Clair had managed to evacuate his raw, unstable garrison undetected until the cautious proddings of Fraser's scouts had shown the west bank to be empty. The American move would have been perfect save for the fatal fires on Mount Independence, lit against St. Clair's strictest orders, a military gaffe for which the more than equivocal Frenchman, La Roche Fermoy, was entirely responsible. Now these blazes—barracks, stores, rations —told Fraser that the east bank was being emptied as well.

Simon Fraser was a tough, seasoned, skillful Scot. He got word to Burgoyne, received his orders, and started in pursuit, crossing to Independence by the bridge of boats which La Roche Fermoy should have destroyed. Fraser was to link up with the Germans, already on the east bank as we have seen, and follow St. Clair on the one road, the cart track that ran southeast to Hubbardton and Castleton, then swinging west to Skenesboro at the very head of Champlain. As to the pursuit up the lake by water, Burgoyne and the Royal Navy would see to that.

So the Scot and his grenadiers and light infantry plunged on into the dark lands where they could guess at the ominous lift of steep, wooded hills that seemed to shoulder one another in the night hush. The moon was high, and in deep pothole valleys ponds and lakes shimmered eerily.

Dawn broke and still the Advanced Corps pushed on. The pace was murderous. Gentleman volunteer Thomas Anburey with the grenadiers of the 29th Worcestershires remembered that this phase lasted from four in the morning until one in the afternoon without any real halts, an exploit that must win admiration from anyone who has ever marched with troops. Sometime during the sweating, steamy hours Von Riedesel appeared. His own troops, who were supposed to link up with Fraser, were hopelessly strung out and there was no telling when a junction might be made. Fraser listened grimly, then decided to push on alone. The baron promised to do his best to catch up. The day ebbed and Fraser was forced to call a halt, with reveille set for three the next morning.

In the soft radiance of a Vermont summer dawn Fraser's van stumbled upon a rebel force that was there only because of two bad blunders. Seth Warner, in command, had been ordered to keep marching and join St. Clair and the main body. Instead, he had halted for the night. Worse, he had neglected to throw out any guards, and the light infantry came in with the bayonet before his men were properly awake. There were flight, surrender, and panic in a lightening terrain where steep sharp hills and thick woods alternated with level clearings not far from the hamlet of Hubbardton.

The picture changed. The rebel force found cohesion, filtered into the woods, massed, struck, and Fraser's force was roughly checked. For some hours the smoke rolled over sunny Vermont meadows, and more and more scarlet figures lay inert on flower-sprinkled grass. The drab rebel lines struck again, began to close about Fraser's left, and a British disaster loomed.

Then from the left rear a fearful din arose. Guttural voices were roaring out hymns. Drums boomed; brasses and oboes sent a deep-toned Lutheran chant sailing out through the hot, smoky air. Von Riedesel had arrived at the point of danger with just enough green-coated Jaegers to bolster Fraser. Action was broken off and British and Germans collapsed, panting and not daring to relax. There was no pursuit. So impressed were both Fraser and the baron that they dug in where they were, admitting that they were fearful of another rebel attack. Two new commanders had had a laboratory demonstration of the more than dangerous rallying power of seemingly beaten American troops.

Gentleman volunteer Anburey set down as his chief lesson of his first action: "I found that all manual exercise (i.e., routine drill) is but an ornament and the only . . . importance it can boast of was that of loading, firing and charging with bayonets." He had caught the difference between drill field and battlefield. Then he concluded, "The exertions of the day had so far wearied me that, drinking heartily of rum and water, I laid down in my bear-skin . . . and did not awake until twelve the next day."

The American survivors of Hubbardton trailed away to the south, caught up with St. Clair, who continued his retrograde movement down to Fort Edward in the open country near the great westerly bend of the Hudson. Fraser and Von Riedesel rested their men, then swung west to Skenesboro, a mere mark on the map by the streamlike beginnings of Champlain.

They found a rested, exuberant army and its always genial, likable commander, who radiated good-fellowship and chuckled richly over the smooth workings of his "Thoughts for Conducting the War from the Side of Canada." The sweep up the last stretches of Champlain had been admirable. The whole Yankee flotilla had been overtaken and either captured or destroyed. Prisoners were still being counted. Stores that the rebels badly needed were now in British possession and were being marked with the broad arrow of the Crown. True, there had been an unexpected clash with the rebels at ruinous long-walled Fort Anne not far down Wood Creek there to the south, and the ancient 9th Norfolks had been roughly handled, but everything was in hand now. The rebels were in the last stages of disorganization and it was hardly worth while trying to make contact with them. Soon Barry St. Leger would be coming down the Mohawk. Sir

William Howe's vast army and flotilla would strike up the Hudson and there would be a joyous meeting at Albany with plenty of wine to toast the decisive victory. There was nothing left now but a brief twenty miles between headquarters and the Hudson, an easy march.

Mention of those twenty miles must have set the more thoughtful officers drumming their fingers on rough pine tables and staring out at the silent menace of the interminable wilderness tangle. Had any of them seen a copy of the *Gentleman's Magazine* of London in which an observant author had described just such country, dwelling particularly on the difficulties of road building? "The trees in their natural state are very close to each other. . . . Fallen trees, lying in all directions . . . are plenty as lamp-posts upon a highway about London, and frequently as thick as lamps upon Westminster Bridge; these being irremoveable, and almost innumerable, the road is continually upon the turn to one side or the other, to get clear of them. . . . About every two or three miles . . . there is a bridge to be made, twenty, thirty or forty feet high, and twice or three times as long, over a creek . . . between two hills."

Those officers who had actually seen the text of the "Thoughts" could also recall Burgoyne's own statement that he greatly preferred the route Champlain–Lake George–Hudson River–Albany to the overland plunge, taking off through the forests from the head of Champlain and Skenesboro, and thence to the Hudson. Yet here he was, talking in charming self-confidence of that same latter route.

Gentleman Johnny seems to have been guided by an evil genius, one Philip Skene, once a major in His Majesty's forces and now proprietor of a vast tract of land about Champlain and Lake George and owner of the yellow fieldstone house that constituted the metropolis of Skenesboro. The value of the ex-major's grant depended on access to the Hudson River, now barred by the same type of wilderness described in the *Gentleman's Magazine*. But if, just *if*, His Majesty's troops could be set to building a road to the Hudson over the Skene acres, then the crafty major would have his Hudson access at no cost or labor to himself. Somehow, he seems to have persuaded Gentleman Johnny to forget about Lake George and its easy water transit and the abundance of British shipping. There was also a ready-made road along the west shore of Lake George. Orders were issued. Artillery and heavy stores might be floated over the lake. The rest of the army was to face those twenty wilderness miles that should have been measured in time and not in distance. Years later Clausewitz wrote that "all time not turned to account, serves the defence," a truth that held long before its utterance. And Burgoyne should have been well aware of the danger of letting an American army catch its breath, even without the recent object lessons of Hubbardton and Fort Anne.

The road building began, horrible, steamy, mosquito-infested work. Almost by inches a military highway was gnawed through the wilderness, and not even the presence of skilled Canadian axmen, imported for the occasion, did much to speed matters. But it was pleasant there at headquarters about the Skene house. There were countless little Canadian carts laden with Gentleman Johnny's wines and choice foods and fresh scarlet-and-white uniforms. Other carts were gallantly freighted with Mrs. Commissary's trunks. The road would be pushed through. There would be a pleasant summertime march to the Hudson and then ho! for Albany, St. Leger, and Howe.

Others besides Burgoyne had thought of axmen. Always, on the fringes of the creeping advance, the still forest air fluttered with the sound of distant blades against distant woods. Patrolling Tories or light infantrymen heard it, looked warily about. There was never anything to be seen. Just the faint noise ahover beyond the close horizons. It patted in Burgoyne's ears as he sat on the porch of Philip Skene's yellow fieldstone house. British officers and Brunswickers looked up from their messes inquiringly. Brass-helmeted grenadiers holding the left of the line at the very fringes of Vermont shivered superstitiously. From dawn until long after dusk the incessant *pock-pock-pock* drifted out, barely audible, inescapable. General Philip Schuyler had found men and axes, had sent them north to add to Burgoyne's days and miles. Trees crashed across trails and others were cunningly felled to crisscross, to interlace with huge trunks already lying there. Heavy boles fell across forest brooks, dammed them, sent sluggish pools of water right and left, creating mucky swamps where a decade or a century of fallen pine needles had provided soft, sure footing. Rocky ravines that had been natural corridors of advance were choked with high-heaped pine and oak. And each log that added its girth to a stack of trunks blocking brook, trail, or ravine would have to be laboriously cut into sections by the men of the advance and hauled aside. A small force of light infantry, of Jaegers could have driven the axmen away. But in the evening cool about the Skene house it probably did not seem worth while, now that the great force released by the "Thoughts" was rolling south.

Strange symptoms, which some British observers had noted the winter before in Canada, were appearing among the German troops. Unquestionably brave and skilled as they were in the field, homesickness and inert despair preyed on them like some silent, insidious fever. Gathered in groups of twos or tens or twenties, they told each other that there was no hope for them; that they would never see the Kinzig or the Main again, never look up to the shaggy crests of the Harz Mountains or climb once more through the Odenwald. From these meetings they crept off to the hospitals to die of no known illness, to succumb to a virtual negation of the will to live. Our observer, Thomas Anburey, noted sadly, "Nor can any medicine or advice you can give them divert this settled superstition . . . men who have faced the dangers of battle . . . without fear, are taken off, a score at a time, by a mere phantom of their own brain. This is a circumstance well known to every one in the army." So far as the record shows, no steps were taken by Burgoyne or Von Riedesel to check this serious drain on the German strength. Perhaps Gentleman Johnny had, what were to him, more serious matters on his mind.

There were the Indians, who could not seem to remember his express injunctions that they were not to play rough. They had been of little use to him militarily thus far in the campaign, save in the matter of screening his advance on Ticonderoga. They galloped off, ears twitching and nostrils aflare, at the least hint of loot. And now they were striking at the rare-met settlers. This was alarming. As the march went south, more and more farms would be found. And, according to Skene, the inhabitants would flock in hundreds to the protection of the royal colors. Already a good many had, and Gentleman Johnny had given them papers attesting to their loyalty, papers that, as in New Jersey, should guard them against any marauders. No one thought of teaching the Indians how to read. They struck when and where they pleased. What weight would a settler give to the King's word if his neighbors were burned out, scalped, and slain?

Tragedy struck close to the Skene house itself. Simon Fraser had a widowed cousin living some miles to the south, and with her was a young girl named Jane McCrae. Jane was engaged to a Tory officer with Burgoyne's column. What better protection could anyone want? Simon Fraser's cousin and young Lieutenant David Jones of Peters' little corps of Tories! Yet Jane's scalp with its long waving hair was brought into camp by a drunken Wyandotte.

Gentleman Johnny was profoundly shaken by this ghastly drama in the forest, aside from its politico-military angle. (What rebel could now be induced to take up his old royal allegiance when a Tory so connected as Jane McCrae was at the mercy of any prowling Indians?) His genuine grief was turned into anger when he received a letter under a flag of truce, signed by Horatio Gates and beginning, ". . . that the famous Lieutenant General Burgoyne, in whom the fine gentleman is united with the soldier and the scholar, should hire the savages of America to scalp Europeans and the descendants of Europeans, nay more, that he should pay a price for each scalp so barbarously taken . . ."

Gentleman Johnny was in a most unenviable position. There can be little question of the sincerity of his concern for the McCrae girl as a person. And he doubtless felt that he had done his best to keep the Indians in check, all that any human could do. But—but—there was the whole question of Indian policy. And now that "meddling old midwife," as he once called Gates, had the audacity to write him, John Burgoyne, in such terms as those cited above and, more, to threaten the widest possible publicity to the McCrae tragedy.

Gates's letter was pompous enough, but purple prose was a medium in which few could outdo Gentleman Johnny. His heavy bulldog jaw probably set in cold anger, he wrote Turncoat Gates: "I condescend to inform you that I would not be conscious of the acts you presume to impute to me for the whole continent of America, though the wealth of worlds were in its bowels and a paradise on its surface." As for the murder, he went on, "Respecting Miss McCrae, her fall wanted not the tragic display you have labored to give it, to make it as sincerely abhorred and lamented by me as it can possibly be by the tenderest of her friends."

Gentleman Johnny could read over these sentences between approving sips of his beloved champagne and reflect that there were dashed few generals in any army who could turn out phrases to match his. But then the wells of inspiration dried up. He had nothing more to say that would still Gates's nickering pen. Lamely the letter ended, for the very good reason that no action against the Indians could be taken. There had been a demand, surely made in all sincerity, for the scalper to be handed over for the most severe punishment. But the repercussions were most alarming. If there were punishment, the Indians would all go home. Burgoyne must have thought of a court-martial, presided over by one of Germain's creatures, in which he would have to explain precisely why he saw fit to alienate such valuable allies of His Majesty. He may have thought, too, of his long line of communications exposed to the lightning attacks of highly disgruntled Indians on their way home to Canada. So no real action was taken, and in his sleep Gentleman Johnny may have heard La Corne St. Luc's harsh voice: "Il faut brutaliser les affaires. Il faut les brutaliser."

Jane McCrae was only one of uncounted thousands of frontier girls to be killed by Indians since the opening of America. But no other single death had such far-reaching effects. It made superb propaganda for the Americans, military and civilian. And it had an immediate and tremendous influence on Whig and Tory alike living near the fringes of the progress of the "Thoughts."

Axmen and Royal Engineers toiled on, and at last there was free passage southward for the army—and for the future yield of Philip Skene's uncounted acres. By August 1 the bulk of the British forces had left the eternal cellar-dank of the forests and stood, with an almost hysterical sense of relief, in the rolling green meadows where the blue glint of the Hudson flowed on its way toward Albany, some forty easy miles away. Victory seemed just ahead. Few men thought of what was behind: twenty miles spanned by forty laboriously built bridges, one of them two miles long. But those twenty miles and forty bridges represented twenty-six lost days since the first quick lunge to Skenesboro.

Junior officers and enlisted men braced themselves for orders that would send a strong, highly mobile force across the river and down the west bank for that joyous meeting with Howe's men and St. Leger's. The orders never came. The troops could only sit and watch while an agonizingly slow procession came out of the west from Lake George. Burgoyne's 138 guns jolted slowly over from the bateaux that had freighted them down the smaller lake day after day. The dullest private could wonder why the heavier guns were worth waiting for. Barring Ticonderoga, such forts as they had seen—Anne, Edward, and George—were so flimsy that their walls could have been breached with rocks. But the guns came on. With them, great wambling cradles, each carrying a bateau, swayed on in the wake of long, horn-tossing ox teams. There were not nearly enough horses and oxen, and hitches and spans had to turn around in the Fort Edward meadows and head back to Lake George for another trip. The days were sliding by again, only now they were labeled August and not July—August, from whose far rim one could look to the end of good campaigning weather.

Other wheeled vehicles struggled over from the west or down the forty-bridge trail, and both enlisted men and the more conscientious officers began to grumble. Back at Skenesboro, Gentleman Johnny had issued strict orders. This army, gentlemen, will have to move fast. So strip down. Send all surplus baggage, clothing, stores back to Ticonderoga. The conscientious officers complied. The enlisted men, of course, had no choice. Back went changes of clothing, personal belongings. And now came this new procession of carts. Thirty of them carried the general's necessities and comforts, and there was a generous allotment for Mrs. Commissary. Unscrupulous lesser officers had followed their general's lead. Influence, forged permits, and sheer brazen impudence swelled the number of flimsy carts and made sure some officers, at least, would be able to approximate their commander's scale of living.

Gentleman Johnny settled himself in the old Smythe house, built from the timbers of the very first Fort Edward, and waited for the massing of all his power. Also, he watched the road that led south very carefully. Several times in the course of the expedition volunteers had left the army in an attempt to slip away as far as New York in search of news of the main striking force that was to come north up the river. So far, no courier had returned.

On the third day of August an exhausted, tattered man stood before Burgoyne and produced from a small quill tight-rolled strips of paper covered with minute script. Gentleman Johnny's well-tended hands spread out the strips and read eagerly. Sir William wrote flatteringly about the capture of Ticonderoga. And the blow north? Sir William's letter struck that blow, a very heavy one, and against Gentleman Johnny. Howe wrote: "My intention is for Pennsylvania, where I expect to meet Washington, but if he goes to the northward and you can keep him at bay, be assured I shall soon be after him to relieve you. After your arrival at Albany, the movements of the enemy will guide yours." With quite unintentional irony Sir William concluded, "Success be ever with you."

Pennsylvania! No hint of a stroke to the north, unless Washington moved into that quarter. And even then Burgoyne was to bear the main force of the American blow until Howe came up to help him out. The sentence about Albany merely meant, "Get there and see what the enemy does." Of the whole plan, nothing remained save Burgoyne and St. Leger, whose roles were minor. The real sting had been removed through Germain's solicitude over his horses and his fears for a lost week end. The "Thoughts" were becoming random thoughts indeed.

And now what could Gentleman Johnny do? His course was simple, since he had only to carry out his orders, as set forth by Germain, and they allowed him no latitude of any sort. Go to Albany! No matter what Howe and St. Leger might do, go to Albany. He knew well enough the fate of any commander who deviated from an order issued by the man who had disgraced the British cavalry at Minden. It is to Gentleman Johnny's credit that he did not panic. It might have been better for him had he shared at least some of his concern with his high brass. Instead he showed himself cheerful, optimistic, and unworried to his troops and their commanders, buttoning the bad news close within him and not even telling the baron of Howe's "intention for Pennsylvania." Supplies were to be gathered, artillery collected from the very last barge on Lake George, and the final leap would be made, brushing aside the last of the rebels, now known to be entrenching on heights near a place called Stillwater, twenty miles down on the west bank. The rebels had not really been much of a bother to date. St. Leger was coming down the Mohawk. The joint forces could look forward to a pleasant and comfortable winter at Albany. Come, now, Howe's move to the south actually didn't make much difference, did it?

Philip Skene was about headquarters again, glowing with reports and sparkling plans. Over to the east, in the Hampshire Grants and western Massachusetts, there were countless armed and devoted Tories waiting only for the appearance of royal troops to rise against their rebel oppressors. Skene had many contacts hither and yon, and his intelligence was sure, unchallengeable. He spoke of a whole Tory corps being added to the expedition. And, more, there were great rebel supply depots at a hamlet called Bennington and more at Manchester, both in the Grants. And these stores included hundreds of fine horses to haul carts and guns, horses to mount Von Riedesel's dragoons, who now crept about unmounted, sunk almost to the level of infantry.

Burgoyne's sanguine mind conjured up glorious possibilities at the thought of more troops, supplies, and, above all, horses added to his force. There were few rebel troops in the Grants, barring the remnants of Seth Warner's command, which had rallied at Manchester after Hubbardton. A large expedition would not be necessary, but such a force ought to be highly mobile, one that could swoop in, seize the stores, and get out. British light infantry seemed cut out for the job, but geography and military etiquette ruled them out.

The German contingent was still spread out to the east as far as Castleton, below Hubbardton, this dispersion being dictated by a hope on Burgoyne's part that New England might be jumpy over the possibility of an invasion of that region rather than a move down the Hudson. So the baron's men were close to the logical jump-off point. If they had been by-passed, with British troops swinging east, military etiquette would have been violated and military honor, a blindly touchy point in that era, would have been mortally wounded. Besides, the baron himself had already heard of horses, stores, and wagons to be had for the taking in the Grants and had asked permission to stage just such a raid.

So to the Germans fell the honor of making this lightning raid. And the nucleus of this force? Baum's now dismounted dragoons, in their boots that weighed twelve pounds a pair, in their heavy cocked hats, long-tailed coats, and with their ponderous sabers and carbines, were chosen to flit with ranger-like cunning through the wooded hills that led on to the Green Mountains. To reinforce them was a body of Brunswick grenadiers, only a little less cumbersome than the dragoons, and two of Pausch's guns were to be dragged along by weakened horses. As an afterthought a handful of picked British marksmen, a body of Tories, and a cloud of Indians were added to cover the advance.

The baron was happy enough about the expedition, but not its destination. His idea was to hit east and north, to a spot called Clarendon, known to contain stores and to be entirely bare of any enemy save for a few militia. But Gentleman Johnny waved the baron off jovially. Manchester was the spot, to the east and *south*. Skene himself had said so, Skene who knew the country and the country people. Von Riedesel was overruled but was not amused. Nonetheless, he offered no further objections at a council there in the Smythe house. Neither did he change the composition of his force. Baum's dragoons would take their place in the line of march.

Before Baum could get under way, a notable addition was made to the army. Down the forest road that led to Fort Anne, her blue eyes round with the wonders that she had seen and her mouth in a wise little button of suppressed excitement, came the baroness. With her were Gustava and Frederica and little Caroline, with gnarled old Jaeger Rockel and the maid Lena in dragon-like attendance. They had had to spend one night on an island where the only shelter was an unfinished cabin, and she had known that something was wrong because the escort, Captain Willoe, seemed disturbed, even when he had seen how Gustava and Frederica and Caroline were asleep on a bed of cut boughs. Such noises during the night. Hissings and crawlings! She really had trouble in getting to sleep and in the morning she found that the island was a rattlesnake sanctuary, and when she saw the castoff skins of those nasty creatures just everywhere—well, she really did make the children hurry through their breakfasts so a start could be made.

So Fritschen and the children settled down at Fort Anne, then moved on to Fort Edward. It was good country and the little girls throve in the pleasant meadows and she learned how to cook bears' paws and found them so good that she wrote home to Wolfenbüttel about them. There were other women at the camp, too, and she liked them very much. There was Lady Acland, whose husband had been wounded at Hubbardton, and a Mrs. Major Harnage and a Mrs. Lieutenant Reynall, and they talked about the country and the children and exchanged recipes and were firmly united in declining to go to Burgoyne's levées at the Smythe house so long as a Certain Person was there.

But the army was about to move. The ladies, Gentleman Johnny gallantly indicated, would be better off at Ticonderoga until it should be safe for them to come to Albany. The baroness found that Lady Acland was more than a little pregnant and spoke to Burgoyne in wide-eyed alarm at the thought of this delicate woman alone at Ticonderoga with painted Indians all about her and all the good doctors with the army. Gentleman Johnny decreed that humanity dictated Lady Acland's presence with the army, and the baroness sailed demurely off. If one woman could go along, so could four. She coaxed skilled workmen to build her a light, strong calash with a waterproof cover, big enough to hold all the Von Riedesel ladies. Gentleman Johnny could start when he pleased. Little Fritschen was quite ready.

Lieutenant Colonel Friedrich Baum and his swift raiding party assembled at Fort Miller on August 11. As their march was about to start, Gentleman Johnny rode up in person and gave Baum a verbal change in objective. He was not to go to Manchester but to Bennington, some miles to the south, where he would find eager Tories, horses, cattle, wagons, saddles, food, and a very shaky militia guard. And since the commander of this vital expedition spoke no single word of English, here was mutual-friend Philip Skene to smooth his path for him.

The unwieldy command lurched off east along the Batten Kill, Lieutenant Bache's little four-pounders and their ammunition wagons already rocking alarmingly on the pitiful road. Burgoyne watched them go, then figuratively dusted off his hands and turned in a wave of optimism to the rest of the army. Once Baum was back from Bennington, there would be horses and wagons galore, cattle to feed the troops. In his own mind he was already at Albany. The whole army was brought to Fort Miller, and Fraser and the Advanced Corps were boated across to the west bank of the Hudson, massing at a spot known as Saratoga, now Schuylerville.

In these busy hours occasional word came in from Baum. No Tories seemed to be materializing. Some horses and cattle were sent in, but the dragoon colonel was having a bad time with the Indians, whom mutual-friend Skene did not seem to be able to control. They terrified the inhabitants of the Hampshire Grants, who began shifting their stock far to the east. The Indians gleefully shot any loose horses and went wild over what herds they met, banging away at them not for food but for the irresistible trophies of sweet-toned cowbells which they tolled joyously as they whooped back and forth to each other. And there were reports of militia massing in the Bennington area, almost fifteen hundred according to some accounts. Nonetheless, Baum was pushing on.

Sometime in the very youngest hours of August 15 an aide woke Burgoyne. There was another letter from Baum, asking for reinforcements at once, but adding no details that alarmed the commander. Through the baron, Gentleman Johnny ordered out the savage Breymann to march with the German Advanced Corps. Probably, through military etiquette, Breymann was the only choice. But his men were nearly as sluggish as Baum's, the call for help might be urgent, and there was the old enmity between the two colonels, the fierce feud that gave little hope that Breymann would strain himself unduly to help out his dragoon foe. Burgoyne's orders to the Advanced Corps contained one inexplicable sentence, one that certainly was not apt to hurry it along. The corps was being sent out "in consequence of the *good news* . . . received from . . . Baum." So Breymann set out on his lightning rescue mission, dragging along two useless guns whose accompanying wagons were further loaded down with extra infantry ammunition. It rained heavily, turning the road into a twisting rope of mud. The column dashed along at the rate of less than half a mile per hour, and Breymann's pedantry was such that he kept halting his men to make them align their ranks in a proper, soldierly fashion.

Some twenty miles ahead, Baum's "good news" was rather hard to make out. He had halted and, strangely, scattered his forces along the little Walloomsac River. He had British sharpshooters here, Tories there, a grenadier post in one spot, a few Jaegers in another, all out of touch with each other and the main body. This was posted worst of all. He built a redoubt on the crest of a very steep round hill and stocked it with his lumbering, booted dragoons. Drive to this same crest today and stand by the tracing of the old earthworks. From the summit there is a fine view of the distant surrounding country. Of the immediate terrain, there is little or none. The hillsides slope away so steeply that the approaches cannot be seen. Virtually hidden are the spots where the various smaller bodies were stationed. Baum stood there, blind, where an enemy force could come within a few yards of his works undetected. And there he waited, increasingly apprehensive as more and more militia were sighted in the lowlands. Clumsy country fellows, of course, but, *verdammt!* there were many of them.

The troops that Baum saw made up one of the oddest armies to appear in the whole war. It was not an American army but a New Hampshire one, raised chiefly through the efforts of John Langdon, Speaker of the General Court. Langdon had pledged his personal fortune, his plate, and his goods to finance this two months' army, raised against the threat of the eastward advance that Burgoyne never made. It was commanded by General John Stark, who after Trenton had retired in a most cantankerous huff to his native state, offended by army routine and by the obliviousness of Congress to Starkian merits. (Hadn't he been first in the field after the nineteenth of April? How about Breed's Hill?)

Now he would accept command, but on condition that there was to be no damned Continental foolishness in the business. He would work with Seth Warner, commander of one of the Sixteen Additional Regiments, but that was because Warner and his men were from New Hampshire or from the Hampshire Grants. Grudgingly he accepted some few hundreds of men from western Massachusetts, brought to the scene by fire-breathing Parson Thomas Allen, Congregational minister of Pittsfield. By the time Baum had dug in, Stark had some two thousand men, many of them with prior service. He might have had more, for Horatio Gates, down at Stillwater across the Hudson, heard of the rallying and sent Massachusetts-born General Benjamin Lincoln with an offer of Continental aid. Stark exploded, was ready to disband his force, but Lincoln's tact and common sense smoothed matters over. He was even shrewd enough to withdraw Gates's

offer and retire from the scene, leaving Stark about as soothed as that
prickly character was ever apt to be.

Through a rain that began to clear by noon, Breymann and his relief
column pushed on. His men were spent and sullen, having passed a wet,
cheerless night in a roadside camp. His horses were in worse shape, since no
fodder could be found for them. The pace was no better than on the fifteenth, and his ammunition carts slowed matters still more by breaking
down with the maddening perverseness of the inanimate.

There was no sign that Baum had ever marched toward the Hampshire
Grants. No sound of action came under the breaking clouds. By the mill
known as San Coick a few wounded men were met and they scarcely clari-
fied matters by giving wildly conflicting statements. Baum was surging
ahead victoriously. Baum had surrendered. Baum's force was wiped out.
Skene, who had ridden back to join Breymann before the final massing of
the militia, was unable to credit the bad reports. Breymann probably hoped
that his archfoe was in serious trouble but was not inclined to favor any
tales of disaster.

The column pushed on. Skene saw a body of armed farmers in a field to
the left, whooped that they were Tories rallying to the Crown, and rode to
meet them, shouting, "Be ye King George's men?" He was answered somewhat tersely by a volley that killed his horse and sent him scampering back
to the protection of Breymann's grenadiers. There were more fields and
more farmers, and Breymann sent his Jaegers slanting after them. The
farmers fired and melted away. Then there were more farmers, firing and
melting. Breymann pushed stubbornly on, taking a good deal of punishment. There was actual cannon fire against the column, and Lieutenant
Spangenberg, commanding Breymann's guns, was horrified to identify the
hostile pieces as those that Lieutenant Bache had trundled out with Baum.
Spangenberg brought his own guns into action, but circling rebels shot
down his gun teams. Breymann noted anxiously that there was more cohesion in the rebel forces and drove his men harder. What he could not
know was that the first enemy bodies he met were scatterings of Stark's
main force, which had overwhelmed Baum almost as completely as Custer
and his troopers of the 7th Cavalry were overwhelmed by Crazy Horse's
Oglalas ninety-nine years later. Now he was striking against Seth Warner's
more compact formations.

Less than a mile from the hill where Baum had made his stupid stand,
Breymann gave up. He had to abandon his guns, a fearful disgrace in those
days, and headed his men back toward the Batten Kill and the Hudson.
Wounded himself, he kept his men pretty well in hand, but as darkness
came, the tail of his column began to fray out. Tough grenadiers, wrecked
by fatigue and by the gloomy menace of the woods that kept erupting more
farmers, fell on their knees, begging for mercy. Others screamed and fled
wildly into the underbrush, where their heavy trappings pinned them until
the exultant men of Stark or Warner disarmed them and sent them on to
collecting-points.

Then relief came. Stark was afraid of losing control of his command in the dark of the woods and broke off the pursuit. The battered Germans limped on with no foe save distance ahead of them. Spent, stung by his wound, Breymann must have seethed with rage as he tallied up his losses. He had started out with some five hundred and fifty men. A night roll call showed nearly two hundred killed, wounded, or prisoner, a ghastly total in any war. No triumphal return to the main army. No horses. No stores. No saddles. No wagons. At least, when all reports were in, Breymann could console himself with the fact that he had done better than the hated Baum. Of that luckless dragoon's force, only nine privates ever rejoined the army, and no officers. Breymann could also reflect that, although wounded and defeated, he was at least alive. Soon he was to hear that Friedrich Baum had died in a farmhouse not far from the round hill where he had dug in, now known as "Baum's Hill."

The morning of the eighteenth found Burgoyne and Von Riedesel in a rather ticklish spot. A bridge of boats had been stretched across the river to link up Fraser's Advanced Corps with the main army. Now a storm had broken the bridge, cutting off Fraser. Then word came in, first of Baum's disaster and then of Breymann's repulse and retreat. All this must have been a staggerer for Burgoyne. Over eight hundred men, all told, lost for good and all, and nothing to show for their efforts. Yet Gentleman Johnny, gleaming in his scarlet and white, rode out to meet Breymann at the head of the 47th North Lancashires, possibly choosing them with a dramatist's eye because their scarlet coats and white facings matched his own colors. When the tormented German remnant appeared, the author-general greeted the haggard men as though they were returning conquerors, though he marred his effect a little by a touch of condescension when he thanked them for "their very pretty little success," further assuring them that the enemy would feel it "most severely."

There was more discouraging news. La Corne St. Luc, perhaps deciding that affairs were not enough brutalized for him really to shine, went back to Canada, taking his son-in-law, La Naudière, and most of the Indians with him. The whole corps had been little use in action, but it was invaluable as a collective eye for seeing what lay beyond the next hill or what might be hidden by the forests. Morally it was most depressing. These savages would never have left a successful army.

Worse news was brewing. Barry St. Leger, with his force of British, Hessians, Tories, and Indians, had bogged down before log-and-turf Fort Stanwix, far up by the headwaters of the Mohawk, and had begun a formal siege. To relieve the fort, a strong formation of Tryon County militia under Nicholas Herkimer, a tower of strength among the valley settlers, pushed upriver and ran blindly into an ambush sprung by Indians and Tories near Oriskany. There was a bloody and indecisive fight in which Herkimer was mortally wounded and both sides fell back. But in the absence of this part of St. Leger's force, Peter Gansevoort, in command at Stanwix, had sent Marinus Willett out in a quick sortie. Willett's men wrecked and sacked the abandoned camps and returned in triumph to Stanwix, loaded with supplies and having suffered no casualties.

Tories and Indians returned from Oriskany in a bad mood. The Indians had lost heavily, particularly the Seneca contingent, and their tempers were not improved to find all their possessions lost as a result of Willett's raid. They began to wonder if they were really in the right war. Faced by their growing restlessness and dangerous edginess, St. Leger tried to hurry the siege, but word was brought upriver of a new American force under Benedict Arnold, whose aim was to relieve Stanwix once for all.

St. Leger finally broke off all action and beat a hasty retreat. This was pure velvet for the disgruntled Indians. They trailed their own allies back toward Oswego, hiding in the woods and starting all sorts of panics and alarms. When jumpy troops or Tories fled or tried to form in open country, the Indians gleefully plundered the abandoned camps, making off with the soldiers' packs, with officers' belongings. Even St. Leger's personal traveling wine cellar fell into their hands. There were more sinister manifestations. It was noted that white stragglers were heard of no more, that scalps which had certainly not come from the Oriskany fight dangled about Indian waists. The command finally staggered into Oswego, and it was obvious that Barry St. Leger would not meet Gentleman Johnny at Albany. Two thirds of the "Thoughts" had evaporated in the wilderness air.

Nonetheless, Gentleman Johnny would keep on down the Hudson. He had to, and was well aware of that fact. Not long after Bennington he wrote Germain a letter of dignified complaint. He wanted very much to withdraw to Fort Edward, since "no operation, my Lord, has yet been undertaken in my favour. . . . But my orders being positive to 'force a junction with Sir William Howe' I apprehend I am not at liberty to remain inactive." He had to go on. In the same letter he sketched the undreamed-of dangers that lurked in the east and dipped his pen in the purple-ink well. "The Hampshire Grants, a country unpeopled and almost unknown in the last war, now abounds in the most active and rebellious race on the continent and hangs like a gathering storm upon my left." He could have included all points of the compass without overstating his case. In Hoffman Nickerson's vivid phrase, "The sands of the invasion were running out."

At last there were thirty days' supplies in hand. On September 15, 1777, Von Riedesel led his Brunswickers and Hessians across the bridge of boats over the Hudson to join the British. It was a magnificent fall day and the combined armies passed in review before their commander, bands playing, colors flying under the deep blue bowl of the sky. Gentleman Johnny, with his dramatist's mental eye on an invisible audience, swept off his hat and shouted, "Britons never retreat." The bridge of boats was broken up, severing the last link with Canada. The final act of his tragedy was beginning.

CHAPTER XXII

". . . nor did I hear a despairing word"

THE Congress was in a most unhappy, apprehensive frame of mind in the late July days of 1777. The news of the fall of its cherished Gibraltar at Ticonderoga had dropped on it with a staggering impact. There was talk of treason and John Adams muttered darkly that things would not mend until the country had hanged a few generals. The Ticonderoga shock was dulled a little by the unchecked sweep south of the invasion "from the side of Canada," a far more ominous portent. Then there was the case of the British force in New York. Something decidedly big was brewing, for the enemy commander-in-chief, Sir William Howe, had sailed off with a great fleet and convoy bearing his choicest regiments. Mists off Sandy Hook swallowed up every hull and sail. It was certain that sails and hulls would reappear, but there was no telling at what point on the long, long coast line Sir William would turn up to pour his scarlet columns ashore. So the Congress worked on, lifting its collective head to peer north toward Burgoyne, to stare east and south in quest of Howe.

There was another gnawing irritation in congressional minds, an irritation that grew steadily. This stemmed from the seemingly endless stream of foreign soldiers, of real or pretended service, who clanked into the rose and white of the State House, more than ready to take over command of the army, graciously relieving the well-meaning but non-military Washington and his rather comical amateur generals. Such claimants might be vague in giving details of their own actual military service, but they were usually most definite in the matter of pay, allowances, and other emoluments.

There had been La Roche Fermoy, a self-styled genius. His conduct at Trenton had been more than dubious. His gross negligence at Mount Independence had made matters much easier for Burgoyne and for Simon Fraser's move to the east shore of the lake. Or take the recent case of Philip-Charles-Jean-Baptiste Trouson du Coudray. *He* had arrived fully expecting to take over all the United States artillery on the strength of a letter from Silas Deane, American commissioner at Paris. Du Coudray's qualifications seemed excellent and he naturally regarded the Deane letter as a bona fide appointment. *But* such nominations and appointments lay in the hands of Congress, not in those of well-meaning Silas Deane. Was the whole United States army to be officered from a Paris lodging? And look at the effect on the army!

To install Du Coudray meant the shelving of Henry Knox. High officers, on hearing the rumor of the appointment, snatched for the nearest pen and sheet of paper. Nathanael Greene wrote a violent protest. John Sullivan sent in his hotly worded resignation, to take effect on the Frenchman's installation. Knox himself acted with more restraint, merely saying, "Though my country is too much pressed at present [for me] to resign, yet perhaps this campaign will be the last." His Lucy wrote with all the stiff hauteur of her office-holding Tory background: "Who knows but I may have my Harry again? This I am sure of, he will never suffer anyone to command him in that [artillery] department. If he does, he has not the soul which I now think him possessed of."

There was a letter from Washington, informing the Congress that Knox was "one of the most valuable officers in the service and who, combatting almost innumerable difficulties . . . has placed the artillery on a footing that does him the greatest honor." A rather vague inspector's appointment was finally found for Du Coudray, but the whole situation was a most uneasy one and continued so until the Frenchman was drowned at a peaceful river crossing in September. And now *another* group of Gauls had arrived!

The leader of this group had had a most perilous voyage from France. Not only had his family violently opposed his coming to America, but Louis XVI had forbidden it and even gone so far as to issue a *lettre de cachet* which, if served, would have sent another victim to the Bastille. There had been a secret flight, a sailing from the Spanish port of Los Pasajes, and a long voyage with the ever-present chance of capture by British ships patrolling the American coast.

He had finally landed at Charlestown in South Carolina and he wrote to his young wife, usually addressed as "Dear Heart," that he had been at once "covered with civilities" and felt as much at home as though he had been twenty years in the country, a figure that he often used as standard of comparison. He set out for Philadelphia, some nine hundred miles away, having first bought carriages and horses, and pitted his not quite twenty years against New World trails. Horses went lame, carriages broke down, and there were long miles to cover on foot, but the young traveler felt the true intoxication of being in a land where people not only talked of liberty but fought for it.

It is doubtful if he knew very much about this fight, its basic origins, its justifications, or the arguments against beginning it in the first place. Emotion, not reason, had started him on his long journey, and the compulsion lay in his having heard, while on garrison duty at Metz in northeastern France, of the Declaration of Independence. His mind was prepared in advance by the currents of liberal thought then sweeping Europe for the ideals expressed by that Declaration, and he does not seem to have delved very deeply beyond the surface ideas.

Yet now he was learning at first hand more than he could ever have obtained by long hours of thought and meditation over the Declaration. Disillusionment never seems to have shadowed his mind. He told Dear Heart that, "the farther north I go, the more I like this country and its inhabitants. There is no kindness or courtesy that I do not receive, though many people hardly know who I am." Then, lest his own family think him too exultant, he changed his tone a little, for "you are away, Dear Heart . . . and there is no happiness for me far from you." He sent kisses to the children, those poor children who "have a vagabond father, but a good fellow at bottom, and a good father, who loves his family very much and a good husband, too, for he loves his wife with all his heart." But with all his protestations and his pinings which he probably set down in all sincerity, the New World and its struggles were to swallow him up for many long years.

And so to Philadelphia came Marie Joseph Paul Yves Roche Gilbert du Motier, Marquis de Lafayette. With him, as chief companion, was huge, German-born ascetic Jean de Kalb, a self-styled baron and a self-made Frenchman. De Kalb came frankly as a soldier of fortune. Little time was needed to change him from adventurer to patriot.

Their reception by Congress struck them both as "more like a dismissal than a welcome." James Lovell of Massachusetts, one of the few members of Congress who spoke French, was delegated to interview them. Lovell was a sincere but uncomfortable sort, obsessed later with a dream of supplanting Washington with Horatio Gates. He talked to the marquis and the baron in the street and seems to have set a precedent for some future congressional quizzings. Did they have any authority from Mr. Deane? Deane, it seemed, had specific orders from Congress to obtain skilled French engineers and that was all. Evidently the memory of Du Coudray, La Roche Fermoy, and others was rankling. "It seems," observed Lovell, "that French officers have a great fancy to enter our service without being invited." Then, according to one of Lafayette's party, "He left us [in the street], after treating us, in excellent French, like a set of adventurers."

Despite this seeming crustiness, born of bitter experience, Lovell must have been favorably impressed. As for the young marquis, he drew up, perhaps at Lovell's prompting, a petition to the Congress. "After all the sacrifices I have made I have the right to insist upon two favors," he concluded, "(1) to serve at my own cost and (2) to begin my service as a volunteer." According to military usage of the time, a volunteer served where he was assigned, usually as an aide and with no troops under him. Thus Lafayette was offering the astounding proposition of serving without pay and without command.

There were debates and mutterings in committee. Then on July 31 Congress passed the following resolution:

> Whereas The Marquis de La Fayette, out of his great zeal to the cause of liberty . . . has left his family . . . to offer his service to the United States, without pension or particular allowance, and is anxious to risk his life in our cause: Resolved that his service be accepted and that in consideration of his zeal, his illustrious family and connections, he have the rank and commission of major-general in the army of the United States.

This made the fullest of full amends for previous chilliness, though Gentleman John Burgoyne would doubtless have approved of the passage concerning the "illustrious family and connections." No damned nonsense about merit, sir!

The marquis made a touchingly boyish acknowledgment. "The feelings of my heart, long before it became my duty, engaged me in the love of the American cause. . . . I shall neglect nothing on my part to justify the confidence which Congress of the United States has been pleased to repose in me. . . . I wish to serve near the person of General Washington till such time as he may think proper to entrust me with a division of the army. . . . I am, Sir, with the sentiments which every good American owes you, Your most obedient servant, the Marquis de La Fayette."

On August 5 there was a dinner in Philadelphia and someone was thoughtful enough to see that the marquis was among the guests. In later years Lafayette told of the gathering and of the chief guest. From his bearing and manner the young Frenchman picked out Washington at once, without any indication from his host. The two met, and Washington, like Lovell, was rather aloof. Another confounded foreigner to tell us how to run the war. The marquis may have had advance warning. At any rate, Washington sized him up quickly, found himself warming more and more to this odd young man who wanted no rank and no pay, whose rather prominent eyes actually grew moist as he spoke of the American cause. The Virginian's final capitulation was complete. The marquis should look on the commander-in-chief's quarters as his own. He would be one of the general's military "family" or staff. There was a friendly suggestion that, as an American soldier, the marquis would know how to adapt himself to the customs, manners, and scale of living of a republican army. Then they parted, but a deep, enduring friendship sprang from that meeting.

Some ten days later the marquis, having bought uniforms, horses, camp equipment, reported to the army at its camp near Neshaminy Bridge in Bucks County, Pennsylvania. He found a desperately ragged army, ill equipped and with no notions of drill and tactics. He may have noted, too, that it was ready to move to the coast should the mysterious Howes, William and "Black Dick," materialize with their fleets. At the same time it was looking over its shoulder to the north. So far as it knew, Burgoyne was still moving and Bennington was not yet fought.

Washington was rather fearful of the effect of the American army of 1777 on this young officer fresh from the meticulously equipped and trained French troops. Might not the very first glimpse discourage the newcomer hopelessly? In 1780 the commander-in-chief was to keep Rochambeau from inspecting the American forces along the Hudson for that very reason. But the marquis' only comment was, "C'est pour apprendre et non pour enseigner que je suis ici."

That first glimpse must have been a good deal for Lafayette to swallow. The troops were, he said later, "tolerably armed and still worse clad [and] presented a singular spectacle. In this particoloured and often-naked state, the best dresses were hunting shirts of brown linen. Their tactics were equally irregular. They were arranged without regard to size, except that the smallest men were in the front rank. With all this, there were good-looking soldiers conducted by zealous officers." And among them, the marquis settled down for a longer stay than he had probably foreseen.

The marquis did much to make the army and the Congress forget men like La Roche Fermoy, La Marquisie and other supercilious troublemakers and paved the way for a great number of serious, able, and devoted Frenchmen. There were Gîmat and Galvan, Du Plessis and Fleury, the unhappy but resolute Marquis de La Rouërie, who clung to the incognito of "Armand," the engineer Duportail, the Marquis de Malmédy, and many like them.

De Kalb, though his later services were to be great, got off to a very unpromising start. He had a contract from Silas Deane specifying that he should be a major general. The Congress was not impressed but soon found that in De Kalb they had no idealistic suppliant begging only for a chance to serve. The colorful baron had a very clear idea of his own worth and brought the legislators up short. He informed them that they could do one of two things. They could commission him major general with suitable pay and emoluments. Or they could pay his passage back to France, where—note this, messieurs—he would bring civil suit against Deane and, by implication the Congress, for breach of covenant. There seemed to be an uneasy feeling that the baron would be able to make his suit stick. In September they commissioned him major general.

Sir William Howe was still afloat somewhere out of sight, his three hundred ships rolling and heaving under a blistering sun. The main fear in both the Congress and the army—and the great hope of royal sympathizers —was that, having made his distracting disappearance, Sir William would suddenly materialize in some spot that would enable him to join hands with Burgoyne's push from the north. Then there were strange and undeniable reports of the whole fleet being seen off the Virginia capes, and John Adams began to worry about Charleston in South Carolina and wrote Abigail of his high regard for the Carolinians. Then he had more news and on August 23 wrote her again: "It is now no longer a secret where Mr. Howe's fleet is . . . it is arrived at the head of Chesapeake Bay. . . . His march by land to Philadelphia may be about sixty or seventy miles. . . . If Congress had . . . debated a month, they could not have concerted a plan for Mr. Howe more to our advantage than that which he has adopted." He comments shrewdly, "He gives us an opportunity of exerting the strength of all the middle States against him, while New York and New England are destroying Burgoyne. . . . Never was so good an opportunity for my countrymen to turn out and crush that vaporing, blustering bully to atoms."

Sir William's "Intention for Pennsylvania" shocked most of the British Army as profoundly as it encouraged, perhaps unduly, most Americans. He had immobilized for nearly six weeks some eighteen thousand of the best British and Hessian troops, had kept them below decks in grilling

August weather. Scurvy and fever had broken out. Nearly three hundred horses had died on the voyage, and those he was able to disembark at Head of Elk on upper Chesapeake Bay were termed by a disgruntled officer "Carrion." And, like Burgoyne moving sluggishly up there in the north, he had wasted time. If he had really wanted to take Philadelphia, there were far quicker routes that he might have chosen. Indeed, it is hard to see what he hoped to gain by the capture of that city, but he seems to have been obsessed with that idea, much as the mere hope of possessing Richmond dominated McClellan's thinking in 1862. Neither seems to have realized that the destruction of Washington's army in one case and Joe Johnston's in the other were the true objectives.

And the architect of this great plan of 1777? None other than the American general, Charles Lee, a rather pampered prisoner in British hands, who undertook to show Howe the way to defeat Lee's own adopted army. Sometimes Lee seems to have felt that his advice was a purely intellectual, professional exercise, a discussion between two bluff old soldiers. At others, he tends to claim that his aid to the enemy was nothing but just being fair all around. It was, he wrote, "not only justifiable but [I am] bound in conscience to furnish all the lights I can to enable 'em to bring matters to a conclusion in the most compendious manner and consequently the least expensive to both Parties." If such reasoning is obscure, it is at least typically Lee.

Sunday, August 24, began with rain, which stopped not long after sunrise, and Philadelphia turned out en masse to line the still-shining sidewalks of Front and Chestnut streets, for General Washington was to lead his army through the city, to lead it south to meet Howe and Cornwallis and Von Knyphausen.

There was a small advance guard and then the commander-in-chief, dressed in his finest blue and buff and mounted on his best horse. With him rode Henry Knox and Tench Tilghman, the young Marquis de Lafayette and other aides. The Philadelphia Light Horse followed, then the Virginia dragoons of George Baylor and Theodorick Bland. The clack of hoofs, the rustle of horsehair plumes gave way to the drumming tramp of the infantry, the steady grumble of artillery wheels.

For more than two hours Washington's men passed through the cobbled streets, the main army of the United States. It had begun to take on an identity of its own. On the sidewalks people could recognize individuals who a year, two years ago had been vague names. Nathanael Greene, his asthma plagued by the summer damp, brought on his division, marching twelve abreast, and there was the pastor-turned-soldier, Peter Muhlenberg, leading his brigade with massed fifes and drums shrilling and rattling in the center. George Weedon headed more Virginians, and watchers whispered that his men called him "Joe Gourd" from his custom of measuring rum from a gourd in his Fredericksburg tavern. There were William Woodford, Virginia again, and Christian Febiger, the Dane, known to the army as "Old Denmark." Everyone knew Anthony Wayne, of course, the gilded young squire from nearby Chester County, and there were murmurs of admiration for Lord Stirling. Fat Benjamin Lincoln rode by, back from his mission into the Hampshire Grants to soothe John Stark, and Philadelphians may have wondered if all Massachusetts men were built to Henry Knox's vast pattern.

Philadelphia and other war-theater cities would see these men again and again, these citizen soldiers who were slowly shaping into what might be termed the "first team." There were, of course, important faces missing. Horatio Gates was in the north, in full command against Burgoyne, having craftily jockeyed able Philip Schuyler out of the picture. Fierce, unrestrained Benedict Arnold was north too. Most important of all, Daniel Morgan had marched eight hundred of his riflemen—Pennsylvanians, Marylanders, and Virginians—up to the Hudson. But it was a respectable force, some eleven thousand men, that filed through the broad streets, a river of bobbing muskets, slanted sabers, and jolting fieldpieces. On only two other occasions in the rest of the long war would the main army of the United States march out to meet the enemy in the field.

Many onlookers were impressed. John Adams wrote to Abigail: "We now have an army well appointed between us and Mr. Howe and this army will be immediately joined by ten thousand militia, so that I feel as secure here as if I was at Braintree, but not so happy. My happiness is nowhere to be found but there." Yet Adams found imperfections in the march-past. "Our soldiers have not yet quite the air of soldiers. They don't step exactly in time. They don't hold up their heads quite erect, nor turn out their toes so exactly as they ought. They don't all of them cock their hats; and such as do, don't all wear them the same way." It's odd that Adams' rustic eye was not caught by the one pathetic attempt at uniformity; by order, the troops had cut green sprigs and stuck them in their hats.

An American officer, now a prisoner of war on parole, stood at the London Coffee House at the corner of Front and Market streets and was surprised at how much of the shabbiness extended to the high brass. "Even in General Wayne," he noted, "there was . . . a considerable falling off. His quondam regimental, as colonel of the 4th battalion, was, I think, blue and white, in which he had been accustomed to appear with exemplary neatness; whereas now he was dressed . . . in a dingy red coat with a black, rusty cravat and tarnished laced hat." This paroled officer thought more of the men in the ranks than did civilian John Adams. "Though indifferently dressed," he reported, "[they] held well burnished arms, and carried them like soldiers, and looked, in short, as if they might have faced an equal number with a reasonable prospect of success."

Whatever the prospects were, the army marched out to meet them. In a day or two there were more boots echoing over the cobbles, and Brigadier General Francis Nash led his brigade of North Carolinians through the city, his long-striding men pressing hard to overtake the main body. After them came John Sullivan, ablaze to wipe out the onus of an ill-fated attack on Staten Island not long before.

Washington and Howe approached each other slowly, their columns dark on the Pennsylvania and Delaware roads, like arrows whose barbed heads were the skirmishers, driven on by the shafts of the main bodies. And so the two forces came closer and closer to the placid ripples of Brandywine Creek, with Painter's Ford in its middle reaches and Chadd's some two miles downstream. On the morning of the eleventh of September, young Elizabeth Coates and three other girls "were walking in the road opposite to Father's, close by Polly Buckwalter's Lane." They were hailed by a group of horsemen, a patrol thrown out on the road to Kennett Square by General William Maxwell and his Jerseymen. One of the men called, "Girls, you better go home." Elizabeth asked, "Why?" The answer was terse but illuminating. "Because the British regiments are coming up the road." "We looked down the road," Elizabeth remembered, "and saw them in great numbers opposite Becky Lynde's."

What the girls saw was probably a vanguard of Tories under Major Patrick Ferguson, a gifted man as well as a skilled soldier, who was later to fight out his life on a stone mountain in the Carolinas. Behind him were thick ranks of scarlet, with the 23rd Welch Fusiliers well in the van. To the four girls scurrying out of danger, this force must have seemed as strong and endless as a biblical host.

Unfortunately the American command viewed it in the same light. Actually it was a holding force under Von Knyphausen, backed by more British and Hessians. The bulk of Howe's power was slipping away to the north in a long, deadly curve, crossing Brandywine's West Branch at Trimble's Ford and the East Branch at Jeffries', the latter being a good three miles upstream from quiet Painter's Ford, where Bland's dragoons watched the approaches to the American right. This whole move threw an ominous shadow out of the past, the same circling movement that had begun the real action on Long Island. As at Long Island, the blow was to fall on the American right rear. And, as at Long Island, it would strike the luckless Colonel Samuel Miles and his Pennsylvanians, who held the farthest extremity of the line under the even more luckless John Sullivan.

The Congress, along with the citizens of Philadelphia, waited, half fearful and half hopeful, for news. All through the eleventh the sound of distant gunfire rustled through the streets, shivering almost gently along the high windows of the State House, against the rose-brick fronts of dwellings. Tidings were slow coming in, but bit by bit the picture unfolded.

Howe and Cornwallis had looped back of Sullivan's right, pouring down from Sconneltown and out of the woods by Osborne's Hill. The surprise was complete, and a roll-up of the whole American line seemed inevitable, with units breaking up and a stream of fugitives, wagons, and gun teams boiling east down the road to Chester. Washington, very tardily alive to the great danger, had sent Greene's whole division of Virginians racing over the four miles that lay between him and Sullivan's routed men. There was hard fighting in a defile not far from sleepy Birmingham Meeting House, with the Virginians falling back slowly and in good order until nightfall ended the action.

The American left had been badly hit after the main attack developed, but Wayne, in command here, withdrew grudgingly from ridge to low ridge until, as on the right, darkness forced a halt in hostilities. There had been a general retreat toward Chester, and disorganization spread evilly over the dark countryside. Through broken units Washington moved with Greene's still solid division, which butted on through the torrent of panic like a heavy log in a flood. At last the whole army had trailed over the bridge at Chester Creek and halted a little beyond the village of Chester itself.

Many of these bare details filtered through into the city. Close on to midnight of September 11, day of battle, Washington tried to write a full report to John Hancock, president of the Congress, but understandable fatigue put the task beyond him. Colonel Timothy Pickering of Salem, Massachusetts, finally drafted the dispatch, which glossed over very little. He read it aloud to Washington, who rallied, particularly at Pickering's closing line. "Notwithstanding the misfortune of the day, I am happy to find the troops in good spirits." The commander-in-chief himself extended the sentence to read: "and I hope another time we shall compensate for the losses now sustained."

In view of the defeat, these words seem almost deluded in their optimism, but actually there were many bright splashes across the otherwise somber record. Sullivan's collapse had been largely due to the fact that his men were too green to maneuver to meet the British onslaught. But old units like the indestructible Delawares had stood firm. A few new formations, notably Colonel Walter Stewart's Pennsylvania State Regiment, had shifted ground smoothly and met their first fire well. Greene's march with his Virginians had been a minor epic. "Joe Gourd" Weedon's brigade had covered the four miles to Sullivan in forty-five lightning minutes and had gone into action fighting hard, this being in marked contrast to Breymann's half-mile-per-hour rate on his way to rescue Baum at Bennington.

Brigade and regimental commanders had shown initiative and improvisation that were utterly lacking a year ago. Weedon, Woodford, Muhlenberg, the Irish-French Thomas Conway, the Pole, Casimir Pulaski, had been able to rally apparently routed men and keep them steady and dangerous. As for the young marquis, he had gone ahead with Greene and Washington and, having no command, had pranced blithely among Sullivan's retreating ranks, urging them to turn and stand. A British bullet caught him in the thigh and he faced capture or death, escaping only because Major de Gîmat got to him in time and threw him back onto his horse. It was a severe though not dangerous wound and he was able to write about it the next day, telling Dear Heart that "messieurs les anglais favored me with a gun-shot that wounded me slightly in the leg, but it is nothing, dear Heart, for the ball didn't touch bone or nerve." At least it was to immobilize him for some six weeks.

As for the army as a whole, it shook itself together while still virtually in full flight. Men got their breaths, took weary note of the good order of Greene's Virginians, and by regiments and companies re-formed as though by some military capillary attraction. Captain Enoch Anderson of the unquenchable Delawares remembered with grim pride that all through that night "I saw not a despairing look, nor did I hear a despairing word. We had solacing words always ready for each other—'Come boys, we shall do better another time.'—Had a man suggested or merely hinted the idea of giving up,—he would have been knocked down, and if killed it would have been no murder."

Another point which passed unnoticed but which may have been more important than any of the others was that a Rhode Islander took a Virginia brigade into action, that a Pennsylvanian held the left with New Jersey troops. Did no one remember the bellows of rage in 1775 when men from one town refused to be commanded by a man from another?

But in Philadelphia the Congress knew only what Washington had reported and could only cling to the brave ending of his dispatch. John Hancock, receiving the message at four in the morning, called the members to an early meeting. Iz Putnam was to send fifteen hundred Continentals down from Peekskill. Appeals were sent to Philemon Dickinson, to William Smallwood, and Mordecai Gist to sweep up all the militia they could. Some enlightened soul thought of the Brandywine troops themselves and an order was issued to send at once thirty hogsheads of rum "in compliment . . . for their gallant behaviour." Each man was to draw one half a gill per day until the supply was gone.

There was the future of Congress to consider. The army was obviously going to pull back deep into Pennsylvania, leaving Philadelphia at Howe's mercy. If Howe came on, it was resolved "that if the Congress shall be obliged to remove, Lancaster shall be the place at which they shall meet." The enemy was still at Chester, fifteen short miles away, but somehow the members showed no immediate anxiety to get out of his probable path. Eliphalet Dyer of Connecticut stated tartly, "We are now very Sulky and determined not to move for him if we can help it . . . you know we Scorn to fly."

While the army retreated and Congress unaccountably waited, a "feast of letters" from Braintree arrived for John Adams in which Abigail breathed fire. "We are no wise dispirited here." (Probably by the news of Burgoyne's advance.) "We possess a spirit that will not be conquered. If our men are all drawn off and we should be attacked, you would find a race of Amazons in America." Native genius was finding ways of replacing goods that were no longer imported. She wrote John of grinding cornstalks into molasses. "It answers very well to distill and may be boiled down to sugar. . . . 'T is said four barrels of juice will make one of molasses." As for herself, "Why should we borrow foreign luxuries? . . . I feel as contented when I have breakfasted on milk as ever I did with Hyson or Souchong. . . . As yet I know nothing of hardships. My children have never cried for bread nor been destitute of clothing. Nor have the poor and needy gone empty from my door, whenever it was in my power to assist them. Heaven grant that I may continue to receive its [heaven's] blessings. One of the greatest is that I can subscribe myself wholly yours." Stubborn Captain Enoch Anderson of the Delawares would have found a kindred soul in Abigail Adams.

Tardily Congress began to prepare to move. Its invaluable records were handled most haphazardly, if not downright shiftlessly. Some papers were sent vaguely up the Schuylkill in a shallop. Others were buried on a nearby farm with the full knowledge and consent of the farmer. This method of disposition was probably safe enough, but no one seems to have boggled over the fact that that farmer was a deeply suspected Tory, later one of the two men to be hanged for treason in Pennsylvania.

Such more than cavalier treatment of vital records is hard to understand on the part of a body made up of so many lawyers. But it was an age where security in the modern sense was little regarded and papers were handled recklessly. Lord North, George III's Prime Minister, once lost a highly confidential document which was finally found fluttering about on the floor of his watercloset. As late as Queen Victoria's time, Lord Salisbury was called upon to turn over an ultra-top-secret paper and answered casually that it must have been in the pocket of an old coat that he had given away sometime before.

When the Congress finally did go, it was in no concerted exodus. John Adams was wakened at three on the morning of the nineteenth, eight full days after Brandywine, by James Lovell, who told him that the bulk of the members had gone and that Howe's advance guard might be expected any time. With a Mr. Marchant, Adams called for horses and set out, not stopping for breakfast. Lancaster had been set as the rallying point for all members, but the town lay too close to the army and they finally ended up at York. John Adams wrote to Abigail that he was "lodged in the house of General Roberdeau, an Israelite . . . who with his sisters and children and servants does everything to make us happy. We are highly favored. No other delegates are so well off." Thus the delegates dug in at York—which they often confusingly called Yorktown—and for a year it was to be the virtual capital of the United States.

While the delegates had dallied in Philadelphia, the two opposing forces sparred rather warily off to the west of the city in the rolling country that lies between the East Branch of Brandywine Creek and the upper reaches of the Schuylkill. It is an interesting commentary on the recovery of the American army from its defeat along the Brandywine fords that Washington was actively seeking contact with the advancing Howe. Casimir Pulaski, newly appointed to a title that matched his handsome, magnetic elegance—commander of the horse—pushed out vigorously, with Anthony Wayne and William Maxwell of New Jersey close behind. Contact was made on the sixteenth with Hessian Jaegers and grenadiers, with the former, trained for irregular as well as formal fighting, appearing to fine advantage. They ducked "behind fences, around the fields and woods . . . to demonstrate to the enemy [the Americans] their superior marksmanship and their skill with the amusettes [rifles]," according to the Hessian captain, Baurmeister.

The main rival bodies came up near White Horse Tavern and another major battle loomed close. But the weather suddenly broke in a terrific storm that immobilized both armies, a storm that probably reached hurricane proportions with floods of rain. The same Baurmeister wrote to the Right Honorable Lord, Gracious and Mighty Colonel von Jungkenn in Hesse Cassel on the Fulda River, "I wish I could give you a description of the downpour. It came down so hard that in a few minutes we were drenched and sank in mud to our calves."

Fighting was out of the question. Muskets were flooded; pans ran with water. And the favorite Anglo-German bayonet could not be used since the hurricane blew directly in the men's faces. Washington withdrew from the field, intending to pull back a few miles, give the muskets a chance to dry out, and then strike back at Howe. But the drive of the rain had beaten the American army as effectually as Howe's force could have, or rather the combination of rain and faulty equipment. The standard cartridge pouch, or cartouche, of the day was an oblong of thick leather with a heavy lid or flap closing it at the top and overlapping widely at the sides. Properly greased and cared for, these pouches were reasonably waterproof. But most of the American pouches on that September day were hastily cobbled affairs made to a faulty pattern. Often the lids were short, with a gap at both sides that simply funneled water into the pouches. As a result, virtually all the ammunition carried into this interrupted action by the American troops was ruined. "A most terrible blow to us," as Henry Knox wrote mournfully. So instead of more action there was a long march through the downpour, two wet night encampments, more marching until the supply depots at Reading Furnace were reached and the now dry pouches refilled.

As for Howe, he pushed easily on, reached the Schuylkill. There a foraging party blundered into a spot called Valley Forge and an unguarded American depot. Gloating, the officers in command checked off the tally of supplies seized or destroyed. "3,800 Barrels of Flour, Soap and Candles, 25 Barrels of Horseshoes," they recorded in chuckling satisfaction. "Several Thousand tomahawks and Kettles and Intrenching Tools and 20 Hogsheads of Resin." All this was a drop in the bucket for the British but of vast importance to the shabby little army which at that moment was making a wide swing, a killing march of nearly thirty miles over bad roads and across breast-deep fords.

Another disaster, this time through enemy action and not weather or random raiders, struck the Americans on the twentieth. The usually alert Anthony Wayne had been detached to hang about the White Horse Tavern-Warren Tavern area, watching for a chance to hit at the British rear. His night bivouac was apparently well chosen near Paoli Tavern and his security measures seem to have been at least adequate. Yet somehow a force of nearly five British battalions and a troop or two of the 16th Dragoons managed to slip up through the night. Before attacking, the British commander, Major General Grey, ordered his men to withdraw their flints. There would be no chance of a trigger-happy Briton spoiling the surprise. Wayne's men were rushed, overwhelmed with nothing but the bayonet. He handled himself and his men very well but could do little beyond withdrawing. The losses were at least seventy prisoners, some hundred or more killed. Eight loaded wagons with their teams were lost along with a thousand muskets. By some miracle the four priceless field-pieces under Wayne were rescued. This action, known as the Paoli Massacre, is still dragged out from time to time to show British brutality. Actually it was an extremely smart, well-planned, and well-executed coup carried out against a usually alert and able enemy with no known excesses on the part of Grey's men. In fact, the victim, Wayne, was virtually to duplicate this feat two years later at a British fort up the Hudson.

This action at Paoli ended everything except maneuvering for the time being. By the twenty-sixth a semi-permanent camp had been formed by Washington at Pennybacker's Mill (modern Schwenkville) on Perkiomen Creek, a tributary of the Schuylkill. That same day Cornwallis led British and Hessian grenadiers into Philadelphia "amidst the acclamation of some thousands of the inhabitants," as the Engineer Montrésor remarked, adding in all honesty, "Mostly women and children." The rest of the Anglo-German force stayed outside the city at Germantown, now a part of Philadelphia.

The loss of Philadelphia was something that had been universally feared by the Americans, military and civilian. Now that the city had actually fallen, men blinked and looked at each other in surprise. The effect was as though a prize fighter had taken a dreaded blow to the chin, only to find that, far from knocking him out, it barely jarred him. The young nation, its Congress and its army were still functioning. As for the British, their seizure of Philadelphia did them little good. To be where they were, they had had to undergo a ghastly sea passage, a grueling march up from Chesapeake Bay and Head of Elk, and a hard battle. And still the American army was very much in existence. The useless city was all that Howe had to show for a whole summer's campaign.

More than twenty miles up the Schuylkill the American army shook itself as it took mental stock. As after Long Island, there was a growing tendency to blame most mishaps on the commander-in-chief, not only in the ranks but among the brasses of varying heights. Timothy Pickering, now adjutant general, was watering his horse at a ford in company with Nathanael Greene. As the two mounts gulped and sloshed their muzzles about, the Salem man said frankly, "Before I came to the army, I entertained an exalted opinion of General Washington's military talents, but I have since seen nothing to enhance it." Greene, remembering Wash-

ington's hesitations about Fort Washington in '76, and forgetting that he
himself might be thought chargeable with the commander-in-chief's delay
in making up his mind about that fatal stronghold, answered, "Why, the
General does want decision." It was very easy to recall shortcomings, easy
to forget the unswerving purpose of the march through the Jerseys, the
bold moves about Trenton and Princeton.

De Kalb was even more strongly critical. He wrote his patron, the Duc
de Broglie, that the Virginian was "the most amiable, kind-hearted and
upright of men." However, he was "too slow, too indolent and far too
weak." There was also a "tinge of vanity" in him, a tendency to overestimate himself. "In my opinion," the baron went on, "whatever success
he may have will be owing to good luck and to the blunders of his ad-
versaries . . . I may even say that he does not know how to improve
upon the grossest blunders of the enemy."

All this was honest, if manifestly unfair, opinion. Greene was clinging
to fears bred by past errors of commission and omission. Pickering was
rendering snap judgment. So, too, was De Kalb, who seems, as well, to be
judging Washington as though he commanded trained, veteran troops,
perfectly equipped. But others besides this trio were wondering.

There was no need to wonder. The commander-in-chief, his force built
up by militia arrivals and by the appearance of Alex McDougall with
nearly a thousand New York Continentals to more than he had at Brandywine, was considering the British position. Spies and scouts told him that
the main force was massed about Germantown, a village of little houses
and almost fortlike stone mansions that straggled along the road that led
south toward Philadelphia. There were councils of war and many of the
generals listened rather aghast at the commander-in-chief's thoughts. Never
mind about Brandywine. Forget Paoli. Let's not live with our past defeats.
Learn from them. Bearing all this in mind—we, the beaten, supposedly
scattered army—attack!

The plan was an ambitious one. In effect, the army was to be split in
two. One heavy column under Sullivan was to strike down the Germantown Road. The other, headed by Nathanael Greene, was to come in from
the east, joining Sullivan at a crossroads deep in the British-Hessian
position. Perhaps it was too ambitious, the sort of coup to be undertaken
only by the best of troops handled by the best of staffs. The thousands of
newly arrived raw militia who made up part of the army did not seem to
be the best tools to use on such a military structure. There were other
disadvantages. The Germantown Road ran broad and well paved, but few,
if any, side roads ran out of it for a good part of its length. Liaison between
Sullivan's advancing men would be difficult. Greene would be out of touch
with the rest of the army until he actually made contact at the crossroads,
where School House Lane and Luken's Mill Lane cut the great street.
Nonetheless, the plan was adopted and few murmurs concerning indecision were heard.

The country sloping generally south toward Philadelphia is dotted with peaceful, leisurely names: Chestnut Hill and Mount Airy and Mount Pleasant. There are Paper Mill Run, Lime Kiln Road, Market House, and the already mentioned School House Lane and its continuation, Luken's Mill Lane. Into this setting poured the main American army, its commander-in-chief riding with John Sullivan.

The march began at three in the morning from the camps almost twenty miles away, for Washington seems to have counted on a dawn surprise to offset the known disadvantages. Spreading east and west along the Germantown Road came Sullivan's men, tramping over fields, plowing through buckwheat patches, filtering under orchard trees. General Francis Nash was there, entering his second and last action at the head of his North Carolinians and following Lord Stirling, as did William Maxwell and his Jerseymen. Wayne brought his Pennsylvanians through the meadows east of the road.

East again, far away on the Lime Kiln Road, came the second striking force, with Nathanael Greene urging his men on. Staff had underestimated the distance to be covered on this curving highway and the Rhode Islander was more than fearful of being late. His brigade commander labored with him: Alex McDougall and his New Yorkers; Charles Scott and Adam Stephen and the ex-pastor, Peter Muhlenberg, with their Virginians.

It was the fourth of October and a fall mist rose with the sun, throwing an eerie, golden pall over the countryside. Then contact was made on the slopes of Mount Airy and all at once the contagious intoxication of victory swept through the attack. Camps were overrun, knots of light infantry and grenadiers formed, broke, formed and broke again. There were ugly, sullying moments when Wayne's Pennsylvanians smashed into the British right and began to remember Paoli, "striking down many of the poor wretches who were Crying for Mercy" (something that the British emphatically had not done in that night surprise). Wayne and his officers struck at their own men with their swords, finally ended the slaughter.

Mist thickened more and more. Twenty yards away a moving company might be grenadiers or North Carolinians, and action grew confused. British drums beat the retreat and suddenly Sir William Howe, riding up from headquarters in the rear, found himself in the unusual and shocking position of being surrounded by British fugitives. Britons remembered his swinging his stick and shouting, "Form! Form! I never saw you retreat before!"

Then a bad American mistake was made. At the east of the main road the great house of Tory Benjamin Chew loomed through the mist, a veritable stone fortress in the fields. A handful of flying men of the 60th Royal Rifles took refuge in the mansion, barricaded themselves securely, and opened with musketry on all passing troops. Some of Maxwell's Jersey men tried to rush the house, but the fire was too heavy. And the American command was presented with a military problem for which past experience had in no way prepared it. Maxwell's men were supposed to drive ahead and reinforce Sullivan, already meeting heavier opposition farther down the Germantown Road. How to dislodge those men of the 60th? Henry Knox, the widest-read book soldier, was consulted. His memory brought little that was useful except for a disastrous tag that one should never leave "an occupied castle" in one's rear. Therefore, this stone citadel should be reduced. Guns were brought up, but their shot merely bounced off the walls. Infantry that should have been otherwise employed kept a steady fire on the shuttered windows. Colonel John Laurens of South Carolina and the young Chevalier de Mauduit du Plessis gathered up straw, drove in a window with reckless courage, and tried to set fire to the interior but failed. Knox's guns and Maxwell's muskets blazed on and on, always futilely. It is easy to be wise after the event, but it seems obvious that the proper course would have been to leave a small holding force to watch the Chew house and send Knox and Maxwell on to the heart of the fighting.

The mist did not lift. British resistance stiffened markedly. In the confusion and ghastly visibility American units fired on each other. Victory turned into panic and the rolling meadows of Germantown were covered with retreating men, many of them in actual flight not from the enemy so much as from the deadly menace of the fog.

Down on the Lime Kiln Road, Greene had made as good time as could have been hoped for, but his route had been a good four miles longer than Sullivan's. His spent men were hit by a mass of fresh British troops sent out by Howe. There was blind fighting and the Rhode Islander nearly lost some of his guns. It was obvious that the two-pronged attack had failed and Greene ordered a retirement. Casimir Pulaski came up with a small cavalry force to guard the retreat. His green troopers were unexpectedly charged by the veterans of the British 16th Dragoons, broke, and galloped on through Greene's so far orderly ranks. New Yorkers and Virginians, thinking that Pulaski's helmeted men were British, had a moment of panic but finally steadied. Thomas Paine, who rode with Greene's staff, reported that "the enemy kept a civil distance behind us, sending every now and then a shot after us and receiving the same from us." The retreat went on quietly. Off to the west, Sullivan's men, recovering at least a semblance of poise, were also quitting the field with little British interference. But the men on the Germantown Road and those on Lime Kiln Road were deadly tired. They had marched a good sixteen miles to enter the action, and now orders were sending them on to their older camp at Pennybacker's Mill, a further twenty-four miles on top of two hours and a half of tough combat. Even rugged Captain Enoch Anderson, whose Delaware company had been with Sullivan, was impressed. "Here we old soldiers had marched forty miles," he wrote. "We eat nothing and drank nothing but water on the tour."

The cost was a heavy one. The American losses in all categories amounted to almost one thousand men, with General Francis Nash of North Carolina among the dead. The British total was about one half that of the Americans. Yet, as Wellington said of Waterloo, "It was a damned close-run thing."

If there had not been that lamentable delay at the Chew house; if divisions had not stumbled into each other in that blinding mist; if the leading waves of the attack had not run short of ammunition; if the American cavalry had been better prepared to keep liaison between units right and left of the Germantown Road; if the army timetable had permitted Greene to arrive just a little earlier—— Cancel out any one of these adverse factors and the British *might* have been driven into the Schuylkill.

But this defeat, for it can only be counted one, had consequences far out of proportion to its immediate, local importance. The heartening effect on the army of near victory may be taken for granted. But in other parts of the world thoughtful, if not necessarily benevolent, men were watching. The British historian, Trevelyan, felt that "eminent generals and statesmen of sagacity, in every European court, were profoundly impressed . . . that a new army, raised within the year, and undaunted by a series of recent disasters, had assailed a victorious enemy in its own quarters and had only been repulsed after a sharp and dubious conflict. . . . The French government, in making up its mind whether the Americans would prove to be efficient allies, was influenced almost as much by the battle of Germantown as by the surrender of Burgoyne."

This is probably overstating the case. Germantown showed, certainly, that a beaten American army was apt to be the most dangerous army. But this had been demonstrated time and again, Germantown being merely the largest-scale example of bouncing off the ropes to date. Nonetheless, added to Burgoyne's surrender soon to come, it undoubtedly helped to weight the scales still more. And to get the flavor and importance of that surrender, we must go back a little in time to witness the final act of Gentleman Johnny's autumnal tragedy.

CHAPTER XXIII

" . . . hangs like a gathering storm upon my left"

WHEN the bridge of boats across the Hudson was broken, Gentleman Johnny Burgoyne had actually cut his last tie with Canada, as he had in effect by his first move south from Fort Edward. What amounted to a brand-new war had begun, and past achievements counted for nothing. The whole structure of the "Thoughts" was gone except for the dwindling force of British and Germans. Gone were any dreams of a dazzling, tripartite stroke that would end the war. British grenadier and Hessian Jaeger now had one inconclusive and inescapable objective: to carry out Germain's directive and reach Albany. No officer or

man of the expedition seems to have thought beyond that point. It would
have been mere futile speculation if they had.

There was no lack of signs to tell the youngest Brunswick drummer boy
that a new field was being entered. In the carefree pre-Bennington days
it had been hardly worth while to think about the living enemy. Success
could be measured by the slow miles left behind the laden columns. Indians and the few light troops who had pressed deeper south on either
bank of the Hudson brought back contemptuous reports of what rebel
patrols they had met. The clumsy farmers fled at the sight of a scarlet coat
or a paint-streaked face; they threw down their rusty muskets and begged
for mercy at the sight of the smallest force.

There had been a marked difference since Bennington. Outposts, British,
Indian, or German, were fired on at night. Sometimes a dawn relief, marching out to make a routine change of posts, found no waiting comrades
grumbling out friendly insults about the slowness of that relief. Instead
there were huddled, silent bodies struck down by some swift, hard blow
out of the night. Reports came in to headquarters of scraps of paper
fastened to stiffening bodies, with scrawled, clumsy letters spelling out
"For Jane McCrae."

Now on the west bank of the Hudson it was worse. Dawn and dusk
spat out orange musket flashes. Then the day became no safer than the
night. A foraging party of nearly thirty men sent out to dig potatoes close
to the army was shattered and the attackers melted away into the forest
tangles. Where a picket of six men had been considered ample not long
ago, twenty to thirty were now needed.

The character of the countryside was changing too. There was still the
wilderness, but where fields broke the age-old tangles they formed a mellow
green setting for well-built houses with wide-shouldered barns, squat, durable gristmills and sawmills, instead of the frontier cabins of the Hampshire Grants and the lake settlements. Thomas Anburey marveled at Philip
Schuyler's "handsome and commodious dwelling-house . . . exceedingly
fine saw- and grist-mill and, at a small distance a very neat church with
several houses about it. This beautiful spot was quite deserted. On the
grounds were great quantities of fine wheat, as also Indian corn." All of
this harvest was at once converted to military uses. Even with nearly a
month's supplies in hand, Burgoyne was taking no chances of running out
of grain and fodder. "Thus," mused the gentleman volunteer, "a plantation . . . thriving and beautiful in the morning, was before night reduced
to a scene of distress and poverty. What havoc and devastation is attendant
on war."

One grimly familiar feature remained unchanged. There was a fairly
narrow plain edging the flow of the river and beyond it a long line of
rugged, wooded heights. From these heights streams and brooks plunged
down to join the Hudson, each cutting wide, deep channels spanned by a
bridge where the wretched road crossed. Unseen hands had wrecked these
bridges, and once more the army halted to listen to the wheeze of saw and

the rap of maul and hammer as the engineers struggled, as they had in the wilderness below Fort Anne, to build something at least strong enough to bear the weight of Burgoyne's guns, ammunition wagons, supply wagons, and of course the thirty-odd carts whose contents enabled the commander to take the field as a gentleman should.

One mile a day and a halt. Two miles and a halt. A mile and a half and a halt, rolling up the accumulated mass of time that was not being turned to account. Brass-fronted helmets, still glossy bearskins, cracked leather skullcaps, scarlet coats and blue, brownish linen overalls that had generally replaced the parade-ground white of regulation breeches—in a multicolored stream Gentleman Johnny Burgoyne's army, antlike, worked south. To the left the Hudson flowed on, deep autumnal blue toward the far bank, muddy brown and black where the supply barges hugged the west shore. September was ripening, and already scarred German faces were softening at the sight of swamp maples that masked themselves in an almost transparent scarlet glow. Broken-nailed hands reached out toward birches where golden leaves were climbing like flames among the green.

Safe in the heart of the army, the baroness's calash swayed along, four sets of round, Teutonic blue eyes wide with surprise at this first hint of the dreamworld of color that was to come. Little Fritschen, a soldier's daughter as well as a soldier's wife, knew very well what the shrunken size of the columns meant. No one needed to explain to her the significance of the breaking of the bridge of boats. And as she rode along, Rockel on the box and Lena and another maid helping her with the children, she was calmly congratulating herself on her good luck. She would always think of herself as lucky. Looking back on the whole of her time in North America, she claimed firmly, "If I had not taken advantage of the chance to join my husband [at Fort Anne], I would have had to remain behind in Canada for three long years." Of course fall was coming on and she had sent all her own clothes and the children's, except for a small summer wardrobe, back to Ticonderoga long ago. But despite the wilderness, the dwindling army, the snapping of communications, the uncertainty about rations, and the approach of cold weather, she still "cherished the sweet hope of victory and of coming into the promised land." So, no doubt, did Mesdames Reynal and Harnage and the increasingly gravid Lady Acland, as well as the hundreds of women (some say thousands), British, German, and Canadian, who shared the fortunes of the humbler elements of the army.

The march down the Hudson was not only slow. It was blind. Unbelievable as it may seem, Burgoyne had only the shadiest idea of where the rebel army was, how strong it might be, and what its military potential was. No longer was he screened by Indians, invaluable in picking up bits of information that headquarters could weave into a coherent picture. The few who stayed with him hung useless on his flanks and could not be induced to go forward. Canadian light troops and Tories showed the same tendency. To make matters worse, the very terrain sealed the eyes of the British command. The narrow river plain over which the army marched so haltingly was pretty well cleared of trees, but rolling shoulders of land jutting out from the wooded heights just at the right hung like shaggy curtains masking what lay beyond. Some of the stream beds were veritable canyons, like the Great Ravine, and held a threat of ambush to limit the range of scouting parties. No dominant hill towered over the army to afford an observation post. If an agile Jaeger or light infantryman climbed a great oak or pine to its very top he only looked into more branches, more festoons of leaves.

Then Burgoyne and his men, British and German, waking in the river meadows where coils of mist rose wavering, heard a new sound, the ghostly patter of unseen drums, like mouse feet scurrying over a hollow flooring, alien drums somewhere off to the south, many drums. At least they now knew in a general way where the enemy was.

There was hasty and not too thorough reconnoitering. Cart paths were found leading inland to the shelf-like heights on the right. In the center there was a clearing, an abandoned farm of some dozen acres with a weed-girdled cabin, the holdings of one Freeman, whose unharvested wheat rippled in the wind. On the left, by the river, the main road cut across the Great Ravine and another cart path led inland from it toward the Freeman lands and other smaller clearings.

The farm and the clearings seem to have dazzled Gentleman Johnny. If he could get his forces to them, particularly the broad Freeman farm, his men could fight like civilized beings instead of whacking about among trees and copses and swamps and bush-choked watercourses. He issued his orders, to the bewilderment of military students ever since.

To begin with, he split his forces. Simon Fraser, still full of the fire that had driven him on to Hubbardton, was to take the massed British and German grenadiers and light infantry, circle in and toward the heights, and then head south over a foul road that touched Freeman's western fields. Gentleman Johnny himself would bring on the line companies of the 20th Lancashires, the 21st North British, the 62nd Wiltshires, and the 9th Norfolks across the Great Ravine and pour them out into Freeman's fields, where those veterans, he felt, would really come into their own. Down on the river road the baron would take his place with the Riedesel, Rhetz, and Specht regiments, backed by Georg Pausch's guns.

This division of forces was bad. What was worse was that they would be completely out of sight of each other. They were all to start southward and then, when it was guessed that they were about abreast, with wide spaces of broken country between the components a signal gun was to be fired and the whole force, in theory, would sweep forward. It is hard to see the plan as anything but a desperate, gambling lunge, its details conditioned by an inexcusable contempt for the enemy.

Before dawn on September 19 the columns formed under the eyes of the 47th North Lancashires and the Hesse-Hanau grenadiers, detailed to stay behind as guard over the bateaux that grated against the riverbank. Other eyes were watching. Over on the east bank, men of an American patrol were staring, unseen, across the river, climbing trees for a better view of the Anglo-German camp. Soon they dropped from the trees, left the bank, and streaked south, bursting with their news. They did not need to hurry. Once more Burgoyne was presenting his foes the inestimable gift of time, for it was not until nearly eleven that his three columns separated, lost touch with each other, and began their lumbering, blundering march.

Gentleman Johnny's farthest advanced elements in the center did not reach the north edge of the Freeman clearing until about a quarter to one. A strong infantry picket in faded scarlet coats poured out of the woods, took open order near the Freeman cabin, and nosed eagerly ahead. There was motion under the trees to the south where vaguely seen men in fur caps and long rifles were gliding. Somewhere among the dense boles an unearthly, horrible gobbling sound broke out, thick, throaty, and yet somehow carrying. Then the south woods echoed to the sharp crack of rifles. Every officer in the picket was struck down. Sergeants and privates toppled and the clearing was suddenly dotted with lithe men in hunting shirts, rifles ready. Daniel Morgan's men had struck the first blow.

The rush of the rifles, probably not much over company strength, carried them across the clearing, where they collided, almost fatally, with the main body under Burgoyne. They managed to break off, fled to the shelter of the south woods, and the bulk of the British command occupied the Freeman fields, which ran east and west some three hundred and fifty yards. There was no enemy in sight, but the eerie, nerve-racking gobble wailed on among the trees. The sound would probably have lost none of its chilling mystery had the British known that it was Dan Morgan's own highly individual way of rallying his companies, many of which had been badly scattered in their march through the woods.

The southern woods were no longer empty. More and more fur caps and hunting shirts filled the spaces between the trunks. Men with slung rifles could be seen climbing squirrel-like to the upper branches. Rifles flashed again, were joined by the duller tones of muskets as newcomers, with a uniform coat here and there, closed up with Morgan.

It was a worse than awkward situation for a commander trained in formal war. There was nothing solid to strike against, no way of estimating the strength of the enemy. Nonetheless, Burgoyne faced the swelling fire calmly and ordered the signal guns to be discharged to tell Fraser on the right and Von Riedesel on the left that the grand march had begun. Actually he had reached the high-water mark of the invasion. Never would Englishman or Brunswicker pass that southern edge of the Freeman farm.

Burgoyne's men, firing as best they could at tree-masked targets, suffered heavily, especially the 62nd Wiltshires. Lieutenant James Hadden and other officers of the Royal Artillery brought on their guns. Marksmen in the trees shot down the gun teams, picked off the cannoneers and gunner officers before a piece could be loaded. There was a sudden rush of infantry and gunners to the shelter of the north woods, leaving the guns silent. Morgan's men and Joseph Cilley's New Hampshire Continentals swarmed into the open, only to find the picture exactly reversed. Now the British were firing from cover on men in an exposed, rolling meadow. Drums beat. The turkey call gobbled out its demoniac message, and the field was silent save for the dull thud of boots as the Americans yielded the ground and the British reoccupied it.

Thus the pattern of the day was set. For three hours and more the scene repeated itself, with the two forces driving each other back and forth over the trampled ground. British losses mounted alarmingly. Of the gunner officers, only James Hadden remained alive, bareheaded since a rifle bullet carried off his skullcap. Thomas Anburey saw his friend, Lieutenant Don of the 21st North British, take a shot through the heart and spring from the ground "nearly as high as a man." The infantry lines closed and closed as gaps were torn in their ranks. Companies were melting to platoons. Weary, hungry, bewildered, dressed in grotesquely patched clothes that might well have stifled the last spark of regimental pride, British officers and men were magnificent. They gave ground with snarling reluctance, drove forward again in solid, shouting rushes over the heaped scarlet bodies that marked an earlier stand. Then they stood, unflinching, to face the blizzard of aimed rifle fire that was, to them, almost a new form of warfare.

They had seen rifles before. Some of the units had faced Morgan's men along the Boston lines. But now, for the first time in the war, rifles were used properly against regular troops. The slow-loading bayonetless weapons were backed by the quicker muskets of the New Hampshiremen. When the British companies went in with the bayonet (that move which had been so fatal to riflemen at Long Island) Morgan's companies melted away into the woods where pursuit was impossible, took their time about reloading, and came back to their posts at the edge of the clearing. They fired carefully on the trim ranks of the British companies. They picked off officers. Mounted aides bearing orders were brought down at once. And yet Burgoyne's men broke only under heavy pressure, re-formed at once, and swept back into action.

Ominously, as at Hubbardton, the arc of American fire worked in sinister flashings wider and wider about the British left. The rifles cracked on. Gentleman Johnny, a superb, calm figure in scarlet and white, called to his men in level, undisturbed tones, chuckling richly from time to time. Bullets cut his coat and he laughed down from the saddle, showing the rents to the nearest private. His hat was pierced and he only waved it above his head. But the fire was creeping more and more about the left, and the British hold on the clearing was growing shallower.

Suddenly there was a new din off at the left. Men of the 9th Norfolks turned sweat-soaked yellow facings toward the sound. Hoofs pounded in the distance. Drums boomed, music blared out, and a Lutheran hymn swelled among the trees. A few officers and men broke ranks, staring, as they saw the baron's sky-blue and buff, saw the tossing heads of Pausch's

gun teams, and in the distance the white facings of the Rhetz regiment.
The Hanau guns skidded on a long slant down a hideous ravine, bumped
to the bottom, strained at the ascent. In an instant they were engulfed
in a wave of scarlet coats, British officers and privates heaving at the wheels
along with the Hanau gunners, manhandling the heavy pieces to the level
ground, where smoke hung thick over tattered scarlet ranks.

The guns went into action. The Rhetz regiment came up on the British
left and the fighting slowly ended as the last rays of the September sun
faded from Freeman's fields. Once more a British force had been saved
from highly possible destruction by the arrival of German troops on its
left. Once more history would repeat itself, on the eighteenth of June,
1815, when Von Bülow brought the first of Blücher's men up on Wellington's left in a Belgian meadow near a village called Waterloo.

Drum and turkey call faded away off to the south. British and Brunswickers dropped to the ground, utterly spent. Darkness thickened and
footsteps padded up stealthily from the British rear. Soon the Indians
were reaping an undreamed-of harvest of scalps from dead and wounded,
from American, Briton, and German, with a fine impartiality.

Burgoyne returned to his headquarters beyond the Great Ravine and
seems unaccountably to have been swirling in the intoxicating air of victory. It may have been due to his own display of unquestioned courage
and gallantry on a hard-fought field and the memory of the unshakable
bravery of his troops. An extra bottle or two of champagne may have helped,
added to the unfailing cheering section of one provided by the still present
Mrs. Commissary. The next day the bright halo still hovered in his mind
and he wrote General Powell, in command at Ticonderoga, "We have had
a smart and very honorable action, and are now encamped in front of
the field, which must demonstrate our victory beyond the power of even an
American news-writer to explain away."

There was little, on the American side, to explain. Burgoyne's losses
had topped the six-hundred mark, killed, wounded, and prisoners. The
unfortunate 62nd Wiltshires had only some sixty men fit for duty. Of the
Royal Artillery, only James Hadden and eleven gunners were left of the
forty-eight who had trundled the guns into action. As for the triple advance, so plausibly set forth by Burgoyne, the strongest element, Fraser's
combined Anglo-German Advanced Corps, had hardly come into the action
at all. The baron's advance along the river had been called off and his men
luckily diverted to save Burgoyne at the very last moment.

Yet to his men he was still Gentleman Johnny. Sergeant Robert Lamb
of the 9th recorded that the general "shunned no danger; his presence
and conduct animated the troops, for they greatly loved the General . . .
he maintained . . . serenity, fortitude and undaunted intrepidity." Lieutenant William Digby said that "General Burgoyne was everywhere and
did everything that could be expected from a brave officer . . . we were
all in good spirits and ready to obey with cheerfulness any orders the
general might issue."

There was fog over the Hudson Valley for the next day or two. Burgoyne hesitated, got ready to push ahead again, called the move off, and finally dug in, following roughly the farthest line of advance from Fraser on the high ground to the west to the baron down by the river. At least he now knew from prisoners fairly accurately where and how strong his opponents were.

The American army was dug in on the heights of Stillwater, a very short distance, militarily speaking, from the British lines. And they were dug in very well under the eye of a skilled, well-trained soldier whom the Congress had given the rank of colonel-engineer, an unusually high grade for one of the "learned branches" of the service. His name was Thaddeus (or Tadeusz) Kosciusko, destined for a long and honorable career as an American soldier.

In command was Major General Horatio Gates with Benedict Arnold as leader of troops in the field, at least in theory. On the nineteenth of September Gates's forces probably totaled some seven thousand men, many of them, according to Continental standards, well seasoned. Militia was flocking to him in encouraging numbers, only in this category he had suffered an unnecessary and exasperating loss. Into the camps about Stillwater on the eighteenth of September had marched the utterly unpredictable John Stark with most of the men with whom he had won Bennington, men from New Hampshire and the Hampshire Grants, a most valuable addition. In the morning they arrived. At noon John Stark led them all out again, heading them across the Hudson and along the roads that led home. The reason? It may be remembered that this force had been enlisted for two months at the time of Burgoyne's potential threat to New England. Now the two months were up to the very day, and home the whole force went, despite the fact that a battle was obviously brewing. It is very likely that as they took the road again on the nineteenth they could hear the gunfire swelling up from the Freeman farm area, a sound which in no way took the edge off their determination to observe the letter of the law in the matter of their enlistments.

The events of the nineteenth could well have brought a wave of optimism, fully equal to that of Burgoyne, over the whole of Kosciusko's fortifications. Instead, on the twentieth and for some days thereafter, there was marked apprehension. Supplies were very slow in coming. Ammunition was so low that Gates worked it out as some forty rounds per man, barely enough for one day's careful fighting.

As far as the action in the Freeman clearing went, Americans could reckon that they had inflicted nearly double the losses that they themselves had suffered. Yet there were ominous memories. At the start of the engagement Morgan's men had become so separated, so widely scattered, that the Old Waggoner himself believed that his cherished rifle corps was wrecked hopelessly. There had been bad management farther back of the lines. Ebenezer Learned's brigade, which had been sent out to back up Morgan, Henry Dearborn, and Cilley, had blundered far away from the fighting and had come into feeble contact with Simon Fraser and the Advanced Corps, well to the west of the proper destination. Other lesser snafus had interfered with the effectiveness of the riposte to Burgoyne.

There were strained relations among the high brass. Gates and Arnold, who had been full of mutual admiration at an earlier period, were now sparring hotly. The latter had been recalled in the midst of the action of the nineteenth and was in a furious mood. If this move of Gates was made tactlessly—though it is hard to see how one could be tactful with Arnold—it was undoubtedly wise. Arnold's obsession for combat would probably have led him to enter the action in person—a spot where a general in his position never should be—and very possibly he might have drawn his troops in a suicidal rush against the ever stubborn and dangerous British. Nonetheless, Arnold is usually given the lion's share of credit for the American success, an historical handout that is rather hard to justify even when made by historians of the rank, say, of Trevelyan or the late Christopher Ward.

For one thing, the swirling action across the clearings shows no sign of any one guiding hand. In retrospect it looks very much like a regimental commander's battle, if not a company commander's. Skilled over-all command, such as Arnold is supposed to have exercised, could well have done other things, such as sending a holding force against Von Riedesel on the river road or launching a sudden drive toward the lightly guarded supply boats in the river. For another thing, there is no direct documentation tying Arnold in with any American fighting. James Thomas Flexner, in his *The Traitor and the Spy*, cites excellent evidence to show that Arnold was at all times back at headquarters with Gates.

Nonetheless, pro-Gates cliques and pro-Arnold cliques formed and their friction added to the general uneasiness.

The action of the nineteenth has been given a multitude of names—Bemis Heights, Stillwater and Saratoga—much as Waterloo has also been called the Battle of La Belle Alliance and of Mont St. Jean. Since it was fought largely on the Freeman acres and was to be followed by another engagement on substantially the same terrain, these encounters will be referred to here as the First and Second Battles of Freeman's Farm rather than as Bemis Heights, Stillwater, or Saratoga. Actually the name is not very important save for identity. What matters is what happened on those two occasions and during the days immediately following them.

There is no doubt about Burgoyne's intent after the nineteenth. For on the twenty-first another messenger from the south managed somehow to worm through the American lines to his quarters. There was word from Sir Henry Clinton this time, and it set Burgoyne's thoughts flowing along still more sanguine channels, quite a different effect from that produced by his last message from the south that spoke of Sir William Howe's "Intention for Pennsylvania."

From New York Sir Henry wrote, "You know my good will and are not ignorant of my poverty. If you think 2000 men can assist you effectually, I will make a push at Montgomery in about ten days. But ever jealous of my flanks if they make a move in force on either of them I must return [to New York] to save this important post. I expect reenforcement every day. Let me know what you wish."

There is a good deal of overreading on Gentleman Johnny's part to draw much hope from Clinton's letter. A force of two thousand men making a limited stroke up from New York could probably have helped him very little. The objective, Fort Montgomery, lay well below West Point in the tangled highlands of the Hudson with such picturesquely named crests as the Dunderberg, the Timp, and the Torne nearby and Popolopen Kill flowing below it. The British seizure of this fort could hardly benefit Burgoyne. Clinton's reference to his own "poverty," used in a military sense, must have told Gentleman Johnny that the two thousand was the maximum effort to be expected. Yet there was a reference to "reenforcements" to encourage him, particularly as he had no way of knowing that Germain had cut these to the bone. He decided to wait and see what effect Clinton's move would have on Gates.

So the halted invasion dug in still more solidly and a period oddly resembling 1915–18 trench warfare set in. It was a grueling time for the British and Germans. The Americans, numbers now growing daily and supply problems quite well solved, grew bolder and bolder. There was nightly sniping. Small raids were thrown out toward the Great Ravine. Anglo-German rations were draining away alarmingly. The horses were forced to eat leaves from the trees, which, while flaming in increasing magnificence, were very poor fodder. The nights rolled dank fogs over the lines, and Burgoyne's men shivered in their light clothes and thought longingly of winter equipment now stored at Ticonderoga.

There was little sleep for anyone and nerves began to crack under the strain as they did in the trenches of France. Desertions, particularly among the Germans, increased alarmingly. Conscientious officers were busy day and night, grew gaunt, haggard, and shaky. The baroness, now installed with her children in a fairly comfortable log house, noted that the baron went days on end without a chance to change his clothes or sleep for more than a few minutes. Characteristically, she made no mention of her own light summer wardrobe, which must have been less than adequate.

Sounds had plagued the invaders ever since Skenesboro. There had been the ghostly pock-pock of Schuyler's axmen blocking the way south. Then there had been the woods beyond Freeman's farm thick with the gibberish of Morgan's turkey call. Now the nights were made hideous by howling dogs. Orders were issued that all dogs were to be tied up. Strays were to be shot on sight. But was that the howling of dogs? Someone fired a shot in the dark and found that he had brought down a lean, mangy wolf drawn from the far northwest with scores of others by the scent of the hastily buried dead. The nightly ululation went on. Men heard the scratch

of ghoulish claws about shallow graves, caught blue-green glints of noc-
turnal eyes. It did not do to be wounded and abandoned between the lines.

There were other signs to set a thoughtful man recasting his ideas of
the enemy. Anburey, out on patrol one night, pushed through a ravine
where some of the fighting of the nineteenth had taken place. There he
found unburied American bodies, one of them a woman, her stiffened
fingers still clasping a double handful of cartridges. Was the stalled invasion facing an army or a nation in arms?

Bad news came from the north and east, the very spot whose inhabitants, as Burgoyne had written earlier to Germain, hung "like a gathering storm upon my left." The storm broke. Capable General Benjamin
Lincoln, operating from the Hampshire Grants, sent detachments totaling
some fifteen hundred men against the lines of communication, such as
they were. Colonel John Brown (Yale, class of 1771) swooped down on
Mount Defiance and Mount Independence, sweeping up several hundred
prisoners, although he was not strong enough to attack Ticonderoga itself.
Other coups were launched at the upper Hudson, and Burgoyne's fleet
of bateaux came under frequent sniper fire. On all sides pressure was
growing stronger. It was high time for Clinton to make his move up the
Hudson.

The deep blue of the slow-bending Hudson reflected colors blazing
brighter and brighter as October came down the valley on the northern
winds—pure gold and maroon and crimson and honey-yellow. Walking
under the flaming trees about the ever strengthening works near Stillwater,
Horatio Gates blinked behind his spectacles and assayed his position with
deceptive Pickwickian benevolence.

He had relieved Benedict Arnold of all command as the upshot of the
endless quarrels between the two men. The relief had been ordered with
a minimum of tact and generosity, for largeness of spirit was scarcely an
outstanding characteristic in the make-up of Horatio Gates, and as a result
Arnold ranged about the camps in the high-explosive mood which could
be expected from his turbulent make-up. This frame of mind may have
struck Gates as regrettable, but he could congratulate himself on having
solved for the time being, at least, a major command problem.

With the rest of his officers he could feel quite content. Among them
were no Greenes or Waynes, but there was a solid core of conscientious,
competent, and utterly reliable brigade and regimental commanders. Dan
Morgan and Henry Dearborn were standouts, with their tough fighting of
the nineteenth to back up their previous records of service about Boston
and on the march to Quebec. With them stood John Glover, with passage
of the East River and the Delaware behind him, and William Whipple
of New Hampshire, a signer of the Declaration of Independence. John
Fellows had brought a highly useful brigade of Massachusetts militia to
match the part-time soldiers from the Albany district—known to the

army as Albanians—who followed Abraham Ten Broeck. John Brooks of Massachusetts and Alexander Scammell of New Hampshire were to their regiments what the senior officers were to their brigades.

The matter of numbers was also soothing to Gates's mind. More than twenty-five hundred militia now ranged along Burgoyne's flank and rear. Directly under Gates's control were probably some seven thousand effectives. Of these, only about twenty-five hundred were Continentals, but the militia undoubtedly contained an important leaven of men who had served earlier in the war.

Another very strong card in Gates's hand was his military estimate of the opposing commander. Gentleman Johnny was an inveterate gambler and "perhaps his despair may dictate to him to risque all upon one throw," wrote Gates to Governor George Clinton of New York. "He is an old Gamester and in his time has seen all chances." This knowledge probably determined Gates to keep pressure on the invaders, but to wait for some desperate move on their part, to see if, in poker terms, the "Old Gamester" would put all his chips on the table while trying to draw to an inside straight. This psychology was sound.

Meanwhile, in the Anglo-German works, indecision was being fatally mixed with bewilderment. The alertness of the Americans and the tumbled, wooded terrain kept intelligence to a minimum. One German officer, more enterprising than most of his fellows, pushed out some thousand yards beyond his own lines in the hope of seeing at least something of the enemy, but saw nothing on his whole trip save the endless screen of bushes and undergrowth. In the ranks times were harder and harder for the men. Rations were cut and cut again. Scant food, lack of rest, and icy nights were reducing them to the point where sleep no longer restored them and food did not strengthen. Hangings for attempted desertion increased. Even officers felt the pinch and subalterns grumbled about paying one pound for a bottle of bad gin.

No news came from the south concerning Sir Henry Clinton's move. News did come from the north, and it was all bad. John Stark had suddenly resumed his private war with the Crown, issuing from the fastnesses of the Hampshire Grants and nobbling up the garrison at Fort Edward. Something had to be done. But what?

On October 7 the Baroness von Riedesel was up early. There was a busy day ahead of her, for she was to be hostess at dinner for Generals John Burgoyne, William Phillips, and Simon Fraser. The dinner was never given.

By noon Gentleman Johnny had launched his weirdest and least comprehensible move of the whole campaign, and fifteen hundred men, supported by the few remaining auxiliaries, stood waiting under the October sun among the golden stalks of a wheat field south of the Freeman clearings. On the right, covered by the auxiliaries, was the young Earl of Balcarres with his British light infantry and the 24th South Wales Borderers in their willow-green facings. The center was made up of a strange formation drawn seemingly at random from most of the German units.

On the left, at the edge of a steep slope, stood Major Acland with his British grenadiers.

The precise objective of this force is still vague. It was far too strong to be the "reconnaissance in force" that Burgoyne called it. It was far too weak, numerically, to mount a real assault. But there the contingent stood waiting under the intense blue of the fall sky with the valley trees ablaze about them. The Old Gamester had drawn his cards at random and was pushing out his chips without counting them.

Sometime after two o'clock the deluge broke in a series of heavy blows. Enoch Poor's brigade swept up the slope on the British left and smashed Acland's grenadiers. Far off to the right the dreaded turkey call began to gibber and gobble, and Morgan and Henry Dearborn struck in at Balcarres' rear. Against the center poured Ebenezer Learned's brigade, and the Germans sagged, rallied, then broke. The wheat field was thick with the rattle of musketry, and the long stalks hissed against running legs, were trampled to paste under heavy boots. Bullets keened through the soft air to rap with an endless hollow thudding against tree trunks.

Burgoyne, the baron, and Fraser tried to rally their units, some of whom preserved fair order, but riflemen high in the branches sent lead drilling after them. Burgoyne's hat and scarlet coat were ripped. The baron faced the deadly fire courageously but had to fall back with his Germans. Simon Fraser, toiling ceaselessly with Balcarres to re-form the light infantry and the Welsh Borderers, suddenly doubled up in the saddle, fatally shot through the belly by Rifleman Tim Murphy of Morgan's command. The rout was complete and Burgoyne's survivors streamed off toward the fortifications in the rear that had been built with so much labor during the weeks of waiting.

There were two fairly strong works in advance of the main line, the so-called Balcarres redoubt and the Breymann redoubt. Into the first poured the young earl and much of his command to strengthen the garrison that was already there. But the Germans thudded doggedly on over the rough ground, making blindly for the main works and leaving the bitter Von Breymann and his grenadier garrison unsupported.

The American pursuit was slow in getting under way but soon gained momentum. During or shortly after the wrecking of the Brunswickers in the center General Benedict Arnold had made his appearance in action, with no command of his own and entirely against orders. Bursting in among Learned's men, many of them from Connecticut like himself, he either urged them on or went along with them. But once before the redoubts, he unquestionably took charge. First he threw Learned's men against the Balcarres redoubt and met a more than hot reception, for the garrison, along with the light infantry and the 24th, fought back violently. The attack died out and Learned's command, along with men from other units, sheltered behind tree stumps and kept up a steady fire.

This type of fighting was too slow for Arnold, who swung over to his own left, cleared out the space between Balcarres and Von Breymann, and

316 FROM LEXINGTON TO LIBERTY

then hurled some of Morgan's men at the Germans. Many of Von Breymann's men fired a token volley into the air and then fled for the nearest
sally port. The rest were swept away by rushes that surged over the walls
and through unguarded gates. Von Breymann, in a black fury, turned
his sword against his own flying men in a last effort to check them. A
musket thudded and Von Breymann lay dead, shot down by some unknown Brunswick grenadier.

Through the autumn dusk, where muskets flashed red-orange, Arnold
rode his great bay horse through a sally port and into the works. A retreating
Jaeger fired, and the bay and the general crashed to the ground. The bay
was dead. Arnold was to be out of action for a long time, wounded once
more in the same leg that had been struck in the swirling blizzard about
Quebec and the Lower Town. When he next took the field it was against
his own people.

As for Benedict Arnold's final outburst in American uniform, it is rather
hard to see just what he had accomplished. It may be that he did actually
give the needed impetus to the attack on the center, back there in the
wheat field, or that he drove on the pursuit, though it does not seem that
Learned's men needed any leadership beyond what they had to begin with.
With both flanks and his center gone, Burgoyne was soundly beaten, his
army finished as a combat entity. Arnold's two bravura charges against the
redoubts—the first of which failed completely—seem only to have increased
American casualties, particularly since Von Breymann's men were apparently on the point of flight anyway. These two slashes at the redoubts
played no part whatsoever in the outcome of the day. As a further footnote
to Arnold's participation, Thomas Anburey, an eyewitness at the Balcarres
sector, places Arnold's wounding there and not at Von Breymann's. If the
gentleman volunteer reported correctly, Arnold's part shrinks still more.

Darkness and Gates's prim conservatism forbade further American action
in the blind tangle of the terrain, and most of the Anglo-Germans fell back
to the Great Ravine and the nearby works, probably stunned beyond
thought or even fear.

The god of war and the god of chance had totted up the results of Gentleman Johnny's last gamble and shown him the score. On the night of the
eighth, despite Germain's rigid orders to go to Albany, despite flamboyant
outbursts that "Britons never retreat," the remains of the army formed in
a pouring rain and began a perilously slow, lurching march north along
the Hudson, the Von Riedesel ladies following in the faithful calash. No
lights were shown; orders were given in a whisper. The men stumbled on
through the streaming night, trying to keep their thoughts away from the
crowded hospitals and their sick and wounded friends abandoned to the
enemy. They also tried not to think, as rain poured down brass-fronted
helmets or turned bearskin caps into sodden horrors, of the long train of
artillery that had been dragged so far, that had played so little part in the
campaign, and that still clanked and rumbled in the heart of the column.
If only those guns and caissons had been left behind, the wretched horses

could have been loaded with supplies from the bateaux and the army would not have been tied to the river and to the dead-slow movement of the clumsy craft. But Gentleman Johnny still clung to his guns. He also clung to his string of personal carts.

There were long halts that could have been fatal if Gates had been more active. When the march started, supply wagons sank hub-deep in the mud and had to be abandoned. In the dark hours, shots, cries, exultant whoops came from the river, and the spent, marching men could tell themselves that wandering rebel patrols had snapped up another bateau loaded with priceless supplies. The sixty-odd miles to Ticonderoga and safety stretched away, endless.

At Saratoga, Gentleman Johnny made a beeline for Philip Schuyler's country house, the same that Thomas Anburey had so admired away back in early September, now seeming a lifetime ago. The baron, Phillips, and others urged Burgoyne to keep going, to get across the little Fish Creek to high, easily defended grounds. Pressure on the British rear, where the remains of the grenadiers held on doggedly, was increasing. Time was wasting. The baroness fumed over the delay and wrote home that Burgoyne spent his nights "in singing and drinking and amusing himself with the wife of a commissary, who was his mistress, and who, as well as he, loved champagne."

Not till the tenth did the army cross Fish Creek, where it dug in by a deep elbow bend of the creek not far from its junction with the Hudson. But Gates was moving too. On the eleventh and twelfth Morgan and Learned were over Fish Creek. Gates held his main body on the south side of the creek. British sentries could peer out, if they cared to face the incessant musket and rifle fire from the enemy, and see John Fellows' Massachusetts militia just across the Hudson. The route to the north, via Fort Edward and its fords, was still open, they thought. But on the thirteenth the twisting road on the west bank of the Hudson was suddenly crawling with skirmishers and the higher lands beyond were thick with deft-moving columns. John Stark, ever unpredictable, had slammed the last escape door. The curtain had come down on the final act of Gentleman Johnny's tragedy. There remained only the brief epilogue, to be spoken among the glowing leaves of the autumnal trees.

Horatio Gates opened negotiations with Burgoyne, beginning with rather sweeping terms. Then the victor's temper underwent a change that the beaten command could not grasp. Actually it was caused by the un-pleasant news of Clinton's tardy move up the Hudson that involved the American loss of Fort Montgomery and the burning of Esopus, now Kings- ton, on the Hudson. Gates need not have been alarmed, since the hostile stroke petered out far below Albany. His terms were accepted by Burgoyne, who held out on only one very minor but highly typical point. The docu-ment to be signed should not be called "The Capitulation of Saratoga." The word offended Gentleman Johnny's sensitive literary ear and he substituted the more sonorous title, "The Convention of Saratoga," and until the end of the war released the prisoners they were known as "The Convention Troops."

The terms were generous, owing probably to Gates's fear of Clinton rather than heart-warming magnanimity on his part. Arms and equipment were to be turned over to the Americans, with some exceptions, and the whole contingent was, under the convention, to be marched to Boston to await transportation to England in British bottoms. Of course they would never fight again. Or so said the solemn pact.

With the signing a fearful hassle was hatched. First of all, Gates far exceeded his powers in negotiating the surrender and in giving terms. In his place, Washington would at once have deferred to the Congress, as the treatment and disposition of the defeated army lay in the province of that body. But Gates was not Washington and sailed gaily ahead as though he were a chief of state. For another thing, the Boston area was set aside as the indefinite home of several thousand beaten troops, nearly half of them alien, a term which cannot be applied to British troops in America. The Massachusetts authorities were not consulted, were given very little time to provide facilities and accommodations for these Convention Troops. Suffering and hard feelings were to result. Then again, His Majesty's Government was not asked if it had the tonnage available for the final transfer to England. And since Burgoyne, a mere commander of a subsidiary force in the field, had signed for the Crown, it would have been only too easy for a minister of Germain's rather dubious standards to repudiate the whole transaction and ship the troops back to the American theater of operations. Congress, too, was not legally bound to back up Gates and certainly did not appear to advantage in its treatment of the prisoners.

So the unfortunate convention troops languished in Cambridge and Rutland in Massachusetts until the late fall of 1778, when they were shipped overland on a frightful march that took them to the Charlottesville area in Virginia. There they stayed until 1781, when many of them were shifted into Maryland and Pennsylvania to wait out the last shadows of war.

While in Cambridge the troops were sent into delirious joy by the actual arrival of British transports off Boston, ready to take them to England. In a blow that seemed needlessly cruel the transports were turned back by the American authorities, on the loudly expressed belief that Sir Henry Clinton really planned to transship the convention army to New York to add to his own force there. For years this belief has been held up as one further proof of the essential meanness of the Congress, of their oaf-like inability to accept assurances on the part of a gentleman like Sir Henry Clinton that there was no thought of such a base act on his part. Unfortunately the Clinton papers, made available for research during recent years, show clearly that that was precisely what the British High Command planned to do. The transports were to load in Boston and then head directly for New York.

But all this lay in the future. The immediate moment was October 17, 1777. The Anglo-German troops formally laid down their arms close by the grass-grown ruins of an old fort built by Baron Dieskau, a Saxon general in the French service, in the 1750s. This ceremony of stacking arms was a very touchy one in the eighteenth century, another of the interminable points of "military honor" that confused thought in and out of action. To glide past this sore spot, Gates ordered (and deserves a bright mark for his thought, whatever its motive) that no Americans were to be present during the stacking.

The two generals met, with Horatio Gates gravely gracious in unadorned republican blue and Gentleman Johnny in his very brightest scarlet and glossiest white, topped with a fantastically plumed hat. British and Germans noted that Burgoyne seemed actually to be enjoying himself, as though he were acting out the part of a heroic, vanquished chieftain in one of his plays. He bowed to Gates. "The fortune of war, General Gates, has made me your prisoner." Gates returned a sweeping bow. "I shall always be ready to bear testimony that it has not been through any fault of your Excellency."

Then the pair, theatrically side by side, reviewed the passage of that army, now weaponless, that had started up Champlain in a dazzle of scarlet and blue and brass. The British troops were sullen and silent. They never did make good prisoners and all through their captivity were as self-assertive and cantankerous as the most arrant Yankee. The Germans passed by, docile, as they were to be until their final release. Panache could hardly have been expected from them, at least so far as the men in the ranks were concerned. Virtually shanghaied by their ruler, shipped off to a distant war that in no way concerned them and which they could not understand, looked down upon by their allies, deprived of credit where credit was due, a prey to an almost psychopathic homesickness, they accepted defeat as stolidly as they would have taken victory. Indeed, barring the possible chance for individual loot, defeat or victory was the same and merely meant an end to campaigning.

So these lost, homesick thousands forded the Fish Creek on their way to surrender. As a possible unconscious and pathetic effort to stake out some kind of claim in this alien land, they lugged with them, unlike the British, uncounted numbers of forest pets. Young deer minced daintily along by the companies, secured by light collars and leashes. Bear cubs matched their pigeon-toed shuffle to the weary swing of gaitered legs. Foxes glided close by their masters and imp-faced raccoons perched on loaded knapsacks. These were the sole, and pitiful, spoils of the campaign.

There must have been a moment of shock to the British as well as to the Germans when they came upon the ordered ranks of Gates's army, when they marched past Morgan's men or John Glover's or Ten Broeck's Albanians. They had seen the Americans before, but rarely en masse. There had been clusters of cowed prisoners, scattering waves of fugitives drifting toward the nearest cover, or half-seen patrols. The forests had spilled wide waves of Yankees out into clearings, and cannon smoke had thinned to reveal riflemen shifting position.

Now the haze of war was gone and they looked on line after endless line of the men who, with the powerful aid of the wilderness, had beaten them. Some marchers felt they they were looking on a new and strange race. There were many old men, brought out by the call for militia. There were boys still a year or two away from the razor, and there were Negroes standing in rank as free men. Much of the clothing looked antiquated, a little more than rustic, to European eyes. Wigs seemed huge and oddly shaped. And what sort of an army was it where a uniformed officer was a rarity?

But there were other things to notice. A century and more of different living conditions and diet had bred a taller race. Faces, the Germans noted, were lean, as lean as the rangy bodies. Paunches were very few. Coats might be shabby, but muskets were well cared for.

And there was the silence, broken only by the wail of the British field music playing "Yankee Doodle" far ahead. Many of the British officers had dreaded being marched through a jeering, undisciplined mob which might hurl clods and stones as well as barbed taunts. But the American ranks were impassive, motionless, even among the most haphazard militia levies. This silence was ordered by Gates, to match his gesture in allowing the defeated army to stack arms out of sight, and it is greatly to his credit. And the order was carried out by thousands of men who could have had no trouble remembering the blastingly scornful adjectives applied to them by these same men in scarlet and blue and green. Such compliance was even more to their credit.

Sometime after the passage of the troops a solid calash with a waterproof cover rocked out of the old German lines, bearing the Von Riedesel ladies, with Lena and Rockel, into captivity. A revelation awaited the determined little baroness. "In the passage through the American camp," she wrote, "I observed with great satisfaction that no one cast us scornful glances. On the contrary, they all greeted me, even showing compassion in their countenances. . . . When I approached the tents, a noble looking man came toward me, took the children out of the wagon, embraced and kissed them, and then, with tears in his eyes he helped me also to alight. 'You tremble' he said to me, 'fear nothing.' 'No,' replied I, 'for you are so kind and have been so tender toward my children, that it has inspired me with courage.' "

The baroness was taken to Gates's tent by her rescuer and there found Gentleman Johnny sharing ecstasies of flamboyance with Horatio Gates, victor and vanquished being in the highest of spirits. Then her guide said, " 'It may be embarrassing to you to dine with all these gentlemen; come now with your children into my tent, where I will give you, it is true, a frugal meal, but one that will be accompanied by the best of wishes.' 'You are certainly,' answered I, 'a husband and a father, since you show me so much kindness.' I then learned that he was the American General SCHUYLER."

It is good to remember that his hospitality followed the family to Albany, where the Schuyler town house was put at their disposal, and from it the baron and the baroness started off with the calash on their long journey to Cambridge, where Riedesel Avenue still perpetuates their name.

News of the convention hopped erratically along the American seaboard, more slowly across the Atlantic. Horatio Gates snatched up a pen and wrote, almost boyishly exultant, to Mrs. Gates down in Virginia. "Dear Mabby: The voice of fame, ere this reaches you, will tell how greatly fortunate we have been in this department. Burgoyne and his whole army have laid down their arms and surrendered themselves to me and my Yankees." Figuratively lapping his chops, he listed the various titles included in his bag, as well as their connections by birth or marriage. Then somewhat vindictively he concluded, "If Old England is not by this lesson taught humility, then she is an obstinate old Slut, bent upon her ruin."

Gates also seems to have placed much reliance on that same "voice of fame" which he mentioned to Mrs. Gates to inform other interested people, but in one most important instance he failed to reinforce that voice with a confirming letter. No longer boyish, but with his ever present streak of pettifogging meanness uppermost, and possibly dazzled by visions of weaseling into the Supreme Command and even a dictatorship, he utterly neglected to report to Washington. The latter learned by accident of Burgoyne's final disaster nearly two weeks after the surrender and was properly shocked. Yet he had the greatness of spirit to write Gates a letter of congratulation on the "signal success." And his rebuke was probably as mild a one as any commanding general ever wrote under such circumstances. "I cannot but regret that a matter of such magnitude and so interesting to our general operations, should have reached me by report only, or through the channel of letters, not bearing that authenticity, which the importance of it required, and which it would have received by a line under your signature, stating the simple fact." It is a further measure of Gates that he did all he could to prevent and then delay the dispatch of his no-longer-needed forces to the main army.

Gentleman Johnny's failure became known in England by slow degrees. Horace Walpole, no admirer of Burgoyne, noted in early November that "Arnold has beaten the vaporing Burgoyne." In this he was undoubtedly relying on rumor traveling the route Ticonderoga–Quebec–London. His crediting Arnold with the victory is interesting, though it in no way backs up the claims made by and for Arnold. Rumor kept on rumbling, and awkward questions were being put to Germain in both Houses.

Definite news was in by December 2, and the reception, in at least one case, was startling. In the town of Frome in ultra-English Somersetshire the happy villagers "made great rejoicing" under the firm impression that Gentleman Johnny, with his Norman-French surname, was a French general, subdued by some proper Briton.

Under attack Germain wove and twisted and side-stepped. He may well have felt as he had in that court-martial in 1760 when old Colonel Sloper was pointing at him as the coward of Minden. But Germain probably did not worry too much. He had a very thick skin, was solidly entrenched in the party in power, and, although the phrase did not exist then, knew very well in principle that "the buck is passed down, never up." Burgoyne, not Germain, must do the explaining.

CHAPTER XXIV

". . . you might have tracked the army . . . by the blood of their feet"

ON October 12, 1777, the Delaware River from Chester, below Philadelphia, down to Newcastle and Reedy Island was thick with ships flying the British colors. Admiral "Black Dick" Howe had brought his warships and transports to the very spot where they might have landed Brother William's troops in early August instead of at Head of Elk, far up Chesapeake Bay.

And the British fleet and army were faced with another task that would have been far easier had an August attack been made. Sir William had to feed his army now that he had finally brought it to Philadelphia. He must have felt qualms as he looked over what maps he had and noted that most of the roads that led from the rich interior and over which his supplies must come were peculiarly vulnerable to blocking and raiding by those scarecrow rebel formations that had no military right to exist. However, a good part of their nuisance value could be canceled if the Delaware were opened from Philadelphia to the sea.

With the fleet at hand, the problem seemed easy. The channel was obstructed by chevaux-de-frise, notably at Billingsport and at Hog Island, the latter destined to rise from muddy oblivion to fame as a shipbuilding center in two twentieth-century wars. Just beyond Hog Island lay a horrible tract of muck, flattered by the name of Mud Island and crowned by ill-sited Fort Mifflin. On the Jersey side of the channel at Red Bank (now a National Park), Fort Mercer commanded the river. Above all these works were a few small American armed ships.

The chevaux-de-frise went easily enough, but there was serious trouble with the two forts. Mercer was held by Colonel Christopher Greene, Nathanael's cousin and a veteran of the march to Quebec. With him were some four hundred seasoned Rhode Island Continentals and the young Chevalier de Mauduit du Plessis, who had made that starkly cold-blooded attempt to fire the Chew house at Germantown with John Laurens. Du Plessis was a trained engineer and made some last-minute changes in the fortifications. The blow was struck by Graf von Donop and some two thousand Hessians, seemingly an extravagant force to use against Mercer. But the Rhode Islanders were steady, Greene's leadership was inspired, and Du Plessis' changes led the Hessians into blind ditches and the attackers finally withdrew. They lost nearly four hundred men—the strength of the garrison—and among them was Von Donop, shot down between ditch and parapet.

Fort Mifflin was brought under fire from land and sea after an unaccountable lapse of over two weeks, and for five days it underwent a savage bombardment. Colonel Samuel Smith, late of Smallwood's Marylanders, was in command with Major Simeon Thayer of Rhode Island, who took over later when Smith was wounded. The fort was battered to pieces. Nearly two hundred and fifty American casualties were incurred, but it was not until darkness fell over the Delaware on November 15 that Thayer and his survivors slipped away to Fort Mercer, which was soon after abandoned by Greene and Du Plessis. The Delaware was now British from Philadelphia to the sea, but over one month had been dribbled away by the British command and Smith, Thayer, Greene, and Du Plessis had written another chapter on American capabilities for Howe and Cornwallis to read.

Militarily the year was over. In early December, Sir William Howe stirred himself and took the road to the northwest with the bulk of his army in one last attempt to lure Washington into a formal battle. The two armies came into contact at Whitemarsh, out the same road beyond Germantown down which Washington's men had marched to their potential success in October. There were some firing, desultory skirmishing, and then Howe tramped his men home to Philadelphia. More days had been wasted, more supplies and munitions consumed. And the American army still lived.

Since the Germantown fight, Washington's force had grown appreciably. He could now count up some eleven thousand effectives, of which over eight thousand were Continentals. From the north had come General James Varnum of Rhode Island with his brigade. Horatio Gates had reluctantly released some of his Saratoga victors, and into Washington's camp poured John Glover's brigade, minus its leader, for the tough, stocky Marbleheader had been assigned the duty of seeing that Gentleman Johnny and all his men reached the Boston area. John Paterson brought in his Massachusetts command. Henry Dearborn and Daniel Morgan were back with the main army, the echoes of the Freeman clearings still loud in their ears.

But much of this strength was illusory. Enlistments, particularly those of the Maryland and Virginia men, were due to expire, and the clouds of utter dissolution that had hovered over the Morristown camps the year before rolled up even more heavily. Brandywine, Germantown, and the succession of subsequent skirmishings had gnawed away at the equipment of every soldier. Clothes were more than ever a festooned mass of tatters. Two and sometimes three men shared the same riddled, threadbare blanket. Immobilization through lack of shoes was becoming alarming. On one occasion a call was sent to Morgan's rifle corps for outpost duty. Out of the six or seven hundred men present, less than two hundred could march. Pressed as the army was for hard money, Washington offered a prize of ten real dollars to the man who could devise some acceptable "substitute for shoes, made of raw hides."

The states were not helping intelligently. The nation was still too young to grasp the idea of a common pool of supplies. Patrick Henry sent up a load of clothing, not for general distribution but for the Virginia troops alone. Most other states acted as narrowly. The old days when South Carolina shipped money and supplies to New England, when Long Island farmers drove herds over the road to Boston, seemed forgotten, out of date.

It was an over-all shortage, and no one military item seems to have been in better supply than another. Rations were as scarce as shirts. Yankee Henry Dearborn wrote sorrowfully in his diary: "This is Thanksgiving Day . . . but God knows we have very little to keep it with, this being the third day we have been without flour or bread, and are living on a high, un-cultivated hill, in huts and tents, lying on the cold ground." Then he re-flected sturdily: "Upon the whole I think all we have to be thankful for is that we are alive and not in the grave with many of our friends." Sergeant Ebenezer Wild spoke for the enlisted men's "poor thanksgiving—nothing but fresh beef [he probably means freshly slaughtered beef] and flour to eat, without any salt, and but very scant of that."

It was not that food was lacking. But poor organization, transport diffi-culties, the tendency of many potential suppliers to hoard for their own use, to keep a watchful eye on the black market—as some Americans did from 1941 to 1945—sealed up the end of what might have been a horn of plenty. Washington still had a fairly free hand for commandeering, a measure that revolted him. But now he had to act. He told George Read of Delaware to buy when he could, but if people refused to sell provable surpluses, seize them. And Read was to watch out for "unfriendly Quakers and others notoriously disaffected" and bear down on them. However, "obtaining these things from Quakers and disaffected inhabitants is recommended, but at all events get them." The wretched trickle increased negligibly.

As the army was the implementation of the will of many Americans, so the Congress was the expression of that will. Like the army, the Congress in late 1777 still held together somehow, dreamed up ambitious plans, made blunders, acted heroically, acted pettily, quarreled internally and sectionally, interfered with the army, sometimes with the very best intent, often nar-rowly. Comfortably lodged at York, it was not popular with the troops. It has been an easy and favored target for later historical snipings. But it held together, struggled along through the inevitable cloud of human error, never quite sure what its true powers were, often bewildered by the exasper-ating disregard with which, one time or another, each of the thirteen states shrugged off the rulings of its own elected delegates.

Yet in the dark year of 1777, lightened only by victory over Burgoyne, the Congress came up with one vitally important matter of finished busi-ness. Since the very earliest days of association there had been no clear-cut concept of just what that association really meant. Men spoke of the "new nation." But was it that? Were not the states actually political entities, loosely allied with one another? Many men thought so, felt that they were participating in a league of states, not in a single leagued state, that Massachusetts was in alliance with Delaware and North Carolina with Pennsylvania.

As far back as June 1776, Richard Henry Lee of Virginia had sought a solution, proposing that "a plan of confederation be prepared and transmitted to the respective colonies for their consideration and approbation." A committee to draw up "Articles of Confederation and Perpetual Union" was set up under Farmer John Dickinson. The question was sheer dynamite, and more discreet and less devoted men might well have ducked it. State-minded men in every colony howled that in even considering such a step the delegates were far exceeding the powers granted them. In committee and in meetings of the whole Congress the vital question was gnawed at, worried, growled over. At last, on November 15, 1777, the Articles of Confederation were adopted and sent on to the various states for ratification, which did not come completely until the spring of 1781.

These Articles were makeshift. They dodged and side-stepped issue after burning issue but somehow held to a general course—"Perpetual Union." Most powers were vested in the states themselves, not in the Congress, for "each State retains its sovereignty, freedom and independence, and every power, jurisdiction, and right which is not by this confederation expressly delegated to the United States in Congress assembled." This left the Congress dependent on the collective will of the states. It could declare war but could not wage war unless each member state backed it. It could borrow money but was given no source of revenue to pay it back. The Congress could not levy taxes. It could only requisition money from the states but could not demand it. In brief, the Congress was authorized to ask for anything that it thought necessary and the states were empowered to slap down any request they saw fit.

Weak and unworkable as those Articles were, they were like a mash that ferments slowly, undergoing chemical changes that are almost imperceptible but ever present. Out of them finally came the Constitution of the United States of America. Without them, or a reasonable facsimile thereof, there might have been no Constitution and hence no nation. They were the first hesitant step toward the unity that was to come, the unity that was to bend under countless unseen stresses and strains down to the present day, to bend and always spring back.

This done, most members of Congress scattered to their respective states. By December a bare score of delegates were in York, and of that twenty-odd only Eliphalet Dyer of Connecticut and James Duane of New York had service that dated back to fateful 1775. This handful, then, was a very raw and green expression of the will of America. Newcomers, they had seen little, if anything, of the commander-in-chief or of the army that was the implementation of that will.

That army was under heavy pressure again, but from its own Congress and not from Sir William Howe. That gentleman seemed content to bask in the comforts of Philadelphia, letting his forces enjoy such embers as might glow out from the hearth of the High Command. Washington was obviously too weak to attack, and winter quarters were in order. But just where the quarters should be located brought civilians baying and bawling. The army should move into Delaware, south of Howe; it should take post in the Jerseys, in western Pennsylvania, or along the Hudson. Many men feared British and particularly Hessian depredations if Washington moved away from their particular area. Doubtless some claimants had a shrewd eye on the profits accruing to the inhabitants of an American-occupied district, though with national credit low as it was, this could hardly have been a determining factor.

Military men had their own ideas, and the final site was an obvious compromise, with all the weaknesses inherent in such give-and-take.

Twenty-odd miles to the west and a little north of Philadelphia the Schuylkill ambles pleasantly along on a generally east-west course, dipping a little to receive the waters of Valley Creek as the lesser stream flows up from the south. East of the creek the ground rises rapidly to a height of some two hundred and fifty feet and straightens out into a rolling two-mile plateau, which was quite heavily wooded in 1777.

There was little to orient this plateau angle formed by creek and river. It was north of the spot called Paoli, where Wayne had been so bloodily surprised in September. There was a ford across the Schuylkill leading north to an area so rich that early settlers had called it the Fat Lands of Egypt and the crossing was still known as Fatland—or Fatlands—Ford. The chief feature was an old forge on the ravine-like creek, and hence the Valley Forge was as good an aiming point for a traveler as any other.

Toward this angle and plateau, as mid-December sharpened and powdery snow began to sift through pine and oak branches, headed the army of the United States.

The choice of Valley Forge as winter quarters for this slowly shredding army has been hammered about unmercifully. Some have pointed out the advantages of the plateau, with its fine observation point covering the lower lands to the east, the terrain over which an attack would probably come. Flanks could be supported by creek and river, and the roads, for the period and area, were good enough for maneuver or retreat, especially if shallow Fatland Ford were bridged. Others saw it as a deathtrap. Major General Baron Johann de Kalb filled his powerful lungs and let out a roar of protest. "The idea of wintering in this desert can only have been put into the head of the commanding general by an interested speculator or a disaffected man," he fulminated. The dismay of General James Varnum of Rhode Island sprinted alongside that of the baron. "I have from the beginning viewed this situation with horror! It is unparalleled in the history of mankind to establish winter-quarters in a country wasted and without a single magazine [supply center]." Thomas Anburey, passing through with the convention troops, Virginia-bound, in 1778, saw the abandoned site and thought that a relatively small force could have bottled up the American army quite easily and forced a surrender. But, pro or con, the choice had been made.

It was only thirteen miles, a good day's march from Whitemarsh, the last permanent camp to Valley Forge, but those miles stretched away before the forlorn army until they covered a week. Baggage wagons with most of the tents and heavier equipment had gone astray. Snow fell, changed to sleet, to rain, and the soldiers huddled in what shelter woods could afford. The temperature slid down the thermometer, and the bare morasses called roads froze stone-hard with knife-edge ruts to slice viciously at rag-bound feet. The tentage arrived, but the roads had to soften a little before a real march could be made. Softening is relative. When the main army did push on, the ghastly stenciling of Trenton was repeated and Washington said that "you might have tracked the army . . . to Valley Forge by the blood of their feet."

On the afternoon of December 19 the columns saw ahead of them the upsloping plateau, crowned at its western end by a conical hill bristly with trees. If any of the marchers knew the hill's name, their being on Mount Joy might have struck them as ironical.

Already engineers moved, dotlike, staking out lines for the camps of the different units. But most of the soldiers were beyond caring. They staggered to their appointed places, lit campfires, and huddled about them in fathomless apathy. There was nothing but bleak wilderness about them. For rations they had only the scanty scraps left in their haversacks, and there was no stir or bustle about the quartermaster's wagons. Even the fires were a doubtful comfort. Wet, broken shoes that edged too close to the flames and coals would soon dry, shrivel, and split. Carefully wrapped rags might char and char until the whole foot bandage fell away. Yet there is no record of shattered men slipping away through the dense mask of trees on this nineteenth of December.

And so the army of the United States began its winter, a winter, as the late Christopher Ward wrote, "whose story has been told and told again, but not once too often."

There were days of huddling under tents whose worn fabric only filtered the northwest winds that swept the plateau and the narrow valley of the creek, whose pegs pulled out of the frozen ground and let dank canvas fall on the sodden inmates. You can trace the very lines of the tents today, following the careful markers along slope and plateau and even down the sides of the steep valley to the creek below. Markers and names are worth looking at, increasingly worth looking at as the country they helped build speeds through rougher and rougher times. Here at the east end is where Parson Muhlenberg camped, his black robes and white pulpit forgotten in his new congregation of four enduring Virginia regiments. Did sturdy "Joe Gourd" Weedon think of his comfortable Fredericksburg tavern as he saw his present guests, the 2nd, 6th, 10th and 14th Virginia staring hollow-eyed at the road over which supply wagons would—might—someday come?

There are Paterson's Massachusetts men beyond Weedon, and more Bay
Staters with Ebenezer Learned joining on. Perhaps the echoes of that rush
on the German center in the Hudson River wheat field, of the roar and
clatter about the abatis of the Balcarres redoubt, came down on the north
wind to sweep over their tents and spread the old, never-forgotten sounds
to their neighbors, John Glover's men.

So the roster goes. Enoch Poor and Anthony Wayne; William Woodford
and more Virginians by Mount Joy; Lachlan McIntosh and his North
Carolinians down by the Schuylkill, and John Sullivan near Fatland Ford.
No battle was fought here. Nothing very much happened. Men simply
endured here, kept alive here and, by living and enduring, kept the army
that was the instrument of their cause alive. And in this there is a deep
glory.

Tents could not be used through a whole Pennsylvania winter, and orders
went out from the very first day that huts were to be built, conforming to
an exact pattern. And the materials for such huts? There it was, growing
along the plateau, down by creek and river, so details of axmen went out,
felled the trees, split them into boards. The work would have gone more
rapidly had there been more axes, but there was no great supply depot to
fill requisitions for hundreds of blades and helves. Plank by plank the huts
went up, fourteen by sixteen feet for the ground plan, six and a half feet
high, steep slab roofs, cat-and-clay chimneys, and slab doors. The work
would have gone more rapidly had there been more nails, more hammers.
And it would have gone more rapidly had men not staggered as they swung
an ax against a trunk or kneaded clay to stop up the chinks in the walls. Yet
the hut city grew to at least partial completion and at last the commander-
in-chief felt free to leave his tent not far from the east bank of Valley
Creek and move into the gray fieldstone house close by the junction of the
creek and the Schuylkill.

For endless days food was a haunting nightmare that always hovered back
of the eyes of any man in authority, whether he commanded a division or a
squad. On the twenty-first a small issue of salt pork was made to some of
the brigades. Then the flow dried up. Empty bellies spread the infection
of mutiny, an odd, typically American mutiny where regiment after regiment took up a dull, monotonous chant that drummed across the plateau
and funneled down narrow Valley Creek, an endless rhythmic chant of "No
meat! No meat!" But still desertions were few.

There were other plagues almost as dangerous as starvation. Soap was
as rare as meat, and bruised, split feet became infected. Foul rags worn next
to the skin set up an itch that only soap and water could cure. Camp
fevers spread. Some of the huts, for lack of proper nails or tools to shape
pegs, were built partly underground, and their sunless, damp interiors
hastened the work of infection and disease.

Dr. Albigensis Waldo, surgeon to the 1st Connecticut of Jedediah Hun-
tington's brigade, had been in the field since April 1775 and must have been
well hardened to what campaigning could do. Yet he was moved enough by

what he saw to enter a vivid description of a probably typical man in his journal: "There comes a soldier, his bare feet are seen thro' his worn-out shoes, his legs nearly naked from the tattered remains of an only pair of stockings, his Breeches not sufficient to cover his nakedness, his Shirt hanging in Strings, his hair dishevell'd, his face meagre; his whole appearance pictures a person forsaken & discouraged. He comes and cries with an air of wretchedness and despair, I am Sick, my feet lame, my legs are sore, my body covered with this tormenting Itch."

There was even a shortage of water in the Valley Forge camp. The plateau held no springs, and it was a weary, disheartening chore for one, say, of Joe Gourd's men to limp a mile or more with a heavy bucket, fill it at the creek, and lurch back to camp with it. And for the start at least, there seems to have been no system of water discipline set up. A letter writer complained sadly that the "warter we had to Drink and to mix our flower with was out of a brook that run along by the Camps, and so many a dippin and washin in it which maid it very Dirty and muddy."

Ingenuity helped a little. John Sullivan's men down by the Schuylkill found beds of fresh-water clams and mussels and, barefoot, trod them out of the mud during thaws. Nathanael Greene, who came of a highly practical family, evolved what he called a "firmity" of wheat and sugar, possibly in paste or dried cake form. It might, he thought, be a very good substitute for meat. How successful the firmity was is not told, but there is no record of it in the Greene diet after Valley Forge.

Some food trickled through, over and above the scant issues that kept life alive, in time for Christmas, and Surgeon Waldo rejoiced at tasting mutton and grog again. But for long periods flour—which the men baked into a sort of hardtack—and frozen potatoes made up the bulk of diet.

Clothing was going fast. Officers mounted guard in old, padded dressing gowns or in blankets slung poncho-wise. Money, if a soldier or officer had any, was of little use. Colonel John Laurens, a wealthy man, sadly watched his last pair of breeches disintegrate, and Surgeon Waldo took darning lessons from the adjutant of the 1st Connecticut. The men were far worse off. Observers saw a guard standing his post properly and presenting arms smartly while standing on his hat to keep his nearly bare feet out of the snow.

And yet there was plenty of food available and there were clothes, or at least cloth from which clothes could be made. Any real flow, however, was bottlenecked by a system of procurement and purchase that almost amounted to genius in its inefficiency. And there were the teamsters. Most of these were civilians, organized and farmed out by civilian wagonmasters. They were probably more unthinking than conscienceless, but it often happened that to lighten a load the teamster would drain the brine from a barrel of salt beef, with quick spoilage resulting. Others were given wrong destinations and dumped priceless grain sacks into empty, muddy fields to spoil. Here and there drivers merely became fed up with a mired hitch and dumped what they carried by the roadside. Lacking grain and hay, the artillery and cavalry horses died off quickly and it began to look as though the army might become completely immobilized. There was, however, surprisingly little hijacking.

Regimental orderly books of bygone wars are apt to make dull reading. In them some officer on duty at regimental headquarters, usually a lieutenant, laboriously copied down the orders sent to his unit from higher echelons—from brigade, from division, and from army—as well as those orders issued by his own colonel and applying to the regiment only. There are no explanations, no amplifications or illuminating asides, the barest possible bones of military routine.

But when such books are read between the lines of fading, often awkward script, when they are read against a background of known happenings and conditions, they become vividly alive.

Here, for example, is the orderly book of the 2nd Virginia for the Valley Forge period, a small, tattered pocket-size book opening from bottom to top. Its thick, softish brown cover is scored with flourishes and doodles, with practice signatures that show how a succession of lieutenants in a hut among the bare dogwood trees tried out the nibs of fresh quill pens.

The 2nd formed part of George Weedon's brigade, stationed next to Peter Muhlenberg's at the east end of the army line. Since October 1777 it had had a new colonel whose name we have noted back in pre-war Boston. His men called him "Old Denmark," Christian Febiger, the quiet, capable, steadfast Dane of Breed's Hill and the march to Quebec. The opening page of the orderly book kept for Febiger by his juniors is captioned "Head Qr. Valley Forg Jany 8, 1778" and begins by stating that the "Major Genl. for to morrow" is the "Marques La.Fait." Later on, one B. D. Calb is named, obviously the explosive Baron de Kalb.

The first entry records that eight men from every brigade in the army "are to parrade to morrow Morning 9 OClock percisely," or, in modern terms, to "fall in." There is nothing illuminating here, nor is there in a following specification: "Such men are to be Selected as know how to Thresh and that are in full health." But other records show that large quantities of stored, unthreshed grain had been found in the neighborhood, and this must have been the detail that spent a week preparing the grain for milling and subsequent issue to the army. The "full health" item shows that such a condition could not be taken for granted. And the whole entry helps refute a charge often made that Washington and his men were pretty supine at this period and did not exert themselves to explore possible sources of supply.

The next lines run through this book and subsequent ones like a rubber stamp. "The Comder in Chief is informed that gaming is again Creeping into Camp . . . he therefore in a most Solemn terms declare that this Vice . . . Shall not when detected escape Escemplary Punishment." This was an unending and unsuccessful war that Washington fought stubbornly. The all-prevalent "Itch" that Surgeon Waldo noted came in for action: "he

Orders and directs the regtl. Surgeons to Look attentively into this matter & as soon as the men who are infected with this disorder are properly disposed in Hutts to have them Anointed."

Later some resourceful officer has found the means for improving camp cookery a little and "The Brigade Qr.Masters are to attend to morrow for the Iron Ovens for their Brigades." This is a small thing, but at least some of the troops will no longer have to bake their hardtack, or "fire-cake" as it was then called, on hot stones by an open fire. Health should improve.

There is a continual coming and going of bodies of troops for outpost duty. They will watch for signs of British activity, hold up civilians trying to slip down into Philadelphia to sell forbidden produce in that rich cash market, and sometimes clash with British patrols. "A Detachment of 300 men are to parrade at 9 OClock to morrow morning . . . to relieve Colo. Morgan's [Rifle] Corps prepared for a weeks Comd." (Comd—Command—in modern terms, "detail.")

The shortage of soap has been mentioned, and steps are taken to remedy that. Certain officers are to "fix upon a plan for collecting the dirty tallow & saving the ashes for the purpose of making soap." Leather, whether in shoes or cartridge boxes, needs attention and so officers are to employ "proper persons to boil the oil out of the feet of the bullocks & preserve it . . . this Oil to be put in casks & delivered to the Qr. M. Genl." In other words, neat's-foot oil is being manufactured and the mention of hoofs shows that some fresh beef is coming in for the troops. There must be no wastage of any part of the slaughtered animals. "The Commy. [commissaries] are therefore directed to spare the Head and pluck together & the Qr.M. are to see the different Compy. [companies] draw it in turn." "Pluck" was an over-all term for the livers, kidneys, heart, etc.

Something in the way of supply is obviously coming in to Valley Forge, but not enough to keep the more desperate soldiers—or those serving under inefficient supply officers—from foraging on their own. "The numerous Instances of peaceable Inhabitants being plundered & grossly abused . . . demand the severest examples . . . no mercy should be shown the Offender."

Soapmaking is on the agenda again and each officer "is to See that his men carry the ashes of each Hutt to a particular spot . . . where a Covering is to be erected that will keep them dry."

The all-important shoes are still posing a problem and it is ordered "That the Brigadiers on the present Exegency send an Officer . . . into the Country to exchang Hides for shoes, Hides at 4d a pound & shoes at 10s the pair." This seems to be an essay into pure barter and must have been typical of many transactions during the war.

Young Captain Henry Lee of Virginia has been down into the plains with his cavalry, the genesis of the later famed "Lee's Legion," and the captain would be celebrated in the near future as "Light-Horse Harry" Lee. The pen strokes in Old Denmark's orderly book seem firmer and blacker as the unidentified duty officer records that "The Commr. in Chief returns his warmest thanks to Capt. Lee and the Officers and men in his troop for the victory . . . gained over a part of the Enemies Dragoons, who Trusting in their Numbers & Concealing their March by a Circuitous Rout Attempted to Supprize them in their Qrs." But after this entry the "Commr. in Chief" takes a sharper tone and "positively forbids the Burnings of the farmers fences Enjoins Itt on all Officers to Use their Indeavours to bring to severe punishment those that shall Offend therein." Almost identical orders can be found in the books of nearly every Civil War general, Union or Confederate. "You've got to remember," Major General Melville Goodwin, U.S.A., said in effect, "that troops are always troops."

Late in January cloth came into the camps in thick bolts. At once brigade orders stated that "Taylors of each Regt to be excused from other duty & to be employed in making up the Cloths of their respective Regts." And Colonel Febiger echoes this in the next paragraph, calling on all company commanders "immediately to make a return of all the Taylors in their respective companies."

Brigade sutlers were appointed to sell liquor to the troops and a strict ceiling set on the prices to be charged:

> Peach Brandy by the Quart, 7 shillings six pence
> | | by the pint | 4 | " | | |
> |---------|--------------|---|------|-------|-----|
> | | by the Gill | 1 | " | three | " |
> | Whiskey | by the Quart | 6 | " | | |
> | | by the Pint | 3 | " | six | " |
> | | by the Gill | 1 | " | | |

It seems odd to find vinegar listed at 2/6 "ye Quart" among the beverages, but it had been known for ages as a powerful anti-scorbutic and was part of the ration of the Roman legions in Caesar's time.

Courts-martial on all levels crowd the pages until the reader wonders how the officers forming them could find time for their regular duty. Floggings are listed in grim recital for trade with the enemy, abuse of civilians, and for attempted desertion. Here are thirty lashes ordered, fifty, three and even five hundred, with the ghastly instruction "to be laid on well, on the bare back."

On into February 1778, when some accounts would lead one to believe that most of the problems of clothing had been solved, Christian Febiger notifies his officers that the mustermaster will inspect the regiment. The men "will appear as neat as Circumstances will admit; their Blankets slung —Beards shaved & Guns in Good Order—Officers Commanding Companies will Order those men who have shoes to procure wood for those who have not." It is typical of Febiger that he closes his orders with an injunction to the officer of the day, who "will particularly see that the Sick men do not Suffer for [lack of] fire."

Many of the huts were damp and most roofs leaked. Straw for bedding soon became foul, as anyone who has slept in French greniers will remember. But fresh straw was not easy to find and wagons to haul it still harder.

Stifling his strong distaste for seizure, the commander-in-chief orders all brigadiers "to Send out A Sufficient party properly officered to procure Straw & Impress waggons to hall it to Camp . . . and make an eaquell Distribution thereof to the Respective Regts. according to the Number present."

These entries contain little, save by inference or surmise, of the real, endless strain of those days. Sometimes the pages flow along in such a routine that the reader is brought up short by Febiger's mention of shoeless men in February or the need for forcibly seizing not only straw but wagons in which to haul it.

But the strain, the tension, the grinding hardships were very apparent to those who issued the orders and to those who recorded them, setting them down with cold-cramped fingers in a leaky, drafty "Hutt" on the plateau. To no one were they more apparent than to the tall, reddish-haired man who lived in the fieldstone house down by the junction of creek and river. On March 1, 1778, from "Head Qrs. V. Forge" he put something of what he felt on paper and issued it to the army. An officer of the 2nd Virginia copied it, as was regulation, in the orderly book, the spelling suggesting that someone in the "Hutt" read it aloud to him as he wrote.

The Commander in Chief takes this occation to Return his warmest thanks to the Virtuous Officers & Soldiers of this Army for that perservering fidelity & Zeal which they have Uniformly Manifested in all their Conduct their fortitude not only under their Common hardships Incident to a Military Life—But also Under the additional Sufferings to which the peculiar Situation of these States has Exposed them Clearly proves them men worthy of the Envyable Privilege of Contending for the rights of human nature—The freedom and Independence of their Country. The recent Instance of uncomplaining patience, during the late scarcity of Provisions in Camp is a fresh proof, that they possess to an eminent Degree, the pride [word is unclear] of Soldiers and magnanimity of Patriots. . . . Defects in the Comys. Department Contingences of weather . . . have Subjected and may again Subject us to a deficiency for a few days, but Soldiers, American Soldiers will despise the meanness of Repining at such trifling strokes of Adversity. . . . He is convinced, that faithful Officers and Soldiers, associated with him, in the great work of Rescuing their Country from Bondage and Misery, will continue in the display of that Patriotical Zeal which is capable of Smothering every difficulty and Vanquishing every Obstacle.

He had come to John Sullivan's town of Portsmouth in New Hampshire in the last month of 1777 and had astonished the citizens, themselves not unaccustomed to display, by disembarking in a scarlet uniform with deep blue facings. To the bright coat was pinned the glittering sunburst of the Order of Fidelity awarded by the Margravate of Baden-Durlach, a decoration more showy than coveted. After him came three aides, similarly dressed, and a cynical wasp-waisted greyhound called Azor. The scarlet and blue, innocently assumed to be the regulation uniform of the United States, was worn by Baron Friedrich Wilhelm Ludolf Gerhard Augustin von Steuben, who had come to this country to offer his services to the new nation. He also had a mission from the Comte de St. Germain to discover what in the name of a thousand pipes of a thousand devils was happening to all the weapons sent through Hortalez et Cie. to the United States. The reported wastage was extravagant.

Soon the baron presented himself to the Congress at York in Pennsylvania. He made an excellent impression, and those members still present goggled understandably over his dossier, which was fortified by a letter from shrewd, benevolent Benjamin Franklin in Paris. All this showed that Baron von Steuben was a very renowned soldier indeed, had served for long years in the wars of that master of wars, Frederick the Great of Prussia, rising to the rank of lieutenant general. This was not as high as it sounded to the congressmen, since the equivalent grade in the American service was brigadier.

Actually the point was academic, since the whole dossier was as valid as a torn-up rain check. The baron had served under the great Frederick but had never been more than a captain. Further, the Prussian service had dropped him from its rolls more than fourteen years before and, prior to stumbling into the present assignment, he had been only a hungry, out-of-work soldier. All this Franklin knew. But he had somehow sized up the baron as a most valuable man for the American army, realized that without high rank he would merely seem to Congress just another La Roche Fermoy, and hence cheerfully lent himself to the deception.

So the Congress welcomed him, the more so in that he did not want rank, preferring, as he said, to serve as a sort of attached volunteer. Also, having basked in the presence of Frederick the Great, he could only accept service under Washington himself.

In late February the baron came to Valley Forge, and Washington, agreeably shocked by the unassuming, self-effacing tone of the baron's letters, rode out some miles to meet him. The veteran of Frederick's wars and the tall Virginian met, took to each other at once, and from that moment the army of the United States began to take on a new and vastly improved character.

Von Steuben, on the other hand, was disagreeably shocked at what he saw in the Valley Forge camps and commented later that no troops he had ever known would, or could, have held together under such conditions. And this former member of the rigid, rank-conscious Prussian Army was unpleasantly startled to note that American officers of this supposedly republican army insisted on honor guards and servants far beyond anything he had known before. He also objected to some of the higher officers living, miles away from their hutted troops, in comfortable houses. Then he set to work.

He had some French, very little English, and had to rely on his secretary, the young Frenchman Pierre Duponceau, Colonel John Laurens, and Lieutenant Colonel Alexander Hamilton to sift his ideas of drill from German

o French to English. Before he uttered his first command he started to
write out a simplified drill that eventually was to range from the manual
of arms to "The Manner for Entering a Camp." Whether he realized it or
not, he and his aides were setting down the very first standard drill regulations for the United States Army.

The pages were laboriously copied out, distributed through division to
brigade to regiment and company, and through the chill nights and dank
dawns a great many junior officers in drafty huts must have cursed the luck
that sent this seemingly verbose German to Pennsylvania. In the 2nd Virginia they were copied into a notebook marked carefully "Bot at Trenton,
Septre. 30th, 1777," and the first entry begins, "Regulations for the Exercise & Evolutions of the Continental Army. By His Prussian Majesty's
Lieut. Genl. Barron Starben. The Inspectors of Brigades are to Assemble
Majors Capts and one Lieut. from each company . . ."

This partial entry leads into the baron's approach to the actual task of
teaching. He was given a group of one hundred men to use as control
guinea pigs and began drilling them, starting with such fundamental points
as the placing of the feet. He cut the drill for loading muskets, which often
ran to over twenty counts, to ten. He altered the march step, probably
changed the "position of the soldier at attention," smoothed off the movements for right-face and left-face, and also lectured on discipline and military courtesy. And he profoundly shocked many of Washington's officers,
who had been brought up in military life on the British pattern. One of the
basic points of that creed was that actually drilling troops was infra dig,
that only sergeants and corporals should do such menial work. (This attitude has carried into the twentieth century. A British cartoon of 1916
shows a Blimpish colonel being taken over a submarine by a naval officer;
pointing to the myriad dials and gauges and tubes, he says carelessly, "Of
course you have a sergeant who understands these things.") So the American officers of 1778 were appalled to see Von Steuben actually take a
musket from an unhandy private and show him how the command "Order
firelocks!" should be executed. Worse, they found that this Prussian martinet not only expected them to take part in drills but got Washington to
insist upon it.

When the first hundred guinea pigs were thought satisfactory, they were
returned to their commands to act as models and another hundred were
detailed. Early and late the baron labored over this, encouraging, demonstrating, roaring out a horrible mixture of tongues, a sort of pidgin of
French, German, and English. Captain Benjamin Walker, late of the 4th
New York, sometimes acted as the baron's interpreter, and to him the exasperated Prussian would turn, his frustrated voice splitting, "Viens,
Valkaire, mon ami! Sacré. Goddam die gaucherie of dese badauds. Je ne
puis plus. I can curse dem no more." So "Valkaire" would take over the
cursing detail.

The lessons went on from the simple school of the soldier to the squad,
the platoon, the company, the regiment, until whole brigades were ma-

neuvering smoothly. Had they been able to operate earlier in such econom
of time and space, Sullivan might have been able to form his men quickl
enough to prevent the disaster to the American right at Brandywine. As i
was, a new American army was born on the bleak plateau of Valley Forge

From the highest echelons down, the healing hand of the baron may b
detected. And from his orders and suggestions as much may be read a
between the lines of an orderly book, but in this case not what the army wa
doing, but what it had *not* been doing before. He ran adjutants' school
made guard mount a formal ceremony. Apparently before his coming n
one had thought to synchronize watches. Now headquarters time was to b
standard. Divisions would regulate by headquarters, brigades by divisions
and regiments by brigade.

The physical aspects of life underwent a change for the better. To re
place Thomas Mifflin, who seems to have been too much occupied witl
political intriguing and personal matters, Nathanael Greene was appointec
quartermaster general. Greene's distaste for this work was profound and sin
cere. Quite understandably he thought of himself as a combat officer, anc
the new duties, assigned in addition to his divisional command, struck him
as dull and onerous. He protested vigorously and then threw himself into
his new work.

He had been brought up in a large, close-knit empire of family busines
and his early training paid off. A problem might be strange and compli
cated, but he knew how to approach it. Paper inventories showed that
numerous categories of supplies existed, but no one seemed to know where
This did not satisfy Greene. Wheezing and limping over the misty coun
tryside, the ex-Quaker set himself the job of finding out. He struck pay dir
by searching where others had merely thrown up their hands.

He reported angrily: "We find the property of the continent dispersed
. . . not an encampment, route of the army, or considerable road but
abounds with wagons, left to the mercy of the weather. . . . Not less than
3000 spades, shovels . . . tomahawks have lately been discovered . . . a quan
tity of tent-cloth, after having laid . . . in a farmer's barn and unknown to
the officer of the department, was lately discovered and brought into
camp."

Decades ahead of his time, Green was unconsciously creating the job of
salvage officer.

Food came in, now flooding the camps, now drying up into reluctant
trickles. The last vestiges of starvation were wiped out, not through the
efforts of the commissary, but by what might be called an act of God.

Sullivan's men down by the Schuylkill had early learned to supplement
their rations by treading shellfish out of the mud. One spring day soldiers
noticed a dark ruffle sweeping upstream, a deeper ruffle than any wind
could cause. There was a subdued humming in the air, an unbroken, whispering murmur. The surface of the river was cut as though by thin black
knife blades, and men began to shout excitedly. Shad were running in the
Schuylkill, shad in uncounted thousands, choking the narrow stream from

bank to bank, leaping clear of the water, being forced onto the shore by the immeasurable pressure about them.

Armed with pitchforks, rakes, shovels, with broken branches, soldiers from all over the camp plunged into the stream, began heaving shad onto the soggy grass of the shore. Eager hands brought baskets, barrels, salt, and the harvesting went on. There were cries that the school would soon run out of reach. Hoofs drummed along the softening ground, and Henry Lee, now a major since his successful clash with British dragoons, sent his mounted troopers into the stream above the blunt point of the run and had them mill their horses about. The upstream rush was checked as the frightened van of the shad tried to turn back, and a long stretch of the river became a boiling cauldron of fish.

There was fresh shad to eat. There were tons of shad to be salted down. A seemingly inexhaustible supply depot writhed and jumped and twisted in the Schuylkill.

The ultra-masculine severity of the Valley Forge camps underwent a gradual softening. Martha Washington bowled up from the Potomac to become chatelaine of the gray stone Potts house by the Schuylkill. Colonel Elias Boudinot of New Jersey thought her position a rather lonely one and recorded that she was "almost a mope for want of a female companion" and straightway summoned Mrs. Boudinot to the camp.

But the hostess of Mount Vernon was as gallant a campaigner as her husband, threw herself cheerfully into the odd life of the plateau and the valley. She thought that the Potts house was far too small, so she had a dining cabin built at one side. There were the men to think about, and she became a familiar figure, basket over her arm, flitting from door to slab door of the hospitals, giving out what passed for delicacies in those grim days, stopping by the worst cases, and always leaving a warm smile and some remembered word in the stark wards that became momentarily brighter for the memory of her passage through them. She also learned, from a local housewife, how to darn the general's stockings.

She was the general's hostess for visiting civilians as well as the gaunt officers. A party of Quaker women came seeking a pass through the lines from Washington and "sat with his wife (a sociable, pretty kind of woman) until he came in. . . . We had an elegant dinner which was soon over, when we went out with the General's wife, up to her chamber."

Local girls appeared, Walkers and Beavers and Moores and, as everywhere, a little court grew up about this First Lady of the Land. There were afternoon and evening gatherings to which her charm—so different from the mobcapped domesticity of later portraits—drew the officers, young and old. Nathanael Greene came, and bulky Henry Knox. Von Steuben and eager young Pierre Duponceau could be seen there, Tench Tilghman and Alexander Hamilton. Fox-haired Lafayette was devoted to her, as was the rather frigid Baron de Kalb. Gimat and Fleury and Du Plessis came to drink tea or coffee, crowding into the little rooms beside Anthony Wayne, John Sullivan, and the flamboyant Pulaski. Managing these assorted groups was a task to try any hostess, as there was no room for dancing, card-playing was ruled out as an example to the rest of the army, and no liquors were served. But day after day the visitors came, ever drawn by the gracious personality of Martha Washington.

As the weather grew better and buds showed on maple and dogwood, other wives appeared. "Lady" Stirling came to join her husband, thought by many to be the finest military figure in the army next to Washington, and set up housekeeping in the Stirling quarters west of Valley Creek. Lucy Knox, now nearly as fat as Henry, came to live just south of Mount Joy and added her lively, if sometimes unbridled, wit to the camp. Nathanael Greene told his Kitty that Henry and Lucy struck him as a perfect married couple.

Kitty Littlefield Greene was one of the earliest arrivals, coming all the way from Rhode Island with the infant Master George Washington Greene, quite a feat of juvenile travel until one remembers the Von Riedesel trek. Somehow or other Kitty Greene had acquired a respectable stock of textbook French, and soon the Greene house, near the junction of the King of Prussia Road and the Gulph Road, was invaded by a wave of French officers, homesick and desperately hungry for even a whisper of their own tongue. Pierre Duponceau, later to be an American citizen and an outstanding member of the Pennsylvania Bar, wrote that Madame Greene was "handsome, elegant and accomplished," an opinion apparently shared by De Ternant and De la Colombe. The mysterious "Armand," Marquis de la Rouërie, was often in attendance, with Gîmat and the others.

It is probable that with the arrival of the feminine contingent officers and men were more careful about shaving, about dressing their hair and prinking out their worn clothes as much as possible. But there were feuds and strong dislikes that flourished among these married, as well as single, "men in barracks" and with which even the tact of Martha Washington could not cope. Von Steuben and De Kalb, both born on the same side of the Rhine, had fought on different sides during the Seven Years' War and heartily detested each other. William Smallwood of Maryland was forever fulminating against non-Marylanders, against the stream of foreign officers, and grew apoplectic over the failure of Congress to give him his second star. William Alexander went into violent tantrums at sly digs about his claim to the title of Lord Stirling. Von Steuben, forgetting his cherished feud with De Kalb, accused Lafayette of plotting against him, jeered openly at his youth and inexperience. Luckily the young marquis deftly turned off the German's barbs, and the drillmaster was forced to fall back on his pièce de résistance, De Kalb.

This was hardly an ideal atmosphere in which to introduce a pair of stormy petrels, two men who had brilliant records for starting nerve-racking jangles in the smoothest milieu. Benedict Arnold, slowly recuperating from his wound of the Von Breymann redoubt, came down into Pennsylvania to hasten his convalescence. As soon as weather permitted he ordered the army commissary to whip up a banquet to which he invited some twenty guests, ıcluding the commander-in-chief. From Washington he received a surrisingly terse refusal to which were added a few pointed and quite natural ɛmarks concerning the relatively lavish scale that the Connecticut major ɛneral seemed to think appropriate. Whether or not this set the tone for ıe rest of the army, Arnold had very few acceptances from the high brass. ınthony Wayne and Lafayette did go so far as to stop by the trestle tables ıid out under the cherry trees and drink a glass of wine with Arnold, but ıen passed on to their own affairs. The marquis seems to have made no ɔmment, but the handsome Wayne, forgetting that he had at least gone ırough the motions of accepting Arnold's hospitality, later released some Jasts that must have blistered the bark of the trees of Valley Forge. He ad of course had some chance to observe Arnold during the Canada cam- aign and since then must have had a good deal of gossip, possibly of ;atesian origin, drummed into his ears. Wayne concluded his tirade, "The ırty, dirty acts which he has been capable of committing beggar all de- ɛription and are of such a Nature as would cause the Infernals to blush." he effect of the cold-shouldering of Arnold's invitation, from the com- ıander-in-chief down, added to the comments of Wayne and others, sent ıe more than touchy general into a long-burning blue rage and may have ɛen a contributing factor to his later sinister actions.

After Arnold another major general came stalking into camp. Charles Lee ad finally been exchanged against the British general, Richard Prescott. he gaunt, big-nosed, hollow-cheeked man was not in a happy mood. It is ɔssible that he did not want particularly to be exchanged, as he may have ɔund the attention paid to his various infallible schemes for the certain ɛstruction of the American army by Sir William Howe to be flattering. .nd he felt that his military honor was badly bruised at being exchanged ɔr a mere Prescott. In his own mind Charles Lee was worth Burgoyne, ʿith perhaps Von Riedesel and a brigadier or two thrown in, in terms of ıartial value. Nonetheless, he wrapped himself in magnanimity and sent Vashington a "Plan for the Formation of the American Army in the least ;xpensive Manner Possible," adding modestly that "I have taken it into my ead that I understand it better than almost any man living." He also wrote Ienry Laurens, now president of the Congress, "I am well and hope always ıall be well with General Washington—and to speak again vainly I am ɛrsuaded (considering how he is surrounded) that he cannot do without ıe." This self-effacing statement was followed by a very broad suggestion hat Congress had better go right ahead and make him (Lee) a lieutenant ɛneral. Why not? Lee assured that body that he would have held that rank ·y now had he thrown in with the Russians, the Poles, or the Portuguese ıstead of with the Americans.

So he came into the camp and began to preach the most extraordinary loctrine: that, when you came right down to it, American troops could ıever defeat British troops, no matter how heavily the latter were outnum- ·ered. He looked upon the highly improved though by no means perfect ıilitary machine which Von Steuben, De Ternant, and Greene had built

up and sneered at it. In the absence of Charles Lee the army had gon
utterly to pot. He considered Washington and remarked to Elias Boudino
that the Virginian was not fit to command a sergeant's guard. From all thi
it may be inferred that Charles Lee was again enjoying himself thoroughly

Throughout this same winter Quaker-flavored Philadelphia took on th
raffish, uneasy self-assurance of a boom town. Sir William Howe's army
quite willing for action but well enough pleased that there were no majo
operations in sight, settled down contentedly. Of the nearly twenty thou
sand men of this army, no one settled himself more gratefully or prepare
to enjoy himself more deeply than a slim, girlishly handsome young office
named John André.

Made prisoner along the Richelieu in '75 and then a captive at Carlisle
deep in the Pennsylvania wilderness, he had been exchanged and nov
swam like an exotic tropical fish in the hectic, unreal stream of life in occu
pied Philadelphia. Sometime after his release he had purchased a captain'
commission in the 26th Camerons, exchanging the blue facings of the 7tl
Royal Fusiliers for the pale yellow of his new Highland unit. He may hav
felt a little chagrined at being denied the jaunty swish of a kilt, which hi
graceful carriage would have managed admirably, but since the summe
of '76 that garment seems to have been ruled out as a too naïve defens
against the North American climate and particularly North American mos
quitoes and black flies. But at least André could preen himself in well-cu
breeches.

Attached to the staff of Major General Charles Grey, and hence free
from the menial maelstrom of regimental duty, he had been an onlooker a
Brandywine. At Germantown he had had the supreme satisfaction o
actually leading an intoxicating charge on horseback, sword drawn, agains
the disintegrating rebels, whom he held in increasing contempt. Charle
Grey, a genial but ultra-tough veteran with a strong predilection for tota
war as opposed to Howe's half measures, thought highly of his young aid
and his estimate of the enemy.

Life had a very pleasant savor in the nostrils of Captain John André
There were fine three-story brick houses for officers' quarters and he him
self shared one with his chief, a handsome house on the south side o
Market Street between Third and Fourth. It was the property of an absente
rebel, one Benjamin Franklin. The young captain admired the house. H
also admired the owner's library to the extent of making several volumes hi
own, along with a portrait of Franklin by Benjamin Wilson. This last iten
he graciously gave to his chief in subtle compliment to the latter's taste
(Long generations afterward a Grey descendant sent the portrait to Americ
and it now forms part of the White House collection.)

What a city Philadelphia was and what scope it gave to André's mani
fold gifts. The boxlike theater on South Street was reopened and officer
and Philadelphians paid anywhere from fifty cents to a dollar to marvel a
The Deuce Is in Him or *Douglas* or *The Citizen*. The captain was happil

home here, writing rhymed prologues, painting really fine scenery, designing costumes, and sometimes acting himself, turning in performances
at his detractors sniffishly termed mediocre.

Then there was the amusingly provincial society of the town, where
rebels still resident and Tories seemed hypnotically to follow the ton set
by André and other sophisticates. Some of the sophisticates must have had
trouble in explaining a few manifestations of the Old World culture and
charm. There was the Hessian General von Knyphausen. Among other
eccentricities he had the rather startling habit of dispensing with a knife
and smearing butter onto his bread with his scarred, splay thumb. There
were balls and routs, and all the officers of the occupation forces were delighted with the standard of pulchritude set by the provincial girls, whom
they rated much higher than those of New York. When the Schuylkill
froze there were skating parties, with bonfires along the banks to flicker out
across scarred ice and the silver glint of skates. Enough snow fell to allow
for sleigh rides that gave opportunity for fascinating tête-à-têtes while the
runners sang through the crust and the span of horses tossed their heads
in the frosty night air. André had a pretty turn for verse and could sing
French, German, and English ballads to his partner, stressing a line with
a glance or gesture while Philadelphia eyes gleamed in response to him over
soft furs.

An officer and a man of honor must keep up his end of the social glitter,
and there were balls given by the army at Smith's City Tavern on Lodge
Alley by Second Street. There were excellent music, gourmet fare, and a
wealth of candles at these evenings. But was there a whispering current
circling just under the ceiling? Did the voices of Caesar Rodney and John
Adams and James Duane and Christopher Gadsden still cling to the walls,
ringing memories of long, sober talks about the doings around Boston and
whether a certain tall, sandy-haired Virginian would accept command of
the New England army? But couples on the floor or at the buffet could not
have heard them in that gay winter of '77–'78. Nor could they have been
heard at dinners tendered by the officers at the old Penn mansion out where
Spring Garden Street now meets Twentieth.

There was so much, too, to amuse a wise, tolerant man of the world. Sir
William Howe set the pace for the life of the army. After patiently accepting a local pinch hitter or two, his heart throb of Boston and New York
days, Mrs. Loring, appeared and was set up once more as the "Sultana."
She went everywhere with Sir William, and a young captain of the Camerons could smile discreetly back of his hand, turn a neat epigram to some
trusted friend as the most proper Philadelphians opened their doors to "La
Loring." They had to, if they wanted the prestige of receiving Sir William
as a guest. She could be seen, too, at the gaming tables, where her striking
blond hair glittered to match the piles of sovereigns and guineas on the
green cloth. She was prominent at horse races on the Common, cheering
on handsome young Banastre Tarleton of the dragoons on whom she probably had a bet. One could laugh tolerantly over the Sultana and the

gambling, just as one could give a man-of-the-world loan to reckless office
who ruined themselves at cards and had to sell their commissions a
creep home to England.

One could also make a neat comparison between Watteau's "E
barquement pour Cythère" and the hurried pairing off of officers of
grades with frail Philadelphians in emulation of Sir William. It was all
warm, human, and amusing, even if the square-toe type of Briton and H
sian indulged in a disapproving "Tschk-tschk!" And what if the men d
grow so lax that guards were not properly posted, if looting of rebel a
Tory alike went on, notably by the Germans? One hardly needed a gua
against the rebels. As for the aggrieved citizens, why, they ought to
sophisticated enough to know that such things always went on when y
had troops in a town.

To be sure, sanitary matters were badly handled. Horses were stabled
private houses, even in that barnlike brick affair called the State House th
Philadelphians held in such veneration. Holes were cut in the floors a
manure and rotting straw bedding were swept through them into the cell
and left there to stew in unholy ferment. But an occupied city was rea
only a camp, and camps had stunk to the high vaults of the sky since cam
first began. So it was nothing to concern oneself about.

It was much pleasanter to think about the local belles, rebel or To
They fluttered so acceptably at the sight of the gallant young captain
Scots in his pale yellow facings and colored delightfully over one of h
neatly turned rhymes. There was lovely Peggy Shippen, whose father, E
ward, was a renowned jurist with a fine library and picture gallery. A
there was another Peggy, still more fascinating, Peggy Chew. André mu
have seen her father's big stone house out on the Germantown road, t
same house about which Washington's attempted offensive had split. B
there could be nothing serious with any of these charmers, of course. T
slim captain, so determinedly an aristocrat, had narrowly missed being co
demned to a tradesman's life in earlier years, and a provincial marria
might set him slipping back into that degraded status.

With the coming of spring, highly disquieting apprehensions filled t
mind of this captain of Camerons, aide to Major General Charles Grey. S
William Howe was to be allowed to return to England for good and it w
only natural that Grey should accompany him. In that case, John Andr
junior captain of his regiment, would have to sink to the drab monotony
company duty, and the doors of headquarters would be closed with S
Henry Clinton, cold and dour, in command of the army. This possibilit
simply could not be faced. In some way an adroit, agile, resourceful, amu
ing, and charming young man must make himself appear indispensable t
Sir Henry.

CHAPTER XXV

". . . never had I beheld so superb a man"

IT was May 5, 1778, and the sun was dipping behind the rolling land masses west of Valley Forge, sending rays slanting across the deep slash of Valley Creek and over the plateau with its clusters of huts that looked almost pastoral in the darkening green of their setting. In dozens of commands aides were reaching for pen, ink, and sand, as a new order had come down from headquarters and it must be entered at once. Quills scratched busily, setting down the caption: "General After Orders 6 OClock pm." The lines flowed on across the pages of uncounted orderly books:

> It having pleased the Almighty Ruler of the Universe propitiously to defend the cause of the United States of America and finally by raising us up a powerful friend, among the Princes of the Earth, to Establish Our Liberty and Independence upon lasting foundations; It becomes us to Set apart a day, for fully acknowledging the Divine Goodness, and celebrating the important event, which we owe to his Benign interposition. . . .

The "important event" was duly celebrated the next day. Out onto the grand parade of the plateau marched the army of the United States. Physically, it looked about as it always had looked. There were patches and cobbled-up rags. Such actual uniforms as had reached the camp merely added to the general nondescript appearance. Boots were rather better than usual, thanks to the efforts of Greene and his predecessors. Muskets were well polished and nearly every man had a bayonet, save for the riflemen, whose weapons would not take the blade.

Individually, then, there was little change. But taken as a whole, the force that moved out onto the plateau was so completely altered that it must have struck an observer who had been away for some months with a shock that was breath-taking.

As late as Germantown, just the September before, the army en masse, or even subdivisions of it, had not been able to maneuver. To go into action in column, the men marched in double or even single file. This, as may be easily gathered, took up valuable road space and had the effect of lengthening any distance that had to be covered. If a regiment were in line facing south and found it necessary—as at Long Island and Brandywine—to change that line to face west, the individual soldiers had to be trailed off in a great arc, headed about in the proper direction, and then somehow butted and shoved into the desired position. Not all outfits were as badly trained as this. It is likely that the Delawares and Smallwood's Marylanders could move quite smartly. But this was of little advantage if the rest of their brigade or division were not following their procedure.

Now all companies were marching four abreast, which cut the length of their road space by four compared with the old Indian-file method. Muskets were at a uniform angle and the step was crisp and regular, utterly unlike the ragged, uneven gait that John Adams had mentioned to Abigail as characteristic of the army as it passed through Philadelphia on its way to Brandywine and disaster.

Fifes and drums whipped out the rhythm and there even seems to have been a band or two. Commanders rode at the heads of divisions—Greene and Sullivan and Stirling and, ecstatically happy, Lafayette. Brigadiers brought on their commands. Colonels and company officers swung their units into place and, square by square, Washington's men snapped to a smooth halt to the accompaniment of crisply grounded arms. Nothing like this had ever been seen on the American continent, save when performed by British, French, or German troops.

More was to come, for the mere marching in brigade or regimental column was simply a means to an end. Selected units broke into motion, melted from column into line, flowed back into column again. A whole regiment marching south in column broke neatly, took up a position in line facing east. There was firing in company volleys, firing by files, so the reports beginning at the right rattled along smoothly to end at the far left. Henry Knox, jouncing heavily in the saddle, brought on his guns in a rocking, swaying line. Subordinate officers like Colonel Thomas Proctor of Pennsylvania sent their six-pounders into swift action, the gunners unlimbering, firing, and limbering again while fifes squealed away and drums cracked out the time. Then the infantry were at it again, changing front, forming square, breaking into a double, four abreast.

And all this was the work of Baron Friedrich von Steuben and the officers who toiled with him. He does not seem to have been surprised at his achievement, for he was shrewd enough to judge accurately the caliber of men with whom he had to deal. To a friend in Europe he wrote that in training German soldiers all he had to do was to tell them what to do. With Americans, he said, he first had to explain *why* a given order was necessary, *what* it was supposed to accomplish. Then not only compliance but comprehension came quickly.

So the tough old German unveiled the 1778 model of the American army under the May sun while a breeze up the Schuylkill rippled through the thickening green of maple and oak and dogwood. This model was by no means perfect. Could it have been held together it would have quickly been polished by combat into a formidable fighting force. But, as always, the leaves were falling from the calendar and soon this militia unit that looked so promising would start for home. Later the Continental regiments would shred out. But Von Steuben's leavening would last to help out with the later formations.

There was a great marquee pitched at the crest of the slope, with tables spread, and at the end of the review invited officers swarmed into it. Martha Washington seems to have presided, with Kitty Greene—who referred to the feminine contingent as "the fair intruders"—Lady Stirling, and Lucy Knox to help her. There were good meats to carve and probably fresh shad from the Schuylkill flanked with a few early vegetables—"garden sauce" in those days—and white bread and passable claret. It was an undreamed-of spread for Valley Forge—"Lucullus dines with Lucullus."

There were games afterward, and Dr. Albigensis Waldo was moved to verse by the green turf and warm sun and possibly the claret:

> One choix at Fives are earnest here
> Another furious at Cricket there.

(The "choix" or "choice" [choosing up sides?] seems to indicate a team. "Fives," still played in England, is much like modern handball.) Races were held on horseback and on foot. There was a stocking-foot race, and young Lieutenant John Marshall of Colonel Henry Heth's 3rd Virginia won it handily. He was wearing a pair of new stockings with white heels that his mother had sent up to him from Virginia and, after the race, he became famous in the army as "Silver Heels." In later years a far different fame was to be his as Chief Justice of the Supreme Court of the United States of America.

The celebration was over at last, marking the end of the gayest hours that Valley Forge had known since that mid-December day when the army, with numbed shoulders and smarting feet, had first sighted the plateau from the Paoli Road. And by now even the most distant outposts knew the true nature of the "important event" that had been celebrated. Encouraged concerning the life expectancy of the new United States by the victory over Burgoyne and the amazing rally that produced Germantown, France had agreed to form an alliance with those states. French funds and supplies would now be available in generous amounts. The French army and the French Navy would participate wholeheartedly. Lafayette, Duportail, Gîmat, Du Plessis, Fleury, and the others were no longer foreign officers with the American army. They could look on themselves as the advance guard of that F.E.F., the French Expeditionary Force, whose participation in American waters and on American soil was promised soon.

Joy over this vital announcement was not uniform. Many men felt that the French monarchy would merely use its intervention to oust the British from all North America and establish a French empire from the Arctic to the Gulf of Mexico and the Mississippi. Older Americans remembered bitterly the French officers who had led the murderous scalping and burning raids that had terrorized all the frontiers in the old days. Bigots cursed an alliance with a Catholic power on any count.

It is likely, too, "troops always being troops," that there was a good deal of grumbling in the ranks. The American soldier usually detests

parades and field days, no matter how attractive they may be to the high
brass and applauding women. There is no record of it, but it is a very safe
bet that many a Valley Forge hut rang with disgusted oaths as men rubbed
musket-chafed shoulders and soaked weary feet, wishing loudly that the
French King would mind his own goddamn business and not come nosin'
where he wasn't wanted.

Even before Von Steuben's work had been begun the country and the
Congress were mulling over the problem of what to do with the army.
There were many murmurs, sometimes rising to full-voiced shouts, that
first of all it ought to be given a new commander-in-chief. The motives back
of this hoped-for change were mixed. John and Sam Adams felt that
Washington was becoming too much of a national idol, that he might
emerge as a dictator or even as the first in a dynasty of American monarchs.
That they and others felt this way shows that they had fallen far short of
even a rudimentary estimate of the man. Others, particularly in the army,
clamored that Washington and defeat were synonymous and that the
real victorious genius, the vanquisher of Burgoyne, was present and ready
to take over. At such suggestions, Horatio Gates, now president of the
rather ludicrous Board of War, simpered deprecatingly but put in no dis-
claimer. There seems, however, to have been no plot, no concerted move
to oust Washington, despite the legend that has grown up around the so-
called "Conway Cabal." But talk, civilian and military, persisted.

As to the use of the army itself, the Board of War came up with probably the most beetle-brained military plan of the century. Lafayette was
to go north, pick up a strong army en route, and invade Canada. Civilian
minds of the Board might conceivably have thought such a move feasible,
but Horatio Gates was president and Thomas Mifflin sat with him. Unless
there was bad faith somewhere, it is inconceivable that these two generals
could have lent themselves to such military moon-raking.

Nonetheless, the young marquis, delighted at having a command of his
own, fell in with the plan and Baron de Kalb was assigned to go along
with him. It is characteristic of the temper of the times, and especially
of the Board of War and the Congress, that Washington was kept utterly
in the dark concerning this Canadian move until it was announced as
under way. Of course nothing came of it. The marquis and the baron went
as far as Albany, only to find that there were hardly any troops for them
to command and that no steps whatsoever had been taken to equip and
supply such an expedition. By mid-March, De Kalb and Lafayette were
back at Valley Forge. It is a tribute to Washington's command of himself
and to his unconscious magnanimity that Lafayette's part in this plan in
no way damaged relations between the two, since it was largely hatched
through the marquis's importuning of the Congress and the Board to be
allowed to command something, no matter what.

But the growls against Washington and these machinations of Gates
and his Board members lay far behind that May day when the new army

was unveiled in celebration of the French alliance. Now the question of what to do with the army became more and more important. And for the first flexing of American muscles tempered by the master trainer, Von Steuben, the commander-in-chief turned to the young marquis.

This turning nearly led to tragedy. Lafayette was given something over two thousand men, among them Poor's New Hampshire brigade and Potter's Pennsylvania militia. Covering them was a unique force under Captain Allan McLane. A wealthy young Delaware firebrand, he had organized a strange partisan corps of riflemen, light horse, musketmen, and some twoscore Oneida Indians. With this command he had butted and slashed and hacked against the British and Hessian outposts through most of the winter. His losses were light, his blows sharp, and his intelligence usually timely and accurate.

Down in Philadelphia, Sir Henry Clinton, ready to take over from comfortable Sir William Howe, heard of Lafayette's move that had brought him to the east bank of the Schuylkill below Matson's Ford. Sir Henry considered the Frenchman's strength, his known dispositions and probable course, and decided to move against him. To capture the marquis, particularly in view of the recent French alliance, was worth a gamble on many counts. Clinton felt that he had put the matter far beyond the realm of gambling by starting out with a force more than twice the size of Lafayette's, intending to strike in on him from two different directions on the ground called Barren Hill. So sure was Sir Henry of success that he actually sent out invitations to a dinner in Philadelphia "to meet the Marquis de Lafayette."

McLane's corps spotted the movement, found a hidden road to the rear, and when Clinton's two wings, under Generals Grant and Grey, converged on Barren Hill, dragoons and grenadiers charged into empty lines. The marquis had slipped away to a fine position across the river at Matson's Ford, and the British, in disgust, tramped back to Philadelphia.

So the marquis and his men returned to camp intact. Soon they and the rest of the army would take the road again, and this time there was to be no blind launching into a void, no mere waiting to see what would happen.

The end of Sir William Howe's reign in North America was celebrated by a day-long pageant at the Wharton estate, just upriver from Philadelphia. The display, intended to extol the virtues of gently born people, was hideously expensive, garish, and greatly admired by officers and Philadelphians, even though its closing moments were marred by Allan McLane's men starting great oil fires beyond the British works and whooping in oafish derision. So in this atmosphere of tawdry tinsel Sir Henry Clinton took over command of the British forces on North America and pondered, as he had been pondering ever since the first rumors of a change in command were current, over what to do next.

His intelligence concerning important American moves was as patchy as Howe's had been. He was better served, however, by overseas sources and had word via swift packets that a powerful French fleet under Admiral Count d'Estaing had sailed from Toulon, convoying some four thousand troops. The destination of this armada, he was told, was the mouth of the Delaware.

Of course the treaty between France and the United States provided for direct French intervention only in case of a declaration of war between France and England, but Clinton and his advisers decided shrewdly, and correctly, that that declaration would coincide closely with the arrival of D'Estaing off the Delaware capes. For a while, at least, France would have control of the seas. Clinton's Philadelphia forces had been badly weakened by orders from London to send troops to the British West Indies against a possible French descent on those rich islands. The New York garrison could not come to his help so long as French ships closed the sea approaches, and dour Sir Henry had no trouble in foreseeing that he could be overwhelmed among the rose bricks and tree-shaded streets of Philadelphia by a combined Franco-American assault.

Clinton was hardly a great soldier, but he never lacked decision. He made up his mind quickly that he would have to cut his losses and transfer his army to New York before D'Estaing's sails were sighted. But he had another problem. The Americans would reoccupy Philadelphia at once, and he had to think, as he and Howe had had to think two years ago in Boston, of the horde of Loyalists who had flocked to the city after Brandywine.

It was a hard conclusion to reach but he unflinchingly ruled that the Tories and their goods must go by sea to New York. The Anglo-German troops would have to face a long march from the Delaware to the Narrows by Staten Island with Washington's army hanging on his left flank. Orders were issued and by June 16 the evacuation of Philadelphia began.

Such a move takes a long time to get under way, and with the very first steps the military Geiger counters of watching Americans began to click like a field of crickets. Through farmers ostensibly coming into town to trade, through the tireless Allan McLane and his band, news was funneled back twenty miles and more to the gray stone house by the Schuylkill. By the first of June the facts were in Washington's hands and he was presented with a commander's dream, the chance of hitting a strung-out enemy from the flank with a strong, compact force. In many ways it suggested Robert E. Lee's missed opportunity to hit McClellan during the latter's march across Lee's front from the Chickahominy to the James in 1862.

The situation called for action. The American force now was rather stronger than Clinton's and the British were limited to two avenues of retreat. The first led up the Delaware to Trenton and thence to Princeton and New Brunswick on the Raritan. The other lay through a scattering of crossroad towns and hamlets, Haddonfield, Mount Holly, Crosswicks, and

Monmouth Court House (now Freehold, New Jersey), and thence to Sandy Hook or Perth Amboy.

As in the past, Washington hesitated, called councils of war, which the irreverent young Alexander Hamilton compared to gaggles of midwives. These gatherings were further complicated by the presence of Charles Lee, on whose experience and knowledge many of the still amateur officers leaned heavily. Lee at once proclaimed that he was "passionately opposed" to any move against Clinton. Let him reach New York. It would be a good riddance. And did any of the gentlemen present really think that Americans could stand up to British grenadiers? No. The thing to do was to sit tight at Valley Forge and see what happened.

Many officers trailed along with Lee. Henry Knox agreed, possibly a little unsure of himself since his blunder at the Chew house in Germantown. Even Von Steuben advised against any attack. With his usual courtesy Washington asked the opinion of a handsome, quite junior brigadier who had sat through the bursts of pessimism with angry detachment, ostentatiously reading a book while sound men like "Scotch Willie" Maxwell, Enoch Poor, and William Woodford glumly backed Lee. Young Anthony Wayne slammed down his book and snapped out his advice: "Fight, sir." Nathanael Greene, Lafayette, and John Cadwalader closed ranks with him, a determined minority of four.

Time was ebbing. Already a priceless military opportunity for the Americans had budded, flowered, and died. Evacuation had begun, and for long hours Clinton's army was split by the Delaware River, half on the east bank, half on the west. But no move was made and the Anglo-German force was into the Jerseys and toiling over the sandy roads.

The retreat was not an easy one. The weather turned unseasonably hot and humid, with clouds banking swiftly to split in heavy downpours that left the countryside asteam with a choking miasma. British and Germans slogged along in their heavy uniforms, their backs bent under packs that sometimes weighed as much as eighty pounds. On roads where the sand was so fine as to be almost liquid, men sank ankle-deep, slipped, skidded. Hats, helmet, coats, breeches became shapeless, sodden wrappings plastered onto chafed bodies. As in Burgoyne's move down the west bank of the Hudson, there were broken bridges to repair, veritable causeways to be built, and there were no less than fifteen hundred wagons to jar and jolt over the bad roads. The rate of march was understandably often less than six miles per day. American formations began to appear on the flanks, Philemon Dickinson's militia and Dan Morgan's rifles, the latter watching the right of the retreat.

Clinton could not know that these bodies were largely for observation, nor could he guess the ultra-timid counsels of Charles Lee. Gatherings of militia and riflemen might be the prelude to an all-out attack on him. Such an attack would come from the north and west and might catch him in broken country if he stuck to his first choice of routes, that heading toward New Brunswick on the Raritan. So he abruptly changed his orders, decided to push north and east through Monmouth Court House and thence to Sandy Hook, where transports could ferry his men and wagons to New York.

In the meantime Washington had been growing more than dubious over Lee's defeatist advice. On June 23 he left Valley Forge with the bulk of his force, crossed the Delaware at Coryell's Ferry. By the twenty-fifth he was slanting southeast through Rocky Hill and Kingston, his men well stripped down in contrast to the overladen British and Hessians. His mind was made up. A strong force must strike Clinton's rear guard. If this developed profitably, the main army could join in. Already Generals Charles Scott and Maxwell were quite close to the British line of march, along with Philemon Dickinson and Dan Morgan. Washington would back them with a strong brigade under an aggressive leader. Enoch Poor's New Hampshiremen were ready and available. Thinking of a proper combat commander, Washington's mind must have gone back to Wayne's terse advice at various councils of war. Anthony Wayne was to take charge of the whole group. But there remained the question of over-all command, a major general's job. And here military etiquette waggishly and exasperatingly entered the picture.

Charles Lee was second only to Washington in the tables of organization. Out of courtesy the command was offered to him. Fortune smiled briefly and bleakly on the American army. Lee was disdainful of an assignment that struck him as very minor. He announced loftily that the job was "a more proper business of a young volunteering general, than that of the second in command of the army."

Lafayette was delighted. An important, independent command with good troops and a notable fighting brigadier under him! With Wayne and Poor's men he set out for Englishtown, a short five miles from the Anglo-Germans at Monmouth Court House. He was on high ground and the visibility was not bad, save for the steam that the hot sun drew up after recurrent heavy showers. Coolly elated, he would gather quick intelligence, make his dispositions, and back up the belief which he shared with Wayne and Greene that American troops, properly trained and led, were not necessarily inferior to European professionals. The prospect glowed in his mind.

There were hoofbeats from the west, and into the Englishtown camp, properly escorted, rode Charles Lee. Back at main headquarters he had suddenly awakened to the fact that the little French boy was at the head of a force of nearly six thousand men, close to half the army. The forward command at once became the most desirable thing in the world, no mere trifle to be fobbed off on a young volunteering general. More than that, his own military honor and that of other senior major generals would be damaged beyond hope of repair if that command were not immediately entrusted to one Charles Lee. He wrote about it stridently, talked loudly, and for reasons which probably can never be quite cleared up the commander-in-chief reversed himself. Lee was to go out at once and take over,

Washington asking only that Lafayette's feelings were to be spared as much as possible. And now Lee had arrived in Englishtown.

To place in command here a man who was opposed to any offensive, who despised the troops he was to lead, was, in small compass, like sending in a quarterback who has no belief or confidence in the plays he is supposed to call. The Swiss Henry Jomini was to write a generation later that "an unwilling commander is half beaten before the battle begins." And Lee was replacing a man who was more than willing.

Toward evening of the twenty-seventh Washington rode on past Englishtown, saw what he could of Clinton's dispositions, and returned to Lee. The commander-in-chief had made up his mind. The advanced guard was to move out at dawn to attack. The rest of the army, not too far in the rear, would move up, ready to throw in its weight as matters developed.

Darkness came on. The marquis, now with no true command but accepting the new turn of events cheerfully enough, asked Lee for specific orders. Wayne came up with the same question, as did "Scotch Willie" Maxwell. The new commander of the advance did not seem disposed to talk. He muttered vaguely about lacking intelligence, about having no plans, and then turned in for the night.

His subordinates, properly aghast, could only wait and listen as the night wore on. What they heard was faint but by no means reassuring. The sandy ground muffled noises, but the still night air must have brought them the sound of slow hoofs, of creaky wheels as Clinton's fifteen hundred wagons started down the road that led to Middletown and Sandy Hook.

After midnight a messenger came from Washington, who was afraid that the enemy might slip away in the darkness; he wanted Philemon Dickinson to make contact with his militia. Grudgingly Lee obeyed the order. But at four o'clock on the morning of the twenty-eighth, when Lafayette boldly invaded Lee's tent, he found that the angular general still had no ideas, had taken no measures to back up Dickinson in case he ran into trouble.

There was no lack of room for trouble. Clinton had started his immense wagon train for Sandy Hook, as the night sounds had indicated. With them was the bulk of the Hessians under Von Knyphausen. But the rear guard still hung about Monmouth Court House, the very cream of Clinton's army. There were three fine brigades of British infantry, two strong battalions of British grenadiers, all the Hessian grenadiers, the Coldstreams, two battalions of British light infantry, the 16th Dragoons and John Simcoe's excellent Tory light horse, the Queen's Rangers. And Dickinson was taking Jersey militia against them.

Reports began to come from Dickinson. He was lightly engaged and the whole British force seemed on the move. Word must have reached Washington, for as the sun began to catch the treetops off by Monmouth, specific orders came down to Charles Lee. He was to attack at once; the rest of the army was already moving to his support.

There was no disputing what this meant. Drums began to mutter, fifes shrilled out, and the American advance began to move. There was "Dickie" Butler and his Pennsylvanians, William Woodford bringing on his Virginians, James Varnum swinging his Rhode Islanders into line. Sometime during the course of the march Wayne and Lee rode out ahead and found the lands about Monmouth empty. Clinton had gone. Then either Wayne or Lee spotted a low-hanging plume of dust smothering the treetops in the middle distance, an infallible sign of troops on the move. Lee reckoned that it would take some two thousand men to kick up such a cloud and, reasoning that the two thousand were the last of the rear guard hurrying to overtake Clinton and the rest, ordered Wayne to cut them off. Wayne was to take six hundred of his Pennsylvanians and two field guns for the job.

Wayne gathered his men and guns, swept out in a wide arc to clear the dust-choked woods. He hit unexpectedly into a rather loose formation of laggards, broke them easily, and then brought up against more solid units. He took position at the edge of a curious long depression, half swamp and half ravine, to the west of Monmouth and called on Lee for support. With that message, about the last coherent move of Lee's force evaporated into the sweltering air of June 28, 1778.

Charles Lee, master of the art of war, scattered his units over the broken terrain like confetti spilling from a sack. There was no plan of attack, no direction, and most of the details of this part of the day may be reconstructed only by surmise and conjecture. Regiments and brigades marched and countermarched. No orders seem to have reached the hazy firing line where Clinton's pressure was increasing. Officers of every grade consulted, improvised, advanced, fell back solely in accordance with what a given man could see. Companies rushed up to reinforce troops in unthreatened positions. Men under attack were left unsupported simply through lack of a single guiding hand. Lafayette urged Lee to order a general advance and received the frightening reply, "Sir, you do not know British soldiers. We can't stand against them!"

On the edge of the ravine where he had first halted, Wayne only knew that Charles Scott had brought his Virginians somewhere up on the left, but not in close touch. Ahead was a thick fringe of advancing British infantry. Suddenly the scarlet coats parted and through the gaps pounded a line of horsemen in green jackets faced with blue and probably wearing vizorless hussar busbies. John Simcoe had thrown the hussars of the Queen's Rangers at the Pennsylvanians. In the past a sudden dash of cavalry had been enough to scatter large, well-posted bodies of Americans. But this was the present, not the past. And Von Steuben seems to have taught his pupils something about receiving a cavalry attack.

Colonel Richard Butler in the center kept calling to his men to hold their fire. Then there was a dry, clicking sound as hundreds of hammers were drawn back, a sharp command, and flame licked along the Pennsylvania ranks. Before the smoke could rise in the dead, stifling air Wayne could be heard trumpeting, "Have at 'em with the bayonet!" The whole line swept forward, found that the charge of the Ranger hussars had been broken, that galloping horses, some of them riderless, were plunging back through the British infantry, carrying those formidable fighters with them.

Wayne checked his pursuit, ordered Colonel Eleazar Oswald's Connecticut gunners to bring their fieldpieces to bear on the still retreating hussars and the confused infantry. One minute to re-form his men and he could press on with the other American units that must be closing in on his right and left.

There was nothing on his right and left. Charles Lee had ordered a retreat, apparently without bothering to notify any units save those nearest him. Here and there officers had seen the start of the retrograde move and had conformed to it without knowing why the order had been given or what spot, if any, had been designated as a rallying point. Wayne sent riders after Lee, but the only answer they brought back was that the ugly, angular man "would see General Wayne later." The Pennsylvania force was badly scattered, but Wayne managed somehow to get it off the field with Oswald's two fieldpieces bumping sturdily along in the center.

The course of the retreat lay along the Englishtown road, beginning with fairly open country and then plunging into low hills cut by another of those swampy ravines and with a long causeway to traverse. The American force poured back, some units keeping admirable order and others close to a *sauve-qui-peut*, bewildered men who did not feel that they had been beaten and who were pardonably unsettled by this sudden change in the tide. Charles Lee rode with the retreat, and the confusion of this part of the day fogs his own behavior and bearing. Some who saw him thought he was in a panic. Others, probably more accurately, noted that he seemed utterly self-possessed, possibly a little amused, as though he were thinking, "See what I meant about facing British troops? What did I tell you?" His method of proving his point was rather drastic but quite in character.

To add to the discomfort of the distracted men, the heat, which had been notable for the last day or so, now outdid itself. Humidity was fearful, the air a stifling blanket about faces and nostrils. The thermometer soared close to one hundred. Officers and soldiers began to collapse, still willing to fight but utterly played out, while the heat waves shimmered over the sticky grass and danced among motionless trees.

Then some men in the van of the retreat saw dust clouds coming toward them down the Englishtown road. There may have been a moment of sheer panic fathered by the thought that Clinton had somehow managed to get a force across the line of march. But there was no spread of scarlet under the choking pall, no glimmer of murky brass. Someone recognized a huge white horse and remembered that it had been a present from Governor Edward Livingston of New Jersey to the big man in blue and buff who handled the mount so easily. Soldiers stopped to stare and then to cheer. The young marquis, his sloping forehead running with sweat, forgot the shame of abandoning the field, was suddenly unaware of the deadly heat. "His presence stopped the retreat . . . his calm courage, roused to animation by the vexations of the morning, gave him the air best calculated to excite enthusiasm." Washington's arrival was a sight that the Frenchman never forgot, and he told and retold how the Virginian rode "all along the lines amid the shouts of the soldiers, cheering them by his voice and example and restoring to our standards the fortunes of the fight. I thought then, as now, that never had I beheld so superb a man." George Washington may have had grave faults as a commander. But as a leader he was close to flawless. Here was no waving of a white plume, no hysterical appeal to emotions, no exerting of mass hypnosis. He had only to show his unshakable courage, his matchless integrity and devotion, and their combined alchemy touched men from New Hampshire and Rhode Island, from Maryland and Virginia, Pennsylvania and North Carolina, and made them one with him and his convictions.

There was an encounter with Charles Lee, who was furiously called upon to explain the why of his movement. Accounts of the meeting rest largely on vague hearsay, but it does seem that just for once the ironclad self-control that reined in Washington's naturally quick temper cracked. The Virginia general, Charles Scott, later recalled: "Yes, he swore that day till the leaves shook on the trees. Charming! Delightful! Never have I enjoyed such swearing before or since. Sir, on that memorable day he swore like an angel from heaven!" Whatever Washington did say was surely strong enough. Later Lee wrote to the commander-in-chief, speaking of "an act of cruel injustice" which required "reparation." Washington answered quite sharply and Lee demanded a court-martial. This was granted, and at the end the second-in-command of the United States Army was suspended for a year. Still later he wrote most insultingly to the Congress, which wearily resolved that there was "no further occasion for his services in the army of the United States," and Charles Lee passed out of the picture for good and all. But all this lay in varying depths of the future.

Taking command from Lee, Washington gave a quick look down the Englishtown–Monmouth road. Just west of a bridge that spanned a swamp ravine he found Walter Stewart's 13th Pennsylvania and Nat Ramsay's 3rd Maryland, the very last of the retreat. They were coming on in good order, but less than two hundred yards behind them was a wall of dust that bulged with scarlet. Bright bayonets gleamed through, and in the van could be seen the brass helmets of the 16th and 17th Dragoons, eager for the final coup de grâce.

Out of the welter of the American side appeared Anthony Wayne, smeared with dust and smoke and calmly furious over what had happened so far. Relieved, Washington gave him command over Stewart and Ramsay. Wayne's orders were simple. Just hold a line until Washington could reform the rest of the army behind him. Then the dragoons were on the Pennsylvanians and Marylanders. Stewart was wounded in the clashing turmoil. A saber blow struck down Ramsay and he was a prisoner. The line gave way, but in good order. Drums beat behind it and dust sifted in from the west. Wayne was bringing up Varnum's Rhode Islanders and the tough New Yorkers of Henry Livingston's 4th, and a new stand was made back of a thick hedge that closed off an orchard. The 3rd and 7th Pennsylvanians were up and part of a Virginia regiment.

Back of Wayne's little force the rest of the army was gathering. There was Lord Stirling on the left and the eager young marquis, beside himself with the joy of his command, in the center. Wheezing in the dust that plagued his asthma came Nathanael Greene. Wheels rumbled and Henry Knox's gunners came jolting up. More guns pounded off to the right and Lieutenant Colonel Edward Carrington, a fine Virginia artilleryman, took up a daring position on the far right, across Wemrock Brook, where his fire could cover Wayne's front.

This was truly a new army. Infantryman and gunner came into action under fire, quietly shepherded by Von Steuben, who thought that they closed up into line "with as much precision as on ordinary parade and with the . . . intrepidity of veteran troops." He must have regretted, as he watched his pupils, that he had backed Lee in recommending that Clinton be allowed to slip away undisturbed. Other eyes saw what was happening, eyes that may have been skeptical about the value of all that wheeling and marching and pacing on the Valley Forge plateau. Alexander Hamilton admitted that never until that day had he "known or conceived the value of military discipline."

And every scrap of discipline, courage, and will to fight was needed. Clinton was throwing in everything he had, perhaps hoping to deliver that one, necessary knockout blow to American military power that should have been each British commander's objective since the nineteenth of April in 1775. The light infantry and the hard Scots of the 42nd Black Watch were launched against Lord Stirling, but Richard Parker's 1st Virginia, Joseph Cilley's 1st and Alexander Scammell's 3rd New Hampshire extended Stirling's left and struck the skullcapped light infantry and the bonneted Scots in the flank and forced them to withdraw.

Then Greene was hit, over on Washington's right. Masses of fur-capped British grenadiers, with the temperature at one hundred, pounded down on him, were backed by Hessian grenadiers in their towering brass helmets. The Coldstream Guards came on. Through the fog of the assault could be seen the yellow facings of the 37th Hampshires and the 44th Essex. Scarlet coats and blue were dropping on the trampled grass, probably as often stricken down by the wicked heat as by gunfire. Edward Carrington's pieces across on Comb's Hill joined in, caught the British attack in the flank, and sealed its fate.

It was fearful fighting. Despite the inhuman heat, despite the endless, killing march from Philadelphia, Clinton's men came on and on until the sun or American fire took them out of action. The British were superb, the Hessians nearly as good. They fell back only on command. They strode into the worst fire as steadily as the flow of Wemrock Brook off on their left. Their drill was so perfectly maintained, their alignment so true that a single shot from one of Carrington's guns knocked the leveled muskets from the hands of a whole front rank. This is usually cited as indicating the accuracy of the Virginian's fire. That fire was as good as could be wished for, but that round must have been a lucky one, its effect being due to the meticulous precision of British troops in action.

Now Wayne was to take the main shock of the attack with his men down by the hedge, well in front of the American center. A fine combat officer, Lieutenant Colonel Monckton, originally of the 45th Derbyshires, was given a magnificent grenadier battalion, formed it almost within musket shot of Wayne and his men, then brought it on in a furious charge. Again the long weeks of drill told and Wayne's whole line held its fire. His files could hear him calling, "Steady! Wait for the word, then pick out the king-birds." Fire was held to within forty yards and then the hedge erupted. Down went the grenadiers, with Monckton falling dead so close to the hedge that some Americans were able to worm through, bring his body into shelter along with the battalion colors.

By now both sides were staggering with heat and exhaustion. Men died right and left under the touch of the sun or collapsed, helpless, with purpling faces while sweat pattered down on scarlet coats, blue coats, or on mended threadbare homespun. But Sir Henry Clinton was not through. Somehow he rallied another long wave of attackers, pressed on close despite losses, and managed to work around the right and left of the seemingly endless hedge.

Wayne was outflanked on both sides. Calmly he ordered a withdrawal which went on in very good shape until his men reached Lafayette's formations. By giving up his orchard position he had lost nothing, since, as noted, he was well in advance of the main American lines. His movement to the rear was a simple one. But it is certain that a year ago, a few months ago, his men could not have carried it out, as few of the movements of the day could have been executed at an earlier period.

Clinton fell back. Washington searched and beat the fields for troops fresh enough to launch a counterattack. He found William Woodford's Virginians and Thomas Clark's North Carolinians. But the term "fresh" is only relative. Woodford's men and Clark's were willing enough, steady enough, but light was failing before they could be brought into action.

During the night Sir Henry withdrew, satisfied that he had insured the safety of his immense baggage train, now well on its way to Sandy Hook. Actually, if there were a victor, it was that same dour, surly British commander-in-chief. He had had to fight harder than he had expected, after Washington's arrival, but what he had dreaded most, being caught in a ten- to fifteen-mile-long column of retreat, was now averted forever. In a few days the force entrusted to him would be back in New York and he could draw a breath of relief for the first time since receiving word of the expected approach of D'Estaing with his French ships and tough, wiry French soldiers.

The American commander-in-chief, having seen that his force was properly disposed for the night, found a tall figure in blue and buff stretched out under an apple tree without cloak or blanket. Washington paused, then lay down under the same tree, spreading his own cloak over himself and the exhausted Marquis de Lafayette.

So sleep settled over the battlefield of Monmouth. The American army, thanks to its Germanic tutor and to the quiet power and inspiration of its Virginia leader, had never fought harder or better.

CHAPTER XXVI

". . . his intention of offering his services to . . . the British"

BACK at the camp at Englishtown from which the army had sallied out into the plains below, the commander-in-chief issued an order. All ranks were to "wash themselves and appear as decent as possible" and then "publickly unite in thanksgiving to the supreme Disposer of human Events for the Victory which was obtained . . . over the Flower of the British Troops." This was fair enough, for if the "human Events" which transpired in the sandy stretches about Monmouth Court House had hardly been a victory, the American fighting man, alone or en masse, had shown himself to be at least the equal of the best British troops on that day.

But now the British and Hessians were gone, safely on their way to New York, and contact had to be set up again. On July 1, 1778, Washington started his army once more over the old trails along which men had stumbled and staggered through sleet and blizzard and stabbing sunlight since '76. The route lay through New Brunswick and Acquanock, through Paramus and Kakiat (modern Ridgewood and West New Hampstead, New Jersey), and thence across the state line to Haverstraw Bay on the west bank of the Hudson, facing Ossining.

So the two armies lay watching each other in virtually the same positions they had occupied in 1776, and a marked change in the pattern of the war had begun. No one, American or British, could have predicted it, but never again would the main American army go into action. Never again was Washington to lead it against the principal British force. From now on the war was to be a matter of detachments, of expeditions, of relatively small bodies operating often far from the parent army.

For the moment Sir Henry Clinton felt that he was not strong enough to mount an offensive across the river. To Washington and his generals the approaches to Manhattan seemed far too formidable to be rushed, particularly as such an operation meant the crossing of a river navigable far beyond Haverstraw. Of course if one had control of the sea, something like Howe's operations that led to the fall of Manhattan in '76 might be attempted. But lacking that——

For a moment it almost looked as though sea control were within reach.

The intelligence that led Clinton to give up Philadelphia had been correct. On July 8 watchers off the Delaware capes spotted the glimmer of sail-cloth, golden in the summer sunlight, made out the broad black hulls of French ships. Charles Henri Hector, Comte d'Estaing, had arrived with a dozen powerful ships of the line and a few frigates, along with the ac-curately reported four thousand French troops. Ten days earlier, and D'Estaing would have caught Clinton at the most delicate part of his evacuation of Philadelphia, and in that event the disaster to the British would have been limited only by one's imagination.

D'Estaing cruised up the coast after communicating with Washington, then on the march to Haverstraw, and suddenly sighted a target the value of whose destruction was enough to stagger any navy mind. In the angle between the west shore of Staten Island and Sandy Hook lay "Black Dick's" British fleet, in a bad position and heavily outnumbered and out-gunned by the French. The new alliance began to function with a speed and smoothness that set both American and French hearts skipping many beats. The passage between Staten Island and the Hook was unknown to the French navigators, and they feared a mass grounding that would have given the game at once into Admiral Howe's hands. Very well. Washington sent a horde of pilots scudding out to the French fleet, and D'Estaing and his officers began soberly to tot up the tally of this most desired victory over the ships of heartily detested Albion.

The pilots had other ideas. The ships, they claimed, were too deep-draft to manage a channel that was partially blocked by a sandbar. Angry French officers stormed at them, and D'Estaing offered up to fifty thousand gold French crowns to the man who would take the leading ship over the bar. But the pilots planted their sea boots on the deck and closed their ears to all arguments, so the French admiral spent eleven agonizing days drooling at the sight of Howe's ships lying at anchor, helpless but out of reach.

There were other allied projects that could be undertaken and, to Wash-ington's joy, D'Estaing listened eagerly. There was the town of Newport in Rhode Island, lightly held by the British but capable of being built up quickly into an invasion base against New England. A plan was drawn up, agreed to by all parties, and the first true Franco-American coup was launched, in splendid augury of things to come.

General John Sullivan was hurried overland to Rhode Island with two first-rate brigades to reinforce the troops already watching the Newport British. The French fleet, with its accompanying white-coated infantry, set sail for Narragansett Bay to close in from the sea, and Americans held their breaths in delighted anticipation of the joint hammer blow that was to fall on the enemy.

Everything went wrong. The French fleet raised Newport without op-position, but Sullivan, touchy as ever, became involved in a fearful quangle-wangle with D'Estaing, himself none too easy a character, that actually threatened the new alliance. A reinforced British fleet appeared out of the eastern end of Long Island Sound, and D'Estaing put to sea to engage it. A terrific storm scattered both navies, causing such damage that the French admiral, probably wisely, headed to Boston with all his men-of-war and transports to refit. No, he would not return to Newport to renew the attack. French Admiralty orders, issued before he had sailed for America, strictly limited the time that he could spend on the Atlantic seaboard and now he was due in the West Indies. The French Government merely looked upon the United States as one of several theaters of war in which the British might be met.

Admiralty orders and D'Estaing's obedience to them were logical enough, but the disappearance of the French from the Rhode Island area discouraged many Americans and gave the Francophobes an exceptionally juicy bone to tooth. What did I tell you? They're not going to help us. All they've done so far is to get John Sullivan into a tight place at Newport and then run off and leave him.

This was true, but inevitable in a war where one ally was trying to operate with ironclad orders at a distance of three thousand miles and more. Sullivan was left to face a strengthened British force, and there was a clash on Newport's gemlike island. The New Hampshire general handled his troops very well. There was a gallant and successful stand against hard Hessian attacks by a regiment of Rhode Island Negroes under Christopher Greene, a feat which confounded those who held that Negroes could not stand against white men. (It will be recalled that there were some who swore that Americans could not stand against British.) Night fell and, following an old pattern, John Glover's Marbleheaders wrote a coda to the day's work by silently ferrying Sullivan's whole force up Seaconnet Passage to Tiverton and the mainland.

Militarily, the rest of the year idled on in neutral. Above Haverstraw Bay, Washington's men fared quite well, for them. Food was at least sufficient and units that went short could only blame their own inefficient supply officers. Shoes were still in short supply, but October brought cases and cases of uniforms from France, blue coats and brown, both faced with red, waistcoats and breeches. Despite the insistence of the less meticulous historical artists on the "regulation Continental blue and buff," thousands of men from colonels to rear-rank privates found themselves irresistibly drawn to the brown-and-red combination and said so as loudly and as often as possible. To keep the new garments from being torn to bits by eager claimants in bargain-counter rushes, the Congress had to decree that the issue be made by lot. As a result, Pennsylvania and New Hampshire regiments, along with Hazen's Canadians, strutted in brown-and-red coats, sniffing smugly at the rest of the army, which was forced by chance into blue.

So as a result of this French shipment most of the troops were able to appear in fairly respectable military garb. Yet that garb was incomplete. Hats, boots, and blankets were, as Washington glumly reported to the Congress, "sadly lacking." This was not surprising. Something always was lacking. The army of the United States was ever to be in the position of Mr. Reginald Wilfer in *Our Mutual Friend*, who, when he managed to acquire a new hat, found that his coat was shabby and, when blessed by a new coat, discovered that his smallclothes or boots needed replacing.

Winter drew on and the army was broken up and spread in a great arc of camps that swept up from Middlebrook in New Jersey, not far from the old Monmouth battlefield, on through to West Point and Fishkill in New York and east to Danbury, Connecticut. The men hutted themselves as they had at Valley Forge and, as at Valley Forge, were blessed with a quite mild winter, the sufferings at that Pennsylvania camp having been due to rations, supplies, and equipment that would have been inadequate almost anywhere in the Temperate Zone.

This new disposition of the army did not imply inactivity. Constant watch had to be kept against possible Anglo-German raids from Staten Island across into New Jersey, where "Scotch Willie" Maxwell patrolled. There was Westchester County, on the mainland just above Manhattan, which was turning into a sort of no man's land, raided and gutted and harried by both sides, where the inhabitants of both persuasions took advantage of the turmoil, as happened in many other areas, to hack away at neighbors in fulfillment of feuds generations old. As far up as Tappan a body of Colonel George Baylor's 3rd Continental Dragoons was surprised by a British force under General Charles Grey, the patron of elegant Major John André. That the affair may be well held up as a model for a night swoop of mobile troops against mobile troops was by no means appreciated in the American army, and there were once more loud howls of "Massacre!" as there had been after Grey's surprise of Wayne at Paoli. Other British demonstrations, notably at Fishkill, kept the high brass nervously alert. More fires flared up, far out of the reach of the commander-in-chief, and British landing parties burned Fairhaven in Massachusetts and took cattle from the none-too-prosperous inhabitants of Martha's Vineyard. Such coups, along with other later forays, actually backfired on the raiders, since they brought the war vividly home to areas that might have merely dozed on, with an academically benevolent eye on such gazettes and rumors as reached them. Now recruiting was stimulated in the wake of each enemy raid and provisions and supplies flowed more freely to the main army.

Along with all such perplexities, the usual blizzard of slack-time problems blew strong about Washington's powdered head. The customary flow of requests to resign swelled as more and more officers took stock of their own particular situations, personal and military. Some felt that they had served long enough. Others were in an impenetrable fog of sulkiness over not being promoted with the alacrity which they felt their talents merited. There was even a school of thought that held that from now on the French would—or should—fight the war and that America no longer needed an army in the field. Many of these requests, especially in the first category, were sound. General Alexander McDougall had kept a frail body in the field through long years solely by will power. General John Glover, remarkable on many counts and above all for being one of the few officers in the army to fight off promotion, was also in bad health and his Marblehead family faced economic disaster without him. Many pleas to be allowed to resign were as valid as McDougall's and Glover's. But the bulk of such petitioners, along with this limping but stalwart pair, stayed on until the end of the war terminated their services.

Then there were men of high rank who had been removed from command—*dégommé*, the vivid French phrase—pending courts-martial or congressional inquiries. Some of these, now cleared, stormed back to the army and demanded a command suitable to their various grades, thus threatening to oust juniors who had carried on for one or more campaigns in the vacated rank but without promotion. Two such were Philip Schuyler and Arthur St. Clair, who had had to answer for the loss of Ticonderoga the summer before. There was always room for Schuyler, who held no field command, but reinstating St. Clair meant the virtual demotion or resignation of the almost irreplaceable Anthony Wayne. These military knots could hardly be sliced through in a moment, and their loosening wasted Washington's time and kept officers and men alike in a state of unhealthy jitters.

There was also the main British Army to watch, its possible major moves to be countered. That army remained passive, to the surprise of most Americans, who had had no opportunity to appreciate the profound change that had taken place in the nature of the war since the French alliance and the arrival of D'Estaing's fleet. No longer were hostilities aimed solely at imposing the will of the Crown on the most outrageous of rebels. The war had turned, so far as the British were concerned, into a hemispheric affair, if not global; had become a resumption of the centuries of strife between continental powers whose alignments were always changing so bewilderingly. England now had to watch the West Indies and the rich colonies there. The Mediterranean could not be forgotten, nor the Indian Ocean. If the Dutch suddenly popped in along with the French, the Java Sea must be kept in mind. And there was always a chance, as there was to be in the days of Napoleon, Wilhelm II, and Adolf Schicklgruber, of a cross-Channel invasion of the British Isles themselves, and troops could no longer be poured lavishly into the British base at New York. The roulette wheel of war had spun and spun since those days when King George's ministers felt that three or four regiments sent to Boston would quickly bring the transatlantic turmoil into a properly obedient and respectful calm.

During this winter of 1778–79, Washington rather worriedly noted that Sir Henry Clinton, far from being aggressive on any large scale, had "become reduced to the spade and pick-axe for defense." So far as the record may be read, neither Washington nor any of his generals could be aware of the great sweeping policy change on the part of the British Government, the complete reappraisal. London had decided to call off all important operations in the North. The Southern states were now the British target, although headquarters were to remain in New York City.

There were reasons, some sound, some definitely shaky, for this shift in British focus. For one thing, an expedition sent to Georgia or South Carolina by water could be shifted easily from the mainland and used against any French coup in the West Indies, a much-dreaded and highly possible development. And Southern campaigns could be reinforced from those islands if the situation permitted. It is easy to overlook the drain that the West Indian commitments imposed on the British command in North America even before the French alliance. Going down the roster of British troops serving here, little notes keep cropping up against this unit or that. From 1776 on, whole regiments, or substantial elements of them, keep slipping away to the South. Here are the 16th Bedfordshires, the 28th Gloucestershires, the 30th East Lancashires, the 35th Sussex, the 40th South Lancashires, the 46th Duke of Cornwall's Light Infantry, the 49th Royal Berkshires, and so on, heading at one time or another to the Indies or to Florida.

A will-o'-the-wisp once again danced and pirouetted before the eyes of British planners in New York and in London to back up reason with an ephemeral wish. It will be remembered that one of the contributing factors to Burgoyne's downfall was Philip Skene's eternal tale of thousands of Loyalists just over the next hill, only waiting for the arrival of His Majesty's troops before springing to arms and wiping out the shabby rebels. So now dozens of advisers narrowed their eyes wisely and nodded their powdered heads. Here, gentlemen, is the South, with Loyalists present in overwhelming numbers. No doubt we should have dipped into this capital earlier. A landing, a show of the royal colors, and the rebel forces, such as they are, will melt into the swamps of the Combahee and the Santee. A new phrase was coined: Beat the Americans with Americans. Organize and equip the Loyalists, support them with royal troops, and the whole South will fall. Such reasoning was blind to the fact that the Tories so far had never been militarily effective, save on the smallest of scales, that they had shown no talent for organizing themselves, and that they had never materialized in the field in important numbers.

This emphasis on the South put a vastly increased burden on Sir Henry Clinton and his staff. Troops could not be sent too lavishly from New York without laying that base open to a sudden coup by Washington. Yet the new theaters of the Indies and the Southern states clamored. Sir Henry set his jaw and plunged into the necessary details, very possibly giving silent thanks that he had accepted the strong suggestions of Major General Charles Grey, now on his way to England, that efficient young Major John André become a member of headquarters staff. Pens swished over soft paper, aides drew up lists, tore them up, made fresh ones, and at least five thousand troops were sent to St. Lucia in the West Indies and a mixed force of British, Hessians, and Tories—some thirty-five hundred in all—

embarked, their target Savannah, Georgia, or, in the phrasing of Dickens' Mr. Willet, "In the Salwanners, in America, where the war is."

With this second expedition a new spring had been wound up in the war, and when that spring finally relaxed, a British army marched, weaponless, between rigid ranks of French and American troops on Virginia soil.

If an uneasy inactivity hung over the main theaters of war, hot fires burned along the fringes of the new nation. The kindling of these fires and their eventual extinction were important in the whole picture and, directly or indirectly, played a part in the eventual outcome of the struggle. Yet the conflagrations seem to belong rather to the slow, relentless surge that finally opened up the West clear to the Pacific. The pattern was as old as North America, the inevitable clash between red man and white.

Out of what is now Kentucky came George Rogers Clark at the head of a tough little band and, in a long campaign that can hardly be matched in our history for sheer, raw endurance and courage, wiped out British posts at Vincennes in present-day Indiana and at Kaskaskia in modern Illinois. These posts were neither strong nor militarily dangerous, but they served as supply bases and propaganda centers for the Indian tribes that were making life almost impossible along the south bank of the Ohio River. With the elimination of Vincennes and Kaskaskia, the Indian menace slackened noticeably.

So in the Mohawk Valley in New York a local war that had a life of its own, apart from the struggle between England and the United States, flared hideously. And here the Indians were solidly backed by Loyalists and Crown forces, supplied, paid, equipped, and often accompanied into the field by them. But looking over the record, it is hard to feel these bitter hostilities were much more than an extension of the eternal fight between the Johnsons, Butlers, and others, with their feudal forest empire, and the independent settlers. One may quite safely read "farmer" for "rebel" and "the Johnson Empire" for the Crown. Local feuds hung onto the larger issues and in many cases dominated them.

As for the Indians, they would have been on the warpath regardless of Johnson and Butler proddings. To them the whites who held the North, who clung to lakes and rivers and built few settlements and fewer towns, were the people to tie to, be they French, as in the beginning, or the later British. Such whites were their allies against the ever-pushing settlers to the south, against those men who were slowly eating into the Indian lands and hence eroding the savage way of life. The red man could live with the trapper, the *voyageur*, the *coureur de bois*. But the man who built a cabin and owned a plow; the people who felled the forests, who built roads and brought in wheeled vehicles—these were the Indians' mortal enemy, no matter how friendly the cabin builder or road maker might be by nature or how pacific his intentions.

So bullet and flame were to rage up and down the Mohawk Valley and crackle on south to the end of hostilities between the United States and England. Like the menace against which George Rogers Clark marched so gallantly, the strife in New York State had, at bottom, little to do with words spoken or written in the rose-and-white State House in Philadelphia in 1776.

The main American army breasted the flow of the winter months quietly enough, as bland a winter as American soldiers were to know as long as the war lasted. Dr. James Thacher, surgeon from Barnstable in Massachusetts, who had known Breed's Hill and the siege of Boston, was now with the main army after long service in the North. The Journal which he had begun in January 1775 continued to grow, and in it he set down the life of his camp, just as he had recorded doings at Ticonderoga and Albany, where he had tended that most troublesome of patients, General Benedict Arnold.

But one of the most significant facts of army life, and indeed of his own, he passed over with little comment beyond the actual record. He had long been attached to hospitals and now seemed to feel that his advancement, professional as well as military, would go faster if he obtained a post as a regimental surgeon. This quest took him several months, but he finally landed the much-desired berth. He was formally assigned to Colonel George Gibson's 1st Virginia Regiment of General Peter Muhlenberg's brigade. It is quite possible that back in '75 or '76 Thacher would have thrown a king-size tantrum had he been asked to fill in for a week or two with a New Hampshire regiment or even one from western Massachusetts. And his potential patients would surely have bellowed as loudly as he. But in the year 1778 we see this Cape Cod doctor settling himself amicably among Virginians and receiving a "polite invitation to take my quarters in the marquee with Colonel Gibson and his lieutenant-colonel William Brent."

In his camp near Fishkill in the shadow of Mount Beacon on the east bank of the Hudson, Thacher's pen flowed on. Owing to the distance from New York, the doctor felt "secure from the annoyance of the dogs of war," which pleased him well enough, but he felt that all regimental officers were slacking off too much, to be contracting "a habit approaching to dissipation," giving suppers "with music and dancing through half the night. These are the favorite amusements of the Virginia and Maryland officers, but they do not accord [James Thacher must have frowned sternly as he wrote these words] precisely with my own views of time well spent." Nonetheless, he does not seem to have been too much of a wowser about such matters, for "I am frequently enticed to a participation in their banqueting revels." One night he dined with Peter Muhlenberg and "as usual, closed the evening with music and dancing." No mention is made of partners in these dances.

Later the Barnstable doctor called on Lafayette, who was just getting over a fever "and was in his chair of convalescence." He was politely and affably received and seems to have been much taken with the young Frenchman, noting particularly his "fine, animated hazel eye." Back in quarters, Thacher jotted down, "Considering him a French nobleman of distinguished character, and a great favorite of General Washington, I felt myself highly honored by this interview."

Thacher's camp was moved into New Jersey and he witnessed some beautiful fireworks provided at Pluckemin by General Henry Knox and later attended a splendid ball, "opened by his Excellency General Washington, having for his partner the lady of General Knox." The ex-bookseller and his Lucy were quite as pleased as their guest, Dr. Thacher. Henry commented that it had been "a most genteel entertainment, given by self and officers. Everybody allows it to be the first of its kind ever exhibited in this state at least. We had above seventy ladies, all of the first ton in the state . . . danced all night—an elegant room."

Later the surgeon was actually bidden to dine with the master and chatelaine of Mount Vernon, to see him and his wife at close range. James Thacher must have taken great care with his uniform, hat, and polished boots before presenting himself at the John Wallace house, which still stands in present-day Somerville, New Jersey, not far from Middlebrook, now Bound Brook. An earlier caller had remarked that Washington "had nothing extraordinary about him, which I had expected." The Barnstable surgeon arrived "with the secret hope of discovering in his features some peculiar traces of excellence, which distinguishes him and elevates him above his fellow mortals." He was not disappointed.

> These expectations are realized in a peculiar manner in viewing the person of General Washington. His tall and noble stature and just proportions—his fine, cheerful and open countenance—simple and modest deportment—are all calculated to interest every beholder in his favour, and to command veneration and respect. He is feared even when silent, and beloved even while we are unconscious of the motive. . . . In conversation, his excellency's expressive countenance is peculiarly interesting and pleasing; a placid smile is frequently observed on his lips, but a loud laugh, it is said, seldom, if ever, escapes him. . . . Mrs. Washington combines in an uncommon degree great dignity of manner with the most pleasing affability . . . [she] has ever been honored as a lady of distinguished goodness, possessing all the virtues which adorn her sex, amiable in her temper and deportment, full of benignity, benevolence and charity, seeking for objects of affliction and poverty, that she may extend to the sufferers the hand of kindness and relief.

This is a fine firsthand impression of Martha Washington, one that Thacher would never amend or modify. And note the effect that the commander-in-chief made upon his guest. The latter is seized with no sudden impulse to snatch up a sword and charge a battery. Instead, the words "respect" and "veneration" occur. This conservative Cape Codder is deeply impressed by a leader, not by a beau sabreur.

Nathanael Greene, now unwillingly, doggedly, and devotedly filling the office of quartermaster general for the whole army, had fine quarters on the Raritan River between Middlebrook and Somerville in an already aged brick Dutch farmhouse where he and Kitty Greene held court. The former Derrick van Veghten place was a magnet for the French officers, as the little house in Valley Forge had been, and for many Americans as well. Nathanael, writing to Jeremiah Wadsworth of Connecticut, able commissary general of purchases, reported, "We had a little dance at my quarters a few evenings ago. His Excellency and Mrs Greene danced upwards of three hours without once sitting down," a feat which neither Nathanael nor Martha Washington seems to have found the least bit out of the way.

Thacher called on Von Steuben, dug in at the Abraham Staats house close by the Raritan, and along with Washington and some twoscore other officers saw the whole army defile in a nearby field while the old German watched maneuvers and evolutions with a martinet's eye. The review must have been well done, for Thacher wrote that it afforded "the commander-in-chief and the spectators the highest degree of satisfaction." Then his mind turned to the one man who was the mainspring of the whole assemblage. "On this occasion we cannot but pride ourselves on the conspicuous figure exhibited by our commander-in-chief. While mounted on his noble bay charger, his stature appears remarkable; and being a good horseman, he displays a lofty carriage, and benign dignity of demeanor, and I hope not to incur the charge of undue partiality, when I say his appearance was incomparably more majestic and dignified than either of his illustrious visitors." These visitors were Conrad Alexandre Gérard, first minister of France to the United States, and Don Juan de Miralles (whom Thacher boldly renders as "Mirrilliars"), minister of Spain, which country was trying agonizingly to get into the war in order to damage England but without in any way encouraging republican rebels in the Americas.

It will be noted that the doctor does not mention Lafayette at any of these gatherings. That eager young soul had sailed for France on a sort of quick home leave during which he hoped to influence the court to come in with heavy ships and powerful regiments, not merely shiploads of brown jackets faced with red.

Thacher's time was by no means spent entirely in wining with his new Virginia friends or in basking in the presence of the great. Von Steuben descended upon him, asking for a detailed list of the sick and disabled of the army. The baron also wanted to know how these cases were quartered, what therapy was being used in various types of illness. Then he dragged Thacher off for a tour of the hospitals and greatly impressed the Cape Codder with his grasp of field treatment. "He is held," wrote Thacher of the German, "in universal respect . . . The continental army has improved with great rapidity under his inspection and review."

June of 1779 found the army on the move again, trailing away over the wearily familiar roads across New Jersey and back to the Hudson. This was no routine shifting of ground, for Sir Henry Clinton had suddenly moved up the river, seizing the commanding height of Stony Point on the west bank and Verplanck's on the east. Dr. Thacher and his fellow officers noted that the two points commanded King's Ferry, an important link in the American supply route that ran from New England to the main army. They could also see that from the two points, now being rapidly fortified, a strong attack could be launched against West Point, some ten miles up the river. There was unwonted optimism in the American army, and Thacher wrote that many officers "expressed a strong desire that the royal troops would afford an opportunity to try our strength and courage. Should this be the event, the struggle must indeed be violent and the slaughter immense."

But the British aim seems to have been to draw Washington into a general action and as the latter showed no signs of taking the bait, Sir Henry Clinton returned to New York, leaving what he thought to be adequate garrisons at Verplanck's and Stony Point. In doing so, he set the stage for an American counterpunch that would be slowly and carefully prepared and brilliantly delivered, although its effects could be only local.

While the Northern theater seemed to be settling into a bed of blackening embers, bright little flames began to curl and twist about the Southern fringe of the nation. At first these flames did not seem to be very important, an uneven creeping of brush fires that could be slapped at without taking the national eye from the Northern embers.

The thirty-five hundred men Clinton had sent south had landed and seized the port of Savannah in Georgia in the last days of 1778. A body of Georgia militia under Major General Robert Howe of North Carolina had been pushed aside and more British troops under Major General Augustine Prevost came up from Florida to join the original landing force. Sunbury fell and Augusta, high up on the Savannah River on the South Carolina border.

Names already familiar began to appear again on the American side. Port Royal, on one of the Sea Islands on the southern brim of South Carolina, was attacked and once again Brigadier General William Moultrie held his ground as resolutely as he had at Fort Sullivan in Charleston Harbor in '76. Andrew Pickens, brigadier general of South Carolina state troops, collided with a Tory formation at Kettle Creek and routed it.

But the flames crept and crept up the Southern fringe. There was a futile American attempt to retake Augusta. Down from the North came deceptively fat Major General Benjamin Lincoln of Massachusetts with about one thousand Continentals and threw his strength into a renewed attack on Augusta. Prevost, an exasperatingly resourceful leader, took advantage of Lincoln's move toward the Savannah River and slipped into Charleston. Lincoln faced about, headed for the coast, and Prevost craftily abandoned Charleston, having accomplished his objective of pulling the principal American force away from Augusta. There was a chance of catching the British force as it retreated, but Lincoln's stroke at Stono, south of Charleston, was roughly handled and Prevost's men trailed safely away to

Savannah, and for a few deceptive months there were embers in the South as well as the North.

Other flames, unseen, unsuspected, and sinister, had begun to burn under cover, but so far no odor of singeing, no faint crackling could be noticed in the spring air of Philadelphia, where Major General Benedict Arnold was in command. Still plagued by his twice-wounded leg, Arnold set himself up in great state in the Penn mansion, with a fine carriage and a houseful of liveried servants. Such an establishment, which made many old acquaintances wonder how he could possibly afford it, may have been in part Arnold's own tribute to his exalted rank and services. He may also have thought it necessary as a setting for the beautiful Philadelphia girl whom he had married on April 8, the same Peggy Shippen who had been one of the belles of the city during the British occupation and who seems to have sighed, unrequited, over that fascinating young John André.

Arnold was supremely happy with his Peggy and with the state in which he and she lived. But Peggy and the joint way of life were the one bright spot in an otherwise murky picture. That damned Congress kept asking him questions, demanding that he settle his accounts that involved the expenditure of public funds. Other questions kept arising out of his Philadelphia command, and some of these reached beyond Congress to the army itself. There were matters like giving unauthorized people passes to go into British-held New York, like the use of public wagons for private ends. And people were saying that, by using his power as commander of the area, he had bought goods very cheaply and then resold them at a vast profit to the Philadelphians. There were many other charges and half-charges that kept cropping up in the Congress and the army. Some of them seem to have been undoubtedly true. Some were relatively blameless and sanctioned by the usage of the times.

From the very beginning of his military career people had found that to differ with Benedict Arnold was to insult him; that even the mildest question brought forth not an answer but a blazing counterattack. He had brawled with Ethan Allen over the command of that first seizure of Ticonderoga in 1775. The Massachusetts General Court had issued him a Massachusetts commission as colonel. But when that august, if somewhat frigid, body asked for an accounting of funds disbursed by Arnold, their request only drove him into a flaming rage.

Now, in Philadelphia, he was demanding a court-martial to answer charges against him that went back to 1776, and the military lawyers were only too happy to oblige him. But movements of troops, the unwieldy mechanism of military law delayed matters, kept them dragging on and on. Things were not proceeding according to Arnold's pleasure, and hence, in his mind, their course must have been not only wrong but deliberately vicious.

So he fretted on in Philadelphia, the discomforts of gout adding to the misery of his slow-healing wounds. He and Peggy lived more lavishly than ever and seemed, to possibly jaundiced patriot eyes, to be cultivating the most notorious and wealthy Tories. When he had first come to Philadelphia, soldiers had cheered him in the streets. Now they made coarse sounds when they sighted him, and once a pack of possibly drunken militia actually chased him, bad leg and all, and were only held off by the general's pistols. This was no atmosphere in which a man like Benedict Arnold could live from day to day.

Sometime early in May 1779 a dealer in porcelains and crockery named Joseph Stansbury was summoned to the Arnold mansion. Stansbury, by discreet use of varying oaths of allegiance, had managed to flourish quite notably during the war years, though it was common report that his real allegiance was to the Crown. But with his latest oath he felt no qualms about calling on General and Mrs. Arnold and probably rubbed his hands on his way to the old Penn mansion. Peggy's tastes were expensive and Stansbury may have had visions of selling some elaborate dinner service.

His reception was a shock to him, though not an unpleasant one. The general, Stansbury said later, "opened his political sentiments respecting the war carrying on between Great Britain and America, declaring his abhorrence of a separation of the latter from the former. . . . General Arnold then communicated to me, under solemn obligation of secrecy, his intention of offering his services to the commander in chief of the British forces in any way that would most effectually restore the former government and destroy the then usurped authority of Congress, either by immediately joining the British army or co-operating on some concerted plan with Sir Henry Clinton."

The china dealer was both shaken and delighted. To act as go-between, which was what Arnold wanted, was risky, but if things worked out, not only would the Crown be restored in America, but one Joseph Stansbury could look to a luscious reward, perhaps even a title, for his part.

It took some planning, but Stansbury went to New York, got a severe case of jitters as he thought things over, and then opened his mind and heart to a red-hot Tory named Jonathan Odell, preacher and, like the china dealer, a poetaster. Together they managed to contact the head of the British Intelligence, himself a rhymester of note, Major John André, now unshakably fixed in the esteem of Sir Henry Clinton and secure against any possible return to regimental drudgery.

For some time past André had been mulling over the possibility of approaching some high American general via a bridge of gold. Many names had been suggested and then discarded, but by some odd quirk the one name that had never been even considered was Benedict Arnold's. So here was a rich prize handed to young André, a prize that he may have regarded as only the just due of a man who had so much conscious charm, who could turn such neat verses and keep the rather heavy, unimaginative Clinton in good humor.

A code for future communications was devised, channels mapped for their transmission, and a suitably flattering answer to Arnold concocted. It probably amused André to know that Mrs. Arnold was an old admirer of his. This might make negotiations easier, since she was not only aware of her husband's plans but heartily approved and encouraged them.

The correspondence started, and André found to his slight chagrin that he was dealing with no fiery idealist but with a hardheaded practical businessman who wanted heavy monetary rewards, figured down to the last halfpenny, rank in the British Army, and possibly a title for his services.

At the other end, Benedict and Peggy were shocked at the haggling, niggling ideas of the Crown. Code letters became rather sharp and at last were terminated with nothing settled. André thereupon closed the Arnold-André file for good, he thought. But the fires were still burning, though masked and hidden. So far no stench arose from them.

BOOK 4

". . . like men who are determined to be free"

ANTHONY WAYNE sniffed the sunlit July air that rolled gently south on the broad blue tide of the Hudson and knew that life was once more tingling and effervescent. Ousted from his command of the Pennsylvania line by the return of the lusterless though steadfast Arthur St. Clair, and unwilling to displace Will Irvine from brigade command, the handsome young Anthony had been drifting about, restless and irritable. Now he found himself tabbed for a job that everyone, including himself, knew to be tailor-made for him.

Since '77 an effort had been made to create a sort of *corps d'élite* in the American army, a body to counter the always formidable British light infantry. "Scotch Willie" Maxwell had commanded the first effort in '77, and Charles Scott of Virginia had headed such an outfit in '78, but little had come of these ventures, though no blame may be attached to either Maxwell or Scott.

Now in '79 a real combing had been given the forty-six slender battalions under Washington's command and four regiments of about three hundred and forty men each had been formed. These men had been carefully picked and some of them could count four solid years under arms and their memories dated back to the road between Lexington and Charlestown, to Breed's Hill and Long Island and the Hollow Way. None had put in less than a year. As for the officers, Washington himself had passed on the qualifications of them all, from ensign up.

On July 15 the commander-in-chief and Von Steuben reviewed this body, the first formal grouping of American light infantry, and under command of Brigadier General Anthony Wayne. The new leader had issued orders prior to falling in that every man was to be "fresh shaved and well powdered," fully equipped and provided with rations for twenty-four hours. Each noncom must have an espontoon, a sort of short pike or spear, and the officers were to be equipped with cutting swords, not mere flumadiddles to glitter on parade. The whole body was probably quite well uniformed, since the issue of French blue or brown coats could hardly have worn out by this time.

The caliber of the men of the light infantry has been indicated. The officers were worthy of the troops they led. Here at the head of the 1st Regiment stood Colonel Christian Febiger with steady François Louis de Fleury as second-in-command and Major Thomas Posey of Virginia serving as major. In later years Posey would rise to the rank of major general and serve as the second governor of the Indiana Territory. These men commanded both Virginians and Pennsylvanians.

Then there was the 2nd—Pennsylvania, Maryland, and Delaware—under Colonel "Dickie" Butler, Lieutenant Colonel Sam Hay, and Major Jack Stewart, a Marylander. The 3rd lined up behind Return Jonathan Meigs, Isaac Sherman, and Henry Champion, Nutmeggers all, as were their men. The mixture of states in the same unit, a manifestation always heartening to any man of the time who looked forward to permanent union, was repeated in the 4th, where Lieutenant Colonel William Hull mingled his own Bay Staters with North Carolinians under Major Hardy Murfree, who would one day give his name to the town of Murfreesboro on Stone River in Tennessee. Nearly a century later, Americans were to battle savagely near that town and along that river, the issue being that same Union here represented by Febiger's men, by Butler's and Hull's.

The inspection went off smoothly and old Baron von Steuben, blinking in the strong summer sun that was reflected from the river, must have felt a deep glow of satisfaction as he watched the picked companies maneuver. No doubt the men felt a fine thrill of that professional pride which comes from being part of a smoothly working military machine. Their performance would be something to talk over as they lounged away the long July afternoon that surely would be theirs after this interesting but routine inspection.

Orders snapped out, drums beat, and the light infantry regiments filed off inland, thinking of their shady tents and the waiting camp kettles. They did not reach their tents. Instead, the whole body turned off, swinging with a glitter of bayonets under the deep green of the trees that edged the road leading west and then south, skirting the cool, shaggy mass of Bear Mountain.

The inspection was not routine. The whole assembly and the subsequent march had been top secret and amazingly well kept in that category. Some men had undoubtedly known that slim young Major Henry Lee and his Legion troopers had been scouring the country to the south, that Captain Allan McLane and his irregulars had been setting up road blocks, turning back country people from the projected line of march. Every dog within earshot of the road had been seized and brought into camp or reluctantly dispatched by a musket ball. Turning west, each man had been issued a square of white paper to tuck onto his hat. The march went on, curving south as the sun dropped, and the seasoned veterans must have begun to guess their objective—newly captured and fortified Stony Point—and the timing of the march and the issue of the white papers strongly suggested that most hazardous and dreaded military operation, a night attack.

Darkness fell and the road narrowed, sometimes forcing the command to go in the clumsy single-file formation. Prior to Von Steuben's teachings, that had been the only formation most of them had known. They threaded the crest of Degaffles Rugh and breasted the slopes of the Donderberg. There was no straggling allowed. Even at a halt men could not leave the ranks unless shepherded by an officer. More details began to sift through. No muskets were to be loaded. The objective was Stony Point and the attack would be in silence and in utter darkness.

Part way toward the Point, which was to be approached from the rear and the inland sides, Anthony Wayne met Henry Lee and was told that the whole countryside was quiet. This must have been highly heartening to the young Pennsylvanian, since it indicated that the garrison at the Point was still ignorant of danger. American success was utterly dependent on surprise, and Wayne probably had Washington's grave words deep in his memory: "Knowledge of your intention, ten minutes previously obtained, blasts all your hopes." The Virginian could have said five minutes just as truly.

Wayne knew that the garrison consisted of well over six hundred men. There were the 17th Leicestershires with their grayish-white facings, the 63rd Manchesters, deep green, the grenadier company of the 71st with their Highland bonnets, blue-and-red gunners of the Royal Artillery, and the green-coated Loyal Americans. The commander of the fort was Lieutenant Colonel Henry Johnston, an alert, aggressive soldier. With the slightest warning this garrison could handle about anything that was thrown at it.

Back in Washington's camp at New Windsor, just above West Point, there was little sleep. Officers paced about, tried to doze, held their watches to shaded lanterns or slanted them in the glow of dying fires. Sometime before dawn Major Benjamin Fishbourne of Pennsylvania, Wayne's chief aide, thundered into camp shouting for the commander-in-chief. A crumpled sheet of paper was produced and the Virginian read:

> Stoney Point, 16th July, 1779
> 2 OClock A.M.

Dear Gen'l:
> The fort and garrison with Col. Johnston are ours. Our officers & men behaved like men who are determined to be free.
> Yours most sincerely,
> Ant'y Wayne.

Gen'l Washington.

Later other details came to deepen the feeling of almost reverent thanks that must have filled Washington and his associates. Only one man of the whole garrison had escaped, for the coup de main had run off like clockwork. Wayne had been knocked out by a scalp wound while clambering over the walls but had soon recovered. François de Fleury's Gallic élan had made him first to leap into the works and cut down the British flag. Christian Febiger, always in the forefront, had personally taken Henry Johnston prisoner. Later Wayne and Old Denmark exchanged swords, and those same blades today are in possession of the two families.

Washington had been gravely worried about a feature or two when the attack was first planned. He dreaded losses and now learned that only fifteen Americans had been killed and some eighty wounded. Then there had been the haunting question of how the Americans would behave if the attack were successful. The commander-in-chief could recall how some of Wayne's men had gone utterly out of hand and shot or bayoneted surrendering British and Hessians at Germantown in memory of the surprise at Paoli. Many men felt that the slaughter of Sheldon's dragoons up the Hudson had been wanton. With these memories strong in their minds, justified or unjustified, how would Wayne's men act in the heat and tension of a night attack? The answer to this probably gratified Washington more than any other detail of the night's work. No prisoners had been harmed.

Still panting from his exertions of the march and the attack, Febiger, the Dane, somehow found pen and ink in the captured fort and wrote his wife, a Carson of Philadelphia, telling "My Dear Girl" that "at 12 o'clock last night we stormed this Confounded place, and, with the loss of about fourteen killed and forty or fifty wounded, we carried it. I can give you no particulars as yet. A musquet ball scraped my nose. No other damage to 'Old Denmark.' God bless you. Farewell, FEBIGER."

A few days later he gave her fuller details, adding that as a result of the *coup de main* Clinton had moved up the Hudson in force. The Dane did not seem particularly disturbed, closing his letter with the statement that if "he intends for our Fort, I think he will be damnably drubbed, as this most glorious affair has given double vigor and spirit to our men."

Febiger could have added, "to our whole country." The taking of the fort actually was of local importance only, and a little bit dimmed by a failure to accomplish a similar stroke at Fort Lafayette across at Verplanck's Point the same night. Indeed, Stony Point was dismantled and evacuated a few days later. But the moral effect was very great and Congress had gold medals struck to commemorate it.

Long before Anthony Wayne's spectacular coup had been planned, hot, bitter appeals for help had been pouring in to Washington from hamlets in the Mohawk Valley and the wild stretches that reached south from it to the Pennsylvania border and beyond. The Johnsons and the Butlers with their aptly named "Destructives" had been lashing the whole area with scourging raids. Joseph Brant and his Indians had thrown themselves into the burning and butchery with a zeal that made the Tory bands seem almost benevolent.

Such appeals could not be overlooked. Most of the settlers were opposed to the Crown and must be protected somehow. Besides, the Mohawk Valley and its neighboring lands constituted an invaluable granary from which the American army drew supplies. So a daring double movement was carefully drawn up, studied, and approved. One fairly large body of Continental troops was to move north out of Pennsylvania to the New York border. There it would meet a smaller group whose route lay south from Canajoharie on the Mohawk, along Lake Otsego, and thence down the Susquehanna.

The objective of this twin stroke was quite simply defined by the commander-in-chief. The country of the Six Nations was to be invaded with "the total destruction . . . of their settlements and the capture of as many prisoners as possible," the last to be held as hostages, "the only kind of security to be depended upon."

The country of the Six Nations extended roughly from Lake Ontario down to the Susquehanna, bounded by the Catskills on the east and Lake Erie on the west. This was no wigwam civilization, for the tribes had their towns, built solid houses, sometimes of stone, and had vast orchard tracts that showed years of cultivation. Politically, these Indians were fairly well advanced, with a sort of constitution and a code of laws. Had the tribal organization matched other phases of their development, the Six Nations might have marched peaceably beside the incoming white settlers. Unfortunately the women tended the fine village farms and all matters of husbandry. The men were above such sordid tasks. War—which was apt to mean indiscriminate raiding—and hunting alone were worth the attention and thought of the braves. With them, governed by such traditions and customs, peace was impossible, so against the Six Nations marched the double expedition.

Command of the larger American force that was to move north was given to John Sullivan, supported by an unusual array of subordinate officers. There were Henry Dearborn and Enoch Poor. Edward Hand was there and Joseph Cilley, along with the inextinguishable "Scotch Willie" Maxwell. Some two thousand seasoned troops marched with them, including a detachment of Dan Morgan's Rifle Corps.

The massing of this force began as early as May, but June had thickened the forest trees before the march actually began. The territory was virtually untouched, and Sullivan had to hack out a road through twenty-five miles of virgin timber, "as there had never been any before, only an old Indian path," and there were wheeled vehicles and pack animals and even cannon to be tugged along.

The first Indian village, Chemung, struck the invaders with amazement. It contained "between 30 & 40 Houses, some of them large and neatly finish'd; particularly a Chapel and Council House." Chemung went up in a "Glorious Bon-fire and wide fields of grain and vegetables were ruin'd." This is a brutal account to read today, but it must be remembered that from such villages came the painted men who burned and slew and tortured up and down the Mohawk and the Susquehanna. So the scorched-earth policy was well applied.

The commander-in-chief's injunction about prisoners and hostages seems to have been overlooked. At Chemung and at subsequent villages Sullivan's men found only empty streets and houses, for the simple reason that no attempt at surprise was made. Each dawn a cannon shot not only roused the army but sent its echoes rolling far along streams and rivers, sifting through woods and over cornfields. And on the march the regiments proceeded "with drums beating, fifes playing and colors flying." And all this suggests that Sullivan did not want prisoners. He was an old hand himself, and with him were tough, skilled men like Dearborn and Cilley and Maxwell. They must have realized that great trains of prisoners would require guards, and guard details would quickly sap the strength from the whole command, leaving it horribly vulnerable.

On August 22, 1779, Sullivan's scouts sighted the other half of the expedition, which was moving south under General James Clinton of New York. This body of some fifteen hundred men had had as tough a march as Sullivan's but had eased much of the way through ingenuity. Clinton had followed watercourses and lakes, had dragged barges on wheeled frames over the portages. When the column found low water at the south end of Lake Otsego, Clinton's men dammed the flow until there was enough depth to float the flatbottoms.

Sullivan and Clinton struck hands and started out together from Tioga, and the earlier pattern of the march repeated itself. There was Onaquaga, "one of the Neatest of the Indian towns . . . with good log houses with Stone Chimneys and glass windows." It was burned, of course, but there had been glass windows and stone chimneys at German Flats and Stone Arabia by the Mohawk. Dearborn's men and Poor's and Clinton's saw Queen Esther's Flats and French Catherine's Town, where they gutted fields of "Cucombars, squash, turnips, Pompions" and, of course, fine corn, some ears being two feet long. In such country, with vast gardens ready for the harvest, the ration problem hardly existed, although one day Henry Dearborn noted, "I eat part of a fryed Rattle Snake . . . which would have tasted very well, had it not been Snake."

Day followed monotonous day, the same sequence of deserted Indian towns, burning houses, and fields to be laid waste. Men with farms of their own were glum as they hacked down the fruits of the squaws' labors and lamented over the rows of "beans, cucumbers, Simblens [i.e., pattypans; i.e., summer squash] watermelons . . . such as cannot be equalled in Jersey."

Near the site of present Elmira, New York, the columns struck the first sign of resistance, a neat ambush laid for them by a large body of Indians and Tories. Green men might have walked into slaughter, but not John Sullivan, Henry Dearborn, or William Maxwell. The ambush was sidestepped, then shattered. Henry Dearborn tersely summed up this action of August 29, 1779: "The Enimy . . . left the field . . . with precipitation & in great confusion pursued by our light Infantry about 3 miles." The victors were by no means squeamish about the enemy, Lieutenant William Barton of the 1st New Jersey recording that some riflemen had found dead Indians the day after the fight "and skinned two of them from their hips down for boot-legs; one for the Major and one for me."

Rejoicing in the victory that had cost only three American dead, the twin commands pushed on. The Seneca metropolis of Kanadaseagea with its eighty houses and wide orchards was burned. Up in flames went Schoyere and Canandaigua, Honeoye and Kanagha; Genesee—or Chinisee, as some diarists rendered it—was the high-water mark, or rather the high-fire mark, of the expedition and the old town of nearly one hundred and thirty buildings flared into the September sky, some twenty miles below modern Rochester.

The columns parted near the Pennsylvania border and Sullivan reported to Washington that, except for one town far beyond Genesee, "there is not a single Town left in the Country of the Five [sic] Nations." There were thanks from the commander-in-chief and from the Congress. No one seems to have asked about the lack of hostages, one of the prime reasons for the long raid, nor about what the uncounted surviving braves of the wasted lands would do now. The wretched inhabitants of the Mohawk Valley would soon be able to answer the last question with piercing emphasis. Burned out, starving, the Indians raided more savagely than ever. Like the British commanders, Washington's army had conquered hostile territory, but the hostile army still lived.

So for the campaigning season in the North for 1779, the commander-in-chief could set down Stony Point and, to a certain extent, the blows against the tribes on the profit side of his military ledger, even if the over-all returns were not great.

British-held New York, a garrison town in which the civil authority was thoroughly subordinated to the military, was a grim enough place for the average American, no matter how loyal to the Crown he might be. For one thing, the sight of fire-gutted houses and the ineradicable tang of charred wood and brick were depressing in themselves and conflagrations kept breaking out, some of them threatening to match the awful blaze of 1776. The streets were full of soldiers, and while any Loyalist could look with pride on the scarlet coats and bearskins of the British grenadiers, the Hessians and the Waldeckers and the Anspachers, along with the droves of staring peasant women who had accompanied these uneasy allies to the New World, struck an alien note. Also, they smelled to a degree that was noticeable even in the relatively bathless eighteenth century.

Even the King's forces were looked upon sometimes with apprehension, if not downright fear, especially the Royal Navy, so vital to the British hold on the continent, for the ships needed crews and from time to time strong press gangs swept into the town from the water front and combed the streets. Not only did they snatch up the destitute, the unemployable, but also sober clerks and even small merchants, and hustled them away to indefinite service on sloop or frigate. And there was no redress.

Some Loyalists throve and made money through these feverish days, but many lived hand to mouth and were driven to accept the scanty "King's Dole," meager enough reward for a man who had ruined himself through belief in the Crown. It must have been hard not to turn bitter as men saw how some people fared. Graft and corruption made fortunes for those, British and American, who were so placed that they could take advantage of glittering opportunities. There were the barrack-masters and quarter-masters and paymasters, some of whom were able to retire after a year's service in New York. The army needed fuel and so did the citizens. Forests in Westchester, on Manhattan itself, on Long Island were cut down. The Loyalist owners received little or nothing for their felled trees, but the full rates were charged to the Crown. And there was profit, too, in selling fire-wood to civilians at famine prices.

Loyalists eagerly hired out wagons and horses for army use, charging a low rate which they rarely were paid. And once a wagon and a horse became incorporated in an army column, the owner was not apt to see either again. Housing fell under military control, and owners or renters were dispossessed without warning to make way for a man who knew someone who knew someone who knew someone and was willing and able to pay for the privilege of that acquaintance.

And a Loyalist might ask of what benefit was this military and naval occupation when by the year 1779 the city of New York was under virtual siege, or at least blockade, by the rebels.

Yet an even-tempered, agreeable, adaptable man could live quite happily on Manhattan Island. There was the cheerful young merchant, Robert Townsend, not quite turned twenty-six, who brought in food staples and even luxuries from the Long Island farms and in turn exported unheard-of delicacies from Europe and the Indies to still prosperous men in Brooklyn or up at Oyster Bay or down by the placid reaches of Great South Bay. Young Townsend had strings of pack horses and a staff of reliable men who understood merchandising and were knowledgable about what manor owners or resident British officers would buy.

Pleasant-looking, a good conversationalist, always well dressed and affable, he was a familiar figure in the shops about Hanover Square and William Street and Wall Street. British officers hailed him when he came into the Navy Coffee House run by Alexander Grant down by the Battery. He was welcome at Sign of the Indian King on Wall Street and at Charles Rouba-let's City Tavern at 115 Broadway, where dinner for two could run as high as eight pounds, and six apples sold for one pound four shillings.

Robert Townsend had other assets. Gifted with a neat turn of the pen, he wrote articles for James Rivington's *Royal Gazette* and even for discriminating magazines published in London. Flitting from shop to coffee-house to officers' lodgings to headquarters, he saw and heard a great deal and incorporated it into bright, chatty bits for Rivington. It soon became known that an officer gained professionally and socially by being mentioned in the *Gazette*, and Townsend's sources of information swelled.

Some of his information followed a less orthodox course. His chief courier, Austin Roe, kept the Townsend pack trains on a quite regular shuttle service deep into Long Island. As a rule, the horses were laden with bona fide merchandise, duly covered by British passes. But often his saddle-bags held a special shipment, say a few reams of fine writing paper. Such a package was quietly dropped off somewhere near Setauket on the north shore, well east of Oyster Bay, addressed to John Bolton, c/o Abraham Woodhull.

Retrieving the paper by night, Woodhull covertly made his way to the beaches where armed whaleboats lay hidden, under command of a big, cloak-muffled man who moved catlike despite his size. The cloaked man took delivery of the package and sailed north across the Sound, finally heading in by the beaches at Fairfield in Connecticut or at Black Rock, now part of Bridgeport.

Once ashore, the whaleboat leader went into Fairfield, where he found a slim, handsome man—one of the finest-looking in the army, if John Trumbull's crayon sketch is to be trusted—wearing a crested, vizored helmet and dragoon's jacket of dark blue faced with white. So Caleb Brewster, captain of Continental Artillery, turned the package over to "John Bolton"—cover name for Major Benjamin Tallmadge of the 2nd Continental Dragoons.

Whether the news from Robert Townsend was hidden, written in invisible ink, among sheaves of fine paper or was to be found in a seemingly innocent letter about commercial and family affairs or masked in elaborate code, Tallmadge deciphered when necessary and sent it on by relays of his dragoons to the commander-in-chief, who would soon be reading of troop movements in New York, of possible blows against the American army, of the arrival of fresh British troops, or of new fortifications up by the King's Bridge.

This intelligence channel seems to have been Washington's first and only serious effort to insure a regular flow of information from the heart of the enemy country. In the past he had merely used itinerant spies, had counted on interrogation of prisoners and deserters, on news brought in by advanced patrols. Little sensational ever traveled this secret road from Robert Townsend to George Washington, but the system afforded a reasonably accurate picture of day-to-day life in occupied New York, which must have helped vastly in building up an idea of Clinton's intentions.

Robert Townsend continued his outwardly carefree and happy life in New York, always with a noose about his neck, until the end of the war. The secret was so admirably kept that it has taken quite recent researches to reconstruct the system, notably the studies of the late Carl Van Doren and of Morton Pennypacker. There are still many dark corners to be illuminated, and it is possible that the future may show that James Rivington, the printer, always regarded as an ultra-Tory, was actually a co-worker of Townsend.

Winter quarters for the army were once more in prospect, and a gradual move, unit by unit, began, with the familiar heights of Morristown as the objective. Farseeing officers made their own preparations, possibly thinking that the coming season might be as easy as the winter of 1778–79. From Second River, near Newark, Christian Febiger wrote to his wife in Philadelphia that he had "drawn an Elegant Suit of Cloathing, Blue and Red with white Vest Coat and Breeches, with Buttons Lineing thread and silk but no Mohair and I dare not have it made up here for fear the damn'd Taylors will Spil it." He asked her to buy him silver epaulets and "silver veluum" for buttonholes "as I am determined to be as neat as any Officer in the Army." He also drew "½ lb green Tea 2 lbs Chocolate and 9 lb Sugar and 5 Gallons of Spirit."

These lines sound as though Old Denmark and his colleagues were actually looking forward to the Morristown months. The reality must have been a distinct shock. By mid-December Colonel Henry Jackson's Massachusetts men, who formed one of the exasperatingly hard to place Sixteen Additional Regiments, trailed wearily into the Morristown area, ending a march which had begun far back at Providence in Rhode Island. With them, pen busy as ever, was Dr. James Thacher, transferred from his earlier berth with Virginia troops. "Our baggage," said Thacher, "is left in the rear, for want of wagons to transport it. The snow on the ground is about two feet deep and the weather extremely cold; the soldiers are destitute of both tents and blankets and some of them are actually barefoot and almost naked." Later the baggage arrived, but it was "very difficult to pitch tents on the frozen ground." No bread for over a week, nothing but poor beef without salt or vegetables.

Howling blizzards swept over Morristown, and the doctor and his friends were "roused from sleep by the calls of some officers for assistance; their marquee had blown down and they were almost smothered in the storm, before they could reach our marquee, only a few yards [away]." Many soldiers "were actually covered while in their tents and buried like sheep under the snow." But the hutting went on, fine growths of walnut and oak furnishing the material. Men gasped in the bitter winds, snow hissed down onto exposed necks, and skinned knuckles tightened on ax handles. The only redeeming feature was that frozen wood cuts more easily that unfrozen. The remaining uniforms and shoes went to pieces rapidly during this grinding labor. One may wonder how many regimental commanders had the foresight to issue an order like that of Febiger's. "I have first to request you not to permit one of our men to wear their new Cloaths untill the hutts are done, the propriety and necessity of which I am convinced Experience will show." Yet even Febiger was forced to write about his men, "their barefooted Situation I have reported to the Board of War, but nothing can be done."

Food, as at Valley Forge, grew more and more scanty, and Washington ruefully wrote to Philip Schuyler that the army lived on "every kind of horse food but hay." Nathanael Greene, who had seen about all there was to see of the war, was so shaken that he exclaimed, "Poor fellows! They exhibit a picture truly distressing—more than half-naked and two-thirds starved. A country overflowing with plenty are now suffering an Army, employed for the defence of everything that is dear and valuable, to perish for want of food."

So for Morristown in the winter of 1779–80 one may recall every distressing feature of Valley Forge, with the addition of bitter cold and deep snows. The days were like a musical theme repeated, but with sinister undertones added. And through all this the commander-in-chief had to struggle to keep his army up to strength, to induce the ever present flood of time-expired men to re-enlist. He even had to weaken himself to send troops to the South to reinforce Benjamin Lincoln after the latter's failure at Savannah in conjunction with D'Estaing. The bulk of the Virginia line under General William Woodford started for South Carolina, and no doubt many of the men at Morristown envied them. Such envy was without justification.

For the past two years the army had emerged from winter duty in quite good shape. From Valley Forge it had come storming out with fire in its eye and an arch to its tail to perform more than creditably at Monmouth, despite Charles Lee's mishandling. In 1779 it had been very much on its toes and had at least managed to keep Sir Henry Clinton off balance, while putting on truly professional shows at Stony Point and Paulus Hook, to say nothing of the Sullivan-Clinton expedition.

But now there was no happy advent of spring into the Morristown camp, no sudden flood of provisions and no miraculous run of shad. As late as April 12, 1780, Washington was sadly writing from his cramped quarters in the Ford house—now 230 Morris Avenue—"We have not at this day one ounce of meat, fresh or salt in the magazine," and he had to add that he knew of no shipments on the way. In late May, James Thacher noted ominously, "Our poor soldiers are reduced to the very verge of famine; their patience is exhausted by complicated sufferings, and their spirit almost broken." The Connecticut line mutinied virtually en masse, and force had to be used in the shape of Pennsylvania troops to break up the movement. There were to be other mutinies later, all owing principally to the question of supply.

So 1780 opened dismally and, except for occasional flashes that induced a return of optimism, ticked off the remainder of its twelve months in an atmosphere of steady American discouragement. Washington and Greene strove as mightily as ever. The Congress backed them reasonably well but, as in the past, could only recommend what the various states should do for the common weal. And each state showed a maddening tendency to wait and see what its neighbors might contribute before taking its own slow and usually reluctant steps. Why should New Hampshire, for example, furnish supplies and men and money when Pennsylvania or Virginia might be duplicating and thus rendering unnecessary New Hampshire sacrifices?

The command problem was as knotty as ever, if not more so. At one period there were only two officers above the rank of colonel in the Morristown camp, the rest, representing every state, either being on detached service or on furlough. Thus the whole weighty burden lay on Washington's shoulders. It seemed to occur to no one, least of all to the commander-in-chief himself, that a spot of home leave might benefit him and the army. The resignation flood kept on. John Sullivan, keen and aggressive as ever, and tough-spirited to the end, finally broke down and had to retire from the service. Alexander McDougall was still on deck, as was John Glover, but their physical condition limited their usefulness. Then two gleams of light appeared. The first, and possibly the brighter, was the tart resignation of Charles Lee. This was accepted eagerly, and the acceptance—firm, final, and uncompromising—sent Lee into a fit of Roman-candle outbursts of rage. The other was the announcement that Major General Benedict Arnold was fit to take a field command again. The unpredictable general seemed eager enough to serve until the final results of inquiries and courts-martial concerning his affairs became known. The written blowing up which Washington was called on to administer was the product of deep thought on the part of the commander-in-chief and, read against the stacks of evidence that elicited it, seems mild enough today. However, it only threw Arnold, as might have been predicted, into a black fury that was repressed, at least for a time.

Far to the south matters looked no better for the American cause. In the fall of '79 Clinton had withdrawn the British force that had held Newport for so long and added it to the New York garrison. Then in late December of the same year he turned over the New York command to Von Knyphausen while he and Cornwallis with some eighty-five hundred crack troops embarked, shielded by Arbuthnot's fleet. No one doubted the destination, and Americans could only hope that Clinton would meet the same reception at Charleston that Howe had met in '76.

History did not repeat. Clinton landed below Charleston, called for troops from Savannah and from Florida, building his strength up to some thirteen thousand men, marched inland to the Ashley River, and from the land defenses of Charleston, Governor John Rutledge could see scarlet British and blue Hessians moving across the flats toward the approaches to the city.

To face them, Benjamin Lincoln had in hand some forty-five hundred, including the men whom William Woodford and others had marched overland. Rutledge made a frantic appeal for North and South Carolina militia, but there was little response, on grounds which must be admitted as at least reasonable. There was said to be smallpox in Charleston, a plague that was peculiarly virulent in the Carolinas. And many devoted men were beginning to find that slavery was by no means an unmixed blessing. It has been noted earlier that the Carolina Negroes were held to be far closer to the jungles, much less tractable, than their fellows farther north. Slave owners who might have been eager to answer the call to arms simply did not dare leave their holdings, small or large, to the mercies of the slaves.

Benjamin Lincoln was caught in a two-way squeeze. He was a good soldier, a sound commander, and realized that his best chance of keeping the war in the South alive was to yield Charleston, which surely was no use to any army that did not command the sea, and take his force into the back country, where Clinton and Cornwallis would have to come after him. He was the victor so long as his army was intact.

Charleston reacted with shortsighted, if comprehensible, violence. Politically and from an organizational standpoint the city *was* South Carolina, or so many Charlestonians felt, and not without reason. Heavy pressure, including some actual threats of violence, greeted the least suggestion of the army heading up toward the Santee. So Benjamin Lincoln accepted the siege and made such preparations as he could to meet the final onslaught. But the citizens whirled about again as the British lines drew closer and Lincoln prepared for all-out resistance. The city must *not* be damaged, must not be evacuated, and the city authorities actually massed local troops to oppose defense or flight.

The outcome was obvious. On May 12, 1780, Lincoln was forced to surrender with his entire army. This disaster was probably in the cards in any event, for it is highly doubtful if this weak force could have survived in the open country, particularly if the energetic Cornwallis had commanded the pursuit. It is quite likely that, in their seeming obstructionism, the Charleston authorities were actually being farsighted in yielding to *force majeure* and thus keeping intact their city, which meant so much to the state.

But at one blow the governmental mechanism of the state was swallowed up by the capture of so many leading rebels. The organization of the South Carolina Continentals was wrecked for a long time to come. Name after revered and respected name was included in the horribly long list of prisoners, civil and military. Men who might have rallied a whole district were now in enemy hands. With them were William Woodford and his Virginians, who may well have wished that they had been left to freeze through the awful Morristown winter. They were high-quality troops whom the country could not well spare.

So in this one stroke virtually the whole South, from Georgia to the Virginia border, lay open to the royal arms. Or so it seemed on the surface. But under the surface lay a fine, hard core of leaders who had not been involved in the surrender and they could command thousands like themselves. It would take time for such men to emerge, but that emergence was to be brilliant.

The Congress and the High Command undoubtedly appreciated, at least to a certain extent, the extreme gravity of Southern events. There were conferences and consultations on how to repair the damage. Measures would be undertaken. But in the meantime the rest of the country seems to have viewed the disaster as still just a conflagration on the far fringes of the land. In the Middle and Northern states recruiting dragged on and the men who stayed with the army set their chins and tried to do what they could with what they had. Christian Febiger, who luckily for him had not gone along with the other Virginians to South Carolina, felt that his command needed bracing and humbly petitioned the Board of War for permission to recruit a band. He was willing, he said, to bear the initial expense himself, to be reimbursed if his experiment were successful but not otherwise. He mentioned "4 Clarinetts and Violins, 2 Bassoons and Bass Viol, 2 French Horns." He added that such a group sent into the towns would help bring in enlistments. On his own copy of the letter he noted later, "presented the above and was utterly refused."

He returned to the charge later, hedging his requests to the extent of four fifers and four drummers, the men to be properly uniformed. He hoped that "The honorable the Board of War will permitt me, as the Uniform of my Regt is blue fac'd with red and it is customary to have the drums and fifes in Reverse Uniform to the Regt to grant me the Order for red Coats fac'd with blue." And this time Old Denmark triumphantly noted, "presented and Granted." It may be assumed that the picked men, most of whom had been present in the wild, dark sweep at Stony Point, could momentarily forget bad news, bad rations, and bad shoes as, behind their massed fifers and drummers, they stepped out in swinging rhythm to defile before their foreign-born colonel who had made himself an American.

And before the fall of Charleston a thudding courier galloped up to the Ford house in Morristown with a most special letter for the commander-in-chief. It was headed, "At the entrance of Boston harbour, 27th April," and began, "Here I am, my dear General, and in the midst of the joy I feel in finding myself again one of your loving soldiers . . ." The letter ended with an assurance that "you will easely know the hand of your young soldier, LAFAYETTE."

The commander-in-chief was visibly moved, according to all accounts, by this letter. The return of the young Frenchman must have done a great deal to lighten the somber frame of mind in which he could not help finding himself, may have made him hope that somehow Charleston would not fall, that there might be another manifestation of the benevolence of Providence, "however little we deserve it." And there was much more in that letter to make him hope, for the distant future if not for the immediate, for Lafayette had written, "I have affairs of the utmost importance that I should at first communicate to you alone."

On May 10, just two days before the curtain slid down on the defense of Charleston, the Marquis de Lafayette galloped up the hill road leading to Morristown, his uniform thick with Jersey dust that must have seemed as familiar to him as the dust of his own native Auvergne, which today comprises the departments of Puy-de-Dôme, Cantal, and part of the Haute-Loire. James Thacher observed with New England restraint that "The safe return of this respectable personage is a matter of joy and congratulation."

To term Lafayette's news as "affairs of the utmost importance" was another understatement. His mission had been successful. Six powerful French naval vessels, six thousand crack troops under command of Major

General Count Donatien de Rochambeau had been earmarked for service in America. Not only that, but by now they must have sailed and should sight Newport by June. And more, this force was under strict orders to co-operate with the Americans, having the capture of New York as its prime objective, to stay in America until "Mission completed" could be written. This was to be no hit-and-run expedition hampered by home-side orders such as had shackled D'Estaing. And for a last, bewildering detail, Rochambeau and his men were to place themselves under Washington's command.

This was more than the commander-in-chief had ever hoped for, more than the nation had dreamed up in its optimistic moments. When the shock of the loss of Charleston struck Washington, the thought of Rochambeau and his veteran regiments must have cushioned the blow a little, must have kept him from the endless, tormenting thoughts that beset any commander whose forces have suffered a bad setback: should he have sent more men to Lincoln in the first place; should he have ordered him to stay inland and not try to hold a port city against an enemy that controlled the sea; should he have gone down there himself to take command? Now such futile reflections were dimmed as Lafayette spoke of Lauzun's Legion, of the Royal Deux-Ponts, the Bourbonnais, the Saintonge, and the Soissonnais regiments, some of which dated back to the days of pike and arquebus.

Of course these formations were still at sea. Weeks must pass after their landing before they could be sent into action. But there actually seemed a future to be planned for, a country to be rallied behind the new allies. Such thoughts could take Washington's mind off the present for a little, keep him from wondering too much about how regimental quotas were to be filled, or why—a most puzzling affair—General Arnold, a combat soldier from the ground up, suddenly appeared bored at any talk of a field command and urged that he be given the housekeeping post up at West Point on the Hudson, far removed from any possible action. Arnold further mentioned the matter to Philip Schuyler, to Robert R. Livingston and other New York State notables, who seemed delighted with the idea of having him in command of that Hudson key fort.

Sometime in mid-May, Major General von Knyphausen, in charge in New York, was rather puzzled to receive a not too explicit letter delivered to him by that most discreet purveyor of china and porcelain, Mr. Joseph Stansbury of Philadelphia. The Hessian officer must have known a little about previous dealings with Mr. Stansbury and his principal, who now was reopening the earlier negotiations and asking to meet with a British "officer of confidence." In the absence of Clinton and André, Knyphausen felt able to make only a noncommittal reply. In the first stages of the correspondence Arnold would probably have torn his none too placid disposition to shreds at such a rebuff, and Stansbury would surely have received a heavy verbal cuffing at being the messenger with bad tidings. Now the unpredictable general seemed anxious to establish himself, to cement his contacts in New York.

Back Stansbury went to New York, bearing with him top-secret documents concerning possible American moves, detailed news of the coming French force and its composition. Later he sent plans of Sound forts, of works at Fishkill, added a few notes on the best means of storming various Hudson River forts and such lighthearted trifles.

In late June, Clinton and the ever attendant André reappeared in New York, along with such troops as had not been left with Cornwallis for the final mop-up of the Carolinas and the total subjugation of the South. Knyphausen turned over all the material received through Stansbury with relief, and the industrious Major André took over that file, which a year ago seemed closed forever. The same types of letters began swooping circuitously between Philadelphia and New York, and now Arnold often signed himself "Gustavus" while André clung to the not particularly masking pseudonym of John Anderson.

Arnold was more and more emphatic that a great blow could be struck on behalf of long-suffering humanity by such high-principled men as himself, André, and Clinton through ending the bloody, useless, and unrighteous war. "The mass of the people are heartily tired of the war and wish to be on their former footing. . . . The present struggles are like the pangs of a dying man, violent, but of short duration," wrote Arnold piously. And he spoke of his hope of getting the West Point command.

Clinton became more and more interested and thought very highly of the idea of turning West Point—and the control of the Hudson—over to the British. With a glance at future public reaction Sir Henry also figured that he "could point out such plausible measures as would ward off all blame and suspicion" from his obliging correspondent in Philadelphia. And of course an "ample stipend" would be paid.

This last suggestion brought up a few more tizzies. Arnold was interested in Sir Henry's precise definition of "ample." Then came more shrewd business dealings or just plain haggling. The general from Connecticut wanted a certain number of pounds per head for every American soldier that he, as commander at West Point, was able to turn over to the British prison hulks. And there must be a lump sum in addition to this. So the letter writing went on between "Gustavus" and "John Anderson," with the former now eager, now coy, now disdainful as the final financial arrangements were outlined, rejected, slashed, increased. But so far, through the hot summer weeks, nothing was actually settled. In the meantime Arnold was prudently turning his possessions into cash and banking the amounts received in British-held New York through various useful and obliging agents.

It is worth noting that, with all the laxity that prevailed in British and most other headquarters of the time in security matters, no leak of these protracted and highly important negotiations seems to have occurred. Smiling, pleasant, and inwardly trembling, Robert Townsend caught no hint of them as he went from coffeehouse to tavern to officers' quarters in quest of news that might appear over his own signature for James Rivington's *Gazette* or over that of Culper, Jr., his code name, for "John Bolton."

CHAPTER XXVIII

"If Mr. James Anderson . . . from New York should arrive at your quarters . . ."

A PEARLY, cottony fog blanketed the waters south of the state of Rhode Island and the Providence Plantations, and the great flotilla that flew the golden lilies of France moved cautiously past No Man's Land, Martha's Vineyard, and Cuttyhunk through hot July days. There was ample reason, even without the fog, for this slow progress. Swinging up from the great southern arc of its course, the armada had sighted and hailed coasting vessels, and the news that they gave was not of a nature to reassure Count Donatien de Rochambeau and his officers. In the South, Charleston had fallen. Might there not have been similar American disasters in the North? It would scarcely be amusing for French ships of the line, frigates, and transports to drop anchor in a supposedly friendly port only to find the British colors flying over the wharves and British ships clearing for action.

Close to the Vineyard, American pilots came on board. Claude Blanchard, chief commissary of the French Expeditionary Force, seized one of them and shouted in vast relief when "he told us that the Americans were still masters of Rhode Island. . . . He was a good man and displayed intelligence."

There were more fogs, more nights of riding at anchor, but at last the French fleet put in at Newport and boats shoved off, laden with white-coated and gold-braided officers, to receive the warm welcome that their new allies must surely be preparing for them. But something had gone wrong. Rochambeau and his staff must have felt like guests dropped by a stupid taxi driver at the wrong apartment house in the wrong street of the wrong city. They wandered in a daze through handsome Newport in a cloud of "*Mais enfins*," "*Incroyables*," and "*Par exemples*." There was no red carpet spread out, no V.I.P. program laid on. Rochambeau wrote restrainedly to the Minister of War, "There was no one about in the streets; only a few sad and frightened faces in the windows." But he managed to get hold of some local dignitaries and identified himself and mentioned the size and mission of his command. It was not until the evening of the following day that "all the houses were illuminated, the bells rang out and there were fireworks."

Count Guillaume de Deux-Ponts—who could just as accurately have been

called Graf Wilhelm von Zwei-Brücken—was a little discouraged. "A coldness and reserve appear to me to be characteristic of the American nation;
they seem to have little of that enthusiasm which one would suppose be-
longs to a people fighting for its liberties, and indeed they seem little suited
to inspire enthusiasm in others," he wrote rather glumly. Then with a
mental "Courage, mon vieux," he added with a firmer touch, "But these
considerations shall not in the least change my resolution, and they occupy
my thoughts less than my reflections upon our military and political situation."

All in all, the French force could hardly have landed under circumstances less calculated to promote the alliance. Another international fiasco
seemed brewing to match the confusions and misunderstandings that had
attended D'Estaing and his fleet. But the snafu was quickly straightened
out. General Billy Heath, who had managed to win Gentleman Johnny
Burgoyne's esteem when the ex-farmer from Roxbury was in charge of the
Convention Troops in Boston, had been delegated by Washington to act as
official greeter. Delayed on the way to Newport, he now threw himself into
the task of erasing the first unpleasant impression which the French had
surely received, and he succeeded magnificently. He was indefatigable in
securing proper camp sites for the disembarking regiments; he located
water supplies, arranged for the purchase of provisions, and smoothed over
the remarkably few rough spots between the townspeople and the newcomers.

He also saw to it that important civilians from adjoining states met the
French brass. President Ezra Stiles of Yale College, who years ago had interested a young Quaker named Nathanael Greene in expanding his education, dined with Rochambeau and solved the language barrier by con-
versing in Latin. The Count, he thought, "spoke it tolerably."

William Channing came to town and was greatly impressed. "The
French Troops are a fine body of men, and they appear to be well-officered.
Neither Officers nor Men are the effeminate Beings we were heretofore
taught to believe them. They are as large and as likely men as can be produced by any nation."

The plainer citizens of Newport looked on the disembarking regiments
and were as impressed as Channing. And it must be said that there was
plenty of reason for their reaction. Here was the flower of the French Army,
beautifully and practically equipped men, mostly in white uniforms. There
was the Royal Deux-Ponts, whose lieutenant colonel of the same name
wrote with such misgivings about the morale of the Newportais. Raised in
the then French Rhine provinces, they wore white-lined blue coats with
bright yellow facings and cuffs. The 41st Soissonnais were in white with
vivid crimson trimmings, the 85th Saintonge used white with green, and
the 13th Bourbonnais white with black. But the real gasps of admiration
must have been for the cavalry of the Legion commanded by Armand
Louis de Gontaut, Duc de Lauzun, a Casanova croyant et pratiquant.
These troopers had seen hard service under the duke in the swamps and

forests of Senegal. Now they pranced through Newport in black hussar busbies, white-plumed and gold-laced. Their light blue jackets were trimmed with yellow and their yellow breeches were piped with white. Over their jackets they slung blue pelisses edged with black fur. The Legion officers glittered still more, substituting cherry-red breeches for the troopers' yellow, marten-fur busbies instead of felt, and there were crimson baldrics and tiger-skin trimmings to their saddlecloths. Many of the Legion's three hundred men were Poles, who carried long, glittering lances, a weapon never before seen on the continent, and the rest were genial Irishmen whose long, curved sabers clanked against their stirrup irons as they rode by.

Certainly no one in Newport or Providence had ever dreamed of such martial panache. Even the French gunners in their more sober gray had their coats trimmed with bands of deep scarlet velvet. And yet with all this display there was an air of quiet efficiency, and plain-minded Americans were pleased to note that, save in Lauzun's Legion, there was very little difference in dress between officers and enlisted men.

So Saintonge and Bourbonnais and the rest paraded on the gemlike little American island in Narragansett Bay while the gleaming copper drums of the regiments pounded out the rhythm of "The Huron March." And yet while the always slow process of debarkation went on, tragedy threatened to smash down on these colorful allies of the United States of America.

Samuel Culper, Jr., had word of it and sent the warning over the secret intelligence road to John Bolton at Fairfield in Connecticut. A powerful British fleet was assembling at the west end of Long Island Sound. British and Hessian troops were pouring aboard transports at Whitestone. There could be only one objective: to catch Rochambeau half ashore and half afloat, a situation in which even his fine troops would have been helpless.

There was no naval force big enough to interfere with this water-borne attack, and yet something had to be done. Washington, tipped off by John Bolton in the person of Major Benjamin Tallmadge, began scrambling his troops about, setting heavy columns in motion as though massing for an attack on New York. He also gave fictitious written orders to several trusted agents in the hope that they might fall into Clinton's hands. American regiments crossed to the east bank of the Hudson, marched, counter-marched for no good reason that they could see, and they cursed head-quarters, footsore James Thacher setting down his own complaints in his diary.

The British flotilla started east up the Sound. Probably Benjamin Tall-madge at Fairfield and Abraham Woodhull across at Setauket and Caleb Brewster at Black Rock watched its progress in agonized helplessness. Then, remarkably, the great mass of ships countermarched, headed back for Whitestone. Clinton was taken in by Washington's maneuvering and had called home ships and troops against an attack on New York that was never intended. Off in Rhode Island, Rochambeau's men continued their de-barkation undisturbed.

The tragedy that had been enacted in the marshy plains about Charleston between the Cooper and the Ashley rivers might still seem to be part of a fringe war to the people of more distant states. But events were piling up like thunderheads that would break in the near future, and then the fringe—if it had ever truly been one—would become one with the whole fabric. The names of the prisoners who had been enmeshed in the fall of Charleston were written off on the ledgers of war, gleefully by the British, grimly by the Americans. The list was a long one, and even today the pages of Heitman's *Historical Register* make sad reading for American eyes with the ever recurring notation against officer after officer: "taken prisoner at Charleston, 12th May, 1780." Their part in the war was over. But the British were stirring and this time no hesitant Howe or Burgoyne with his rash indolence led them.

One week after the fall of Charleston, Cornwallis, quite on his own at last, slipped the leash on his command and started it northwest through South Carolina. Scarlet-coated British infantry, Von Bose's blue-and-green Hessians, a cloud of cavalry, British and Tory, white-jacketed for the hot weather, crossed the sluggish Santee at Lenud's Ferry and spilled into the heart of the state.

Detachments pressed on to the Congaree, up the Saluda to the frontier post of Ninety Six. Others followed the Santee to its junction with the Wateree and went north up the latter, with the soft green contours of the High Hills of Santee on their right, until they came to Camden, close to the dead center of South Carolina.

The Tory unit known as the British Legion, along with a few troops of the tough, battle-wise 17th Dragoons, followed the fantastically plumed helmet of handsome young Banastre Tarleton. This would have been a formidable force in any event. Now its military value was at least doubled through the lucky capture, near Charleston, of a herd of fine, swift horses that could walk away from and outlast the usual country-bred type known locally as tackies.

In an area called the Waxhaws, close to the North Carolina line, Tarleton overtook a body of Virginia cavalry under Colonel Abraham Buford and virtually wiped it out. Cries of "Massacre!" are very apt to occur in any engagement where the casualities of the vanquished are out of all proportion to those of the victor. Records of this clash are conflicting, but it is difficult not to feel that, here in the Waxhaws, Tarleton and his men were, to say the least, unrestrained, a characteristic of most of Tarleton's victories. He was an accomplished, gifted man and an excellent cavalry leader. But he seems to have had the killer instinct to a marked degree, a trait which crops out in some men of all nations in all wars. A parallel to Tarleton may be found in the leader of Hodson's Horse in the Indian Mutiny of 1857, although the type seems to be quite rare among the British.

Feeling that South Carolina was now pacified, in the sense used by Julius Caesar in his *Commentaries*, Tarleton rejoined Cornwallis at Camden on the Wateree. The next move, he thought, would be into North Carolina, a mild sort of practice march. Then would come Virginia, and all the states south of the Potomac would bask in the glow of the Crown.

Ready to push off for his true base in New York, Sir Henry Clinton received the stream of reports telling of Cornwallis' progress. In the cool elegance of the Brewton house in Charleston he composed a report to Lord George Germain. "I may venture to assert that there are few men in South Carolina who are not either our prisoners or in arms with us." This was a neat and modest way of saying "Mission accomplished." He could have amplified his report by adding that the prisoners included most of the political leaders as well as militia and Continental officers. From a military as well as a civil standpoint the magnets that had drawn the state out of the Crown orbit were gone.

It might have been quite possible to bring South Carolina back to its old allegiance. But as in Rhode Island, New Jersey, and Pennsylvania, the Crown officers seem not only to have employed every known way of alienating the Carolinians but to have invented new ones when the old stand-bys ran out or became stale and uninteresting.

Plundering and abuse of the inhabitants went on unchecked. Known rebels who took the oath of allegiance—and there were many such—found that they were not allowed to own weapons to defend themselves against marauding bands or possible slave uprisings. More, as time went on, they found themselves looked upon as true subjects of the Crown, liable to draft for military service and thus forced to fight against their former associates. Slaves were snapped up by the type of grifter, who flourished so happily in New York, and shipped off for sale in the West Indies. Many ex-rebels began comparing notes with staunch Tories who were suffering from nearly all the same grievances as themselves, and between rebel and Tory a slow bond grew. They, too, were being brought together by a common experience. Sir Henry's report to the slippery Germain looked neither below the surface nor into the future.

Sir Henry sailed for New York, leaving Cornwallis to mature and execute the plan designed to bring all the South back to the Crown. But Cornwallis, alert and active in the pleasant valley of the Wateree, suddenly found that another, more immediate problem faced him. An American force was moving down from North Carolina in the rather pathetic hope of driving Briton, Hessian, and Tory down to the Santee and thence to the coastal swamps.

Weeks before, the nucleus of this American expedition had been sent south with a rather vague notion of somehow relieving the pressure on Lincoln, then still holding out in the Charleston area. Qualitatively, it was excellent, consisting of the always formidable Delaware and Maryland Continentals, backed up by the infantry and cavalry of Armand's Legion. The able, experienced Baron de Kalb was in command, with many excellent subordinates, including William Smallwood, now a major general, who had done so well at Long Island and White Plains, and Colonel Otho

Holland Williams, also of Maryland, whose service dated back to 1775. Quantitatively, it amounted to only a few hundred men.

Those men had made a killing march. The heat had been, and continued to be, fearful. Insect life was maddeningly plentiful, especially "the tick, a kind of strong, black flea which makes its way under the skin. . . . My whole body is covered with these stings," De Kalb wrote his wife in France.

The column had no transport and the men had to live off the country, which was thinly settled. A soldier wrote, "We marched from Hillsborough . . . without an ounce of provision being laid in at any one point, often fasting for several days together, and subsisting frequently upon green apples and peaches; sometimes by detaching parties we thought ourselves feasted, when . . . they seized a little fresh beef and cut and threshed out a little wheat; yet, under all these difficulties, we had to press forward."

Charleston fell, Lincoln was a prisoner, and command of the Southern Department suddenly dropped on De Kalb's shoulders. The Congress, sitting at Philadelphia, may have thought that it would not do to have a foreigner in such an exalted command; it may have been that few members knew De Kalb personally, he never having courted political favor; or perhaps that body felt that De Kalb needed a sure, guiding mind over him, the touch of a gifted master of war. That master was ready to hand, and Horatio Gates was ordered south. It is to Gates's credit that he took the assignment, for he had no illusions about the American weakness in that area. He wrote that he was to take over "The command of an army without strength, a military chest without money, a Department apparently deficient in public spirit, and a climate that increases despondency instead of animating the soldier's arm."

In late July 1780 he took over from De Kalb at Hollinsworth's Farm on Deep River in North Carolina, bringing with him Virginia militia under Lieutenant Colonel Charles Porterfield. Major General Richard Caswell, remembered from his activities against the Highlanders at Moore's Creek Bridge in '75, came in with a body of North Carolina militia, bringing Gates's force to a little over three thousand. With this body he set out, apparently supremely confident of overwhelming Cornwallis near Camden in South Carolina.

He might have added more and quite valuable strength, for on the march south two very shabby-looking, exhausted, but highly pugnacious South Carolinians reported to him. One was very small, frail, and limped badly from a still healing ankle fracture. The other was taller, lean, saturnine. The taller man later admitted that the pair did not make a very glittering appearance; they had made their way laboriously up from the coast through country thick with British and Tories and their personal possessions consisted of "one rusty horse-fleam." But they assured Gates that if he would only authorize it they could raise quickly a large body of horsemen quite capable of acting as efficient mounted infantry. The conqueror of Burgoyne was indulgently tolerant as he waved off their proffer; he had, he said, no need of any mounted troops. So Lieutenant Colonel Francis Marion and

Major Peter Horry had to sit out Gates's coming operation. It was the last bit of leisure this pair was to enjoy till the end of the war.

Gates pushed cheerfully south, piling blunder onto blunder. Of the two possible routes to Camden, he chose the longer one, which led through desolate country, despite the pleas of his officers that the other road was not only shorter but tapped an area where supplies could be found. His men staggered on, purged with the scant diet of green fruits and corn. Otho Williams noted that the men "were breaking ranks" on the march and were "much debilitated." De Kalb and Williams tried to call Gates's attention to the fact that of the whole force only the Marylanders and Delawares, along with Armand's men, had been in action before. They further showed him accurate returns in a vain attempt to correct the commander's oddly swollen notion of his own strength, but all this was waved aside as Marion and Horry had been. To De Kalb, Gates said loftily, "Sir, there are enough for our purpose."

There was a final night march with the dysentery-racked men falling out by the dozen. Pinewoods threw the flankers into confusion right and left of the column. Then close to dawn came a heavy collision. Cornwallis had been moving north astride the road that led to the Waxhaws. He had the Royal North Carolinians, the British Legion, and the Volunteers of Ireland, a very rugged outfit recruited mostly on the Philadelphia water front during the British occupation. The 33rd West Ridings linked up with the Irishmen, and beyond them were the 23rd Welch supported by light infantry. In reserve, the tireless Scots of the 71st waited, with Tarleton and his British and Tory dragoons ready to charge.

American collapse was almost instantaneous. The raw militia broke in panic and streamed north along the Waxhaws road. The left and the center caved in completely, when Tarleton drove his dragoons, sabers bright in the sun and brass helmets gleaming, into the rear. Only on the right was there any serious fighting. The gigantic De Kalb, well seconded by General Mordecai Gist, commanded the Marylanders and the Delawares there. Attacks by solid Tory formations, led by ugly Lord Rawdon, were smashed and smashed again. De Kalb took the offensive and his men went in with the bayonet, yelling, broke the lines opposite them, took scores of prisoners. The baron and his men thought that they were winning. Gates had not bothered to notify them of the collapse of the rest of the army, hidden from sight by the dust and smoke and by the contours of the land. Nor would Gates ever send word, for he himself was in flight with the others, in a pelting gallop on a famous race horse that finally carried him into Charlotte, North Carolina, a good sixty miles from the action.

De Kalb and his men only knew that pressure on them was increasing, though probably no one realized that Cornwallis had now thrown the bulk of his force against the shrinking six hundred. Still sublimely convinced that they were winning, the Delawares and Marylanders fought on, giving and taking heavy punishment. Fighting became hand to hand. De Kalb's horse was killed and he fought on with his saber while bayonets stabbed and musket butts swung in deadly hammer blows. Then the baron was down while leading a counterattack. Tarleton's dragoons swept in from the rear and the fight was over. Formations broke up, scattered for woods and swamps, leaving De Kalb mortally wounded on the bloody grass.

Gates, in his supreme optimism, had issued no orders for a possible retreat, had indicated no rallying point. Harassed by Tarleton and his cavalry, the fugitives staggered on toward the North Carolina border. The action had taken place on August 16. By the nineteenth Gates could survey what was left of his army. Guided, it seems, chiefly by instinct, it had rallied at Hillsboro, far in the north of the state, and amounted to some seven hundred men, most of them without equipment, many without weapons, seven hundred out of the force of three thousand with which Gates had started out to conquer the South.

Morally as well as militarily this was one of the most crushing reverses that the American army ever faced in any war. There was no longer any army worthy of the name to oppose the royal troops. Virginia lay open, and beyond Virginia were Maryland and Delaware and Pennsylvania. No force existed to implement the moral action taken at Philadelphia on July 4, 1776. For what could a Southern patriot hope, on what could he rely? The war in the South seemed over.

Yet was it? A few days after the action of August 16 a British and Tory column was convoying a long line of prisoners down the banks of the Wateree to the Santee. Out of thick woods and swamps there suddenly burst a cloud of horsemen, not uniformed and carrying every imaginable type of weapon. The column was crumpled up, most of the prisoners released, and, like a puff of light smoke, raiders and prisoners vanished into the depths of South Carolina. Francis Marion and Peter Horry had decided to go on with the war even if Horatio Gates had thought their services useless. It was the first flicker of a widespread uprising whose survivors would at last see British ships, loaded with troops, sail out of Charleston, as they had sailed earlier from Boston and Philadelphia. But all this lay in the future. Men could think only of Gates and the wreckage of his army and the dashed hopes of the patriots of four states.

In late September 1780 the country in general and the army in particular were still reeling from the impact of Gates's defeat at Camden and the full knowledge that events to the south could no longer be thought of as occurring on a distant fringe. In Westchester County, just above Manhattan Island, a new tension was felt, a tension so strong that it may have acted as an anesthetic against the bad news. The whole area had for months been turned into a torn and murderous no man's land, ravaged by patrols from both armies, by guerrilla bands of uncertain sympathies but of an unquestioned thirst for loot of all kinds. Solitary travelers, civilian or military, were more than likely to be waylaid. Small patrols, British, Tory, and rebel, were often wiped out and the attackers were as apt to be in tattered civilian clothes as in uniform.

Across the northern fringe of this area the commander-in-chief rode with a suitable escort, bound for Hartford in Connecticut, where he was to have his first conference with Rochambeau and the senior French officers. It seems odd that Rochambeau, having landed at Newport in July, should only now be meeting the man under whom he was to serve. Washington probably delayed the interview, hoping from day to day that there would be something at least a little encouraging to tell his new French subordinate, some concrete evidence of progress on which future joint operations might be based. There was little visible improvement anywhere, but the conference could be delayed no longer.

Such considerations were important, but they were beyond the concern of those men charged with the task of making sure that no guerrilla raid, no sudden British coup fell on Washington during his passage to and from Hartford. There seem to have been no tip-offs that such a stroke was being considered, but the greenest dragoon trooper could grasp the horrible implications to the army and the country should the commander-in-chief fall into British hands.

As a part of the over-all security measures Major Benjamin Tallmadge was out with a strong detachment of the 2nd Dragoons. As he rode along through the bright hours of September 23, the wind off the Sound rippling his horsehair plume and the folds of his blue-and-white uniform, he surely had a good deal on his mind in addition to the safety of the commander-in-chief.

Major General Benedict Arnold, now in charge at West Point, had been deluging the officers at the advanced posts with letters, buttery, flattering letters unlike Arnold's usual terse, rather angry style. There had also been demands to furnish Arnold with data on all confidential agents in order, of course, that he might keep all intelligence threads in his hands. This was something that Tallmadge could easily side-step, since details of the Brewster-Woodhull-Townsend chain could be released only by Washington himself. Culper, Jr., while not being specific, was obviously uneasy about some current trend, just uneasy enough to alert Tallmadge.

There had also been a rather strange letter from Arnold to the major. "If Mr. James Anderson, a person I expect from New York should arrive at your quarters, I have to request that you will give him an escort of two horse to bring him on his way to this place, and send an express that I may meet him. If your business will permit I wish you to come with him." Tallmadge may have thought that he was being asked to take a good deal on faith in forwarding an unvouched-for man fresh from British-held New York.

There was little definite to worry about, but the major, in later days, told Historian Jared Sparks, "With Arnold's character I became acquainted while . . . he resided in New Haven and I well remember that I was impressed with the belief that he was not a man of integrity. The Revolution coming on . . . we all seemed, as if by common consent, to forget his knavish tricks."

The patrol ended peacefully and Tallmadge returned to his quarters, where a thunderbolt, wrapped in a letter from Dragoon Lieutenant Colonel John Jameson, was waiting for him. Some militiamen had picked up a suspicious character and brought him to Jameson's quarters at North Castle. The suspect's name was John Anderson. John Anderson, not the James of Arnold's letter. But known intelligence data, added to conjecture, sent Tallmadge galloping off to North Castle.

His superior, a capable Virginian, received him courteously. Yes, the man John Anderson had been brought in and there was something very wrong about the whole matter. In Anderson's stockings had been found detailed plans of the West Point forts, data on ordnance there, and summaries of confidential instructions issued by the commander-in-chief. The strange thing was, Jameson thought, that some of the documents seemed to be in Arnold's handwriting and the prisoner had a pass signed by Arnold. There was forgery involved. As for any danger to West Point, why Arnold himself had had the heavy chain that blocked the river hauled ashore for repairs and had scattered the garrison of the forts to the four winds to cut firewood for the coming winter. Did that look as though Arnold, in the best position to judge, had scented any threat?

As for the papers, Jameson had sent them on by courier to Washington, now on his way home from Hartford, with an explanatory letter. No, the major could not question John Anderson. He was, at that very moment, on his way to Arnold's quarters on the east bank of the Hudson and, frankly, Jameson would not care to be in the man's shoes when Arnold questioned him. Oh yes, and a copy of the letter to Washington had also gone on to Arnold.

At these disclosures, Tallmadge, with his specialized intelligence background, very respectfully and very firmly hit the ceiling. He urged his superior, "in private and in the most friendly manner," to recall the prisoner to North Castle and by all means to stop the explanatory letter to Arnold. What the major told Jameson "greatly agitated" the latter, who, nonetheless, clung to military procedure. Arnold was his superior and any decision about Anderson must be left to him.

This whole interview remains fogged in mystery, since Tallmadge wrote later, "I have deliberately concluded never to disclose the circumstances which relate to this event." There is an unexplained and highly tantalizing hint of action outlined by Tallmadge in his scant words, "I suggested a plan which I wished to pursue, offering to take full responsibility on myself, and which, as he [Jameson] deemed too perilous, I will not further disclose." It is highly possible that the suggestion was that Tallmadge should take a strong force of dragoons, surround the Beverly Robinson house, where Arnold was quartered, and place the general under arrest. No other course of action fits Tallmadge's words and Jameson's refusal.

At last a compromise, highly unsatisfactory to the major, was reached. Jameson sent dragoons after the group guarding John Anderson, but utterly refused to recall the letter to Arnold. The prisoner was brought to regimental headquarters at Old Salem, where he did not strike his guards as any particular prize. Lieutenant Joshua King of Massachusetts, who had been a fifer at Lexington in '75, thought he looked like "a reduced gentleman" with his days-old beard, worn and dirty clothes, and unkempt hair. Nonetheless, King fitted him out with a complete change and summoned the troop barber. Refreshed and much sprucer, the prisoner appealed to King and asked permission to write a letter to Washington, who would at once see the absurdity of further detaining not mere John Anderson but actually the exalted adjutant general of the British Army, Major John André. To this, King agreed.

In the meantime, as hours slipped away, the gods of chance must have been chuckling happily as they fouled up the timetables of the couriers Jameson had sent to Washington and to Arnold. The first had counted on cutting into Washington's line of march at Danbury in Connecticut, but the commander-in-chief and his party had taken a different route west, returning from the conference with Rochambeau. So the courier, in not too much of a hurry, came back to Old Salem, the papers undelivered. Lieutenant Solomon Allen, bearer of the copy to Arnold, had turned back to Old Salem on the recall of André and his guard. Now the pair had to be rested and started out again, the packet for Washington, which now included André's letter, being directed to the Beverly Robinson house, where the commander-in-chief was sure to check in.

Allen was first to reach the Beverly Robinson house, well ahead of the second courier, and found Arnold at breakfast with his military family. Much relieved, he delivered the letter and all his ridings about became nothing but weary memories in his mind. Communications were always slow in those days, and there was no reason for him to feel uneasy that the prisoner had been taken on the twenty-third and the news of the capture delivered to Arnold two whole days later.

Arnold read the letter from Jameson announcing the capture of one John Anderson. He at once ran upstairs for a quick word with his wife and then left the house, telling his aides, David Franks and Richard Varick, that he had to go across the river to West Point. He dropped quickly down the steep bank to the landing where his military barge, fully manned, always waited him. There he told the coxswain to drop far down-river to the anchorage of H.M.S. Vulture, having "particular business from His Excellency to the Captain" of that ship.

Arnold's appearance on the deck of the armed sloop was a heavy blow to the captain, Andrew Sutherland, and to Beverly Robinson, an unswervingly staunch Tory and owner of the house that had sheltered Arnold. Sutherland and Robinson knew that, days before, Major John André had been slipped ashore to confer with the American general. They also knew precisely why the meeting had taken place, and when the watch on deck had sighted the military barge they had fully expected to congratulate André on a difficult mission well performed.

Arnold's story staggered them. He had not been able to find boatmen willing to row André from the meeting place to the *Vulture*, so at Arnold's urging the major had been slipped across the Hudson in civilian clothes and bearing the most damning of papers, this being directly against Clinton's strictest orders. And now, caught as he tried to slip down the east bank into the British lines, André was a prisoner.

The turncoat general did not seem to share their horror. To him, André was expendable. There was no chance of handing over West Point now, but just the same, Clinton was receiving a rare prize in the person of the renowned Benedict Arnold. News of the defection would shake the rebellion to its foundations.

Back on the east bank of the Hudson, Washington finally appeared with his suite and was given the papers found on André along with the explanatory letter. From here on events moved predictably. All American secret agents ducked for cover, including Robert Townsend and his aides, fearing that Arnold had enough data to enable Clinton to hang them. Luckily he didn't, or he surely would have used it. But it was a frightening time for them all and for the men with whom they worked.

West Point was strengthened, and men were rushed to it under Anthony Wayne. Of course Clinton tried desperately to secure the release of his adjutant general, claiming that he had entered the American lines in good faith and at the invitation of an American general. But he could not argue away the fact that that entry into the lines had been for the express purpose of perfecting a plan in conjunction with a now avowed traitor, to wreck the army of the United States. So André was brought across the Hudson to Tappan and there court-martialed in the Old Dutch Church. Under military law the verdict was inevitable—death by hanging.

If events had been predictable, the conduct of one person was not. The charming, frivolous, foppish Major John André, with a lifetime of genteel scheming for his own ends back of him, should have fallen into an abject, blubbering state of funk. But somehow the intense heat of his predicament called forth unsuspected reserves of high courage, of sheer gallantry. He was as charming as ever, talked gaily with his guards, seemed to welcome visits from various officers, wrote verses, and made clever little sketches. Through the whole army there ran an open wish that somehow the verdict might be reversed.

Tallmadge burst out, "By heavens, Colonel Webb, I never saw a man whose fate I foresaw whom I so sincerely pitied. . . . He . . . seems to be as cheerful as though he were going to an assembly. I am sure that he will go to the gallows less tearful of his fate and with less concern than I shall behold the tragedy." And Benjamin Tallmadge spoke for many Americans with those words.

On October 2, 1870, the sentence was carried out and the prisoner remained calm as ever. With the fifes and drums beating out the "Dead March," he commented pleasantly to his immediate escorts, "I am very much surprised to find your troops under such good discipline, and your music is excellent."

The ubiquitous James Thacher made a somber entry in his ever swelling diary. "Major André is no more among the living. I have just witnessed his exit. . . . He betrayed no want of fortitude, but retained a complacent smile on his countenance and politely bowed to several gentlemen whom he knew. . . . Informed that he had an opportunity to speak . . . he said . . . 'I pray you to bear witness that I meet my fate like a brave man.' . . . The wagon now being removed from under him, he was suspended and instantly expired." So this surprising metamorphosis of John André endured until the final tightening of the noose, and the tragic grief that was felt at British headquarters was matched in the Hudson River camp of his enemies.

In New York, very much alive and very much at liberty, Benedict Arnold was busily cashing in on his venture into treason. It is likely that the rewards so graciously bestowed upon him in no way came up to his earlier calculations. But now he had nothing with which to bargain. West Point was firmly in American hands, doubly and trebly alerted. And he could not walk out on his new connections, since the only other road he could take would lead him straight to the gallows. So he had to be content with what was actually in hand: a commission as brigadier general in the British Army (he had been a major general in the American); the rather odd sum of 6,315 pounds sterling—no shillings or pence mentioned—in a lump; an annual pension of five hundred pounds for Peggy; British commissions for three sons by his earlier marriage to Margaret Mansfield of New Haven; pensions of one hundred pounds per annum for each of his children by Peggy, and there would be five in all. This hardly constituted a windfall, but Arnold had no more leverage to apply at the moment.

While the country and the army were rallying from the shock of Arnold's treason and shuddering at the thought of what would have happened had strong British forces pushed up the Hudson to find the West Point garrison scattered and the forts defenseless, the new allies were digging themselves in at Rhode Island and the Providence Plantations.

The French High Brass was more than impatient that no role had been assigned the white-coated regiments, that Washington, at the Hartford conference, had talked in generalities, and that no French officers were invited to take a size-up look at the American army. In this last, Washington was undoubtedly wise. Even to American eyes the troops looked in bad shape both as far as equipment and numbers were concerned. It may have been feared that one glance at the mixed masses of Continental and militia would have so shocked the professional French that they would at once have whistled up their fleet and gone scudding back to France.

Young Comte de Fersen, Swedish aide to Rochambeau, wrote his father, "Our position here is a very disagreeable one. We are vegetating at the very door of the enemy in a most disastrous state of idleness and uncertainty. . . . We are of no possible aid to our allies. . . . We are even an expense to them because by paying cash for our provisions we depreciate their paper money." These were trying times for an active young staff officer, but De Fersen was to see vastly worse ones in years to come, days that would find him disguised as a coachman driving a fugitive King of France and his pretty, empty-headed Queen in flight from their own people. (This trip would end at a town called Varennes and then double back straight to the steps of the guillotine.)

Yet Rochambeau, despite his impatience, seems to have understood at least something of Washington's problems and through them the problems of the nation and loyally deferred to them. A better commander of an allied army could hardly have been found. Later the Marquis de Ségur, who lived through the Newport days and would later survive the retreat of a French army from Moscow, thought that Rochambeau seemed "to have been purposely created to understand Washington and to be understood by him and to serve with Republicans . . . his example more even than his authority obliged us scrupulously to respect the rights, properties and customs of our allies."

As for the army as a whole, it settled itself very comfortably and happily at pretty Newport, "which," an officer wrote, "must have been one of the most agreeable spots in the world and . . . even now with so many houses destroyed by the British . . . it is still a charming place of residence." Some homesick men suddenly found that the island and the country about it were very like Normandy and were cheered by the resemblance. Rochambeau was quartered in the Vernon house, with Aide Fersen at Robert Stevens' in New Lane. Fabulously handsome and lupine De Lauzun was at the Hunters' at the corner of Mary and Thames streets.

The regiments were barracked all over the island, across on the mainland, with some camps reaching as far up as the little town of Providence with its handsome brick Brown College. This spreading of veteran professional troops, of a strange tongue and clinging to a church that was highly suspect in the eyes of most Americans of the day, should have been dynamite. So far as the records show—and there is no reason to doubt them—the union between these professional fighters from all parts of France and the untraveled Rhode Island country people may be termed almost idyllic.

Part of the answer to this lies in the lines of the extract from De Ségur. The sense of this is amplified by the Abbé Claude Robin of the Soissonnais regiment. Rochambeau seems to have drilled it into the heads of all ranks during the long voyage that the French must be on their best behavior. The poilus of 1780, according to the abbé, were "mild, careful and moderate and in the course of our long sojourn, not a single complaint was lodged against them . . . when this line of conduct had been maintained for a few weeks a complete revolution in the spirit of the people was noticed. Even the Tories and Loyalists could not help loving the French." This is high praise, but the record on both sides bears it out.

Rhode Islanders played their part, too. Local leaders saw to it that there was no profiteering, usually the chief source of trouble between troops and civilians, at home or abroad. There seem to have been no fights between these strange-looking and strange-spoken troops and the ultra-independent and self-sufficient Rhode Islanders. And if, as the Abbé Robin says, there were no complaints against the troops, neither was Rochambeau's headquarters deluged with spurious claims for damages. This friendly occupation stands out as a model for both soldier and townsman.

A more severe test lay ahead for part of the French Expeditionary Force. The glittering Duc de Lauzun and his French-Irish second-in-command, a man so handsome that even beside Lauzun he was known as "le beau Dillon," took the hussars and lancers of the Legion far off into Connecticut, to the forest capital of Lebanon, which some French rendered as "le Baron." It was a tearful parting, apparently, but away the troopers rode, plunging into forest tracts such as none of them had ever imagined, though many of them could recall the horrors of tropical Senegal. The whole countryside, as it appeared to these Europeans, was a wilderness with wide forest tracts opening to show a little town, then closing until ten or fifteen miles of unbroken green and brown suddenly revealed another.

Here was a wonderful setting for isolation, loneliness, boredom to fray tempers, magnify petty incidents into intolerable insults, produce neuroses, or, in French military slang of a later day, "le cafard." Lauzun himself wrote in the early days of his stay, "Siberia alone can be compared to Lebanon. It is composed of a few cottages scattered in the midst of a vast forest."

The impact of these outlandish troops must have been something for the Lebanese to stand up to. Newport had always been a sophisticated spot, but rustic Lebanon! Here were long lances twinkling in the wide grassy street, hussar busbies, sky-blue and yellow jackets, cherry-colored breeches, glittering sabers, fur-trimmed dolmans and pelisses. And, by regulation, all the troopers wore mustaches, and the newly joined, still too young to sprout such adornments, had them painted on their upper lips with shoe blacking. This must have been a startling sight in a clean-shaven country. What a chance for the local sprigs to rough up some of these strutting fops and macaronis.

But the miracle of Rhode Island was repeated. The Legion settled itself with an almost Yankee adaptability in little Lebanon. Lauzun himself became a noted squirrel hunter, and when Major General the Chevalier de Chastellux, Yankophile and author of delightful memoirs of his American years, visited him, the chevalier was taken out on a squirrel safari which he dignified into "la Chasse."

Aged Governor Jonathan Trumbull, whose tenure of office dated back to Crown days, gave dinners to the French officers, and De Chastellux left a vivid sketch of "this small, old man in the antique dress of the first settlers in the colony approaching a table surrounded by twenty hussar officers and without either disconcerting himself or losing anything of his formal stiffness," saying a long blessing before seating himself. De Chastellux might have added that Trumbull helped along the alliance by rigidly curbing any profiteering.

To this day the French are remembered at Lebanon. Headquarters house, still standing, is known as the "war office." Barrack sites are still pointed out, along with wells that French and Poles and Irishmen dug. The Legion seems to have had a band of some sort, and the troopers staged musical rides "pour épater les bourgeois." Officers and men poured into Alden's Tavern, sometimes riding their American mounts right up to the bar, where, says tradition, the horses were served a good tot of New England rum, the riders apparently preferring the imported West India brand. When the tavern site was excavated some years ago, quite a haul of foreign coins was made, pieces from all over Europe that must have slipped down through the planking as hussar or lancer clattered in, calling like the new-born Gargantua, "A boire! A boire!" and scattering money broadcast.

None of this has anything to do with the progress of the struggle of the thirteen states and their allies, on the surface. But when the troopers rode out in the late spring of 1781 to join the white-coated fantassins for the long march that was to end on the peninsula between the York and the James, they knew, as did the foot soldiers, that they were leaving friends, that they would meet more friends when they joined the soldier sons of the people among whom they had lived. Sleek court noble like Lauzun, weathered campaigner like Artillery Chief d'Aboville, non-com from the valley of the Aisne, private from the banks of the Rhone, friendly Pole and rollicking Irishman, they had all done their part to make a strange alliance glow with efficient warmth. And so had every official, townsman, or countryman in the Rhode Island-Connecticut billeting areas. The story of Yorktown might have been different had sullen, resentful allies stood, side by side but apart, before Cornwallis' works.

CHAPTER XXIX

"I only lament that my abilities are not more competent . . ."

THE months of 1780 were falling slowly into the discard, piling up into a somber heap that represented the blackest period that the new United States had so far known. In the North affairs seemed hopelessly static, the few events that did take place being only for the worse.

In the South, still under the pall of Gates's disastrous sally toward Camden in South Carolina, decay seemed to be setting in fast. Cornwallis' grip on the states from Georgia on to the Virginia border appeared unshakable. Yet he and his lieutenants were embarking on a course that could hardly be better calculated to shake, if not actually weaken, the British hold.

The harsh measures that loomed so ominously after the fall of Charleston increased. Tarleton raided and ravaged suspected areas, burned and destroyed without apparently inquiring too closely whether the inhabitants were Whig or Tory. Major Wemyss, detached from the 63rd Manchesters to lead Tory formations, struck north along the coast into the Georgetown section, killed off flocks, smashed the hand looms on which most of the country people depended for clothing, killed, burned, and looted. Other raider leaders, like the Connecticut Tory, Major James Dunlap, took the rather extreme view that, as the Revolution in the North had started largely among dissenters, any church that was not Church of England marked the congregation as atrocious rebels. Such buildings were burned, men hanged out of hand, houses destroyed, and stock killed or driven off. Since many staunch Tories were equally staunch Presbyterians, this policy only served to create new rebels. From Ninety Six to the sea, destruction and death mounted. Winter was coming on, and hundreds of Carolinians could shudder as they felt its approach and thought of vanished herds and looked upon smashed looms.

Severity also reigned in Charleston, and many of the leaders who had been duly paroled found themselves shipped suddenly off to St. Augustine in Florida. Once there, they were faced with a demand to subscribe to a new and far more sweeping oath. This was protested bitterly, and men like Christopher Gadsden were confined in St. Augustine Castle. Confiscation of property went on unchecked and became a delightful source of revenue to the hangers-on who followed the army.

South Carolina was by no means passive under this treatment, and little by little, as the shock of the Gates defeat wore off and the policy of the Crown became more and more severe, a sort of Maquis movement came into vigorous being. Small bands, formed for mutual protection against British and Tory raiders, took the field, found others operating like themselves, swelled into larger bodies, became little armies whenever a real leader appeared.

Such leaders were by no means lacking. First and foremost was the frail, swarthy, eagle-nosed Francis Marion, whom Gates had so slightingly dismissed. Colonel Thomas Sumter, handsome, full of panache, recklessly brave, became a natural rallying point. He might have been the one key figure in the resistance movement, but he was possessed of an independence of spirit, a hatred of authority and control so deep as to make John Stark seem like a robot. Colonel Andrew Pickens pretty well matched Marion and Sumter in daring, skill, and devotion. As time went on, the state was divided among this trio, unconsciously at first and then formally, with Marion covering the coastal areas and ranging inland, Sumter the central portions, and Pickens the west, although these spheres of influence were naturally rather fluid.

All of them understood very well, Marion best of all and Sumter probably the least, the vital difference between guerrilla bands and organized armies. Roughly speaking, your true army has two objectives, the first being to destroy the enemy and the second to take and hold territory. The guerrilla band that properly understands its mission does not hold ground. Its key technique is the side-stepping of open combat, the eroding of enemy forces and supplies. It hits and runs, unless in overwhelming strength, and the most important item is the running, the getting away after striking.

So up and down the state and sometimes well into North Carolina, little evasive actions were fought at Flat Rock, at Thicketty Fort and Rocky Mount, Hanging Rock and Old Iron Works. As a rule, these were successful when the various bands stuck to their true mission. Disaster usually fell upon them when they tried to act like formal armies.

Taken action by action, these clashes amounted to little. In the aggregate they seriously impeded any notions that Cornwallis might have had about pushing on north. Then in October an almost impromptu blow struck the Crown forces with dizzying impact. Major Patrick Ferguson, a British officer highly respected by both sides, led a force composed entirely of Tories into the western reaches of the highlands and found himself on a long, high, wooded hill shaped something like an aircraft carrier minus its "island" and lying in both the Carolinas. It was known as King's Mountain, and there on the seventh he was hit by a slightly smaller force of backwoodsmen mainly from present-day Tennessee and West Virginia under Colonel Isaac Shelby and "Nolichucky Jack" Sevier. Ferguson was killed and his command wiped out, a spectacular victory marred by the hangings of a good many Tories rightly or wrongly suspected of having committed similar outrages on rebels in the past. Adding this sudden stroke to the incessant needle stings by Marion, Sumter, and Pickens, Cornwallis began revising his roseate notions of an easy, pleasant march north and went into winter quarters at Winnsboro, well west of Camden and the Wateree.

So with the struggle dormant in the North, that area really became the fringe and the formerly isolated threads in the South wove themselves into a whole fabric. It would have taken supernatural clairvoyance to see this from Washington's headquarters in the brick-and-stone De Windt house at Tappan. Yet the commander-in-chief moved as though he were clearly aware of the change in the geographical focus of events.

First of all, it was obvious that Gates must be relieved after his Camden debacle. In the past such appointments to commands that must, for reasons of distance if no other, be virtually independent had been made by the Congress. It was that body which had named Gates to take charge of the Southern theater, and in doing so Washington had not even been consulted. Now the laurels of Saratoga were withered on the brow of Burgoyne's conqueror and the members of Congress probably felt a little diffident about masterminding the choice of a successor to Gates.

Up at West Point, now happily freed from his hated quartermaster duties, Nathanael Greene was settling himself for the winter and was eagerly awaiting the arrival of his Kitty. The season would pass pleasantly, he thought, on this eagle perch far above the autumnal flow of the Hudson. His family would be with him and, professionally, he would be commanding troops again. There would be plenty to do, strengthening West Point, seeing that new levies were raised and the old formations kept up to scratch for the operations that were bound to come with the spring of 1781.

A courier rode up to the cliff post, was waved through by the various sentries. A rider from the commander-in-chief did not have to bother with formalities, once identified. Soon Greene was staring at a letter that bore Washington's flowing signature. "By a letter . . . from his Excellency the President of Congress . . . I find it has been their pleasure to appoint an officer to command" the Southern theater. "It is my wish to appoint you. . . . Besides my own inclination to this choice . . . it concurs with the wishes of the delegates from the three Southern States. . . . I have only to add, that I wish for your earliest arrival, that there may be no circumstances to retard your proceeding to the southward."

This appointment, made by Washington and endorsed by the Congress, especially the Southern delegates, was an expression of trust such as had fallen to very few Americans, as Greene was well aware. He answered promptly, "I only lament that my abilities are not more competent to the duties that will be required of me, and that it will not be in my power on that account, to be as extensively useful as my inclination leads me to wish. But as far as zeal and attention can supply the defect I flatter myself my country will have little cause to complain."

As events turned out, there were to be no causes for complaint. Washington had chosen the best-fitted man in the whole army for the job, despite Greene's disclaimers. The Rhode Islander had had extensive combat service. In addition to this, his recent long months as quartermaster had given him a deep insight into the problems of maintaining an army as well as commanding it in action.

There were other considerations that must have sent Greene limping up and down his West Point quarters, rubbing his high forehead in perplexity. The Southern command was looked upon as a military graveyard. Lincoln had certainly found it so, as had Gates—although the former would undergo a last-minute resurrection. Could Greene expect anything better? He was to take no troops with him. Instead, his command would consist of the feeble wreckage of Gates's army, probably less than a thousand men fit for duty.

The prospect of leaving West Point for such an assignment could not have been very pleasing despite the honor. And besides, Kitty was on the way to join him, would arrive in a day or so.

Characteristically, Greene passed none of his doubts and worries and private disappointments along to Washington. He hung about West Point to the very last minute and then left for army headquarters, ironically missing Kitty by the narrowest margin. There were last-minute instructions at headquarters, and Von Steuben was detailed to go along with him to help out in any role that Greene might see fit to assign. Then the new commander of the Southern theater was on his way.

On December 2, 1780, Greene took over from Gates at the little town of Charlotte, North Carolina. This was a touchy situation, as Gates, in natural disappointment and irritation, might have made the transfer of command difficult and unpleasant. But whatever Gates's faults were, he showed not the least pettiness on this occasion and behaved as though Nathanael Greene were graciously conferring a favor on him by taking his place. Greene was considerate, tactful, and in every way possible spared the feelings of the defeated general whom he was relieving. The interchange of compliments and courtesies greatly impressed Otho Holland Williams, whom Gates had distressed so much in the pre-Camden moves, and he commented that "it was an elegant lesson of propriety, exhibited on a most delicate and interesting occasion."

Gates finally rode off, and Greene called for reports on the handful of wraiths given him to conquer three states and wipe out Cornwallis' army. Headquarters were in the courthouse, which loomed importantly over the thirty-odd houses scattered about the red-mud streets of Charlotte. It had a lofty cupola and was raised high above the sloping ground by a series of solid brick pillars, with a wide gallery surrounding the main or second floor. Along this gallery clanked officer after officer, to be closely questioned by the wheezing ironmaster from Rhode Island.

The reports could be made quickly, since there was little detail involved. On paper, Greene could tot up about twenty-three hundred men, of whom over nine hundred were Continentals. But under the heading "Present and fit for duty" the grand total reached less than eight hundred. Then his mind, trained in logistics through his quartermaster service, had to dig into the question of how the men were equipped, fed, armed, and clothed. His subordinates were first astounded, then delighted. Colonel William Polk of North Carolina, acting quartermaster for the little command, marveled that Greene "by the following morning understood them [supply problems] better than Gates had done in the whole period of his command."

Greene, too, marveled, but not with pleasure. There were only three days' rations in the whole camp. Most of the wheeled transport had vanished at Camden, as had Gates's artillery. There was no cash in the military chest, and if there had been there was little to buy in the bone-stripped countryside. The men looked worse than the reports. Clothes were mere tatters. Shoes, as always, were deplorable. Morale was very low, and hence the camps were filthy, badly sited, and ill guarded. Yet Greene, riding in his blue and white along the ridges and through shallow valleys, could shelve his quartermaster's mind and bring his military gifts into play and realize that qualitatively the command might amount to something. The Continentals were none other than the Delawares and the Marylanders, and the past told him that they could be brought up to a high rating very quickly. The militia looked shaky and ragged, but there were many self-reliant, tough North Carolina riflemen among them, with a fine leavening of Georgians.

His greatest asset, one that Gates had very thoroughly overlooked, was the high level of his subordinate commanders. There was the cavalryman, Colonel William Washington, a man of known competence. And Greene could well remember how Lieutenant Colonel Edward Carrington had brought up his guns on the right flank at Monmouth to shatter a heavy enemy attack. Otho Williams the new commander had probably met back in '75, when the Marylander had marched into the Boston lines with Cresap's riflemen. There was another fine Marylander, John Eager Howard, a man of extended service who was later to marry the fascinating Peggy Chew of Philadelphia. This was an unbroken list of quiet, seasoned standouts, a group that any commander would fight and scheme and plot to have under him.

He could listen to them with confidence as they told him of other competent officers, so far unknown to him, men like the dashing William Richardson Davie of North Carolina, who on paper needed a little vouching for. Davie had fought at Long Island. After that ghastly defeat he had felt that the war was lost and had gone back to the brick college at Princeton in New Jersey to finish his interrupted studies. Thence he had returned home to practice law, convinced that a great deal of good could be done by a skilled attorney in the unsettled days sure to follow on the American collapse, in which he reluctantly believed. What he saw after the fall of Charleston told him that for a while the days of law were over, and he returned to the field. Greene took to him at once and, sizing him up, appointed him quartermaster in place of William Polk, who felt himself too old for the job. Davie bucked and fought, as Greene himself had done when Washington made Greene quartermaster general. He wanted to stay in combat, just as Greene had. Davie protested that, among other things, he knew nothing about money and accounts. "Don't concern yourself," said Greene pleasantly. "There is no money and hence no accounts."

There was no need for Greene to introduce a newcomer to the theater, a huge man in fringed buckskins who climbed stiffly up the gallery steps to headquarters. Arthritis, on top of a very natural disappointment at having his magnificent work against Burgoyne completely overlooked, had kept Dan Morgan in retirement since '79. Now, belatedly made a brigadier, he came creakily into the field again, racked by pain in all his joints but grimly resolved that the Old Waggoner would "crack his whip once more."

Nor did Greene have to give much biographical data in telling his officers that Lieutenant Colonel "Light-Horse" Harry Lee was on his way to the Carolinas with his Legion of several hundred men, horse and foot. They had been newly equipped in Virginia, and the commander thought that the sight of plumed leather helmets, green jackets, white breeches, and knee boots would be a fine tonic for the army. Probably most of Greene's officers thought that Lee's troopers would go straight under William Washington's skilled hand. But the Rhode Islander had other ideas of the use of the Legion. And as early as his second day at Charlotte he wrote a letter to a South Carolinian whom Gates had treated with negligent condescension.

The Great Pee Dee flows southeast through the hills of the Cheraws, just below the North Carolina line. Through plains and swamps it wanders

rather vaguely on toward the sea, and between the Black Mingo and the
Little Pee Dee it is joined by Lynches Creek. At this junction, river and
creek, aided by lesser confluents, form a big island. In 1780 this island
would probably have been barely discernible from the air, since it and the
country on all sides of the river were thick with pine and oak. From the
ground a traveler came upon it suddenly with its living waters flowing
moatlike about it. It was called Snow Island, and people were beginning to
compare it to Athelney, Alfred the Great's secret base against the Danes in
Somersetshire, for here was the fortress without walls that sheltered Francis
Marion and his men.

From Snow Island, Marion sallied out against Cornwallis, against Tory
concentrations, snapping up a convoy here, ambushing a patrol there, striking quickly, melting away, striking again. True to the laws of guerrilla warfare, places did not interest him. Do damage and get out was Marion's
unvarying rule. Gifted with an Indian's sense for the country, he rode
through dense forests and shunned roads and trails. Whenever he could,
he used fords or swam his horses across streams. When he had to use a
bridge, his men stacked blankets over the planks to deaden the thump of
hoofs. The British came to dread him, and strong detachments had to be
wasted just guarding convoys. Supply routes had to be altered, and the
merest rumor that Marion was abroad set commanders of garrisons bellowing out alarms, firing into the empty darkness, and demanding men and
more men to cover that part of the convoy line assigned to their care. Three
times Cornwallis added to the garrison at Nelson's Ferry, a vital spot on the
Santee, simply because Marion was thought to be in the neighborhood.
But each time, Marion was striking somewhere else and then threading back
to Snow Island.

The numbers of men at Snow Island varied from a dozen or so to a
hundred or more, depending on Marion's needs and the temper of the
countryside, and his personnel was constantly changing. But a small, hard
knot of lieutenants was nearly always with him. Peter Horry, who had gone
to Gates's camp with Marion, was there, along with several others of his
name. There were Postells, Conyers, Vanderhorsts, Doziers, Jennerets, and
Mouzons. In this preponderance of French Huguenot names were Jameses
from Wales, a galaxy of Jameses, so many of them that some had to be distinguished by locale, as in the case of John James of the Lake.

It was an odd band under an odd leader. Leader and band were particularly notable in this area of vicious fighting, this almost intra-tribal war,
in that Marion allowed no reprisals, cracked down hard on wanton killing,
and would permit no looting of any sort, except of royal stores, which were
carried back to Snow Island and there pooled for the benefit of all. His
theory was that one day the war would be over and surviving rebel and Tory
would have to live side by side, an impossible situation if legacies of hatred
and revenge were piled up against that time.

To Snow Island came the letter that Greene had written in the brick-
pillared courthouse in Charlotte, the bearer having been intercepted by

Marion's sleepless patrols that girdled a wide tract about the river refuge. Greene had begun: "I have not the honor of your acquaintance, but am no stranger to your character and merit." Then he outlined some ideas of his own on guerrilla warfare which the taciturn Marion thought eminently sound. Here, obviously, was a man to work with. And, as an earnest of Greene's faith and confidence in the Lord of Snow Island, Henry Lee's Legion was at that moment on the march to join the band.

The job of finding Marion was a tough one. Lee and his men ranged down from the Cheraws and found no trace of the Swamp Fox, as he was beginning to be known. There were open, grassy tracts to cross, great stands of pine and oak, ghastly swamps and river crossings where quicksands might be feared. By luck Lee stumbled onto one of Marion's foraging parties and was brought to Snow Island. It was fortunate for the Virginian that Marion was still there, for he had a habit, while keeping the island as a permanent base, of moving off with his command to the heart of some fearful swamp farther up the river, off by the Santee or along the Black Mingo.

To mix troops trained in formal warfare with a roving band like Marion's was a bold experiment on Greene's part. But the swarthy little South Carolinian and the florid Virginian seem to have understood each other at once. Together they plotted a raid on a strong British post at Georgetown on Winyah Bay, one that would blend guerrilla mobility with cohesion of regular troops.

It was a typical Marion operation, and Lee's eyes must have bulged as the silent little man, eternally sipping his favorite vinegar, set the wheels turning. Messengers slipped away from the island with a seeming aimlessness. Then in a January dusk the Great Pee Dee came alive. From hidden creeks, from landings by ruined plantations, from a dozen streams and backwaters floated a procession of boats rowed or poled by old men, by women, by weedy boys. There were great barges built to carry plantation produce down to the sea. There were small ferries, canoes, clumsy dugouts, brought into sudden existence by a terse word from Francis Marion.

Water-borne, the two commands set out. The blow at Georgetown turned out to be only a partial success, but it was vastly important in that it did show that regulars and irregulars could work together, that both Marion and Lee had the elasticity of mind to learn and to adapt. Lee's troopers were shown how far and how fast and how silently a large body of men could move if certain conditions were observed. The guerrillas saw and appreciated the value of formal march discipline. When the two groups finally returned to Snow Island, each had gained greatly in knowledge without losing any of its own particular virtues. In this first raid the foundations for future profitable joint operations were laid.

Up at Charlotte, Greene considered what lay before him and how best to face it. Some of his officers spoke wisely about going into winter quarters, but Greene waved such suggestions away. He had seen troops rot through too many winter camps to think of subjecting this force to such a test.

Pacing up and down the courthouse gallery, looking south and east and west over the down-sloping ground that led to the main British Army and its chain of posts, he realized that he was not strong enough to attack Cornwallis at Winnsboro. Then he came to a decision that violated every principle of war, that had lost New York to the Americans and had led to Burgoyne's downfall. He would split his little army in two.

Part would be shifted down to the Cheraws to train and refit. The other section would go west and west again, to the country between the Pacolet and the Broad, just inside the South Carolina border, a long sixty or seventy miles, and the Old Waggoner would lead it. Greene could spare him only about six hundred men, but the core of the force was made up of the tireless Marylanders and Delawares under Colonel John Eager Howard, and more militia was expected to pick up the column once it had started.

Greene and Davie and Carrington and the army engineer, Thaddeus Kosciusko, watched the tough handful march out under Dan Morgan. Greene was taking a fearful calculated risk, for his hope was that Cornwallis would, in turn, split his army and give Morgan at least a fair chance of beating that detachment and thus lessening the over-all odds against the Americans. If Cornwallis did not fall for what was really a decoy move and struck up at the Cheraws with his whole force, the Southern campaign and possibly the war might be over. But Greene could count on Marion and Sumter and Pickens to send him word of any major British undertaking.

Daniel Morgan, rigid in the saddle from arthritis, took his men west, crossing the Catawba while William Washington's white-coated helmeted troopers covered the advance. The Old Waggoner, while always offensive-minded, had a fine seasoning of experience to temper that trait. Now in his thoughts was a letter from Greene that counseled, "Put nothing on hazard. Retreat is disagreeable, but not disgraceful. It is not our business to risk too much." With all this, Morgan agreed.

In the last days of December, Lieutenant Colonel James McCall with over two hundred and fifty South Carolina militia joined Morgan and at once was sent with William Washington to strike at a Tory body that was operating like the Mohawk Valley "Destructives" along Fairfort Creek. Militia infantry and Continental cavalry worked well together. The Tory force was wiped out and Washington curved on south across the Tyger and the Enoree almost down to Ninety Six on the Saluda before turning back. It was a good shakedown cruise for the militia as well as the dragoons, and Morgan was pleased. Then he began hastily to regroup his forces as the new year of 1781 opened. Colonel Andrew Pickens sent him word that some eleven hundred men, infantry, cavalry, and artillery, under Banastre Tarleton were astir and moving up via the Enoree.

Down in the Winnsboro area Cornwallis had received reinforcements under Major General Alexander Leslie and could now see that his adjutant's reports listed some four thousand men. They were quality troops. A brigade of the Guards had marched up the Wateree to join him; he had elements of the 16th Bedfordshires, the 33rd West Ridings, the 71st High-landers, the individualistic Welch of the 23rd, Hessian infantry and Jaegers, Tarleton's British Legion with a few troops of the 17th Dragoons and some Tory outfits. These last seem to have contained very few Carolinians, for, as so often happened, the presence of royal forces had not produced any great Loyalist rush to the colors, despite glowing hopes and promises. Corn-wallis' Tories were mostly units recruited in the North, of respectable length of service, and could be rated first-line troops.

Morgan's move to the west had been quickly noted, but for a while there was no British counterstroke. This passivity was not the bemused indolence that had marked Howe and others. Cornwallis was genuinely puzzled and perplexed. The split of Greene's forces was highly unorthodox and reck-less, and the new picture called for close staff analysis. Then the British commander saw that if he forgot Morgan and struck at Greene the Old Waggoner could sideslip west to the post at Ninety Six and thence slide east down the Congaree and the vital Santee area. Similarly, if he went after Morgan, Green could drive straight south toward Charleston. So, as Greene had hoped, he had to split his army as his adversary had done.

Tarleton was the man to handle Morgan, and some rather pungently terse letters passed between the cavalryman and Cornwallis. "Dear Tarle-ton: If Morgan is . . . anywhere within your reach, I should wish you to push him to the utmost. . . . No time is to be lost." "My Lord: I must either destroy Morgan's corps or push it . . . toward King's Mountain." "Dear Tarleton: You have understood my intentions perfectly." So, it may be added, had Dan Morgan.

Tarleton set out, as reported by Pickens. Cornwallis left Leslie with a holding force at Camden and swayed slowly north, where he would be in a position to mop up the wreck of Morgan's certain rout and then hit east at Nathanael Greene.

By January 17 Morgan had chosen the spot where he wanted to meet Tarleton. It was a wide, level stretch covered with virgin timber—pine and oak and chestnut—the trees growing so far apart and the ground about them so clean that horsemen could easily ride among the boles. In more peace-ful days this parklike area had been used by drovers to rest and graze cattle that were being driven east to market. Its nature and name were repeated over and over in the state, but of all the old pasturages, this one alone, almost in the shadow of King's Mountain, is remembered—the Cowpens.

There was no support for either flank, and the winding course of Thicketty Creek barred escape to the east and the loops of the Broad hemmed in the north. On this plain were two low hills, one behind the other, the southern rise being the higher. To many of Morgan's officers this choice seemed suicidal. But Morgan knew Tarleton and counted on no finesse from him, just a head-on, smashing assault. He also knew the merits and demerits of hastily raised militia and wanted to give his levies no thick woods or swamps to flee into. He put them where they would have to fight or be sabered. In this last estimate he showed that he had been away from the army too long. The Carolina and Georgia militia were green. But the Virginia levies held a large proportion of ex-Continentals. They would prove to be about as steady as men in regular service.

Early in the morning of the seventeenth he posted his little army. Out in the flatlands toward the flow of the Pacolet were Carolinians and Georgians, many of them riflemen, under the tireless Andrew Pickens, now ready for his first formal battle. On the southern, and higher, hill Morgan placed the cream of his force, Howard's Marylanders and Delawares, flanked right and left by Virginia militia. Out of sight, down the reverse slope of the lower northern hill, William Washington's dragoons stood ready to mount, bridles over their arms, chatting idly with McCall's North Carolinians, who were held in reserve.

From the hill where Howard's men were stationed, the foreground, tree-studded, stretched away south to the blue twinkle of the Pacolet like a stage setting. There were the oaks and the pines, there the double lines of drab militiamen and the roll of the river far beyond them. A Delaware file closer could look down as though from a balcony seat as Banastre Tarleton made his dramatic entry into the stage of the Cowpens. There he was, with his plumed helmet and a handful of white-coated troopers. His sword winked as he pointed out the American skirmish line, obviously ordering his men to clear the field. Rifles began to crack, and one saddle was empty, five, a dozen and more. The troopers rode out of sight, with Tarleton storming at them for retreating without orders. Down among the trees and along grassy stretches drab figures rose leisurely and sauntered back to the second line, where Pickens received them.

Now the near bank of the Pacolet was thick with troops advancing in line of battle. Off to the left front the skullcaps of the British light infantry flickered. Inward came the green coats of the infantry of Tarleton's Legion, and beyond them the blue facings of the 7th Royal Fusiliers. Hoofs beat faintly in the distance, and from the hill, brass could be made out as British dragoons rode up on either flank. From Howard's hill the scarlet and white and green array looked like a parade of toys, sinister toys that swelled and swelled into threatening dimensions. Marylanders watched the long lines come on, probably reflecting sourly that it was about time for the militia to panic.

The panic never came. Every militia move had been explained in advance by Dan Morgan himself to the militia privates as well as officers. This accounted for the easy withdrawal of that first line which had driven off Tarleton and his dragoons. Now Pickens was quietly reminding his men to hold their fire until "killing distance" was reached. As at Breed's Hill—how many long years ago?—raw men created their own fire discipline, loosed, as Morgan had asked earlier, two controlled, shattering volleys, and then fell back toward Howard's men.

Marylanders, Delawares, and Virginians could see them coming in good order across their own front, muskets and rifles carried easily. It was something to remember, up there on the hill, that almost casual withdrawal across and then behind Howard's men. But then, hadn't the Old Waggoner told the militia men they'd be quite safe between the two hills? There was nothing to fret a man if Dan Morgan had said they'd be safe.

There was one moment of peril. The militia from the far right had the longest distance to cover, and a bugle blared and Howard's men gasped as they saw the flash of sabers and heard the pound of hoofs as Tarleton's dragoons swung in onto the last of the retirement. But there were other bugles on the field that day. Out from the dead ground between the two hills poured Washington's cavalry, struck Tarleton's riders in the flank and broke them utterly, re-formed, and, their immediate job done, withdrew.

The spectator role was over for the men on the south hill. The British, despite their losses and the repulse of the dragoons, had taken the militia withdrawal for flight, an opinion for which, unfortunately, there was ample precedent. Tarleton's whole line swept upward, shadows slanting long on the crisp, browning grass. There was hard, desperate fighting as Howard's men stood firm against skilled, unwavering attacks while oily smoke rose lazily toward the thin January sun.

Tragedy hung black in the sky when an American order to wheel was misunderstood and led to a withdrawal on one wing. This could have been fatal to unsteady troops, but Howard's battle-wise men took in the situation, conformed to the unintended movement, and soon were in good formation, puzzled but unshaken, in the space between the two hills. The attackers saw only the empty crest and took the short retirement to mean flight. They began to yell piercingly, as they had at the first American withdrawal at the Hollow Way in '76. They imagined a rout and pressed forward. Their ranks broke and good order was lost. Topping the rise, they stared down at Marylanders, Delawares, and Virginians, who were now advancing, bayonets aslant. To add to the American line, Pickens' militia, having curved back to the two hills, now reappeared. Captain Kirkwood's slim Delaware battalion moved against the British right and the whole picture was changed.

Men in red and green were breaking, throwing down their arms. Up came the bonnets of the 71st Scots, but militia riflemen finally wrecked their stubborn stand and Major Archibald McArthur handed over his sword to Andrew Pickens. In the rear, Tarleton tried to rally his dragoons for another charge, but they had had enough and, discipline or no discipline, wheeled about and started for the rear. Then Washington's troopers were among them, driving them farther and farther out of action. The pursuit swirled on, and at one moment the two leaders, Washington and Tarleton, were wheeling and circling about each other, cutting and thrusting. Washington's horse was wounded and finally American trumpets sounded the recall.

Among the trees by the Pacolet, Sergeant Major William Seymour of the Delawares leaned panting on his musket and reflected that the victory could be "attributed to nothing else but Divine providence, they having 1,300 in the field of their best troops and we not 800 of standing troops and militia." In his modesty he seems to give no credit to the uncommon toughness and skill of his comrades, Continentals and militia, or to excellent handling from company level upward. There was a military box score for Seymour to set down almost reverently. "One Major, thirteen Captains, fourteen Lieutenants, nine Ensigns and five hundred and fifty private men, with two field-pieces and four standards of colors" had been taken. All in all, since these figures were low and do not include killed and wounded, Tarleton had tossed away nearly 90 per cent of the men with whom he had started to "destroy Morgan's force."

Daniel Morgan had a tough, cool mind. He had just won a striking victory, but he knew that Cornwallis was astir somewhere to the south with an army that he could not hope to match. He began a steady retreat, slanting off northeast toward the fords of the Catawba. It was a rugged hike, with one hundred miles covered over killing terrain, "very difficult marching, being very mountainous," in the opinion of veteran Sergeant Major Seymour.

This move was a vital one. Cornwallis, on learning of Tarleton's defeat, figured that Morgan would do precisely what he should not have done, that the Old Waggoner, dizzy with success, would hang about in the King's Mountain-Cowpens area. Counting on his opponent doing the wrong thing —a very dangerous course to follow in war or commerce or sports—he struck out into the void, found that he had missed his quarry, and was immediately faced with a very tough decision.

A Gage or a Howe would have fallen back to Camden and Winnsboro. But Cornwallis was a far bigger man than those two. He knew that since his apparent conquest of South Carolina he had twice lost his left wing, first at King's Mountain and now at the Cowpens. To fall back would dishearten his army, terrify the Tories, and set all rebels snapping and snarling at him from Ninety Six to Winyah Bay.

So in camp at Ramsour's Mills on the upper Catawba he made up his mind. A naturally aggressive man, he would go after Morgan. But to catch up with him, he would have to move very fast and he had lost the cream of his light, mobile troops at the Cowpens. No matter. He would strip his army to the bone and drive it relentlessly. Two days were spent in burning wagons and stores. No tents were to be used. Rations were destroyed, except for what the men could carry. Unlike Gentleman Johnny Burgoyne, he included himself in this peeling down. More, he had the heads of all rum casks staved in and gave permission for just four wagons to come with the column to carry medical supplies, the sick, ammunition, and salt. This was grim work and resulted in over two hundred desertions, mostly Hessians. But it served notice that a new kind of British commander was in the field.

On the last day of January, 1781, he started, and now his plan had expanded beyond Morgan. He would try to dispose of Greene as well and, if he could not bring about an open action, would hit for the fords of the Dan River, which curved shallowly down from Virginia into North Carolina and back into Virginia again before joining the Roanoke. His intelligence assured him that the Dan crossings, today thick with textile mills, would be a deathtrap for Greene. There were not, he was told, enough boats available to ferry even a fraction of the rebel army to safety, and the fords were not usable save at low water. Drums beat, cavalry trumpets rang out, and the pursuit was on.

News of Morgan's victory took nearly a week to reach Nathanael Greene in the Camp of Repose in the Cheraws. A lesser man would have been elated, ordered up rum for the troops, and sent a congratulatory letter to the Old Waggoner. But the Rhode Islander, while thoroughly appreciating the value of the Cowpens, saw quickly that victory could end in disaster if Morgan's little force were caught. With a dozen or so dragoons he set out at once across country to join Morgan, a reckless dash through Tory-infested country that could have ended fatally, though Greene did not seem to appreciate the acute danger of his course.

Before leaving, and by courier once he had started, he fired out machine-gun blasts of terse orders. The Cheraw army under the South Carolinian general, Isaac Huger, must start north toward the Dan at once. Edward Carrington, now acting faithfully as quartermaster, must go ahead of Huger to round up everything on the Dan that would float, to set civilians to building boats. Greene had seen the crossing at Trenton and remembered the key point of Washington having scouted the Delaware long before for floating stock. Lee's Legion, planning raids with Marion up to the Congaree, was recalled to the main army. Marion was told to harry the Santee while Pickens, on his own again, operated between Ninety Six in the west and the High Hills of Santee on the east.

Huger and Morgan finally joined forces and started on the seventy torturing miles to the Dan. It was in February, the worst of all possible months. There was rain that turned into sleet and sleet that clotted into wet, sticky snow. At night the roads froze stone-hard and deep ruts became long, reddish-brown sword blades. With the day, the surface bogged down into deep mud where feet slithered and worn shoes fell apart. These were tough men and they could have walked away easily from most British commands.

But now Cornwallis was cracking his whip, and the British soldier, formidable at all times, is never more dangerous, never finer than when the chips are down. There were obscure brushes at fords, fierce gallop-and-hack encounters in sloppy fields and among the blackjack growths. There was no shaking off the pursuit, no time to catch a breath and plan a little. This was a new kind of war, and past experience of British pressure could not help Greene. He was equal to meeting changed situations.

Near the Dan the Rhode Islander formed a small highly mobile and carefully picked force of not quite seven hundred men. There were Washington and his dragoons, the troopers and infantry of Lee's Legion still fresh after their march up from Marion's lairs, some Virginia riflemen and Continental infantry. Greene offered this command to Morgan, but ague and arthritis had finally combined to take the Old Waggoner out of the war for good, and the choice fell on Otho Williams.

The mission of this command was simple to explain, staggeringly difficult to execute. Williams trailed his troopers and foot soldiers off to the west, let Cornwallis see him, and then slanted north. At once General O'Hara of the Guards was sent after him with a strong detachment, and Cornwallis, thinking that Williams was actually part of the main American force, changed the course of his march slightly, away from Greene's route and toward the west. Day after dripping day, through ink-black nights when British patrols charged British patrols and Americans fired on Americans, Otho Williams hung on, his double aim being to keep his little band between Greene in the east and Cornwallis in the west, while never allowing himself to be drawn into any major action. Horses died; men died. Rations ran out and soldiers gnawed at dried alligator meat, a dubious delicacy that even the poorest settlers thought fit only for their lean, yellow hounds. O'Hara's men suffered equally with Williams', and the guardsman from Ireland matched the Marylander in endurance, skill, and toughness.

Through an early-morning mist among the blackjacks some five days after he had set out on this thin-ice mission, Williams had word from Greene. Most of the army had crossed the Dan into Virginia near Boyd's Ferry and Irwin's, not far from its junction with the Roanoke. With Lee's cavalry covering his rear, Williams moved cautiously north. Tarleton's dragoons were keeping in sight of Lee's green-coated troopers, but the Virginian was not worried. His own men were still well mounted, while the British cavalry was reduced to weedy little tackies that could be easily outridden. Darkness came, and the roads began to harden again. Another rider from Greene brought more news. The main army was over the Dan to the last man. Williams could forget about O'Hara and join Greene.

The little command rode on through the darkness toward the curving river and safety, some forty miles away. The men, especially the infantry, were staggering with fatigue, for, as Sergeant Major Seymour wrote, "we marched for the most part both day and night . . . so we had scarce time to cook our victuals." Henry Lee remembered that no tents were used and that "The heat of the fires was the only protection from rain and sometimes snow. . . . The single meal allowed us was always scanty . . . being bacon and corn meal." But at last the river was reached and crossed. The retreat to the Dan was over.

Cornwallis kept on, but the swollen river was before him and, as at the Delaware, all boats were at the opposite bank. Bracing himself with the thought that from Virginia south to Florida not a single American soldier was in arms against the Crown, he trailed south to Hillsboro, apparently feeling much as McClellan did when, after Antietam, he trumpeted out that Robert E. Lee had been driven from Union territory. In 1862 McClellan overlooked the fact that Lee's army still existed. Cornwallis, in 1781, seems to have shown the same blindness about Greene. Moreover, in considering the Carolinas and Georgia as entirely Crown territory, such names as Marion, Sumter, and Pickens slipped his mind.

Actually he had plenty to worry about without dwelling on such unruly, if distant, characters. The countryside had been picked to the last crumb of supplies. His main base was hundreds of miles away in another state. There was no handy depot from which to draw material to replace what he had destroyed at Ramsour's Mills before starting on his gambling chase of Morgan, Huger, and Greene. He could hope, however, for recruits to make up for his not inconsiderable casualties. Hillsboro was looked upon as deep in a Tory heartland, and he issued a proclamation so florid that Burgoyne might have been proud to claim it. "Wheras it has pleased the Divine Providence to prosper the operations of His Majesty's arms," it began, then went on to speak of His Majesty's dearest wish, that of "rescuing faithful and loyal subjects from the cruel tyranny under which they have groaned." And as an indulgent afterthought Cornwallis almost coyly suggested that those faithful and loyal subjects would not be unwelcome if they flocked into Hillsboro and the royal standard, particularly if they just happened to have with them their arms and, let us say, ten days' provision.

The Tories answered this appeal in surprising numbers, and royal officers were justified in feeling that here at last was the great Loyal rising that had been predicted and hoped for since '75. But above the Dan in Virginia, as weeks went by, Greene was stirring again. Andrew Pickens reappeared in the theater to worry the countryside. Light formations under Captain Kirkwood of Maryland interfered with foraging parties and patrols. Henry Lee's horsemen swooped south and broke up Loyalist formations hurrying to join Cornwallis. On one of these forays Tory Colonel Pyle and his men, riding along the reedy banks of the Alamance, mistook Lee's green-jacketed men for Tarleton's. Accepting Pyle's error, the Legion cavalry virtually allowed itself to be passed in review at close range by the unsuspecting Tories. Then, whether by secret signal or common impulse, Legion sabers and pistols were out and Pyle's men were shot, stabbed, hacked, and routed. Details are very hard to piece together, but this action bears all the earmarks of a bloody massacre, as complete and cold as anything that Tarleton ever devised or executed. All that may possibly be said in extenuation is that Lee, outnumbered, was in a very tight spot and had the choice of acting as he did or risking the total loss of his troopers.

This wrecking of Pyle's men, hardly one of whom escaped unhurt, added to the more routine incursions of Pickens and Kirkwood and others, completely checked the rush of Tories to join the royal colors. Early hopes fading, Cornwallis wrote Germain that his force was isolated "among timid friends and adjoining to inveterate rebels." Some major step had to be taken, since, to add to his other troubles, a reinforced Greene was moving his whole army down into North Carolina.

The whole war in the Southern theater was Nathanael Greene's—and victory, stalemate, or crushing defeat rode on his broad shoulders. But men hundreds of miles away were thinking and acting in his support. Up at New Windsor on the Hudson, where a mercifully mild winter was reigning, the commander-in-chief was striking and parrying at the usual blitz attacks that were always his. There had been frightening disturbances in the Pennsylvania and Jersey lines that had to be faced—mutinies, they have usually been termed, although the word "strike" might describe them rather better. There were efforts to get a French fleet into action against General William Phillips, Burgoyne's old second-in-command, now exchanged and in the field again. He was raiding into Virginia, in conjunction with another British general named Benedict Arnold, who was demonstrating his undying love for America by relentless use of fire and sword. The naval attempt was one more allied fiasco, owing not to French reluctance but rather to lack of unity of command.

In Philadelphia a familiar figure was backing Greene materially as Washington was morally. Christian Febiger, out of combat service for a while, was sending endless brigades of wagons south through central Virginia. His letter-book for those days shows how Alexander Perkings (sic) wagon contained "9 saddles; 110 sword-blades; 4 Quoilers [horse-breechings]; 44 Carabine Bucketts." John Logwood had 104 swords; 251 pr. of horse-shoes and two hay-screws. James Willson and John Lawrence stowed away 400 camp kettles between them while another pair loaded 89 tents and 300 canteens.

In late February the Dane wrote direct to Greene of the arrival of a French ship and how he and a Dr. Skinner had assembled "Cloathing for Lee's Corps compleat as also Sadles and other Accoutrements. I am now packing up 2000 Coats 2000 shirts . . . and every moment expect a Quantity of hunting Shirts." He added cheerfully that he himself was obliged "almost to attend the greasing of a Waggon . . . for want of money to pay a Laborer."

At Charlotte in Virginia old Von Steuben was running a recruit camp that was sometimes nearly empty, at others bulging with volunteers. The geographical imminence of danger, the lure of short-term enlistments and cash bounties for service seem to have dictated the size of Von Steuben's command and the number of men he could send on to Greene from the north.

This support, moral and physical, may well have seemed merely theoretical to the Rhode Islander as he moved south of the Dan. His whole force showed a paper strength of over four thousand, but of these less than fifteen hundred were Continentals and some of these were raw, hastily sent on by Von Steuben from Virginia. It was not a very manageable body as a whole, but Greene felt that to remain static was as bad as defeat. Besides, he had only to look at his calendar to know that perilously soon the enlistments of great sections of his militia would run out, and experience told him of the futility of hoping that such men would stay a day longer than was called for by their contract.

So south he went, the troopers of Washington and Henry Lee screening the advance, tangling with mounted Tories at a ford, striking Tarleton's dragoons, recoiling. By March 14, the whole army came down to a spot that Greene had carefully marked as a possible and desirable field for action during the retreat to the Dan.

It was only a spot on a map near the headwaters of Reedy Fork, which ran east to join the Haw River, which, in turn, later flowed into the Cape Fear as the latter ran on to Wilmington and the sea. There was a hill topped with a fair-sized brick building that justified the map entry "Guilford Court House." South, the ground sloped away with ragged lawns and a few saplings to tell of an earlier attempt at landscaping the courthouse premises. Beyond lay some clearings framed by quite clean woodland and a road that trickled weakly south again and leading toward another map spot, New Garden or Quaker Meeting House, some twelve miles off. This place was not important in itself, but for the moment it assumed the stature of one of Vauban's forts, for about it Cornwallis was camped.

It was hoped that Cornwallis would accept the challenge of the Americans' presence so close to him, a challenge like that of a boy jumping into a bull ring. If not, he must be decoyed into the open and onto the ground of Greene's choice.

The American commander was a seasoned veteran but, unlike many old-timers, he was always willing to learn. Reports of the Cowpens action taught him a lot. Moreover, as he surveyed his chosen ground from the pathetic lawns of the courthouse, he had phrases of a letter, written by the now retired Dan Morgan, clear in his mind. "You have a great number of militia," the Old Waggoner had written. "If they fight, you beat Cornwallis, if not, he will beat you. Put the militia in the center with some picked troops in their rear . . . to shoot down the first man who runs."

On the morning of the fifteenth Lee's cavalry was sent south down the wood road, hoping to draw out Cornwallis. Greene busied himself in posting his men. Following Morgan's ideas, he stationed his willing but green militia well to the front, astride the road and at the edge of the farthest clearing, flanked by what veteran troops he could spare. Washington's troopers stood by their mounts just in the rear, to be joined by Lee's horsemen on the latter's return. Virginia militiamen made up the second line, a few hundred yards behind the first, with woods on all sides of them. On the courthouse hill, a little to the right rear of the militia lines, stood the backbone of the force, Virginians under Isaac Huger and Marylanders led by Otho Williams. Blocked out on a map, these dispositions seem rather like an off-scale blueprint of the preliminaries of the Cowpens. To them Greene added another Morgan touch. Alone, he rode along the militia lines, speaking quietly and confidently to the raw men. Nothing to worry about. Wait till the enemy were within what Andrew Pickens had called "killing distance." Then two volleys. Greene held up two gloved fingers to stress his point. After that the militia work was done for the day and the men could file off as at the Cowpens and form again behind the Continentals. The general rode back to the hill, leaving the militiamen alone but somehow comforted back of the rail fence at the edge of the clearing.

Lee's sally against Cornwallis had been a marked success. His troopers had stumbled onto a column of Tarleton's dragoons in a narrow, steep-banked road. There the Legion men pretended flight, rallied, wheeled, and charged, breaking up the enemy formation completely. There was no pursuit. Lee had seen what he wanted to see and "retired precipitately" to report to headquarters that Cornwallis' whole force, nearly two thousand strong, was moving rapidly north along the road. Then he took his place in the battle line.

Few of the North Carolinians back of the rail fence had been in action before, and their first glimpse of the enemy en masse must have been frightening, despite Greene's calm words. Fanning out to the attack came Von Bose's blue-coated and silver-helmeted Hessians, the flat, cock-feathered bonnets of what was left of the 71st Scots, the scarlet and blue of the Welch, and the scarlet and deep red of the 33rd West Ridings. There were blue-coated gunners trundling two light fieldpieces over the rough road. Through the trees could be seen green-coated Jaegers, skullcapped light infantry, and two full battalions of the Guards themselves. In the rear, probably a little crestfallen after their brush with Lee, rode Tarleton's dragoons.

The scarlet-and-blue lines left the woods, started across the clearing toward the rail fence. Men could hear the crunch of boots, the irritable snap of British drums beating out the commands, and the rumble of gun wheels. The hush was almost theatrical there in the bright, clear noon, with the high sun melting the nippiness from the March air. Suddenly along the fence rifles and muskets ripped out and the hush fled off among the trees. Blue coats and scarlet pitched to the ground, but the lines still came on, with the drumbeats worrying and snarling. The Anglo-German line halted, fired, and then charged, bayonet points low, into the rolling smoke. The charge was not carried through. Hessian and Englishman stopped, staring in sudden hypnosis at the steady line of muzzles still carefully balanced on the rails. Sergeant Robert Lamb of the 23rd Welch said later, "They were taking aim with nice precision . . . a general pause took place; both parties surveyed each other a moment with anxious suspense. Colonel Webster then . . . said, 'Come on, my brave Fusiliers.' . . . They rushed forward amidst the enemy's fire. Dreadful was the havoc on both sides."

The North Carolinians did not wait to receive the charge. Obediently they had loosed the two rounds as Greene had requested and, as soon as their hammers had fallen, they broke and poured back through the second line. The Virginians of this line, posted as they were in thick woods, could not offer such solid resistance, and the fighting swept on to the hill south of the courthouse. The British grenadiers were in, and the Guards. A green Maryland outfit broke under the scarlet menace of the Guards, and the American line swayed dizzily. With a toss of horsehair crests Washington's dragoons caught the Guards in the rear, broke them with bright sabers beating out the tempo of the charge, ripped their ranks apart. Howard struck the Guards' flank with his veteran 1st Maryland and Kirkwood's inexhaustible Delawares and rolled them onto the advancing grenadiers.

This part of the fight swirled and eddied up and down the hill, but each of Howard's rushes sent the fringes of the melee closer and closer toward the heart of the British Army. Cocked hats, bearskin caps, bandaged heads were mixed inextricably to a deadly accompaniment of gunshots, stabbing bayonets, and high-swinging musket butts.

On a slight rise to the south Cornwallis had to make a lightning choice that would have staggered most commanders. He could trust to luck that the American impetus that was gaining with every minute would peter out before bursting through his lines. Or he could—— He took the hard but militarily sensible course and ordered his own guns to play at once on the fighting, tangled mass of scarlet and drab that was surging nearer and nearer, electing to inflict a few casualties on his own men rather than hold his hand and accept the far heavier ones, and the possible loss of his army, that would have followed a break-through by Howard. The Royal Artillery blasted away. Briton and American were struck down. But slowly the two masses drew apart.

Perhaps a swift follow-up by Greene would have turned this action into an utter rout for the British. But Greene could not gamble. A victory might so wreck his little army that it would cease to exist as a military force. He watched Howard break clear and fall back. Off on the left, riflemen and the Legion infantry were standing off the drives of Von Bose's Hessians and Jaegers. The sun was dropping behind the wooded hills to the west and there were no American reserves. Making a decision that was nearly as hard for a commander as that of Cornwallis, he ordered a retreat. It was carried out, still under heavy fire, but "it was conducted with order and regularity," as a British eyewitness recalled.

So Cornwallis, after a halfhearted attempt at pursuit, was left in possession of the field and could technically claim to be the victor. That he was able to make such a claim rested largely on his decision to fire on his own men as well as on the Americans. (Similar decisions were made by American commanders in World War II when the need for haste compelled them to send their own infantry over uncleared mine fields.) But it was almost as costly a victory as Cowpens was a defeat. He could count 25 per cent casualties, including Colonel Webster, who had brought on the Welch by the rail fence, now mortally wounded, and General O'Hara of the Guards, severely wounded. Worse, he had incurred these casualties for nothing, since, with a further weakened force, he was still as far from any base as he had been before, supplies of all kinds were running out, and Nathanael Greene, the loser, still had an army in the field.

The American retreat was leisurely and carried only some four miles west along Reedy Fork. Greene rested there a night or so and then made his way on to the little Speedwell Iron Works, not far to the north on Troublesome Creek. Greene had hard work ahead of him. His battle casualties had been far less than the British, but each tick of his fat, gold watch marked the departure for home of one or ten or a hundred militiamen whose time was up or who felt that there was no sense in just hanging around a camp with a lot of officers telling them what to do. Soon he had little left save for his indestructible Continentals, Washington's men, and the Legion horse and foot.

Nathanael Greene had perhaps lost a battle but he had won a campaign. Cornwallis, after a day or two about Guilford Court House, shook himself together, left such wounded as could not be moved to Greene's care, and started for Wilmington on the coast at the mouth of the Cape Fear River. The local Tories, from whom he had hoped so much, had failed him utterly, and his victory at Guilford Court House seemed to chill them still more. Had he tried to strike inland and return to Winnsboro in South Carolina, he stood a fine chance of being cut to pieces on the long march. Only at the port of Wilmington could he hope to refit and revictual his command. Actually he was going far, far beyond Wilmington, and his march was to carry him at last to the little brick house sheltered under the bluffs at Yorktown, looking out on the York River in Virginia.

Greene started to follow this retreat to the coast, then checked himself. His true mission, as he saw so clearly, lay in the Carolinas and, leaving the West Ridings, the Welch, the Scots, the Guards, and the Hessians, along with Tarleton's command, to trail away with Cornwallis, he began laying plans for an American move south. And his first step was to rush letters off to Thomas Sumter, Andrew Pickens, and Francis Marion.

The theater into which Greene planned to move was, at first glance, confusing, whether viewed from the terrain itself or worked out on a map. Yet essentially it was fairly simple. The British military hold on South Carolina was based on a long chain of posts and strong points that lay like a great inverted T on the land. The bar of the T stretched east and west, from Charleston on the coast to Ninety Six in the deep interior, and followed rather roughly the course of the east-west rivers and the roads that paralleled them—the Santee, the Congaree, and the Saluda, which were virtually one stream whose name changed from district to district. The upright followed the Wateree north from its junction with the Santee to the main inland base at Camden, beyond which the river took the name of Catawba. There were various minor lines running off from the broad strokes of the T, such as the route to British-held Georgetown on Winyah Bay far north of Charleston and posts such as Orangeburg, well south of the Santee-Congaree route.

Along bar and upright of the T moved vital British traffic. If Greene could break this flow somewhere in the center, the east and west ends might be rolled up. So he decided to strike at Camden. On paper he hardly had the strength for such a coup, but he hoped to nullify British military power by having his invaluable auxiliaries, Marion and Pickens and Sumter and their fellows, launch guerrilla blows at various points up and down the T, thus choking off any flow of reinforcements to the points against which he wished to move.

So the plan was formulated, the first instance in the war of intelligent teamwork between regular and irregular. Let the irregulars tie up road and river, if only temporarily, while the regulars moved against the larger garrisons. On the use of the regulars, Greene placed one strict limitation. They must be hoarded. A drawn battle, a stand-off, with his own troops still in hand, was far more desirable than any field victory that left him triumphant but with losses that immobilized him or left him too weak to meet a possible counterstroke. Perhaps this lesson had been drummed into him at Guilford Court House, where he had been content to leave the field less damaged than his adversary, beaten on paper but with his aim achieved. Perhaps the idea had been in his mind before he took over from Gates. He could not afford actual victory which might easily nullify overall success.

Greene's plans were kept secret from all save his highest brass. Marion, Sumter, and Pickens were notified by word of mouth rather than risk the capture of a courier bearing written orders. To Francis Marion, who had been exploding like a small but highly disturbing string of firecrackers along the bar of the T, Greene sent Captain Daniel Conyers, who served as liaison officer between the two. Conyers found the Swamp Fox sitting among the hummocks of a loathsome, moss-draped swamp, quietly sipping his vinegar, and to him sketched out the general plan of campaign.

This met with Marion's complete, if taciturn, approval. As an added fillip, Conyers told him that Harry Lee's whole Legion, which had worked so well with the irregulars before, was being sent to join him, along with Captain Edward Oldham's company of Marylanders. The suggested target for the combined force was Fort Watson, a little below the spot where the Congaree became the Santee. This, too, Marion found to his liking.

On April 6, 1781, Nathanael Greene broke up his camps and the struggle for South Carolina began.

CHAPTER XXX

"We fight, get beat, rise and fight again"

DESPITE the bright glare of continued activity that came up from the South, the eyes of the commander-in-chief and most of the nation were focused on the main British force on Manhattan Island. It was there, in the opinion of the majority, that the really important blow, the combined Franco-American coup, would fall. Washington's army could be easily concentrated, and it was, militarily speaking, a short march from Rochambeau's headquarters at Newport to the Hudson.

Yet by a sort of capillary attraction American strength began oozing south down the fringe to that area that had become, though largely unrecognized, the main fabric of the war.

In late February a picked body of Continentals was started for Virginia, some twelve hundred men in all, to help General Peter Muhlenberg and his Virginia militia to checkmate the devastations of Arnold and Phillips. The very composition of this force—indeed, the make-up of commands everywhere—showed an alignment that would have set the whole country screeching with rage a few years before.

In South Carolina a Rhode Islander fighting for the recovery of that state. Along the Hudson a Virginian feared a coup at the Northern states, feared it so much that it was with a distinct wrench that he sent these twelve hundred down into his homeland to protect it. The twelve hundred were picked light infantry under Colonel Joseph Vose (Massachusetts), Lieutenant Colonel de Gîmat (France), and Lieutenant Colonel Francis Barber (New Jersey). The men were drawn from the New England states and New Jersey, and at the head, marching to the rescue of Virginia, rode another Frenchman, the young Marquis de Lafayette.

By early March he was at Head of Elk, the old landing place of Sir William Howe back in '77. Thence, stripping his command down much as Cornwallis had done at Ramsour's Mills, so far to the south, he moved swiftly to Fredericksburg in Virginia, his men streaming in past many of the same houses that in 1862 were to shiver to the artillery of Ambrose Burnside and Robert E. Lee.

He had trouble on the march. Hot weather, of an intensity new to most of his men, came on and they began to desert in alarming numbers. The tall marquis at once showed that, while he might be quite new as an independent commander, he had learned to understand the psychology of American troops. Instead of bursting into a Gallic or even a Burgoyne-like harangue, he quietly made a few unemotional points. He was heading, he told the men, toward a hard campaign against superior numbers. He stated further that he himself was going, even if he had to ride alone; that while he hoped his command would stay with him, any soldier who really wanted to go home had only to apply for duty back along the quiet Hudson. Had the marquis ever read *Henry V*? His thought suggests

> . . . he who hath no stomach to this fight,
> Let him depart; his passport shall be made,
> And crowns for convoy put into his purse.

Desertions stopped and Lafayette braced himself for the coming ordeal, which looked tougher and tougher as the days went on. It had been first hoped that he might meet Greene coming north. Instead he learned that the ex-Quaker had swung to the south and that Cornwallis was heading up into Virginia to join Arnold, now in local command as a result of the sudden death of stout old William Phillips. The young Frenchman and his light infantry were to meet a real test.

While Lafayette was moving into Virginia the campaign in South Carolina was assuming a pattern that was to hold pretty consistently to the end of the war. Greene pushed steadily toward Camden, the northern end of the T upright, which was held by Dracula-faced Lord Rawdon with well-drilled Tory formations and part of the 63rd Manchesters.

South and east of Greene, slipping down to the T bar where Fort Watson lay on the north bank of the Santee, Marion and Lee were discussing ways and means for reducing that base, a quite important supply center. The pair found plenty to talk about. Watson lay secure on the crest of an old Indian mound with high palisades and three lines of felled and sharpened tree trunks, forerunners of modern barbed wire. The attackers had no artillery to breech the walls. To offset this lack, they built a wooden tower higher than the fort and garnished it, in the phraseology of the day, with riflemen. Since this tower commanded about every corner of the fort, the garrison surrendered, and one important link in Lord Rawdon's communications with Charleston and other points was knocked out. There was no thought of holding Fort Watson, which would have tied up valuable men, so Marion and Lee took their combined forces into the Santee swamps and set about planning more harassment of the enemy.

North, up the vertical stroke of the T, matters did not flow as smoothly. Close to Camden, Greene took up a position much like that at Cowpens and Guilford Court House, a low, oval hill with approaches over flat ground. On April 25, two days after the fall of Fort Watson, Lord Rawdon came up from Camden to meet the challenge.

Greene met him with Kirkland's Delawares, Otho Williams' Marylanders, Huger's Virginians, and Washington's cavalry, along with some North Carolina militia. For a moment it seemed as though the Cowpens might be repeated. But there was a misunderstood order, as at the Cowpens, without the quick adjustment made on that earlier battle. Washington's dragoons charged successfully and then broke far too deep into Rawdon's rear, got themselves bogged down with an unwieldy mass of prisoners, and were not at hand when they might have turned the fight upside down in the Americans' favor.

There was a sullen but orderly retreat up the sandy road that led north past Rugely's Mills and the site of Gates's defeat the year before. Philosophically Greene wrote to the Chevalier de la Luzerne, "We fight, get beat, rise and fight again."

Yet the pattern persisted. Rawdon had won a clear victory but had paid heavily for it. He fenced about, trying to get through the light infantry and cavalry screen that shielded the American army, but soon gave it up. Sumter was out with his men along supply routes. Marion and Lee had taken Fort Watson, and the problem of supplies and reinforcement seemed beyond him. On May 11, Lord Rawdon came to a decision, burned Camden along with such matériel as he could not take with him, and abandoned this main northern post of the British chain. Once more, Greene had lost a battle and achieved his objective.

The Camden garrison tramped south down the T upright toward the bar of the Santee. Rawdon's march was slow and things began to happen ahead of him. Out of the swamps rushed Marion and Lee once more and struck at Fort Motte, which covered the junction of the Congaree, the Santee, and the Wateree. Like Watson, Motte fell, owing chiefly to the ingenious use of fire arrows in the hands of the guerrillas. The American colors were hardly raised over the Motte house when Nathanael Greene, who with a small escort had circled on ahead of Rawdon's retreat, rode in.

There were more moves ahead. Regretfully he said that he must split up the smooth-working team for the moment. Marion's men were to ride east and north through the pine country, into the cypress lands, and out among the palmettos by the shores of Winyah Bay and Georgetown. Guerrilla pressure there, at the far northeast of the British chain, would be most healthy, Greene thought. Marion nodded silently, whistled up his leathery companions, and rode off. As for Harry Lee with his Legion and Oldham's men, Greene wanted them to hit out west and north for Fort Granby at the spot where the Broad and the Saluda became the Congaree. And the main army? With Rawdon plodding south, Greene planned to take his men west and west again, clear to Ninety Six, the far west anchor of the bar of the inverted T. Soon Fort Motte was deserted, and Lord Rawdon could only glower at its wrecked works as he led his old Camden command down to the Santee and thence east. He would not halt until he reached Monk's Corner, not far from Charleston.

Greene trailed his striking force up the Congaree, up the Saluda toward Ninety Six, but the irregulars working with him kept exploding along the Santee, south into Georgia and east to the fever swamps of the coast.

This combination was ideal, given the none-too-powerful means at the Rhode Islander's disposal. Alone and unsupported, Greene must have met quick disaster. Without him serving as a solid anvil against which the lighter hammer blows of the irregulars fell, the bands of Marion and Pickens and Sumter must have been little more than irritants to the British, if indeed they had been able to keep the field. Together, regular and irregular were shaped into a key which Greene was skillful enough and patient enough to turn in the lock that was finally to shut the British from all the South.

Marion, Lee (who when detached from the army must be classed with the Swamp Fox as a partisan), and Andrew Pickens studied the countryside, the people, the enemy, and shaped each move to conform to Greene's master pattern. Sumter, able as the best, persisted in morrising off on his own, striking here, striking there, with no regard for the activities of the others. He was, however, of great value in keeping the spirit of rebellion alive in the districts where he operated and often tapped fertile supply centers for the benefit of all.

So while Greene was approaching Ninety Six, blows that were not too important in themselves were struck. Marion, darting to the coast, drove the British from Georgetown. Up the Congaree, Henry Lee took Fort

Granby. Andrew Pickens dropped down into Georgia and struck at Augusta. The going was tough and Lee raced his Legion to join him, mounting an infantryman behind each trooper for greater speed, a trick that he had learned from Marion. On the way the Legion scouts found that at Fort Galphin, near Augusta, was gathered a great quantity of stores, including the annual Crown gift to the western Indian tribes, a handout that was supposed to keep the savages in the field against the rebels. Galphin was taken easily, and Lee gloated over a rare haul of arms, powder, blankets, rum, and salt. This was a double gain. The American army could use all this. And the Indians, sulking like spoiled children over the non-appearance of their accustomed subsidy, began to slide away from Crown influence. Augusta, when Lee reached it, proved a tough assignment, but he and Pickens clung grimly about the works for two weeks and finally received the surrender.

Sumter came brilliantly into the field, brought his hard-riding and hard-fighting men down to Orangeburg, south of the Santee on the north fork of the Edisto River, and forced its surrender.

This made bad reading in Charleston. After Guilford Court House, in March, the British posts had stretched unbroken from Ninety Six to the sea, north to Camden and south to Augusta in Georgia. Now in mid-May this chain had melted. Lost to the Crown were Camden, Watson, Motte, Granby, Nelson's Ferry, Georgetown, Orangeburg. In all of South Carolina there remained nothing in Crown control save the Charleston area and Ninety Six, and Greene was moving against the latter with a little army that had been beaten in its two formal engagements.

Ninety Six, so called, it is said, because it was just ninety-six miles from an Indian center on the Keeowee to the west, was well garrisoned and superbly commanded by a New York Tory, Lieutenant Colonel John Harris Cruger. Greene opened a formal siege on May 22 under the skilled guidance of Engineer Thaddeus Kosciusko. It was hard going. Operations dragged on into June, past mid-June. Then on a clear hot night, bright pin points began to burn on the crests to the east. Greene read the warning message of the signal fires, grimly accepted another mark in his seemingly endless defeat column, and retreated hastily, but in good order. The very next day, onto the plains about Ninety Six marched Lord Rawdon with a strong British column made up of his earlier formations and fresh troops who had recently arrived at Charleston. Cruger and his Tory garrison were saved, after having staged one of the most brilliant defensive feats of the whole war.

So there was one more loss for Greene but, as after Guilford Court House, after Hobkirk's Hill, his objective had been obtained. Rawdon demolished the works at Ninety Six, and the last inland British post in the South was given up. The far west end of the T bar was gone.

Summer began to burn hotter and hotter from the highlands of the west, along the river valleys, and over the swamps of the coastal plains. Greene and Rawdon marched and countermarched, feinted and sparred. Lee's

Legion, which had joined the main command during the siege, was always in the van, trying to cut in ahead of the retreat as Rawdon, along with Cruger's force, struck south and east down the state.

March and maneuver went on under fearful conditions. A British officer, remembering swamps with their organ hums of mosquitoes, difficult crossings of the Congaree and lesser streams, wrote later of "forced marches under the rage of a burning sun . . . sinking under the most excessive fatigue, not only destitute of every comfort, but almost of every necessity . . . totally destitute of bread . . . the country afforded no vegetables for a substitute. Salt at length failed . . . only resources were water and the wild cattle they found in the woods." These were mostly troops brought up to formal warfare, but the scarlet column staggered on, manfully meeting conditions that might have slowed down Marion's men or Sumter's.

Greene's pursuit was facing the same conditions. In three weeks his men covered well over three hundred miles through wicked country under burning-glass heat that set the savannas dancing and turned swamps into suffocating ovens. The unquenchable Delaware captain, Robert Kirkwood, still following the path into which he had first turned in the far dawn of 1776, said that "rice furnished our substitute for bread. Of meat we had literally none." Fortunately the wet country was alive with booming frogs whose legs formed the chief rations for the Legion and the light infantry. Alligators were eaten thankfully. "Never had we experienced so much sickness at any one time as we did now. Nearly one half of the army was disabled by wounds or fever," was Light-Horse Harry Lee's summing up.

Lord Rawdon had reoccupied Orangeburg down on the Edisto forks. Weak as he was, Greene hurriedly drew plans to drive Rawdon and his men from the town, and for a moment it seemed as though the two armies would stagger into action like two exhausted, punch-drunk middleweights flailing feebly at each other. But supply conditions and the hard Carolina sun intervened. In the past, formal armies had religiously gone into winter quarters. Now another touch was added to this strange Southern war. Greene and Rawdon sought summer quarters, and the former could reflect that, of his original T, only the bar was left.

In the summer of 1918 a desert column composed mostly of Arabs and commanded by a long-jawed British archaeologist made its scorched, harrassed way out of the sands and the sun to a deep canyon cleft in a range of naked red mountains. The cleft was called Rumm, and in it lay deep, cool shade, running crystal streams, grass that was softly emerald to desert-blinded eyes. "Later, when we were riding inland, my mind used to turn me from the direct road, to clear my senses by a night in Rumm," wrote the Englishman T. E. Lawrence. The spell of the place was strong on him and on every Arab rifleman and on every British Lewis-gunner in that column which plunged from desert death to the life-giving shade and water and grass of the canyon cleft.

So in the summer of 1781 Nathanael Greene's army staggered from the

choking, miasmic plains and the scummy flow of falling river and swamp
into the fresh emerald lift of the High Hills of Santee. The little range,
never higher than two hundred feet, begins some twenty miles up the east
bank of the Wateree and undulates south until its last round crest looks
down to the union of the Congaree and the Santee. The soil is sand and
clay, yet somehow rich, and corn- and cotton fields lie basking along crest
and slope. There are cool groves and clear-running streams and springs.

Out of swamp and canebrake and moss-hung cypress tangles came North
and South Carolinians, Marylanders and Delawares and Virginians. They
rolled on the soft, springy grass, buried their sun-cracked faces in glasslike
springs, and drank as they had never dared drink in the polluted waters
below. On shaky knees they dug their heels into soil that did not quake or
squelch under them. They flung themselves under clean oak and chestnut
groves that did not loose gray hordes of mosquitoes to whine about sweat-
soaked necks. The men of that little army were to remember the High Hills
of Santee as Lawrence and his column looked back on Rumm.

The kindly hills snatched fever-ridden men from the grave. The clean soil
and the healing drift of the soft wind cured festering wounds and swamp
sores. Sleep under clear stars that were not fogged by marsh effluvia undid
the damage caused by heat, long marches, and bad, scant food. William
Davie, whom Greene had so shrewdly appointed commissary, sent food and
rum down along the road that followed the crest of the hills. Soon
Nathanael Greene had an army again.

The High Hills of Santee and the life that flourished there apparently
were too sybaritic for the tough commands of Lee, Marion, and Sumter.
Under Greene's orders they combined, with Sumter working smoothly in
harness for once, struck south and south again, smashing into the strong
British post at Monk's Corner on the Cooper River, not far above Charleston itself. They took over a hundred prisoners, a good two hundred horses,
and a long string of wagons, invaluable for Greene's transport-starved army.
And the remains of the Corner garrison withdrew to the Charleston area
while still another British post was marked off in the books of Lord Rawdon's staff as lost.

Monk's Corner accounted for, Lee's Legion clattered back to share the
delights of the High Hills of Santee with its fellow units. Sumter moved
west to guard the Congaree crossings by Friday's Ferry. Francis Marion with
all his Horrys and Postells and Ogiers and Jameses and Conyers nipped
away at his vinegar by once formidable Nelson's Ferry on the Santee, while
he spoke in monosyllables of future moves with his chief lieutenant, Peter
Horry.

Down at Orangeburg the British sat quietly, recuperating under less favorable conditions than their enemies. Lord Rawdon, shattered in health,
tossed up his command and sailed for home. He was not to reach it for a
long time, his ship being snapped up by a French flotilla under a French
sailor of whom no one knew very much, a quiet, skilled man named
De Grasse. With Rawdon gone, still another British commander faced

Greene, Lieutenant Colonel Alexander Stuart of the 3rd East Kents, the famous Buffs.

Then the summer rains came. The Wateree and the Congaree and the Santee, the Broad and the Saluda and the Edisto, the Enoree and the Combahee and the Great Pee Dee swelled, burst their banks. The lowlands were flooded and the High Hills of Santee stood out like a green island chain above the waterlogged flats. Until the floods went down, there could be no further action in the South.

In the commander-in-chief's Hudson River headquarters high officers read the reports that drifted up from Nathanael Greene in the Carolinas, documents that well serve as models for any officer in a subordinate berth keeping the top echelons informed. Some officers were a little discouraged that there were no more victories like the Cowpens to chalk up, but Washington, Knox, and men of similar discernment who could see the picture in the large were delighted with Greene's accomplishments. Still, there seems to have been a general feeling that his theater was, at most, a profitable side show. The real axis of attention must be the North.

Yet, like little blobs of quicksilver, more and more strength trickled away toward the Potomac and across it to join other blobs. Cornwallis' whole strength was now in Virginia, and young Lafayette was feinting quite skillfully before the scarlet advance. But feinting cannot be kept up forever. Such a maneuver is useful only as preparation for snapping out a hard punch once the enemy is properly deceived, and for launching such a blow the marquis did not have the power. His men plodded, advanced, fell back, sideslipped across the very ground over which, some eighty years later, other armies were to move. Fredericksburg and the Wilderness, the Rappahannock, the Rapidan, the North Anna, and the banks of the James saw marching men in a preview of other far mightier and more deadly hordes that later generations were to launch.

To help out Lafayette, Anthony Wayne and the Pennsylvania line, now reconstituted and no longer strike-minded, were sent south. Over a thousand men followed the handsome Wayne, a mere trickle that would have been lost in the armies of Grant or Lee or Jackson or Meade, but in 1781 an important reinforcement. Qualitatively, Wayne's contingent rated very high. Most Pennsylvania linemen were of long service, tough, resourceful veterans, and they were led by men like Richard Butler and Walter Stewart. Thomas Proctor's nine guns of the 4th Continental Artillery rolled and jolted along with them.

Wayne joined Lafayette at Fredericksburg, and here a nasty situation could have developed. The marquis was a full major general; Wayne, though only a brigadier, had seen far more service than the slant-browed young Frenchman. But the Pennsylvanian struck hands with Lafayette and placed himself under his orders as completely as Rochambeau had subordinated himself to Washington. The two commands moved east. Cornwallis, conservative for the moment, withdrew to the neighborhood of Williamsburg to watch developments. He had very little to worry about. Even if Greene should come north to join the other Americans in Virginia, the British commander had only to whistle up a British fleet and shift his troops by water to any spot on the coast that might seem profitable. That, Cornwallis could reflect, was what command of the sea meant.

As the month of June 1781 flooded over the continent and looked benignly down on Nathanael Greene and his men relaxing gratefully among the High Hills of Santee, drums were beating and cavalry trumpets were blowing along the lower edges of New England. The drums rolled and throbbed past Newport's Redwood Library and were echoed strongly on the mainland across the Seaconnet Passage. The trumpets blared out among the forest trees about Lebanon over in Connecticut. The armies of France were about to march at last.

On June 9th, Bourbonnais and Royal Deux-Ponts were ferried across to Tiverton and struck out gaily along the road to Providence, gaitered legs swinging in unison and tall colored pompons aslant in their little cocked hats. Soissonnais and Saintonge followed. D'Aboville's long train of artillery clanked and rumbled over the hard highways, and supply and ammunition wagons stirred the whitish dust with their heavy ironbound wheels.

There was a long wait for regrouping at Providence, and then the true march began early on the morning of the nineteenth. Day by day the stages of the journey were marked off in orderly books and diaries, by De Chastellux and Blanchard and the Abbé Robin, who marched with the Soissonnais. There were Waterman's Tavern and Plainfield and Windham, Bolton and Hartford and Farmington, and each little town or pin point on the map saw the long, swinging white columns appear in the eastern distance, swell into full scale through a village street to the rataplan of French drums and the blare of field music, then shrink and shrink under their dust clouds across plain or ridge to the west.

As at Newport, French discipline on the march or in camp set American eyes bulging, especially the eyes of ex-servicemen who had done a little marching themselves. The inhabitants were unmolested and no couriers overtook the army after a halt with saddlebags abulge with damage claims.

Baron's Tavern in Connecticut—and by now the villages had lances and busbies and long sabers to stare at as well as the lean, quick-stepping infantry—and Break Neck Hill and on to Newtown. For old soldiers, it was not so much of a march, just from Narragansett Bay to the Hudson—or so officers and men in the columns thought. They could begin to look forward to the end of the hike when they actually crossed into New York State and halted at North Castle, where the head of the column may have been met by Lieutenant Colonel John Jameson of the 2nd Continental Dragoons. This was in the first week in July, and any day now the French van would sight the Hudson, and tented camps would flourish along its banks through long, restful days. No marcher could know that a letter was on its way from France to the American commander, a letter that was to turn schedules and plans and timetables upside down. No one could look far to the middle spaces of the Atlantic and know that a heavy fleet flying the gold lilies of France was setting a course for the West Indies. Who could guess that, among those islands, the Duke de St. Simon was issuing orders to the regiments of Gâtinais, Agenais, and Touraine in garrison there? There might be a halt by the Hudson, but that would be all. Actually the march of the French had hardly started.

Lacking that same knowledge, Washington and his ideal ally, Rochambeau, had come to no conclusion about where and how the Franco-American armies were to be employed. The original directive of the French had pretty well specified New York and the main British army there. This marched very closely with Washington's thoughts. Again and again he reminded Rochambeau that "Your Excellency will be pleased to recollect that New York was looked upon by us as the only practicable object under present circumstances."

The Frenchman had other possibilities in mind but loyally left any final decision to Washington. Rochambeau's willingness to concede found the Virginian by no means hidebound about the New York objective. "Should we be able to secure naval superiority, we may perhaps find others more practicable and equally advisable" was a thought that he stressed to his co-worker.

As the march went on to the King's Bridge, where Lauzun's Legion saw a snatch of action in backing up General Benjamin Lincoln, and finally to Verplanck's Point, just across from Stony Point, many French officers had their first glimpse of their new commander-in-chief. De Chastellux had already hymned Washington almost extravagantly. Now Cromot du Bourg witnessed his meeting with Rochambeau and himself was received "with the affability that is so natural to him. He is a very fine looking man. His bearing is noble in the highest degree and his manners are those of one perfectly accustomed to society." General Mathieu Dumas confessed, "We had been impatient to see the hero of Liberty. His dignified address . . . won every heart."

Not a traveled man, Washington seemed to know instinctively how to address the French Army. His official bulletin welcoming them to the Hudson is a model of understanding, and the closing lines reached right down to the ranks. "The regiment of Saintonge is entitled to particular acknowledgments, for the spirit with which the men continued and supported their march without one day's respite."

In fact, the whole march had been remarkable, and Commissary Claude Blanchard was able to write to Admiral Barras that it had been completed "without leaving a man behind us, except ten love-sick soldiers from the regiment of Soissonnais who wanted to return to see their sweethearts at Newport." Anyone who has had service in the field can appreciate the feat of moving some five thousand men over two hundred and twenty miles in eleven days with only ten stragglers to report.

The Abbé Robin, surveying the American army as a whole, noted that it had "no regulation uniform, only perhaps the officers and some of the artillery." He was *épaté* by omnipresent hunting shirts, which he called *casaques avec des franges* and found ideal for campaigning, adding wisely that "troops are intended for action and not for show." In World War I and World War II foreign observers were struck by the amount of personal equipment issued to American troops. But in 1781 the good abbé threw up his hands in astonishment "at finding in their tents, where three or four men live, not over forty pounds of baggage." Certainly Washington's men could not have been called overgadgeted. There were more exclamations over the commander-in-chief's methods of shifting his troops to conceal their true numbers. "Now with a few soldiers he forms a Spacious Camp and spreads a large number of tents. Then again with a large number of men he reduces his tentage and his force [apparently] almost vanishes." In this, of course, Washington had had long practice, having been compelled from the start to hide his weakness or mask his strength from friend and foe alike. At the moment that the abbé was writing, there were probably less than seven thousand Americans in the area.

The question of what to do hung unresolved over the Franco-American camps, but the needle of action pointed more and more steadily to Manhattan. Report after report came to Washington's headquarters that Cornwallis had embarked along the Chesapeake and was sailing for New York. If true, this move would clinch Manhattan as the coming theater of action, and Washington and Rochambeau weighed various courses. But both were too experienced to build precipitately on what amounted to rumor. They planned but did not commit themselves.

Then on August 14, 1781, while the sun dipped toward the green-topped palisades across on the Jersey shore and gilded the slow sweep of the Hudson, a courier raced to Washington's headquarters with news that set his younger aides whooping and pounding each other on the back. A vast weight fell from Washington's shoulders, and his usually impassive face must have lightened to match the sunset across the river.

Count François Joseph Paul de Grasse had cleared the West Indies with no less than twenty-nine combatant ships. With him rode a mass of transports into which had been packed, at then French Haiti, the Gâtinais, Agenais, and Touraine regiments, together with artillery and some cavalry. Destination? The reaches of Chesapeake Bay.

Now the objective was obvious. Americans and French were to march together overland to Virginia and join Lafayette and Anthony Wayne. With De Grasse controlling the local waters, the three regiments from Haiti under the Duke de St. Simon could slip up the James and add their weight to a combined attack against Cornwallis. The whole setup seemed to work out smoothly, like a neat, mathematical formula. Smoothly, that is, *if* De Grasse could keep control of the seas. If he failed, Cornwallis could either be heavily reinforced or else whisked out of danger by a British fleet. And *if* the joint operations could be carried out promptly, for there was a little teaser hidden in the news to the effect that De Grasse and St. Simon must not remain on the coasts of North America after October 15, 1781. This was a tacit reminder that the French as well as the British were fighting a nearly global war. A further *if*—whether the overland march could be made—offered a problem, simple on the surface, but formidable. Most of Washington's troops were from the Northern and Middle states and they were quite vocal in indicating that they did not wish service in the South, largely through a widespread belief that the climate was dangerously unhealthy. And, lastly, *if* such a march could be financed. The American treasury was at an all-time low. Rochambeau had only what was left of the military chest with which he had landed a year ago.

Time alone would tell if De Grasse could nullify British naval efforts and if the joint operations could be completed before the October deadline. As to the other ifs, Washington, laboring diligently, managed to persuade the army to march. Finances proved a far knottier problem. Financial wizard Robert Morris had ruefully to say that he could see no possible supply of hard money until late autumn, and if the congressional printing presses began turning out more paper money, the new issue would further depress such tender that already had ranged from forty to sixty paper dollars for one in specie. Solution came from an unexpected quarter. Rochambeau, after a weary huddle with his army treasurer, came quietly to Washington. The military chest contained French livres amounting to some forty thousand dollars. If Rochambeau's American commander would do him the honor of taking one half of this sum—— The march could begin.

It is more than surprising to note that through all this time Sir Henry Clinton had remained passive in New York, without making the slightest attempt to interfere with Franco-American doings just up the Hudson. Patiently he watched the sudden wave of activity and continued to sit on his hands. Boats were being collected all along the river just out of British reach. Great wheeled frames to carry massive flatboats were seen trundling heavily hither and yon. Such symptoms had been noted before and did not seem worth bothering about now. Details of French and Americans appeared in New Jersey, opposite Staten Island, and began building huge ovens, permanent affairs that could have baked bread for thousands of men over a long period of time. They were, of course, a blind. It is doubtful if they took in Sir Henry Clinton to any marked degree, for he made no attempt to interfere with the work. As a precaution he went on strengthening the New York defenses and, as a possible countermove to the Franco-American concentration above him, he seems to have toyed with the idea of a water-borne offensive against Rhode Island, of all places.

In the third week of August the banks of the Hudson thundered and rumbled as the armies prepared to cross. Field guns and the bulky pieces of D'Aboville's siege train had to be manhandled down to the water. Henry Knox's guns and limbers and ammunition wagons slammed their ironbound wheels against boulders and over stony ground. Tossing their heads and neighing in protest came the horses of the gun teams and the heavy wagons, the light-stepping mounts of Lauzun's men. Barges and longboats and rafts bobbed underneath the sloping banks by King's Ferry, began their tireless shuttle across the broad surge of the river, to bring up for unloading "at the foot of the western slope of Stony Point where there are heavy boulders of granite rock, scatterings of glaciers of long ago, long spent," as Washington wrote to a friend in Virginia.

Battery by battery, troop by troop, and company by company, the two armies made their way to the west bank. "We finished crossing on the 25th [of August]," reported Commissary Blanchard. "It was long because the river is wide and had to be crossed on rafts. I was there on the 25th and saw most of the troops and the baggage pass. General Washington was also there; they had arranged for him a time schedule of the crossing which he examined with the closest attention. . . . He pressed my hand with much affection as he left me."

For long hours the river, navigable for the heaviest ships then afloat, had been jammed with helpless boatloads of troops, horses, and equipment, and still Clinton sat comfortably in New York. Not a ship cleared for an up-river sail, not a troop or company felt out the allied lines. In Franco-American reports and letters there is no hint of the nearly unbearable tension that must have been felt by every American, every Frenchman during the dangerous crossing. Yet that tension must have been there, drawing thousands of eyes south with each faint murmur or rumble that might tell of an enemy blow. Only afterward did tightly held breaths go out in a great "Ooof!" of relief. The elder Deux-Ponts marveled, "An enemy, a little bold and able would have seized the moment of our crossing the Hudson, so favorable for him, so embarrassing for us, for an attack. His indifference and lethargy at this moment is an enigma that cannot be solved by me."

There was a final massing, a last rearrangement of troops, and the French march-tables began to note more odd names to match those already entered in New England. Pompton was neatly written in and Whippany, Bullion's Tavern and Somerset, until the stone barracks by the flow of the Delaware were sighted, and Trenton heard French voices as earlier it had heard English and Hessian tones.

The American contingent headed the long procession, picked battalions of light troops drawn from many parent units. Leading the army and these shock troops were innumerable faces that had become familiar since the first lurid rays of wartime, faces that had been streaked by the smoke of Breed's Hill and Long Island, the Hollow Way and Trenton and Monmouth, the tragic struggles north of the St. Lawrence. Edward Hand was there and Timothy Pickering and Henry Dearborn. Benjamin Lincoln commanded a division and Moses Hazen, James Clinton, and Elias Dayton led brigades.

New England troops predominated, with a strong leavening from New York and New Jersey, but battalion commands were mixtures that melted state and sectional lines. Alexander Hamilton, now turned infantryman, led Nutmeggers as well as New Yorkers, and South Carolinian John Laurens marched at the head of a mixed group of Massachusetts, Connecticut, and

New Hampshire men. The 2nd Field Artillery, under the over-all command of Henry Knox, followed John Lamb of New York and Ebenezer Stevens of Massachusetts. The engineer train, drawn from New York and Connecticut, took its orders from the Chevalier Louis Lebique Duportail, whose American service went back to the early summer of 1777. The picked might of America was on the road with that of France.

On September 2 the American column passed through Philadelphia, and Dr. James Thacher, without whose presence no campaign could have been complete, bewailed the fact that "the streets being extremely dirty . . . we raised a dust like a smothering snow-storm . . . this was not a little mortifying, as the ladies were viewing us from the open windows of every house." He lingered on in the city the next day to watch the passage of the French, recording their fine appearance in "white broadcloth, faced with green," which suggests that he saw only the tireless Saintonge regiment, the others having different facings. He was impressed that the French not only had the usual fifes and drums but also were "furnished with a complete band of music, which operates like an enchantment."

On the fifth the commander-in-chief, having watched the passage of his joint command, followed along with his staff. His steady ally, the Comte de Rochambeau, who was becoming a fast, personal friend as well as fellow soldier, elected to drop down the river by boat. Rochambeau wanted to have a look at the old forts where Lieutenant Colonels François de Fleury and de Mauduit du Plessis had so distinguished themselves back in '77, along with Colonel Christopher Greene, the latter now dead in an obscure scuffle in Westchester County. It may be that, in addition to satisfying his military curiosity, Rochambeau's mind craved distraction, as Washington's must have also.

The march had so far been a model for future commanders to study, but it had value only in connection with the whereabouts of De Grasse and his fleet, and the only hints that had come in so far had been hotly disturbing to Rochambeau and his Virginian superior. Coast watchers had reported masses of sail on the horizon from time to time, but there had been no sure identification. Soon it was known that more British warships had put in at New York, then that the combined enemy fleets under Admirals Hood and Graves had cleared the port and set a course south. Silence from De Grasse could very well mean that Hood and Graves had met and overpowered him or driven him far off course, which would have been just as bad.

The forts were duly and probably hastily inspected, and Rochambeau's craft headed for Chester on the right bank of the Delaware. As the little party neared the Chester landing, the Frenchmen could see an unmistakable figure in blue and buff, tall, erect, commanding. Cromot du Bourg, the glittering Lauzun, Baron Jean de Closen of the Royal Deux-Ponts stared at the approaching wharf, their Gallic aplomb a little shaken. The man in blue and buff had snatched off his hat, leaving his powdered head bare to the sun, and was waving his headgear wildly. Then he whipped out a handkerchief and snapped it to and fro. This was a Washington whom they had never seen. Probably a little alarmed, Rochambeau leaped ashore only to find himself swept up in a quick embrace. *Mais qu'est-ce que se passe, hein?*

There were a few quick words. Papers rustled in the warm air and French hats soared high. Admiral de Grasse was safely into the Chesapeake with twenty-eight powerful ships. Already the three thousand men of the Gâtinais, the Agenais, and the Touraine regiments were pouring ashore. Now Cornwallis was sealed in from the sea. St. Simon's three thousand, added to the men under Wayne and Lafayette, could contain him from the land approaches to the Yorktown peninsula. For the first time since 1775 a real American victory, offensive and not defensive, was just over the horizon.

There were General Orders to issue to the armies. "As no circumstance could possibly have happened more opportunely in point of time, no prospect could ever have promised more important successes." These closing words were read out to regiments and battalions, with the reminder that there was still work ahead: "Nothing but our want of exertion can probably blast the pleasing prospects before us."

The water routes were clear, and it was decided to embark the armies on Chesapeake Bay and float them to the James. There was an appalling shortage of boats, but busy agents combed the shores, raking up battered little schooners, sloops, eighteenth-century versions of bug-eyes, and even open craft.

On September 8 the leading columns reached Head of Elk in excellent shape. The weather had been highly favorable on the whole, rations had kept pace with the march, and to most of the marchers soldiering must have seemed a good life for the moment.

Far to the south, beyond Chesapeake Bay, beyond the twist and flow of the rivers that fed into it, beyond the curving Dan and the Deep and the Yadkin and the Pee Dee, American troops and British were experiencing a far grimmer kind of soldiering on that same eighth day of September.

CHAPTER XXXI

"Done in the trenches before Yorktown, in Virginia . . . G. Washington"

THE move began while the cool night air of August 22–23 flowed among the trees that fringed the High Hills of Santee. Alexander Stuart with his British and Tories was astir not far from the junction of the Wateree and the Congaree, a bare eighteen miles, buzzard flight, from Nathanael Greene's camps, where word had come in that the English commander seemed not unduly concerned about an enemy move, possibly counting on the still flooded country to act as a shield.

Greene had other ideas. Through a growing August dawn his North and South Carolina militia filed along the spine of the High Hills, heading north and always north away from Stuart. Otho Williams and John Howard brought on their ever present Marylanders. Lee's Legion marked a long, green path over the yellow-white of the sandy roads, and Wade Hampton's troopers took to the rolling fields to make way for Robert Kirkwood's Delawares.

The route was agonizingly familiar to many of the marchers, who could remember only past defeats without recalling that those defeats had added up to victory. Nathanael Greene, riding along with the sun stronger and stronger on his right and probably hoping that a return to the lowlands would not make his asthma worse, could point out landmarks to the Marquis de Malmédy, who had recently joined his force.

At Camden, the column now swung abruptly south down the west bank of the Wateree and came at last to Howell's Ferry, halfway up the Congaree, and there was news of the enemy, who had marched away east down what passed for the Charleston road along the Santee. Here Greene's men waited and rested by the cool flow of the river until sunrise of September 4 set them on the road again. The march up the Wateree and down its west bank had been quite leisurely. Now feet in broken boots, in deerskin moccasins thudded endlessly under live oak and cypress and through the gray moss beards of swamps, covering twenty-nine miles in two days. Light troops and cavalry had been sweeping ahead, and Robert Kirkwood brought word to Greene about a place called "Eutaw Springs where Lay Col. Stewart [sic] with the British Army Consisting of 2,000 men." This was a rather stronger force than Greene commanded, since so many enlistments had run out in the High Hills, and included not only the formidable John Harris Cruger and his old Ninety Six command but excellent cavalry under Tory Major John Coffin, once of Boston in Massachusetts.

But new strength was coming to join Greene. While he lay at Laurens' plantation, less than twenty miles from Eutaw Springs, the countryside began to stir. Out of the wilderness to the south of the Santee rode a frail little man in a skimpy coat of reddish country cloth and a skullcap marked with the silver crescent of the 2nd South Carolina Infantry. The cap was charred on one side, souvenir of an occasion when the wearer had rolled into a swamp campfire while asleep and had been snatched out in the nick of time. Francis Marion had never bothered to replace it, since it still covered his head and that was all he asked of it. It was as much a part of his uniform as the little sword, firmly rusted into its scabbard, that dangled by his saddle.

After Marion came long strings of horsemen and foot soldiers shepherded on by the usual Horrys and Postells and Jameses. They had just finished a fabulous march far down toward Charleston, where they had gone to the rescue of guerrilla leader William Harden, trapped by British and Tories along the Pon-Pon. Now Harden was saved, the march was over, a round trip of more than four hundred miles through enemy country and without the slightest loss. What orders had General Greene to give?

Greene, frowning over long columns of figures by candlelight that shimmered on the sluggish Santee, saw that this new force raised his numbers, at least on paper, fairly close to Stuart's. To the swarthy, taciturn Swamp Fox he proposed a novel idea. The guerrilla command was substantial and had acquired respectable cohesion for irregulars. It could take its place, under Marion's command, in formal battle line, at least for the engagement that Greene was sure was coming. Marion was not taken with this arrangement. He probably foresaw that, once embedded in the main army, he would have trouble getting his men out. They would, if they stayed long enough, reach a vulnerable point of no return, a period during which they would have lost their old skills without having acquired new ones. But he trusted and respected Greene. If that was what the Rhode Islander wished, then Marion's men would take their places with the militia that Andrew Pickens had brought down, with the levies of William Henderson and Jethro Sumner. Thus for the moment the swamp men were transformed into ordinary line soldiers.

So while far to the north French and American infantry were crossing the Brandywine fords on their way to Head of Elk, Greene's command moved out of the Laurens plantation and headed for Burdell's Tavern, sometimes called Plantation, a little above the objective, Eutaw Springs.

At Guilford Court House and at Hobkirk's Hill, Greene had maneuvered to force an attack by the enemy on ground of his own choosing. Here for the first time he was boldly taking the offensive, seeking the enemy out. Militarily he was beginning a new chapter.

Eutaw Springs, today close to the shores of Lake Marion, a body of water formed by modern damming, derives its name from two puncture holes in the earth that pour out the waters of an underground river and flow to the Santee via Eutaw Creek. In 1781 a fine brick house, two stories and an attic, stood close by the steep-banked creek, close to the twin springs. It had a fine sweep of garden and looked out onto a wide clearing which was palisaded and split by an east-west road that forked off toward Charleston. There were oaks and cypress all about this parklike property, and by the creek bank blackjacks grew thickly. It must have been a peaceful, pleasant spot with the sun dappling down through the wide-spaced trees, the murmur of the Santee joining in with the endless gurgle and whisper of the springs. The calm of the place could hardly have been ruffled when the air shivered to the jar of wagon wheels and gun wheels, when cavalry horses picketed under the trees whinnied and bounced echoing kicks off each other's ribs, when nearly two thousand men in scarlet and green and white coats shouted and laughed and squabbled within the palisade.

Lieutenant Colonel Stuart of the Buffs was an alert, energetic soldier, but

something of the tranquillity of Eutaw Springs must have lulled him a
little. There was excuse for this, for scouts and intelligence brought him no
news of the proximity of Greene and Marion and De Malmédy and Williams. "Notwithstanding every exertion being made to gain intelligence of
the enemy's situation, they rendered it impossible by waylaying the by-
paths and passes through the different swamps," he explained later. As it
was, he felt so secure that on the very early morning of the eighth he sent
a few hundred men, without arms and guarded only by a small knot of
cavalry, down the road that led to Burdell's and Greene's camp to prowl
some old plantings and bring back potatoes and greens. While this group
was grubbing away, two American deserters came into the British lines and
gave Stuart ominous news. The Rhode Islander was at that very moment
leading out his men. This so clashed with the British commander's own
notions that he went into a quite respectable huff and had the pair
locked up.

Something buzzed in the back of Stuart's mind, however, and trumpets
blared in the sunrise. Out of the palisade rode able John Coffin with both
horse and foot and headed up the road toward Burdell's. Soon there was
movement on the road, among the trees right and left, still cool in the
green light of the dawn. Men were running toward him, unarmed men
who had been rooting up potatoes and garden sauce. There were mounted
men behind this spray of fugitives, mounted North Carolinians under
Colonel James Armstrong.

Bostonian Tory Coffin thought he had struck the core of Greene's advance and charged ahead with both infantry and cavalry. However, he had
met only the far outer fringe and Armstrong fell back, a move which Coffin
saw and misinterpreted. What he could not see farther up the road was the
infantry of Lee's Legion, with the green-clad troopers in the woods to their
right and Henderson's South Carolinians to the left. Coffin came on after
Armstrong, as Harry Lee remembered, "with a degree of recklessness which
indicated either his ignorance of its [our] strength and the presence of the
main body, or his contempt for the [our] service."

Coffin was quickly disillusioned. Along the road and in the dew-soaked
woods American drums beat and American cavalry trumpets rang clear.
Legion and militia moved in smoothly; Henderson's men held their fire,
then loosed it. The Legion infantry went in shouting with the bayonet,
drums rattling urgently. Some of the Legion cavalry under Major Joseph
Eggleston made a cautious circling movement, then smashed hard into
Coffin's rear, using the same combination of judgment and dash that was
to distinguish one Major General Joseph Eggleston Johnston nearly a century later. Coffin's foot soldiers were routed and his cavalry driven back to
the palisade.

By the brick house and its twin springs Alexander Stuart was now thoroughly alerted and his reaction was quick and efficient. The broad en-
closure was alive with swift-moving men. The Buffs took position on the
right, their flank resting on the steep bank of Eutaw Creek. A little ahead

of them the light infantry and the grenadiers were posted in the thick black-jack growth under a very tough major named Marjoribanks, the seeming daintiness of whose patronymic was rendered then, as now, Marshbanks. Cruger's steady Loyalists were astride the road that cut the estate, with the 63rd Manchesters and the 64th North Staffordshires extending the lines south. Coffin guarded the floating left flank with those of his men who had not been in that first bold dash up the road toward Burdell's.

From the west Greene was coming in fast. De Malmédy brought on the center with Marion and Pickens. Lee and Henderson covered the flanks, and back of this solid line hurried Wade Hampton, Williams, and Sumner, while William Washington and Robert Kirkwood closed in the rear.

Both sides moved forward, and soon the trees of the Eutaw Springs estate waded in a smoke tide that coiled and eddied about their brown trunks. Under heavy attack Greene's center was swept away, Marion's men, as was to have been expected, acting a little uncertainly in their first stand-up fight. Only Lee and Henderson stood firm. Watching road and smoke-filled copse and open fields filled with wavering men, Greene sent in Jethro Sumner and his North Carolinians. The American line was not only re-established. It began to go forward.

The Legion infantry went in with the bayonet again. Henderson was wounded, but Wade Hampton took over at once and kept the pressure increasing. Right, left, and center, Stuart's men sagged, began to break, while drums beat frantically and bullets kept up a rap-rap-rap, hollow and eerie, against the tree trunks. Then Greene gestured urgently, and on came the elite of his army, Williams' Marylanders and Kirkwood's Delawares.

The British line caved. Men were pouring down the road that led east along the Santee in unashamed flight. Only on the British right, there among the blackjacks by Eutaw Creek and its pitch-roof banks, was there a stand. Major Marjoribanks and his skullcaps and bearskins seemed rooted, unshakable and immovable. William Washington took his helmeted troopers in a wild, slanting charge against them, only to have his men shot down in the sunny patches of the thick blackjack tangles.

Word was sent to the Marylanders and the Delawares to bear left and hit Marjoribanks' flank and rear, but for once this part of the command could not answer. The men had smashed through into the camps that Stuart's men had left standing, had found cooked food, equipment, clothing, and, worst of all, rum casks, and had gone completely out of hand. Back on the road to Charleston, Stuart instantly sensed a change in the tempo of the fight, rallied his fugitives, and brought them in fair order back into the clearing. There were confused scuffles about the brick house, a last charge or two, and Greene once more realized that he could not afford a victory.

Through baking, shimmering air where dust and smoke hung like a Narragansett fog he withdrew his men and left the field to Stuart and his taut-stretched troops. One more push might have left the Rhode Islander with a real textbook conquest. But also it might have turned his army into a skeleton force, and for all he knew, there was a fall campaign for which to prepare and then more operations that could carry on through 1782 and into 1783.

So the field was left to Stuart. That sturdy fighter, like Cornwallis after Guilford, Rawdon after Hobkirk's Hill and Ninety Six, held his ground for a few hours and buried his dead, including that superb leader, Major Marjoribanks. Then he took the long hot road back to Charleston.

There was no way for Greene to have known or guessed it, but Eutaw Springs was the Monmouth of the Southern campaign. Never again would the two little main armies meet in combat. There was no more thought of re-establishing the chain of British posts from the coast to Ninety Six. Even Wilmington in North Carolina, there at the mouth of the broad Cape Fear, was given up, and the only spots where the royal colors now flew or were ever to fly again were Charleston and Savannah, kept there by the grace of the Royal Navy. The whole T was gone.

Nathanael Greene, in the short months from January to September, had taken the fragments left him by Gates and, while never actually winning a major battle, never having enough men, enough supplies, enough money, had won a tremendous campaign. Calmly he had done what he could with what he had. And he had seen and utilized resources to which Gates had been blind and to which many other American generals would have been blind. Under him, or rather with him, the local forces of Marion and Sumter and Pickens and many other lesser-known country leaders had been utilized to the full. As has been cited before, he could not have existed without them, nor they without him. But Greene was the man who recognized this interdependence and developed it to its utmost.

The war, of course, was not actually over in the South. Well into 1782 there was to be bushwhacking. Raids would be executed and bodies of men were to dash into bloody combat. The war between Whig and Tory, irrespective of the armies, flared on more and more bitterly without the least regard for military operations. Much of this animosity, and indeed the feeling that kept many partisan bands in the field, had its roots in local troubles that antedated the war. Some historians have even suggested that they may be looked upon as continuations of the century-old struggle between Cavalier and Roundhead in England.

But they had no effect on Greene's lines, which finally came to rest in an arc about Charleston. Reports sent by courier to the commander-in-chief were dated at such odd spots as Rantowle's Creek or Wappetaw, the Pon-Pon or Round O, and in them Nathanael Greene spoke modestly of his accomplishments and asked that a little more help be sent him for the hard campaign that must come in 1782.

While fighting eddied about the brick house near Eutaw Springs and then drifted sullenly away toward Charleston, the troops of the Duke de St. Simon were settling themselves on the low peninsula between the York and the James. Boat by boatload they were slowly joined by their fellow

countrymen who had made the long march west and then south from Newport under Rochambeau.

They moved under skies that were now cloudy, now miraculously clear,
with the sun riding high in a deep blue setting, much as the hidden future
held bright lights and deadly shadows for so many of them. Young Louis
Alexandre Berthier, as the years unfolded, was to become chief of staff to
Napoleon, with the titles of Marshal of France, Prince of Wagram and of
Neuchâtel. Charles Pichegru would command French republican armies,
oppose Bonaparte's climb to power, and die mysteriously. That sturdy
Gaul, Charles MacMahon, was to live out a peaceful life, but his son, Edme
Patrice Maurice de MacMahon rose to be not only Marshal of France but
second President of the Third French Republic. With the fleet, Honoré
Ganteaume would rise to admiral under Napoleon. In the jungle slime of
the South Pacific twentieth-century Americans were to be familiar with
names left there by Louis Antoine de Bougainville and Jean François de
La Pérouse. The latter died on the island of Vanikoro, now familiar to millions under its theater pseudonym of Bali H'ai. These men and many others
had long stretches of bright, even dazzling sunlit life ahead of them.

A little more than a decade away clouds would roll in, ominous and
final, for others. Mauduit du Plessis died horribly in a slave uprising in
Santo Domingo. In Paris, tumbrels rumbled and the slick blade of the guillotine clanked to mark the exit of the elegant Duke de Lauzun, of "Le
Beau" Dillon and De Billy-Dillon. To the scaffold went Count de Custine
and the Viscount Alexandre de Beauharnais, whose lovely Creole widow,
Josephine, drew bitter criticism from her friends for marrying a scrawny-
looking Corsican gunnery officer named Bonaparte.

But all that lay in the future, and in the light and shadow of September
1781 any military-minded Frenchman could look forward without too much
apprehension to a brisk campaign against Messieurs les Anglais, who had
shut themselves up so securely at Yorktown, across the peninsula. The more
thoughtful found their optimism tempered by a small black patch of uneasiness that fluttered batlike in the backs of their minds. Count de Grasse
had long since taken his combat fleet out to sea. There were rumors that
he had met Hood and Graves, but no reports of the outcome. They could
console themselves that, while bad news takes wings, the good idles and
dawdles on the way.

On the fourteenth the Franco-American camps about the flush of the
Williamsburg bricks and the cool white of its doorways were shaken out
of their routine duties by insistent drumbeats. West of the College of
William and Mary, St. Simon's men hurriedly adjusted baldric and bayonet
slings, formed into rigid lines. A little group of horsemen, too spread out
and too small for any patrol, was coming at a hand-gallop through the
camp of the Virginia militia without drawing rein. Sergeants, gripping their
espontoons rigidly at company flanks, kept dutifully impassive but could
not help wondering at all this *tohu-bohu*. Monsieur le Duc de St. Simon

himself was hurrying up, plumes stirring in the soft fall air. Perhaps ce sacré Cornwallis had mounted himself a sortie, quoi!

The horsemen were nearer and the end files could make out at least one man, perhaps more, in the familiar uniform of the Bourbons. But in the lead was an enormous man who seemed to be in blue and buff, a tenue as faultless as that of the American "Vayne," with whom they were now familiar. And voyez, here came galloping to meet them, the young Marquis de Lafayette in his American uniform, along with Monsieur le Gouverneur de la Virginie, Monsieur Nelson.

The blue-and-buff man had dismounted, as had the young marquis, and they were embracing each other like two Frenchmen. Now St. Simon had come forward and there were introductions of the most formal. Now the Comte d'Autichamp of the Agenais was being presented and De Rostaing of the Gâtinais and the Vicomte de Poudens of the Touraine. Ah, now one knew what it was that agitated itself! The large man was none other than that "Vasinton," of whom they had heard even in the West Indies, and the Frenchman with him could only be Monsieur le Comte de Rochambeau! Through the Agenais and the Gâtinais and the Touraine, men clapped their cockaded hats on their bayonet-tipped muskets and raised them high, cheering.

It must have been a chokingly emotional moment for Washington. After a few quiet days spent at Mount Vernon, his first glimpse of his beloved estate since early '76, and in the congenial company of Rochambeau, De Chastellux and others, he had pushed on hard for the neck of the York-town peninsula and the camps that flowed inland from it about Williamsburg. He had ridden in, after setting a killing pace, to be met first by Lafayette and then by the newly arrived French, glittering in their smart efficiency.

But there had to be a letdown. No man could tell him a single, sure word about De Grasse and the rumored action against the British. The scattering of the French fleet would have been a fearful blow. Nearly as bad would have been the British interception of another fleet under Admiral Barras, bound south out of Newport with the bulkier pieces of French ordnance and tons of salted beef for the American army.

There was a formal dinner that night, and the massed bands of St. Simon's regiments played for the guests, featuring an excerpt from André Ernest Modeste Grétry's Lucille. It was a jovial, convivial evening for the juniors. The seniors, with Washington, must have been distrait. Disaster to De Grasse and Barras meant at best one more inconclusive campaign that would damage the British little and would profoundly discourage the people of the United States and the court of France. During the year, with great ceremony and jubilation, the Congress of the United States had signaled the ratification of the Articles of Confederation, which bound the old thirteen colonies into a unit, bound them loosely, perhaps, but at least gave a fairly firm platform for some future, tighter bond. Ratification would be meaningless without the force of arms to back it up.

There never was such a sunrise as that of September 15, 1781, breaking over the Yorktown peninsula. The first rays reached Washington, then spread through camp and bivouac, along the brick streets of Williamsburg, and everywhere those rays were matched by the light that glowed suddenly in men's eyes. Admiral de Grasse, unexcitable Auvergnat that he was, had sent word that he was back in Chesapeake Bay. There had been a brisk engagement with Hood and Graves and, far out of sight of land, guns had thundered and wooden walls had rung to the impact of cannon balls. Now Messieurs les Anglais were gone, scattered, driven north. And more, Barras' fleet from Newport was safe and on its way to the closest anchorages along the James. So strong was the radiance of the news that men forgot to notice that, after all, there had been no sunrise, that a steady, gentle rain was falling.

That one action off the Virginia Capes, little noticed save in detailed histories, unseen save by the relatively few participants, was to turn out to be the single, decisive engagement of the whole war. It is ironic that not one American soldier had taken part in the quick, brief climax of six years of struggle, almost equally so that not one of the men so laboriously brought over and so strictly maintained by Rochambeau had pulled a trigger in effecting it. Yet there the record stands. The French had seized control of the seas for the allies and would hold it just long enough.

Yet that control would have meant nothing had there not been on the Virginia peninsula the armies of St. Simon and Rochambeau, armies which formed the larger part of Washington's command by a considerable margin. And those same French could not have been there had not, year in and weary year out, American men and women in unnamed thousands grimly followed Washington and, still more important, followed the ideals and the aims which he embodied for them, for those who marched with him, for those who had but briefly glimpsed him, for those to whom he was but a steady-burning spark of hope and quiet inspiration. To the country he was not a blaring trumpet call. Rather, he was a throwing back of the head, a stiffening of the spine, a clearing of the eye. His was that spirit guiding Nathanael Greene's pen when the Rhode Islander wrote to the French minister, De la Luzerne, not complaining but merely stating a fact, "We fight, get beat, rise and fight again."

The last depression spent, Washington was alive with plans. He must see De Grasse, make sure that the admiral would do everything in his power to speed the fall of Cornwallis. De Grasse sent up the James a neat little captured English vessel, named for George III's Queen, Charlotte. With Rochambeau and the joint staffs, the commander-in-chief sped far down Chesapeake Bay until the walls of *La Ville de Paris*, De Grasse's flagship, towered cliff-like above them.

Washington surely had never seen such a ship, and neither, probably, had Rochambeau. Mounting some one hundred and twenty guns, it was the largest warship then afloat, relatively comparable to the *Musashi-kan* and the *Yamato-kan* of the World War II fleets of the world. Its figurehead at the bow and its vast glassed galleries astern were alive with fine carving and aglitter with gold. With his first glimpse of this colossus the last of Washington's doubts must have vanished. If any lingered, De Grasse dispelled them. The admiral showed a gratifying tendency to interpret ironclad orders from the Ministry of Marine very liberally. He would blockade up the bay. Yes, he would send ashore what powder he could spare. Some eight hundred marines would start up the James at once.

With the lightest heart that he had known, probably since he started out with Braddock's doomed column in 1755, certainly since the first whisper of real trouble that came with the Sugar Act of 1764, Washington took his grateful leave. Adverse winds that bounced the *Queen Charlotte* about like a floating cocked hat set both Washington and Rochambeau afret with impatience, and four full days passed before they reached the combined camps once more.

Then the pair started working. Cornwallis had thrown up fortifications across the York at Gloucester Point and there was a chance that he might have enough small craft at hand to ferry his army over and escape. Once on the other bank, he could drive up through Virginia, into Maryland and Pennsylvania, and possibly effect a junction with Clinton. If Rochambeau objected that thus Cornwallis would be without base and supply line, Washington could assure him that other armies on the North American continent had moved farther and under worse conditions. "Joe Gourd" Weedon now faced the Gloucester lines with some Virginia militia. Not enough. Lauzun and his French and Irish and Poles would move there at once along with De Grasse's marines. The Duke de Choisy, who had distinguished himself at the siege of Cracow in Poland years ago, was given command of the area.

Down from Head of Elk on the Chesapeake that improvised flotilla slipped on endlessly. Men from New England and New York and New Jersey swarmed ashore along the James, mingling with Virginians and Marylanders and Pennsylvanians, with the Soissonnais, the Gâtinais, and the Royal Deux-Ponts. Engineers of both armies traced out lines. D'Aboville's guns, Henry Knox's guns were manhandled ashore and dragged off over thick, sandy roads by horses, by ox teams, and by sweating cannoneers to the solid, fascined casemates that were waiting for them. Already howitzers and fieldpieces were slamming, adding to the incessant din of wheel and voice and clanking shovel. Yet underlying all the clamor, the air seemed hushed, as though thousands of ears were listening for the bell that would ring down the final curtain on Yorktown, one more act in the drama that had begun six years ago.

Actually the decisive bell for the last of all curtains had already been rung far out to sea by De Grasse. Other bells were to ring under the touch of Washington and Rochambeau. Few would take any of these clangings as final, and most men would wait months for the curtain to rise on at least one more act.

On September 30, 1781, scouts reported that the British had silently evacuated their most advanced posts, and the allied armies butted closer to the main defenses of Yorktown. This British move was due to Cornwallis' realization that he simply did not have enough men to cover such an extensive zone of defense as he had first marked out and that no more reinforcements could come to him. Wryly he could appreciate more than ever the importance of control of the sea.

He still had one possible avenue of escape and an invaluable channel through which supplies could be funneled by foraging parties through the still open door of the Gloucester area just across the York River. But on October 3 the Duke de Choisy rolled forward his combined force of French and Americans, close to the Gloucester works, a move in which Banastre Tarleton and one of his convoys were badly mauled by a sudden charge of Lauzun's lancers and hussars. The Gloucester door had been slammed forever.

Day in and day out the big guns of the besieged and the besiegers roared and stunned. It was probably the heaviest artillery concentration that the continent had ever known or would know until Ambrose Burnside massed his Union guns along the Rappahannock, just across from Fredericksburg, in 1862.

Dr. James Thacher, looking after allied casualties in the front lines, had a "fine opportunity of witnessing the sublime and stupendous scene which is continually exhibited. The bombshells . . . are clearly visible in the form of a black ball in the day, but in the night, they appear like a fiery meteor with a blazing tail, most beautifully brilliant, ascending majestically from the mortar . . . and gradually descending to the spot where they are destined to execute their work of destruction." Those who have been under modern artillery fire may be surprised to learn that these shells made no noise at all in their passage until the down flight began, accompanied by a barely audible whistle.

On the night of October 14 white-coated French began quietly massing in their gloom-filled trenches on the left of the allied line. Off on the right, a hum, buzz, and rattle hung over the American works. A two-pronged assault was to be launched against enemy redoubts that enfiladed the allied lines and gave James Thacher and his colleagues far too much work to do. There was an empty, chilling hush that hung heavy over the assault groups. Then—slam-slam-slam-slam-slam-slam! Six cannon, fired in rapid succession, gave the signal. As he led out the flank companies of the Royal Deux-Ponts and the Gâtinais, Count Guillaume des Deux-Ponts found that "that moment seemed to me very sweet, and was very elevating to the soul and animating to the courage." Over on the right, young Alexander Hamilton and the devoted Frenchman, De Gîmat, brought on the mixed companies of American light infantry.

With bayonets fixed and muskets empty, the allied assault troops swept on through the darkness, stumbling over the rough ground but keeping very fair order. Surprise seems to have been complete, and the two enemy works were taken quickly and smartly. The supposedly excitable and impetuous French had been a little slower than their allies in taking their objective, since they had methodically and calmly halted their columns to allow their sappers and engineers to rip down abatis and other obstructions. The coldly efficient Americans, on the other hand, had gone through the entanglements with a whoop and a rush, throwing aside book and precedent in their unbridled eagerness.

The next day Cornwallis wrote dismally to Clinton, ". . . the enemy carried two advanced redoubts by storm. . . . My situation now becomes very critical; we dare not show a gun to their old batteries and I expect that their new ones will open tomorrow morning. . . . The safety of the place is, therefor, so precarious that I cannot recommend that the fleet and army should run any great risk in endeavoring to save us." The last faint stars of hope were winking out in the battered streets of Yorktown and across at Gloucester Point, where Lieutenant Colonels John Graves Simcoe and Banastre Tartleton sadly watched the black-clad farrier sergeants knock in the heads of horses that starvation had rendered useless. Did anyone in the British camp glance at a calendar and shiver as he saw the approach of October 17, the very day on which Burgoyne's men had marched out as prisoners back in '77?

Like a boxer whose eyes and brain are clouding over under a succession of jarring punches, Cornwallis launched a weak counterattack against the French lines which was beaten back with little important damage done. Then in desperation he tried to embark his men in barges and flatboats, hoping that somehow he could pound his way through De Choisy, his French and Virginians. But a gale swept down the York River, "almost as severe a storm as I ever remember to have seen," commented New Jersey Colonel Elias Dayton, and the boats were laboriously sculled back to the Yorktown landings and safety.

On the morning of the seventeenth, French and American artillery thundered into fullest action. There were 24-pounders and 18's and 16's. There were mortars and howitzers, even little coehorns, which were much like World War I trench mortars. Knox and D'Aboville were throwing every available bouche-à-feu against the British works. Dr. Thacher reckoned that fully one hundred pieces of all weights were engaged that morning. "The whole peninsula trembles under the incessant thunderings of our infernal machines," he wrote in awe, adding that there was almost no answering fire.

It must have been difficult for gunners and observers to make out the British works. The haze of a lovely Virginia October day was thickened by heavy gouts of cannon smoke, by clouds of soft earth hurled skyward. Somewhere about ten o'clock on that anniversary morning of Burgoyne's surrender the air cleared a little opposite the left end of the French gun positions. Cannoneers began yelling, pointing gray arms with their deep red velvet cuffs toward a suddenly seen sector of the British line known as the "Horn Work." Scarlet showed vaguely through the thinning haze, and D'Aboville's gunners could make out one little British drummer, alone against the sky, manfully hammering out some drumbeat message whose meaning was lost in the pounding voices of the guns. Fire slackened and the boyish figure drummed on. He was beating the request for a parley, and Lieutenant Ebenezer Denny of the 4th Pennsylvania, grasping the intent of the staccato roll, thought that he had "never heard a drum equal to it—the most delightful music to us all."

A bigger, heavier man appeared on the parapet by the diminutive drummer in his shabby grenadier cap and waved a white handkerchief. There was a moment of stunned unbelief through the American and French lines, though every man must have expected such a denouement sooner or later. An American officer ran forward, met his British opposite number as the latter slithered down the face of the Horn Work. The handkerchief was used to make a blindfold, and the Englishman was led into the forward works.

Back at Williamsburg, the commander-in-chief was busily writing letters. Later he meant to ride out and watch the morning's bombardment, but first he wanted to arrange for the use of the William and Mary buildings for military purposes. There was also the question of York River pilots for De Grasse. As he wrote, gunfire down by Yorktown seemed to be slacking off a little, but it was nothing to notice. Probably D'Aboville and Knox were shifting to new targets. Up to Washington's quarters galloped a sweating dragoon courier with a letter. The Virginian broke the seal, read it, and was on his feet in an instant, staring and staring. "Sir"—the flowing script may have wavered before Washington's eyes—"I propose a cessation of hostilities for twenty-four hours, and that two officers may be appointed by each side, to meet at Mr. Moore's house, to settle terms for the surrender of the posts at York and Gloucester. I have the honor to be, Sir, your humble and obedient servant, CORNWALLIS."

George Washington had rallied swiftly and coolly from many an adverse blow. Now the hand of success had fallen stunningly on his back, and the effect must have been almost as numbing as, say, the sight of Charles Lee's unbeaten men in full retreat from Monmouth. But he soon shook off the impact of the news. John Trumbull came running in answer to the commander-in-chief's summons, and John Laurens joined him. Connecticut and South Carolina pens scratched, and at last an answer to Cornwallis was approved. "An Ardent Desire to spare the further Effusion of blood, will readily incline me to listen to such Terms . . . as are admissible," the main paragraph ran.

Couriers went out with this reply, with warnings to commanders in all parts of the allied line. Slowly the gunfire died away. In the lines of the Bourbonnais, swarthy infantrymen cautiously climbed to the parapet of their trench system, looked about unbelievingly. Far to the right, where Lafayette commanded, men of Major Nathan Rice's Massachusetts-Connecticut battalion worked out into the warm air, peered at the silent British lines, and then stretched out gratefully in the sun, yawning in luxury in spots where a man could not have lived a few hours ago. Throughout the day men walked cautiously, as though afraid that a sudden move, a loud noise might shatter the brittle-seeming hush that hung over the peninsula. Descendants of all these men—French, British, and American—were to step as dazedly through the hours of November 11, 1918. Night fell and the air cleared, showing a sky "decorated with ten thousand stars." The peace of mind of some of the wearier men was disturbed by showers of meteors that sailed across the black bowl above them, frighteningly suggestive of a fresh onset of explosive shells. Dawn came and the hush was still unbroken and men began to believe in it and in its duration.

There were more parleys, exchanges of letters, and sometime before noon on the nineteenth Washington, Rochambeau, and Barras, the latter filling in for the unfortunately ill De Grasse, rode to a deserted British post close by the York River. British officers joined them with a packet of papers signed by Cornwallis and his Royal Navy representative, Thomas Symonds. Washington's firm surrender terms had been accepted. He spoke quietly to one of his aides, who wrote at the foot of the document, "Done in the trenches before Yorktown, in Virginia, October 19th, 1781." Then the commander-in-chief took a pen and signed himself simply, "G. Washington." Rochambeau and Barras added their signatures and the surrender became *fait accompli*.

There was little that was dramatic in this writing of a few lines, this sifting of fine sand across the glistening ink. But these pen strokes called into being a clashing, glittering finale, a set piece at once as gorgeous, sharp, and solemn as the first trigger drawing on Lexington Green, far off in April 1775, had been half seen and hesitant.

Bright sun on the noon of October 19, 1781, poured down on the fields of the peninsula, the gnawed and trampled fields where the armies of France and the United States had drawn their hard arc about the doomed tobacco port of Yorktown. The allied camps were aboil with men shuttling about as drums beat out their urgent clamor. In the calm air that was rich with the smell of trampled grass and wood smoke and tobacco and oiled leather, company after company formed. Sergeant majors called roll, the usual terse snap of their voices tightened by excitement. Men answered to their names in the Saintonge regiment, in Colonel Goose van Schaick's 1st New York, in the Bourbonnais, and in Colonel Joseph Vose's Massachusetts battalion.

Somewhere along the road that led up to Yorktown, Baron von Steuben looked at his watch, compared it with Benjamin Lincoln's. Off to the left Baron de Viomenil checked the time with the Marquis de Chastellux. The bark of the roll calls faded out. The fields were quiet. On the far fringes carriage wheels grated, hoofs clopped, and dainty slippers, stout country boots hissed through the brown grass as the civilians of the countryside pressed cautiously forward, eager to see and yet fearing to be caught up in the irresistible sweep of marching men that might start at any moment.

Drums slammed out. Full-throated music sailed up from the French lines into the gentle air, gay, soaring notes as bright and as clear as the gleaming instruments of the bands. Citizens and their wives and daughters cried out at the toss of the tasseled batons of the drum majors, at the mellow tinkle of the timbrels, a sound that was new to them.

The fields began to flow. Here came the blue and white of the Royal Deux-Ponts. Then there was white and white and white, seemingly endless white of the Agenais and the Soissonnais and the Bourbonnais and the Gâtinais and their fellow regiments, slashed over with violet and black and clear yellow and rose and crimson and dark green. White broadcloth legs were masked to mid-thigh with black gaiters, and bright cockades swayed among the lifting bayonet glints. The long columns, garnished with clouds of mounted officers and aides, swung off toward the road to Yorktown, halted at its flat western edge, dressed expertly to a smart, precise rattle of grounded arms.

To the east, drabber troops were on the move, headed by bands that, to the ears of one American observer, "played moderately well." To watch these men with their bronzed faces ride by, march past with swinging stride, was to leaf through a directory of military America. There rode Lafayette with Vose and Wyllys and Rice and Laurens, bringing on their hard-bitten New Englanders. James Clinton led out New Yorkers under Goose van Schaick and Van Cortlandt, Jersey men with Elias Dayton and Ogden, Rhode Islanders with Olney. The quiet elegance of Anthony Wayne ushered in the Pennsylvanians of Walter Stewart and Dickie Butler. There were Virginians with Thomas Gaskins, Marylanders swinging on under the command of Mordecai Gist and Peter Adams and Alexander Roxburg. Ironbound wheels clanked, harness hissed and jingled, and the Continental artillery rumbled out with Henry Knox and John Lamb and Edward Carrington, the latter released by Nathanael Greene for this campaign in Carrington's native state.

The flow was dazzling, hypnotic. Swarming men and women stood on tiptoe, trying to catch a glimpse of Parson Muhlenberg or the Georgia general, Samuel Elbert, the Chevalier Duportail, rigid Baron von Steuben, or the Canadian Moses Hazen, men of whom they had heard or read, men under whom missing sons or husbands had served.

There was a deep murmur from the massed bystanders, a rising tide of welcome and wonder as these people saw their own massed army for the first time. A light breeze picked up the swelling murmur, deepened it, underscored its meaning, brought with it echoes of earlier years, until the sound became a living recitative of the so far brief history of the people of the United States and of the army that embodied its will.

There were sinister undercurrents, starkly somber passages that muttered of divided counsels, of a state withholding supplies and men and money for fear that another state might benefit or the common group of states grow too strong. There were oily, plausible echoes to tell of glib men plotting to make a profit out of starving, ragged troops. There were harder tones to be heard which recorded plots and downright treason and betrayal.

Furtive, slinking tempos were beaten out to mark desertion and flinching
and faintheartedness in the field and at home. In the murmur could be
caught the voices of men crying out in defeat and confusion at Long Island
and in the wild panic by Kip's Bay. Desperation and defeat along the St.
Lawrence were there, the threnody of hopeless misery of New Jersey and
Pennsylvania winters, flight along the Brandywine and the bitter frustration of Monmouth. There were the voices of recruiting officers in towns
and villages of every state, hopelessly pleading for men to come and fill
up the skeleton companies of the distant and seemingly forgotten army of
the United States. A terrible record was droned out, a record that might
have been fatal.

But there were other passages of the recitative, memories of voices back
in another decade and in this decade shouting that there must be no more
Virginians or New Englanders or Carolinians, that all were Americans.
Repeated were the muffled, uneasy, and yet steady tones of minutemen
waiting on a score of village greens through an April night in '75. The
rowlocks of the Marbleheaders creaked as they saved a beaten army to fight
again. Icy ruts thudded under gun wheels along the winter road to Trenton,
and unseen forests crackled as men glided among the trunks to close in
on Burgoyne, and these sounds rattled in unison with the night sweep
of American infantry up the slopes of Hudson River forts or the pound
of American troopers in a Carolina meadow.

So harsh, jarring notes and bravely triumphant notes told their story of
a people and its army, an army whose men were far too few and were
always just enough.

Now that army was halting on the east side of the road to Yorktown,
facing its French allies with the deserted enemy works looming somber on
its right. Drums began to beat, orders snapped out, and right and left the
waiting ranks bristled to attention. There were hoofbeats far off to the
American left, then a cloud of light dust and horsemen appeared, heading
on down the long lane of regiments and battalions where bayonets flashed
upward in salute. There on a huge bay horse, gleaming in blue and buff,
rode the one man who was, the one man who could have been, the living
embodiment of those hard, drab ranks to his right, who could have welded
them to the white-and-blue men on his left. From the beginning George
Washington had met every blow, stood up under every discouragement,
every frightening disaster that the army as a whole had known. With that
army he had eked out the slim rewards of fate and had never allowed them
to dazzle him, to sweep him into disastrous error or vainglorious rashness.
He had been well seconded, but through the very nature of the man and
the great office that he held, he had had to meet debacle and triumph alone,
assay them—and go on, still alone. Now he rode in Virginia sunlight toward
his greatest glory, still calm, still assaying, and still ready to go on, alone,
at the head of the men whom he had led for so many years.

Rochambeau rode a little behind him, and the Virginian knew that
without the Frenchman and his legions he would not be moving toward

the silent works of Yorktown. The steady Frenchman knew that without his tall companion his American venture would have landed him in a bottomless morass of disaster. And both realized to the full that without the French fleet, represented by Admiral Barras, riding just behind them, their joint campaign could easily have come to nothing.

The hoofs clopped on. Washington turned to take his post at the far right of the American line, with Rochambeau and Barras facing him on the French flank. The whole rolling plain lay waiting in the midday hush that was broken only by the endless murmur of the crowds and the restless stab of a hoof at the powdery soil.

Then from Yorktown, lying inert and sullen off by the river, sad drums began to roll. Out of the works rode a scarlet group heading for the double hedge of allied troops that lined the rough highway. In the lead was a well-set-up darkly handsome man with a frank, ready smile, Brigadier General Charles O'Hara of the Guards. He seemed a little uncertain as he trotted on through the warm air that was tense with expectation. He looked right and left and then edged his horse over toward Rochambeau. The Count, surprised, said nothing but pointed to the opposite side of the road, and O'Hara, flushing a little at his own faux pas, swung his mount about, presented himself to Washington.

The commander-in-chief was, as usual, courteous but impassive. He acknowledged the introduction. But where was Lord Cornwallis? It seemed that his lordship was indisposed that day, probably a *maladie diplomatique* or rather *militaire*, and had named Charles O'Hara as deputy to offer the surrender in his name. Washington inclined his head gravely. In that case, deputy should surrender to deputy and, turning in his saddle, he named General Benjamin Lincoln to act for him. Lincoln edged his mount forward, the scuffling hoofs sounding loud in the hush. Then the man from Hingham in Massachusetts spoke quickly to O'Hara.

The British Army and its auxiliaries were to march out between the French and American to an open field beyond the far end of the French lines. There its leaders would find Lauzun's cavalry drawn up in an arc within which the beaten army was to stack its arms, re-form, and march back to Yorktown for further orders. O'Hara nodded and the brief interview was over.

Off by the battered works, drums snarled away, louder and louder. There were movement and color by the main sally port and music overlaid the drumbeats. Out the defeated army came, company by company, battalion by battalion, most of them men who had crushed Gates at Camden, driven furiously after Greene's feeble command in the long retreat to the Dan, fought him to a standstill at Guilford Court House, and then made the killing march from Wilmington up into Virginia.

There were the blue coats of Von Bose's Hessians, Von Voit and Von Seybothen's Anspachers, and Ewald's green Jaegers. The music played on, and there were the first of the British emerging sullenly from the works. The Germans had gone on at their usual crisp step and in solid formation, but American observers noted that the British "marched through both armies with a slow pace." Their ranks were not trim and it was obvious that a good many marchers had been at the rum casks in defiance of orders. On they came, their names and their uniforms invoking memories that went back to the first occupation of Boston. There were the 17th Leicester-shires and the 23rd Welch, the 33rd West Ridings and the remains of the 71st Scots. Men who had served in the early days about Boston could place the white facings of the 43rd Oxfordshires, who had arrived just too late for Breed's Hill, but relative strangers were the 80th Royal Edinburgh Volunteers. Men of the grenadiers, light infantry, and line companies came on, their feet dragging and their shoulders slumped. Even the bands were affected and played, as an American noted, "not military marches, but of certain airs, which had in them so peculiar a strain of melancholy . . . which . . . excited sentiments far different from those I expected to enjoy."

Then they came out into the great arc that was fringed by Lauzun's lances and sabers; they found the Hessians and Anspachers neatly stacking their arms according to surrender terms. When the turn of the scarlet ranks came, muskets went clattering furiously into a disorderly heap despite the halfhearted remonstrances of their officers. Drummers staved in the heads of their drums, brave with the bright regimental coats of arms. Infantrymen snatched up their muskets and smashed the butts on the ground, kicked away their fine leather cartridge cases with their brass emblems. The whole performance was cut from the same cloth as the outbursts at the Saratoga surrender and in keeping with national character. Englishmen have many virtues, and one of the most notable is that they make lamentably bad prisoners of war, as their military guardians from Cambridge in 1777 to Colditz in 1945 have learned.

At last the men of Cornwallis' command were marched off to begin the long route that was to take them over trails that, years later, Lee and Jackson and Grant and Sheridan were to know. The trails led across Virginia and through Ashby's Gap in the Blue Ridge to Winchester in the Shenandoah or to Frederick in Maryland.

On the plains about Yorktown the music was gay and soaring again as the French and American armies filed away, quietly joyous, to their quarters. For the commander-in-chief there was a bit of military courtesy to be discharged and he gave a dinner for Charles O'Hara of the Guards, a possibly ticklish ordeal which seems to have gone off more than smoothly, owing, perhaps, to the easy polish of the guardsman. John Trumbull, present at the table, greatly admired his poise and his even dignity.

Later the commander-in-chief excused himself. The American army had just played its part in a striking victory and he must report what had been accomplished to that body which had first raised that army and placed it under his care and made him accountable for it to the nation.

So his report to the Congress dealt with that army and not its commander, as must have seemed only reasonable to him. With Trumbull and John Laurens to help him, he finally came up with a draft that seemed suitable to him. "I have the Honor to inform Congress, that a Reduction of the British Army under Command of Lord Cornwallis, is most happily effected. The unremitting Ardor which actuated every Officer and Soldier in the combined Army in this Occasion, has principally led to this Important Event, at an earlier period than my most sanguine hope had induced me to expect. . . ."

CHAPTER XXXII

"With a heart full of love and gratitude, I now take leave of you"

WHILE the true importance of Cornwallis' surrender became apparent to America and the rest of the world fairly soon, for many months it was regarded as a great victory, but not *the* great victory. Once again a British army had laid down its arms and Cornwallis had joined Gentleman Johnny Burgoyne as a general defeated in the Americas. But other British forces remained, very strong about New York and potentially dangerous in the Carolinas. So, to most minds, Yorktown simply meant, "Two down and two to go."

In 1782 the armies of the United States, France, and Great Britain carried on the same sort of existence that they had so often before, and life became a carbon copy of other years.

The French under Rochambeau, having wintered pleasantly in Virginia, made their colorful progress north to the general area where Washington's main strength now lay along the Hudson. In time and at the inevitable gesture of events, they tramped smoothly east and at last embarked for home at various New England ports. During this period Rochambeau had worked faithfully as ever with Washington, both leaders hoping for the arrival of a French fleet that would make possible that one, final joint assault on Manhattan which had been their objective from the start.

The record of this post-Yorktown era, as set down in orderly books and letter books, might have covered 1777 or 1779 as well as 1781–82. Enlistments were difficult. Officers resigned, squabbled about rank, memorialized the Congress and Washington concerning grievances that were often very flimsy and more often very real.

On Manhattan, Sir Henry Clinton still sat tight, watching and waiting for some Franco-American move. Then in 1782 he resigned wearily and went home to England, his place being taken by Sir Guy Carleton, one of the ablest and surely the wisest of the many fine soldiers doomed to serve under Howe and Clinton.

In the South, Nathanael Greene kept the field against the British at Charleston and Savannah. Reinforcements were sent him and the nation was treated to the sight, unbelievable a few years before, of Pennsylvania troops under St. Clair and Wayne operating as far away as Georgia— American troops serving in another part of America, not regional levies transported to a foreign, loosely allied state. But there was never strength for a large-scale move against the British-held ports. Skirmishes and scuffles dragged on and, as always, cost lives, among them that of young John Laurens, who had led New Englanders in Virginia. In the back country the old, dreary, bloody internecine struggle continued, quite apart from the war, a struggle of extermination so bitter that Greene wrote, "Not a day passes, but there are more or less who fall a sacrifice to this savage disposition. The whigs seem determined to extirpate the tories, and the tories the whigs."

Yet events were moving toward a definite end. They came so slowly, seemed, each in itself, so inconclusive, that they passed little noted until the slow climax was reached. There was no one blazing moment to cele- brate, to set the whole nation whooping and roaring in delirious exultation. The curtain was falling imperceptibly on the drama of America, and as it sank by slow degrees, the audience was still seated, the cast was still on the stage, while stage hands ripped down the scenery and backdrops, item by leisurely item.

Here and there were solid portents for thoughtful men to note. Dr. James Thacher, still with Major Nathan Rice's battalion up the Hudson near Newburgh, opened his worn diary to August 5, 1782, and began to write, perhaps a little unsteadily, "Flags are passing and repassing from this post to New York and back every day, and several gentlemen have been permitted to come out of that city. By the intelligence which they bring . . . commissioners are sent from the court of London to Paris, where they are to meet French and American commissioners for the important purpose of negotiating a general peace. May God grant them success in bringing to America an honorable peace and national independence."

Later it became generally known that peace would be concluded and that the foundation of that peace was American independence. But there was so much uncertainty, reports of so many snarls and hitches in the negotiations, that men could hardly point to a given day and say, "From now on, it's all settled." Late in the year the British gave up Charleston and Savannah and sailed away to the West Indies. But in New York the same formidable army lay ready under Guy Carleton's hand. Other troops could join them there. The Southern ports could be reoccupied. All that could be surely said was that for the moment matters military were static.

The year 1783 repeated the weary, indecisive pace of its predecessor. News from abroad pointed rather negligently to some approaching decision, as it had in the past. When in April the final treaty that acknowledged the independence of the United States was presented to the Congress for ratification, there was jubilation on a moderate scale. Everything had come so gradually that the fine edge of triumph had been worn away and now people were saying that they'd known all along that this was just what was going to happen. It is probably as well that the denouement was slow. The new nation was able to face its utterly staggering and unplanned future in a reasonably sober mood. And besides, Sir Guy Carleton still held New York with fleet and army. He looked very permanent there, despite the exodus to Europe and to Nova Scotia of thousands upon thousands of Tories who would not or who dared not stay and face the new order.

Spring and summer idled down the calendar. Fall crept over the country. Then in November more and more letters passed between Washington and Carleton, and soon what was left of the already disbanding army of the United States was on the move, ready to take over Manhattan Island in the wake of the departing British.

It was December 4, 1783. Sir Guy Carleton's warships and transports lay in the lower harbor, ready to clear New York for the last time. On the Battery the flag of the new nation with its thirteen bold stripes and thirteen bright stars stood out bravely over the north bastion of Fort George. The city of New York was quiet, still shaken emotionally by the entry of the last of the army of the United States during the final week of November and by its first glimpse since 1776 of the commander-in-chief who had left its streets, beaten, and now returned to them in triumph. Through the thin sunlight of a December noon, officers of many ranks were riding along Broad Street, along Pearl Street, converging on gambrel-roofed Fraunces' Tavern with its fanlighted doors and gables. Their heads were carefully powdered, their swordhilts polished, and as they dismounted they gave a surreptitious flick of a handkerchief to their boots or snapped invisible fluff from blue uniform sleeves, glossy-new or shiny-worn.

Slowly the big room to which they had been invited filled up. Baron von Steuben was there and Alex McDougall. Vast Henry Knox took up an ample corner—280 pounds by the Newburgh scales against Washington's 220—along with James Clinton. Henry Jackson, who had commanded the Massachusetts troops on their entry into New York, clanked in. One by one they trooped to the long room, the higher officers who were still with the army in the dying weeks of 1783.

Along one side of the room stood a table with cold cuts and hot joints, decanters of wine and pyramids of glittering glasses. But no one edged up to the table or sent wine gurgling into a glass. The officers sat about in restless quiet, exchanged brief snatches of conversation, fell silent, ventured another remark or two, were silent again. Battle-scarred fingers drummed on white-clad knees. Tense and strained, they were waiting for their host, who had summoned them to the last council they would hold with their commander-in-chief.

Benjamin Tallmadge, erect and handsome, crested helmet tucked correctly under his left arm, suddenly saw blue and buff in the passage outside. With the others he rose quickly, and George Washington entered the room in a complete hush that was broken only by the commander-in-chief's slow tread. There was an inclination of Washington's powdered head, a few barely audible words of welcome, a muffled patter of response. Some officers shifted their feet awkwardly, cleared their throats. Host and guests were like a pack of strange children suddenly thrown together in an unfamiliar room.

Washington gestured toward the platters and decanters on the table, but only one or two officers edged forward. They saw him dab food onto a plate, pick up a fork, then set them both down. The commander-in-chief had often seen his subordinates at a loss, but never before had they seen him so utterly adrift. Finally he filled a wineglass shakily and gestured again. One by one the glasses were brimmed. Tallmadge and McDougall and Jackson and the others held their glasses, staring woodenly at them. Someone raised his hand in warning.

The commander-in-chief was speaking, speaking in a tight, throttled voice they had never heard before. The words came out with difficulty and he was blinking with each syllable. "With a heart full of love and gratitude, I now take leave of you." The words came out slowly and carefully. "I most devoutly wish that your later days may be as prosperous and happy as your former ones have been glorious and honorable." He raised his glass.

Here and there a man managed to stammer out some kind of response, drank, added again to the confused mutter that rose in the long room. Their commander-in-chief was speaking once more, fighting out each word while his cheeks glistened unashamedly, matching those of his guests, from tough old Von Steuben to young Benjamin Tallmadge. "I cannot"—the sounds struggled out—"I cannot come to each of you, but shall feel obliged if each of you will come and take me by the hand."

The room swayed toward him. First was Henry Knox, who, with the absent Nathanael Greene, had been an ever secure prop through the blackest of days. The ex-Boston bookseller blindly put out his hand. Washington started to reach for it, but memories of the old years overwhelmed him and he impulsively threw his big arms about his chief of artillery, held him close.

One by one the officers stumbled by, were received in the same accolade, simple, unaffected, and immeasurably sad. Benjamin Tallmadge, one of the last in line, later spoke for every guest present. "The simple thought that we were then about to part from the man who had conducted us through a long and bloody war, and under whose conduct the glory and independence of our country had been achieved, and that we should see his face no more in this world seemed to me utterly insupportable."

Then the commander-in-chief strode from the room, turned at the door with high-lifted arm, and was gone. His officers were left to their own thoughts and memories of the man and of the many men who had deserved the same accolade but would have to wait for it on the other side of the grave.

The commander-in-chief's ordeal was not over. Cocked-hatted and cloaked, he passed through a guard of honor at the door and took his last salute as a soldier of the United States. Then he hurried for his barge, waiting at Whitehall Ferry, but a solid wall of New Yorkers hemmed him in, cheered as they had cheered his entry in November. People along that choked lane to Whitehall remembered his tense, set face, the convulsive clenching of his jaw muscles as he saw mothers holding up children for a hasty glimpse of that tall Virginia planter who had once stood before the Congress and said, "I do not think myself equal to the command I am honored with."

He was in his barge, ready to push off for Paulus Hook, where horses awaited him for the trip that was to take him through Philadelphia and on to the Potomac. Oars dipped and the barge drew away from the shore.

When Washington had first humbly taken command of the little army that stood for the expressed will of most Americans, he committed himself and them to stand in battle against the might of a whole empire. Yet the struggle had hardly been one of nation against nation. Rather, it had been a rallying of people in support of ideals and beliefs that were common to nearly as many Englishmen as Americans. The clash had come because a small powerful clique in England had veered sharply away from the centuries-old drift toward representative government and back to feudalism. Such disparity of aims could not exist within one empire. The absolutist rule *had* to strike down the frightening rising toward popular government across the Atlantic. And those in America who clung fiercely to opposing ideals *had* to resist.

Now the struggle was over, won by democracy over absolutism rather than by Americans over Englishmen. And in that victory the power of absolutism died forever in England.

Washington's thoughts may well have been following such a course as his barge headed for Paulus Hook. Did he see, as well, that the war had been but a mere incident in the long struggle against absolutism? As his little army had flung itself, alone at the time, against a vast power that was reverting to darker political ages, so now the new country, feeble and ill organized and vulnerable as that army, stood alone in a world where most rulers hoped for the extinction of this bold essay into living democracy.

Whether this emergent nation "so conceived and so dedicated" could survive in such a world lay in the hands of those who had stood out for the rights of man from the first ominous threats against them. George Washington may have felt that he had done his part in upholding the cause of freedom through eight long years of command in the field. His service to the country could reasonably be considered at an end.

But as in 1775, when every section of the land had turned to him for leadership, had seen in him the embodiment of all that was best in national ideal and aspiration, so before long America would seek him out again. One more long span of eight years of selfless leadership was to be exacted from him as President and commander-in-chief. His would be the task of calling forth the spiritual forces of the nation, of maintaining the struggle for liberty and justice against enemies within as well as without, of establishing for all time a beacon light for mankind to shine not only on all America but to send its rays to every corner of the globe where men cherish a belief in the right to live in freedom. For none knew better that freedom is never static, that it must be won again and again, than the tall Virginian as his men rowed him on toward Paulus Hook.

August 22, 1954
Beverly, Massachusetts

Index

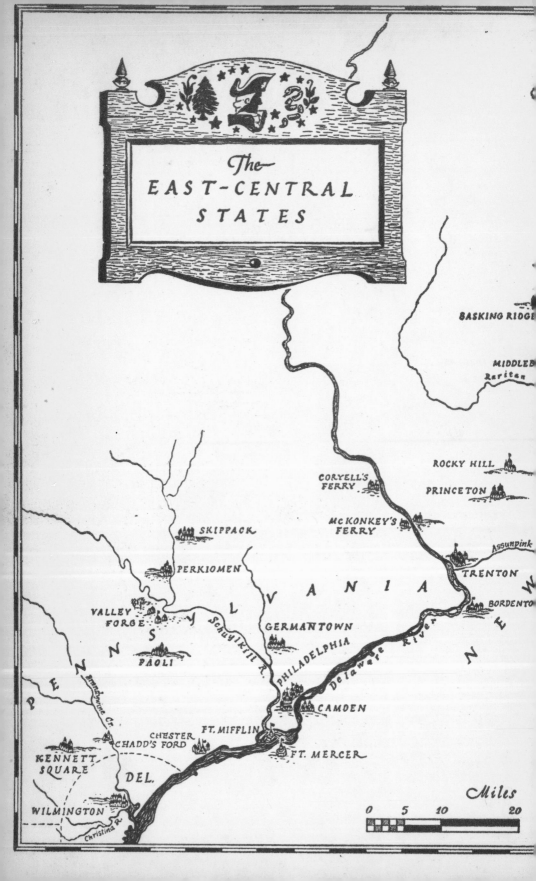

The
EAST-CENTRAL
STATES

BASKING RIDGE

MIDDLEB
Raritan

ROCKY HILL

CORYELL'S
FERRY

PRINCETON

McKONKEY'S
FERRY

SKIPPACK

Assunpink

PERKIOMEN

TRENTON

V   A   N   I   A

BORDENTO

VALLEY
FORGE

Schuylkill R.

GERMANTOWN

N
E
W

PAOLI

PHILADELPHIA

Delaware River

KENNETT
SQUARE

Brandywine Cr.

P
E
N
N
S
Y
L

CHESTER
CHADD'S FORD

FT. MIFFLIN

CAMDEN

DEL.

FT. MERCER

WILMINGTON

Christina R.

Miles

0   5   10   20